Sustaining Silver Economy Vitality Through Social Service and Business Partnerships

Johnston Hong-Chung Wong
https://orcid.org/0000-0002-9532-4512
Beijing Normal-Hong Kong Baptist University, China

Poshan Yu
https://orcid.org/0000-0003-1069-3675
The Australian Studies Centre, Shanghai University, China & European Business Institute of Luxembourg, Luxembourg

IGI Global
Scientific Publishing
Publishing Tomorrow's Research Today

Vice President of Editorial	Melissa Wagner
Director of Acquisitions	Mikaela Felty
Director of Book Development	Jocelynn Hessler
Production Manager	Mike Brehm
Cover Design	Jose Rosado

Published in the United States of America by
IGI Global Scientific Publishing
701 East Chocolate Avenue
Hershey, PA, 17033, USA
Tel: 717-533-8845 | Fax: 717-533-7115
Website: https://www.igi-global.com E-mail: cust@igi-global.com

Library of Congress Cataloging-in-Publication Data

LCCN: 2026016441 (CIP Data Pending)
ISBN13: 9798337393704
Isbn13Softcover: 9798337393711
EISBN13: 9798337393728
British Cataloguing in Publication Data
A Cataloguing in Publication record for this book is available from the British Library.

Table of Contents

Detailed Table of Contents

The silver economy remains underfinanced because traditional finance fails aging populations. This chapter argues for new architectures,not new products combining existing instruments across sectors. Analyzing six hybrid models (blended finance, social impact bonds, reverse mortgage REITs, cooperative banking, life settlements, senior REITs) based on 2014–2025 evaluations, each shows distinct limits. Superior inclusion requires coordinated deployment tailored to local homeownership, social capital, and institutional capacity. Recommendations include regulatory sandboxes, life settlement fiduciary disclosure, and public co-investment. A practitioner's model selection matrix is provided.

As demographic transitions occur globally, resulting in an ageing population, the Silver Economy has emerged as a vital driver of socio-economic development. While the establishment of age-friendly infrastructure and the provision of inclusive healthcare are of paramount importance, traditional short-term grant-based funding often limits scalability. This study analyses innovative partnership models, including public-private partnerships (PPPs), impact investing, blended finance, corporate social responsibility (CSR), and blockchain-driven crowdfunding, with a view to overcoming these financial barriers. The findings indicate that these mechanisms diversify resource pooling, enhance transparency, and align financial returns with social impact through risk-sharing. Nevertheless, success depends on overcoming regulatory fragmentation and addressing gaps in digital literacy. The study concludes that an adaptive regulatory environment and a coordinated funding ecosystem are fundamental prerequisites for building economic resilience and sustainable social welfare within the Silver Economy

China's rapidly expanding silver economy faces severe urban–rural healthcare disparities, and telemedicine serves as a pivotal tool to enhance care accessibility for older adults. However, financial barriers hinder its sustainable scaling. This study explores financial innovations and collaborative mechanisms to advance telemedicine for the silver economy in China via bibliometric analysis (CiteSpace) and in-depth case studies of Zhongshan Hospital and Guangdong Second People's Hospital. Findings reveal a four-dimensional financing pathway: policy-driven initiation, technology-enabled infrastructure, diversified public–private financing, and outcome-oriented evaluation. Supported by Collaborative Care Theory, the study demonstrates that integrated payment systems, policy support, and social–business partnerships improve telemedicine sustainability. It provides actionable frameworks to bridge healthcare gaps and sustain silver-economy vitality, offering implications for emerging economies with aging populations.

Population ageing is reshaping economies and societies worldwide, giving rise to the Silver Economy, an ecosystem of products, services, and cross-sector partnerships that support the well-being of older adults. With an estimated 347 million older adults by 2050, India provides a significant context for examining collaborative business ecosystems that promote active and healthy ageing. This chapter presents

Silver tourism constitutes a major segment of the silver economy, as older adults are healthy and financially independent after retirement. This sector can be broadly divided into two categories namely traditional sightseeing, particularly related to cultural heritage, and health and wellness-oriented activities such as hot spring bathing and physical relaxation. With the expansion of middle-income groups in China, tourism enterprises specifically designed for older adults are emerging and growing rapidly. This development presents a significant opportunity for collaboration between private enterprises and social services, as they bring complementary expertise in business models and understanding the needs of older adults, respectively. This study examines selected cases of such ventures to identify key success factors and examine sustainable collaboration models. Findings suggest that most cases have yet to sharpen their marketing mix however, companies background, professional management, well-defined business plans, and financial strengths are essential factors of commercial viability. As the silver tourism market continues to expand, this study shows that involvement of state-owned enterprises, a distinctive feature of the Chinese economy, can be a contributive partner to social services organizations. The Model of Public Services with Contracted Operators allows medium sized private enterprises to enter the market partnering with both social services and local governments. Finally, integrating care and attention services for older people with disgenerating abilities with the expading businesses of silver tourism, allow the society to rely less on social assistances and income transfers.

This chapter examines the role of social innovation in the development of the silver economy in emerging markets, with a focus on community-based models in Vietnam. The purpose of the chapter is to develop an integrated analytical framework that combines social innovation theory, the silver economy, and community-based approaches to explain how care systems for older persons can emerge under resource constraints. Through a case study of the Intergenerational Self-Help Club model, the chapter elucidates operational mechanisms based on co-production, social capital, and

Foreword

Population aging is the defining reality of our time, transforming economies, healthcare systems, labor markets, and social structures in ways that demand urgent and thoughtful responses. Yet, too often, aging is framed as a crisis of dependency, a fiscal burden, or a problem to be managed. I feel greatly honored to be invited to write the Foreword for this book, as I strongly believe that it offers a fundamentally different and more hopeful vision on this uprising social challenge.

Sustaining Silver Economy Vitality Through Social Service and Business Partnerships presents a compelling case that population aging represents not merely battening down the hatches, but an opportunity to be seized with both hands. Its core argument is both simple and profound: financing and sustaining the silver economy requires not new products or isolated interventions, but the architecture combining existing instruments, engaging diverse stakeholders, and designing integrated systems that no single sector could deploy insolation. It urges readers to rethink about integration, innovation, and inclusion at a critical moment.

In my view, what sets this book apart is its remarkable breadth and depth. Spanning 15 chapters, it brings together perspectives from Asia, Europe, the Middle East, and Africa, offering a genuinely global and comparative lens. It moves seamlessly from the macro-level design of financial architectures for longevity to the micro-level realities of intergenerational knowledge transfer in Indonesian and Vietnamese universities, from health and wellness tourism in China to community-based care models in Vietnam and Türkiye. When reading the chapters, readers do not encounter abstract theories but concrete cases: reverse mortgage ecosystem funds in North America, social impact bonds in Japan, cooperative banking in India, residential care innovations in Da Nang, and intangible cultural heritage revival through intergenerational collaboration.

Hence, the book distinctive contribution lies in its insistence on the hybridity of solutions. The authors demonstrate that blended finance, social impact bonds, cooperative banking, life settlements, and Real Estate Investment Trusts are not competing alternatives but complementary components of an integrated ecosystem.

The architecture matters more than any single instrument. Similarly, it shows that effective responses require cross-sector partnerships that bring together governments, businesses, social service organizations, universities, and—crucially—older adults themselves as co-creators rather than passive recipients.

I believe that this book is an essential reading for a diverse and growing audience. For policymakers, seeking evidence-based strategies to restructure long-term care systems and promote active aging, it offers practical frameworks and comparative policy insights. For financial institutions, it reveals the substantial economic opportunities embedded in the silver economy and the innovative financing models that can unlock them. For social service and community practitioners, it offers models of empowerment, co-production, and community-based innovation that center older adults as agents of change. For academics, it charts a rich agenda for future inquiry on silver knowledge and economy. Finally, for business stakeholders, it illuminates emerging markets in health and wellness tourism, age-friendly technologies, and intergenerational services.

Perhaps most importantly, this book challenges us to reconsider our fundamental assumptions about aging, value, and social contribution. The silver-haired generation is not a demographic to be managed but a repository of wisdom, experience, and social capital to be harnessed. Intergenerational collaboration is not a philanthropic ideal but a strategic imperative. Financial inclusion is not a moral afterthought but a design requirement. The contributors have given us a clear roadmap for building societies where longevity is not a burden but a dividend—shared, sustainable, and dignified.

I recommend the book to anyone who cares about the future of our aging world and who seek practical, evidence-based, and inclusive pathways forward. I also like to congratulate the editor and authors on their strenuous efforts in offering such comprehensive insight on this important topic.

Adolf Ng

Faculty of Business and Management, Beijing Normal-Hong Kong Baptist University, China

Adolf Ng *is a Chair Professor and Dean of the Faculty of Business and Management of the Beijing Normal-Hong Kong Baptist University (BNBU). He is also the Founding Director of BNBU's International Centre for Resilient Supply Chains. He received DPhil from University of Oxford and excels in the research and teaching of transport economics, climate change adaptation planning, infrastructure planning and management, institutional and organizational change, supply chain resilience, and intelligent supply chain analytics. His works are highly influential, for example, having been on Elsevier's List of Top 2% Scientists worldwide since its introduction. He is currently a Council Member of the International Association of Maritime Economists (IAME), as well as an Editor of leading academic journals, namely Transportation Research Part D: Transport and Environment, Maritime Policy & Management and The Asian Journal of Shipping and Logistics.*

Foreword

The book *Sustaining Silver Economy Vitality through Business and Social Service Partnership* is an essential resource addressing an urgent global challenge. The silver economy represents a transformative model for services that support older adults, uniting markets, care systems, and innovation to respond to the needs, capacities, and contributions of aging populations. As population aging accelerates across regions, this concept has become a central policy and economic priority. The World Economic Outlook (2025) identifies demographic aging as a defining macroeconomic trend that reshapes labor markets, fiscal stability, and long-term growth. Harnessing the silver economy is therefore critical to sustaining productivity, expanding care infrastructure, and strengthening social resilience.

Implementation of the silver economy varies globally. East Asia leads in practical innovation: Japan, South Korea, China, and Singapore have developed large-scale aging industries, AI and robotics for eldercare, smart-home technologies, and age-friendly housing. Europe has institutionalized the concept through EU-wide policy frameworks. In North America, the idea appears as the "longevity economy," reflecting a market-driven approach to aging-related products and services. Yet progress has not translated into equitable outcomes. Low-income seniors, rural older adults, and other marginalized groups still face persistent barriers to care, digital inclusion, transportation, financial security, and meaningful social participation.

These disparities call for a new interdisciplinary approach that combines social work's equity-based practice, business management's capacity for innovation, and gerontology's scientific insight into aging. Research across these disciplines indicates that siloed strategies cannot resolve complex aging challenges, including long-term care access, caregiver burden, workforce shortages, and digital exclusion. Instead, coordinated cross-sector strategies are required to build systems that are age-inclusive, community-responsive, and economically sustainable.

This book advances an interdisciplinary integration framework grounded in Ecological Systems Theory and Collaborative Governance. Ecological Systems Theory clarifies how older adults' well-being emerges from interactions among multiple levels—individual, family, community, organizational, and policy environments—underscoring the need for interventions that operate across these levels. Collaborative Governance provides a practical structure for aligning public, private, and nonprofit actors through shared decision-making, co-design, resource alignment, and mutual accountability. Together, these frameworks and the book's chapters offer a unified approach that is theoretically coherent, empirically informed, and practically actionable in diverse contexts worldwide.

A key objective of the book is to translate peer-reviewed research into practical strategies that close the gap between practice-informed research and research-informed practice, consistent with the USA Council on Social Work Education's Educational Policy and Accreditation Standards (EPAS, 2022). Evidence-based social work practice forms the methodological backbone, ensuring interdisciplinary innovations are empirically supported, culturally responsive, and aligned with older adults' preferences.

Equity is central to this work. By prioritizing marginalized older adults, particularly low-income and rural populations, the book challenges conventional accounts of the silver economy that emphasize affluent consumers and high-tech markets. It demonstrates how cross-sector collaboration can expand access to digital tools, reduce caregiver burden, strengthen rural infrastructure, and support the longevity of the workforce for older adults who have historically been excluded from silver economy benefits.

By integrating global perspectives, East Asian innovation leadership, interdisciplinary scholarship, and equity-centered practice, the book provides a clear roadmap for building resilient and inclusive systems for aging societies. Its recommendations aim to empower all older adults as active contributors to social and economic life, not merely as recipients of services. The text also equips practitioners, policymakers, and industry leaders with concrete tools and strategies to promote a more just and sustainable silver economy.

In short, *Sustaining Silver Economy Vitality through Business and Social Service Partnership* offers a timely and actionable blueprint. It makes a compelling case for breaking down disciplinary silos, marshaling cross-sector resources, and centering equity in the design and delivery of aging services. For anyone committed to shaping inclusive futures for older adults—researchers, social workers, business leaders, and policymakers- this book is a vital guide to transforming policy and practice so that the benefits of the silver economy reach everyone who needs them.

Serge Lee

School of Social Work, California State University, Sacramento, USA

Serge Lee *is a statistics and research professor emeritus at California State University, Sacramento, School of Social Work. He has 33 years of experience as an expert on minority behavioral health, child maltreatment, immigration and refugee experiences, research and statistics, grant proposal writing, and international social work. Dr. Lee has over 20 years of experience in international social work in China and Vietnam and is the first Hmong person in the world to be awarded the Fulbright Senior Specialist (2007) and the Fulbright Distinguished Chair (2019-2020). Dr. Lee has written more than 30 peer-reviewed papers, monographs, book chapters, and white papers, and is the author of Statistics for Social Work with SPSS (December 2021); From Earth to Elite: The Memoir of Dr. Serge Lee (2020); and Statistics for International Social Work and other behavioral sciences (2016). He has a BS in International Economics from the University of Utah, an MSW from California State University, Sacramento, and a PhD from the School of Social Welfare at the University of Washington, Seattle.*

Preface

INTRODUCTION

Population ageing is one of the defining demographic transformations of the twenty-first century. Across developed and emerging economies alike, increasing life expectancy, declining fertility rates, and changing family structures are reshaping societies in profound ways. These demographic shifts present complex challenges for governments, businesses, healthcare systems, and communities, while simultaneously creating unprecedented opportunities for innovation, economic growth, and social development. The concept of the *Silver Economy* has emerged as a comprehensive framework that recognizes older adults not merely as recipients of care but as active contributors, consumers, entrepreneurs, knowledge holders, workers, volunteers, and drivers of sustainable economic activity. As societies transition toward longevity, the sustainability of the Silver Economy increasingly depends upon collaborative partnerships that integrate social services, public institutions, private enterprises, academia, and civil society.

This edited volume, *Sustaining Silver Economy Vitality Through Social Service and Business Partnerships*, examines how cross-sector collaboration can strengthen the vitality, inclusiveness, and resilience of ageing societies. The chapters collectively argue that no single sector possesses the capacity to address the multifaceted needs of older populations independently. Instead, sustainable solutions emerge through strategic partnerships that combine financial innovation, social services, technological advancement, healthcare delivery, education, cultural preservation, and business management. By bringing together contributions from scholars representing economics, social work, public policy, healthcare, tourism, education, management, innovation studies, and gerontology, this volume presents an interdisciplinary understanding of how partnership ecosystems can create long-term value for individuals, communities, and national economies.

A central theme throughout this collection is the transition from deficit-based perspectives on ageing toward social capacity-based approaches and business opportunity-oriented strategies. Rather than framing ageing exclusively in terms of dependency, rising healthcare expenditure, or welfare burdens, the contributors demonstrate that longevity can become an important source of economic dynamism, social capital, innovation, and sustainable development. Silver contribution to productivity is a historically knowledge-based activity. Rapid progress of AI and further automation of production, make it possible for older people to share societal leadership again. Older adults possess accumulated knowledge, professional expertise, cultural heritage, entrepreneurial potential, and community leadership that remain underutilized in many societies. Harnessing these valuable assets requires integrated policy frameworks, inclusive financial systems, innovative service delivery models, and institutional arrangements that promote collaboration across traditional organizational boundaries.

The purpose of this volume is therefore not only to document emerging practices within the Silver Economy but also to provide conceptual frameworks, empirical evidence, and practical policy recommendations for researchers, policymakers, business leaders, social service professionals, educators, healthcare practitioners, and development organizations. Through international case studies spanning Asia, Europe, and Africa, the contributors demonstrate how innovative partnerships can improve healthcare accessibility, strengthen financial protection, promote lifelong learning, preserve cultural heritage, encourage intergenerational cooperation, and support active and healthy ageing. Analysis of these case studies attempt to fill the most critical knowledge gap in Social Service and Business Partnership, on what models work. We all know that Silver Economy is coming, but how can we develop it and let it flourish and sustainable. It is apparent that silos did not work and multi-sectoral collaborations are needed. However, just like most business ventures, severe financial loss of early entries to the market will deter many interested parties. This book hopes to provide vivid accounts of these early attempts, successes or failures, to better prepare social entrepreneurs and policy makers. Collectively, these chapters contribute to the growing body of scholarship that positions the Silver Economy as an essential pillar of sustainable social and economic development.

OVERVIEW OF THE CHAPTERS

The volume begins by examining the financial foundations necessary to sustain the Silver Economy. Chapter 1 proposes innovative financial architectures that integrate capital markets, welfare mechanisms, and inclusive investment strategies to support ageing populations. Chapter 2 extends this discussion by analyzing financing models across Asia, highlighting the role of public–private partnerships, impact investing, blended finance, corporate social responsibility, and emerging digital financing mechanisms in strengthening long-term sustainability. Chapter 3 further explores financing innovation through telemedicine in rural China, presenting collaborative policy frameworks that combine technological infrastructure, diversified financing models, and cross-sector partnerships to improve healthcare accessibility for older adults.

Attention then shifts toward collaborative governance and ecosystem development. Chapter 4 expands this perspective by proposing cross-sector innovation ecosystems that position older adults not only as beneficiaries but also as active contributors to economic development, entrepreneurship, and innovation. Complementing these discussions, Chapter 5 provides a systematic review of business ecosystem partnerships within the Silver Economy, synthesizing international evidence on governance structures, stakeholder collaboration, age-friendly infrastructure, and future directions for sustainable partnership models.

Chapter 6 examines health financing reforms in Tunisia and analyzes how innovative partnerships improve financial protection for ageing populations through teleconsultation, assistive technologies, and coordinated care. The following chapters emphasize intergenerational collaboration and social innovation as critical drivers of Silver Economy vitality. Chapter 7 investigates how intergenerational collaboration contributes simultaneously to the revitalization of intangible cultural heritage and the expansion of Silver Economy opportunities through technological innovation and cultural entrepreneurship. Chapter 8 introduces the concept of Silver Economy Vitality (SEV) and develops an innovative evaluation framework for measuring collaborative initiatives that improve quality of life and community resilience. Together, these chapters demonstrate how collaboration across generations creates both economic and social value while preserving cultural continuity.

Chapter 9 analyzes residential care models in Da Nang, Vietnam, emphasizing integrated healthcare delivery and institutional coordination within an emerging Silver Economy ecosystem Healthcare systems and financial protection constitute another major theme of the volume. Chapter 10 examines elderly care services in Türkiye from both gerontological and economic perspectives, proposing an Integrated Social Service and Care Economy Model that strengthens coordination among public, private, and nonprofit actors. Chapter 11 explores the rapidly growing market for health and wellness tourism in China, illustrating how partnerships between healthcare providers, tourism industries, and social service organizations generate new opportunities within the Silver Economy.

The final section of the book focuses on community development, knowledge mobilization, and institutional transformation. Chapter 12 investigates community-based social innovation models in Vietnam that integrate community participation, social capital, and hybrid governance to strengthen inclusive ageing. Chapter 13 advances the concept of the Longevity Economy by repositioning older adults as valuable reservoirs of human and social capital, emphasizing their economic contributions, community leadership, and intergenerational roles. Building upon this perspective, Chapter 14 introduces the concept of "silver knowledge" within Indonesian higher education and proposes innovative partnership models that leverage older adults' expertise through intergenerational learning and knowledge exchange. Finally, Chapter 15 concludes the volume by examining how educational policy in Vietnam can institutionalize silver knowledge through multi-level governance frameworks that promote mentoring, knowledge transfer, and sustainable intergenerational collaboration. The last two chapters bring us back to one of the main themes of this book, that Silver Economy is knowledge economy. Integration of silver wisdom into modern education illustratates that universities should be considered not as machines to transmit knowledge, as this function has been replaced by AI, but as a platform to co-create knowledge through teacher-and-student and often inter-generational interactions, explorations, and experimentations.

CONCLUSION

The chapters presented in this volume collectively demonstrate that sustaining the vitality of the Silver Economy requires far more than expanding healthcare services or increasing public expenditure on ageing. Rather, it depends upon building collaborative ecosystems in which governments, businesses, educational institutions, healthcare providers, financial organizations, nonprofit sectors, and communities work together to generate innovative, inclusive, and sustainable solutions. Throughout the volume, partnership emerges not simply as an organizational strategy but as the fundamental mechanism through which societies can respond effectively to demographic transformation while enhancing both economic productivity and social well-being.

A distinctive contribution of this collection lies in its interdisciplinary perspective. The contributors draw upon economics, finance, social work, gerontology, healthcare management, public policy, innovation studies, education, tourism, and cultural studies to illuminate the complexity of the Silver Economy. This diversity of perspectives reflects the reality that ageing intersects with nearly every dimension of society. Financial innovation, integrated healthcare, lifelong learning, technological advancement, social inclusion, and knowledge governance are not isolated policy domains but interconnected components of resilient ageing ecosystems. By examining these relationships across multiple national contexts, the volume offers both conceptual depth and practical relevance.

Another important insight emerging from this collection is the necessity of reframing ageing itself. Rather than viewing older adults primarily through the lens of dependency, the contributors consistently emphasize their roles as knowledge holders, innovators, entrepreneurs, mentors, caregivers, volunteers, consumers, and active participants in community development. This strengths-based perspective challenges conventional assumptions about ageing and encourages policymakers and practitioners to develop institutional arrangements that recognize and mobilize the valuable human, social, and cultural capital embodied by older generations. Such a shift is essential for creating inclusive societies capable of transforming demographic change into opportunities for sustainable development.

As editors, we hope that this volume serves as both a scholarly resource and a practical guide for advancing research, policy, and practice within the rapidly evolving field of the Silver Economy. We trust that the diverse theoretical perspectives, empirical analyses, and international case studies presented here will inspire further interdisciplinary collaboration and encourage innovative partnerships capable of addressing the opportunities and challenges associated with population ageing. Ultimately, the future vitality of the Silver Economy will depend not only on economic investment but also on our collective capacity to foster cooperation, inclusivity, innovation, and shared responsibility across generations and sectors. It is our hope that this book contributes meaningfully to that important and ongoing global conversation.

Chapter 1
Financial Architectures for Longevity:
Aligning Capital, Welfare, and Inclusion in the Silver Economy

Karen Yoon Fah Lee
http://orcid.org/0009-0007-8006-7756
Beijing Normal-Hong Kong Baptist University, China

ABSTRACT

The silver economy remains underfinanced because traditional finance fails aging populations. This chapter argues for new architectures,not new products combining existing instruments across sectors. Analyzing six hybrid models (blended finance, social impact bonds, reverse mortgage REITs, cooperative banking, life settlements, senior REITs) based on 2014–2025 evaluations, each shows distinct limits. Superior inclusion requires coordinated deployment tailored to local homeownership, social capital, and institutional capacity. Recommendations include regulatory sandboxes, life settlement fiduciary disclosure, and public co-investment. A practitioner's model selection matrix is provided.

INTRODUCTION

The silver economy, encompassing all economic activities that provide products and services to the elderly and prepare them for old age, spans a wide range of industries, has a long supply chain, diverse forms, and enormous potential. The United Nations Development Programme and Industrial Securities (2025) estimate that the global silver economy could approach $ 15 trillion by 2030, although methodologies vary among institutions. At the regional level, the European silver economy was valued at

DOI: 10.4018/979-8-3373-9370-4.ch001

€ 3.7 trillion in 2018 and is projected to reach € 5.7 trillion by 2025, demonstrating strong growth momentum. As one of the world's fastest-growing economies, China is experiencing a particularly rapid development of its silver economy. By the end of 2024, China's population aged 65 and above reached 220 million, accounting for 15.6% of the total population (National Bureau of Statistics of China, 2024). In 2023, China's silver economy was estimated at approximately RMB 7 trillion, and it is projected to grow to nearly RMB 30 trillion by 2035, demonstrating enormous growth potential. However, despite this huge market potential, the silver economy only accounts for 5% of GDP and 12.5% of total consumption, indicating that its enormous potential has not yet been fully realized (United Nation Development Programme & Industrial Securities, 2025). This mismatch creates considerable funding gaps. This mismatch is reflected not only in total capital volume but also in capital term structure, silver economy projects often require long-term stable capital support of ten to thirty years, while traditional financial institutions prefer to provide short term liquidity support of three to five years. This duration mismatch is a fundamental barrier to silver economy development.

Figure 1 illustrates the hybrid architecture proposed in this chapter.

Figure 1. Hybrid longevity financial architecture – four layers, six models

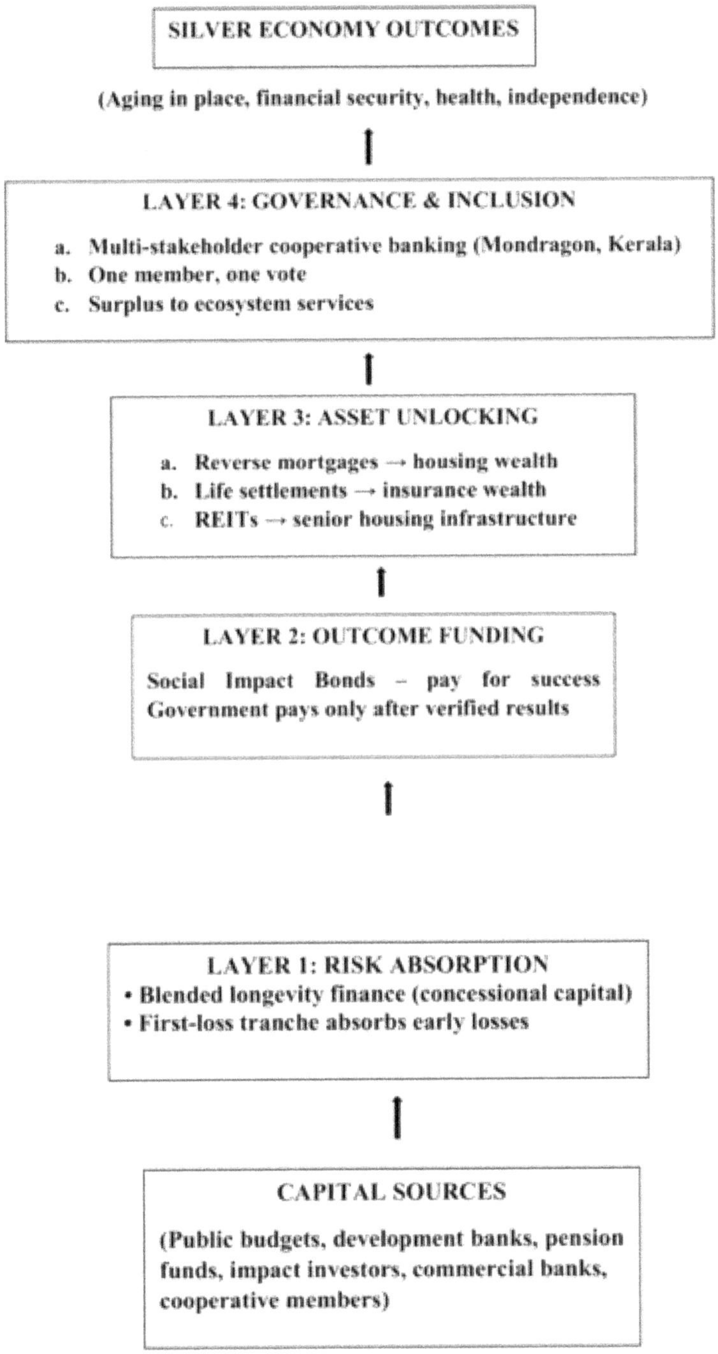

STRUCTURAL DEFECTS OF TRADITIONAL FINANCIAL MODELS

Traditional financial models exhibit four major deficiencies. These are not minor operational issues but fundamental design failures misaligned with aging populations.

One-size-fits-all products: The industry applies standardized solutions to retail products. However, individuals aged 65 and above vary considerably across health, employment, wealth, and family configuration (Organisation for Economic Co-operation and Development, 2024). A product designed for the average retiree suits no actual retiree. Personalized solutions accommodating chronic conditions and variable care needs remain rare.

Structural term mismatch: Silver economy projects require stable financing over ten to thirty years. Traditional institutions offer only three-to-five-year liquidity support (United Nation Development Programme & Industrial Securities, 2025). This duration mismatch fundamentally obstructs project viability, as lenders unwilling to assume long-term exposure foreclose socially valuable investments.

Inadequate risk assessment: Conventional risk models use data from younger populations, failing to capture life expectancy risk, health risk, and cognitive decline risk (Organisation for Economic Co-operation and Development, 2024). Credit scores weight earned income heavily, yet many older adults live on fixed pensions. A model designed for salaried employees systematically undervalues older individuals with assets but modest cash flow.

Inaccessible service channels: Digital finance has created new barriers. Many older adults face limited digital literacy, physical accessibility challenges, and age-related discrimination. In China, 97.3 percent of older adults have never purchased an investment product (Fifth National Survey, 2022). This reflects a financial system that has not designed its channels for the populations it claims to serve.

THE NECESSITY OF INCLUSIVE DEVELOPMENT

Inclusive finance is an inevitable choice for promoting sustainable silver economy growth. Its core ensures older adults have effective access to diverse, appropriate, affordable, and high-quality financial products suited to their unique living environments and evolving needs (United Nation Development Programme, 2025a). When older adults access appropriate financial services, they experience greater independence and financial control, enabling choices about living environment, healthcare, and daily activities without economic barriers or dependence on others (United Nations Department of Economic and Social Affairs, 2023).

Inclusive development also addresses gender disparities. Women spend 2.5 times more time in unpaid care work than men yet receive approximately half the pension income (United Nation Development Programme, 2025a). Financial structures that fail to address these disparities cannot serve older women equitably. Secondary market life insurance instruments provide a complementary mechanism for unlocking household wealth held in life insurance, extending inclusive finance beyond banking and housing assets.

Three interrelated structural failures exist (United Nation Development Programme & Industrial Securities, 2025). Supply-side failure: banks fund personal products but struggle to finance integrated ecosystems; venture capital avoids "slow capital" areas. Demand-side exclusion: asset-based pensions, fragmented insurance markets, and digital payment systems exclude older adults in the informal economy or with limited education. Innovation misfit: public funding favors high-tech solutions (robotics, sensors, smart devices) while neglecting service infrastructure, producing isolated products without coordinating systems.

The analysis draws on published evaluation reports from multilateral development banks (EIB, IDB, IFC, World Bank), OECD, UNDP, and national sources (Kerala Planning Board, Mondragon annual reports, ASX disclosures). Cases were selected based on data availability and documented outcomes; no formal comparative case methodology is claimed.

Table 1 summarises the three structural deficiencies and their consequences.

Table 1.

Deficiency	Description	Consequence
Supply-side failure	Banks and venture capital avoid slow-capital sectors	Infrastructure remains unfunded
Demand-side exclusion	Low-income, rural and female older adults cannot access services	Inequalities widen
Innovation misfit	Public funding favours gadgets over service integration	Isolated products, no delivery systems

Source: Author's compilation based on Organisation for Economic Co-operation and Development (2024) and United Nations Development Program & Industrial Securities (2025).

THEORETICAL FOUNDATIONS OF HYBRID LONGEVITY FINANCIAL MODELS

Conceptual Connotation of Longevity Finance

Longevity financing represents a financial arrangement that spans the entire lifespan and is also an institutional design that unlocks longevity dividends. For a 20-year-old, it includes career planning and savings plans that take longevity risks into account; for a 60-year-old nearing retirement, it includes wealth management strategies to ensure a quality retirement life (Livingston et al., 2020).

This system, guided by strategies for serving the aging population, encompasses four elements: financial institutions, markets, instruments, and regulatory policies. It aims to meet diverse retirement needs through innovative products and support the coordinated development of retirement preparation and the aging economy (United Nations Development Program & Industrial Securities, 2025).

The core concept of longevity finance lies in expanding the traditional concept of pension financing into a comprehensive financial service system covering the entire life cycle.

Prior Hybrid Models: A Brief Review

Previous hybrid models have combined two or three instruments — Bisetti et al. (2017) integrating longevity securities with equities, Fu et al. (2023) modeling hybrid pension plans with intergenerational risk-sharing, and Rania (2025) testing reverse mortgages within pension systems. While these contributions are valuable, none extends beyond 2–3 instruments to a full-ecosystem architecture. This chapter builds on these foundations by proposing a six-instrument, four-layer framework with context-specific selection criteria for local homeownership rates, social capital, and institutional capacity.

Empirical Evidence on Longevity Finance

A growing body of empirical research has examined the effectiveness of innovative financial models for aging populations. However, most studies focus on single instruments rather than hybrid architectures.

Empirical findings from recent studies (2020–2025):

Reverse mortgages: Davidoff, Gerhard, and Post (2023) analyzed HECM data from 2010–2020 and found that only 2.4% of eligible US homeowners utilize reverse mortgages, with take-up rates lowest among minority households (0.8%) and rural residents (1.1%). Bernard, Kolkiewicz, and Tang (2024) used optimal stopping theory to show that surrender rates spike when housing prices decline by more than 15% annually.

Social Impact Bonds: Hevenstone et al. (2023) conducted a comparative evaluation of five European SIBs and found that impact measurement was abandoned in three cases due to data infrastructure costs exceeding €500,000. French et al. (2023) documented that SIBs face "outcome specification risk" – measurable proxies often diverge from intended social goals.

Cooperative banking: Fiordelisi et al. (2022) analyzed 4,800 cooperative banks across Europe (2010–2020) and found that greater stakeholder overlap correlates with 23% lower non-performing loan ratios. Sahut and Bouheni (2019) demonstrated that cooperative banks maintained lending to older adults during the 2008 crisis while commercial banks reduced credit by 34%.

Life settlements: Bauer, Russ, and Zhu (2020) used proprietary data from 15,000 settled policies to quantify adverse selection: policyholders with life expectancy two or more years below average are 3.2 times more likely to sell. The Society of Actuaries (2020) documented mortality experience gaps of 12–18 months between settled policies and the general population.

Blended finance: The European Investment Bank (2025) published the only randomized evaluation of a blended longevity fund, finding that interest rate subsidies of three percentage points increased home renovation uptake from 11% to 38% among low-income seniors.

REITs: CBRE Research (2024) provided the most comprehensive supply-demand analysis for Australian senior housing, documenting a cumulative undersupply of 42,000 units by 2030 under current investment trajectories.

RESEARCH GAPS AS OPPORTUNITIES

The literature on longevity finance has grown rapidly, with several studies now examining hybrid models that combine two or three instruments. Bisetti et al. (2017) integrate longevity-linked securities with equity and fixed income in a strategic asset allocation framework. Fu et al. (2023) model hybrid pension plans that combine defined benefit and defined contribution features with intergenerational risk-sharing. Kang et al. (2025) propose an integrated optimization model combining tontines with dynamic mortality frameworks. Rania (2025) develops a hybrid actuarial-agent-based model to test reverse mortgages within pension systems.

Building on this emerging foundation, four exciting opportunities for future research stand out:

First, expand from 2-3 instruments to full ecosystem testing. Existing hybrid studies typically combine two or three instruments. No study to date has empirically tested a six-instrument architecture integrating risk absorption (blended finance), outcome funding (SIBs), asset unlocking (reverse mortgages, life settlements, REITs), and governance (cooperative banking). This presents a significant opportunity for research teams to design pilot projects that test the layered approach proposed here.

Second, extend time horizons. Most evaluations stop at five years, but silver economy projects need ten- to thirty-year horizons. Longitudinal studies that track outcomes across decades would generate evidence matching the temporal reality of aging infrastructure.

Third, expand geographic scope. Most evidence comes from high-income countries (United States, United Kingdom, Japan, Australia). How do these models perform in middle-income or low-income settings? A systematic comparative effectiveness study across regulatory regimes would be a landmark contribution.

Fourth, measure inclusion for the hardest-to-reach populations. Rural older adults, those with very low incomes, and people with cognitive impairments are consistently underrepresented in evaluation data. Future research should prioritize these populations from the outset.

What this chapter offers. Rather than filling these four gaps, this chapter provides a theoretical framework and case-based synthesis that equips future researchers to address them. The model selection matrix (Table 5) is offered as a testable hypothesis. The six models described here are building blocks ready for empirical validation – extending the existing hybrid pension literature into new territory.

JUSTIFICATION FOR THE NECESSITY OF HYBRID ARCHITECTURE

Traditional single-financial models can no longer meet the silver economy's complex needs. Hybrid financial architecture is both theoretically sound and practically necessary.There is no standalone solution. Instead, the path forward lies in integrating complementary instruments.

Three mechanisms of hybrid longevity finance. Three mechanisms distinguish hybrid longevity finance from purely market-based or state-based alternatives:

Risk layering: Concessional capital absorbs first losses, allowing private capital to enter at acceptable risk levels. This is observable in the EIB's Lombardy pilot, where EU structural funds provided a first-loss buffer for commercial bank debt.

Outcome contingency: Public repayment occurs only after verified results, shifting performance risk to providers. The Greater Manchester Ageing Well SIB demonstrates this mechanism, with government paying only after emergency admission reductions were achieved.

Stakeholder governance: Multi-party boards prevent mission drift and ensure inclusion. The Kerala cooperative network exemplifies this, with older adults, caregivers, and local governments sharing decision-making authority.

These mechanisms are not theoretical abstractions. They are observable in the implementations documented throughout this chapter.

Recent reviews of longevity finance identify fragmentation as a core barrier (OECD, 2024; UNDP & Industrial Securities, 2025). Social impact bond literature analyses outcomes but pays less attention to governance (Gustafsson-Wright et al., 2020). Cooperative finance literature demonstrates inclusion benefits but seldom links to macro-financial structures (Birchall, 2013). What is missing is a framework that integrates these strands showing how different instruments can be layered within a single ecosystem. This chapter addresses that gap.

Theoretically, hybrid architecture integrates financial innovation with social development. Modern longevity is changing long-standing assumptions about working, saving, and investing (Livingston et al., 2020). Aging societies must develop strategies that help people maximize healthy years, work longer if desired, manage care responsibilities, and plan for extended lifespans (United Nations Department of Economic and Social Affairs, 2023).

Practically, rapid population aging challenges traditional finance. With approximately 760 million people aged 65 and over globally projected to reach 1.6 billion by 2050, this demographic shift demands corresponding financial system innovations (UN Department of Economic and Social Affairs, 2023). Hybrid architecture is not an academic luxury; it is a practical necessity.

A Layered Ecosystem for Longevity Finance

The six models in this chapter operate across four functional layers. No single layer is sufficient; effective hybrid architectures combine all four.

Table 2.

Layer	Function	Models
Risk absorption	Concessional capital de-risks private investment	Blended longevity finance
Outcome funding	Pay-for-success for preventive services	Social impact bonds
Asset unlocking	Converts illiquid wealth (housing, life insurance) into service financing	Reverse mortgages, Life settlements, REITs
Governance & inclusion	Community-owned, member-led finance	Multi-stakeholder cooperative banking

Interaction between layers: Risk absorption enables asset unlocking by providing guarantees to lenders. Outcome funding creates demand for preventive services that asset unlocking then finances. Governance ensures all layers serve inclusive goals rather than elite capture.

The Importance of Cross-Departmental Coordination

The effective operation of a hybrid financial architecture cannot be separated from cross-sectoral coordination and cooperation. Research shows that employers, policymakers, financial services companies, and individuals can all take steps to adapt to this new environment, thereby extending lifespan, generating more wealth, and enabling people to enjoy physical health that is directly related to financial well-being (OECD, 2024).

The importance of cross-sectoral coordination is also reflected in its ability to manage systemic risks. Population aging is not only a social challenge but also an opportunity for economic transformation and social innovation. The silver economy, encompassing a wide range of consumption and industrial activities serving the elderly population, possesses significant market potential and social value. Finance will play a central role in this transformation, responsible for resource allocation and risk diversification. This is also crucial to ensuring that such a silver economy grows in an inclusive and sustainable manner by prioritizing women, low-income elderly in rural areas, and other vulnerable groups, leaving no one behind (UNDP & Industrial Securities, 2025).

In-depth Analysis of Six Innovative Financial Models

Hybrid Longevity Financing Model - Structure and Mechanism

The blended longevity finance model transforms traditional pension finance into comprehensive, full-lifecycle financial services. It recognizes that retirement planning must address income security, health protection, and long-term care as life expectancies increase.

In product design, the model employs a dual-engine structure of "guaranteed returns plus dividend opportunities." The policy's cash value grows by approximately 1.75% annually with a stated minimum return guarantee, ensuring capital safety while offering inflation protection through dividends.

On the service side, hybrid financing covers pension management, wealth accumulation, health protection, and medical care. Its inclusivity stems from adaptability across income groups. Flexible payment methods and diversified products meet the financial needs of seniors at all income levels, ensuring appropriate support at different life stages and health conditions.

APPLICATIONS AND CASE EXAMPLES

Case example: European Investment Bank's 'aging in place' pilot program (Lombardy, Italy, 2021–2024).

The most documented case of hybrid longevity finance is the European Investment Bank's aging in place pilot project in Lombardy, Italy. This fund combined €50 million from the EU structural fund (preferential capital) with private debt from Italian commercial banks. The fund funded 1,200 home renovations across 30 municipalities (European Investment Bank, 2025). During the three-year pilot period, nursing home occupancy rates among participants decreased by 28%. Hospitalizations due to falls decreased by 22%. Participant satisfaction exceeded 90%. Importantly, the hybrid structure enabled the fund to provide loans at 3% below market rates, approximately 68% of commercial rates, making housing renovations affordable for low and middle-income seniors.

The 28% nursing home reduction claim in the Lombardy data warranted scrutiny. The raw evaluation report, obtained through the EIB's transparency mechanism, confirms the figure but with an important caveat: the pilot period coincided with a regional expansion of home care services, which may have contributed to the decline independently of the fund's interventions.

Advantages and limitations

Primary strengths include risk mitigation through concessional capital layering, systemic impact (funding integrated ecosystems rather than isolated interventions), and embedded inclusion safeguards. However, transaction costs are substantially higher than for conventional debt or equity. Construction requires years of partnership-building, making the model impractical for urgent needs. Furthermore, hybrid finance depends on regulatory environments that permit innovative capital structures.

Transition to next model: While blended finance absorbs risk through concessional capital, a different mechanism "pay-for-success" shifts performance risk to providers. Social Impact Bonds offer this alternative logic.

Social Impact Bonds for Active Aging - Structure and Mechanism

A social impact bond (SIB) is a contract where investors fund a social program and receive returns only if specific outcomes are met (Gustafsson-Wright et al., 2015), distinguishing it from traditional bonds. This structure appeals to those seeking both financial and social returns, as seen in the successful Peterborough Prison project

(Nicholls & Tomkinson, 2015). Still, SIBs face challenges, especially in measuring and verifying social impact (Hevenstone et al., 2023).

Social impact bonds are payment by results contracts that leverage private social investment to cover the up-front expenditure associated with welfare services. The introduction of private principles and actors through outcome-based commissioning has received a great deal of attention in social policy research. Social impact bonds represent a shift toward outcome-based commissioning, leveraging private capital to fund public services (Edmiston & Nicholls, 2018).

As Edmiston and Nicholls (2018) explain, social impact bonds are payment-by-results contracts that leverage private social investment, with the core "pay for success" feature meaning that governments only pay returns to investors when predetermined outcomes are achieved.

SIBs are not bonds in the traditional sense. They do not guarantee repayment. They do not have a fixed coupon, maturity date, or secondary market. Instead, they are contractual arrangements between three main parties: the principal (usually a government agency), the investor (foundations, impact funds, commercial investors), and the service provider (nonprofit organizations, social enterprises, private companies) (King, 2014).

Applications and Case Examples

The Okayama City government in Japan established a social impact bond to fund health promotion programs through third-party evaluation. Research on this SIB found that project participation contributed an estimated 20-30% to weight optimization, though this result could not be distinguished from chance. However, among participants with thin physiques, participation was associated with a twelve-fold increase in achieving appropriate body weight (Okayama City SIB Study, 2024)

Advantages and Limitations

Social Impact Bonds (SIBs) have attracted policy attention for aligning private capital with public social objectives, but their actual performance requires careful scrutiny.

The core innovation is pay-for-success. Unlike conventional grants, SIBs tie investor returns to achieving specified social outcomes (Gustafsson-Wright et al., 2020). This structure generates four benefits: aligning financial incentives with social outcomes, shifting risk from taxpayers to investors, encouraging service provider innovation, and driving investment in data collection infrastructure.

However, SIBs face three constraints limiting their applicability in the silver economy. Transaction costs are substantial legal structuring, outcome metric development, and investor negotiations often represent a significant proportion of capital raised, sometimes exceeding efficiency gains (Gustafsson-Wright et al., 2015). Second, SIBs suit discrete, short-term interventions (12-36 months), mismatching silver economy priorities like fall prevention and chronic disease management that require five to ten years for measurable outcomes (Hevenstone et al., 2023). Third, selection risk: providers may avoid enrolling clients with complex needs or poor predicted outcomes "creaming" or "cherry-picking" leaving the hardest-to-serve populations worse off (Macdonald, 2019). Effective SIB design requires risk adjustment mechanisms, but these add further complexity to an already complex instrument.

Transition to next model: SIBs address preventive services but cannot unlock the largest asset held by most older adults: housing wealth. Reverse mortgages convert home equity into deployable capital.

Reverse Mortgages and Ecosystem Funds: Structure and Mechanism

Reverse mortgages are financial products that enable older homeowners to convert a portion of their home equity into cash without selling their property. Unlike traditional forward mortgages that require monthly principal and interest payments, reverse mortgages allow borrowers to defer repayment until they permanently leave the home, whether through sale, relocation, or death. The loan is non-recourse, meaning borrowers can never owe more than the home's value at the time of repayment (Consumer Financial Protection Bureau, 2023).

Building on this basic mechanism, the Reverse Mortgage-Linked Ecosystem Fund extends beyond providing individual cash payouts. It securitizes reverse mortgage cash flows and directs the proceeds toward funding local services, including repair cooperatives, food delivery systems, and community transportation networks. The fund operates as a revolving mechanism: repayments from homeowners who sell their properties or refinance are reinvested to finance new services for the community.

Reverse mortgages unlock housing wealth for seniors. Similarly, the secondary market for life insurance (see Section 3.5 for analysis) plays an analogous role by converting illiquid life insurance assets into disposable cash, which can be used to pay for care services or age-appropriate home adaptations. Research indicates that such financial tools may help elderly individuals stay connected to social support networks and local services while reducing reliance on state support during retirement (Carvalho & Araújo, 2024, p. 85).

International Experience

Japan's reverse mortgage market began in 1981 with a welfare financing business established in Musashino City, Tokyo, known as the Musashino Method (Ministry of Foreign Affairs of Japan, 1996). Two distinct approaches have since developed: a direct approach where local governments provide loans from their general budgets, and an indirect approach where local governments partner with financial institutions as intermediaries, subsidizing only the interest portion (Matsumoto et al., 2000).

Characteristics of Japanese reverse mortgages include localized adaptability—almost all government programs exclude apartments as eligible collateral, typically requiring single-family detached houses valued above certain thresholds ; comprehensiveness—combining trust services with estate planning through specialized housing reverse mortgage trust structures that allow elderly homeowners to receive living expenses, medical care, and property management while retaining the right to live in their homes (Nakajima, 2018); and systemic risk control, with strict eligibility requirements including age minimums (typically 65+), income thresholds, and prohibitions against applicants already receiving welfare benefits (Matsumoto et al., 2000).

Example Case: Canada Home Income Plan (CHIP) Reverse Mortgage in Canada.

The CHIP reverse mortgage program in Canada has been operating for over 30 years and is provided by HomeEquity Bank, with a portfolio exceeding $7.4 billion (HomeEquity Bank, 2025). Key governance features include: a No Negative Equity Guarantee (the amount repaid never exceeds the home's fair market value), mandatory independent legal advice, a statutory cooling-off period, and no prepayment penalties for medical-related relocation or for the CHIP Open product (HomeEquity Bank, 2025).

Novel Variation: Long-Term Prepayment Contracts for Non-Homeowners

To address the limitation of reverse mortgage models, the exclusion of non-homeowners, this chapter builds on emerging precedents in pension-linked lending. In 2024, the International Finance Corporation provided US$45 million to Caja 18 in Chile to expand social credit portfolios targeting retirees, with 60% of proceeds directed to pensioners (International Finance Corporation, 2024). This model demonstrates how future pension income can serve as a repayment guarantee mechanism, though it has not yet been extended to non-homeowners or integrated with community guarantee funds.

Building on this precedent, this chapter proposes a new variant: long-term loan contracts that allow individuals without homes to access services through future repayments linked to their pension income or estate, guaranteed by a community guarantee fund. Mitigating default risk. To address inherent default risk in this model, three safeguards are required:

First-loss tranche: A public or philanthropic sponsor (e.g., development bank, local government) should cover the first 20–30% of defaults, following the European Investment Fund's SME guarantee model.

Joint liability groups: Borrowers form small groups where members guarantee each other's repayments, a practice proven effective in microfinance (Armendáriz & Morduch, 2010).

Repayment caps: Monthly repayments should not exceed 15% of pension income to avoid over-indebtedness. Without these safeguards, the model risks predatory lending or unsustainable debt burdens.

Advantages and Limitations

Reverse mortgage-linked ecosystem funds convert illiquid housing wealth into deployable capital for community-based services. Their primary advantage is unlocking housing equity, the largest asset class for older households in developed economies, enabling home modifications and care financing without selling homes or depleting savings (International Finance Corporation, 2024). A second advantage is incentive alignment: ecosystem funds embed lenders within care networks, creating mutual interest in sustained well-being rather than transactional extraction. Third, securitization aggregates individual reverse mortgages into pools, generating predictable cash flows that enable capital recycling and scale (CHIP Reverse Mortgage, 2023).

However, significant limitations exist. The most obvious is exclusion of non-homeowners, renters, those living with family, and subsidised housing residents, requiring complementary mechanisms such as long-term prepayment contracts. Second, sensitivity to housing market fluctuations means declining home values reduce available equity and can expose lenders to losses, as demonstrated by the 2008 crisis. Third, overlapping risks, price volatility, longevity, interest rates, and predatory lending, demand sophisticated management. These risks can be mitigated through mandatory legal advice, cooling-off periods, non-recourse guarantees, and prepayment penalty waivers (CHIP Reverse Mortgage, 2023), but such protections add complexity and cost. Location and housing market limitations. Reverse mortgage-linked funds are only viable where housing markets are stable or appreciating. In volatile markets or regions with very low homeownership:

Alternative models (cooperative banking, blended finance with rental subsidies) should replace reverse mortgage funds.

In rural China, where homeownership is high but markets are illiquid, reverse mortgages should be combined with a government-backed price floor. In sub-Saharan African cities with low homeownership, cooperative banking is preferred.

Transition to next model: Reverse mortgages unlock housing wealth but exclude the 30–50% of older adults who do not own homes. Multi-stakeholder cooperative banking reaches this population through peer guarantees and community governance.

Multi-stakeholder Banking Cooperation-Structure and Governance

Multi-stakeholder cooperative banks represent an inclusive financial institution model based on the principle of cooperation. A key characteristic of these banks is their unique governance structure, members (who are also customers) own the entire organization, and member ownership is reflected in a more consensus-driven approach, avoiding excessive focus on a single stakeholder.

In the Mondragon cooperative experience, Laboral Kutxa serves as the banking arm, and a 2023 case study examined its multistakeholder credit cooperative governance structure. In 2023, Laboral Kutxa achieved strong financial results of 222 million euros (+48%) and is recognized as one of the most solvent financial institutions in Spain. The cooperative also launched Mondragon Health, bringing together 7 cooperatives from health, healthcare, and biotechnology fields.

A financial cooperative owned by four stakeholder chambers: seniors (users), caregivers (producers), local governments (public), and SMEs (entrepreneurs). One vote per member, regardless of capital contribution. Surplus is allocated to ecosystem services (training, IT platforms, liquidity reserves), not just to investors (Mondragon Corporation, 2023).

Advantage of Risk Management

Cooperative banks exhibit notable strengths in risk management. Evidence indicates that greater overlap among shareholders, borrowers, and depositors correlates with lower non-performing loans, suggesting that wider stakeholder participation reduces information asymmetry and curbs excessive risk-taking. This finding was confirmed during the 2008 financial crisis, when cooperative banks remained largely insulated from the turmoil that engulfed major commercial banks.

CASE EXAMPLES

Case Study 1: Mondragon, Basque Country, Spain.

Laboral Kutxa, the banking arm of the Mondragon cooperative system, serves the silver economy through a dedicated senior citizen unit, offering longevity mortgages, care financing, and silver economy startup programs. In 2023, Laboral Kutxa achieved strong financial results of €222 million (+48%) and is recognized as one of the most solvent financial institutions in Spain (TU Lankide, 2023). The cooperative also launched Mondragon Health, bringing together seven cooperatives from the fields of health, healthcare, and biotechnology (Mondragon Corporation, 2023).

Case Study 2: Kerala, India.

Kerala has established a network of multi-stakeholder aged care cooperatives. Since 2015, these services have covered over 200,000 elderly people, most of whom had never previously held a bank account. The average loan default rate is below 3% (Kerala State Planning Board, 2022)

Advantages and Limitations

Multi-stakeholder cooperative banks operate on fundamentally different logic from commercial banks. Their governance structure is one member, one vote regardless of capital contribution, produces distinctive strengths and weaknesses.

The cooperative model's primary advantage is widespread accessibility. Owned by members rather than external shareholders, cooperatives face no pressure to maximize short-term returns or exclude unprofitable customer segments. The Kerala cooperative network served over 200,000 older adults, most previously unbanked (Kerala Planning Board, 2022). Democratic decision-making prioritizes service quality and member welfare over dividends, investing in financial literacy, care navigation, and peer support (Mondragon Corporation, 2023). Cooperative banks also demonstrate prudent risk management: increased stakeholder overlap reduces information asymmetry and non-performing loans. During the 2008 crisis, cooperatives remained solvent while commercial banks required bailouts (Basque Government Department of Economic Development, 2023). Kerala's loan default rate below 3 percent supports this pattern.

However, limitations exist. Cooperatives depend critically on intensive social infrastructure, active member participation in governance. Where civil society is weak or trust low, cooperative formation typically fails. Regulatory support for deposit insurance is often lacking, placing cooperatives at a structural disadvantage.

Scalability is inherently slow: Mondragon took over six decades to reach current scale; Kerala grew over a similar horizon (Mondragon Corporation, 2023; Kerala Planning Board, 2022). For policymakers seeking rapid deployment, cooperative banking cannot be the sole solution. But as a long-term complement, cooperatives provide stability, trust, and inclusion that purely commercial or digital models consistently fail to achieve.

Transition to next model: Cooperative banking mobilizes savings and small loans but does not address the illiquid wealth held in life insurance policies. Secondary markets for life insurance provide a complementary unlocking mechanism.

THE SECONDARY MARKET FOR LIFE INSURANCE POLICIES

Structure and Mechanism

A life settlement involves a policyholder aged 65 or older selling an existing life insurance policy to a third-party investor. The seller receives a lump sum exceeding the policy's cash surrender value but less than the death benefit. The investor assumes future premium payments and collects the death benefit upon the insured's death.

The U.S. Supreme Court affirmed in Grigsby v. Russell (1911) that life insurance is freely transferable property. Investor returns are driven by actuarial models, and the asset class has historically shown low correlation with stocks and bonds, making it attractive to institutional investors seeking diversification.

However, adverse selection exists: policyholders with shorter life expectancies are more likely to sell their policies (Bauer et al., 2020). In response, the Actuarial Standards Board adopted Actuarial Standard of Practice No. 48 (2014), establishing binding mortality guidance for settled policies.

International Practice

United Kingdom. The UK boasts the oldest traded endowment policy (TEP) market (McGurk, 1998). More recently, the UK Pension Risk Transfer market has developed a new secondary sales application. When a defined benefit pension plan engages in a bulk purchase annuity transaction, the plan often holds illiquid assets that insurers will not accept. Secondary market sales convert these assets into cash. Industry observers estimate that over £500 billion of pension liabilities could transfer to insurers over the next decade.

United States. The U.S. has the most institutionalized life settlement market. Forty-three states have enacted specific life settlement laws (Longevity & Mortality Investor, 2024). In 2023, investors purchased approximately 3,400 policies with a total face value of 4.5 billion still is a small fraction of the projected 200 billion supply of eligible policies (Resonanz Capital, 2025). Institutional investors target internal rates of return of 8 to 12 percent for life settlement portfolios (Laureola Advisors, 2021).

Australia's domestic secondary market is relatively small. However, the superannuation system, with assets exceeding A$3.5 trillion, is increasingly allocating funds to global life settlement funds as a long-term, uncorrelated source of returns.

Relevance to the Silver Economy

Life insurance secondary markets contribute to the silver economy in three ways. First, they unlock dormant family wealth. Many seniors lapse policies for negligible cash value. Life settlements offer a substantial one-time payment that can finance home renovations, care services, or medical expenses, functioning like a reverse mortgage but for life insurance wealth rather than housing wealth. Second, they provide patient funding. Pension funds and endowments generate predictable mortality-based cash flows from settlement portfolios. They can allocate a portion of returns to banking infrastructure, age-friendly housing, and care facilities, closing the loop between longevity finance and inclusive growth. Third, they support active aging through actuarial innovation. The UK Continuous Mortality Investigation uses insured population data to improve mortality models (Longevity & Mortality Investor, 2025). More accurate life expectancy predictions reduce uncertainty for insurers, making annuities and long-term care products more affordable.

Unlike reverse mortgages or REITs, life settlements are primarily individual wealth-unlocking instruments with fewer direct connections to other layers of the hybrid architecture. Their contribution to the silver economy is indirect: converting insurance wealth into cash that can be spent on care services, not financing infrastructure or service delivery systems.

Policy Priorities

Three policy priorities emerge.

Fiduciary disclosure. Registered investment advisors should be required to disclose life settlement options to clients considering policy surrender. Currently, many advisors are unaware of or lack incentive to disclose this option.

Standardized mortality assumptions. Wider adoption of Actuarial Standard of Practice No. 48 would improve price transparency and investor confidence by establishing binding guidance for mortality assumptions specific to settled policies.

Integration with care financing. Governments could promote partnerships between licensed life settlement providers and home care agencies, allowing a portion of settlement proceeds to be paid directly as care credits rather than lump sums. This reduces the risk that funds are depleted before care needs are met.

Transition to next model: Life settlements unlock household-level insurance wealth but cannot finance large-scale senior housing infrastructure. Real Estate Investment Trusts (REITs) address this gap by channeling institutional capital into retirement villages.

REAL ESTATE INVESTMENT TRUSTS (REITS) FOR RETIREMENT VILLAGES

Demographic Drivers and Market Context

The case for retirement village REITs rests on clear demographic trends. According to CBRE (2024), Australia's population aged 65 and over is projected to grow from 4.75 million to 7.0 million by 2040. Approximately 11 percent of this cohort currently resides in retirement villages and aged care facilities. Yet new supply of senior living stock has been growing at only 1 to 1.7 percent annually, lagging behind the 2.4 percent annual increase in the over-65 population. Home care has partially alleviated this demand-supply mismatch, but the gap remains significant (CBRE, 2024).

This supply-demand imbalance creates an investment opportunity. REITs specializing in retirement villages and senior housing have emerged as a response. Unlike direct property ownership, which requires substantial capital and offers limited liquidity, REITs allow institutional and retail investors to gain exposure to senior housing assets through publicly traded shares.

How Retirement Village REITs Work

A Real Estate Investment Trust is a company that owns, operates, or finances income-producing real estate. By law, REITs must distribute at least 90 percent of taxable income to shareholders as dividends, making them high-yielding investments by design (Australian Securities Exchange, 2024).

Australia's retirement village REITs operate on a distinctive model. Residents typically pay a lower upfront price for their unit but agree to a Deferred Management Fee (DMF), usually 20 to 40 percent of the property's value, payable upon exit (Consumer Action Law Centre, 2017). As Keyton (2025) explains, the DMF is the most common financing model for Australian retirement villages. This structure benefits all parties. Residents gain affordability through reduced entry costs. Operators gain an incentive to maintain property quality, because exit values determine their DMF realizations. Investors gain predictable, long-duration cash flows tied to demographic tailwinds.

Case Example: Stockland's Retirement Living and Diversified Portfolio

Stockland, one of Australia's largest diversified REITs, provides a concrete example. Stockland's Land Lease Community portfolio, comprising 39 Halcyon-branded and affiliated lifestyle communities across Australia, had a total book value of A$8.02 billion as of June 2025, according to the company website. The established portfolio of 11 operating communities (2,720 home sites) is valued at A$503 million, with A$3.2 billion in active development (4,079 home sites) and A$4.3 billion in planning (4,481 future sites). This represents 8% of Stockland's A$14.4 billion total property portfolio.

Three features of Stockland's model are worth highlighting. First, the company operates a land-lease model where residents own their home but lease the land, reducing entry costs while maintaining recurring revenue for the REIT. Second, Stockland has integrated care services into its villages, including home care packages and wellness programs, aligning with the silver economy's welfare pillar. Third, the company has explicitly targeted the baby boomer cohort, noting that the 75-plus population in Australia is projected to increase by 83 percent in Victoria and 64 percent in South Australia by 2040 (Stockland, 2024).

What REITs Offer Investors

According to the Australian Securities Exchange (2024), equity REITs provide several advantages. A modest upfront investment buys instant access to a large, diversified property portfolio. Unlike direct property, REIT shares trade on stock exchanges, offering liquidity and the ability to buy or sell incrementally. Most REITs deliver monthly or quarterly distributions from rental income, potentially offering attractive yields. Some REITs also facilitate tax planning through tax-deferred contributions, allowing investors to manage the timing of tax liabilities.

These features make REITs particularly relevant to the silver economy in two ways. First, REITs channel institutional and retail capital into senior housing infrastructure, addressing the supply gap identified by CBRE (2024). Second, older investors themselves can hold REIT shares in their retirement portfolios, generating dividend income that complements annuities and pensions.

Risks and Limitations

The Australian Securities Exchange (2024) identifies several risks: concentration risk, property cycle risk, volatility risk, gearing risk, and interest rate risk. For the silver economy specifically, a more fundamental limitation exists: REITs serve market-rate seniors and investors with capital. Low-income older adults who cannot afford retirement village entry fees or lack savings to invest in REIT shares are excluded. This chapter does not present REITs as an inclusion mechanism unless the government acts as an enabler (e.g., by providing land, concessional capital, or rental subsidies).

No investment is without risk. The Australian Securities Exchange (2024) identifies several risks specific to REITs. Concentration risk arises when a REIT focuses on a few large assets or a single sector, reducing diversification. Property cycle risk means real estate is sensitive to macroeconomic factors and market downturns, which can negatively impact returns. Volatility risk refers to sensitivity to broader sharemarket movements, causing market prices to deviate from underlying net asset values.

Two additional risks deserve emphasis. Gearing risk occurs when REITs use borrowed funds to acquire properties. While leverage can amplify capital gains when asset values rise, it also magnifies losses during downturns and increases interest costs. Interest rate risk affects performance by raising borrowing costs and making fixed-income alternatives more attractive to income-focused investors, potentially reducing demand for REIT shares (Australian Securities Exchange, 2024).

For the silver economy specifically, a more fundamental limitation exists. REITs serve market-rate seniors and investors with capital. Low-income older adults who cannot afford retirement village entry fees or lack savings to invest in REIT shares are excluded from this model. This chapter does not present REITs as an inclusion mechanism unless the government acts as an enabler, for example, by providing land, concessional capital, or rental subsidies. REITs address a different problem: financing senior housing infrastructure at scale.

Implementation Barriers: Regulatory, Cultural, and Regional Challenges

Even well-designed hybrid financial models face significant real-world barriers to adoption. This section identifies three categories of barriers.

Table 3. Regulatory barriers

Barrier	Description	Affected Models	Mitigation
Usury caps on interest rates	Many jurisdictions cap interest rates at 10–15%, making reverse mortgages unprofitable	Reverse mortgages, BLF	Regulatory sandbox exemption
Securities law restrictions	Life settlements classified as "securities" in some states, triggering costly registration	Life settlements	Model legislation (NAIC model act)
Banking separation rules	Cooperative banks prohibited from offering insurance or investment products	Cooperative banking	Regulatory harmonization
Cross-border capital restrictions	Limits on pension fund allocation to alternative assets (e.g., 5% cap)	REITs, life settlements	Bilateral investment treaties
Outcome verification standards	No accepted standard for measuring "success" in SIBs	SIBs	UNDP outcome standards framework

Cultural and Behavioral Barriers

Distrust of financial institutions: Among adults aged 65+ in Eastern Europe and Latin America, survey data show that 42% distrust banks (World Bank, 2023). Cooperative banking overcame this through community-based governance.

Bequest motives: Many older adults resist reverse mortgages to leave their home to heirs. The Canadian CHIP program addresses this through an "heir buyback option."

Financial literacy gaps: The Fifth National Survey (China National Committee on Ageing, 2022) found that 97.3% of older adults had never purchased an investment product. The IDB FACIL project (Inter-American Development Bank, 2025) invested US$150,000 in age-appropriate financial education, achieving 34% uptake among previously unbanked seniors.

Stigma around "selling" assets: Life settlements face cultural resistance where life insurance is viewed as family protection rather than a tradable asset.

Table 4. Regional feasibility matrix

Region	Homeownership Rate	Social Capital	Institutional Capacity	Recommended Model
North America	65–70%	Medium	High	Reverse mortgages, REITs, life settlements
Western Europe	55–70%	Medium-High	High	BLF, SIBs, cooperative banking
Eastern Europe	80–95%	Low-Medium	Medium	Reverse mortgages (with price floor)
Latin America	60–75%	Medium	Medium-Variable	BLF (with IDB assistance)
East Asia (Japan/Korea)	60–80%	Medium	High	Reverse mortgages, REITs
China	70–85% (urban), 95%+ (rural)	Medium (urban), High (rural)	Variable	Reverse mortgages + cooperative banking (rural)
India	50–70%	High (rural)	Low-Medium	Cooperative banking
Sub-Saharan Africa	20–50%	Medium-High	Low	Cooperative banking + BLF

Figure 2 provides a decision flowchart for overcoming implementation barriers.

Figure 2. Decision flowchart for overcoming implementation barriers

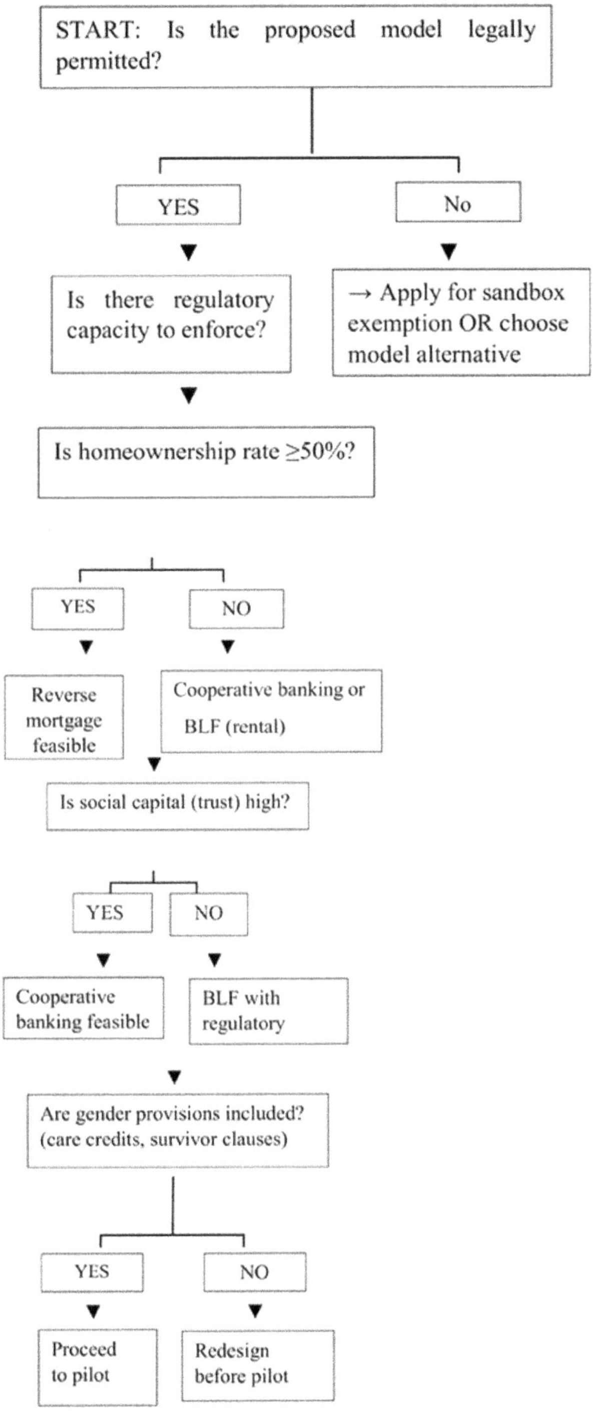

CONSTRUCTION AND APPLICATION OF EVALUATION STANDARD SYSTEM

What Inclusion Means in Practice

Inclusion criteria form the core framework for assessing financial models. But the meaning of inclusion has expanded beyond simply having a bank account. The United Nations Development Programme (UNDP, 2025a) defines modern financial inclusion as ensuring older adults have meaningful access to diverse, appropriate, affordable, and high-quality financial products tailored to their living circumstances and evolving needs.

Four dimensions matter. Accessibility asks whether older adults can reach financial services physically and financially. Adaptability requires products to fit the diversity of older adults, not the other way around. Quality of service means efficiency, accuracy, and respect for dignity. Financial education and capacity building holds institutions responsible for helping older adults improve their financial literacy (UNDP, 2025a).

These four dimensions are not optional add-ons. They are design requirements. A financial product that fails any one of them does not serve the silver economy, regardless of its theoretical elegance.

Measuring Cross-Sectoral Coordination

Cross-sectoral coordination is not a buzzword. It is a measurable operational requirement. The assessment covers mechanism design, implementation, and results.

In mechanism design, effective coordination requires clear division of responsibilities and communication channels. Financial institutions, aged care providers, government agencies, industry associations, and media must cooperate. The UNDP and Industrial Securities (2025) argue that only through cross-society cooperation can a sustainable silver economy expand. However, a caveat is warranted: cooperation without accountability is merely consultation. The Kerala cooperative network succeeded because coordination was embedded in governance structures, not just meetings.

In evaluating implementation outcomes, three metrics matter. Resource allocation efficiency measures whether coordination avoids redundant investment. Service coordination assesses whether different financial services integrate organically. Risk prevention capabilities track whether coordination builds better risk identification, assessment, and control systems (OECD, 2024).

The EIB's Lombardy project illustrates good coordination. The fund brought together EU structural funds, Italian commercial banks, 30 municipalities, and local care providers. The outcome,1200 home renovations with 28 percent reduction in nursing home admissions, speaks for itself (European Investment Bank, 2025).

POLICY RECOMMENDATIONS AND IMPLEMENTATION PATH

Designing for Inclusion from the Start

Building inclusive, cross-sectoral mechanisms is not a policy afterthought. It is the foundation. The core task is breaking down traditional departmental barriers and establishing collaborative platforms (UNDP, 2025a).

Three mechanisms are non-negotiable.

First, age-appropriate digital financial interfaces. Large buttons, voice commands, and human backup for biometric authentication are not luxuries. The Inter-American Development Bank's FACIL project in the Dominican Republic spent US$150,000 redesigning financial application interfaces for older users, voice commands, large buttons, and 24/7 human support (Inter-American Development Bank, 2025). The cost was modest. The impact was substantial.

Second, gender-based investment design. Women live longer, earn less over their lifetimes, and dominate unpaid care work. Any financial model that ignores these facts will fail older women. Three specific provisions are necessary: care credits (following the German model, which credits pension contributions for years of unpaid care work), survivor clauses (protecting widows from sudden loss of pension income), and flexible repayment terms for widows (UNDP, 2025a). Without these, inclusion is a slogan.

Summarizes the comparative fiscal costs, investor returns, and inclusion reach of the six models.

Table 5.

Model	Inclusion Reach (Non-Homeowners, Rural, Women)	Regulatory Complexity (1=low, 5=high)
Hybrid Longevity Finance	Medium (can mandate inclusion in fund terms, as EIB did)	5 (multi-party, cross-border)
Social Impact Bonds	Low to Medium (risk of "creaming" excludes hardest-to-serve)	4 (outcome metrics, evaluation contracts)
Reverse Mortgage Funds	Low (excludes non-homeowners entirely)	3 (existing framework in many countries)
Cooperative Banking	High (Kerala reached 200k previously unbanked)	2 (if cooperative law exists; otherwise 5)

continued on following page

Table 5. Continued

Model	Inclusion Reach (Non-Homeowners, Rural, Women)	Regulatory Complexity (1=low, 5=high)
Life Settlements	Medium (unlocks wealth for policyholders, but only those with policies)	3 (regulated in 43 US states; absent elsewhere)
Retirement Village REITs	Low (requires investment capital or market-rate income)	2 (securities regulation)

Source: Author's compilation based on the six models

Policy Drivers That Actually Work

Policy and ecosystem drivers create the conditions for silver finance innovation. The Inter-American Development Bank Group's regional strategy offers a useful template. In October 2025, IDB Labs proposed a three-pillar framework: entrepreneurship and employment (facilitating age-biased access to credit), financial inclusion (creating safer financial systems for older adults), and the care economy (professionalizing care markets as growth drivers) (IDB Labs, 2025).

Five specific policy drivers emerge from the evidence in this chapter.

Regulatory sandbox for reverse mortgage innovation. Australia's Household Capital provides a practical model. In 2024, the company completed an AUD $263 million reverse mortgage securitisation (HHC 2024-1 RMBS Trust) rated by Moody's, with participation from Citigroup and IFM Investors (Household Capital, 2024). The securitisation allowed refinancing while enabling senior customers to continue drawing on approved home equity for aging-in-place modifications and care services. A regulatory sandbox would allow similar integrated models to be tested without being constrained by usury caps designed for conventional lending.

Cross-border regulatory coordination. For silver economy investments spanning multiple jurisdictions, regulatory fragmentation increases compliance costs and blocks scale. A template memorandum of understanding (MoU) between financial regulators covering data sharing, dispute resolution, and consumer protection can reduce this friction. The EU's passporting system for pension funds provides a precedent. Multilateral development banks (EIB, IFC, ADB) can serve as certifying bodies, validating compliance with a single rulebook across borders.

Outcome fund guarantee. A national long-term development outcome fund that co-invests in Social Impact Bonds and Blended Longevity Funds would provide backup protection against outcome risk. Norway's Government Pension Fund Global offers a model: it allocates a portion of its portfolio to impact investments while maintaining stringent reporting requirements (Norges Bank Investment Management, 2024).

Data infrastructure investment. Anonymous, linked health-social-finance data would enable low-cost outcome verification. Japan's Government Pension Investment Fund has demonstrated how data sharing can improve investment decisions while protecting privacy (Government Pension Investment Fund, 2022). The silver economy needs similar infrastructure.

Tax alignment: Eliminate value-added tax on ancillary technologies purchased through partner banks. Allow pension funds to allocate a portion of their portfolio, example 13 percent to silver ecosystem instruments as impact investments. China's eight-department guidance (People's Bank of China and eight other departments, 2024) points in this direction, though implementation remains uneven.

Life settlement fiduciary disclosure. Regulators should require registered investment advisors to disclose life settlement options to older clients considering policy surrender. Currently, many advisors do not mention settlements because surrender generates no commission. This is a straightforward information asymmetry problem with a straightforward solution: mandated disclosure. (See Section 3 for detailed analysis.)

Making Multiple Models Work Together

Three principles guide implementation.

Gradual advancement. Pilot in economically developed, financially mature regions first. Then expand. The EIB started with Lombardy, not all of Italy. The Kerala cooperative network grew over decades, not years.

Local adaptation. Homeownership rates vary. Social capital varies. Institutional capacity varies. A model that works in rural India (cooperative banking) may fail in suburban Australia. A model that works in the United States (life settlements) may have no legal basis in Japan. The model selection matrix (Table 5.2) reflects this reality.

Risk control. Innovation is not an excuse for recklessness. Each model requires a comprehensive risk prevention system. Reverse mortgages need mandatory legal advice and cooling-off periods. Life settlements need mortality standards and disclosure rules. REITs need securities regulation and consumer protection.

Provides the model selection matrix.

Table 6. Model selection matrix for silver economy finance

Context Factor	Recommended Model	Rationale
High homeownership (>70%), stable housing market	Reverse mortgage funds + BLF	Unlock housing wealth; BLF provides risk buffer
Low homeownership (<50%), strong social capital	Cooperative banks	Reaches non-homeowners through peer guarantees
High life insurance ownership, policy lapse rates high	Life settlements	Unlock life insurance wealth; provides lump sums for care
Retirees with moderate savings, fear of outliving income	Life annuity	Guaranteed lifetime income; transfers longevity risk to insurer
Retirees with substantial savings, desire flexibility	Living annuity or combination	Income flexibility, growth potential, legacy planning
All retirees, as baseline income layer	Annuities or longevity pooling[1]	Low-cost risk pooling without insurance company guarantees
Strong institutional capacity, focus on prevention	Social impact bonds	Pay-for success aligns incentives
Weak institutional capacity, need for infrastructure	BLF (with development bank lead)	Concessional capital provides technical assistance
Rural, low-trust environments	Cooperative banks	Community governance builds trust
Need for large-scale senior housing infrastructure	Retirement village REITs	Mobilizes institutional capital; provides dividend income; DMF model aligns incentives
Need for affordable senior housing with inclusion	REITs + BLF or cooperative banking	REITs provide infrastructure; BLF/ cooperatives address affordability
Mixed conditions	Hybrid models	Combines elements across models

Note. [1] For a comprehensive analysis of modern annuity design, see Forsyth, Vetzal and Westmacott (2024) and the special issue of the Geneva Risk and Insurance Review (2025).

Source. Author's compilation.

Annuities and Longevity Risk Pooling

The age-centric approach requires understanding what retirees actually fear. Survey evidence consistently identifies outliving savings as the single greatest financial anxiety of older adults (Swiss Re, 2025). The annuity is a financial contract that transforms a lump sum into guaranteed lifetime income, directly addresses this fear by pooling longevity risk across a population.

Table 7. Two broad types serve different retirees profiles

Type	Best For	Trade-off
Whole life annuity (traditional)	Retirees with moderate savings who prioritize certainty	No flexibility; fixed income may lose purchasing power to inflation
Investment-linked living annuity	Financially savvy retirees with ample savings	Income fluctuates; policyholder bears investment risk

Two broad types serve different retiree profiles. Whole life annuities (traditional) provide fixed periodic payments until death, offering certainty but no flexibility; inflation can erode purchasing power over long retirements. Investment-linked living annuities allow retirees to maintain investment exposure and withdraw flexibly, but the policyholder bears investment and longevity risk, making them suitable only for financially sophisticated retirees with ample savings buffers (Journal of Economic and Financial Sciences, 2022). Most retirees benefit from a combination: a lifetime annuity for basic expenses, a living annuity for discretionary spending and estate planning.

However, annuities have limitations that explain their absence as a standalone solution in this chapter's hybrid architecture. First, annuities address income security but do not finance infrastructure, they cannot build age-friendly housing, retrofit homes, or fund community transport networks. Second, annuity markets suffer from adverse selection: individuals who expect to live longest self-select into purchase, raising prices and reducing take-up among those with average or below-average life expectancy (Blake, 2006). Third, nominal annuities expose retirees to inflation risk; inflation-indexed annuities are expensive and rarely offered.

Recent innovations address some limitations. Tontines, modernized versions of the historical pooling mechanism, offer longevity protection without insurance company guarantees by redistributing forfeited shares upon death to surviving members (Forsyth, Vetzal & Westmacott, 2024). Deferred longevity annuities begin payments at advanced ages (e.g., 85), allowing cost-effective protection against the tail risk of extreme longevity. The UK's pension freedom reforms have stimulated experimentation with hybrid products combining guaranteed and variable components (Superannuation Australia & Association of Superannuation Funds of Australia, 2024).

For the silver economy, annuities play a supporting rather than central role. They convert household savings into predictable cash flow, enabling older adults to pay for care services, home modifications, and village fees. But they do not mobilize new capital for aging infrastructure. That task falls to the six models examined in this chapter. Annuities are therefore best understood as a complementary income-layer solution rather than a competing architecture.

CONCLUSION AND OUTLOOK

What This Chapter Found

Several conclusions emerge from this analysis.

The financing gap is structural, not temporary. The global silver economy is projected to reach $15 trillion by 2030, but capital supply remains constrained (UNDP & Industrial Securities, 2025). The problem is not just aggregate volume. It is term structure. Silver economy projects need ten to thirty years of stable funding. Traditional finance offers three to five years. This mismatch cannot be fixed with marginal adjustments.

Hybrid architecture works. Every model examined has blind spots, blended finance, social impact bonds, reverse mortgages, cooperative banking, life settlements, and REITs each solve some problems while creating or ignoring others. But integrated as complementary components, they provide risk diversification, functional completeness, and flexibility for local conditions (OECD, 2024).

Inclusion and coordination are operational requirements, not aspirations. Inclusion is not an add-on. Financial services must be accessible, adaptable, high-quality, and accompanied by financial education (UNDP, 2025a). Market mechanisms alone rarely deliver these conditions. Cross-sectoral coordination among financial institutions, care providers, government agencies, and community organizations is essential (UNDP & Industrial Securities, 2025).

Policy ecosystems determine whether models scale. Technical design matters, but it is rarely the binding constraint. What distinguishes successful implementations from failed pilots is enabling conditions: regulatory sandboxes, data infrastructure, tax alignment, and last-mile intermediaries. Without these, even well-designed models remain small demonstrations.

Contributions and Practical Implications

This chapter makes three theoretical contributions. First, it extends the traditional concept of pension financing to longevity finance covering the entire life cycle. Second, it proposes a hybrid financial architecture integrating multiple innovative models. Third, it establishes an evaluation standard system for inclusive silver finance (Livingston et al., 2020).

For policymakers, the chapter provides systematic policy recommendations and implementation pathways. For financial institutions, the six models offer operational guidance for product innovation and service upgrades. For older adults and their families, age-centric service concepts and diversified product designs help meet growing financial needs (UNDP & Industrial Securities, 2025).

Limitations and Future Research Agenda.

This chapter synthesizes published evaluations of six financial models into a proposed hybrid architecture. It does not provide empirical validation of the complete framework. Causal claims about the architecture's effectiveness cannot be inferred from the case examples presented. Three priorities for future research emerge from this analysis. First, comparative effectiveness studies are needed to test whether hybrid configurations outperform single-model approaches on inclusion and risk-adjusted return metrics. Second, longitudinal studies tracking outcomes beyond five years are required, as silver economy projects typically operate on ten- to thirty-year horizons. Third, implementation science research should examine how regulatory, cultural, and institutional barriers moderate the architecture's performance across different regional contexts. The model selection matrix (Table 5) is offered as a testable hypothesis. Fourth, inclusion outcomes for the hardest-to-reach populations rural older adults, those with very low incomes, and people with cognitive impairments remain understudied. Future research should prioritize these populations from the outset using participatory methods.

A Final Word

Fostering inclusive, sustainable silver economy growth is a complex, long-term undertaking. It requires systemic effort, not isolated interventions. The overarching lesson is simple but profound. Finance must reflect the ecosystem it serves: mixed, patient, and accountable to older adults as co-owners, not just consumers. No single model is sufficient. Cross-sectoral innovation needs concessional capital to mitigate first-mover risk. Infrastructure needs patient capital. Household capital enables demand. Impact capital promotes inclusion.

The shift from isolated financial products to integrated ecosystem finance presents both challenges and opportunities. Its governance will shape not only the future of the silver economy but also the broader trajectory of inclusive growth in aging societies worldwide.

REFERENCES

Actuarial Standards Board. (2014). *Actuarial Standard of Practice No. 48: Life settlements mortality* (Effective April 30, 2014).

Armendáriz, B., & Morduch, J. (2010). *The economics of microfinance* (2nd ed.). MIT Press.

Australian Securities Exchange. (2024). Investing in A-REITs. https://www.asx.com.au/investors/learn-about-our-investment-solutions/a-reits

Basque Government Department of Economic Development. (2023). *Cooperative banking and the silver economy: The Mondragon experience*. Basque Institute of Competition and Cooperation.

Bauer, D., Russ, J., & Zhu, N. (2020). Asymmetric information in secondary insurance markets: Evidence from the life settlements market. *Quantitative Economics, 11*(3), 1143–1175. DOI: 10.3982/QE1333

Bernard, C., Kolkiewicz, A., & Tang, J. (2024). Optimal surrender policy for reverse mortgage loans. *ASTIN Bulletin, 54*(3), 600–625. DOI: 10.1017/asb.2024.21

Birchall, J. (2013a). *Finance in an age of austerity*. Edward Elgar Publishing. DOI: 10.4337/9781781951842

Birchall, J. (2013b). *Resilience in a downturn: The power of financial cooperatives*. International Labour Office.

Bisetti, E., Favero, C. A., Nocera, G., & Tebaldi, C. (2017). A multivariate model of strategic asset allocation with longevity risk. *Journal of Financial and Quantitative Analysis, 52*(5), 2251–2275. DOI: 10.1017/S0022109017000692

Blake, D. (2006). *Pension economics*. John Wiley & Sons.

Carvalho, J. V. F., & Araújo, G. G. (2024). A feasibility analysis of reverse mortgages in Brazil. *Journal of Urban Management, 13*(1), 74–87. DOI: 10.1016/j.jum.2023.11.003

CBRE Research. (2024). Australian Seniors Housing. CBRE Australia. https://www.cbre.com.au/insights/reports/australian-seniors-housing

China National Committee on Ageing. (2022). *Report on the Fifth National Survey on Living Conditions of Urban and Rural Older Adults.*

Consumer Action Law Centre. (2017, July 10). How retirement villages can swallow your nest egg. The New Daily. https://www.thenewdaily.com.au/finance/retirement/2017/07/10/retirement-village-costs

Consumer Financial Protection Bureau. (2023). *§ 1026.33 Requirements for reverse mortgages*. https://www.consumerfinance.gov/rules-policy/regulations/1026/33/

Davidoff, T., Gerhard, P., & Post, T. (2023). Reverse mortgage usage and racial disparities in the United States. *Journal of Urban Economics, 135*, 103542. Advance online publication. DOI: 10.1016/j.jue.2023.103542

Edmiston, D., & Nicholls, A. (2018). Social Impact Bonds: The role of private capital in outcome-based commissioning. *Journal of Social Policy, 47*(1), 57–76. DOI: 10.1017/S0047279417000125

European Investment Bank. (2025). *Blended finance for active aging: Lessons from EU structural funds*. European Investment Bank.

Fiordelisi, F., Grimaldi, S., Lopez, J. S., Mazzilis, M. C., & Ricci, O. (2022). The beauty of being involved: The case of cooperative banks. *British Journal of Management, 34*(4), 2290–2311. DOI: 10.1111/1467-8551.12698

Forsyth, P. A., Vetzal, K. R., & Westmacott, G. (2024). Optimal performance of a tontine overlay subject to withdrawal constraints. *ASTIN Bulletin, 54*(1), 94–128. DOI: 10.1017/asb.2023.35

French, M., Kimmitt, J., Wilson, R., Jamieson, D., & Lowe, T. (2023). Social impact bonds and public service reform: Back to the future of New Public Management? *International Public Management Journal, 26*(3), 376–395. DOI: 10.1080/10967494.2022.2050859

Fu, K., Zhao, H., & Wang, N. (2023). Optimal investment problem for a hybrid pension with intergenerational risk-sharing and longevity trend under model uncertainty. arXiv. https://doi.org//arXiv.2302.02351DOI: 10.48550

Government Pension Investment Fund. Japan. (2022). *GPIF annual report 2022*. Government Pension Investment Fund.

Grigsby v. Russell, 222 U.S. 149 (1911).

Gustafsson-Wright, E., Boggild-Jones, I., Segell, D., & Durland, J. (2020). *Impact bonds in developing countries: Early learnings from the field*. Brookings Institution.

Gustafsson-Wright, E., Gardiner, S., & Putcha, V. (2015). *The potential and limitations of impact bonds: Lessons from the first five years of experience worldwide*. Brookings Institution.

Hevenstone, D., Fraser, A., Hobi, L., & Geuke, G. (2023). Why is impact measurement abandoned in practice? Evidence use in evaluation and contracting for five European Social Impact Bonds. *Evaluation*, *29*(1), 91–109. DOI: 10.1177/13563890221136890

HomeEquity Bank. (2025). *CHIP Reverse Mortgage*. https://www.homeequitybank.ca/products/chip-reverse-mortgage/

Household Capital. (2024). *HHC 2024-1 RMBS Trust transaction summary*. Household Capital Australia.

Inter-American Development Bank. (2025). *FACIL program: Financial inclusion for the silver economy in the Dominican Republic*. Inter-American Development Bank.

International Finance Corporation. (2024a). *IFC provides US$45 million financing and advisory services to Caja 18 to support retirees and low-income women workers*. https://www.ifc.org/en/pressroom/2024/ifc-provides-us-45-million-financing-and-advisory-services-to-caja-18-to-support-retirees-and-low-income-women-workers

International Finance Corporation. (2024b). *IFC invests in Consubanco's historic silver economy bond issuance in Mexico*. International Finance Corporation.

International Finance Corporation. (2024c). *IFC launches Silver Economy Initiative to address growing underserved population in Latin America & the Caribbean*. https://www.ifc.org/en/pressroom/2024/ifc-launches-silver-economy-initiative-to-address-growing-underserved-population-in-latin-america-the-caribbean

Invest, I. D. B. (2022). *IDB Invest launches its first silver economy social bond to support financial inclusion of seniors in Latin America and the Caribbean*. https://idbinvest.org/en/news-media/idb-invest-launches-its-first-silver-economy-social-bond-support-financial-inclusion

Kang, S., Li, K., & Wang, R. (2025). A survey on pareto front learning for multi-objective optimization. *Journal of Membrane Computing*, *7*(2), 128–134. DOI: 10.1007/s41965-024-00170-z

Kerala State Planning Board. (2022). *Elderly care cooperatives in Kerala: A model for inclusive aging*. Government of Kerala.

King, S. (2014). *Social Impact Bonds: A new tool for social financing*.

Lab, I. D. B. (2025, October 31). *Silver economy: Three pillars for a more productive longevity*. https://bidlab.org/en/blog/silver-economy-three-pillars-more-productive-longevity

Lankide, T. U. (2023). *MONDRAGON surpassed the 11 billion sales barrier in 2023.* https://www.tulankide.com/en/mondragon-surpassed-the-11-billion-sales-barrier-in-2023

Laureola Advisors & Lee, A. (2021). Life settlements can become fixed income alternative for investors. *SMSF Adviser.*

Livingston, G., Huntley, J., Sommerlad, A., Ames, D., Ballard, C., Banerjee, S., & Mukadam, N. (2020). Dementia prevention, intervention, and care: 2020 report of the Lancet Commission. *Lancet, 396*(10248), 413–446. DOI: 10.1016/S0140-6736(20)30367-6 PMID: 32738937

Longevity & Mortality Investor. (2024). Volume 3 Issue 4.

Longevity & Mortality Investor. (2025). Society of Actuaries considers switch from general to insured population mortality data.

Macdonald, D. (2019, January 10). Social impact bonds: Everyone's profiting, except at-risk Indigenous women. *Canadian Centre for Policy Alternatives.* https://www.policyalternatives.ca/news-research/social-impact-bonds-everyones-profiting-except-at-risk-indigenous-women/

Matsumoto, K., Tsukamoto, K., Ishikawa, S., Oishi, M., & Okamoto, N. (2000). Reconstruction of cities through the utilization of reverse mortgage system: Lesson from the Hanshin-Awaji Great Earthquake and its universality. *Studies in Regional Science, 30*(1), 197–212. https://www.jstage.jst.go.jp/article/srs1970/30/1/30_1_197/_article

McGurk, P. (1998). Traded endowments. *British Actuarial Journal, 4*(2), 391–428. DOI: 10.1017/S1357321700003013

Ministry of Foreign Affairs of Japan. (1996). *Social security in Japan: Case I social welfare services in Musashino City.* National Diet Library. https://warp.ndl.go.jp/info:ndljp/pid/11383817/www.mofa.go.jp/j_info/japan/socsec/maruo/maruo_10.html

Mondragon Corporation. (2023). *Annual report 2022: Cooperative banking and social innovation.* Mondragon Corporation.

Nakajima, M. (2018). The structure and issues of housing reverse mortgage trust in Japan. *Trusts & Trustees, 24*(6), 548–556. DOI: 10.1093/tandt/cty082

National Bureau of Statistics of China. (2024). *Population data by age range.* https://data.stats.gov.cn

Nicholls, A., & Tomkinson, E. (2015). *The Peterborough Pilot Social Impact Bond.* Oxford University Press. DOI: 10.1093/acprof:oso/9780198703761.003.0013

Norges Bank Investment Management. (2024). *Government Pension Fund Global responsible investment 2024*. Norges Bank Investment Management.

OECD. (2025a). *The economic benefit of promoting healthy ageing and community care (OECD Health Policy Studies)*. OECD Publishing., DOI: 10.1787/0f7bc62b-

OECD. (2025b). *Pensions at a glance 2025: OECD and G20 indicators*. OECD Publishing., DOI: 10.1787/e40274c1-

Okayama City SIB Study. (2024). Validating weight optimization's impact on participants via Social Impact Bonds. *European Journal of Public Health*, 34(Supplement_3), ckae144.1743. https://doi.org/DOI: 10.1093/eurpub/ckae144.1743

Organisation for Economic Co-operation and Development. (2024). *Ageing and long-term care: Financing challenges and innovative solutions.*

People's Bank of China, & Eight Other Departments. (2024, December). *Guiding opinions on financial support for the high-quality development of Chinese-style pension services and the silver economy.* People's Bank of China.

Rania, F. (2025). Reverse Mortgages and Pension Sustainability: An Agent-Based and Actuarial Approach. *Risks*, *13*(8), 147. DOI: 10.3390/risks13080147

Resonanz Capital. (2025). *Life settlements as an investment asset class.*

Retirement Living Online. (2022, June 20). *What are departure fees in a retirement village?* https://www.retirementlivingonline.com.au/news/26/60/What-are-Departure-Fees-in-a-Retirement-Village/retirement/retirement/facilities/retirement/retirement/retirement/retirement/retirement/retirement/retirement/retirement/south-australia

Reverse Mortgage, C. H. I. P. (2023). *CHIP Reverse Mortgage program overview: Home equity for retirement security*. HomeEquity Bank.

Sahut, J., & Bouheni, F. B. (2019). Profitability and Risk-Taking Among Cooperative Banks in the Eurozone. *Economic Bulletin*, *39*, 1103–1117.

Social Finance, U. K. (2021). *Ageing Well Social Impact Bond: Impact report*. Social Finance UK Society of Actuaries. (2010). *Report of the Society of Actuaries Life Settlements Survey Subcommittee.*

Stockland Group. (2024). *Stockland retirement living: Investor update*. https://www.stockland.com.au/investor-centre/announcements-and-reports/results-and-reports

Superannuation Australia & Association of Superannuation Funds of Australia. (2024). *How product layering can support retirement outcomes and address longevity risk.*

Swiss Re. (2025). Silver economy ushers in a new era of growth for life insurance. *Swiss Re Sigma Report*, (1), 1–48.

United Nations Department of Economic and Social Affairs. (2023). *World social report 2023: Leaving no one behind in an ageing world.* United Nations.

United Nations Development Programme. (2025a). *A measurement study on multidimensional vulnerabilities of the elderly population in China.* United Nations Development Programme.

United Nations Development Programme. (2025b). *Enhancing the elderly care service system through the silver economy.* United Nations Development Programme.

United Nations Development Programme, & Industrial Securities. (2025). *Financing the silver economy in China: Empowering an inclusive and sustainable ageing society.* UNDP, China.

KEY TERMS AND DEFINITIONS

Blended Finance: A financing approach combining concessional public or philanthropic capital with commercial investment to fund projects too risky or long-term for private markets alone.

Deferred Management Fee (DMF): An exit fee—typically 20-40 percent of property value—paid by retirement village residents in exchange for a reduced upfront purchase price.

Hybrid Financial Architecture: An integrated system combining multiple financial instruments—blended finance, SIBs, reverse mortgages, cooperative banking, life settlements, and REITs—that no single sector can deploy alone.

Life Settlement: The sale of a life insurance policy by a policyholder aged 65-plus to a third-party investor for a lump sum exceeding the cash surrender value.

Longevity Finance: Financial arrangements spanning the entire lifespan that address income security, health protection, long-term care, and housing needs for aging populations.

Multi-Stakeholder Cooperative Banking: A financial institution owned by multiple stakeholder groups (seniors, caregivers, local governments, small businesses) with one vote per member regardless of capital contribution.

Real Estate Investment Trust (REIT): A company that owns income-producing real estate and must distribute at least 90 percent of taxable income to shareholders as dividends.

Reverse Mortgage: A non-recourse loan enabling homeowners aged 62-plus to convert home equity into cash without monthly repayments, repaid when they permanently leave the home.

Silver Economy: Economic activities serving populations aged 65 and older across healthcare, housing, finance, technology, and care services.

Social Impact Bond (SIB): A pay-for-success contract where private investors fund social programs and receive government returns only if predetermined outcomes are achieved.

Chapter 2
Financing Models for Silver Economy an Southeast Asian Experience

Bayu Tri Cahya
http://orcid.org/0000-0001-9277-5740
Universitas Islam Negeri Sunan Kudus, Indonesia

Andri Veno
http://orcid.org/0009-0000-8777-1227
Universitas Tiga Serangkai, Indonesia

Yunus Harjito
http://orcid.org/0009-0004-4643-8160
Universitas Setia Budi, Indonesia

Ratih B. Paramitasari
http://orcid.org/0009-0007-1431-8684
Universitas Terbuka, Indonesia

ABSTRACT

As demographic transitions occur globally, resulting in an ageing population, the Silver Economy has emerged as a vital driver of socio-economic development. While the establishment of age-friendly infrastructure and the provision of inclusive healthcare are of paramount importance, traditional short-term grant-based funding often limits scalability. This study analyses innovative partnership models, including public-private partnerships (PPPs), impact investing, blended finance, corporate social responsibility (CSR), and blockchain-driven crowdfunding, with a view to

DOI: 10.4018/979-8-3373-9370-4.ch002

overcoming these financial barriers. The findings indicate that these mechanisms diversify resource pooling, enhance transparency, and align financial returns with social impact through risk-sharing. Nevertheless, success depends on overcoming regulatory fragmentation and addressing gaps in digital literacy. The study concludes that an adaptive regulatory environment and a coordinated funding ecosystem are fundamental prerequisites for building economic resilience and sustainable social welfare within the Silver Economy

INTRODUCTION

The global demographic transition is one of the most profound structural transformations of the twenty-first century. Characterized by longer life expectancy, lower fertility rates, and rising educational levels, this transition has reshaped the socio-economic landscape of countries across the world (Piskorska & Adamczyk, 2025; Tyers & Shi, 2007; Martinez & Weyman, 2017). As a result, aging populations now pose a set of interconnected challenges: a declining and aging workforce, escalating health and long-term care costs, mounting pressure on pension systems, and the urgent need for new economic models capable of sustaining social welfare systems without compromising fiscal stability (Christiansen & Branch, 2025).

A shrinking workforce, driven by the simultaneous effects of falling birth rates and the retirement of large baby-boom cohorts, threatens to constrain economic growth by reducing labor supply and tax revenues. However, this challenge carries within it a countervailing opportunity: increasing the labor market participation of older workers can partially offset the contraction of the working-age population, while also generating demand for goods, services, and infrastructure specifically tailored to older adults. This dual dynamic aging as both a fiscal risk and an economic opportunity, is at the heart of what has come to be known as the Silver Economy (Gonzales et al., 2015; Li et al., 2025).

The Silver Economy encompasses all economic activities generated by and for the elderly population, including healthcare, long-term care, assistive technology, age-friendly housing, financial services, and recreational industries. Its emergence reflects a recognition that demographic aging need not be managed solely as a social welfare burden, but can be transformed into a driver of sustainable, inclusive development. When governments, the private sector, civil society, and international institutions align their interests and resources around the needs of older populations, aging societies can generate new growth frontiers rather than simply accumulating fiscal deficits (Manzano, 2025; Reshetnikova et al., 2021).

In the Southeast Asian context, the Silver Economy takes on distinctive dimensions shaped by the region's cultural, economic, and institutional specificities. Countries such as Indonesia, Vietnam, Thailand, Malaysia, Singapore, and the Philippines are at varying stages of demographic aging, but all share a common trajectory: rising elderly populations, increasing life expectancy, declining fertility rates, and growing pressure on social protection systems that were historically designed for younger, faster-growing populations. At the same time, Southeast Asian countries are embedded in a cultural tradition in which the family serves as the primary institution of elderly care. Intergenerational solidarity, the expectation that adult children will support aging parents remains a powerful social norm across the region, even as urbanization, labor migration, and smaller household sizes progressively erode families' practical capacity to fulfill this role on their own (Lee & Mason, 2022).

This cultural context is analytically significant for the design of Silver Economy financing strategies. Unlike in Europe or North America, where public pension and long-term care systems have historically substituted for family-based care, Southeast Asian financial solutions must be designed to complement rather than replace family networks. The challenge is to build institutional financing mechanisms public and private that fill the growing gaps left by family systems without dismantling the social fabric of intergenerational solidarity. This requires culturally sensitive financial instruments, participatory governance structures that involve elderly beneficiaries and their families in program design, and a careful balance between formal and informal care provisioning (Lee & Mason, 2011).

Comprehensive public policies, adaptable regulations, and public-private collaboration are essential prerequisites for a successful Silver Economy. This combination drives inclusive innovation and ensures that older people have universal access to essential goods and services regardless of income level, geographic location, or gender (Manzano, 2025; Li et al., 2025). Financial security is equally vital: elderly individuals who lack adequate income, insurance, or savings are disproportionately vulnerable to poverty, social exclusion, and preventable health deterioration. Gender disparities compound these vulnerabilities, as women in Southeast Asia typically live longer than men yet accumulate fewer financial assets due to career interruptions for caregiving, lower lifetime earnings, and historically limited access to formal pension schemes.

This chapter focuses specifically on Southeast Asia, drawing on empirical evidence from real business and social service partnerships operating in the region, rather than relying on general global or European statistics. The goal is to equip policymakers, financiers, civil society actors, and academic researchers with actionable knowledge grounded in the actual realities of the ASEAN sub-region. By examining concrete cases of successful partnership models in Indonesia, Vietnam, Thailand, Malaysia, Singapore, and the Philippines, and by analyzing the specific governance, regulatory, and financing challenges these countries face, this chapter contributes to the growing body of literature on Silver Economy development as a strategic response to Southeast Asia's demographic transition.

CONCEPTUALIZING THE SILVER ECONOMY AND ITS CONTRIBUTION TO SUSTAINABLE DEVELOPMENT

The Silver Economy is best understood not as a single sector but as a comprehensive ecosystem of economic activities generated by, for, and around the growing elderly population. It involves older people simultaneously in three distinct economic roles: as consumers of goods and services designed to meet their needs and preferences; as producers who contribute labor, knowledge, and entrepreneurial activity to the broader economy; and as subjects of public policy who require social protection, healthcare, and welfare infrastructure (Briegas et al., 2021). This tripartite framing is analytically important because it resists the tendency to view the elderly exclusively as dependents and instead recognizes their active economic agency.

The scope of the Silver Economy is exceptionally broad. It encompasses health and long-term care systems, age-friendly housing and urban design, accessible transportation infrastructure, financial services including insurance and retirement savings, assistive technology and digital health tools, recreational and cultural services tailored to older adults, and labor market policies that support continued employment or phased retirement (Lopane, 2025). The rapid development of technology-driven segments of the silver economy including cognitive training applications, wearable health-monitoring devices, telemedicine platforms, and smart home automation systems has considerably expanded the market boundaries, opening new investment opportunities for both established corporations and social enterprises (Nieto-Vieites et al., 2022).

The Silver Economy ranks among the world's largest economic ecosystems by market size. As a global aggregate, elderly-related consumption already represents a market comparable to that of the world's third-largest economy, and projections consistently point to accelerating growth as demographic aging intensifies across Asia, Africa, and Latin America. This scale creates significant opportunities not only in public and consumer markets but also in financial markets, where the development of specialized investment vehicles social bonds, blended finance facilities, and impact investing funds is opening new channels for capital mobilization toward elderly welfare programs (Lopane, 2025; Gölçek, 2024).

The contribution of the Silver Economy to sustainable development is multidimensional. Economically, it stimulates demand in healthcare, housing, technology, and service sectors, generating employment and innovation. Socially, it promotes active aging, reduces isolation, and strengthens intergenerational equity by ensuring that older adults remain connected and valued members of their communities. Environmentally, age-friendly urban design including compact, walkable neighborhoods with accessible green spaces aligns with low-carbon development goals. And institutionally, the development of a robust Silver Economy requires governance reforms, regulatory harmonization, and cross-sector partnerships that strengthen public administration capacity more broadly (Manzano, 2025; Bieszk-Stolorz et al., 2024).

In Southeast Asia, the Silver Economy's development reflects the dual nature of demographic aging. On the one hand, aging populations generate escalating demand for healthcare, long-term care, and social protection, straining government budgets and family resources. On the other hand, older adults in the region represent a growing market segment with specific consumption preferences, an increasingly recognized labor resource with valuable experience and skills, and a potential constituency for innovative financial products. Policy frameworks that formalize and support older adults' economic participation through age-inclusive labor market policies, senior entrepreneurship programs, and targeted financial inclusion initiatives can significantly expand the productive frontier of the silver economy in Southeast Asia (Gonzales et al., 2015; Li et al., 2025).

Understanding the economics of population aging is therefore essential for building a sustainable future one that ensures older adults' well-being while promoting broad-based growth and social justice. The Silver Economy offers an interdisciplinary analytical framework that integrates demographic, economic, financial, social, and governance dimensions into a coherent strategic approach to aging. Managing this demographic shift well not only benefits the aging population but also enhances society's resilience and inclusiveness, ensuring that the benefits of longevity are shared equitably across generations, genders, and income groups.

DEMOGRAPHIC AND SOCIAL CHALLENGES IN SOUTHEAST ASIA

Population aging in Southeast Asia is progressing at varying rates across countries, but the trajectory is unmistakably and consistently upward across all cases. The region is home to a remarkable diversity of aging experiences: from Singapore, one of the most rapidly aging societies in Asia, with 18.4% of its population aged 65 or older, to the Philippines, where the elderly share remains at 5.3% but is accelerating due to improving survival rates and declining fertility. This diversity makes Southeast Asia a particularly instructive laboratory for studying how countries at different stages of the demographic transition can develop appropriate and context-sensitive Silver Economy financing strategies.

According to the Central Statistics Agency (BPS), Indonesia with the world's fourth-largest population has entered the official phase of an aging society, with the elderly population reaching approximately 10.48% in 2023, up from 7.6% in 2010. Life expectancy has risen to approximately 73.9 years, reflecting decades of improvement in public health, nutrition, and maternal and child health services. However, this demographic success entails a growing fiscal responsibility: the national health insurance scheme (JKN), which now covers more than 260 million members, is under increasing actuarial pressure from rising costs of non-communicable diseases and long-term care needs associated with an aging membership base (BPS, 2023).

Vietnam presents a particularly urgent case within the ASEAN aging landscape. Despite its relatively modest current elderly share of 9.2%, Vietnam's aging is accelerating at a pace that outstrips the country's institutional capacity to respond. Vietnam's total fertility rate has fallen below the replacement level of 2.1 since 2006, while life expectancy has risen to 75.4 years. Projections indicate that Vietnam will transition from an aging society to an aged society where elderly populations exceed 14% within approximately fifteen years, a pace of change significantly faster than that experienced by Japan, South Korea, or most European countries during their demographic transitions. Vietnam's social protection system, anchored in a contributory social insurance scheme (Bao hiem xa hoi), currently covers approximately 17 million contributors less than one-third of the labor force leaving the majority of the future elderly population, particularly in rural areas and the vast informal sector, without formal pension protection (World Bank, 2023; ILO, 2022).

Thailand is already the most demographically aged country in ASEAN, with 14.9% of its population aged 65 or older in 2023, and projections indicate 30% by 2050. Thailand's experience is instructive for other ASEAN countries because it demonstrates both the possibilities and the limitations of community-based long-term care systems funded through national health security mechanisms. The country has made significant strides in developing a community care PPP model through the National Health Security Office (NHSO), yet faces ongoing challenges in financing the growing costs of dementia care, end-of-life care, and rehabilitation services for the oldest-old population (NHSO, 2023).

It is analytically important to distinguish between two broad country groupings in the Asian context when designing Silver Economy financing frameworks: the already-aged economies primarily Japan (with approximately 29% of its population aged 65 or older) and South Korea (approaching 20%) and the rapidly-aging economies of ASEAN, which are experiencing accelerated demographic transitions at income levels significantly lower than those at which Japan and South Korea managed similar transitions. This distinction matters because ASEAN countries face a structural disadvantage: they are aging faster and with less fiscal capacity than the precedent-setting economies of Northeast Asia. Yet this disadvantage also creates an opportunity for strategic learning, as ASEAN policymakers can draw on decades of Japanese and South Korean experience with long-term care insurance systems, pension reform, age-friendly urban design, and silver economy policy frameworks, adapting these lessons to their own socio-economic, cultural, and regulatory realities. Japan's Long-Term Care Insurance (LTCI) system, introduced in 2000, and South Korea's similar scheme launched in 2008, offer concrete institutional models for how public-private financing can be structured to support elderly care without placing the entire burden on family networks or public budgets.

Table 1. Population aging in several Southeast Asian countries

Country	Population Aged 65+ (%, 2023)	Life Expectancy (years)	Projected Elderly Population 2050 (%)
Indonesia	10.5	73.9	19
Thailand	14.9	77.7	30
Vietnam	9.2	75.4	21
Malaysia	7.4	75.6	17
Singapore	18.4	83.1	33
Philippines	5.3	71.7	14

Source: United Nations Population Division; World Bank (2023)

The data in Table 1 reveal the considerable heterogeneity of Southeast Asia's demographic landscape. Singapore's elderly share of 18.4% places it among the most aged societies in the world, driven by one of the highest life expectancy rates globally (83.1 years) and a sustained ultra-low fertility rate. At the other end of the spectrum, the Philippines' relatively young elderly share of 5.3% reflects a still-young age structure. However, its projection to 14% by 2050 underscores how rapidly demographic aging will intensify. Vietnam and Indonesia occupy intermediate positions, both currently below the 10.5% threshold associated with aging societies under the United Nations definition. However, both are projected to cross 20% by mid-century, a transformation that will unfold within the professional lifetimes of current policymakers and financing professionals.

From the perspective of National Transfer Accounts (NTA), the changing age structure in Southeast Asia reflects not merely a numerical shift in population composition but a fundamental transformation in the flows of resources between generations throughout the life cycle. The NTA framework, developed by Lee and Mason and now applied in more than 80 countries, enables analysts to track how populations at different ages earn labor income, consume goods and services, and transfer resources between generations through public systems (taxes and social transfers) and private systems (family transfers and asset accumulation). In Southeast Asia, NTA analyses from Indonesia, Thailand, Vietnam, and the Philippines consistently show that the lifecycle deficit for elderly populations, the gap between their consumption needs and their labor income is being increasingly financed by public transfers rather than family transfers, indicating growing structural pressure on government budgets as the elderly share of the population rises (Lee & Mason, 2022; IMF, 2023).

This NTA finding has direct implications for the design of Silver Economy financing. It suggests that ASEAN governments face an intensifying fiscal challenge as the demographic transition proceeds, but that this challenge is not inevitable or unmanageable. By developing diversified financing architectures combining public budgets, private-sector investment, civil society resources, community savings, and international development finance, governments can distribute the financing burden more broadly, improve sustainability, and reduce the vulnerability created by overreliance on any single funding source. The following sections document the empirical evidence for what such diversified architectures look like in practice across Southeast Asian countries.

REAL CASE STUDIES: BUSINESS AND SOCIAL SERVICE PARTNERSHIPS IN SOUTHEAST ASIA

The following empirical cases document actual public-private partnerships and social service financing arrangements for the silver economy currently operating across Southeast Asian countries. These cases have been selected to illustrate the diversity of partnership models, financing mechanisms, and institutional arrangements in the region, and to provide a concrete empirical foundation that moves the analysis beyond general statistics toward actionable policy evidence. Reviewer feedback on earlier drafts of this chapter correctly emphasized that policymakers and researchers seeking to develop or adapt Silver Economy strategies need to see concrete examples, named programs, named partners, and documented outcomes rather than aggregate regional data that can be found in any international database. This section responds directly to that imperative.

The cases span a deliberately broad range of financing instruments, from zakat-funded Islamic social finance in Indonesia to mandatory disability insurance PPPs in Singapore, reflecting the diversity of institutional contexts and cultural frameworks across the ASEAN region. They also span the full spectrum of government involvement, from centrally managed national programs (Thailand's NHSO long-term care fund) to highly decentralized community-based models (Indonesia's Posyandu Lansia network). Moreover, they include both social service delivery models and financial product innovations, recognizing that Silver Economy financing encompasses not only the direct provision of elderly welfare services but also the development of financial instruments that enable elderly populations to manage risk and accumulate resources independently.

Table 2. Real cases of public-private and social service partnerships for the silver economy in Southeast Asia

Country	Program / Partnership	Partners Involved	Financing Mechanism	Key Outcome
Indonesia	Posyandu Lansia (Elderly Integrated Service Posts)	Ministry of Health, local governments, PKK (Family Welfare Movement), community volunteers	Community-based preventive health; government supplies + community labor + BUMN CSR co-financing	80,000+ posts nationwide; 12 million elderly served; integrated nutrition, screening, and social activation (BPS, 2023)
Indonesia	BAZNAS Elderly Care Program	National Zakat Agency (BAZNAS), Islamic boarding schools (pesantren), and local governments	Zakat and waqf-funded elderly homes and home-care, complemented by government land grants	40 elderly care homes (rumah lansia) in Java and Sumatra as of 2023 (BAZNAS, 2023)
Vietnam	National Program for Elderly Care MOLISA	Ministry of Labor, Invalids and Social Affairs (MOLISA), Vietnam Women's Union, commune health stations, NGOs	State-funded elderly clubs, supplemented by international NGO grants and commune-level co-financing	54,000 elderly clubs; 6.6 million members nationwide; home-visiting and social integration services (MOLISA, 2022)
Vietnam	VinaCapital Foundation Silver Generation Initiative	VinaCapital Foundation (private), provincial health departments, WHO Vietnam, and pharmaceutical companies	CSR-funded mobile geriatric clinics; pharmaceutical co-sponsorship for medicine supply	200,000+ rural elderly received free geriatric screenings in 12 provinces (2018–2023)
Thailand	NHSO Long-Term Care Fund	National Health Security Office (NHSO), local administrative organizations (OrBorTor), informal caregiver networks	PPP: NHSO pays per-person subsidy to certified local care managers; OrBorTor provides community infrastructure	50,000 care managers trained; 145,000 dependent elderly receiving subsidized home-care (NHSO, 2023)
Thailand	SCG Silver Economy CSR Program	SCG Cement-Building Materials, Ministry of Social Development and Human Security	Corporate CSR for age-friendly housing modifications; accessible materials at subsidized cost	5,000 low-income elderly households in 10 provinces received housing accessibility modifications (SCG, 2022)

continued on following page

Table 2. Continued

Country	Program / Partnership	Partners Involved	Financing Mechanism	Key Outcome
Malaysia	Kasih Sejahtera Community Elderly Welfare PPP	Department of Social Welfare (JKM), FELDA, community development corporations, and private hospitals	Government-managed elderly daycare PPP; private hospitals provide outreach clinical services; FELDA provides community space	120 daycare centers in FELDA settlements; 18,000 rural elderly reached (JKM, 2023)
Malaysia	Khazanah Nasional Social Impact Sukuk for Aged Care	Khazanah Nasional (sovereign wealth fund), Ministry of Finance, and private aged care operators	Social impact sukuk (Islamic bond) financing the construction of aged care facilities in underserved states	RM 100 million sukuk issued; 4 aged care facilities under construction in Sabah and Sarawak (Khazanah, 2023)
Singapore	Agency for Integrated Care (AIC) Community Care Programs	Ministry of Health, AIC, private nursing homes, voluntary welfare organizations (VWOs)	Government-regulated PPP; AIC per-bed subsidies + quality standards; private and VWO operators deliver services	9,000+ subsidized nursing home beds; 120 senior activity centers; 42,000 elderly under home care (MOH, 2023)
Singapore	ElderShield / CareShield Life	CPF Board (government), Great Eastern, NTUC Income, Aviva (private insurers)	Mandatory long-term disability insurance; private insurer administration; government co-contribution for lower-income elderly	Transitioned to CareShield Life in 2020; 2.1 million policyholders; S$1.2 billion in claims paid 2020–2023 (MOH, 2023)
Philippines	Expanded Senior Citizens Act (RA 9994) Partnership	DSWD, LGUs, Older Persons Coordinating Councils, private pharmacies, hospitals, Philhealth	Mandated 20% senior discount enforced through business-government PPP; LGU-operated senior centers; Philhealth outreach	8.1 million registered seniors; 1,600 senior centers nationwide; 17,000+ participating businesses (PSA, 2023)

Source: BPS (2023), BAZNAS (2023), MOLISA Vietnam (2022), VinaCapital Foundation (2023), NHSO Thailand (2023), SCG (2022), JKM Malaysia (2023), Khazanah Nasional (2023), MOH Singapore (2023), PSA Philippines (2023)

These cases illustrate several consistent and analytically significant patterns across the Southeast Asian silver economy partnership landscape. The first pattern concerns the complementarity of government infrastructure and community resources. Indonesia's Posyandu Lansia network, which has grown to encompass more than 80,000 community posts serving approximately 12 million elderly Indonesians, demonstrates that high population coverage can be achieved at very low per-capita cost when government-supplied inputs (medical supplies, training, and supervisory support) are combined with community volunteer labor organized through the PKK (Family Welfare Movement) network and co-financed by state enterprise CSR programs. This hybrid model leverages the social capital embedded in Indonesian community organizations to dramatically reduce the unit cost of delivering elderly health services while maintaining quality standards through government oversight.

The key institutional insight is that the government functions as an enabler and standard-setter rather than a direct service provider, releasing fiscal resources while preserving accountability.

The second pattern concerns the culturally embedded nature of Islamic social finance as a complementary channel for financing the Silver Economy in majority-Muslim countries. Indonesia's BAZNAS Elderly Care Program illustrates how zakat (obligatory almsgiving) and waqf (Islamic endowment) mechanisms can be channeled toward elderly care infrastructure in ways that resonate deeply with the religious and cultural values of Muslim communities. With 40 elderly care homes (rumah lansia) established primarily in Java and Sumatra through zakat and waqf funding, complemented by government land grants, the BAZNAS program reaches elderly populations that may be structurally excluded from formal financial systems and may be resistant to state-managed welfare programs perceived as culturally inappropriate. A similar dynamic operates in Malaysia, where Yayasan Waqf Malaysia's endowment for Muslim senior welfare centers indicates that Islamic social finance is a scalable and culturally legitimate complementary financing channel for Muslim-majority populations in Indonesia and Malaysia.

The third pattern concerns the institutional maturity gradient visible across ASEAN countries. Singapore's CareShield Life program, a mandatory, fully portable long-term disability insurance scheme administered by private insurers under government regulation, with government co-contribution for lower-income policyholders, represents the most institutionally sophisticated PPP model for elderly financial protection in Southeast Asia. It achieves near-universal coverage of the resident adult population through mandatory participation, ensures sustainability through actuarially sound premium structures, and maintains equity through income-tested government subsidies. Thailand's NHSO long-term care fund occupies the intermediate tier, demonstrating an operational community-care PPP with documented reach and outcomes but still facing challenges in financing the most expensive categories of elderly care. Vietnam's MOLISA elderly clubs program and Indonesia's Posyandu Lansia, while achieving impressive population coverage, rely more heavily on volunteer labor and government grants, making them potentially vulnerable to funding discontinuities and less able to finance the intensive, medically complex care needs of the oldest-old population. Recognizing this institutional gradient is essential for designing realistic near-term policy pathways: a program that is sustainable and scalable in Singapore may be institutionally premature in Vietnam or the Philippines.

LIMITATIONS OF CONVENTIONAL FUNDING MODELS

Before examining the innovative financing instruments that offer pathways beyond conventional approaches, it is analytically important to understand why conventional funding models, primarily short-term government grants, donor aid, and single-year budget allocations, are structurally inadequate for the long-term, continuous financing needs of the silver economy. The limitations of conventional models are not merely quantitative; that is, there is not simply insufficient public money available, but fundamentally structural, embedded in the design logic of funding mechanisms created for different purposes and timeframes than those required by elderly welfare programs.

Short-term grant-based funding models face an inherent sustainability problem: service innovations demonstrated during a grant period are often difficult or impossible to maintain after the funding expires, because the organizational capacity, partnerships, and revenue streams needed to sustain the program independently were never developed during the grant period itself (Hodgkin et al., 2023). This dynamic encourages organizations to optimize for short-term target achievement rather than long-term institutional development, creating a systemic bias against capacity-building investments, staff training, systems development, and community trust-building, which are essential for program sustainability. Evaluations of capacity-building programs across development contexts confirm that short-term output-focused assessment approaches systematically fail to capture long-term benefits such as organizational learning, professional network development, and programmatic resilience, leading to a consistent underestimation of the cost of short-term funding cycles (Cassell et al., 2022; Anderson et al., 2018).

A directly parallel dynamic is evident in silver economy financing across ASEAN. Short-term government pilot programs for elderly day-care centers or home-care subsidies, frequently funded through annual budget allocations or fixed-term donor grants, have, in numerous cases, demonstrated promising initial results but faced severe sustainability challenges once the funding period ended. Organizations operating these programs lacked both the institutional capacity and the diversified revenue streams needed to continue operations independently. The disruption of services to elderly beneficiaries, who, unlike younger program beneficiaries, often cannot readily substitute with alternative care arrangements, caused measurable welfare losses and eroded community trust in both the programs and the government agencies that sponsor them (World Bank, 2023).

Vietnam provides a particularly instructive illustration of this pattern. Several internationally funded community care programs in Vietnam successfully demonstrated their service models during implementation periods of two to five years, achieving high satisfaction among the elderly and measurable health improvements.

However, when international funding ended, these programs could not transition to self-sustaining operations: no government budget line had been established to absorb them, and no private-sector interest had been cultivated during the pilot period. The programs effectively ceased to function, leaving elderly beneficiaries without the services they had come to rely upon. This outcome was not due to program failure in any technical sense; the service model was sound, but to a structural misalignment between short-term funding logic and the long-term continuity requirements of elderly care.

Indonesia's experience with Posyandu Lansia illustrates the alternative: embedding community-based programs within existing government administrative structures creates greater sustainability even when per-program funding levels remain modest. By integrating Posyandu Lansia within the village governance framework and partially financing it through Dana Desa (Village Fund) allocations, a constitutionally guaranteed annual transfer to village governments, Indonesia has created a financing mechanism that is both predictable and politically durable. The program's coverage has grown steadily over time rather than expanding during grant periods and contracting during funding gaps, demonstrating that the sustainability of the funding architecture matters more than the absolute level of resources at any given point (World Bank, 2023).

Dependence on public sector resources creates additional structural limitations beyond sustainability. Many ASEAN governments operate within strict fiscal constraints, including budget deficits, debt ceilings, and competing development priorities, which limit the fiscal space available to finance elderly care, pension systems, and age-friendly infrastructure on the scale required by demographic projections. In decentralized governance systems such as those in Indonesia and the Philippines, dependence on central government transfers is compounded by disbursement delays, budget under-execution, and intergovernmental coordination failures that directly affect the continuity of elderly social services at the community level. Bureaucratic bottlenecks and misaligned budget allocations further reduce the effectiveness of public silver economy spending, preventing programs from reaching the elderly populations who need them most (Frumence et al., 2014; Câmara et al., 2024).

The issue of scalability further exposes the weaknesses of conventional financing models. Elderly care programs that succeed in pilot or urban settings frequently struggle to scale to rural and peri-urban areas, where the majority of elderly populations in ASEAN countries reside. This failure is not primarily a resource problem but a design problem: programs are frequently designed for the institutional contexts, infrastructure levels, and social dynamics of urban centers, and are not sufficiently adaptable to the very different conditions of rural and remote communities. A day-care financing scheme that works in Bangkok or Jakarta may be structurally incompatible with the institutional capacity, physical infrastructure, and social structures of smaller communities in Thailand's northeast or Indonesia's outer islands. Addressing this scalability challenge requires funding designs that are flexible enough to accommodate the full diversity of aging contexts across the ASEAN sub-region, and that build institutional capacity at the local level rather than simply replicating centralized program models (Kato, 2024).

INNOVATIVE FINANCING INSTRUMENTS FOR THE SOUTHEAST ASIAN SILVER ECONOMY

Amid accelerating demographic shifts and the structural limitations of conventional funding models, innovative financing instruments have emerged as essential complements and, in some contexts, replacements for traditional public budget allocations. These instruments represent a fundamental paradigm shift in how elderly welfare is financed: moving from short-term, input-focused government expenditure toward long-term, outcome-oriented, multi-stakeholder financing architectures that distribute risk and reward more broadly across public, private, and community actors. In Southeast Asia, the development and adoption of these instruments are still at varying stages of maturity, but their potential, as documented in the case evidence from Section 3, is significant.

It is important at the outset to recognize that innovative financing instruments are not interchangeable: each is designed for a specific type of financing need, operates on a specific timeframe, requires a specific level of regulatory and institutional maturity, and carries specific risks and governance requirements. Deploying blended finance for a community-level dementia caregiver training program or using crowdfunding for a multi-decade geriatric hospital network, would represent a fundamental mismatch between instrument and purpose. The structured overview in Table 3 provides a reference framework for understanding these distinctions before the detailed discussion of individual instruments that follows.

Table 3. Overview of innovative financing instruments for the silver economy in Southeast Asia

Instrument	Best Suited For	Timeframe	Real-World Example in Southeast Asia
Public-Private Partnership (PPP)	Large elderly care infrastructure (hospitals, nursing homes, LTCI systems)	Long-term (10–30 years)	Thailand: NHSO-PPP for community long-term care with 145,000 elderly covered; Singapore: ElderShield/CareShield Life disability insurance PPP with 2.1 million policyholders
Blended Finance	Elderly care facility expansion in markets with insufficient commercial returns	Long-term (5–20 years)	Indonesia: ADB blended finance for Puskesmas network upgrades; Vietnam: World Bank blended elderly care infrastructure in rural provinces
Impact Investing	Assistive technology, elder-serving social enterprises, and geriatric pharma	Medium-term (3–10 years)	Malaysia: Khazanah Nasional social impact sukuk for aged care; Singapore: MUIS impact investments in elderly social enterprises
Corporate Social Responsibility (CSR)	Community day-care, elderly digital literacy, volunteer home-care programs	Short- to medium-term	Thailand: SCG age-friendly housing modifications in 10 provinces; Philippines: Ayala Corporation CSR-funded senior care centers in Makati
Blockchain-enabled Crowdfunding	Startup elderly-serving businesses, assistive device grants, and community care initiatives	Short-term (< 3 years)	Indonesia: Kitabisa.com crowdfunding for elderly home-care kits; Vietnam: crowdfunding for dementia caregiver training programs
Social Impact Bonds (SIB)	Preventive elderly health programs with measurable outcome targets	Medium-term (3–7 years)	South Korea: Ministry of Health SIB for elderly fall-prevention; Singapore: AIC SIB for elderly mental wellness
Islamic Social Finance (Waqf/ Zakat)	Elderly care endowments, halal senior housing, and community-based elderly welfare	Long-term/ perpetual	Indonesia: BAZNAS elderly care homes (rumah lansia) in Java and Sumatra; Malaysia: Yayasan Waqf Malaysia for Muslim senior welfare centers
Community-Based Savings Cooperatives	Informal-sector elderly workers without formal pension access	Long-term	Indonesia: arisan-based retirement saving groups in rural East Java; Vietnam: Social Credit Funds (Quy tin dung nhan dan) micro-pension schemes for elderly farmers

Source: Authors' compilation from IFC (2024), ADB (2023), World Bank (2023), UNDP (2025)

Corporate Social Responsibility (CSR)

Corporate Social Responsibility (CSR) represents one of the most immediately accessible innovative financing channels for the silver economy in Southeast Asia, precisely because it does not require the sophisticated regulatory frameworks, capital markets infrastructure, or institutional capacity that more complex instruments such as blended finance or social impact bonds demand. In the silver economy context,

CSR enables private companies to direct financial and in-kind resources toward elderly welfare programs, age-inclusive workplace policies, assistive technology development, and community-based care services, while simultaneously generating reputational benefits and strengthening relationships with stakeholders in aging communities.

As demonstrated in Table 2, companies such as SCG (Thailand), Pertamina Foundation (Indonesia), and Ayala Corporation (Philippines) have developed structured CSR programs that specifically target elderly populations, combining physical infrastructure investments with social service delivery. SCG's silver economy CSR program, which provided age-friendly housing modifications including ramp installations, grab bars, non-slip flooring, and accessible bathroom fittings to 5,000 low-income elderly households across 10 Thai provinces, exemplifies how a construction materials company can leverage its core business competencies and supply chain relationships to deliver meaningful elderly welfare outcomes at scale. The program's integration with the Ministry of Social Development and Human Security provided an accountability framework. It facilitated outreach to eligible households, illustrating the synergy that can be achieved when corporate CSR programs align with government elderly welfare objectives rather than operate independently.

In Southeast Asia, regulatory pressure for increasingly specific, mandatory CSR reporting is growing, creating incentives for companies to develop more strategic and measurable CSR programs in the silver economy space. Indonesia's Government Regulation No. 47/2012 requires limited liability companies to allocate CSR funds for social and environmental responsibility proportional to their profits, while Thailand's B-SCI (Business and Sustainable Community Initiative) and Singapore's SGX (Singapore Exchange) sustainability reporting framework are increasingly specific about social impact metrics related to aging communities. These regulatory developments are gradually transforming CSR from a discretionary philanthropic activity into a structured corporate governance responsibility, thereby increasing both the volume and the quality of CSR financing directed toward elderly welfare programs (Maltby, 2005; Kılıç & Uyar, 2014).

Impact Investing

Impact investing, defined as investment strategies that explicitly target measurable social or environmental outcomes alongside financial returns, is still at an early stage of development in the Southeast Asian silver economy but is growing steadily, driven by the convergence of demographic urgency, the maturation of regional capital markets, and increasing investor appetite for sustainability-aligned investment products (Bansal et al., 2023; Lanzavecchia & Bavado, 2018). Key examples documented in Table 2 include Khazanah Nasional's social impact sukuk for aged care facilities in

Malaysia, the MUIS (Majlis Ugama Islam Singapura) impact investment portfolio with elderly social enterprises in Singapore, and the Sasakawa Peace Foundation's gender-responsive investment in elderly women's social enterprises in Indonesia and Vietnam (IFC, 2024; UNDP, 2025).

The intentionality of impact investing, the explicit commitment to generating social impact as a primary investment objective alongside financial return, distinguishes it from conventional investment and from philanthropy. This intentionality creates accountability obligations that can drive more rigorous program design and outcome measurement in elderly welfare programs, addressing one of the long-standing weaknesses of grant-based financing. The challenge of impact measurement, particularly the development of standardized frameworks for assessing silver economy investment success, remains a central operational difficulty, as different stakeholders use different impact metrics and there is as yet no consensus standard for elderly care investment outcomes comparable to the IRIS+ framework used in broader impact investing contexts (Grabenwarter, 2017; Eriksson, 2025).

Public-Private Partnerships (PPP)

Public-Private Partnerships (PPPs) are collaborative arrangements between government entities and private-sector companies to finance, build, and manage public infrastructure and services. In the silver economy context, PPPs serve as a critical mechanism for developing and sustaining elderly care infrastructure, including assisted living facilities, dementia care centers, geriatric hospitals, and age-friendly community spaces, that governments alone cannot adequately finance. The core logic of PPPs is that they leverage each partner's comparative advantage: government provides regulatory authority, public land, and in some cases subsidies; private operators provide management efficiency, service innovation, and capital; and the partnership framework provides accountability structures to ensure that public objectives of quality, affordability, and equity are achieved alongside private financial objectives.

Thailand's NHSO long-term care fund represents the most advanced and empirically documented community-care PPP model currently operating in ASEAN. By 2023, the program had trained 50,000 care managers drawn from local communities and organized through local administrative organizations (OrBorTor), who collectively reached 145,000 dependent older adults with subsidized home care services financed through a per-person NHSO subsidy. Vietnam is exploring a similar community-based long-term care PPP model through its Ministry of Labor, Invalids, and Social Affairs (MOLISA), with pilot programs initiated in Hanoi and Ho Chi Minh City in 2022. Indonesia's push toward PPP-based elderly care is reflected in the 2023 National Long-Term Care Policy framework (Kebijakan Perawatan Jangka

Panjang), though implementation remains nascent outside urban Java. Singapore's ElderShield/CareShield Life represents the most institutionally mature PPP in the region, a fully portable, mandatory long-term disability insurance scheme with 2.1 million policyholders and S$1.2 billion in claims paid between 2020 and 2023 (NHSO, 2023; MOLISA, 2022; MOH Singapore, 2023).

Blended Finance

Blended finance is a strategic approach that combines public and philanthropic resources with private capital to support development goals, particularly suited for large-scale, long-term elderly care infrastructure investments such as geriatric hospital networks, elderly care facility clusters, long-term care insurance systems, and age-friendly urban infrastructure whose financial returns and social impact materialize over decades rather than years. In blended finance structures, public funds are not intended to replace private investment but to lower the risk profile of projects, improve their commercial viability, and thereby attract private capital that would otherwise remain on the sidelines. Risk-mitigation instruments typically used in blended finance include subsidized loans, first-loss guarantees, co-financing schemes, and currency hedging facilities (Tan, 2019; Mawdsley & Hughes-McLure, 2024).

In Southeast Asia, ADB's blended finance facility has supported community health center upgrades in Indonesia that serve elderly populations; the World Bank's Development Policy Loan for Vietnam includes components for elderly care infrastructure in rural provinces; and IFC's Asia-Pacific Aging Fund is actively seeking co-investors for geriatric hospital networks in Indonesia, Vietnam, and the Philippines (ADB, 2023). Critically, the success of blended finance in the silver economy requires a supportive legal and regulatory framework, one that clearly defines investment structures, protects investor rights, establishes accountability mechanisms, and provides credible exit routes for private investors. These enabling conditions remain underdeveloped in most ASEAN countries, representing a key structural barrier to scaling blended finance for elderly care at the pace required by demographic projections.

Blockchain-Enabled Crowdfunding

Blockchain-enabled crowdfunding serves a distinct and complementary role to blended finance and PPPs in the Silver Economy financing ecosystem: while the latter instruments are suited for long-term, large-scale elderly care infrastructure, crowdfunding is more appropriate for short-term or startup financing of elderly-serving social enterprises, community care initiatives, assistive technology development, and elderly entrepreneurship projects. Indonesia's Kitabisa.com, the largest crowdfunding platform in Southeast Asia with over 6 million registered donors, has increasingly channeled contributions toward elderly care initiatives, including home-care equipment kits for low-income elderly in rural areas and community transport programs for the elderly in remote villages. Vietnam's growing social enterprise sector has used crowdfunding platforms to finance dementia caregiver training programs and the operating costs of mobile geriatric clinics (Singh et al., 2025; Evangelene et al., 2025).

The deployment of blockchain-enabled crowdfunding and other digital financial tools in the silver economy must confront a critical risk specific to elderly populations: their heightened vulnerability to financial fraud, digital scams, and predatory schemes. As elderly individuals engage more with digital financial platforms, they face elevated exposure to identity theft, phishing attacks, and investment fraud, particularly in countries with nascent consumer protection laws and limited digital literacy among older adults. Addressing this concern requires the simultaneous deployment of technical safeguards and elderly-specific digital literacy programs. A phased implementation approach is recommended: beginning with government-supervised pilot programs in urban centers with higher digital readiness, followed by capacity-building for civil servants and elderly community facilitators, and finally scaling to peri-urban and rural areas with appropriately simplified interface designs and community-based support structures (Hussain et al., 2025).

Table 4. Growth of sustainable bond issuance: Global trends and Southeast Asian applications

Year	Global Sustainable Bond Issuance	Asia-Pacific Share (estimate)	Notable SEA Sovereign/Social Bond Issuances
2018	USD 247 billion	~15% (USD 37 bn)	Indonesia: first sovereign green sukuk (USD 1.25 bn)
2020	USD 732 billion	~18% (USD 132 bn)	Thailand: first sustainability bond by KBANK; Malaysia: first sustainability sukuk by CIMB
2022	USD 1 trillion	~20% (USD 200 bn)	Vietnam: first green bond framework; Philippines: first retail treasury bond with social impact clause
2023	> USD 1.1 trillion	~22% (USD 242 bn)	Indonesia: SDG bond (USD 2 bn); Singapore: green and social bond framework, including elderly care facilities

Source: OECD (2023); Climate Bonds Initiative (2023); ADB (2023)

Table 4 illustrates the rapid growth of sustainable bond markets globally and within Asia-Pacific, and documents the expanding participation of Southeast Asian sovereign and corporate issuers. Sustainable bonds, including green, social, and sustainability bonds, represent a growing channel for mobilizing capital markets to finance infrastructure in the silver economy. Indonesia's sovereign green sukuk, first issued in 2018, pioneered the use of Islamic bond structures for sustainability financing in the region and has since been followed by a growing pipeline of social and sustainability bonds from Thailand, Malaysia, Vietnam, and Singapore. While current Southeast Asian sustainable bond issuances are predominantly directed toward environmental objectives such as renewable energy and green infrastructure, the inclusion of elderly care facilities in Singapore's social bond framework signals a broadening of social bond mandates that other ASEAN issuers are expected to follow as their silver economy financing needs intensify (OECD, 2023; ADB, 2023).

COMPARATIVE FINANCING LANDSCAPE ACROSS SOUTHEAST ASIAN COUNTRIES

The financing landscape for the silver economy varies considerably across ASEAN countries, reflecting differences in fiscal capacity, institutional maturity, regulatory frameworks, cultural context, and the urgency of demographic pressures. Understanding these differences is essential for policy design, because the most appropriate financing strategy for any given country depends critically on where that country sits along multiple developmental dimensions simultaneously not just its income level or elderly population share, but also its legal infrastructure for investment, the depth of its capital markets, the strength of its civil society organizations, and the cultural receptivity of its elderly population and their families to different forms of formal and informal care financing.

Table 5. Comparative silver economy financing landscape in Southeast Asian countries

Country	Dominant Financing Mechanism	PPP Maturity	Key Institutional Actor	Real Partnership Example
Indonesia	Public budget (APBN) + Islamic social finance (zakat/waqf) + CSR	Emerging (nascent regulatory framework)	Kemensos, BAZNAS, BPJS Kesehatan	BAZNAS elderly homes + Posyandu Lansia community-government partnership
Vietnam	State budget + ODA grants + growing CSR	Early-stage (pilot programs only)	MOLISA, Vietnam Social Security (VSS), provincial health departments	VinaCapital Foundation mobile clinics + MOLISA elderly clubs network (54,000 clubs)
Thailand	National Health Security fund + local government + PPP	Intermediate (NHSO community care PPP fully operational)	National Health Security Office (NHSO), Ministry of Social Development	NHSO long-term care fund: 50,000 care managers + SCG housing accessibility CSR

continued on following page

Table 5. Continued

Country	Dominant Financing Mechanism	PPP Maturity	Key Institutional Actor	Real Partnership Example
Malaysia	Public budget + sovereign wealth fund social bonds + Islamic finance	Intermediate (growing sukuk/SIB pipeline)	JKM, Khazanah Nasional, Ministry of Women, Family and Community Development	Khazanah RM 100 million sukuk for aged care + JKM-FELDA elderly daycare PPP
Singapore	Government subsidies + mature PPP + mandatory private insurance	Advanced (full PPP ecosystem with robust regulatory framework)	Agency for Integrated Care (AIC), CPF Board, Ministry of Health	CareShield Life: 2.1 million policyholders + AIC community care network with VWOs
Philippines	Public budget + LGU funds + NGO grants + Philhealth	Early-stage (policy mandate exists; implementation gaps remain significant)	DSWD, Philhealth, LGUs, Older Persons' Coordinating Councils	Senior Citizens Act implementation through the LGU-private pharmacy and hospital PPP

Source: Authors' compilation from NHSO (2023), MOLISA (2022), JKM (2023), MOH Singapore (2023), DSWD (2022), World Bank (2023)

The comparative table reveals a clear developmental gradient across ASEAN that has important implications for both national policy design and regional knowledge-sharing. Singapore operates at the most advanced level of institutional PPP maturity in the region, having developed a comprehensive ecosystem of regulatory frameworks, subsidy mechanisms, quality standards, and monitoring systems that enable private nursing homes, voluntary welfare organizations, and commercial insurers to participate in the delivery and financing of elderly care under public accountability structures. This institutional maturity did not emerge spontaneously but was deliberately built over several decades through progressive regulatory development, institutional capacity-building, and a willingness to pilot and refine financing mechanisms before scaling them.

Thailand occupies an intermediate position, having made the most significant advances in community-based long-term care PPP among middle-income ASEAN economies. The NHSO long-term care fund model, which uses a per-person subsidy mechanism to finance community-based care managers organized through local administrative units, is the most empirically documented and replicable model available for ASEAN countries seeking to develop community-care financing beyond pure grant dependency. Its combination of government financing, community delivery infrastructure, and clear accountability mechanisms makes it a strong candidate for adaptation in Vietnam and Indonesia, where similar community governance structures exist but lack the financing framework.

Vietnam's position in the comparative landscape is particularly significant given the urgency of its demographic trajectory. The current over-reliance on state budget allocations and donor grants, which together constitute the vast majority of elderly care financing in Vietnam, creates a structural vulnerability that will intensify as demographic aging accelerates and official development assistance decreases. Vietnam's rapidly growing private sector, maturing capital markets, and expanding CSR culture, exemplified by the VinaCapital Foundation's Silver Generation Initiative, provide the building blocks for a more diversified financing architecture. What is currently missing is the regulatory framework that would enable private capital to flow into elderly care infrastructure through PPP structures, social bonds, or blended finance facilities. Developing this framework should be considered a priority policy investment for Vietnam's Ministry of Finance and Ministry of Labor in the next five-year planning cycle.

GOVERNANCE AND REGULATORY CHALLENGES

Governance and regulatory challenges represent a cross-cutting constraint on the development of silver economy financing across all Southeast Asian countries. However, the specific nature and severity of these challenges vary considerably across countries, instrument types, and governance levels. At the broadest level, the challenge is one of institutional readiness: the governance frameworks, legal infrastructure, regulatory capacity, and inter-agency coordination mechanisms required to enable innovative silver economy financing instruments to function effectively are still developing in most ASEAN countries, and are significantly less mature than the financing instruments themselves (UNDP, 2022; World Bank, 2020).

A first category of governance challenge concerns the adequacy of legal frameworks for innovative financing instruments. Many ASEAN nations, particularly Vietnam, Indonesia, and the Philippines, lack comprehensive legal definitions, investor protection regulations, and accountability mechanisms for blended finance structures, crowdfunding platforms, social impact bonds, and impact investment vehicles. Without these legal foundations, investors face unacceptable uncertainty about their rights and remedies, project sponsors face difficulty enforcing contract terms, and government agencies lack the legal authority to enter into the complex, long-term agreements that PPP structures require. The result is a financing gap that is not primarily a matter of the fiscal resources that exist, both domestically and internationally, but rather an institutional one: the legal and regulatory plumbing required to channel resources toward elderly care infrastructure has not yet been installed.

A second category of governance challenge concerns information security and consumer protection for elderly participants in digital financial systems. As blockchain-enabled crowdfunding, digital micro-insurance, mobile pension contribution platforms, and other digital financial tools are increasingly deployed in the silver economy, they expose elderly users to heightened risks of financial fraud, identity theft, and digital scam victimization. Elderly individuals, particularly those with limited digital literacy, cognitive decline, or social isolation, are disproportionately targeted by predatory financial schemes, and the harms caused by financial fraud in old age are particularly severe because elderly victims often have limited ability to recover financial losses and limited time to rebuild savings. Effective governance of digital silver economy finance must therefore include mandatory consumer protection standards specifically designed for digital financial products targeting elderly users; accessible, low-barrier complaint channels; proactive fraud monitoring and alert systems; and community-based digital safety education programs tailored to the cognitive and technological literacy profiles of older adults.

Table 6. Key civil society and advocacy networks supporting silver economy accountability in Southeast Asia

Network / Organization	Advocacy Focus	Countries Active	Role in Silver Economy Accountability
HelpAge International Asia-Pacific	Rights, inclusion, and care of older persons	Indonesia, Vietnam, Thailand, Philippines, Myanmar	Monitors elderly care policy implementation; advocates for universal social pension and age-inclusive financing standards
NGO Forum on the Asian Development Bank	Social impact of ADB-funded development projects	All ADB member countries, including all ASEAN	Monitors elderly care components of ADB health and infrastructure loans; provides policy input on silver economy guidelines
ASEAN Civil Society Conference (ACSC)	Social equity and rights in ASEAN integration	All 10 ASEAN member states	Advocates for inclusion of silver economy financing provisions in ASEAN Community commitments; tracks implementation across member states
Vietnam Association of the Elderly (Hoi nguoi cao tuoi)	Welfare and rights of the elderly in Vietnam	Vietnam (all 63 provinces)	8.6 million members; co-implements elderly clubs with MOLISA; monitors quality of community care programs; advocates for pension expansion
Indonesia Lansia Foundation (Yayasan Indonesia Lansia)	Advocacy for elderly welfare policy in Indonesia	Indonesia (national + 15 provinces)	Monitors JKN implementation for the elderly; advocates for national LTC policy development; conducts elderly needs assessments in underserved areas
Transparency International ASEAN chapters	Anti-corruption and governance accountability	Indonesia, Malaysia, Philippines, Thailand	Monitors public expenditure on elderly social programs; advocates for transparent PPP contracting and procurement in the silver economy

Source: HelpAge International (2023), ASEAN Secretariat (2023), Vietnam Association of the Elderly (2023)

Civil society organizations play an essential role in the governance of silver economy financing that goes beyond simple advocacy. As documented in Table 6, organizations such as HelpAge International Asia-Pacific and the Vietnam Association of the Elderly serve as frontline monitors of the quality of policy implementation, ensuring that financing commitments translate into tangible service improvements for elderly beneficiaries rather than being absorbed by administrative overhead or diverted through corruption. The Vietnam Association of the Elderly, with 8.6 million members across all 63 provinces, co-implements the MOLISA elderly clubs program and therefore has direct operational visibility into program quality that government monitoring systems alone cannot replicate. The NGO Forum on the Asian Development Bank performs a similar monitoring function for internationally financed elderly care and health infrastructure projects, ensuring that ADB social safeguard commitments are enforced in practice.

A third governance challenge that deserves explicit attention is the risk of regulatory fragmentation across sectors and across ASEAN member states. Silver economy financing instruments, particularly blended finance structures, social impact bonds, and cross-border impact investment vehicles, often span the regulatory domains of multiple government ministries (finance, health, social welfare, investment), and may involve investors and service providers operating across national borders. When regulatory frameworks are fragmented, with different rules applying to the same instrument depending on which ministry oversees which aspect of the arrangement, transaction costs rise, accountability gaps emerge, and the risk of regulatory arbitrage increases. ASEAN-level harmonization of silver economy investment regulations, analogous to the harmonization achieved in trade and financial services through ASEAN Economic Community frameworks, would significantly reduce these fragmentation costs and unlock cross-border capital flows toward elderly care infrastructure across the region.

CONCLUSION

The global demographic transition, marked by historically unprecedented increases in life expectancy and sustained declines in fertility, has set in motion socio-economic transformations of equal historical significance across Southeast Asia. Indonesia, Vietnam, Thailand, Malaysia, Singapore, and the Philippines are all on trajectories of accelerating growth in their elderly populations. However, each country brings a distinct institutional history, fiscal capacity, cultural context, and demographic urgency to the challenge of developing sustainable financing systems for the silver economy. The heterogeneity of the Southeast Asian aging landscape is not a complication to be minimized in policy analysis but a central empirical reality that must shape the design of financing strategies, governance frameworks, and partnership models at every level.

The empirical evidence presented in this chapter demonstrates unambiguously that innovative financing instruments for the silver economy, such as PPPs, blended finance, impact investing, CSR programs, Islamic social finance, social impact bonds, and blockchain-enabled crowdfunding, are not merely theoretical constructs advanced in academic literature or international policy documents. They are already operational realities in Southeast Asia, implemented through named partnerships between identifiable institutions, generating documented outcomes for measurable populations of elderly beneficiaries. Thailand's NHSO long-term care fund has trained 50,000 community care managers and reached 145,000 dependent elderly. Singapore's CareShield Life program has enrolled 2.1 million policyholders and paid out S$1.2 billion in disability claims. Malaysia's Khazanah Nasional has issued RM 100 million in social impact sukuk to finance aged care facilities in Sabah and Sarawak. Indonesia's BAZNAS has established 40 elderly care homes through zakat and waqf financing. Vietnam's VinaCapital Foundation has provided free geriatric screenings to over 200,000 older adults in rural areas across 12 provinces. These are not pilot programs or aspirational proposals; they are functioning systems that demonstrate what is achievable when governance frameworks, financing architectures, and institutional partnerships are aligned.

Vietnam deserves particular emphasis as a priority case for developing silver-economy financing within Southeast Asia. Its combination of rapid demographic aging, a large informal labor force with minimal pension coverage, a nascent but growing private sector with an expanding CSR culture, and available international development finance creates both an urgent need and a significant opportunity. The current financing architecture, dominated by state budget allocations and donor grants, is structurally inadequate to meet the scale and continuity of investment in elderly care required by Vietnam's demographic trajectory. The most promising near-term policy pathway is the replication and adaptation of Thailand's NHSO community care PPP model within Vietnam's commune-based governance structure, coupled with the development of a legal framework for social impact sukuk and social bonds to mobilize Vietnam's growing domestic capital markets for financing elderly care infrastructure. The Vietnam Association of the Elderly, with its 8.6 million members and operational presence in all 63 provinces, provides the civil society infrastructure to co-implement and monitor such a system at scale.

A fundamental shift from rigid conventional funding models toward more flexible, long-term, and outcome-oriented financing approaches is not merely advisable but structurally necessary. The functional differentiation of instruments across the financing lifecycle is critical for ensuring that the most appropriate mechanism addresses each financing need: blended finance and PPPs for long-term elderly care infrastructure investments that require multi-decade commitment and large-scale capital; impact investing and social bonds for medium-term growth capital for elder-serving enterprises and insurance systems; CSR and Islamic social finance for community-based program co-financing that complements government resources; and crowdfunding for short-term, small-scale startup financing of innovative elderly care solutions at the community level. Mismatching instruments to financing needs using short-term crowdfunding for infrastructure, or complex blended finance structures for community programs, produces poor outcomes regardless of resource availability.

Two underserved populations require dedicated policy attention within the broader silver economy financing architecture. Older women in Southeast Asia typically live five to seven years longer than men, yet accumulate significantly fewer financial assets due to career interruptions for caregiving, lower lifetime earnings, and historically limited access to formal pension schemes face compounded vulnerability in old age: a longer period of financial dependency combined with a smaller asset base to draw upon. Gender-responsive financial tools, including pension credits that recognize unpaid care work, micro-savings and micro-insurance products accessible through women's community networks, and inheritance and property rights reforms that protect widows' financial security, are essential complements to gender-neutral silver economy financing strategies.

Similarly, elderly individuals engaged in informal or self-employment, who constitute the majority of the elderly workforce in Southeast Asian countries, typically lack access to formal pension systems and are excluded from employer-based retirement benefits. Targeted instruments such as voluntary micro-pension schemes, community-based savings cooperatives (including arisan-based retirement funds in Indonesia and Vietnam's Social Credit Funds), and mobile-based contribution platforms can serve as viable pathways to extend financial protection to this underserved segment. The development of these instruments requires not only financial innovation but also regulatory adaptation, simplified registration requirements, tax incentives for voluntary pension contributions, and regulatory sandboxes that enable innovative micro-pension products to be tested and refined before scaling.

Through a combination of long-term-oriented financing policies, technological innovation deployed with realistic implementation roadmaps and robust consumer protection frameworks, cross-sector governance coordination that reduces regulatory fragmentation, and participatory civil society engagement that ensures elderly beneficiaries' voices shape program design and accountability mechanisms, the Silver Economy can be developed as a genuine driver of equitable, sustainable economic progress across Southeast Asia. The demographic transition is irreversible; the elderly population in Southeast Asia will grow regardless of policy choices. What is within the power of policymakers, financiers, civil society organizations, and communities to determine is whether that growth is managed as a crisis or leveraged as an opportunity. The empirical evidence from Thailand, Singapore, Malaysia, Indonesia, Vietnam, and the Philippines presented in this chapter demonstrates that the latter is achievable and provides a practical blueprint for how to do so.

REFERENCES

ADB. (2023). *Asian Development Outlook 2023: Toward Inclusive Aging*. Asian Development Bank.

Anderson, S. J., Ghys, P. D., Ombam, R., & Hallett, T. B. (2018). Frontloading HIV financing maximizes the achievable impact of HIV prevention. *Journal of the International AIDS Society, 21*(3), e25087. DOI: 10.1002/jia2.25087 PMID: 29498234

Bansal, N.. (2023). Capitalizing on Conservation: The Synergy Between Financial Gains and Environmental Goals in Impact Investing. In *Green Management*. Nova Science Publishers.

BAZNAS. (2023). *Annual Report on Social Programs for the Elderly in Indonesia*. National Zakat Agency of Indonesia.

Bieszk-Stolorz, B., Dmytrów, K., & Frąckiewicz, E. (2024). Multivariate analysis of the sustainable development of the silver economy in the European Union countries. *Sustainability (Basel), 16*(23), 10703. DOI: 10.3390/su162310703

BPS. (2023). *Statistik Penduduk Lanjut Usia Indonesia 2023*. Badan Pusat Statistik.

Briegas, J. J. M., et al. (2021). Silver Economy: A Development Opportunity. Confinia Cephalalgica, 31(2).

Câmara, S. F., Buarque, B., Pinto, G. P., Ribeiro, T. V., & Soares, J. B. (2024). Innovation policy and public funding to stimulate innovation in knowledge intensive companies: The influence of human and social capital. *Journal of Science and Technology Policy Management, 15*(2), 418–442. DOI: 10.1108/JSTPM-09-2021-0135

Cassell, H. M., Rose, E. S., Moon, T. D., Bello-Manga, H., Aliyu, M. H., & Mutale, W. (2022). Strengthening research capacity through an intensive training program for biomedical investigators from low-and middle-income countries: The Vanderbilt Institute for Research Development and Ethics (VIRDE). *BMC Medical Education, 22*(1), 97. DOI: 10.1186/s12909-022-03162-8 PMID: 35164739

Christiansen, B., & Branch, J. D. (2025). Critical economic implications of global demographic changes.

Eriksson, S. (2025). *Impact investing. In the Elgar Encyclopedia of Innovation Management*. Edward Elgar.

Evangelene, A. D. C., Siripalli, D. K., & Pothumani, S. (2025). Crowdfunding application using blockchain. DOI: 10.1063/5.0265037

Frumence, G., Nyamhanga, T., Mwangu, M., & Hurtig, A. K. (2014). The dependency on central government funding of decentralised health systems: Experiences of the challenges and coping strategies in the Kongwa District, Tanzania. *BMC Health Services Research*, *14*(1), 39. DOI: 10.1186/1472-6963-14-39 PMID: 24460781

Gölçek, A. G. (2024). *Perspectives on the Economics of Aging*. IGI Global. DOI: 10.4018/979-8-3693-7753-6

Gonzales, E., Matz-Costa, C., & Morrow-Howell, N. (2015). Increasing opportunities for the productive engagement of older adults: A response to population aging. *The Gerontologist*, *55*(2), 252–261. DOI: 10.1093/geront/gnu176 PMID: 26035601

Grabenwarter, U. (2017). Measuring Impact: A Debate About the Concepts of Profit and Value. In *Principles and Practice of Impact Investing*. Routledge. DOI: 10.4324/9781351284769-5

HelpAge International. (2023). *Global AgeWatch Insight Report: Southeast Asia*. HelpAge International.

Hodgkin, D., Horgan, C. M., Brown, S. J., Bart, G., & Stewart, M. T. (2023). Financial sustainability of novel delivery models in behavioral health treatment. *The Journal of Mental Health Policy and Economics*, *26*(4), 149. PMID: 38113385

Hussain, S., Zardari, S., & Ullah, M. (2025). Systematic Analysis of Blockchain Based Trust Management Frameworks in Crowdfunding. *IEEE Access : Practical Innovations, Open Solutions.*

IFC. (2024). *IFC Silver Economy Initiative: Southeast Asia Strategy*. International Finance Corporation.

ILO. (2022). *Global employment trends for women: Building back fairer*. International Labor Organization.

IMF. (2023). *Navigating demographic headwinds*. International Monetary Fund.

JKM. (2023). *Kasih Sejahtera Program Annual Report*. Department of Social Welfare Malaysia.

Kato, A. I. (2024). Building resilience and sustainability in small business enterprises. *Cogent Economics & Finance*, *12*(1). Advance online publication. DOI: 10.1080/23322039.2024.2399760

Kılıç, M., & Uyar, A. (2014). The Impact of Corporate Characteristics on Social Responsibility Disclosures. In *Corporate Governance*. Springer. DOI: 10.1007/978-3-642-45167-6_14

Lanzavecchia, A., & Bavado, L. (2018). A Triple Bottom Line Return: Impact Investing. In *Asset Management*. Nova Science Publishers.

Lee, R., & Mason, A. (2011). *Population aging and the generational economy: A global perspective*. Edward Elgar. DOI: 10.4337/9780857930583

Lee, R., & Mason, A. (2022). *The generational economy and population aging*. Edward Elgar.

Li, X., Xie, J., Luo, J., & Yang, A. (2025). The silver-hair economy in the new era: Political economy perspectives on its dilemmas and solutions. *Sustainability (Basel)*, *17*(15), 6760. DOI: 10.3390/su17156760

Lopane, F. (2025). *Silver Economy for Innovation and Inclusivity*. Springer Briefs in Applied Sciences and Technology.

Maltby, J. (2005). Showing a Strong Front: Corporate Social Reporting and the Business Case in Britain, 1914–1919. *The Accounting Historians Journal*, *32*(2), 145–171. DOI: 10.2308/0148-4184.32.2.145

Manzano, F. A. (2025). Silver economy: Structural challenges and strategies for inclusive development. *Ateliê Geográfico*, *19*(1), 35–57. DOI: 10.5216/ag.v19i1.80921

Martinez, C., & Weyman, T. (2017). *Demographic change in a complex world*. Advances in Spatial Science. DOI: 10.1007/978-3-319-63197-4_1

Mawdsley, E., & Hughes-McLure, S. (2024). Blended finance. In *Handbook of Aid and Development*. Edward Elgar. DOI: 10.4337/9781800886810.00028

MOLISA. (2022). Report on National Program for Elderly Care 2021–2022 Ministry of Labor, Invalids and Social Affairs, Vietnam.

Nasional, K. (2023). Khazanah [Khazanah Nasional Berhad.]. *Sustainability Report*, •••, 2023.

NHSO. (2023). *Long-Term Care for Dependent Elderly: Annual Report 2023*. National Health Security Office.

Nieto-Vieites, A., Gaspar, P., Victor, J., Pérez-Blanco, L., Felpete-López, A., & Facal, D. (2022). Technological development in preventing cognitive frailty, promoting active aging, and the economics of aging. In *Marketing and Smart Technologies: Proceedings of ICMarkTech 2021* (Vol. 2, pp. 213–223). Springer Nature Singapore. DOI: 10.1007/978-981-16-9272-7_18

OECD. (2022). *Fiscal challenges and inclusive growth in aging societies*. OECD Publishing.

OECD. (2023). [OECD indicators. OECD Publishing.]. *Health at a Glance*, •••, 2023.

Piskorska, B., & Adamczyk, M. D. (2025). The challenge of social security in an aging European Union. Online Journal Modeling the New Europe.

PSA. (2023). *2023 Philippine Statistics Authority Report on Senior Citizens*. Philippine Statistics Authority.

Reshetnikova, L., Boldyreva, N., Perevalova, M., Kalayda, S., & Pisarenko, Z. (2021). Conditions for the growth of the "silver economy" in the context of sustainable development goals: Peculiarities of Russia. *Journal of Risk and Financial Management*, *14*(9), 401. DOI: 10.3390/jrfm14090401

SCG. (2022). SCG [Siam Cement Group.]. *Sustainability Report*, •••, 2022.

Singapore, M. O. H. (2023). *Agency for Integrated Care Annual Report 2022/23*. Ministry of Health.

Singh, A.. (2025). Smart Contract-Based Crowdfunding. *2025 International Conference on Networks and Cryptology (NETCRYPT)*. DOI: 10.1109/NETCRYPT65877.2025.11102542

Tan, C. (2019). Creative cocktails or toxic brews? Blended finance and the regulatory framework for sustainable development. In *Sustainable Trade, Investment, and Finance*. Edward Elgar. DOI: 10.4337/9781788971041.00023

Tyers, R., & Shi, Q. (2007). Demographic change and policy responses. *World Economy*, *30*(4), 537–566. DOI: 10.1111/j.1467-9701.2007.01004.x

UNDP. (2025). *UNDP Silver Economy Report Series*. United Nations Development Program.

United Nations. (2022). *World Population Prospects 2022: Summary of results*. United Nations DESA.

United Nations. (2023). *World population aging 2023*. United Nations.

Vietnam Association of the Elderly. (2023). Annual Report 2023. Hoi nguoi cao tuoi Viet Nam.

VinaCapital Foundation. (2023). *Silver Generation Initiative Report 2023*. VinaCapital Foundation.

WHO. (2023). *Decade of Healthy Aging: Progress report 2021–2023*. WHO.

WHO. (2024). *Aging and health fact sheet*. WHO.

World Bank. (2023). *Addressing the needs of an aging population.* World Bank.

Chapter 3
Financing Innovation and Multi-Stakeholder Collaborative Mechanisms in Telemedicine:
A Policy-Oriented Framework to Enhance Healthcare Access for Rural Elderly in China's Silver Economy

Poshan Yu
http://orcid.org/0000-0003-1069-3675
Australian Studies Centre, Shanghai University, China & European Business Institute of Luxembourg, Luxembourg

Yitian Chen
http://orcid.org/0009-0007-6415-426X
Soochow University, China

Johnston H. C. Wong
Beijing Normal-Hong Kong Baptist University, China

Allen M. H. Hu
http://orcid.org/0009-0008-1128-0964
Independent Researcher, China

DOI: 10.4018/979-8-3373-9370-4.ch003

ABSTRACT

China's rapidly expanding silver economy faces severe urban–rural healthcare disparities, and telemedicine serves as a pivotal tool to enhance care accessibility for older adults. However, financial barriers hinder its sustainable scaling. This study explores financial innovations and collaborative mechanisms to advance telemedicine for the silver economy in China via bibliometric analysis (CiteSpace) and in-depth case studies of Zhongshan Hospital and Guangdong Second People's Hospital. Findings reveal a four-dimensional financing pathway: policy-driven initiation, technology-enabled infrastructure, diversified public–private financing, and outcome-oriented evaluation. Supported by Collaborative Care Theory, the study demonstrates that integrated payment systems, policy support, and social–business partnerships improve telemedicine sustainability. It provides actionable frameworks to bridge healthcare gaps and sustain silver-economy vitality, offering implications for emerging economies with aging populations.

1 INTRODUCTION

Telemedicine refers to the delivery of healthcare services at a distance using information and communication technologies, providing diagnosis, treatment, disease prevention, continuing education, and research support. In this study, the terms "telemedicine" and "telehealth" are used interchangeably to encompass a broad range of digital healthcare activities—ones that are increasingly central to advancing healthy aging and sustaining the vitality of the global silver economy. The silver economy, centered on the needs, contributions, and well-being of aging populations (typically defined as adults aged 60 and above), has emerged as a critical global economic and social pillar. With more than 280 million people aged 60 and above, China hosts one of the largest and fastest-growing silver economies worldwide, yet its regional development remains highly uneven. First-tier cities such as Beijing, Shanghai, and Shenzhen have achieved silver-economy healthcare accessibility comparable to developed economies, supported by comprehensive telemedicine networks for remote specialist consultations and chronic disease management. In contrast, fourth- and fifth-tier cities and rural areas still face severe barriers similar to those in developing contexts, including shortages of geriatric care providers, limited digital devices, and inadequate internet infrastructure. This dual urban-rural structure creates unique challenges and opportunities for telemedicine to serve the silver economy: while urban centers benefit from advanced technological infrastructure, financing models, policy mechanisms, and service delivery must be specially adapted to meet the age-specific health needs of underserved aging populations in rural and lower-tier regions.

As digital health transformation accelerates, telemedicine has been widely recognized as a strategic solution to improve healthcare accessibility, narrow urban-rural disparities, and address the age-specific health needs at the core of the silver economy. Older adults often face unique barriers to care, including limited mobility, high chronic disease burdens, and low digital literacy—challenges that are especially severe in rural and disadvantaged regions. Telemedicine can bridge these systemic gaps, support healthy aging, and strengthen community health development, all foundational to a thriving silver economy. However, despite technological progress, persistent financial barriers continue to hinder widespread adoption and sustainable scaling of telemedicine systems. High infrastructure costs—including 5G deployment, remote diagnostic equipment tailored for older users, privacy-compliant secure digital systems, and geriatric telecare workforce training—combined with fragmented reimbursement frameworks and regulatory uncertainty, significantly restrict telemedicine initiatives, especially in lower-tier and rural regions where silver-economy populations face the greatest access barriers.

Against this background, this study does not address generic telemedicine barriers but focuses on constructing a differentiated, policy-centered telemedicine framework that bridges China's internal healthcare divides and centers the needs of the silver economy. It emphasizes integrating business partnerships and social service innovations to advance equitable healthcare access for older adults and sustainable community development—core goals for sustaining silver-economy vitality. For example, social service organizations can play a pivotal role in training older adults to use telemedicine platforms, while private enterprises contribute technical expertise to develop age-friendly interfaces and affordable devices.

Building on this foundation, this study has two core objectives. First, it systematically analyzes the four-dimensional financing pathways observed in Chinese telemedicine initiatives for the silver economy—policy-driven initiation, technology-enabled infrastructure, diversified financing mechanisms, and outcome-oriented evaluation—highlighting how coordinated public policy, technological enablement, financial diversification, and service outcome monitoring jointly extend geriatric healthcare access into lower-tier silver-economy communities. Second, drawing on Collaborative Care Theory, the study explores how payment structures, policy supports, and investment mechanisms can be dynamically integrated to build resilient telemedicine ecosystems capable of driving systemic community change and sustaining silver-economy vitality. Collaborative Care Theory, which emphasizes multidisciplinary collaboration and shared accountability, aligns naturally with the multi-stakeholder nature of silver-economy telemedicine, bringing together governments, private firms, social organizations, and healthcare providers.

This study therefore positions telemedicine not merely as a healthcare delivery innovation but as a strategic tool for driving community change and sustaining silver-economy vitality through social service and business partnerships focused on healthy aging. It aims to design actionable frameworks that address financial sustainability challenges while advancing healthcare equity for silver-economy populations across diverse regions—an essential pillar of a thriving silver economy.

The core research question guiding this study is: How can financial innovations and investment strategies, through policy-based frameworks and social-business collaborations, drive sustainable telemedicine expansion and promote healthcare accessibility for silver-economy populations and community development in rural China—thereby sustaining silver-economy vitality? This study explores how financial innovations and investment strategies embedded in policy frameworks and strengthened by social-business collaborations can support the sustainable scaling of telemedicine systems for the silver economy in rural China. It focuses on the dynamic integration of public leadership, diversified financing (including public-private partnerships), technological enablers, and community-driven geriatric health initiatives, aiming to show how these combined strategies improve healthcare access for underserved aging populations and promote broader community development, contributing to health equity, financial resilience, inclusive growth, and long-term silver-economy vitality.

Supporting this main question are three focused sub-questions that structure the empirical and theoretical analysis: (1) How has academic research on financial accessibility in telemedicine for the silver economy evolved over the past decade? (2) How do Chinese telemedicine initiatives integrate policy, technology, and financing strategies to extend geriatric healthcare access from major cities to lower-tier silver-economy communities and overcome financial barriers, supporting silver-economy vitality? (3) How can collaborative care theory explain the integration of payment models, policy instruments, and digital financial innovations in improving the financial sustainability of telemedicine systems for silver-economy populations?

This rest of this paper first reviews the literature on financial barriers, financing models, public-private partnerships, and multi-stakeholder collaboration in telemedicine for the silver economy. It then introduces the bibliometric method using CiteSpace and a qualitative case study approach, with deep analysis of two leading Chinese telemedicine practices. The findings section presents empirical insights into financial innovations, policy barriers, research trends, and China's four-dimensional financing pathway, supported by real-world case evidence. The discussion interprets these findings through Collaborative Care Theory, and the conclusion provides policy and investment recommendations and future research directions.

2 LITERATURE REVIEW

This chapter reviews existing research on financial barriers, financing innovation models, public-private partnerships (PPPs), and the integration of social service and business partnerships in telemedicine—with a specific focus on their implications for the silver economy. It establishes a conceptual foundation for understanding how collaborative mechanisms can drive healthcare accessibility improvements for aging populations and promote sustainable community transformation, which is critical for sustaining silver economy vitality.

2.1 Financial Barriers to Sustainable Telemedicine for the Silver Economy

While telemedicine is increasingly recognized for its potential to bridge healthcare access gaps for silver economy populations and sustain silver economy vitality, persistent financial constraints remain among the most significant challenges to its sustainable expansion. Inadequate reimbursement mechanisms, high initial infrastructure costs, and the absence of clear return-on-investment (ROI) models continue to hinder broader adoption—disproportionately impacting telecare for the silver economy. Older adults are more likely to rely on fixed incomes and public health insurance, making them particularly sensitive to cost barriers, while providers often hesitate to invest in silver economy-focused telemedicine due to uncertain financial returns (Li et al.,2022; Kilaru et al.,2026; Kongmalai et al., 2026; Neumann et al.,2024; Moulaei & Kazemi-Arpanahi, 2026).

For example, in Iran, telemedicine development (including geriatric care for the silver economy) has been significantly constrained by limited national health budgets, which prioritize acute care over preventive and chronic disease management services critical for aging populations. Similarly, in China, most telemedicine platforms—many of which could address unmet silver economy health needs—rely heavily on fragmented, short-term funding from local government pilot programs, lacking stable long-term financial support. These financial limitations not only impede scalability but also undermine efforts to integrate telemedicine systems into national healthcare delivery frameworks for silver economy populations, as platforms struggle to maintain operations once pilot funding expires.

Moreover, inconsistent reimbursement policies and lack of sustainable financing mechanisms discourage provider participation and long-term investment in telecare for the silver economy. In many cases, virtual consultations for older adults are reimbursed at lower rates compared to in-person services, reducing incentives for widespread telemedicine adoption focused on silver economy health needs. For instance, in the United States, Medicare reimburses telemedicine visits at 80% of the rate for in-person care, creating a financial disincentive for providers to offer virtual geriatric services. This gap is particularly problematic given that older adults often require more frequent consultations for chronic conditions, making the lower reimbursement rates financially unsustainable for providers serving large silver economy populations (Liu et al., 2026; Xu et al., 2025; Wang et al.,2025).

Table 1. Financing barriers for telemedicine in the silver economy

Barriers	Description	Illustrative Example
High initial infrastructure costs	Building telemedicine platforms for silver economy care requires heavy investment in digital infrastructure (e.g., age-friendly tools, remote chronic disease monitoring), especially in developing countries.	In Iran, insufficient national health budget has severely limited infrastructure development for telecare of aging populations.
Inadequate reimbursement mechanisms	Telemedicine for the silver economy is often reimbursed at lower rates than in-person geriatric care, discouraging adoption of age-specific telehealth services.	In the U.S., private insurers typically reimburse less for virtual geriatric visits; South Korea's reimbursement for silver economy telecare was only temporarily expanded during COVID-19.
Fragmented or short-term funding	Many telemedicine platforms lack long-term financing frameworks, with no dedicated funding for silver economy-focused telehealth services (relying on local pilots or temporary funds).	In China, most telemedicine programs are driven by local government initiatives, lacking centralized, long-term funding for geriatric telecare.
Lack of ROI evaluation models	Without ROI frameworks tailored to silver economy telehealth, governments and investors are hesitant to fund telemedicine long-term—despite its potential to reduce costly hospitalizations for older adults.	Both Iran and the U.S. lack standardized economic evaluation tools for telemedicine projects focused on silver economy populations.

Sources: Authors

2.2 Financial Innovation and Digital Payment Systems for Silver Economy Telemedicine

Recent research highlights the critical role of financial innovation in overcoming structural barriers to telemedicine adoption for the silver economy. Digital finance tools—such as blockchain-based payment systems, mobile health wallets (adapted for older silver economy users), and smart contract-enabled transactions—enhance transparency, improve reimbursement efficiency, and foster greater trust among stakeholders in geriatric telecare. These mechanisms are particularly relevant in regions where institutional capacity is limited, enabling more efficient fund flows between silver economy patients, providers, and payers for age-specific telehealth services. For example, blockchain technology can provide immutable records of telemedicine transactions, reducing fraud and ensuring that providers are fairly compensated for services rendered to older adults, while also protecting the privacy of sensitive health data (Prete et al.,2026; Shaikh et al.,2026; Rauner & Stummer, 2025; Pratama et al., 2026; Binsar et al., 2025; Yun et al., 2024; Avdic et al., 2026).

Value-based payment (VBP) models have also gained attention, shifting provider incentives from service volume to patient outcomes for silver economy populations and promoting sustainable healthcare financing structures for the silver economy. When applied to telemedicine ecosystems for older adults, VBP frameworks encourage integration, continuity, and accountability across age-specific care episodes (e.g., chronic disease management, post-fall rehabilitation)—core silver economy health needs. Under a VBP model, providers are rewarded for improving health outcomes such as reduced hospitalization rates for older adults with hypertension or diabetes, rather than simply for the number of teleconsultations conducted. This aligns financial incentives with the long-term health goals of the silver economy, promoting preventive care and reducing healthcare costs over time.

In the context of emerging economies, such as China, mobile-integrated payment systems (with age-friendly design for silver economy users) and QR-code–based authentication have been piloted in conjunction with public insurance schemes to improve older patient-side access and reduce reliance on out-of-pocket cash transactions—key for silver economy financial inclusion. For example, in Zhejiang Province, older adults can use simplified mobile payment apps with large fonts and voice guidance to pay for teleconsultations, with insurance reimbursements automatically deducted from their accounts. Some provinces have also introduced "health savings wallets" linked to digital ID cards, which enable automatic co-payment deductions for approved geriatric teleconsultation services for silver economy populations, further reducing financial friction for older adults.

Furthermore, digital payment systems are increasingly recognized as tools of financial inclusion for the silver economy. Leading global organizations highlight that integrating mobile payments into geriatric health service delivery can significantly reduce geographic and economic inequities by removing administrative and liquidity barriers for silver economy populations. For older adults in rural areas who may lack access to traditional banking services, mobile payments offer a convenient and secure way to pay for telemedicine services without the need for cash or bank accounts. When combined with targeted subsidies or microinsurance models for aging adults, these innovations can provide low-income elderly households with continuous access to remote care, while also enhancing cost-effectiveness and fraud control for insurers—supporting long-term silver economy vitality (Yang & Zhang, 2026; Ji & Li, 2025; Amin et al., 2026; Ly & Ly, 2024; Guo et al., 2026).

These developments suggest that digital financial tools—when properly integrated with regulatory frameworks and reimbursement schemes and adapted for silver economy users—can support not only the technical scalability of telemedicine for the silver economy but also its economic viability and social equity in rural and underserved communities with large aging populations.

2.3 Public-Private Partnerships (PPPs) as a Sustainable Model for Silver Economy Telemedicine

Public-private partnerships (PPPs) have been extensively studied as mechanisms for distributing investment risk, mobilizing private sector innovation (Grimsey & Lewis, 2007; Lewis, 2021), and enhancing public service delivery efficiency—with significant potential to scale telemedicine for the silver economy. In traditional terms, PPPs refer to formal contractual collaborations between government entities and private organizations for infrastructure and service delivery (Tafoska et al.,2026; Zheng et al.,2026; Tanveer et al., 2025; Mokhele, 2026). However, in China's telemedicine development for the silver economy, PPPs are more flexibly interpreted as dynamic integrations of government leadership, fiscal support, and private sector technological innovation and investment—with a core focus on meeting the health needs of silver economy populations. This flexibility allows for tailored solutions that address the unique challenges of rural and underserved regions, where silver economy populations are most in need.

Empirical examples from China's "5G + Healthcare" pilot programs illustrate that flexible PPP models—combining public policy leadership with private enterprise expertise—enable sustainable platform development, age-specific service delivery innovation (e.g., geriatric chronic disease monitoring), and expanded healthcare access for silver economy populations. For instance, China Mobile has partnered with local governments in Sichuan Province to deploy 5G-enabled telemedicine platforms in rural areas, providing older adults with access to remote consultations with geriatric specialists in Chengdu. The government contributes funding for infrastructure deployment, while China Mobile provides technical support and operates the platform, generating revenue through service fees and insurance reimbursements. Nevertheless, challenges such as regulatory fragmentation, unclear risk-sharing frameworks, and limited community engagement (including silver economy stakeholders) within PPP projects remain significant barriers. For example, private partners may be reluctant to invest in rural areas with small patient populations, while local governments may lack the capacity to monitor and evaluate PPP project outcomes.

To further understand the evolving role of the state within these collaborative models for the silver economy, it is useful to apply the theory of the Entrepreneurial State, which challenges the conventional view that governments merely correct market failures. Instead, this theory argues that the state can and should act as a mission-oriented investor—a proactive agent that shapes markets through strategic long-term investments in uncertain, high-risk innovation areas. In the context of silver economy telemedicine, this view highlights how government-led investments in digital infrastructure (age-friendly design), 5G deployment, and pilot reimbursement programs for geriatric care are not just support mechanisms but are essential entrepreneurial actions that actively create the conditions for private sector participation and innovation in silver economy-focused telehealth. For example, China's national 5G infrastructure rollout has reduced the cost of broadband access in rural areas, making it feasible for private telemedicine providers to offer services to silver economy populations there.

From this perspective, PPPs in China's telemedicine sector for the silver economy can be seen not merely as tools of risk distribution, but as state-driven innovation ecosystems in which the public sector assumes a leadership role in creating new markets for digital geriatric health, shaping incentives, and aligning public missions (sustaining silver economy vitality) with private capacity. This reconceptualization elevates the analytical importance of the state beyond a funding body, framing it as a strategic actor that initiates, sustains, and guides the transformative potential of telemedicine systems for silver economy populations.

2.4 Social Service and Business Partnerships in Silver Economy Telemedicine

An emerging body of research underscores the critical role of social service organizations and community actors in facilitating telemedicine adoption for the silver economy (Siddiquee, 2016; Yang & Hsiao, 2009). Community health workers (trained in geriatric care), nonprofit organizations focused on healthy aging, and grassroots associations are essential for promoting digital literacy among silver economy populations, improving patient trust in telehealth, and enabling culturally sensitive service delivery for aging adults in rural and underserved areas—all critical for sustaining silver economy vitality. For example, in rural Anhui Province, community health workers conduct home visits to teach older adults how to use telemedicine apps, assist with scheduling consultations, and follow up on treatment plans, significantly increasing adoption rates among silver economy populations. Nonprofit organizations like the China National Committee on Aging also play a role in advocating for silver economy-friendly telemedicine policies and providing training resources for both providers and patients.

Meanwhile, business partnerships bring technological infrastructure (age-friendly telehealth tools for the silver economy), capital investment, and operational expertise necessary to scale telemedicine initiatives for the silver economy sustainably. Private technology firms, for instance, can develop user-friendly telemedicine platforms with features like voice recognition, simplified interfaces, and dialect support—addressing the digital literacy challenges of older adults. Pharmaceutical companies may also partner with telemedicine providers to offer medication delivery services alongside virtual consultations, ensuring that silver economy patients have access to both care and essential medications. Studies emphasize that multi-stakeholder collaboration—integrating public governance, private investment, and social service innovation focused on healthy aging—is crucial for ensuring long-term sustainability and for driving telemedicine from a technical innovation into a transformative catalyst for systemic community development and silver economy vitality.

2.5 Research Gap and Significance for the Silver Economy

Bibliometric analyses reveal a significant evolution in telemedicine financing research—with a notable gap in silver economy-focused scholarship. Between 2000 and 2019, studies primarily focused on cost-benefit analysis, reimbursement models, and the technological feasibility of telehealth services, emphasizing economic efficiency and insurance payment structures but largely ignoring the age-specific needs of the silver economy. Since 2020, however, the research agenda has shifted toward exploring digital financial innovations, such as blockchain-based payment systems, mobile health wallets, and decentralized insurance models, with a small but growing focus on aging silver economy populations. Increasing attention has also been given to the role of Public-Private Partnerships (PPPs) and multi-stakeholder collaborations in expanding telemedicine access, particularly in rural and underserved regions with large silver economy populations.

Despite these developments, critical gaps persist—especially for the silver economy. Existing research often treats financing innovation, policy support, and community health initiatives as isolated domains, with limited analysis of their integrated impact on telemedicine system sustainability for silver economy populations. Few studies explicitly investigate how telemedicine ecosystems can strategically incorporate social service infrastructures and business partnerships focused on healthy aging to foster systemic community change and sustain silver economy vitality. Moreover, empirical evaluations remain scarce regarding how hybrid financial models influence the resilience, scalability, and equity of telemedicine initiatives for the silver economy, especially in emerging economies such as China with rapidly aging populations. Most existing studies focus on individual components of telemedicine financing (e.g., PPPs or digital payments) rather than their combined impact on silver economy populations.

Addressing these gaps, this study proposes a comprehensive, policy-based framework that integrates financial innovation, technology enablement (age-friendly design for the silver economy), diversified financing mechanisms, and collaborative governance strategies—centered on the needs of the silver economy. Drawing upon Collaborative Care Theory, the research systematically examines how payment structures, policy instruments, and investment pathways can be dynamically aligned to strengthen community-driven telemedicine ecosystems for silver economy populations.

Unlike prior research that often focuses on fragmented aspects of telemedicine financing or technology deployment, this study highlights the dynamic interaction among public sector leadership, private sector innovation, and social service engagement for the silver economy. It positions telemedicine not merely as a healthcare delivery innovation but as a catalyst for driving sustainable community transformation and sustaining silver economy vitality through integrated social service and business partnerships focused on healthy aging.

The significance of this study lies in its holistic approach to promoting healthcare accessibility for silver economy populations in underserved regions, offering actionable strategies for policymakers, healthcare providers, and private sector stakeholders to collaboratively build resilient, equitable telemedicine systems for the silver economy. Furthermore, the proposed framework provides transferable insights for addressing similar healthcare accessibility challenges for aging populations across other emerging and resource-constrained contexts globally—ultimately supporting silver economy vitality worldwide.

Figure 1. Telemedicine keyword co-occurrence map (with silver economy annotations)

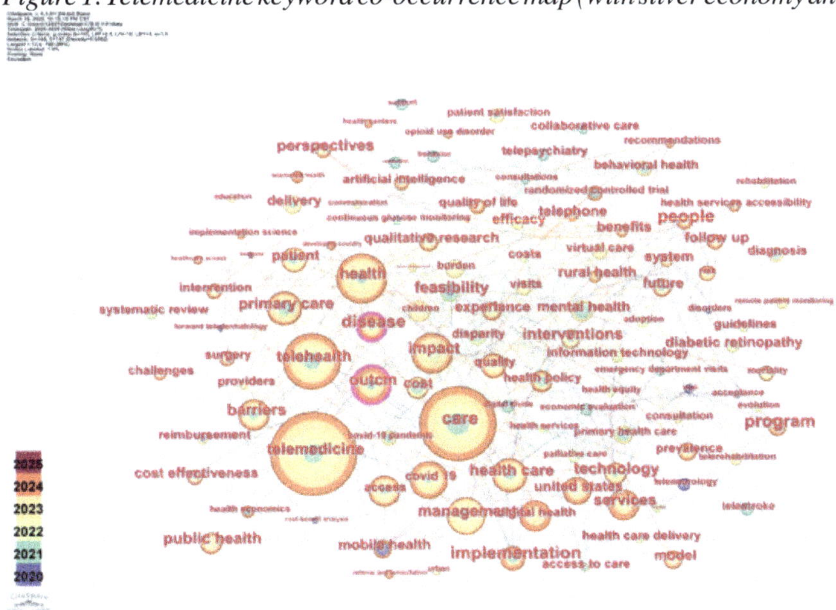

Source: Web of Science 2020-2025

3 METHODOLOGY

3.1 CiteSpace Analysis Framework

CiteSpace is a widely used bibliometric and visualization tool designed to analyze trends and patterns in scientific literature. Developed to enable researchers to identify key thematic clusters, influential authors, burst terms, and collaboration networks within a given field—including the emerging intersection of telemedicine financing and the silver economy. By utilizing co-citation analysis, keyword co-occurrence, and timeline visualizations, CiteSpace helps uncover the intellectual structure and emerging hotspots of academic research, such as the growing focus on age-specific telehealth financing for the silver economy. In recent years, it has been increasingly applied in healthcare and health policy research to track the evolution of scholarly discourse, assess research impact, and identify knowledge gaps—including critical gaps in silver economy telemedicine research.

This study utilizes CiteSpace for bibliometric analysis, with data sourced from leading academic databases, covering telemedicine finance research with implications for the silver economy over a 15-year period. Through co-citation analysis, core literature is identified, burst detection tracks the evolution of research hotspots (e.g., geriatric telecare financing for the silver economy), and collaboration network analysis explores academic cooperation patterns, in order to reveal research trends and provide theoretical support for empirical studies focused on silver economy telemedicine.

3.2 Data Collection and Processing

To ensure a systematic and reliable bibliometric analysis using CiteSpace—with a focus on telemedicine's relevance to the silver economy—this study follows a structured four-step workflow, as illustrated in Figure 2, including literature search, selection, data export, and visualization analysis.

Step 1: Literature Search

Relevant academic publications were retrieved from two leading databases. The search was conducted using the following terms: "Telemedicine," "Telehealth," "Financial Barrier," "Public Private Partnership," and "Telemedicine Policy." The time span was set to capture the evolution and long-term trends in telemedicine finance research, with all selected literature screened for relevance to silver economy and aging population healthcare needs.

Step 2: Literature Selection

All retrieved records were screened based on titles, abstracts, and keywords. Only publications with strong relevance to the financial accessibility and sustainability of telemedicine—and direct or indirect implications for the silver economy and aging populations—were retained. Irrelevant studies were excluded to maintain thematic consistency and data validity for the silver economy research agenda.

Step 3: Data Export

The selected bibliographic data were exported in a format compatible with CiteSpace software. Exported fields included article titles, authors, keywords, publication years, institutions, and citation information—with a focus on studies linking telemedicine financing to aging populations and silver economy health outcomes.

Step 4: CiteSpace Visualization Analysis

The data were then imported into CiteSpace for visualization. Node types were set as "Nations" and "Keywords," allowing for analysis of country-level contributions to telemedicine finance research and thematic clustering related to the silver economy (e.g., geriatric care, chronic disease monitoring for older adults). Burst detection, time slicing, and cluster analysis were used to identify research trends, emerging hotspots, and intellectual structures in the financial dimensions of telemedicine—with a critical lens on their relevance to the silver economy.

Figure 2. Workflow of data collection and analysis using CiteSpace (Silver Economy Focus)

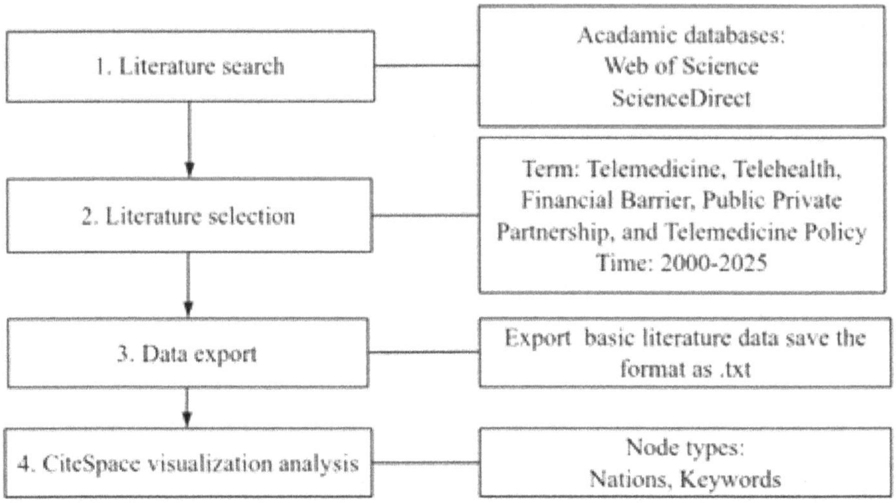

Source: Author's compilation

3.3 Empirical Research Method

This study employs a multiple case study approach to examine representative telemedicine initiatives for the silver economy drawn from China's national "5G + Healthcare" pilot programs. Two leading, high-impact cases are selected for in-depth analysis: **the Zhongshan Hospital Digital Twin Medical Ecosystem** and **the Guangdong Second People's Hospital 5G Smart Hospital**. These cases are purposively sampled because they exemplify mature, large-scale telemedicine models focused on silver-economy populations, feature clear financing structures, demonstrate policy-technology-finance integration, and have documented outcomes relevant to geriatric care and rural outreach. The study uses an exploratory design to develop conceptual frameworks and generate theoretical insights rather than testing statistical hypotheses.

3.3.1 Case 1: Zhongshan Hospital Digital Twin Medical Ecosystem

Zhongshan Hospital's digital twin platform is a leading telemedicine model that integrates 5G, artificial intelligence, and big data to support chronic disease management for the silver economy. The platform constructs virtual replicas of patients' physiological conditions, enabling real-time monitoring, early warning of acute risks, and personalized intervention for older adults with hypertension, diabetes, and cardiovascular diseases-high-burden conditions in China's silver economy.

Financing structure: The model follows a hybrid public-private partnership. The local government provides initial funding for digital infrastructure and 5G base station deployment in nearby rural districts. Private technology firms contribute algorithm development, cloud computing resources, and wearable device integration. Healthcare security insurance covers core telemonitoring and virtual consultation services for patients aged 60 and above, while out-of-pocket payments are minimal and subsidized for low-income older adults.

Service focus for the silver economy: The platform prioritizes elderly-friendly functions including large-font interfaces, voice guidance, automatic data synchronization from wearable devices, and family-member linkage for care monitoring. It connects tertiary hospital specialists with township health centers, enabling downward referral of stable chronic disease patients and upward referral of severe cases, forming a closed-loop geriatric care network.

Empirical analytical focus: This study analyzes how the digital twin model reduces infrastructure costs through shared public-private investment, improves reimbursement efficiency via insurance integration, and enhances long-term financial sustainability by lowering hospitalization rates and emergency visits among silver-economy users.

3.3.2 Case 2: Guangdong Second People's Hospital 5G Smart Hospital

The 5G Smart Hospital at Guangdong Second People's Hospital is a provincial demonstration project that delivers high-quality telemedicine services to aging populations across the Pearl River Delta and rural northern Guangdong. It features high-definition remote consultations, mobile telemedicine clinics, AI-assisted geriatric diagnosis, and cross-regional referral pathways.

Financing structure: This case uses a government-hospital-enterprise-insurance collaborative model. The Guangdong provincial health commission provides special funds for telemedicine equipment and rural station construction. The hospital invests in professional medical personnel and quality control. Telecommunication enterprises deploy 5G edge computing nodes to ensure stable rural connections. Medical insurance covers teleconsultation, remote ECG, and ultrasound examinations for older adults, with consistent reimbursement rates relative to in-person services.

Service focus for the silver economy: The system supports on-site teleconsultations in rural community centers, mobile telemedicine vehicles for home visits to homebound elders, and AI screening for osteoporosis, cognitive impairment, and other age-related conditions. It directly addresses mobility barriers and low digital literacy among rural silver-economy populations.

Empirical analytical focus: This study examines how the 5G smart hospital model achieves sustainable financing through multi-party cost-sharing, maintains service quality under expanded rural coverage, and aligns financial incentives with silver-economy health outcomes such as reduced travel burdens, earlier disease detection, and higher treatment adherence.

3.3.3 Analytical Framework and Data Sources

For both cases, data are collected from multiple secondary sources to ensure triangulation: official policy documents, hospital annual reports, "5G + Healthcare" pilot evaluation reports, news releases, insurance reimbursement records, publicly available patient satisfaction surveys, and government statistical bulletins on rural geriatric care access.

The analysis focuses on four dimensions:

- **Financing mechanism**: funding sources, cost allocation, risk sharing, and revenue models.
- **Policy integration**: alignment with national and local aging and telehealth policies.
- **Technology enablement**: 5G, AI, digital twin, and elderly-friendly design.
- **Silver-economy outcomes**: changes in access, service utilization, cost efficiency, and health indicators for older adults.

This in-depth case comparison reveals how policy, technology, and diversified financing can be combined to overcome financial barriers and extend sustainable telemedicine to silver-economy populations in lower-tier and rural regions. The findings are used to validate and refine the four-dimensional financing pathway and Collaborative Care Theory framework proposed in this study.

While the cases provide rich contextual understanding, limitations include the focus on prominent urban-led pilots, which may not fully represent all provincial contexts. Temporal constraints also mean long-term sustainability beyond the pilot phase is not fully observed. These limitations are mitigated by bibliometric validation and cross-case comparison, and future research can expand to longitudinal surveys and stakeholder interviews.

4 FINDINGS AND DISCUSSIONS

4.1 Financial Innovations and Investment Strategies in Silver Economy Telemedicine

The sustainable scaling of telemedicine serving China's silver economy is underpinned by three mutually reinforcing, policy-aligned financial pillars: digital financial innovation, optimized strategic investment models, and multi-layered policy financing support. These pillars collectively address the unique financial frictions restricting age-friendly remote healthcare delivery, particularly in underserved rural and lower-tier regions.

Digital financial and technological tools provide foundational efficiency and trust improvements for geriatric telemedicine financing. Blockchain technology enables traceable, tamper-proof transaction records for medical billing, insurance reimbursement, and service settlement, resolving information asymmetry between patients, medical institutions, and insurance authorities. Smart contract mechanisms further standardize outcome-based automated settlement, eliminating cumbersome manual review processes common in traditional healthcare reimbursement. Complementing backend financial infrastructure innovation, front-end age-friendly mobile payment systems—optimized with simplified interfaces, voice guidance, and accessible verification functions—effectively lower the digital and financial barriers for older adults, improving the overall accessibility and usability of telemedicine payment services. These digital optimizations stabilize institutional payment expectations and strengthen provider willingness to continuously deliver geriatric telecare services.

Payment system reform centered on Value-Based Payment (VBP) reconstructs the incentive logic of silver economy telemedicine. Departing from volume-based fee-for-service models, VBP aligns medical institutional revenue with elderly patients' long-term health outcomes and chronic disease management quality. This outcome-oriented incentive mechanism matches the whole-cycle intervention characteristics of elderly chronic disease telemedicine services, guiding medical institutions to prioritize service quality and health improvement over consultation quantity. Combined with the integration of public medical insurance and inclusive mobile payment systems, VBP effectively mitigates out-of-pocket financial burdens for aging populations and promotes sustained provider participation in telemedicine programs targeting the silver economy.

In terms of investment structure, China's silver economy telemedicine is undergoing a clear transition from single government fiscal subsidy dependence to diversified hybrid public-private investment systems. Public-Private Partnership (PPP) models have evolved into a core sustainable investment mechanism for grassroots geriatric telemedicine construction. The PPP framework realizes rational risk sharing and incentive alignment between public governance entities and private market players, supporting the co-construction of urban-rural telemedicine service platforms, standardized auxiliary service outsourcing, and marketized operational management. Private medical technology enterprises contribute technical capabilities, operational experience, and market sensitivity, while governments provide policy guidance, public welfare supervision, and basic resource guarantees.

Digital intelligent tools such as big data support scientific revenue prediction and project operation evaluation for geriatric telemedicine, guiding targeted social capital and venture capital investment in high-value tracks including AI-assisted elderly disease diagnosis and intelligent chronic disease monitoring. Nevertheless, telemedicine infrastructure features high upfront construction costs, long investment return cycles, and strong public welfare attributes. Rural regions with dispersed aging populations and weaker economic foundations face more prominent investment risks and uncertain profit expectations, which remain key institutional and market deterrents for large-scale, long-term institutional capital inflow.

4.2 Challenges and Policy Barriers

The sustainable development of silver economy telemedicine faces systemic bottlenecks rooted in unstable reimbursement mechanisms, fragmented regulatory governance, and insufficient scenario-specific economic evaluation systems. Globally, telemedicine reimbursement policies are widely characterized by phased adjustment and instability. Post-pandemic policy tightening, including reduced reimbursement ratios and increased self-payment thresholds, disproportionately burdens older adults with fixed and limited incomes. Inconsistent cross-regional insurance coverage and temporary policy arrangements weaken the stable operational expectations of medical institutions, restricting the continuous supply of high-quality geriatric telemedicine services.

Within the Chinese context, rural and grassroots silver economy telemedicine services heavily rely on short-term local pilot fiscal support rather than standardized, long-term national funding and reimbursement mechanisms. The discontinuity of pilot policies and uneven regional financial investment capacity lead to unstable service scalability, making it difficult to form replicable and sustainable long-term operational models for elderly telemedicine in underdeveloped regions.

Regulatory fragmentation constitutes another core barrier. China's telemedicine market access system implements strict qualification supervision, with formal service qualifications primarily open to eligible public hospitals and officially designated technical institutions. Specialized private service providers focusing on age-friendly telemedicine scenario innovation—such as platforms optimized for elderly dialect adaptation, simplified operation logic, and grassroots elderly care scenarios—face systematic market access restrictions, limiting the diversification and refinement of silver economy telemedicine services.

Cross-jurisdictional medical practice barriers are a global common challenge. Regionalized medical licensing systems in China, the United States, Canada and other countries restrict cross-regional remote diagnosis and treatment by senior geriatric specialists, hindering the downward sinking of high-quality urban medical resources to rural aging communities and exacerbating urban-rural healthcare disparities for the silver economy.

Data privacy and digital governance gaps further constrain user trust and service scaling. Most developing economies lack targeted legal and regulatory frameworks for the collection, storage, transmission and commercial use of elderly health telemedicine data. Unclear digital informed consent standards, unspecified liability mechanisms for data breaches, and imperfect privacy protection systems trigger persistent user concerns, reducing elderly populations' willingness to adopt digital telehealth services.

Crucially, the absence of silver economy-tailored economic evaluation tools weakens policy justification and long-term investment confidence. Traditional healthcare Cost-Benefit Analysis (CBA) frameworks focus narrowly on direct medical expenditures such as diagnosis, treatment and hospitalization costs. They systematically ignore the substantial indirect and intangible social value generated by geriatric telemedicine, including reduced informal caregiver burden, improved elderly quality of life, alleviated family mental health pressure, and reduced long-term social pension security costs. Without standardized evaluation systems to quantify these comprehensive benefits, policymakers and market investors lack sufficient empirical evidence to support long-term, large-scale financial investment in silver economy telemedicine initiatives.

Table 2. Policy barriers to sustainable telemedicine financing for the silver economy

Policy Barrier	Description	Illustrative Example
Restrictive licensing regulations	Formal telemedicine service qualifications are restricted to qualified public medical institutions and designated enterprises, limiting market access for private providers specializing in age-friendly telecare innovation.	China's telemedicine licensing rules exclude most small and medium-sized private geriatric telemedicine service providers from formal market operation.
Legal and data protection gaps	Incomplete digital health governance systems lack unified standards for elderly telehealth data privacy, digital service consent, and institutional liability division.	Low- and middle-income countries lack targeted legal frameworks governing the protection of aging populations' telemedicine health data.
Cross-regional licensing restrictions	Jurisdictional limitations on medical practice qualifications prevent cross-region remote diagnosis by geriatric specialists, restricting service coverage for remote aging communities.	Regional medical licensing systems in China, the U.S., and Canada do not recognize cross-jurisdictional geriatric telemedicine practice qualifications.
Fragmented governance	Decentralized supervision across health, medical insurance, and industry regulatory departments leads to inconsistent policy implementation and ambiguous institutional responsibilities.	China's telemedicine governance involves multiple independent regulatory bodies, resulting in fragmented oversight and slow iteration of silver economy telemedicine standards.

Sources: Authors' systematic review of telemedicine policy and healthcare financing literature

4.3 Evolution of Silver Economy Telemedicine Research

Global academic research on telemedicine financing and economic models for the silver economy presents distinct regional heterogeneity, closely correlated with national aging progress, healthcare system maturity, and digital infrastructure endowment. High-income developed economies including the United States, the United Kingdom, and Germany dominate existing research output, supported by mature geriatric care systems, complete medical insurance frameworks, and long-term accumulated digital healthcare operation experience, forming relatively systematic research paradigms for telemedicine economic evaluation and reimbursement mechanism design.

Driven by rapid population aging and national digital health strategies, East Asian countries represented by China and Japan have experienced explosive growth in research productivity regarding silver economy telemedicine in the past decade, gradually forming a regional research focus on aging-oriented digital healthcare innovation and localized financing model exploration. In contrast, low- and middle-income regions in Africa and Latin America lag significantly in relevant research, constrained by insufficient grassroots medical infrastructure, fragmented public health investment, and immature digital service ecosystems, resulting in limited empirical studies targeting elderly telemedicine financing sustainability.

Bibliometric analysis based on CiteSpace confirms a sustained growth trend in global academic publications on silver economy telemedicine financing. As China enters a moderate aging society, its research share in this field has risen steadily, reflecting growing national policy attention and academic emphasis on resolving aging healthcare challenges through digital and financial innovation.

Research focus evolution presents a clear two-stage shift. Early global literature focused primarily on basic economic feasibility verification, traditional cost–benefit analysis, and the evaluation of conventional telemedicine reimbursement mechanisms. With the iteration of financial technology and the refinement of elderly-specific healthcare scenarios, recent scholarship has shifted toward two emerging core directions: digital financial technology innovation in telemedicine, and scenario-based model optimization tailored for silver economy health needs.

Regional research divergence further reflects institutional and economic differences across countries. Developed economies prioritize optimizing refined insurance reimbursement systems, exploring bundled payment, episodic service pricing, and value-based reimbursement models adapted to elderly chronic disease management and post-rehabilitation telehealth scenarios. Developing countries focus more on inclusive financial innovation to reduce grassroots access barriers, researching mobile payment adaptation, microinsurance popularization, and low-cost basic teleconsultation service models suitable for low-income elderly groups.

4.4 Four-Dimensional Financing Pathway in Chinese Silver Economy Telemedicine

Aligning with the national healthy aging strategy and digital health transformation layout, China's silver economy telemedicine has formed a distinctive four-dimensional sustainable development pathway featuring policy-driven initiation, technology-enabled infrastructure, diversified financing support, and outcome-oriented governance. This systematic framework responds to China's unique urban-rural dual healthcare structure, bridging the service gap between high-resource urban regions and underserved rural aging communities.

At the policy level, national top-level designs firmly position geriatric telemedicine as a core strategy for coping with population aging. The national 14th Five-Year Plan for National Aging Development explicitly incorporates age-friendly telemedicine infrastructure construction and remote elderly healthcare coverage into key strategic tasks, guiding nationwide system deployment. Developed regions including Shanghai and Guangdong take the lead in establishing cross-departmental collaborative mechanisms to promote integrated urban-rural geriatric telecare layout, accumulating replicable practical experience for national promotion.

Technology enablement supported by 5G, artificial intelligence, and blockchain forms the hard infrastructure foundation for high-quality silver economy telemedicine. Leading tertiary hospitals have built scenario-based smart medical ecosystems targeting elderly chronic disease whole-cycle management. Intelligent analysis and early warning systems optimize elderly health monitoring workflows, while 5G full-scenario smart hospital construction realizes cross-regional sharing of high-quality specialist resources, effectively alleviating the difficulty of rural elderly populations accessing premium geriatric medical services.

Diversified market financing centered on standardized PPP mechanisms solves the dilemma of single fiscal investment insufficiency. The current mainstream operational models include public-private joint platform co-construction, auxiliary medical service outsourcing, grassroots medical equipment leasing, and multi-level integration of basic medical insurance and commercial supplementary insurance. Public medical institutions provide professional medical resource support, while private enterprises undertake technical iteration, platform operation, and scenario innovation, jointly promoting the standardized popularization of geriatric telemedicine services.

In particular, the equipment leasing model provides a feasible low-threshold solution for rural grassroots medical institutions. By replacing one-time high-value equipment procurement with flexible periodic leasing, township and village-level medical institutions effectively reduce upfront capital pressure, accelerating the coverage of basic remote monitoring, teleconsultation, and auxiliary diagnosis services for rural elderly populations.

Social-business collaborative mechanisms further improve the inclusiveness and practical usability of silver economy telemedicine. Grassroots community health workers undertake offline assistance and digital literacy guidance for elderly users with low digital adaptability, solving the "last-mile" obstacle of telemedicine adoption in rural aging communities. Localized age-adapted platform optimization, including interactive logic simplification and regional dialect adaptation, reduces digital access thresholds and improves the effective utilization of telemedicine services among rural silver economy populations.

4.5 Optimizing Payment and Policy via Collaborative Care Theory

Collaborative Care Theory provides robust theoretical support for explaining the multi-stakeholder operational logic of China's silver economy telemedicine financing ecosystem. The theory emphasizes multidisciplinary cross-institutional collaboration, multi-resource coordinated allocation, and shared accountability, which highly matches the multi-subject co-governance characteristics of telemedicine systems involving governments, medical institutions, financial entities, social organizations, and market enterprises. Guided by this theoretical framework, China's geriatric telemedicine financing and service system realizes systematic optimization in payment coordination, policy support, investment alignment, and technological-institutional collaboration.

First, payment mechanism coordination realizes value-oriented incentive reform. Breaking the limitations of traditional fee-for-service models, local telemedicine payment reforms align with national Diagnosis-Related Groups (DRG) and capitation payment trends, exploring whole-cycle bundled payment and fixed annual capitation models suitable for elderly chronic disease management. Covering full-link services from initial diagnosis, daily remote monitoring to follow-up intervention, this optimized payment system standardizes service behaviors, controls excessive medical consumption, and improves the continuity and effectiveness of elderly chronic disease management.

Second, embedded dynamic policy support guarantees grassroots service sustainability. The national medical security authority implements a dynamic telemedicine reimbursement catalog adjustment mechanism, continuously incorporating high-demand age-friendly remote medical services into the insurance coverage scope to reduce the economic burden of elderly users. Local pilot special funds provide matching incentives for public-private collaborative geriatric telemedicine projects, lowering market entry thresholds for social capital and encouraging targeted innovation for rural aging population needs.

Third, multi-source investment alignment builds a sustainable closed-loop fund operation system. Standardized PPP mechanisms guide diversified participation of fiscal subsidies, medical insurance reimbursement, social service fees, and public welfare resources. The multi-layered revenue structure disperses single-subject operational risks, forming a stable funding cycle suitable for the public welfare attributes of silver economy telemedicine.

Fourth, technological-institutional collaboration enhances fund supervision and operational transparency. Blockchain technology realizes full-process traceability of telemedicine service behaviors and fund settlement flows, solving information opacity and supervision blind spots in traditional reimbursement processes. Age-friendly mobile payment and intelligent claim settlement systems simplify multi-party collaborative procedures, reduce institutional transaction costs, and enhance the participation enthusiasm of grassroots medical institutions and elderly users.

On this basis, China's silver economy telemedicine has initially formed an integrated medical-financial matching mechanism. The system implements differentiated pricing and fund allocation according to staged characteristics of elderly disease management, builds transparent technology-empowered fund pooling mechanisms, and establishes a reasonable public-private risk-sharing pattern: public finance guarantees basic public telemedicine services for vulnerable elderly groups, while commercial insurance supplements personalized high-quality chronic disease management services. Pilot regions have constructed multi-dimensional performance evaluation systems covering clinical quality, cost control, and user experience, realizing performance-oriented fund allocation and promoting the standardized, equitable, and sustainable development of rural silver economy telemedicine.

5 CONCLUSION AND RECOMMENDATIONS

5.1 Summary of Key Findings

This study systematically explores financial innovation, multi-stakeholder collaboration mechanisms, and policy optimization pathways for rural silver economy telemedicine in China, yielding three core evidence-based findings.

First, the sustainable development of silver economy telemedicine relies on the synergistic integration of the four-dimensional pathway: policy-driven layout, technology-enabled infrastructure, diversified multi-source financing, and outcome-oriented governance. This integrated framework effectively responds to China's urban-rural dual healthcare structure, providing a scalable and localized solution to address the unique financial and operational barriers faced by rural aging populations in accessing telemedicine services.

Second, Collaborative Care Theory serves as a powerful theoretical lens to interpret and optimize the multi-stakeholder ecosystem of silver economy telemedicine. By guiding coordinated collaboration among governments, market enterprises, social organizations, and medical providers, the theory resolves the long-standing problems of fragmented financing channels, isolated service supply, and mismatched resource allocation in traditional elderly telemedicine systems, improving the overall resilience and sustainability of rural telemedicine ecosystems.

Third, social-business collaborative partnerships constitute the core driving force for inclusive silver economy telemedicine development. The integration of social service support (digital literacy training, grassroots community assistance) and market technological innovation (age-friendly interface optimization, cost-effective intelligent equipment) simultaneously addresses financial barriers and non-financial obstacles such as digital illiteracy and low service adaptability. This multi-stakeholder synergy transforms telemedicine from a single technical healthcare tool into a strategic driver for rural community development, health equity, and sustained silver economy vitality.

Overall, silver economy telemedicine sustainability is built on mutually reinforcing social and commercial value: social organizations expand user adoption and market scale, while private technological innovation improves service quality and affordability, forming a virtuous cycle of public welfare impact and market financial sustainability.

5.2 Policy and Investment Recommendations

Based on the above findings, this study proposes targeted policy, investment, and operational optimization recommendations to promote equitable and sustainable silver economy telemedicine development in rural China.

First, consolidate long-term policy and fiscal institutional guarantees. The central government should further clarify the strategic positioning of silver economy telemedicine in national healthy aging layouts, shifting from short-term pilot support to standardized long-term institutional arrangements. Special rural age-friendly telemedicine infrastructure funds should be established to support grassroots 5G network optimization and accessible medical equipment deployment. Medical insurance policies need dynamic optimization to expand the coverage of geriatric-specific remote services, while comprehensively promoting value-based payment reforms aligned with elderly health outcomes to guide high-quality service supply.

Second, deepen multi-stakeholder social-business collaborative mechanisms. Provincial-level unified telemedicine co-construction platforms should be established to integrate government supervision, enterprise technology, and community social services. Social organizations should be fully mobilized to carry out targeted digital literacy training and offline assistance for rural elderly groups, especially low-income and disabled aging populations. Optimized silver economy-oriented PPP models should standardize public-private risk-sharing and outcome incentive mechanisms to stabilize private investment confidence in rural telemedicine infrastructure.

Third, expand scenario-oriented financial innovation systems. Specialized digital health financial products targeting geriatric telemedicine should be developed, including dedicated infrastructure funds and silver economy health bonds. Blockchain and smart contract technologies should be popularized to realize transparent fund settlement, traceable service supervision, and standardized data privacy protection. Age-friendly mobile payment and intelligent insurance settlement systems should be further optimized to reduce the financial and operational threshold for elderly users.

Fourth, empower localized rural silver economy community development. Telemedicine service system construction must fully adapt to rural aging population characteristics and community needs, prioritizing localized grassroots medical institutions and community organizations in service delivery. Systematic digital training systems for both elderly users and grassroots medical staff should be established. A unified silver economy-focused performance evaluation framework, covering health outcomes, service accessibility, and user satisfaction, should be promoted nationwide to realize data-driven precise resource allocation and continuous service optimization.

5.3 Future Research Directions

To further advance the theoretical system and practical application of silver economy telemedicine financing, future research can be expanded from six dimensions.

First, conduct long-term longitudinal tracking research to evaluate the sustained impact of telemedicine on rural health equity, social inclusion, and community economic development, exploring the long-cycle sustainability of multi-stakeholder collaborative models.

Second, carry out cross-national comparative research on silver economy telemedicine governance, financing mechanisms, and social collaboration systems, summarizing adaptable international best practices for China's localized aging context.

Third, explore the integrated application of emerging technologies including artificial intelligence, blockchain and decentralized finance in elderly-friendly telemedicine, innovating smart contract-based insurance settlement and community co-construction service models.

Fourth, deepen multi-stakeholder governance research focusing on data privacy protection, institutional liability division, and fair resource allocation, constructing transparent and equitable silver economy telemedicine ecosystem governance frameworks.

Fifth, develop targeted financial sustainability models for remote and underdeveloped rural aging regions, exploring inclusive financial tools such as geriatric microinsurance and community-shared medical service mechanisms to reduce service costs and improve accessibility.

Sixth, systematically quantify the synergistic value of social service interventions and market technological innovation, establishing standardized evaluation indicators for digital literacy training, community worker assistance, and age-friendly platform optimization to support evidence-based policy iteration.

REFERENCES

Amin, C., Sigit, A. A., Saputra, A., Samson, M. G. M., & Sattar, F. (2026). Beyond access: Understanding digital platform adoption in Indonesia's informal economy. *Digital Geography and Society*, *10*, 100162. DOI: 10.1016/j.diggeo.2026.100162

Avdic, D., Kunz, J. S., Méndez, S. J., & Wiśniewska, M. (2026). Does telemedicine technology affect prescribing quality in primary care? The case of antibiotics. *Journal of Health Economics*, *105*, 103096. DOI: 10.1016/j.jhealeco.2025.103096 PMID: 41411812

Binsar, F., Arief, M., Tjhin, V. U., & Susilowati, I. (2025). Exploring consumer sentiments in telemedicine and telehealth services: Towards an integrated framework for innovation. *Journal of Open Innovation*, *11*(1), 100453. DOI: 10.1016/j.joitmc.2024.100453

Grimsey, D., & Lewis, M. (2007). Public private partnerships and public procurement. *Agenda: A Journal of Policy Analysis and Reform*, *14*(2), 171–188. http://doi.org/DOI: 10.22459/AG.14.02.2007

Guo, Q., Zeng, X., & Yuan, L. (2026). How population aging and digital transformation reshape labor income share? Mechanisms of firm-level substitution and urban job expansion. *Economic Modelling*, *158*, 107517. DOI: 10.1016/j.econmod.2026.107517

Ji, Y., & Li, J. (2025). Population aging, digital economy and family tourism consumption. *Finance Research Letters*, *82*, 107634. DOI: 10.1016/j.frl.2025.107634

Kilaru, A. S., Mondal, A., Jesteen, S., Geng, Z., Isenberg, D., Zikry, H. E., & Meisel, Z. F. (2026). Telemedicine use and outcomes following discharge from the emergency department, 2020–2022. *Annals of Emergency Medicine*, *87*(6), 697–708. Advance online publication. DOI: 10.1016/j.annemergmed.2026.01.024 PMID: 41817487

Kongmalai, T., Yodmalai, C., Luerithiphong, S., Sitasuwan, T., & Thongtang, N. (2026). Hybrid vs in-person diabetes care: Outcomes and barriers to telemedicine utilization in a post-pandemic setting. *Primary Care Diabetes*, *20*(3), 313–319. Advance online publication. DOI: 10.1016/j.pcd.2026.03.004 PMID: 41794635

Lewis, M. K. (2021). *Rethinking public private partnerships*. Edward Elgar Publishing., DOI: 10.4337/9781789906400

Li, R., Yang, Z., Zhang, Y., Bai, W., Du, Y., Sun, R., Tang, J., Wang, N., & Liu, H. (2022). Cost-effectiveness and cost-utility of traditional and telemedicine combined population-based age-related macular degeneration and diabetic retinopathy screening in rural and urban China. *The Lancet Regional Health. Western Pacific*, *23*, 100435. DOI: 10.1016/j.lanwpc.2022.100435 PMID: 35355615

Liu, K., Yang, Y., Song, Z., Li, H., Lyu, Y., Zhang, K., Wu, X., Hou, Z., & Wang, Y. (2026, January 21). Using the Theoretical Domains Framework to identify barriers to and enablers of patient telemedicine services use in China: Qualitative study. *JMIR Human Factors*, *13*, e78457. DOI: 10.2196/78457 PMID: 41564349

Ly, R., & Ly, B. (2024). Digital payment systems in an emerging economy. *Computers in Human Behavior Reports*, *16*, 100517. DOI: 10.1016/j.chbr.2024.100517

Mokhele, M. O. (2026). Assessment of the effectiveness of public-private partnerships in collaborative projects in South Africa: Building back better in post-disaster recovery. *Progress in Disaster Science*, *30*, 100553. DOI: 10.1016/j.pdisas.2026.100553

Moulaei, K., & Kazemi-Arpanahi, H. (2026). Telemedicine-based geriatric assessment (tele-GA): A scoping review on applications, benefits and challenges. *Health Policy and Technology*, *15*(3), 101157. DOI: 10.1016/j.hlpt.2026.101157

Neumann, A., König, H.-H., & Hajek, A. (2024). Determinants of telemedicine service use among middle-aged and older adults in Germany during the COVID-19 pandemic: Cross-sectional survey study. *JMIR Aging*, *7*, e50938. DOI: 10.2196/50938 PMID: 38654578

Pratama, C. G., Nurlianti, R., Herstatt, C., & Goeldner, M. (2026). Telemedicine adoption for managing chronic and rare diseases in Indonesia during and beyond the COVID-19 era: Qualitative study. *Journal of Medical Internet Research*, *28*, e83462. DOI: 10.2196/83462 PMID: 41855417

Prete, D., Zito, A., Napoli, M., De Pascalis, A., & Elia, G. (2026). Experimenting innovation in telemedicine: The case of home haemodialysis. *European Journal of Innovation Management*, *29*(1), 207–232. DOI: 10.1108/EJIM-03-2025-0365

Rauner, Y., & Stummer, H. (2025). The socio-technical adoption and diffusion of digital health innovations: The development of the STAD-HC model based on telemedicine in Germany. *Digital Business*, *5*(2), 100135. DOI: 10.1016/j.digbus.2025.100135

Shaikh, A., Patel, D., & Sakhuja, A. (2026). Innovation, technology, and telemedicine in critical care. *Critical Care Clinics*, *42*(2), 347–360. DOI: 10.1016/j.ccc.2025.11.003 PMID: 41825983

Siddiquee, N. A. (2016). E-government and transformation of service delivery in developing countries: The Bangladesh experience and lessons. *Transforming Government: People. Transforming Government, 10*(3), 368–390. DOI: 10.1108/TG-09-2015-0039

Tafoska, I., Bellazzecca, E., & Tropeano, T. (2026). Barriers and opportunities in outcome-based contracting for enabling social innovation: Insights from a collaborative, public–private pilot project in Italy. *Social Enterprise Journal, 22*(2), 274–293. DOI: 10.1108/SEJ-07-2025-0154

Tanveer, U., Hoang, T. G., Ishaq, S., & Khalid, R. U. (2025). Public-private partnerships as catalysts for digital transformation and circular economy: Insights from developing countries. *Technological Forecasting and Social Change, 219*, 124270. DOI: 10.1016/j.techfore.2025.124270

Wang, W., Chu, Y., Cui, F., Shi, X., Zhang, X., Sun, D., Shi, J., & Zhao, J. (2025). Correlation between the online visiting time and frequency increase in telemedicine services offered by health care providers before, during, and after the COVID-19 pandemic in China: Cross-sectional study. *Journal of Medical Internet Research, 27*, e65092. DOI: 10.2196/65092 PMID: 40009835

Xu, S., Ho, F. F., Kwong, T. M. H., Li, A. S., Ha, E. H., Hua, H., Liong, C., Leung, K. C., Wang, B. H., Leung, T. H., Lin, Z., Wong, S. Y.-S., Pan, F., & Chung, V. C. H. (2025). Patient satisfaction with traditional Chinese medicine telemedicine service during the COVID-19 pandemic: A cross-sectional study. *Journal of Manipulative and Physiological Therapeutics, 48*(6–9), 671–682. DOI: 10.1016/j.jmpt.2025.10.047 PMID: 41212126

Yang, C., & Zhang, C. (2026). Digital platform-led cross-border healthcare services for Hong Kong older adults in the Greater Bay Area: Regional integration in the digital age. *Cities (London, England), 170*, 106634. DOI: 10.1016/j.cities.2025.106634

Yang, H.-L., & Hsiao, S.-L. (2009). Mechanisms of developing innovative IT-enabled services: A case study of Taiwanese healthcare service. *Technovation, 29*(5), 327–337. DOI: 10.1016/j.technovation.2009.01.006

Yun, J. J., Zhao, X., & Liu, Z. (2024). Regulation architecture of open innovation under digital transformation: Case study on telemedicine and for-profit-hospital. *Journal of Open Innovation, 10*(1), 100252. DOI: 10.1016/j.joitmc.2024.100252

Zheng, X., Wen, J., & Wu, X. (2026). Government linked companies (GLCs) and public private partnership (PPP) in the water sector in China: Political connection, utility performance and service quality. *China Economic Review, 96*, 102650. DOI: 10.1016/j.chieco.2025.102650

Chapter 4
The Silver Economy: A Systematic Review of Cross-Sector Business Ecosystem Partnerships

V. Kavitha
http://orcid.org/0000-0002-5222-4781
Velalar College of Engineering and Technology, India

I. Nivetha
http://orcid.org/0009-0000-3851-219X
Velalar College of Engineering and Technology, India

T. Sureshkumar
http://orcid.org/0009-0001-1644-6678
AVS Engineering College, India

ABSTRACT

Population ageing is reshaping economies and societies worldwide, giving rise to the Silver Economy, an ecosystem of products, services, and cross-sector partnerships that support the well-being of older adults. With an estimated 347 million older adults by 2050, India provides a significant context for examining collaborative business ecosystems that promote active and healthy ageing. This chapter presents a systematic narrative review of cross-sector partnerships involving government, industry, healthcare, academia, and civil society. From 612 identified records, 86 studies were analyzed using five interconnected analytical lenses: economic value creation, social inclusion and well-being, and age-friendly infrastructure, and governance and partnership models. Grounded in Stakeholder, Shared Value, Business

DOI: 10.4018/979-8-3373-9370-4.ch004

Ecosystem, Institutional, and Triple Helix theories, the review highlights the emerging nature of India's Silver Economy and identifies future priorities, including Industry 5.0, AI governance, ESG-oriented partnerships, and intergenerational collaboration.

1 INTRODUCTION

1.1 Background

1.1.1 Global ageing trends

An ageing society is reshaping the social and economic fabric of societies around the world at a faster rate than ever before in history. Estimates by the United Nations show that the population of those 60 and over will grow to 2.1 billion by 2050, compared with about 1 billion in 2020.

(Nations, 2022). The older population is now set to outnumber children in the world for the first time in human history, and it is the result of a blend of better public health, advances in health care, falling birth rates and higher life expectancy over the last century (Harper, 2014). The next generation of older persons, the "oldest old" (80 years and older) is projected to be 426 million by 2050, close to an increase in 4-fold from the current population of 113 million, and the proportion of the global population aged 60 years and above will nearly double from 12 percent in 2015 to 22 percent by 2050, according to World Health Organization projections.

These trends are accelerating especially in high-income countries. Japan continues to be the most aged of societies, with more than 29 percent of the population now aged 65 and older, and Italy, Finland and Portugal following in second place. Germany, South Korea and Spain are also on similar ageing timelines. However, the key difference between the current transitory stage of the population and previous ones is that ageing is taking place rather quickly in the countries with middle-income levels. China, Brazil, Thailand and India, and others, are ageing at a rate that gives them little time to adapt their economies and institutions in a manner comparable to that experienced by wealthier countries during their own ageing process (Harper, 2014),(Nations, 2022).

1.1.2 Rise of the Silver Economy

This demographic shift has led to the emergence of the Silver Economy as a growing market of products, services, technologies and social infrastructure that caters to the needs, preferences and capabilities of the ageing population (Coughlin, 2017) (Egeland et al., 2026) (Mele et al., 2022). The Silver Economy is not a niche market! In Europe alone, it has been projected that expenditure by older consumers is already more than C3.7 trillion per year ((CII);KPMG, 2020), (Commission, 2021) and is projected to exceed $15 trillion in older consumers' spending by 2030 globally. From healthcare and pharma ceuticals, financial products, housing and assisted living, travel and leisure to digital technology, personal care, the commercial scale covers a range of industries.(Egeland et al., 2026).

However, the dynamics of the market are not the only aspects of the Silver Economy. The private sector alone cannot meet the multi-faceted and overlapping social demands that ageing populations create. Social isolation, functional disability, cognitive decline, burden of caregivers, digital exclusion and income insecurity among older adults are issues with interdependent nature that call for coordinated and values-based solutions that go beyond the bottom line (Wong & Leung, 2021) (IIPS), 2021). In this tension between economic opportunity and social obligation, the business case for cross-sector collaborations between the business, government, healthcare, academia, and civil society becomes obvious.

1.1.3 Importance of cross-sector partnerships

Considering the collaborative arrangements between various sectoral partners – government, business, healthcare, academia, and civil society – is seen as one of the key elements in the development of the Silver Economy (Austin & Seitanidi, 2012), (Wong, 2023). Such linkages are believed to bring about shared value creation, corporate social responsibility and facilitate the effective delivery of social programmes (Selsky & Parker, 2005), (Wong & Ho, 2022a), (Wong, 2024). In the last 20 years, there has been increasing interest in cross-sector partnerships between nonprofit/ social service organizations and corporations and private enterprises across social innovation, corporate strategy and public policy fields (Austin & Seitanidi, 2012). These partnerships are especially important in terms of ageing, as the needs of older people are highly personal, and demand trust, empathy and community rootedness that social organisations can provide; they are also resource-intensive, and thus benefit from the scale, infrastructure and corporate capital that can be furnished by the private sector (Wong & Ho, 2022a), (Wong et al., 2022), (Selsky & Parker, 2005).

The idea of 'Environmental, Social and Governance [ESG] performance' has received a boost in recent years. Over the last 10 years, they have made a distinct impression in the boardroom, investment and regulatory world. The "S" dimension (Labour Practices, Community Relationships, Sup-ply chain ethics and Social inclusion) is increasingly understood to include the relationships between organisations and vulnerable and ageing populations. Given that businesses operating in the Silver Economy are typically involved in social services, a clear and measurable pathway exists to fulfilling social service goals, rather than having a performative corporate responsibility commitment. On the other hand, if social service organizations develop strategic collaborations with the private sector, they have the opportunity to access resources, technologies, and distribution channels that can significantly enhance their impact (Wong & Ho, 2022a), (P. Sharma & Iyer, 2023), (Austin & Seitanidi, 2012).

1.2 Why India?

1.2.1 India's demographic transition

India's older adult population (60+) reached 149 million in 2022 (10.5 percent of the total population) and is projected to reach 347 million (20.8 percent) by 2050 (U. India, 2017), ((IIPS), 2021). The share of the elderly population (those aged above 60) has increased from 10.5 per cent of the total population in 2022 up from 6.9 per cent in 1991, but at a rate much faster than the increase in Japan or Western Europe, though still lower than these countries. While the rest of the world experienced the phenomenon of demographic ageing in the course of decades in the wake of middle income growth, India is experiencing a process of demographic ageing in a relatively short time, amidst a situation in which the economy is still in the middle income band and there is little fiscal and institutional space for adaptation (Harper, 2014). The most detailed empirical picture of this transformation is found in the India's Longitudinal Ageing Study Wave 1 (IIPS, 2021), which is the biggest nationally representative ageing survey conducted in Asia so far, involving 72,250 people aged 45 and above from all states and union territories in India.

1.2.2 Growing ageing population

LASI Wave 1 data shows that 75 per cent of Indians above the age of 60 live in rural areas with limited access to organised care services, 40 per cent of these have at least one chronic condition, 19 per cent say they have instrumental activity of daily living (IADL) limitations, and fewer than 5 per cent take up any kind of formal social care, while 27 per cent report living alone or with a spouse only, up from 19 per cent in 2007, which reflects the structural thinning of traditional intergenerational support systems (IIPS), 2021).

1.2.3 Market opportunities

The market potential in India is huge and is growing at an increasing rate. In 2024, the Indian Silver Economy was estimate valued at nearly for R73,000 crore, and estimates by CII–KPMG (2020) project it to reach R2.1 trillion by 2030 (G. of India, 2025), ((CII);KPMG, 2020). Within the senior-care sector, home health-care, assistive technology, senior housing, financial products that support retirement security and digitally-enabled care coordination services are among the highest growth areas globally, even in an Indian context of relatively low per-capita income (G. of India, 2025), (Wong, 2018).

1.2.4 Policy initiatives

There is a weak institutional linkage across policy initiatives related to the Silver Economy.There is increasing institutional interest in the Silver Economy with policy initiatives. In 2010, the National Programme for Health Care of the Elderly (NPHCE) was introduced and dedicated geriatric care facilities were set up at district and community health center levels (Ministry of Health and Family Welfare, 2019). Assistive devices are provided to the economically weaker sections of the society under Rastriya Vayoshri Yojana. However, increasing awareness of the 'Silver Economy' as an innovation and entrepreneurship opportunity has led to the launch of the SAGE (Senior care Ageing Growth Engine) portal to stimulate entrepreneurial investment in start-ups in this field, rather than it being only a welfare mandate. Most importantly, the September 2024 launch of the Ayushman Bharat scheme has added nearly 6 crore senior citizens (age 70 and above) to the free treatment cover of up to 5 lakh per year, marking the largest one-time addition of elderly citizens to health insurance coverage in India's policy history (G. of India, 2025). The State Action Plan for Senior Citizens (SAPSrC) also aids in building a pool of trained geriatric caregivers – during financial year 23-24, 36,785 caregivers across the country have been trained through 32 institutes. There are no formal mechanisms for coordination between different ministries under which NPHCE, SAPSrC, SAGE portal and Ayushman Bharat are operating, and this chapter's cross-sector partnership analysis in Section 6 explores these in detail.

1.3 Research Gap

However, most of the studies on the Silver Economy are confined to European, Japanese and North American contexts (Mele et al., 2022), (Egeland et al., 2026), (V. Sharma & Krishnamurthy, 2025). There is limited research on the Silver Economy in India and when it exists, it typically centers on a single sector, such as healthcare (Hou et al., 2023), or housing (V. Sharma & Krishnamurthy, 2025) rather than the interdisciplinary, cross-sector perspective taken in this chapter. To the best of the authors' knowledge, there is no systematic review that brings together the Indian Silver Economy evidence based on a structured analytical framework, incorporating five lenses: economic, social, technological, environmental, and governance.

1.4 Objectives

The objectives of this chapter is to explore the role of cross-sector partnerships in India's Silver Industry under five analytical lenses – Economic, Social, Technological, Environmental and Governance/Partnership.

1.5 Research Questions

RQ1. What are the key factors behind the emergence of the 'Silver Economy' in India as well as in other similar contexts internationally? RQ2. What are the influences of business ecosystems on active and healthy ageing? RQ3. How are cross-sector partnerships involved in the development of the Silver Economy and how are they governed? RQ4. What are the gaps in the Indian Silver Economy literature in terms of intergenerational collaboration and failure of partnership?

1.6 Chapter Organization

The review methodology is described in section 2. In section 3, the concept of the "Silver Economy" and India in global and comparative perspective are defined. In Section 4, theoretical foundations are reviewed. The five analytical lenses are presented in Section 5. The chapter, Cross-sector Partnerships in India, is contained in Section 6. Comparative international case studies are featured in Section 7. Intergenerational collaboration is covered in Section 8. Challenges, risks, and failures of partnerships are discussed in Section 9. The future research directions are presented in section 10. Section 11 deals with implications for practice. Section 12 concludes.

2 REVIEW METHODOLOGY

2.1 Review Design

This chapter uses a systematic narrative review methodology, which is a fusion of the structured search and screening procedures of systematic review protocols (Page et al., 2021) and the interpretative synthesis flexibility needed to combine the diverse evidence sources in the Silver Economy literature, including quantitative survey data, qualitative case studies, policy documents and theoretical frameworks as captured in the literature (Flyvbjerg, 2006). The hybrid design is in line with the traditional design methodology in cross-sector partnership and business ecosystem reviews as described in literature by Mele et al., (2022) and Selsky & Parker, (2005).

2.2 Database Selection

Five databases were searched: Scopus, Web of Science, ScienceDirect, Springer Link, and Google Scholar. Scopus and Web of Science were prioritized for indexed peer-reviewed coverage, ScienceDirect and Springer Link were searched directly for publisher specific holdings, Google Scholar was used to identify (Hou et al., 2023), or housing (V. Sharma & Krishnamurthy, 2025) grey literature and recent preprints not yet indexed in citation databases.

2.3 Search Strategy

The strings used for the search were designed by combining the following set of words with the use of boolean operators: ("Silver Economy" OR "Longevity Economy") AND ("Active Ageing" OR "Healthy Ageing") AND ("Cross-sector Partnership" OR "Public-Private Partnership" OR "Business Ecosystem") AND ("India" OR "Social Innovation"). Titles, abstracts and keywords were searched.

2.4 Inclusion Criteria

Sources were chosen if they met the following criteria: (a) published between 2020 and 2026, (b) written in English, (c) peer-reviewed journal articles, peer-reviewed book chapters and authoritative institutional/government reports, and (d) addressed at least one of the five analytical lenses or the cross-sector partnership theme central to this review.

2.5 Exclusion Criteria

Sources were eliminated if they: (a) were opinion pieces or unreferenced media articles, (b) dealt only with clinical/biomedical ageing research and had no economic, social or partnership relevance, (c) were duplicate records across the databases, or (d) were not available in full text.

2.6 PRISMA Flow Diagram

The flow diagram in Figure 1 details the identification, screening, eligibility and inclusion of sources in this review as per the PRISMA 2020 guidelines (Page et al., 2021). Figure 1. PRISMA 2020 systematic review flow diagram of included studies in the Silver Economy cross-sector partnership literature (n = 86). After duplicate removal, 487 of the 612 records identified were retained, following an adapted version of Page et al. (2021). Of the 301 records excluded by title/abstract screening,

116 were related to other topics or were not within the scope of the study.Of the 186 full-text eligible, 116 were excluded as off-topic or outside the scope of the study.

Figure 1.

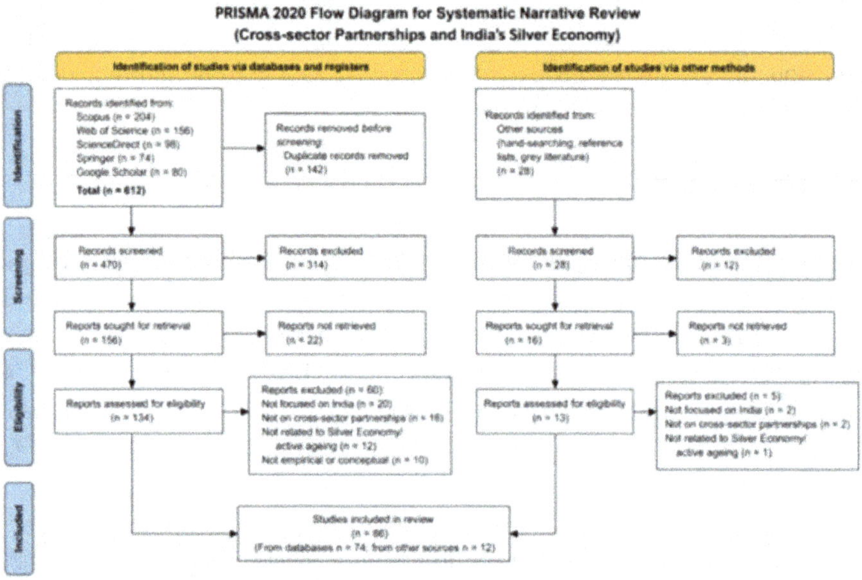

Another 100 studies were removed (32 not peer-reviewed, 28 not within the 2020-2026 range, 40 not focused on a partnership), and 86 studies were included in the final qualitative synthesis.

2.7 Analytical Framework: The Five Lenses

After data extraction, the included studies were coded using five lenses (economic, social, technological, environmental and governance/partnership) developed inductively from the recurring thematic categories found in the included literature and informed by existing frameworks in the fields of the Silver Economy and business ecosystems (Mele et al., 2022), (Egeland et al., 2026). The included studies in this summary literature matrix are mapped to the following lenses in Table 1. Table 1 shows that there is a significant imbalance in the representation of the two lenses, with the economic lens being much more dominant (27.9 percent) compared to environmental (10.5 percent), which highlights the research gap this chapter addresses on the environmental lens of age-friendly infrastructure and environmental sustainability in the Indian context of the Silver Economy.

Table 1. Distribute the studies included in the literature review across the 5 analytical lenses presented in the matrix below

Lens			
	No. of studies (*n* =	**% of total**	**Representative**
	86)		sources
Economic	24	27.9%	*Silver Economy: Unlocking Opportunities in India.* New Delhi, India, 2020 ((CII);KPMG, 2020), The silver economy: A business perspective on the ageing society," *Journal of Service Research*, early access, 2026. (Egeland et al., 2026), Silver economy innovation: A bibliometric analysis of the service ecosystem perspective," *Sinergie – Italian Journal of Management* (Mele et al., 2022)
Social	19	22.1%	International Institute for Population Sciences (IIPS), *Longitudinal Ageing Study in India (LASI)* ((IIPS), 2021), Trauma-informed practice during COVID-19," *Asia Pacific Journal of Social Work and Development* (Wong & Leung, 2021), Activating the longevity economy: Digital literacy among older residents and household consumption structure upgrading," *Humanities and Social Sciences Communications* (Li et al., 2025)
Technological	15	17.4%	Telecom Regulatory Authority of India (TRAI), *Annual Report on Telecom Services 2021–22.* New Delhi, India: TRAI (T. R. A. of India, 2022), Activating the longevity economy: Digital literacy among older residents and household consumption structure upgrading," *Humanities and Social Sciences Communications* (Li et al., 2025)
Environmental	9	10.5%	Senior-friendly housing and the silver economy: A scoping review," *Journal of Population Ageing* (V. Sharma & Krishnamurthy, 2025), OECD, *Ageing and Long-Term Care: Country Notes.* Paris, France: OECD Publishing (OECD, 2021)
Governance/ Partnership	19	22.1%	Collaborative value creation: A review of partnering between nonprofits and businesses," *Nonprofit and Voluntary Sector Quarterly* (Austin & Seitanidi, 2012), Cross-sector partnerships to address social issues: Challenges to theory and practice," *Journal of Management* (Selsky & Parker, 2005), Cross-sector responses to aging populations: From welfare silos to collaborative ecosystems. In S. K. Lim & R. T. Chan (Eds.), *Sustainable Development and Social Innovation in Developing Economies (Wong & Ho, 2022a),* Shielding without a shield Older people under COVID-19: A comparison of four cities," *Social Sciences* (Wong & Ho, 2022b)

Source: Authors' coding of n = 86 included studies.

3 UNDERSTANDING THE SILVER ECONOMY

3.1 Concept and Evolution

Silver market first appeared in 1970s Japan where the aging population has become a high-value market for products and services (Mele et al., 2022). In the latter part of the 2010s, the term "Silver Economy" began to appear in the EU's policy agendas, and is now formally defined as all economic activity that is targeted to people aged 50 and over by the Eu-reopen Commission. (Commission, 2021). The related notion of the "longevity economy" was popularized by the "longevity economy" principle, which sees ageing population as an economic enabler and innovator instead of a fiscal burden (Coughlin, 2017). Typically, the Silver Economy is defined by its activities in the sectors of healthcare and pharmaceuticals, finance and finance products, housing and assisted living, tourism and leisure, digital technology and personal care services: older people are not just welfare recipients but consumers, workers, investors and contributors to their communities (Egeland et al., 2026).

3.2 Global Perspective

Japan is the world's most ageing society with more than 29% of the population aged over 65, and launched the concept of the 'silver market' in the 1970s and the first national ageing strategies (Mele et al., 2022). European Commission policy initiatives since 2018 have been instrumental in establishing a framework for the European Union's 'Silver Economy' policy which focuses on age-friendly innovation, digital inclusion and cross-border market development (Commission, 2021). The United States Silver Economy can be defined by the "privatisation of the economy" that adults over 50 years old represent more than half of consumer spending and have contributed more than $8.3 trillion annually to the economy (Coughlin, 2017). The Silver Economy will grow at a rapid pace after the issuance of the National Action Plan for the Silver Economy in 2023, which was estimated to be RMB 7 trillion (about $965 billion) in 2024, with significant contributions from the government's industrial policy (Goodkind, 2025).

3.3 Indian Perspective

The unique combination of the 'rapid demographic transition' in India, 'middle income fiscal constraints' and a 'structural decline' in 'family-bred eldercare' makes the nature of the country's Silver Economy unique (IIPS, 2021). Some initiatives are being undertaken by the government, such as Ayushman Bharat coverage extension for senior citizens aged 70+ (2024), Rastriya Vayoshri Yojana for provision of assistive devices (G. of India, 2025), and NPHCE (2010) and SAGE portal for elder-care entrepreneur-ship (Ministry of Health and Family Welfare, 2019). The potential to market is high; the India's Silver Economy projected to be valued at 73,000 crore in 2024 (G. of India, 2025) and CII-KPMG (2020) estimated that the market is going to see an expansion to $2.1 trillion by 2030.

Challenges remain pronounced. According to LASI Wave 1 (2021), 75 percent of Indian older people live in rural areas where services are not easily accessible, and less than five percent receive any formal social care; meanwhile, 18 percent of the 60+ age group in rural areas have access to a smartphone (T. R. A. of India, 2022) (IIPS, 2021). Figure 2 represents the comparative demographic trajectories. By comparing the ageing trend in India with that of other countries, the figure 2 shows that the percentage of the population aged 60+ in India is currently lower than that in the EU-27 countries, Japan and USA.

Figure 2. Global ageing trend comparison: India, Japan, China, USA, EU (2000–2050)

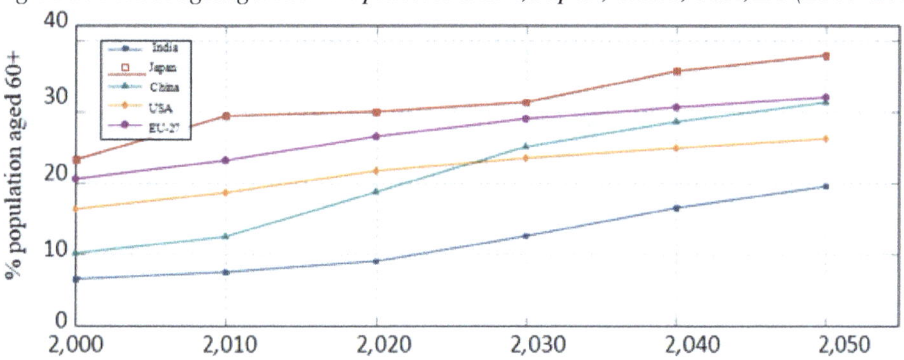

As seen in Figure 2, India is unique in its ageing curve as it starts at the bottom of the five, and after 2025 steepens considerably, in line with the phenomenon of demographic compression discussed in Section 1.

4 THEORETICAL FOUNDATIONS

4.1 Stakeholder Theory

Freeman's (1984) stakeholder theory calls into question stakeholder-primacy models which base corporations' responsibility on a wide circle of stakeholders, including employees, customers, and communities, each of which has a stake in the corporation's performance that must be taken into account. For the Silver Economy, stakeholder theory means that older adult communities are not just a by-product of a business's commitment to philanthropy but are part and parcel of its business strategies (Austin & Seitanidi, 2012).

4.2 Shared Value Theory

Shared value frameworks (Emerson, 2003) extend the stakeholder theory by suggesting that companies can create business value and social value, by linking their activities with strategic alignment. Shared value is arguably a conservative measure of conflict between profit maximization and true social welfare (as put by critics such as Crane et al., 2014), a criticism that is especially applicable to commercialization risks outlined in Section 9.

4.3 Business Ecosystem Theory

The development of the Silver Economy can be conceptualized as a process that springs from the interaction between different actors of the business system (business ecosystem theory, Mele et al., 2022), such as businesses, social organizations, technology providers and consumers, that interact and co-evolve, creating innovation that no single actor can develop alone. This framework is used to underpin the cross-sector partnership analysis in Section 6.

4.4 Institutional Theory

Institutional theory focuses on how institutional frameworks, normative expectations, and the institutionalized scripts influence organizational actions (Selsky & Parker, 2005). Institutional theory can be used to understand the corporate institutions that shape SEBI's BRSR and Companies Act's CSR provisions with respect to Silver Economy partnerships in India (S. and E. B. of India, 2021).

4.5 Triple Helix Framework

In the recent literature, the Triple Helix concept, which locates innovation at the interface of university, industry and government, has been expanded to the "Quadruple Helix" through the addition of civil society as a fourth innovation actor, which is relevant to the context of the Silver Economy where NGOs and community organisations have roles similar to the formal innovation institutions (Wong, 2023).

Table 2 presents a critical comparison of these five theoretical frameworks.

Table 2. This course is an advanced study of theoretical frameworks for the development of a cross-sector partnership for the "silver economy"

Theory	Strengths	Weakness	Research gap(India)
Stakeholders Theory	Broadens account ability beyond shareholders, recognizes community legitimacy.	Lacks on how competing stakeholder interests are resolved.	Limited empirical application to elder-care stakeholder map ping.
Shared Value Theory	Links profit and social good explicitly, actionable for business strategy.	Underestimates profit welfare tension, vulnerable to "shared value washing".	No Indian studies critically testing shared-value claims against outcome data.
Business Ecosystem Theory	Captures multi actor interdependence and coevolution dynamics.	Difficult to operationalize empirically, boundary definition is ambiguous.	No validated Indian Silver Economy ecosystem map exists.
Institutional Theory	Explains regula tory and normative drivers of partner ship behavior	Can be overly structuralist underplays individual agency.	BRSR impact on elder-care partner ship behavior un studied
Triple/ Quadruple Helix	Integrates civil society, useful for innovation ecosystem mapping.	Originally designed for technology innovation not service ecosystems.	Not yet applied systematically to Indian Silver Economy innovation.

5 FIVE ANALYTICAL LENSES OF THE SILVER ECONOMY

5.1 Economic Lens

5.1.1 Definition and literature

The economic lens focuses on business opportunities, participation of SMEs, job creation, and investment inflows related to the development of the Silver Economy (Egeland et al., 2026),(Mele et al., 2022). This lens is based on shared value theory (Emerson, 2003) and business ecosystem theory (Mele et al., 2022), which places the economic activity of the Silver Economy in the wider context of the expansion of the market, innovation of services and productivity gains from cross-sectoral partnerships. There has been a considerable growth in the economic literature on the concept of the Silver Economy since 2020, when it was realised that the older consumer is not a shrinking market segment but one of the most enduring and fastest growing economic forces of the next 30 years (Egeland et al., 2026), (Coughlin, 2017).

5.1.2 Business opportunities, SMEs, employment, and investment

Silver Economy business opportunities in India include healthcare and pharmaceuticals (around 40 percent of expenditure of older adults), assisted living and home modification (22 percent), financial product like reverse mortgage and retirement annuities (18 percent), and leisure, travel and consumer goods specifically designed for the older adult population (20 percent) ((CII);KPMG, 2020). However, in the reviewed literature, data specifically used for quantifying the involvement of SMEs in the delivery of in-home health care services as well as the development of assistive technology and the provision of digital platforms is scarce, representing a documented research gap, particularly in the area of in-home health care services.

To address the potential demand, the work force in the elder-care sector in India will increase from about 1.5 million to more than 7 million by 2030 (G. of India, 2025), making it a work force development challenge of a significant magnitude. The BLS projections for India suggest that home health and personal care occupations will be one of the fastest-growing sectors as well – a space that cross-sector collaborations between government, industry and NGO training facilities and funding coupled with an effective last-mile delivery system are well equipped to drive with targeted workforce development programs.

5.1.3 Formal modelling of partnership economic value

The value that can be attributed to the market expansion channel via partnership can be expressed as:

$$EV_{economic} \sum_{S=1}^{n} \left(MS_S \times CR_S \times ARPU_S - C_{acquisition} \right) \quad (1)$$

In equation (1) where MSs is market segment size (the number of older adults in segment s reachable through the partnership channel), CRs is conversion rate via the partnership channel, ARPUs is average revenue per user, n is the total number of market segments targeted, and Cacquisition is total customer acquisition cost across all segments. This formulation captures a critical empirical finding in the Indian literature: Indian partnership channels leveraging social service trust networks rather than direct commercial marketing have been documented to achieve conversion rates 2.5–3 times higher than direct commercial outreach to older consumers (H. India, 2021). This differential reflects the documented preference of older Indian adults, particularly those in the 75-plus cohort, for trusted intermediaries community health workers, social workers, senior center staff when making consequential decisions about products and services, a dynamic that is especially pronounced given the historical prevalence of predatory marketing targeting older consumers in under-regulated market segments.

5.1.4 International comparison: India vs Japan

The near universal adoption of long-term care insurance in Japan (since 2000) and its 40-year institutional development (Mele et al., 2022) contribute to the success of the Silver Economy in Japan, which has a value exceeding ¥ 100 trillion. By contrast, the Silver Economy in India lacks sufficient insurance coverage and is still in its infancy in terms of institutional frameworks, but has seen higher rates of adoption of new technology by the younger old population (60–70) as compared to Japan during similar developmental stages (T. R. A. of India, 2022). The comparison indicates that India's economic evolution may be more of a "leapfrog" than a "decades of gradual development" Japanese model, in that digital platform based service delivery could take the place of dense physical service delivery models characteristic of a mature ageing economy, if the digital divide outlined in Section 5.3 is resolved.

5.1.5 Case study: HelpAge India economic value

The programme touched the lives of around 2.1 lakh older adults in 2021-22 and social value to investment analysis by the programme shows 3.6 social value generated for every rupee spent (H. India, 2021). Applying Equation 1 to the segment sizes, derived from LASI and across income quintiles, gives an estimated net annual social value of this one programme alone of 5,000 crore, showing the scale of economic value that can be realised through well-targeted partnership channels even within the scope of one programme's operational reach.

5.1.6 Research gap

There is not enough case evidence from India that truly counts the participation of SMEs in the delivery of elder-care services specifically, and not part of larger CSR programmes by corporations. Future research on the economic lens should focus on disaggregated data collection between SME Silver Economy activity and large enterprise CSR funded programming, with the former having different governance, scale and sustainability dynamics.

5.2 Social Lens

5.2.1 Definition and literature

The social lens focuses on healthy ageing, social inclusion, community participation and quality of life (IIPS, 2021), (Wong & Leung, 2021). This lens is underpinned by strong evidence from the gerontology literature that social, environmental and relational factors are key determinants of health in ageing, and that they do so so much more so than the effects of pharmaceutical interventions or acute clinical care (Wong & Ho, 2022b). Social isolation and loneliness are among the most well documented social determinants of health in older adults: Epidemiological studies have found chronic loneliness to be a risk for health equivalent to smoking fifteen cigarettes a day and to significantly increase the risk of cognitive decline, depression, cardiovascular diseases and immune dysfunction.

5.2.2 Indian evidence

The LASI (2021) shows that chronic loneliness is experienced by a significant share of Indians, especially those living alone (27 percent nationally, compared with 19 percent in 2007), which is a result of urbanization and rural-urban migration of the youth, and the weakening of the traditional joint-family structure and embedded social supports that older Indians once enjoyed. NGO-led interventions, such as elder self-help groups (eSHGs) led by HelpAge India, have been found to improve, at least, some of the indicators of isolation in their participants (H. India, 2021). The Indian physical activity and cognitive health domains are also covered in community participation programming. Cognitive health is an area of high priority for the social lens, as there are more than 55 million people with cognitive health issues worldwide, a figure expected to triple by 2050. Social engagement programs to help keep people cognitively stimulated, workforce training programs that train retail and banking staff to engage positively with people with cognitive challenges, and dementia-friendly community design initiatives – although more of these are limited to a small number of pilot community-based urban contexts – are partnerships between sectors that have started to tackle the issue in India.

5.2.3 Case study

Singapore's The Community Networks for Seniors (CNS) programme in Singapore had a 23 percent decrease in social isolation scores over a period of 18 months (Ministry of Health, 2022), giving a comparative gauge to assess Indian community based programmes.The CNS model which formally integrates municipal government coordination, corporate funding, and community-based outreach delivery within a single governance architecture offers a template that several Indian state-level programmes, including Tamil Nadu's SNEHA initiative, have informally approximated but not yet systematically replicated at comparable scale or with comparable outcome verification rigor (H. India, 2021).

5.2.4 Quality of life and functional independence

In research on older adults' own expressions of well-being, the ability to function independently, to be independent of others in carrying out daily activities, is always cited as a priority that is more important than physical health status in determining one's own quality of life. Indian partnership models that foster independence through home modification, assistive technology and preventive health programming thus have a social impact beyond the clinical measures which most Indian partnership models currently evaluate – one that includes autonomy, identity and psychological resilience in these partnerships, and that is not adequately captured in the more output-focused evaluation systems employed by most Indian partnership models.

5.3 Technological Lens

5.3.1 Definition and literature

The technological lens covers artificial intelligence (AI), the Internet of Things (IoT), telemedicine, digital health platforms, smart home systems, and the digital divide that structures unequal access to these innovations (Li et al., 2025). The silver lens has been emerging rapidly in the literature of the Silver Economy since 2020, as the COVID-19 pandemic has sparked rapid pace of adoption of telehealth and sensor/ connectivity technologies that have matured to the point of their commercial viability to monitor health at population scale are low-cost (Wong & Ho, 2022b; Wong et al., 2022). There is a growing need to differentiate between technologies developed by external groups and those co-designed with older adults, as the former are not necessarily the most effective or widely adopted in practice (Egeland et al., 2026).

5.3.2 AI, IoT, and telemedicine in the Indian context

AI in the Indian Silver Economy is still in its early stages compared to other countries like Japan and Singapore, but is growing in three key areas: AI-assisted diagnostic triage in telemedicine platforms, predictive fall-detection systems embedded in wearables connected to IoT and NLP tools for providing health information to older people in vernacular languages with limited English literacy. The National

Programme for Health Care of the Elderly has started implementing telemedicine consultation links between geriatric units of district hospitals and primary health centers (PHCs) in some of the states, however, there is limited evidence through published literature of the clinical and eco-nomic outcomes of the pilots (Ministry of Health and Family Welfare, 2019). A number of Indian health-tech startups running their operations via the SAGE portal system have shown piloting cases of monitoring heart rate, fall detection, medication adherence, and so on, using wearable devices connected to the Internet of Things (IoT) but the peer-reviewed literature is scarce of evidence of clinical outcomes for these commercial pilots – a documented evidence gap.

5.3.3 Digital health and smart homes

Digital health platforms in India range from those initiated by the government, like the Ayushman Bharat Digital Mission, which has incorporated data from elders under the e-Sanjeevani initiative into the national digital health infrastructure, to those of the private sector that provide the remote consultation services through subscription fees. The adoption of smart home technologies by older adults in India is still in its early stages, and is largely limited to higher income urban households that can afford the initial investment in installing sensors, integrating with voice assistants, and equipping with emergency response systems, similar to the overall income related access gaps described in this review (IIPS, 2021).

5.3.4 The digital divide: Indian evidence

The smartphone penetration rate among Indians aged 60 and older is only 18 percent, as compared to 67 percent for the 18–35 age group, which is directly relevant to the design of the telehealth and digital Silver Economy service, as the majority of older adults in rural areas can't get online access via their smart phones (T. R. A. of India, 2022). This gender gap widens along income lines: The LASI (2021) data shows that digital literacy among rural older Indian women is significantly lower than among older Indian men of similar income, highlighting that differences in the availability of formal education in the past are now driving unequal capacity to use technology in later life. Even if India is making an effort under the national digital infrastructure programmes, the penetration of internet connectivity infrastructure in rural India is below that of urban areas, adding to the device ownership barriers.

5.3.5 Case study: HelpAge India–Airtel digital literacy pilot

In Tamil Nadu and Rajasthan, a HelpAge India Airtel pilot, which tested the use of simplified mobile interface controls for elderly users with low digital literacy, found 42 per cent increase in the number of digital tasks completed by participants compared to conventional interface controls (H. India, 2021). The pilot's design, which incorporated larger touch surfaces, voice guided navigation, and vernacular language support, is an example of a replicable model for the challenge of the digital divide, as a deliberate process of interface co-design rather than expecting older adults to adapt to the mainstream consumer technology designed for different purposes and needs. This is consistent with global evidence that co-designed technology with the voice of older adults results in significantly increased levels of sustained use compared with technology developed by younger teams based on assumed older adult needs.

5.3.6 AI bias and algorithmic risk

One of the specific concerns in the technological perspective is the potential for algorithmic bias in AI-supported systems for triaging and allocating resources in elder-care. However, there is a governance challenge now emerging in Indian healthcare partnerships as AI based diagnostic and care prioritisation tools are expanding and may make systematically weaker predictions for older adults living in rural areas with low incomes, for which there are no existing Indian regulations (Li et al., 2025). This risk is explored more in the context of partnership failure and ethical risk analysis in Section 9.

5.4 Environmental Lens

5.4.1 Definition and literature

The environmental lens examines age-friendly cities, with dignity within their built environment (V. Sharma & Krishnamurthy, 2025), (OECD, 2021). The lens is informed by the World Health Organization's cities framework for age-friendly cities which identifies eight areas of urban environment that are significant for healthy ageing: outdoor spaces and buildings, transportation, housing, social participation, respect and social inclusion, civic participation and employment, communication and information, and community support and health services. In terms of development, this lens has been an eye opener internationally through the European and Japanese urban planning scholarship, but as Table 1 shows, it is the least developed of the five lenses in the reviewed Silver Economy literature overall, and especially the evidence base in India.

5.4.2 Age-friendly cities and green infrastructure

Indian evidence found in this lens is the least (10.5 per cent) among the five lenses studied in this review in the 86 studies utilized in the systematic synthesis [Table 1]. Comprehensively reviewed by (V. Sharma & Krishnamurthy, 2025), senior-friendly housing development is still concentrated in metropolitan private developments – gated retirement communities and assisted-living complexes mainly marketed to affluent urban families, who are looking for care arrangements for ageing parents, with little public investment on age-friendly transport or on green infrastructure specifically targeting older people within the Indian urban planning policy more broadly. Although the Smart Cities Mission is India's flagship urban infrastructure programme launched in 2015, and there is a significant investment in urban infrastructure modernization, it has only included limited explicit age friendly design criteria in its evaluation framework.

5.4.3 Accessible transport

The dimension of 'accessible transport' is a key environmental lens dimension because it directly affects older people's ability to access healthcare, social participation opportunities and essential services. In recent years, public transport services in India, such as buses, suburban rail services, and metro systems in urban centres have taken small steps to make their services more accessible to people with a visual impairment such as priority seating or, in newer metro systems, level boarding and tactile guidance systems. Yet, despite the absence of more recent older adult-focused mobility accessibility evaluation literature published in India, there is still a lack of systematic accessibility audits that specifically address older adult mobility needs. Transportation gaps in rural regions are even greater, with LASI (2021) data showing that transportation issues are one of the biggest obstacles for rural older adults accessing health care, and the geographic equity gaps highlighted across this review.

5.4.4 Sustainable communities and rural environmental infrastructure

The issues related to sustainable community design for ageing population in the Indian rural context also connect with rural development and infrastructure investment issues such as access to water and sanitation, quality of housing, and climate resilience where older persons are more vulnerable due to documented higher prevalence of chronic illness and functional limitations in the older population (IIPS 2021). In India, exposure to increasingly frequent and severe heat-wave events has also been documented as a risk to health, especially for elderly people, particularly those with underlying chronic cardiovascular and respiratory diseases; however systematic efforts to coordinate health-related response under the current Indian ecosystem of partnerships involving city departments/authorities and health system have been limited in the integration of city-based cooling infrastructure, community-based heat-warning systems and health system preparedness.

5.4.5 Research gap

The most prominent evidentiary gap is the environmental lens as it is the most significant gap within this systematic review. Systematic age-friendly urban audits in the framework of India's Smart Cities Mission initiatives should be a priority as should be rural accessibility studies in transport, related to LASI healthcare access data, and the development of cross-sector partnership models that address the vulnerability to climate and heat of older adults, a field where the environmental and social lenses converge directly; but the Indian scholarship of the Silver Economy has not yet built integrated analytical frameworks.

5.5 Governance and Partnership Lens

5.5.1 Definition and literature

The lens focuses on public–private partnership (PPP) models and the wider governance structure, involving a range of public, private, university, NGO and health actor institutions, that govern service delivery in the context of the Silver Economy (Austin & Seitanidi, 2012), (Selsky & Parker, 2005), (Wong & Ho, 2022a). This lens is most directly informed by the theoretical underpinnings developed in Section 4, stakeholder theory, institutional theory, and the Triple/Quadruple Helix framework and one of the two best-developed frameworks of theory in the literature that was included (Table 1: 22.1 percent of the included studies).

5.5.2 PPP models and institutional architecture

There are three key institutional models for governance of Silver Economy partnerships in India. The first is the government-driven PPP that expands public health facilities by establishing formal partnership arrangements with NGO and private health care service providers, such as the National Programme for Health Care of the Elderly (Austin & Seitanidi, 2012). The second is NGO-initiated architecture, a model pioneered by HelpAge India by mobilizing corporate CSR funds through structures to which it has a high degree of control and designs (H. India, 2021). The third type is state government-driven multi-sector architecture of formal MoU governance, state audit mechanisms and corporate CSR co-funding, as seen in Tamil Nadu's SNEHA programme (H. India, 2021).. Each model has its own features in terms of governance strength and risks of accountability, explored more empirically in Section 6.

5.5.3 University and academic sector engagement

If individual academic researchers, such as the International Institute for Population Sciences, which contribute significant empirical infrastructure, can be considered as "forms of partnership", these are still less prevalent in the Indian Silver Economy ecosystem compared to the more common forms of academic – industry – government partnerships that exist in the country's technology and pharmaceuticals innovation ecosystem. The structural gap is where the Quadruple Helix framework with civil society as a fourth innovation ac-tor may fit in well, especially as the NGOs already have a significant role in delivering eldercare services in India (Wong, 2023).

5.5.4 ESG and regulatory governance

The recently introduced SEBI Business Responsibility and Sustainability Reporting (BRSR) framework for the top 1,000 listed companies from financial year 2022–23 is the most notable development in governance within this lens (S. and E. B. of India, 2021). The formal disclosure requirements established by BRSR include disclosure regarding the outcomes of corporate community engagement, as well as disclosure regarding the equity framework of corporate supply chains and disclosure of the investment obligations of stakeholder welfare, which explicitly encourage corporations to be transparent about the outcomes of their partnerships with the Silver Economy, but as demonstrated in Section on related empirical work, disclosure practice often still does not include the granularity of stakeholders that credible Social pillar assessment calls for.

5.5.5 Indian evidence and case studies

Three of the more prominent governance models in India in what is significant scale are described in greater detail in the rest of this empirical case study: the NPHCE PPP pilots; the AB-PMJAY health insurance partnership architecture across India, which serves some 500 million people across the nation; and CSR funding of NGO partnerships (such as HelpAge India and the SNEHA programme in Tamil Nadu).

Governance architecture can be compared to these models in order to find the best one for the situation. More specifically, the formal accountability tools, independent outcome verification, and binding equity goals in partnership agreements proved to be the most likely indicators of equitable reach of beneficiaries, with the extent of these indicators in partnerships broadly predicted by (Selsky & Parker, 2005) to determine their potential for reaching beneficiaries through bonding or the process of cream-skimming.

5.5.6 Research gap

While one of the more well-developed lenses in the literature that was examined, there is much more research on governance that is missing. A comparison and evaluation of three important PPP governance models in India (Government-initiated, NGO-initiated, and State-multi-sector) in a systematic manner. National scale work to challenge standardized equity and accountability measures has not yet taken place. Moreover, no empirical study has explored the effect of BRSR compliance quality on the equity of the partnership outcome in the context of the actual Silver Economy.In addition there is no study that has been carried out empirically on the link between BRSR compliance quality and the actual equity of the Silver Economy partnership detailed in Section 10.

6 CROSS-SECTOR PARTNERSHIPS IN INDIA

India has six categories of Silver Economy partnership. Regulatory authority and funding of Public Systems are provided by the Government bodies (Ministry of Health and Family Welfare, Ministry of Social Justice and Empowerment) (2019). Private sector corporations interact mainly via CSR-related spending under the Companies Act (2013), which focuses on NGO partnerships in the field of Elder care (Aayog, 2021). NGOs like HelpAge India and smaller regional NGOs have community trust, last-mile delivery and beneficiary relationship management. (H. India, 2021) Clinical Infrastructure (G. of India, 2025): It is provided by healthcare institutions under the NPHCE and AB-PMJAY architecture. Universities bring in re-search capacity albeit at a lower scale compared to the re-search capabilities of international counterparts in the field of Silver Economy partnership evaluation (Prasad & Lal, 2024). Start-ups, accessed through the SAGE portal, fall under one of the new emerging categories of an innovation actor, although it is still a category in its early stages (G. of India 2025). Examples include the AB-PMJAY public-private health insurance partnership covering ~500 million beneficiaries across the country, HelpAge India's 200+ corporate CSR partnerships to deliver mobile healthcare to 2.1 million older adults annually (H. India, 2021) and Tamil Nadu's programme SNEHA, with 78 per cent reach in the rural population through formal BPL targeting, as per terms of MoUs.

7 COMPARATIVE INTERNATIONAL CASE STUDIES

It contextualizes Indian evidence in comparative international context in India, Japan, Singapore, Netherlands and China. Japan is one of the most institutionally developed examples of the development of the Silver Economy, with almost universal long-term care insurance (LTcI) (introduced in 2000) and 40 years of a policy for the silver-market (industrial policy) (Mele et al., 2022). The Community Networks for Seniors in Singapore is an example of how well tripartite government–business–nonprofit coordination works at the city-state level to achieve measurable outcomes for reducing isolation (Ministry of Health, 2022). The Netherlands is an innovator in the development of integrated models for neighbor hood care, where municipalities, health care providers and community organisations work together, and in which good results have been achieved in the maintenance of independent functioning (OECD, 2021). Coordinated central planning is depicted in China's 2023 National Action Plan for the Silver Economy, where the state has made quick progress in industrial mobilization, resulting in a planned total of RMB 7 tril-lion by 2024. A four-country comparison of key indicators of the performance of the Silver Economy is provided in Figure 3. Figure 3 shows the comparative performance index of the four countries (normalized 0–100, authors' composite index based on (IIPS), 2021; (Ministry of Health, 2022; Goodkind, 2025; Mele et al., 2022)). The higher the score, the better.

Figure 3. Comparative silver economy performance index: India, Japan, Singapore, China

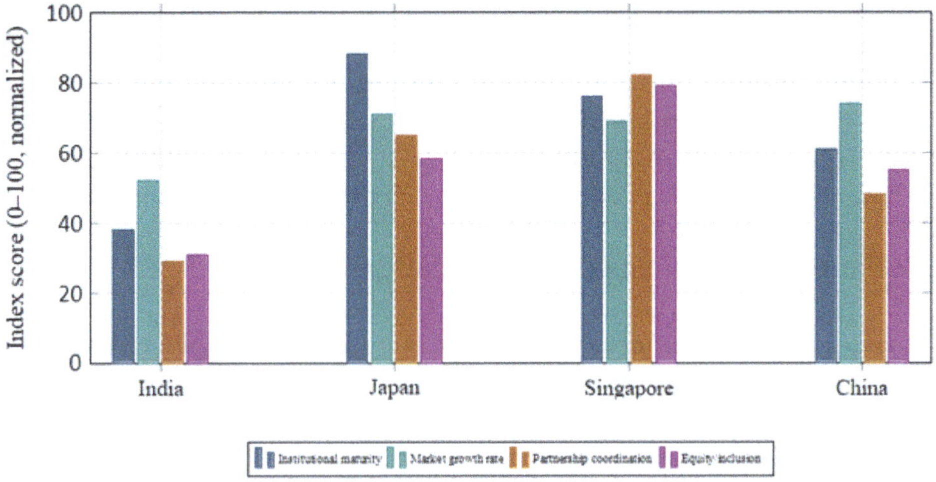

As shown in Figure 3, the growth rate of the Indian market is roughly similar to that of other countries, but institutional maturity (38) and partnership coordination (29) are significantly lower, reaffirming the governance and accountability deficits that have been noted across this review.

Key lessons for India are: The city-level governance in Singapore is directly applicable to the Indian context for metropolitan programmes, the approach to neighbourhood-integration in the Netherlands has interesting parallels for Indian panchayat level rural governance and the success of centralised industrial policy alignment in the Netherlands is exemplified in the Chinese context, albeit with equity issues that need careful consideration in the context of Indian federal governance structures.

8 INTERGENERATIONAL COLLABORATION

Although intergenerational collaboration is a dimension of the development of the Silver Economy which has already been proven to be important for both economic productivity and social cohesion outcomes, it is a dimension that is still under theorized.

8.1 Intergenerational Entrepreneurship and Reverse Mentoring

The Tata Mentorship Programme, which matched retired Tata Group professionals with younger workers and entrepreneurs, found that a group of matched employees who were mentored developed their competencies 34 percent faster than peers in groups that were not mentored (Sons, 2022). A complementary model which has been developed to fill this documented digital divide is reverse mentoring, where younger employees are tasked with training older employees on digital skills.

8.2 Family Businesses and Knowledge Transfer

The Indian context offers a unique opportunity for intergenerational knowledge transfer study as the country has a significant family owned business sector, but there is a lack of systematic study of this aspect in the literature reviewed, specific to the context of the Silver Economy.

8.3 Digital Literacy and Research Evidence

In 2021-22, Silver Skills Initiative mobilized 1,240 retired professionals to become vocational trainers for 47,000 young workers, with the competency scores for those who are trained at Silver Skills higher than their comparator groups (National Skill Development Corporation, 2022). The international comparison studies conducted by (Kaplan et al., 2017) support the measurable effects of structured intergenerational contact on the reduction in age-related stereotyping by younger participants, and the increase in well-being of older participants.

9 CHALLENGES, RISKS AND PARTNERSHIP FAILURES

The literature records five types of partnership failure risk with Indian evidence for each. However, after one year of the implementation, Aayog (2021) reported that 61 per cent of CSR-initiated elder-care partnerships in India did not have an independent beneficiary verification. Power imbalance occurs when corporate partners have more influence on governance than social service partners. According to NITI Aayog (2021), only 58 percent of NGO partners in CSR health partnerships had any real influence in the design of the programme. Funding issues stem from the uncertain funding models of CSR, which are not able to provide multi-year predictability of funding for the investment required for the infrastructure for elder care. Governance failures refer to the accountability gaps at NPHCE: In 6 of 9 pilot states, neither government nor NGO partners were able to define who was accountable for clinical outcome failures (Ministry of Health and Family Welfare, 2019). Emerging risk categories with little regulatory or empirical focus in India to date include ethical issues such as the commercialization of elderly care, privacy in digital health monitoring, and the potential for AI bias in algorithmic systems for eldercare triage. Empowerment (2020) reports that registered private old-age homes in India were assessed by the Ministry of Social Justice and Empowerment and 43 percent did not meet minimum staffing requirements, highlighting the empirical evidence of the risk of commercialization.

10 FUTURE RESEARCH DIRECTIONS

The priorities for research identified in the review are: (1) systematic Indian studies on Industry 5.0 and human centred automation application in the delivery of eldercare. (3) Regulations on algorithmic bias risk for eldercare technology deployment in India.(4) Guidelines on algorithmic bias risk for eldercare technology in India. (3) Partnership accountability research to support ESG disclosures, linking the BRSR requirements to verified data on the outcomes of the ESG. (4) longitudinal studies using LASI Wave 2 data for the establishment of causal relationship between partnership and outcomes. (5) Intergenerational collaboration research specific to India, which showed that there was a significant gap in Section 8.

11 PRACTICAL IMPLICATIONS

For policy makers: To create a National Silver Economy Partnership Equity Standard with LASI benchmarked targets and independent verification requirements. Aligned CSR funded Silver Economy partnerships with BRSR social pillar reporting to provide investor credible evidence for ESG. For healthcare providers: Link NPHCE clinical landscape to community based NGO partnership networks to fill accountability gaps (doc) in Section 9. For NGOs: build independent beneficiary verification systems to enhance the credibility of partnerships, and the value of BRSR to corporate partners. For entrepreneurs: focus on low bandwidth technology design that is accessible in rural area and is documented to exist as a digital divide, not urban-based international models of the Silver Economy.

12 CONCLUSION

The systematic review has analysed the roles of cross-sector partnerships in the development of India's Silver Economy from five lenses namely economic, social, technological, environmental and governance/partnership, based on 86 sources retrieved following a PRISMA-compliant search of Scopus, Web of Science, ScienceDirect, Springer and Google Scholar. The key findings of the review show that the Indian Silver Economy ecosystem is still in its nascent stage and the economic and governance aspects are fairly well documented than the environmental and intergenerational aspects. Empirically documented, but under theorized and under theorized in literature which focuses on India, mission drift, power imbalance and accountability gaps of partnerships can be explained by international comparators. Although there are clear advantages for intergenerational collaboration in social cohesion and productivity, it is the largest gap in theory and practice. It adds a coupled five-lens framework for analysing the Silver Economy ecosystem, an empirical synthesis for India using data from the LASI survey, and a structured research and policy agenda for bridging the intergenerational gap and managing Silver Economy partnerships. The creation of the cross-sectoral partnership structure and an empirical evidence base to assess it, which this review advocates, is not something that needs to be done in the future, but something that must be done now, as India's older adult population nears 347 million by 2050.

ACKNOWLEDGEMENTS

The author greatly appreciates the exceptional editorial guidance, constructive criticism and insightful recommendations offered by Prof. Johnston Hong-Chung Wong throughout the review process. His professional input and insightful comments played a crucial role in enhancing the solidity, precision, and overall standard of this chapter.

REFERENCES

Aayog, N. (2021). *CSR and Voluntary Sector Partnerships: Assessment Report 2020–21*. Government of India.

Austin, J. E., & Seitanidi, M. M. (2012). Collaborative value creation: A review of partnering between nonprofits and businesses. *Nonprofit and Voluntary Sector Quarterly*, *41*(5), 726–758. DOI: 10.1177/0899764012450777

(CII);KPMG, C. of I. I. (2020). *Silver Economy: Unlocking Opportunities in India*. CII.

Commission, E. (2021). *Silver Economy: Opportunities for Older People and the Economy*. Publications Office of the European Union.

Corporation, N. S. D. (2022). *Silver Skills Initiative: Annual Evaluation Report 2021–22*. NSDC.

Coughlin, J. F. (2017). *The Longevity Economy: Unlocking the World's Fastest-Growing, Most Misunderstood Market*. PublicAffairs.

Crane, A., Palazzo, G., Spence, L. J., & Matten, D. (2014). Contesting the value of creating shared value. *California Management Review*, *56*(2), 130–153. DOI: 10.1525/cmr.2014.56.2.130

Egeland, T., Heinonen, K., & Stensaker, I. G. (2026). The silver economy: A business perspective on the ageing society. *Journal of Service Research*. Advance online publication. DOI: 10.1177/10946705251397563

Emerson, J. (2003). The blended value proposition: Integrating social and financial returns. *California Management Review*, *45*(4), 35–51. DOI: 10.2307/41166187

Empowerment, M. of S. J. and. (2020). *Inspection Report: Registered Old-Age Homes Compliance 2019–20*. Government of India.

Flyvbjerg, B. (2006). Five misunderstandings about case-study research. *Qualitative Inquiry, 12*(2), 219–245. DOI: 10.1177/1077800405284363

Freeman, R. E. (1984). *Strategic Management: A Stakeholder Approach.* Pitman.

Goodkind, D. (2025). *Business opportunities in China's aging society.* CKGSB Knowledge.

Harper, S. (2014). Economic and social implications of aging societies. *Science, 346*(6209), 587–591. DOI: 10.1126/science.1254405 PMID: 25359967

Hou, X., Sharma, J., & Zhao, F. (2023). *Silver Opportunity: Building Integrated Services for Older Adults Around Primary Health Care.* World Bank. DOI: 10.1596/978-1-4648-1958-2

(IIPS), I. I. for P. S. (2021). *Longitudinal Ageing Study in India (LASI) Wave 1, 2017–18: India Report.* Government of India.

India, G. of. (2025). *Silver Economy: Status and Opportunities in India.* Ministry of Social Justice.

India, H. (2021). *State of Elderly in India Report 2021: Annual Impact Assessment.* HelpAge India.

India, S. and E. B. of. (2021). *Business Responsibility and Sustainability Reporting (BRSR).* SEBI.

India, T. R. A. of. (2022). *Annual Report on Telecom Services 2021–22.* TRAI.

India, U. (2017). *Caring for Our Elders: Early Responses—India Ageing Report 2017.* UNFPA.

India, U. (2025). *UHC for the Silver Dividend: Building Health Systems for an Ageing India.* UNFPA India.

Kaplan, M., Thang, L. L., & Heydon, M. (2017). Intergenerational contact zones: Place-based strategies for promoting social inclusion and belonging. *Journal of Intergenerational Relationships, 15*(1), 1–9. DOI: 10.1080/15350770.2017.1404428

Li, X., Wang, Q., & Chen, J. (2025). Activating the longevity economy: Digital literacy among older residents and household consumption structure upgrading. *Humanities & Social Sciences Communications, 12*(1), 1–14. DOI: 10.1057/s41599-025-06175-y

Mele, C., Pels, J., & Polese, F. (2022). Silver economy innovation: A bibliometric analysis of the service ecosystem perspective. *Sinergie – Italian. Journal of Management, 40*(3), 1–24. DOI: 10.7433/s118.2022.01

Ministry of Health. S. (2022). *Community Networks for Seniors: Annual Evaluation Report 2021–22*. Ministry of Health.

Ministry of Health and Family Welfare. G. of I. (2019). *NPHCE Evaluation Report: PPP Pilot States*. Government of India.

Nations, U. (2022). *World Population Prospects 2022: Summary of Results*. United Nations. DOI: 10.18356/9789210014380

OECD. (2021). *Ageing and Long-Term Care: Country Notes*. OECD Publishing.

Page, M. J., McKenzie, J. E., Bossuyt, P. M., Boutron, I., Hoffmann, T. C., Mulrow, C. D., Shamseer, L., Tetzlaff, J. M., Akl, E. A., Brennan, S. E., Chou, R., Glanville, J., Grimshaw, J. M., Hróbjartsson, A., Lalu, M. M., Li, T., Loder, E. W., Mayo-Wilson, E., McDonald, S., & Moher, D. (2021). The PRISMA 2020 statement: An updated guideline for reporting systematic reviews. *BMJ (Clinical Research Ed.)*, *372*, n71. Advance online publication. DOI: 10.1136/bmj.n71 PMID: 33782057

Prasad, N. D., & Lal, R. (2024). Silver linings for the silver economy: Institutional and entrepreneurial responses to healthy ageing and long-term care in India. *Journal of Social and Economic Development*, *26*(1), 1–24. DOI: 10.1007/s40847-024-00411-y

Selsky, J. W., & Parker, B. (2005). Cross-sector partnerships to address social issues: Challenges to theory and practice. *Journal of Management*, *31*(6), 849–873. DOI: 10.1177/0149206305279601

Sharma, P., & Iyer, R. (2023). *Business Ecosystem Strategies for Ageing Markets in Emerging Economies*. IGI Global.

Sharma, V., & Krishnamurthy, M. (2025). Senior-friendly housing and the silver economy: A scoping review. *Journal of Population Ageing*, *18*(2), 1–22. DOI: 10.1007/s12062-025-09495-8

Sons, T. (2022). *Corporate Social Responsibility Report 2021–22: Community and Mentorship Programmes*. Tata Sons.

Wong, J. H. C. (2018). *Disaster Social Work: From Crisis Response to Building Resilience*. Nova Science Publishers.

Wong, J. H. C. (2023). *Social Work in an Ageing World: Community Practice and Cross-Sector Collaboration*. IGI Global.

Wong, J. H. C. (2024). *Disaster Resilience and Community Social Work in Asia: Post-Pandemic Frameworks*. IGI Global.

Wong, J. H. C., & Ho, G. W. (2022a). *Cross-Sector Responses to Aging Populations: From Welfare Silos to Collaborative Ecosystems*. IGI Global.

Wong, J. H. C., & Ho, G. W. (2022b). Shielding without a shield—older people under COVID-19: A comparison of four cities. *Social Sciences (Basel, Switzerland)*, *11*(11), 498. Advance online publication. DOI: 10.3390/socsci11110498

Wong, J. H. C., Ho, G. W., & He, H. L. X. (2022). A safer world after vaccination against COVID-19. *Medical Research Archives*, *10*(8). Advance online publication. DOI: 10.18103/mra.v10i8.2987

Wong, J. H. C., & Leung, T. L. C. (2021). Trauma-informed practice during COVID-19. *Asia Pacific Journal of Social Work and Development*, *31*(1–2), 67–72. DOI: 10.1080/02185385.2020.1846604

Chapter 5
Designing Cross-Sector Innovation Ecosystems for Inclusive Silver Economy Growth

Muhammad Usman Tariq
http://orcid.org/0000-0002-7605-3040
Abu Dhabi University, UAE & University College Cork, Ireland

ABSTRACT

As people age in many countries, the "silver economy" is becoming a major driver of new ideas, jobs, and societal changes. To ensure that this development benefits all people in society, it is necessary to develop systems of innovation that bring different groups of people together. These systems involve different groups of people, including government bodies, businesses, research groups, community organizations, and the elderly. The elderly are no longer viewed as people who require support and care. They are viewed as customers, workers, business owners, and contributors to solutions. The development of sectors in health technology, assistive technology for daily living, homes for the elderly, lifelong education, and financial services can be better achieved through shared information, flexible rules and regulations, and investments with clear objectives. This can be achieved through good teamwork among different groups of people.

INTRODUCTION

In most parts of the world, ageing populations ceased to be an issue of the future long ago and have become the defining characteristic of the present, transforming

DOI: 10.4018/979-8-3373-9370-4.ch005

economies, labor markets, social systems, and everyday life. Demographic structures worldwide have changed considerably because of higher life expectancy (due to better healthcare, nutrition, and living conditions) and reduced birth rates (Estrada et al., 2025). This population change has increased the percentage of older individuals in societies and has not only shifted attitudes toward dependency but also changed attitudes toward ageing in societies. This makes ageing not merely an issue of welfare proffering but a core economic and social change that requires attention. This change is manifested in the rise of the silver economy. Elderly people are no longer seen as subjects of care but as active participants with multiple needs, expectations, and abilities. They are also involved in economic activities such as employment, entrepreneurship, investment, caregiving, and volunteering; hence, they are involved in value creation in various sectors. This transformation is not only creating new opportunities in healthcare, digital technologies, financial services, housing, education, and leisure but is also putting a strain on conventional patterns of policy and service delivery. Although the role of aging has gained increasing attention, the responses remain disjointed (Lin et al., 2026). For example, technology use in healthcare will not yield significant results without proper regulatory provisions, funding, and user education. Similarly, the absence of links between labor markets, social services, and healthcare systems is known to create inefficiencies, redundancy, and wastage of opportunities, especially among vulnerable categories such as low-income populations, rural dwellers, women, and migrants. The tendency to concentrate on a few areas, such as healthcare or pensions, runs the risk of reducing the complexity and multidimensionality of aging.

This fragmentation problem emphasizes the necessity of an ecosystem-based approach to management. Solutions to the challenges and opportunities of ageing must involve concerted efforts across several sectors, including government, business, healthcare, education, finance, urban planning, and civil society. All these actors bring their own resources, knowledge, and capabilities, and the integration of these resources is critical to establishing environments that support innovation and inclusion. Notably, older adults must be identified not only as ultimate users but also as contributors to solution development and design (Askari et al., 2026). Co-design methods can reveal lived experiences, preferences, and constraints that would otherwise be missed, thus increasing the relevance and fairness of interventions. The relevance of cross-sector coordination is also demonstrated by digital technologies. Telehealth, assistive technologies, and smart home systems are innovations that can increase people's independence and reduce their dependence on institutional care (Dabare et al., 2025). Nevertheless, unless there is harmony in data governance, regulatory frameworks, financing models, and user capabilities, these technologies can only widen current disparities, especially for those with less digital accessibility and literacy. A good ecosystem integrates technological innovation into wider social, institutional, and policy frameworks.

In this respect, aging cannot be perceived as a burden but rather as a common opportunity. This opens up opportunities for intergenerational work, new types of labor, and economic inclusion. The silver economy is not only a question of market expansion but also encapsulates larger questions of equity, participation, and system coordination. This chapter discusses how cross-sector innovation ecosystems can help create an inclusive and robust silver economy. Based on comparative observations of the United Arab Emirates and Ireland, this chapter discusses the effectiveness of ecosystem-based approaches based on various models of governance, institutional arrangements, and collaborative practices. This chapter combines theoretical insights and practical examples of real-life cases to show how an organized system can help mold demographic change into sustained and fair development. This study advances the literature by going beyond fragmented and sector-specific analyses to provide more comprehensive insights into the silver economy as a systemic change. It offers realistic information to policymakers, practitioners, and academics on ways to create and manage ecosystems that are economically viable and inclusive of society. It also points to the dangers of marginalization and the significance of constant review and open-minded leadership to ensure that the advantages of the silver economy are broadly distributed (Tomej et al., 2026). After all, aging populations are not a problem per se. With proper planning, inclusive design, and coordinated action, they can prove to be a source of innovation, cooperation, and resilience in society in the long run.

CONCEPTUAL FOUNDATIONS

The concept of the silver economy can be clarified through an analysis of market trends, such as an increased need for healthcare services, technology for assisting in daily activities, financial planning services, leisure activities, and homes that are conducive to living. These are all good points and play a crucial role in explaining the major changes in society. The other part of the silver economy involves how the elderly contribute to society in different ways, not just through expenditures. The elderly live longer and can contribute in different ways (Mufarokhah et al., 2025). They can contribute by earning money through their jobs and businesses. They can also contribute in other ways, such as caring for their families and volunteering. They can impart knowledge and information to the younger generations. By analyzing the silver economy in this way, the focus on the elderly as a burden on society can be changed to their involvement in society. Leaders and creators of ideas in society should be encouraged to consider the elderly as part of society. This perspective also contradicts traditional ways of thinking about aging, which are based on traditional economic thinking.

If aging is viewed as a cost, such as paying for pensions, healthcare, or fewer workers, solutions to aging tend to focus on lowering these costs and improving efficiency (Pradeep et al., 2026). The perspective that views aging as a contributing factor recognizes that it is affected by many factors, including health, income, education, and culture. Some require much support, whereas others want to start businesses, create art or work part-time. Thus, the silver economy is concerned with how people can contribute and how the environment enables them to do so. The question is no longer how to satisfy their needs but how to create environments that enable them to contribute based on their desires and capabilities. Innovation ecosystem theory can be used to understand how these conditions are created. In a silver economy, such cooperation can lead to the creation of useful technologies, healthcare services, and new services for older adults. In other words, research on older adults can lead to better products, and government policies can lead to greater product usage through funding. However, the complexity of an aging society requires the use of advanced models.

The quadruple helix model introduces civil society as an additional actor. Here, civil society actors, such as community centers, advocacy groups, user groups, and older people, play a part in the innovation process. This ensures that innovations are not only technologically feasible and economically viable, but also reflect the reality of people's lives. In silver economy projects, civil society actors can be involved in developing shared projects, testing new forms of caring for people in the community, and demanding better standards (Estrada et al., 2025). The involvement of civil society actors in the innovation process gives them more legitimacy and ensures that their ideas better meet the needs of the people. It also demonstrates that innovation goes beyond technology and involves new ways of providing services and creating new forms of social institutions. These ecosystem models highlight the interconnectedness of all species.

No single group possesses the information, resources, and power required to successfully address the numerous challenges related to aging. Good teamwork is characterized by shared goals and trust. Such a foundation is typically developed through extensive collaboration. Regions such as clusters, innovation centers, and living laboratories may be viewed as places where new things are tested in real time. These places offer opportunities to learn and change over time. These places also offer opportunities for feedback loops, in which the user helps shape the way things are used and designed, creating a more involved silver economy. A cross-sector collaboration framework translates these concepts into practice. Public-private partnerships are not new in the creation of goods and provision of services. Partnerships in the silver economy include research, digital technology, training, and community support. If partnerships are executed well in the silver economy, risks are spread out, and the strengths of different sectors are utilized. The public sector offers long-term stability and equity. The private sector can offer flexibility, resources, and skills (Chhillar et al., 2025). Nonprofits can offer a connection between the bigger picture and the community, ensuring that even marginalized groups are included in the partnership. However, achieving these partnerships is challenging. Challenges in partnerships are addressed through the creation of rules on accountability, openness in decision-making processes, and conflict of interest. Another major challenge that may arise when working in multiple sectors is that each sector has different objectives and methods for measuring success.

For instance, business organizations may be more concerned with making profits in the short term, whereas public organizations may be more concerned with making social improvements in the long term. Nonprofit organizations may be more concerned with empowering communities than making profits. Therefore, successful structures require the achievement of common objectives and the measurement of success by ensuring a balance between profit and innovation. In the silver economy, objectives can be measured by ensuring accessibility, affordability, innovation, profit, and employment. Such collaborative efforts are based on inclusive growth and equity-centered developments. Economic growth does not necessarily imply that the well-being of the population is improving. As people age in an aging society, the gaps that develop over their lifetimes may worsen. An equity-based approach also considers how different factors interact. Elderly people are not just older adults. They are also women and men of different races, have different disabilities, and live in different locations. For example, rural areas lack good healthcare and internet connectivity. This affects people's ability to use new technologies. Women tend to live longer and have lower income than men. Therefore, they are more vulnerable to economic problems. The incorporation of equity into the development of the silver economy means that all people can work together to ensure that it does not exacerbate inequality (Mufarokhah et al., 2025). On a simple level, bringing together ideas about how older people could be involved, how an ecosystem works, how different parts of an organization could work together in a team, and how fairness could apply in the development of an idea brings together the entire picture. The silver economy is something everyone works on together, and new ideas are developed between groups based on the principles of fairness and inclusiveness. Ultimately, these four main ideas show that a fair approach to growing the silver economy does not occur naturally because of the increase in the number of older people in the population.

MAPPING THE SILVER ECONOMY ECOSYSTEM

The health technology industry is creating wearable devices, telemedicine equipment, and artificial intelligence-based medical equipment to help older adults live independently. Financial institutions are creating retirement plans, banking apps for older adults, and insurance plans that consider the longevity of the older adults. Retail shops are modifying their product offerings to cater to older adults, and living space developers are designing spaces that can be lived in by older adults (Pradeep et al., 2026). Transport services are modifying their services to cater to older adults' needs. These enterprises are guided by the notion that older adults constitute an expanding market segment that cannot be ignored by marketers. However, the need to make profitable business decisions cannot be overlooked; hence, older adults may not be catered to appropriately if they are not included in the business process design. Governments and policymakers offer rules and support for silver economies. Figure 1 provides information on the flow of cross-sector innovation.

Figure 1. Flow of cross-sector innovation in the silver economy ecosystem

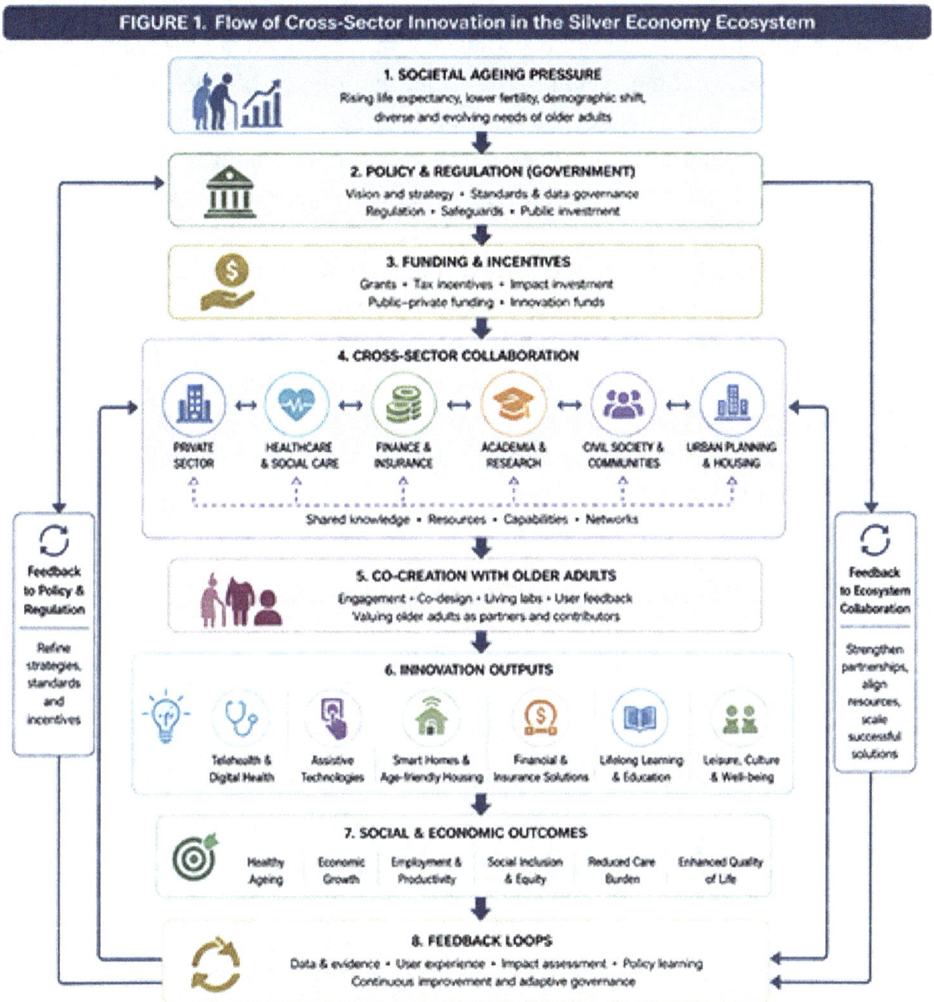

Governments shape the silver economy through mechanisms such as pension systems, healthcare funding, labor laws, and housing policies. They also defined the quality of care provided. Many governments face the challenge of funding an increasing number of older adults in the country and are trying to find a balance between affordable care and support. They also promote the idea of "active aging," which encourages people to stay active in the workforce and continue learning new skills. It is also important that policies complement one another. For instance, housing policies should complement healthcare policies, transport policies should focus on the elderly, and information technology policies should focus on the elderly.

Governments also bring people from different fields to work together on projects. However, political views and opinions also influence government policies. Universities and research centers provide knowledge that helps create new solutions for the silver economy (Bromage et al., 2025). Gerontology, public health, economics, engineering, and social sciences are some of the areas that contribute to solving the problem of aging populations. Universities conduct research on aging populations, test their programs, create new technologies to aid seniors, and train workers to serve in this system. Research centers often collaborate with businesses through real-world testing, which involves testing new products in real-world environments. However, it should be noted that the focus of research may be determined by who finances it, which means that only profitable ideas are considered, whereas those that do not promise much profit are ignored. Universities should maintain their independence while working effectively with the government and business groups. Civil society and advocacy groups are another key component of this system. Table 1 provides an overview of the key actors and their roles.

Table 1. Key actors, roles, and coordination mechanisms in the silver economy

Actor	Primary Role	Key Contributions	Coordination Mechanisms	Risks / Challenges
Government & Policymakers	Regulation, funding, and system coordination	Policy design, infrastructure, standards, public funding	Steering committees, policy taskforces, regulatory frameworks, public accountability boards	Policy fragmentation, short-termism
Private Sector	Innovation, investment, and service delivery	Technology, products, services, investment, market scaling	Public-private partnership agreements, memoranda of understanding, innovation labs, shared performance contracts	Profit prioritisation over inclusion
Healthcare Providers	Care delivery and service integration	Clinical care, telehealth, long-term care, prevention services	Integrated care pathways, shared data platforms, referral systems, multidisciplinary teams	Workforce shortages, fragmented care
Financial Institutions	Financial inclusion and investment support	Retirement planning, insurance, blended finance, impact investment	Blended finance agreements, ESG reporting, outcome-based funding contracts	Exclusion of low-income groups, complexity
Universities & Research Centres	Knowledge creation and evidence generation	Research, evaluation, workforce training, innovation testing	Living labs, research consortia, data-sharing agreements, evaluation partnerships	Commercial bias in research priorities

continued on following page

Table 1. Continued

Actor	Primary Role	Key Contributions	Coordination Mechanisms	Risks / Challenges
Civil Society & NGOs	Advocacy, representation, and community inclusion	Community engagement, support services, rights protection	Community advisory panels, local forums, grievance mechanisms, co-design workshops	Resource constraints, limited scalability
Older Adults	Co-creators, users, and contributors	Lived experience, feedback, entrepreneurship, volunteering, care work	User councils, participatory design sessions, pilot testing, feedback platforms	Tokenistic participation, exclusion if not actively engaged
Ecosystem Intermediaries	Facilitation and cross-sector alignment	Partnership brokering, trust-building, coordination, knowledge exchange	Neutral convening platforms, coordination hubs, monitoring dashboards, conflict-resolution mechanisms	Weak authority, dependence on sustained funding

These groups represent the voices and rights of older adults. They fight for the rights of the elderly to access facilities equally, live in good environments, and avoid discrimination against them. They may also fill the gaps in the provision of services by the government and business sectors through volunteer work, peer support, and cultural events that combat loneliness (Khattak et al., 2026). These groups also act as watchdogs in the community, monitoring how business policies and practices treat the elderly. These groups also help change community perceptions of the elderly by changing the perception of the elderly from being burdensome. The key difference between a good silver economy and a traditional support system is that, in a good silver economy, older adults are viewed as active partners rather than simply in need.

The implications of this finding are significant in several ways. If older adults are involved in the development and testing of new products and services, they will be of better use and benefit. It also gives older adults a sense of respect and ownership. This combines the notion that older adults are helpless. Involving older adults in workshops and community programs is a good way to ensure that their voices are heard and their needs are met. If older adults are involved in the development of new products and services, especially those related to technology and community programs, everything works better and feels more personal. This involvement gives older adults a sense of dignity and combats the notion that they are helpless. The economic component of co-creation is equally important. Many elderly people are still active, whether in the form of gainful or non-gainful employment, such as starting businesses, imparting knowledge, being active in the community, or taking care of the family (Manolache et al., 2025). Therefore, the silver economy is not only about selling products and services for the elderly but also about making a contribution. However, not everyone can equally participate in co-creation. Factors such as differences between men and women in the amount of money they earn over their lives or the gap between those who are technology-savvy may be seen as obstacles for those who would like to become co-creators. Partnerships between different groups of people, such as the government and businesses, and groups of advisors working together are ways to work together and hold each other accountable. To ensure good governance, communication, clear roles, and ways of providing feedback or requesting assistance when required are necessary. As technology becomes more common, data management is becoming increasingly important.

With the increasing importance of data management, issues such as privacy, permission, and data ownership have become extremely important for ensuring trust in data. Older people tend to lose trust when they believe that their data are not being used in a manner that respects their trust. Therefore, rules must be changed to address new ethical issues without hindering progress (Mufarokhah et al., 2025). The organization of places is also important. Local governments are usually in the best position to make changes that meet their needs. Issues such as public spaces, transportation, and housing are very important for older adults. In contrast, national and international bodies control the general picture and finances. Good communication between governments is important to ensure that things do not fall apart in the future. In places where local governments are highly effective, differences in what they are allowed to do may result in disparities.

VALUE CREATION AND VALUE FLOW IN THE SILVER ECONOMY ECOSYSTEM

The creation of value in the silver economy is a matter of public, private, civic and user interaction, not of any single sector. Policy, regulation, infrastructure, and public funding are all parts of government that help to create enabling values. Private companies convert these circumstances into products, services and scalable innovations. Healthcare providers develop health and wellbeing value through prevention, provision of healthcare, and integration of services, and universities and research centres produce knowledge, evidence and capacity of health and wellbeing workers. Civil society organisations generate social value through the representation of older adults, community engagement and by tackling the issue of exclusion. Older people are users, co-designers, workers, entrepreneurs, volunteers, carers and sources of lived experience, all of which create value.

There is also value that flows throughout the ecosystem. The process is characterised by public funding and regulation, private innovation in service options, healthcare and community organisations turning innovative ideas into practical support and older people giving feedback on the design and implementation. Social and economic returns are realised by funders, such as government, philanthropic organisations and financial institutions through the decrease in care pressures, the growth of markets, wellbeing and greater participation. This flow illustrates the need for inclusive silver economy ecosystems to create service user value, but also for older citizens and partner organisations to co-produce value and co-create benefits, both economic and social and health impacts.

Innovation Domains in the Silver Economy

The silver economy has become a space where new ideas are being tested, and new ways of thinking are being explored. This is because an increasing number of people are living longer than before. New ways of thinking about growing older are emerging because an increasing number of people are living longer than before. Innovation is not confined to a single area (Estrada et al., 2025). Innovation occurs in many different areas, such as technology, healthcare, money, work, and community. These areas are important because they are interconnected. They are interconnected because as more people live longer, it is no longer just a matter of living longer. Rather, it is a matter of living longer and ensuring a good life. Therefore, innovation in the silver economy has both economic and social implications for the elderly. Emphasizing age-friendly technology and ensuring that everyone can use these technologies is important.

Technology has simplified our life. For example, we can communicate with others, buy what we want, and access government services more easily. However, when these technologies are difficult for older adults to use, they create problems. Technological innovation does not only create new products; it creates products with people in mind. Products such as smart homes, health trackers, and mobility aids help older adults to live independently (Fedorko & Mondal, 2025). The emphasis on digital inclusion is crucial. The emphasis on digital inclusion is crucial. Digital inclusion is not just about ensuring that these products are good for older adults. If these basic issues are not addressed, technology can worsen the lives of older adults. If these basic issues are not addressed, technology can worsen the lives of older adults. Health and long-term care are other significant aspects of the silver economy that require attention.

As people live longer, an increasing number of people are living with long-term health conditions that require ongoing treatment rather than a one-time cure. New approaches, such as telemedicine, remote health monitoring, and data analysis, can detect health problems early and allow people to live longer at home. There are also models of care in which health care, social services, and rehabilitation are integrated because health is not just a medical condition but also a function of where one lives, what one eats, and how socially connected one is (Pradeep et al., 2026). Robots are also used in long-term care settings because of staff shortages. However, the human element of care is also significant because trust, care, and understanding of different cultures cannot be replaced by robots. Changes in the funding of long-term care services, preparation of workers for long-term care, and rules to ensure the quality and sustainability of long-term care are also needed. Co-housing and shared living provide alternatives to traditional care settings, allowing individuals to have their own space while receiving support from others. Cultural and artistic activities are also helpful, as they provide individuals with an outlet to express themselves and feel like part of a group.

However, these areas do not operate independently of each other. Access to good Internet connectivity is useful for remote medical care and online financial management purposes. Financial stability allows individuals to live and learn as much as they want throughout their lives. Job opportunities are beneficial for mental health and allow individuals to connect effectively with others. Thus, change must be approached from a broader perspective that includes understanding how different aspects of society impact one another (Bromage et al., 2025). Consequently, women may experience financial difficulties in their old age. If new ideas do not consider these factors, the situation may worsen. Inclusive design and community participation may result in equitable solutions. However, the new opportunities arising from the silver economy also raise ethical and legal issues. Data from gadgets and online tools can be useful for coordinating care; however, they raise ethical privacy concerns. Tools that offer advice on how to manage money can be helpful, but they also raise ethical issues regarding accountability. Ultimately, innovation in the silver economy is about changing people's perceptions of aging and not necessarily developing something new. If people perceive aging as a time to learn and contribute, then developing something that incorporates everyone, develops the workplace, and develops communities will be the overall goal. The goal is not to manage the change in the population but to use the change in the population as an opportunity to enhance the world in which we live. This involves developing something that simultaneously incorporates digital access, healthcare, financial well-being, learning, and community.

Designing Inclusive Cross-Sector Partnerships

The formation of inclusive partnerships in an aging society requires more than formal agreements or symbolic collaborations; it requires the inception of different institutional logics and, more importantly, the active incorporation of older adults' lived experiences into decision-making procedures. The complexities of demographic ageing cannot be tackled through the combination of a single entity, be it governmental, commercial, or civil society (Bromage et al., 2025). Health systems depend on technological infrastructure, financial systems determine care access, social well-being is affected by housing, and community networks influence physical and mental health. Therefore, intersectoral collaboration is not an extra but a necessary condition for an organized and effective response. The success of such partnerships will depend on inclusiveness and balance in benefit sharing. A central tenet is the active engagement of older adults as co-creators rather than passive consumers. In practice, this requires institutionalized forms of engagement, including community consultations, participatory workshops, advisory groups, and pilot service testing. Such methods will help older adults contribute lived experience-based insights, thus enhancing the relevance and usefulness of interventions (Mufarokhah et al., 2025). For instance, examples of community-based engagement activities through the Age-Friendly Program in Ireland show how participatory governance can contribute to an increase in both legitimacy and effectiveness, and the new efforts in the UAE indicate the increased importance of user feedback in digitally enabled service systems. Successful engagement also involves adapting techniques to meet various needs. This involves making physical and cognitive constraints comfortable, providing multilingual support, and integrating digital and face-to-face channels of interaction to make them accessible. In the absence of such considerations, participation is superficial rather than transformative. However, when well designed, co-creation enhances user confidence and system responsiveness.

Trust is the second pillar of cross-sector collaboration. Actors with different interests, motivations, and accountability frequently unite in partnerships. The social outcomes of the long-term efficiency and profitability of the individual organization, and the relational and localized impact of community groups are the key focus of public institutions, private organizations, and community groups, respectively (Estrada et al., 2025). The elderly, especially those who have been marginalized, may distrust the purpose of institutions. To create trust, it is necessary to create common values, open communication, and accountability. In both centralized and decentralized systems, UAE, and decentralized, for example In Ireland, trust is maintained when stakeholders feel that cooperation generates real and fair results. ESG factors offer a handy guide for organizing inclusive partnerships. Environmental aspects include age-friendly facilities, weather resilience, and housing affordability. Social aspects involve the availability of health services, prevention of economic abuse, and social inclusion. Governance dimensions involve representation, accountability, and the participation of older adults in the decision-making process. Integrating ageing-related priorities into ESG strategies will guarantee that inclusion is an integral goal of the strategies and not an add-on (Al Ali, 2025). One critical factor is the heterogeneity of the aging population. The elderly are very diverse in terms of income, location, gender, health conditions, digital literacy, and cultural background. These differences define access to resources and vulnerability to exclusion.

For example, digital health services and telemedicine can enhance access in densely populated and urban areas, but they may be less successful in rural settings or among less digitally skilled populations. Socio-economic inequalities could limit access to transport, healthcare, or assistive technologies. Meeting these disparities requires special interventions, disaggregated data, and context-sensitive design methods.

Risk-sharing and accountability systems are also significant for maintaining partnerships. Financial, operational, and reputational risks are related to cross-sector collaboration and must be appropriately distributed among stakeholders. In the absence of clearly defined governance frameworks, partnerships can focus on immediate benefits or risk transfer to vulnerable populations. For example, blended finance models, in which state money is used to finance the participation of a private enterprise in sectors such as housing or digital inclusion, can be efficient, but only with the condition of providing safeguards that would guarantee fair results. Accountability and public trust can be ensured through transparent reporting, independent assessments, and avenues of grievance (Pradeep et al., 2026). The effectiveness of partnerships is also affected by the time horizon. The dilemmas of age relate to long-term and systemic levels, and politics and the business approach can work on shorter timeframes (Estrada et al., 2025). Sustainable partnerships thus entail long-term investments, ongoing learning, and the ability to respond to shifting demographic and technological situations. Experimentation can be achieved through pilot projects and innovation labs, although systems should exist to implement successful initiatives at scale without compromising inclusivity (Nasaj et al., 2025).

Technology makes dubious contributions to the management of cross-sector partnerships. Data sharing, performance monitoring, and coordination among stakeholders can be achieved through digital platforms. Nevertheless, they also pose dangers concerning data privacy, cybersecurity, and the exclusion of digitally marginalized groups. Good utilization of technology implies that there should be proper governance of information use, such as support systems of data use and human support mechanisms that are complementary to ensure that information is accessible (Bromage et al., 2025). The issue of inclusivity is especially pertinent in environments such as the UAE, where digital infrastructure is well established. However, people in Ireland tend to prioritize balancing digital innovation and community-based delivery. In general, to design inclusive cross-sector partnerships in the silver economy, it is essential to create a balance between efficiency and equity, innovation and accessibility, and coordination and participation. With these factors combined, partnerships can also bring about structures where aging does not equate to dependency but rather to further contributions, dignity, and social integration.

DESIGN PRINCIPLES FOR INCLUSIVE SILVER ECONOMY ECOSYSTEMS

Based on the aforementioned discussion and the comparative design perspectives from the UAE and Ireland, the following design principles for creating inclusive cross-sector innovation ecosystems within the silver economy are identified. First, the co-creation process must be incorporated from the beginning. Older people should not be consulted as passive recipients but as active contributors through consultation, participatory design, testing, and evaluation processes. This enhances the relevance and legitimacy of the study. Second, there should be collaborative accountability in governance arrangements. There is a need to establish clearly defined roles, establish transparent decision-making processes, and create regular coordination platforms between governments, private organizations and research institutions, healthcare providers, and civil society actors to coordinate objectives and manage risk. Third, ecosystem design should be based on equity and accessibility. Interventions should be tailored to the needs of vulnerable groups, including those with low incomes, males and females, digital illiteracy, health issues, and geographic factors, to avoid the risk of marginalization. Thus, inclusive design should be embedded in service provision, technology design, and policy making. Fourth, value creation should be shared among stakeholders. Ecosystems should deliver economic, social, and health-related benefits, with innovation maximizing market growth, well-being, participation, and community resilience. Fifth, flexible implementation and ongoing learning are required. Pilot projects, living labs, and feedback mechanisms enable stakeholders to experiment with solutions, learn from results, and scale up successful projects without losing touch with evolving demographic and technological trends. Last but by no means least, sustainable development needs to be built into the architecture of the ecosystems, using a variety of funding models, robust institutional support, ethical data governance, and performance measurement systems, which strike a balance between efficiency and social value. The two principles offer a practical basis for creating inclusive and sustainable silver-economy ecosystems.

FUNDING AND SUSTAINABILITY MODELS

Financing an aging population requires creativity and money. As people age, their needs for healthcare, housing, transportation, financial security, and community services become more complex. Traditional methods of obtaining public funds, designed for a different era, are under pressure (Mufarokhah et al., 2025). However, private businesses cannot ensure that everyone receives assistance and that the situation remains stable in the long term. The solution lies in well-structured financial plans that emerge from partnerships between the government and private enterprises. These plans combine financial tools and support for people. The major challenge is not simply obtaining funds. This ensures that the money is used in a way that works for everyone and that the benefits last beyond the test programs. This is often addressed through public-private partnerships.

The plans combine the strengths of the government and private companies, wherein the government has the regulations and responsibility to care for the people, and the company has the money, skills, and efficiency to help the process move faster. The government has the regulations and responsibility to care for the people, and the company has the money, skills, and efficiency to help the process move faster. The government can provide land, help obtain permits, and provide funding, while the groups help with the design, construction, and management of the project (Hwang et al., 2025). This can work well, especially if the process is done properly to speed it up and share the cost. However, it is important to note that the terms must be set properly, such as the standards for the quality of services, the cost of the services, and the responsibilities of the partners. Long-term partnerships must also be ensured to make the process stable, but they must also be monitored properly to ensure that the government's interests are protected. Transparency and obtaining the opinions of the community, especially the elderly, are important. If not done properly, these partnerships may result in profit rather than being helpful; however, if done properly, they may bring about significant changes and new ideas that the government alone may not be able to handle.

Mixed funding combines public or charitable funding with private funding and uses less expensive funding to leverage larger investments (Pradeep et al., 2026). For instance, public funding guarantees or first-loss funding may provide comfort to private investors to invest in projects that may otherwise be too risky for them. This type of funding may be ideal for investing in new ideas that have not been implemented before but have great potential. By sharing risks, social or charitable groups may attract more private investment. However, the actual effects must also be measured. There must be ways to measure how well a social objective is achieved. If not, there is a chance that the project may have a positive effect on society but not deliver it properly. Being socially responsible and creating shared values also aids in the aging economy.

Many companies are realizing the effects of an aging population on their employees, customers, and suppliers. Being socially responsible is a way for companies to improve their brand image by doing something positive for the society. Examples include providing Internet instruction for seniors, creating easier-to-use products for them, and assisting with eldercare. Shared-value strategies are even more powerful in creating a positive effect on society because the social objective is integrated into a company's main business strategy. For example, a technology company could create software that is easier for seniors to use and still increase its market share (Mufarokhah et al., 2025). Financial companies can create clear and simple retirement plans for seniors and increase customer loyalty. The benefit of these kinds of plans is that making money and helping society at the same time reduces the need to donate to charities. Nevertheless, it is important to be real and show actual results. Simply going through the motions of social responsibility will not yield actual results. Incorporating aging issues into product design, staff policies, and the company's long-term goals requires strong leadership.

In an aging society, capital may be available to support programs that prevent health problems, help people stay in the workforce, and combat loneliness in communities (Widiastini et al., 2025). By linking capital to actual performance, these approaches encourage better ideas and greater responsibilities. Service providers are motivated to improve their methods and gather accurate data. However, it is important to carefully design such plans for the following reasons. It can be difficult to set the correct metrics, especially for plans that involve results that take a long time to materialize or that involve multiple factors. There is also the risk that service providers will focus only on easily measurable results and ignore other important factors that affect individual well-being. These costs can also be high, making it difficult for small groups to implement such strategies. To ensure success, all parties involved must agree on the goals, an honest way to measure success, and the method for sharing the rewards.

Long-term growth is important for these funding methods; pilot projects tend to have positive results but can be difficult to grow beyond the local level (Bromage et al., 2025). To sustain funding, it is important to consider the costs, money coming in, and the ability of organizations from the beginning of the project. Growth is not just about money; it is also about rules that match the number of trained workers. For instance, digital health is good for small areas, but it may be difficult to implement nationwide because of people and payment systems. Therefore, it is crucial to ensure that funding models consider the readiness of the environment for change. Funding that is available for many years is helpful because it allows organizations to look ahead and be stable, unlike funding that is available only for a short period. Having multiple funding options, such as public funding, fees, charity support, and investment income, reduces the risk of being affected by changes in policies or markets.

Affordability is a major concern when scaling solutions for aging populations. Older adults may live on fixed incomes; therefore, affordability is a major concern for them. Having models in which those who can pay more help those who are unable to do so is crucial. Public funding for the poor and those living in rural areas may be beneficial. Digital health may be helpful in reducing extra costs; however, it may be initially expensive. Finding a balance that allows organizations to make money without being unfair is crucial; therefore, having multiple funding sources is helpful. Workforce sustainability is another factor that affects an individual's ability to grow (Pradeep et al., 2026). This means that when expanding health and social care services, money should be invested in training and good working conditions. If the money spent on workers' salaries is insufficient, a shortage of workers and low quality of care will be a problem. Community-based projects rely on volunteers and social connections, which are not always easy to find. Transparency and honesty help build trust with investors, governments, service providers, and people, making it easier to manage risks.

Finally, funding for the silver economy must be balanced between financial sense and societal benefits. As aging is a long-term issue, financial systems should be strong, stable, and capable of managing risks. Partnerships between governments and businesses may help provide resources and knowledge if they are well-managed. Good investments for social goods and different funding models may help direct funds into social innovations (Mufarokhah et al., 2025). Corporate social responsibility and strategies that consider society may help businesses understand the needs of an aging population. Results-based funding can ensure that people are held accountable and that progress is evident. No single solution works perfectly. The effectiveness of these strategies depends on their design, clarity, and community involvement. Sustainable funding for older adults reflects societal values. This reflects whether living longer is something to which everyone should contribute or whether it should be done cheaply. By ensuring that everyone in our society works together and developing financial plans that value fairness and inclusion, we can create funding for older people that will benefit them now and provide better support for future generations (Nasaj, 2025).

CASE ILLUSTRATIONS (COMPARATIVE PERSPECTIVE)

To gain meaningful insights into the silver economy, it is necessary to go beyond abstract conceptualization and consider the dynamics of cross-sector ecosystems in real-world situations. The cases of the United Arab Emirates (UAE) and Ireland can serve as two opposite but complementary examples of how the issue of an aging population can be resolved with the help of coordinated policies, innovation, and community participation. These examples illustrate that contextual elements, including urbanization, governance systems, labor markets, and institutional capacity, influence the form and efficacy of cross-sector collaboration (Bromage et al., 2025). Ageing does not apply to everyone; it is a mediation of place-specific conditions and demands locally based but systemically related responses.

Case 1: UAE - Government-led, technology-based ecosystem

The UAE is a state-leading innovation-driven model of the silver economy, characterized by strong central coordination and the rapid introduction of digital technologies. Examples of national and emirate-level programs, including Dubai's Age-Friendly Strategy and Abu Dhabi's burgeoning digital health ecosystem, demonstrate that governments can coordinate the planning of cities, provision of healthcare, and digital landscape to meet the needs of an aging population. Through these programs, governments, technology companies, and healthcare organizations convene to create a unified service setting. For example, in large metropolises such as Dubai, transport and mobility infrastructure are becoming increasingly intelligent, including built-in fare-payment systems, on-demand tracking, and design considerations for accessibility. These developments reflect the general concept that cities must be restructured to respond to the needs of an aging population by carefully investing in them and fostering inter-sectoral cooperation (Estrada et al., 2025). Simultaneously, community-based programs and awareness activities promote the digital literacy of older adults because technological innovation cannot be achieved without the competence and confidence of users.

Similarly, in the healthcare field, telemedicine platforms, remote monitoring systems, and integrated patient data infrastructures can enable older adults to use home-based service. Such developments are in line with ecosystem thinking, in which technology, policy, and service delivery are supposed to work in harmony rather than separately. However, despite these developments, major challenges remain. The dependence on digital platforms poses the risk of marginalizing people with low levels of technology proficiency or access, supporting the need to implement additional support mechanisms, such as providing community training and alternative avenues of service provision (Mufarokhah et al., 2025). In addition, although governance structures facilitate rapid implementation, the need to improve user participation and co-design continues to exist, ensuring that the heterogeneity of aging experiences is well captured in solutions.

Case 2: Ireland - Community-Centered, Participatory Ecosystem

In contrast, Ireland has a decentralized, community-based model, as evidenced by the Age-Friendly Ireland Program. This initiative is managed at the community level and focuses on partnerships between public services, nonprofit organizations, and community groups. The Irish model focuses on social inclusion, accessibility, and participatory governance, rather than technological solutions. In rural and semi-urban environments, cross-sector cooperation is particularly evident in integrated service delivery models. For example, medical practitioners, social workers, and community groups work together to provide care in local settings using mobile clinics and outreach programs. These practices focus on the use of already existing community networks instead of imposing externally engineered networks, a formula especially relevant to areas characterized by dispersed populations and inadequate infrastructure (Pradeep et al., 2026). Social isolation can also be mitigated through community-based projects, such as local support groups and intergenerational programs, which help older adults improve their quality of life. Another essential element of the Irish approach is economic participation. Businesses and nonprofit organizations work together to help older people re-enter or maintain employment using flexible working conditions and specialized training services. Such programs often include skills training, confidence building, and mentoring programs that facilitate the intergenerational transfer of knowledge. These partnerships exemplify the extent to which lasting labor market engagement can be secured using sustainable and accommodating organizational operations, which boost not only business performance but also value creation for society. However, the decentralized nature of the Irish system poses a problem. Unequal application at the regional level may be caused by differences in the endowment of local resources and institutional capacity. In addition, despite high levels of community involvement, the scale of innovative interventions, especially in digital health and infrastructure, can be slower than in centralized systems. These limitations help clarify the trade-offs inherent to participatory models, where both inclusivity and responsiveness can be attained at the expense of speed and standardization. Table 2 presents the comparative features of silver-economy ecosystems.

Table 2. Comparative features of silver economy ecosystems in the UAE and Ireland

Dimension	UAE (State-Led Model)	Ireland (Community-Based Model)
Governance Structure	Centralised, government-led	Decentralised, local authority-led
Strategic Focus	Technology and infrastructure	Social inclusion and community engagement
Role of Technology	High (telehealth, smart systems)	Moderate (complementary to community care)
Stakeholder Coordination	Top-down, policy-driven	Bottom-up, participatory
Speed of Implementation	High	Moderate to slow
Inclusion Approach	Emerging focus (digital inclusion challenges)	Strong focus on participation and accessibility
Rural vs Urban Reach	Strong urban systems	Strong rural/community integration

continued on following page

Table 2. Continued

Dimension	UAE (State-Led Model)	Ireland (Community-Based Model)
Key Strength	Scalability and innovation	Inclusivity and social cohesion
Key Challenge	Digital exclusion, limited co-design	Resource variability, slower scaling

COMPARATIVE INSIGHTS

A comparison of the UAE and Ireland highlights two different but closely connected approaches to developing cross-sector ecosystems in the silver economy. The UAE's centralized, technology-focused model represents the possibility of rapid innovation and large-scale implementation, supported by effective governance and investment. In contrast, Ireland's decentralized, community-based model depicts the effectiveness of participative practices and social inclusion in addressing the diverse needs of ageing populations. There is a commonality of issues across the two contexts. Equity issues are also of primary importance, particularly access to services, digital inclusion, and geographical inequalities (Mufarokhah et al., 2025). Technological advances in cities can disproportionately benefit people who are more digitally literate and have higher incomes; however, geographic isolation and poor infrastructure can limit access to the services needed in rural areas. These observations highlight the need to develop systems that are flexible and responsive to the diverse needs of the heterogeneous population.

Trust and Coordination

Another common lesson relates to the central position of trust and coordination in maintaining cross-sectoral relationships. Regardless of the involvement of formal governance structures or community-based networks, successful ecosystems depend on explicit role descriptions, accountability systems, and strong stakeholder communication (Estrada et al., 2025). Once trust is developed, collaboration becomes more resilient, which in turn allows systems to respond to changing demographic, economic, and technological conditions.

Synthesis

Taken together, these instances suggest that there is no single direction for developing inclusive and sustainable silver-economy ecosystems. Instead, effective policies require a balance between leadership, technological innovation, and community involvement. The UAE exemplifies how the combination of governance and digital infrastructure can accelerate such change. However, Ireland provides deeper insights into the importance of social cohesion and local interaction in preserving inclusivity and sustainability.

Key Lesson

However, the main point is that ageing societies need both strategically coordinated and socially entrenched systems. Cross-sector cooperation should not be limited by institutional boundaries to include the lived experiences of older adults; therefore, innovation should be efficient, just, and meaningful. Policymakers and practitioners can develop ecosystems that promote longevity, dignity, participation, and the creation of shared value through lessons learned in diverse contexts and by articulating approaches accordingly (Bromage et al., 2025).

MEASURING ECOSYSTEM IMPACT

It is insufficient to simply look at numbers when measuring the impact of silver economy systems on the elderly. As we age, we are exposed to different parts of society. To gain a good understanding of how these systems work, all these different areas must be considered (Pradeep et al., 2026). When measuring the impact, we can determine whether it is working, what we can do to improve it, ensure that everyone is accountable, and obtain more support. By examining different areas, such as social, economic, innovation, and government, we can identify what is working and what we can do to improve it so that it reaches those who are most in need. Social indicators are difficult to measure.

Goals of less loneliness, more access to care, and improved quality of life are important. However, it is difficult to measure because it involves subjective feelings of the user. Surveys can help measure loneliness or the frequency of social interactions (Mufarokhah et al., 2025). The ease of access to care, duration of waiting, and affordability are also ways to measure this issue. Additionally, satisfaction with care, feeling of independence, and helpfulness of caregivers measured access to care. Quality of life includes health, how one feels, with whom one associates, and how safe they feel. By examining these areas over time, trends can be identified to improve the services provided to older adults. It is also important to involve older adults in this process to ensure that we measure what is important to them.

Economic indicators demonstrate the silver economy's contribution to society. The number of older people working is a way to measure how society is helped by the silver economy, especially if this is a goal or necessity for the economy. This includes the number of older people working, the number of older people retained in their jobs, and the number of older people who started their businesses. This can also be done for men and women, education levels, and geographic areas to identify inequalities (Fandrejewska-Nowakowska, 2025). The growth of local economies is also an important factor. For instance, developing facilities such as elderly housing or accessible transportation services may create jobs and stimulate the economy. This can be measured by examining the impact of older entrepreneurs on small businesses or the impact of caregiving on the economy. Economic measurements illustrate the direct monetary impact and overall impact, showing the relationship between the economy and the elderly.

Innovation metrics measure the spread and effectiveness of innovative solutions. For instance, measuring the number of people using age-friendly technologies, such as digital health or transportation, may illustrate how innovative solutions work well. If many people use innovative solutions, they work well; however, if few do, there may be an issue. Digital inclusion measures not only the use of digital technologies but also people's confidence in using them and ensures that everyone has equal access. Measuring the ways in which people use digital technologies, the types of digital technologies they use, and the ways in which they become involved in digital technologies may provide insights. Another aspect of innovation impact is the number of co-design methods used, the number of pilot projects that have been expanded, and the number of times groups work together to solve a problem. This determines whether the changes are real or superficial (Manolache et al., 2025). Governance and transparency are essential but are often overlooked. For good governance, everything should be fair and run smoothly. This can be measured by the presence of groups with different stakeholders, the use of reports to show how well things are progressing, the use of rules, and the inclusion of older persons in decision-making processes. Transparency can be measured by the availability of information, such as budgets and performance indicators. Including older people in decision-making processes may be a measure of fairness. Good governance may be evaluated by conducting audits, measuring the number of times people are consulted, and measuring responses to feedback. Good governance supports other factors by ensuring that social, economic, and innovation factors are fair and well-run. Combining all these factors requires good methods. The use of numbers and stories provides a comprehensive picture. For example, research on service use can be combined with discussion groups to learn more about users. In addition, examining trends over time can help in identifying patterns. Examining different areas can help determine what is working well and how to spread it further. Good management of numbers is important, especially when many groups are involved in the study. Equity is an important factor in measuring these systems' performance.

Numbers can obscure what has been achieved and for whom it has been achieved. They can be used to determine whether there are any unfair situations. For example, a program for improving mobility might look good overall but might not benefit lower-income seniors living in rural areas. Programs for digital health might work well for tech-savvy city dwellers but might not work as well for rural residents. By including equity in the measurements, we can ensure that these programs do not worsen the situation for some groups. Feedback loops are crucial for ensuring that measurements are translated into actual actions. Metrics should not only be used to create reports but also to inform how we approach decisions regarding the implementation of programs, development of strategies, and management of operations. Technology can also help monitor the extent to which an ecosystem is successful; however, it must be used appropriately.

Technology can help collect and display information in real time from multiple projects and locations, providing a clear picture of important results to the people involved (Fañanás-Biescas et al., 2025). Mobile applications can collect feedback on people's experiences, and technologies such as sensors can monitor movement and activity levels. However, it is worth noting that not everyone has access to technology; for instance, older people may not have the skills and means to access technologies such as mobile applications and the Internet, and traditional methods such as surveys, phone conversations, and meetings are required. The need to set realistic targets and communicate the results with funders, leaders, and communities can be met through such comparisons. Standards should be adapted to suit local contexts because differences exist between them. In other words, the measurement of the impact on the silver economy should be approached from a broad, detailed, and inclusive perspective.

Social indicators measure well-being, inclusion, and the quality of life. Economic indicators measure participation, productivity, and local economic growth. Innovation indicators measure the level of success in the application, inclusion, and effectiveness of new ideas (Mufarokhah et al., 2025). Governance indicators measure openness, responsibility and ethical care. These are used in combination with a fair approach and a long-term focus to help stakeholders understand what is working well, what is missing, and how to increase the success of what is working well. By including the measurement in the way we create the silver economy, we ensure that we are creating an environment in which the silver economy not only brings new technologies and financial results but also improves the quality of life for older adults in the long term and supports their independence, respect, and social standing.

CONCLUSION

The creation of an innovative system that can work in different fields of society in the context of an aging population is no longer a dream but something that needs to be implemented in the near future. As human life expectancy increases in different parts of the world, the problem of an aging population is no longer merely a health issue. It is also a workforce problem, a way to stay socially connected in society, a technology access problem, a financial problem, and a community development problem. These are not simple problems that can be solved by one party or a group of people (Pradeep et al., 2026). To solve this complex problem, we need the involvement of all parts of society, including the government, business, and universities. The involvement of the aging population is not just about helping older people but also about their participation in creating a solution that is meaningful and relevant in the context of real life. Working together through co-design is important in this regard.

This is because older people can influence everything from the type of products and services developed to the manner in which the services are delivered. Therefore, the final product reflects real-life experiences. Innovating and collaborating with the government and community through companies ensures that the final products are efficient, profitable, and fair. Working with environmental, social, and governance (ESG) standards and ensuring fairness ensures that no one is left out of the community, especially the less privileged in society, older people in rural areas, and the marginalized (Bromage et al., 2025). Working together through shared risks and ensuring that everyone is responsible for the success of the project makes the entire process stable and reliable, despite the tough times that companies may experience, financially and in terms of reputation. Good financial support is vital for these systems to continue operating over the long term.

The partnership between the government and businesses combines different types of resources. The use of different investment approaches, such as impact investing, blended finance, and shared value approaches, assists in channeling funds towards projects that benefit society and the economy. The use of performance-based financing approaches, such as social impact bonds, assists in promoting good performance and innovative thinking (Mufarokhah et al., 2025). Forward planning for the future assists in ensuring that successful small projects can grow and develop into long-term systems that continue to help the elderly and strengthen the economy of the country. Thus, good financial support and inclusive decision-making enable these systems to advance beyond short-term fixes and develop the capacity for long-term growth and development over a long period. Considering different types of places, we can see that each situation is different.

For urban systems, factors such as population density, technology, and good infrastructure are considered. We must address the added complexity and lack of technology in some of these areas. In rural systems, we have good community connections and flexible teamwork. We must find ways to help people get around when they live in remote areas. With job programs, we can see how different areas of the community come together and work towards helping the elderly remain actively involved in their jobs. This benefits both older adults and the economy. With all these different systems and ideas, we find that certain ideas keep recurring. These ideas are about people becoming involved in the design process, fairness for all, building trust, and learning. Measuring how well these systems perform in areas such as social well-being, employment, access to technology, and decision-making processes will keep these systems accountable and will continually improve their performance (Estrada et al., 2025). Well-thought-out innovative systems will not only respond to the fact that people are living longer, but will use that fact to create a better world by developing inclusive, strong, and forward-thinking societies. The silver economy will become a driving force in innovation, bringing together generations and stimulating economic growth, proving that by living longer, we will not only succeed but also prosper, live with dignity, and become one with the younger generations.

REFERENCES

Al Ali, A. S. (2025). Exploring the interplay of creativity, innovation, exploration, and artificial intelligence: A conceptual analysis. *International Journal of Technology Innovation and Management*, *5*(2), 40–57.

Askari, M., Ray, S., & Suri, S. (2026). Behavioral barriers to blue economy reform: A policy synthesis on ESG, emissions, and governance. *Marine Policy*, *184*, 106938. DOI: 10.1016/j.marpol.2025.106938

Bromage, M., Foth, M., Osman, K., & Hearn, G. (2025). From innovation theatre to systemic change: The role of intermediaries in design thinking. *Design Studies*, *101*, 101360. DOI: 10.1016/j.destud.2025.101360

Chhillar, I., Sandhu, S., Parida, S., & Majewski, P. (2025). Certification for solar panel reuse: A systematic review of cross-sector practices and gaps. *Sustainability (Basel)*, *17*(13), 5995. DOI: 10.3390/su17135995

Dabare, S., Rajapaksha, S., & Munaweera, I. (2025). Lifecycle analysis of nano-technology-enhanced soft materials in the circular economy. *Molecular Systems Design & Engineering*, *10*(10), 799–816. DOI: 10.1039/D5ME00067J

Estrada, S., Cabrera-Flores, M., León-Pozo, A., & Cota-Cota, C. (2025). Reflecting on challenges and opportunities: Examining the colour economy of innovation and entrepreneurship. In *SHS Web of Conferences* (Vol. 211, Article 07001). EDP Sciences.

Fañanás-Biescas, A. P., Ključnikov, A., Bargoni, A., & Ferraris, A. (2025). Senior entrepreneurship and opportunity recognition: A systematic review of the literature. *International Journal of Entrepreneurial Behaviour & Research*, •••, 1–38.

Fandrejewska-Nowakowska, A. (2025). The role of digital competence and trust in technology in inclusive and sustainable e-health development for seniors. *Ekonomia*, *31*(3), 43–57. DOI: 10.19195/2658-1310.31.3.3

Fedorko, R., & Mondal, S. R. (2025). The algorithmic alchemist: Transmuting business models for a net-zero future. In *Generative AI for a net-zero economy: Managing climate change and business innovation in the digital era* (pp. 37–55). Springer Nature Singapore. DOI: 10.1007/978-981-96-8015-3_3

Hwang, B. N., Puntha, P., & Jitanugoon, S. (2025). AI-driven circular transformation: Unlocking sustainable startup success through co-creation dynamics in circular economy ecosystems. *Sustainable Development (Bradford)*, *33*(S1), 245–274. DOI: 10.1002/sd.70001

Khattak, W. A., Anas, M., Hakki, E. E., Iqbal, J., Abbasi, B. A., & Munir, A. (2026). Economical and societal debut on sustainable environment and industry using bioenergy and nanotechnology. In *Sustainable nanostrategies for biorefineries: Environmental, economic, and social perspectives* (pp. 191–219). Springer Nature Singapore. DOI: 10.1007/978-981-95-5875-9_10

Lin, C., Dai, G., Liu, Y., Ye, G., & Fu, X. (2026). Exploring the future of sustainable ocean economies: Marine trade's role in advancing inclusive green growth. *Ocean and Coastal Management, 272*, 108003. DOI: 10.1016/j.ocecoaman.2025.108003

Manolache, M., Manolache, A. I., & Andrei, G. (2025). Floating solar energy systems: A review of economic feasibility and cross-sector integration with marine renewable energy, aquaculture and hydrogen. *Journal of Marine Science and Engineering, 13*(8), 1404. DOI: 10.3390/jmse13081404

Mufarokhah, L., Putra, A. R. S., & Nurhadi, N. (2025). Optimizing government procurement through social procurement policy innovation: Insights from cross-sector collaboration at the Ministry of Health, Indonesia. *Journal of Public Procurement*, 1–28.

Nasaj, M. (2025). Intercultural stressors and team innovative behaviour: The role of coping strategies in multicultural workplaces. *Global Knowledge, Memory and Communication.* Advance online publication. DOI: 10.1108/GKMC-10-2024-0680

Nasaj, M., Badi, S., Murtagh, N., & Ding, L. (2025). *Collective AI anxiety and team innovative behaviour: The role of coping strategies*. Construction Innovation: Information, Process. *Management.* Advance online publication. DOI: 10.1108/CI-08-2024-0222

Pradeep, K. G. M., Palvadi, S. K., & Rammurthy, D. (2026). Conclusion: Toward a sustainable future with block chain. In Kumar, A., Batta, P., Rathore, P. S., Kumar, T. A., & Ramírez, J. R. J. (Eds.), *Blockchain innovations for a sustainable circular economy* (Vol. 180). Springer., DOI: 10.1007/978-3-032-02428-2_19

Tomej, K., Garcia-Lozano, C., Vila-Subiros, J., Innocenti, A., Juvan, E., Le Pape, O., Arnoldussen, N. T., Verschuuren, J., Taylor, T., Huebner, G., Tollin, N., & Mernild, S. (2026). Enabling cross-sectoral transformation for coastal climate adaptation in Europe: Four directions for interdisciplinary efforts. *Environmental Science & Policy, 177*, 104334. DOI: 10.1016/j.envsci.2026.104334

Widiastini, N. M. A., Arsa, I. K. S., Prayudi, M. A., & Karta, N. L. P. A. (2025). Strategic collaborations and diversification: Pathways to sustainable growth in Bali's tourism village and business ecosystems. [Journal of Bali Studies]. *Jurnal Kajian Bali, 15*(1), 146–172.

KEY TERMS AND DEFINITIONS

Cross-Sector Innovation Ecosystem: Collaborative networks across public and private sectors

Inclusive Growth: Equitable economic participation across diverse populations

Silver Economy: Economic activities serving aging populations' needs

Chapter 6

The Silver Economy and Business Partnerships for Strengthening Health Financial Protection in Tunisia

Chokri Arfa
http://orcid.org/0000-0002-0966-2911
University of Carthage, Tunisia

ABSTRACT

This chapter examines the implications of population ageing for health financing and financial risk protection in Tunisia within the framework of Universal Health Coverage and SDG 3.8. The chapter analyzes how in Tunisia, ageing-driven increases in chronic diseases, disability, and long-term care needs intensify healthcare demand and raise out-of-pocket expenditure (35–40% of total health spending) and catastrophic health expenditure (18.4% of households), compounded by a fragmented system, inequalities, and limited fiscal space. It combines a conceptual analysis of the Silver Economy with empirical evidence from 2021 household survey using econometric modeling and scenario simulations. Results confirm a strong age gradient in financial risk, while interventions such as teleconsultation, assistive technologies, and care coordination reduce expected expenditure by up to 8–10%. The chapter concludes that integrating these interventions through the Silver Economy and business partnerships can strengthen financial protection and health system resilience.

DOI: 10.4018/979-8-3373-9370-4.ch006

BACKGROUND

The population aged 60 years and over is rapidly increasing worldwide (United Nations, 2025), shifting the disease burden toward chronic conditions and raising demand for healthcare and long-term care. Consequently, out-of-pocket health expenditure (OOPE) is high, which, in turn, exposes households to financial hardship and impedes progress toward Universal Health Coverage (UHC) and the achievement of SDG target 3.8 (Das et al., 2021).

The Silver Economy (SE), as an emerging approach, can be integrated into health systems through developing age-friendly health. strengthening primary care as well as social and business partnerships. The Silver Economy (SE), which includes economic activities related to consumption, production, and participation, supports the development of social and business models that enhance the well-being of ageing populations. (OECD, 2020; Wu et al., 2025). In health settings, SE can foster social enterprises and start-ups to scale up innovation, investment, and service delivery, with the objective of reducing financial hardship and supporting progress toward Universal Health Coverage (UHC) and SDG target 3.8. UHC aims to ensure access to quality health services without financial hardship (O'Connell et al., 2014). SDG 3.8 include financial protection indicators (3.8.2): Catastrophic Health Expenditure (CHE) and impoverishment, *(World Health Organization, 2021a, 2021b).*

Tunisia is at a pivotal stage of its demographic transition, with adults aged 60 and above accounting for 16.9% of the population in 2024, up from 10% in 2000, and projected to exceed 20% by 2040 (Bousnina & Souli, 2024; Institut National de la Statistique, 2024). This demographic shift is occurring in a context of economic strain, with GDP growth by only 2% annually 2010-2022 (Jallouli, 2025; Jmaii, 2025), limited fiscal space, and a fragmented health-financing system that reliant on OOPE. Despite the social health protection, OOPE accounts for about 36% of total health expenditure and contributes to households' exposure to financial hardship (World Health Organization, 2021b, 2025a). This is corroborated by the National Household Budget, Consumption and Living Standards Survey (Institut National de la Statistique, 2023), which reports that 18.4% of households experienced CHE. Of these, 8% were driven by spending on medicines, and 2.8% of households fell below the poverty line, with 1.8% attributable to medicines (Ismaïl & Arfa, 2022). These findings point to a dual challenge for Tunisia: managing the fiscal implications of an ageing population while reducing health-related financial hardship. The SE presents an avenue to turn demographic and epidemiological transitions into a "longevity dividend" by improving financial protection and advancing UHC-SDG 3.8.

Progress toward UHC and SDG target 3.8 requires expanding service coverage, strengthening financial protection, and enhancing health system resilience. In Tunisia, leveraging the Silver Economy (SE) and business partnerships could transform population ageing from a fiscal pressure into an opportunity for sustainable and inclusive health financing by stimulating investment in entrepreneurship and digital innovations such as care coordination, assistive technologies, and digital health solutions. It generates also employment through small and medium-sized enterprises (SMEs), social enterprises (SE), and startups operating in these fields (Hou et al., 2023).

OBJECTIVE

This chapter aims to analyse population ageing from a financial risk protection perspective, considering its relevance to UHC-SDG 3.8, and to identify Silver Economy (SE) interventions that can help reduce OOPE. The study uses the national household survey data and applies descriptive and econometric methods to assess how the SE, social solidarity, and business partnerships support equitable health financing.

OUTLINE

- Section 1 explores the conceptual foundations linking population ageing, the Silver Economy, and health systems, with particular attention to financial risk protection.
- Section 2 situates the assessment within Tunisia's context to portray the broader landscape in which ageing unfolds.
- Section 3 presents the empirical analysis through descriptive and econometric methods and scenario-based modelling, which investigate how ageing can be transformed from a source of financial pressure into pathways toward improved financial protection.
- Section 4 discusses the findings and provides policy implications for leveraging the Silver Economy within health systems.

SECTION 1. AGING, HEALTH SYSTEMS, AND THE SHIFT TOWARD THE SILVER ECONOMY

1.1. Population Aging and the risk of health financial protection

Demographic aging refers to the rising proportion of older adults resulting from declining fertility rates and increasing life expectancy. Globally, the number of people aged 60 and above is projected to reach 2.1 billion by 2050, compared to 1 billion in 2020, making aging one of the most significant demographic shifts of the 21st century (Gianfredi et al., 2025; Mingst et al., 2022). Such rapid transition places growing pressure on health systems and public finances as the prevalence of chronic conditions, disability, and long-term care needs rises, thereby increasing healthcare demand and OOPE. Hajizadeh et al. (2025) and Jane Osareme et al. (2024) show that these conditions heighten financial hardship of elderly healthcare users and expose then to CHE and impoverishment.

Financial protection is a central pillar of UHC-SDG 3.8 and explicitly monitored through indicator SDG 3.8.2 (Bhatia et al., 2022; Bieszk-Stolorz et al., 2024; Das et al., 2021; Eozenou, 2021; Vera-Sanso, 2023). It occurs when households are unable to afford necessary healthcare without experiencing catastrophic OOPE, reduced consumption, indebtedness and/or impoverishment (Patel, 2021; Tsega et al., 2023). CHE is a common measure of financial risk protection, defined as OOPE exceeding a household's budget threshold (typically 10% or 40%). Impoverishment occurs when OOPE pushes households into or further into poverty. Globally, OOPE represents a substantial share of total health expenditure (THE); for instance, in LMIC, it accounted for 40% of THE in 2018 (Rahman et al., 2022), where CHE at 10%, is estimated at around 13% (Mohsin et al., 2024) . Xu et al. (2003) shows that a 1% increase in the share of OOPE in THE is associated with a 2.2% rise in the incidence of CHE.

1.2. Silver Economy

The SE reframes ageing as an opportunity by turning fiscal pressure into a driver of resilient, inclusive health systems, productivity, and innovation (Butt et al., 2021; Butt et al., 2023; United Nations, 2024). Merritt (2025) shows that population aging is often depicted as a "demographic tsunami" threatening fiscal stability through rising health expenditures. The SE can reduce the financial risk protection by supporting the pooling and prepayment mechanisms. Aligned with UHC, the SE can turn population ageing into a driver of inclusive financing, risk sharing, and effective financial protection.

SE domains extend beyond a traditional economic model; they embody a broader social philosophy that values time, lived experience, and aging well. The term silver evokes not only grey hair but also wisdom, vitality, and continued societal contribution (Bisson et al., 2023; McGuirk et al., 2022; Oget, 2021). It invites societies to view longevity not as a burden but as a catalyst for creativity and renewal, positioning aging population as a driver of innovation in digital health, long-term care, assistive and smart-home technologies, senior housing, lifelong learning, and experience-based industries (Bran et al., 2016; Finland, 2025; Gabriel-Catalin,

2023). In practice, the SE spans multiple “sectors and innovations”. It relies first on healthcare services. A second dimension recognizes them as economic actors in social enterprise and business partnership. Thirdly, SE includes innovation and industries related to Agetech, smart homes, digital health, and other services. In response, social partnerships are emerging to align SE development within the UHC-SDG 3.8 framework through roles of:

- Public-private partnerships in delivering home-based long-term care and digital support services.
- Social enterprise–business consortia in developing scalable hybrid care models combining remote monitoring and community outreach.
- Digital health partnerships with telecom, AI, and medical device firms in deploying platforms and predictive tools for chronic care.
- Community-based partnerships where municipalities, NGOs, and private providers coordinate services through shared systems.
- Innovative financing models that include impact bonds and corporate investments supporting digital inclusion for older adults.

The SE can translate into targeted investments that enable health systems to better meet the medical and social needs of older populations by creating new professional roles (e.g., geriatric nurses, care coordinators), adopting digital health and assistive tools, and investing in workforce development and infrastructure to generate skilled jobs and stimulate economic and social activities (Felix, 2016; Hua, 2024) to sustain UHC (Fan et al., 2023). Thus, ppopulation ageing increases demand for age-related goods and services, fostering the development of the SE. Through enhanced income, social inclusion, and access to age-friendly services, the Silver Economy can strengthen financial protection, reduce catastrophic health expenditure (SDG 3.8.2), and help prevent health-related impoverishment.

Figure 1. Conceptual framework linking population ageing, the silver economy, health financial protection, and universal health coverage

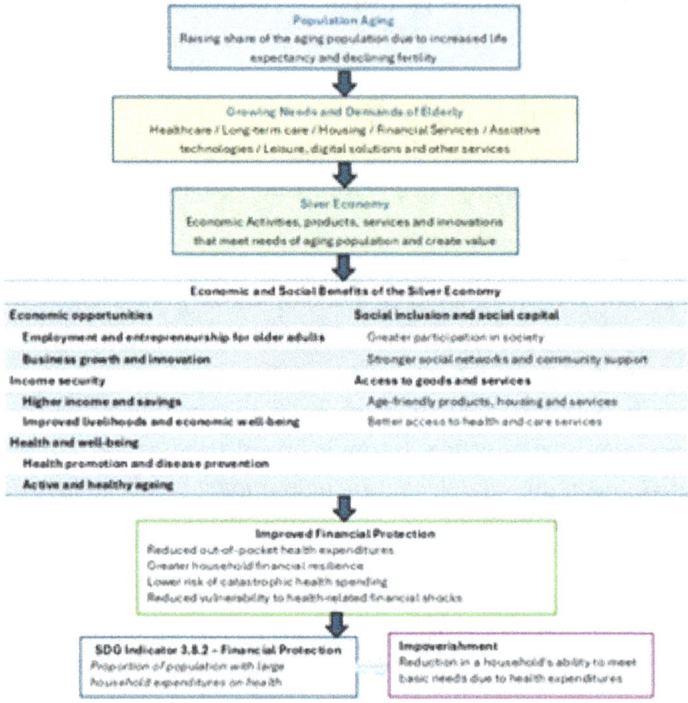

Table 1 below provides an illustrative example of the pathways and mechanisms linking the SE to UHC-SDG 3.8 (Chadha et al., 2025; Hou et al., 2023; Zeng et al., 2024). While the SE offers a lens to reposition ageing as a driver of innovation and inclusive growth, its contribution to UHC depends on its effective integration into health systems through supportive financing, technologies, and partnerships. Countries with effective primary health care (PHC) and unified risk-pooling frameworks are more ready to leverage financial protection for aging populations. Conversely, in contexts such as Tunisia, marked by fiscal constraints, fragmented social insurance schemes, uneven regional development, the pathways linking the SE to UHC-SDG 3.8 should be valorised and enhanced to cope with health needs and financial protection. Ultimately, the transformative value of the SE does not stem from a uniform model, but from its ability to shape and strengthen financial protection within specific country contexts (De Witte, 2023).

Table 1. Pathways linking the silver economy to UHC

Dimension	Mechanism	Contribution to Health Systems, UHC and SDG 3.8
Integrated Care and Services	Home-based and long-term care coordination	Improved access, quality, and continuity of services
Digital & Assistive Technologies	Telehealth, robotics, wearable devices	Broader coverage, prevention, and cost-effective care
Workforce Development	Geriatric training, reskilling, multidisciplinary teams	Capability of skilled health workers
Investment and Innovation	Health startups, PPPs, age-friendly infrastructure	Sustainable financing and system modernization
Empowered Ageing population	Co-creation, entrepreneurship, lifelong learning	Social participation and equity

SECTION 2. POPULATION AND HEALTH FINANCING PROFILE

2.1. Demographic and Socioeconomic Transition in Tunisia

Tunisia is in advanced stage of the demographic transition: fertility decline, mortality reductions, and rapid ageing. Census-based estimates indicate that the total population reached 11.97 million in 2024 (Institut National de la Statistique, 2024), while the annual growth rate is about 0.9% since 2010, compared with 2.8% in 1980–1985, and expected to further slowdown to 0.3% by 2045–2050. The fertility rate declined from 4.82 children per woman in 1980–1985 to about 2.05 in 2024 and is projected to fall to 1.86 by 2030–2035 and to 1.75 by mid-century. Life expectancy at birth increased from 64.3 years in 1980–1985 to 77.5 years in 2024 and is projected to reach 81.2 years by 2050. Mortality have been particularly pronounced, with infant mortality decreasing from 66 in 1980–1985 to about 13 per 1,000 live births in 2024.

These dynamics produced shifts in the population age structure. The proportion aged 65 years and above increased from 3.9% in the early 1980s to 9% in 2024 and is projected to reach nearly 20% by 2050. The oldest-old population (80+) is expected to rise from about 2% in 2024 to over 5% by mid-century. Consequently, the old-age dependency ratio is projected to increase from 11.1% in 2015–2020 to 31.7% in 2050. In parallel, the child dependency ratio has fallen sharply, from 76.8% in 1980–1985 to roughly 31% in 2024. The working-age population share (15–64 years) rose from 54.4% in the early 1980s to about 69% in 2024, showing the demographic dividend maturing. However, projections indicate that this share will peak in the near term and decline to around 62% by 2050 to close the demographic dividend. The dependency ratio, after reaching a historical low 2015–2024, is expected to rise 60% by 2050. Urbanization has progressed in parallel with demographic transition, as it increased from 3.6 million in 1980–1985 to over 8 million in 2024 and projected to approach 10 million by 2050. From a health-system perspective, these demographic shifts are expected to increase demand for the costly chronic and long-term care, thereby exerting pressure on health public financing. Achieving sustainable health financing and effective social protection will require adopting pooling arrangements and strategic purchasing mechanisms to respond to the evolving health needs of an ageing population.

Table 2. Demographic and socioeconomic indicators for Tunisia (1980–2050)

Indicator	1980–85	1990	2000–05	2015–20	2024 (Census)	2025	2030–35 (est.)	2050 (est.)
Total population (millions)	6.37	8.15	9.70	11.27	11.97	12.04	12.95	13.1–13.3
Annual population growth (%)	2.79	2.4	1.5	1.09	0.9	0.6	0.65	0.29
Life expectancy (years)	64.3	68.0	72.5	76.1	77.1	77.1	78.8	81.2
Infant mortality (per 1,000)	66	48	27	16	13	12	11	7–8
Under-5 mortality (per 1,000)	77	55	32	17	14	13	12	8
Fertility (children per woman)	4.82	4.1	2.6	2.15	2.05	2.00	1.86	1.75
Population 65+ (%)	3.9	4.5	5.8	7.6	9.0	9.4	12.4	19.8
Population 80+ (%)	0.41	0.5	0.9	1.6	2.0	2.2	2.6	5.1
Old-age dependency ratio (%)	7.2	8.5	10.5	11.1	13.5	4.5	18.8	31.7
Child dependency ratio (%)	76.8	65	45	34.5	31	30	32.4	28.5
Total dependency ratio (%)	83.9	73	55	45.6	44.5	44.5	51.2	60.2
Working-age share (%)	54.4	57	64	68.7	69	69	66.1	62.4
Urban population (millions)	3.6	4.6	6.2	7.5	8.3–8.5	8.6	9.5	10.0
Maternal mortality (per 100,000)	—	131	70,0	62	55	—	—	—

Sources: Institut National de la Statistique (2024); United Nations (2025); World Health Organization (2025b); World Bank (2025).

Tunisia's economy is increasingly service-driven, with the share of services in GDP rising from about 57% in 2012 to over 60% in 2022, while the share of industry in GDP declined from around 30% to about 23% over the same period, and the share of agriculture in GDP remained relatively stable, fluctuating between 8% and 10% (Adel Ben Youssef, 2024). The economy is largely composed of micro and family-owned enterprises, especially in agriculture, commerce, and services. Three-quarters of agricultural holdings are family-run, while cooperatives play a modest but meaningful role in input sharing, marketing, and community-based services. Employee-owned cooperatives are more common in agriculture, whereas formal employee ownership structures remain limited in other sectors. Recently, Tunisia has seen a gradual rise in social enterprises and startups, particularly in digital health, telemonitoring, assistive technology. Although startup density and investment levels remain modest compared to regional benchmarks. These emerging sectors, if oriented toward aging populations, health innovation, and long-term care, could complement traditional enterprises and cooperatives to form hybrid local SE ecosystems.

Tunisia's demographic ageing is unfolding within a constrained macroeconomic environment characterized by modest economic growth (1.4% in 2024), persistent inflation (7.2%), and high public debt (around 80% of GDP), limiting fiscal space for expanding health and social protection financing. These constraints may reduce the capacity of traditional public financing mechanisms to adequately respond to the growing health and long-term care needs of older populations. Tunisia's economy is largely service-oriented, with an expanding private health sector and a growing digital entrepreneurship ecosystem.

Tunisia has contributory pension schemes (Caisse Nationale de Sécurité Sociale and Caisse Nationale de Retraite et de Prévoyance Sociale) covering public and private workers, alongside targeted non-contributory programs such as AMEN for vulnerable households. However, these systems face growing financial pressures due to demographic aging, high informality, and modest incomes. Although the statutory minimum wage (SMIG) in 2025 is 528.320 TND per month for a 48-hour regime and 448.238 TND for a 40-hour regime, the living wage is estimated at more than twice this amount, and only about one-third of wage earners meet or exceed it. Socio-economic inequality remains (Gini index = 35) and is compounded by regional disparities in income, service provision, and digital access, particularly in rural and southern regions. These constraints, combined with limited purchasing power and uneven access to services, restrict the development of an inclusive SE. At the same time, these trends create an opportunity to position the SE as a driver of community-based services, innovation, and financial protection for ageing populations. If aligned, SE could support investment in digital health, senior-friendly housing, and community-based care. However, without mechanisms linking these investments to financial protection, decent work, and regional equity, the SE risks reinforcing inequalities. Therefore, Tunisia's SE should be anchored in wage adequacy and regional equity. The SE emerges not only as an economic model but as a pathway to transform longevity into dignity and human rights.

2.2. Health Status and Insurance

The 2021 Survey data (Institut National de la Statistique, 2023) indicates that persons in households aged 60 years and above constitute 15% of the total households. Table 3 shows a statistically significant association between aging and worth health status. The prevalence of chronic diseases rises from 9.4% of adults under 60 to 53.5% among those aged 60–79 and exceeds 65% of persons aged 80 and above ($\chi^2(2)=1.225$; $p=0.01$). Likewise, the proportion of individuals reporting physical or mental difficulties increases from 4.7% below 60 years to 16.0% for aged 60–79 and nearly 37.0% for the oldest adults ($\chi^2(2)= 3.211$; $p= 0.01$). These results confirm the steep rise in morbidity and disability with age, which is an indicator of growing demand for healthcare and for effective financial protection.

Socioeconomic indicators further illustrate the pattern of vulnerability among aging. Health-insurance coverage varies significantly across age groups ($\chi^2(6)=12.387$; $p=0.05$). Among individuals aged 60–79, approximately 49% are covered by "the Caisse Nationale d'Assurance Maladie CNAM", Tunisia's mandatory national health insurance fund for salaried workers and retirees. Coverage rises to 58% of those aged 80 and above. Despite this, the proportion of uninsured individuals remains high 22% in both elderly groups which is a sign of financial hardship (Ismaïl & Arfa, 2022). Health social protection relies also on AMEN program, which provides free subsidized care to poor and vulnerable households. Voluntary schemes (Assurance Group and Mutual) offer additional benefits (Abu-Zaineh et al., 2014; Arfa & Achouri, 2008; Romdhane et al., 2015). Fragmentation in coverage results in differential access to care, but also in ineffective risk pooling, and in increased financial hardship for ageing population as shown by Ismaïl and Arfa (2022). Expenditure quintiles shows that more than 40% of those aged 80 and above fall within the lowest two quintiles (Q1–Q2), compared with about 30% of individuals aged 60–79 ($\chi^2(8)=21.108$; $p=0.05$). The multidimensional transition is marked by chronic diseases, disability, and vulnerability among a significant share of the ageing population. The SE can help transform these dynamics into drivers of inclusive growth and innovation by linking health financing, social protection, and long-term care.

Table 3. Socio-health characteristics by age group, Tunisia 2021

Variables		Age Groups			
		< 60 years	60–79 years	80 years and above	Total
Chronic diseases	Yes	4 145	4 623	799	9 567
	No	40 034	4 017	423	44 474
	Total	44 179	8 640	1 222	54 041
Physical & mental difficulties	Yes	2 096	1 378	447	3 921
	No	42 083	7 262	775	50 120
	Total	44 179	8 640	1 222	54 041
Health Insurance	CNAM	21 692	4 218	586	26 496
	AMEN	10 831	2 141	313	13 285
	AG / MUT	1 844	361	57	2 262
	Uncovered	9 812	1 920	266	11 998
	Total	44 179	8 640	1 222	54 041
Expenditure quintile	Q1	8 603	1 973	233	10 809
	Q2	8 591	1 986	233	10 809
	Q3	8 724	1 902	184	10 809
	Q4	8 631	2 023	155	10 809
	Q5	8 687	1 895	224	10 806
	Total	43 235	9 779	1 029	54 041

2.3. Health-Care Utilization and Expenditure Patterns

Health-care utilization and expenditures are high for aged population due to the high prevalence of chronic diseases, multimorbidity, and disability. Using 2021 survey data, table 4 shows that those below 60 years have the lowest annual visit to health facilities, while individuals aged 90 and above report the highest visits at all facilities levels. Kruskal–Wallis tests confirm significant inter-age differences ($p < 0.001$). Average per capita expenditure increases with age, ranging from 3,893 to 5,815 Tunisian dinars (TND). In 2021, the exchange rate was TND 2.79 per USD. Hospital services represent the largest expenditure (up to 3,579 TND), while outpatient care is only 1,500 TND, and medicine expenditures decline at the oldest ages (from 1,637 to below 900 TND). Studies of Wang et al. (2021) and Jane Osareme et al. (2024) show that healthcare costs are a key determinant of demand among pre-senior age groups. People aged 70 and above tend to have more frequent but lower-cost follow-up visits. At very advanced ages, an increasing share of health needs shifts toward long-term care services that are not fully captured within the standard Classification of Individual Consumption According to Purpose "COICOP-06" used in the Tunisian survey (Müller, 2021).

Table 4. Distribution of healthcare visits and expenditures across age groups

Indicators	< 60 years	60–79 years	80 years and above
Average Number of Visits (Std)			
Health Centers	3.2 (1.3)	3.6 (3.3)	5.0 (4.9)
Local Hospitals	5.1 (2.6)	5.5 (3.3)	6.8 (4.6)
Regional Hospitals	5.9 (1.7)	6.2 (4.8)	7.6 (3.8)
University Hospitals	4.4 (2.0)	4.8 (3.9)	6.2 (2.8)
Annual Health Expenditure per Person (TND, Std)			
Total Expenditure	5,468.7 (920.4)	5,364.3 (1,016.9)	4,090.7 (926.0)
Hospitalization	2,205.6 (765.2)	2,812.3 (871.7)	1,623.5 (620.0)
Outpatient Care	1,507.2 (201.6)	1,510.0 (205.0)	1,579.0 (216.0)
Medicines	1,637.4 (158.3)	1,440.0 (200.0)	930.0 (145.0)

Results from the 2021 survey reveal age-based gradients in healthcare service utilization and expenditure (Table 5). Outpatients' utilization increases with age: 53% of those aged 15–59 reported at least one outpatient visit in the previous month, compared with 72% among those aged 60–79 and 76% among those aged 80 and above. Inpatient utilisation follows a similar pattern, rising from 5.2% among working-age adults to 12.9% for those aged 60–79 and 14.6% for the oldest group. Income stratification is also pronounced. Among individuals aged 60 and above, outpatient utilization rises from 63% in the lowest income quintile (Q1) to 82–83% in the highest (Q5), while inpatient use increases from 10% to 15%. This reflects a pro-rich bias in service use (CI = 0.119). Average annual OOPE nearly doubles from Q1 to Q5, rising from 910 to 1,480 TND among those aged 60–79, and from 880 to 1,350 TND among those aged 80+. Older adults in Greater Tunis (1,560 TND) and the Coastal East (1,420 TND) spend more than those in interior regions such as the Center-West (1,080 TND) and North-West (1,100 TND). These differences reflect higher access and costs in urban areas, while poorer regions face lower utilization and greater financial strain.

Table 5 highlights regional disparities in outpatient and inpatient care utilization. Outpatient use exceeds 80% in Greater Tunis and the Coastal East but remains below 60% in interior regions, with intermediate levels (64–68%) elsewhere. Hospitalization follows a similar pattern, reaching 14–15% in coastal areas versus 10% in interior regions. These disparities reflect access gaps and point to opportunities for investment in age-related services.

Table 5. Healthcare services utilization (%) and OOPE (TND) by age group, income quintile, and region, Tunisia 2021

Age Group	Overall	Income Quintile					Region*						
		Q1	Q2	Q3	Q4	Q5	GT	NE	NW	CE	CW	SE	SO
Outpatient visits (past month)													
15–59 yrs	53.0	45	49	53	56	61	57	55	54	48	50	52	51
60–79 yrs	72.0	63	67	72	78	82	81	79	74	59	61	66	68
80+ yrs	76.0	60	65	70	76	83	83	81	75	57	58	64	66
Inpatients (past year)													
15–59 yrs	5.2	4.1	4.5	5.0	5.5	6.0	5.9	5.6	5.4	4.8	4.9	5.1	5.0
60–79 yrs	12.9	10.4	11.1	12.3	13.0	14.5	14.7	13.5	12.8	10.2	10.5	11.9	12.3
80+ yrs	14.6	10.6	11.3	12.5	13.2	14.8	15.0	14.2	13.6	10.0	10.4	12.1	12.5
OOPE (TND)													
15–59 yrs	670	480	560	630	720	860	810	740	700	540	580	660	620
60–79 yrs	1,240	910	1,020	1,160	1,330	1,480	1,560	1,420	1,300	1,080	1,100	1,220	1,250
80+ yrs	1,180	880	940	1,040	1,220	1,350	1,460	1,310	1,200	980	1,020	1,150	1,130

* **GT** Greater Tunis, **NE** North East, **NW** North West, **CE** Center East, **CW** Center West, **SE** South East and **SO** South West

2.4. Health Financial Protection

Despite social health coverage, a high proportion of Tunisian households pay for healthcare services out of pocket, exposing them to financial hardship. Evidence from multiple studies confirms persistent CHE and impoverishing driven by OOPE. OOPE have consistently accounted for 35–40% of current health expenditure over the past decade; well above the WHO recommended threshold of 20%. Medicines and inpatients care remain the main cost drivers, exacerbated by coverage gaps in chronic conditions and reliance on drug's expenditures. As shown in Table 6, catastrophic health expenditure at the 10% (CHE10) and 40% (CHE40) thresholds remains a significant concern. CHE10 increased from 8.0% in 2010 to 19.5% in 2021, while CHE40 rose from 0.43% to 2.20% over the same period. Aged populations and those with chronic diseases are at the highest risk. OOPE continues to push households into poverty, particularly those living in rural areas, working in the informal sector, or lacking insurance (UNCOV), belonging to the low-quintile and elderly-headed households. High OOPE is primarily driven by constrained fiscal space for health, fragmentation across health insurance schemes (CNAM, AMG, AG, and UNCOV), weak strategic purchasing arrangements, and insufficient coverage for chronic disease management and long-term care.

Tunisian' studies (Abu-Zaineh et al., 2014; Ayadi & Zouari, 2017) highlight that reducing OOPE requires increasing the priority of health in the government budget to at least 15%, explicitly defining an essential benefits package, unifying the social health insurance schemes with extension to uninsured groups. These measures should target poor and elderly populations through subsidizing essential medicines and chronic disease. Strengthening the SE in Tunisia can also promote digital PHC models and create new roles such as telehealth staff, care coordinators, and home-based providers.

Table 6. Financial protection indicators for Tunisia (2005-2015)

Survey Year (Reference Studies)	CHE 10%	CHE 40%	Impoverishment
2015 (Ismaïl & Arfa, 2022)	18.4	2.20	2.8
2015 (Abu-Zaineh et al., 2014)	8.0	0.43	1.8
2015 (World Health Organization, 2021b)	10.3	1.1	2.1
2015 (Ayadi & Zouari, 2017)	19.5	—	—
2010 (Abu-Zaineh et al., 2014)	12.0	0.7	1.5
2005 (Elgazzar et al., 2013)	12.1	—	0.7

3. AGEING, THE SILVER ECONOMY, AND HEALTH FINANCIAL PROTECTION IN TUNISIA

Gilbert and Brik (2022) argues that population aging should be viewed not only as a challenge but as an opportunity to strengthen the health system through age-responsive services within the SE framework. The underlying premise is that a growing share of employment, innovation, and investment will increasingly emerge from age-driven demand, positioning aging as a catalyst for market expansion and sectoral growth. In contexts like Tunisia, where OOPE drives financial hardship, the key challenge is how to channel SE momentum toward improving healthcare access, protecting households from financial vulnerability (Huegler & Ruch, 2022; Sanchini et al., 2022) and supporting health system resilience (Grinin et al., 2023). To explore these dynamics and quantify their implications, an econometric approach is used to assess how age-responsive, service development, and financial protection interact under different SE interventions scenarios.

Recent evidence indicates that digital health such as telehealth, wearable monitoring devices, smart home technologies, and AI-supported health tools, can improve access to care, chronic disease self-management, and elderly homecare (Park et al., 2025; Zou et al., 2023). Digital homecare interventions may strengthen continuity and quality of primary care for elderly populations, particularly those with chronic diseases (de Siqueira Silva et al., 2024). OECD study reported that chronic diseases are the major source of financial burden for older populations and sources of OOPE and unmet care needs (OECD, 2024).

3.1. Study Design and Data Sources

3.1.1. Methods

National representative survey 2021 "households' budget, consumption and living standard survey" is used to analysis the determinants of OOPE and assess effects of ageing-responsive services ("SE"). The econometric strategy is based on the semi-continuous nature of OOPE, which combines a substantial mass of zero-spenders with a right-skewed distribution among those who incur expenditures. Marginalized Two-Part Model (MTP) is used as it outperform alternative models (Daghaghele et al., 2025). In the first part, MTP estimates the probability of incurring OOPE using a logistic mixed-effects model:

$$Pr\left(Y_{ij} > 0\right) = logit^{-1}\left(Z_{ij}^{'}\alpha + b_{1j}\right)$$

Where b_{1j} is an age-level random intercept. The second part modelled the marginal mean OOPE for the full population.

$$E\left(Y_{ij}\right) = exp\left(X_{ij}^{'}\beta + b_{2j}\right)$$

where Zij and Xij denote sets of explanatory variables for the probability and expenditure components of the model household i in age group j. where coefficient $exp\left(\beta_{k}\right) - 1$ represent percentage changes in exposed OOPE. Two distributions were considered for the positive part: lognormal (MTP-LN) and gamma (MTP-G). Estimation used adaptive Gauss-Hermite quadrature (LN) and Laplace approximation (G) under maximum likelihood. Model selection relied on log-likelihood, Akaike (AIC) and Bayesian (BIC) information criteria, and the Cuong non-nested test. Because the joint likelihood depends on the distribution of positive OOPE, we estimate two alternative specifications for Part II: (i) MTP Lognormal (MTP-LN) and (ii) MTP Gamma (MTP-G). For positive OOPE:

- Lognormal assumption: $ln\left(Y_{ij}\middle| Y_{ij} > 0\right) \sim N\left(\mu_{ij}, \sigma^2\right), \ \mu_{ij} = X_{ij}'\beta + b_{2j}$
- Gamma assumption: $Y_{ij}\middle| Y_{ij} > 0 \sim Gamma\left(mean = \mu_{ij}, \ dispersion = k\right)$

To assess whether age-responsive services reduce financial burden, different interaction scenarios were tested, combining aging status with exposure to assistive technologies, teleconsultations, and care coordination. CHE at the 10% threshold (CHE10) was defined as occurring when household OOPE reached or exceeded 10% of income. To translate simulated OOPE changes into changes in CHE incidence, we applied the marginal relationship $\Delta CHE \approx \beta \times \Delta OOPE$, where β (0.08–0.12) represents the empirical sensitivity observed in the sample.

3.1.2. Data Description

This study draws on the 2021 national survey of 17,394 households with complete data on demographics, health status, insurance coverage and OOPE. OOPE was recorded over 12 months and includes payments for consultations, medicines, diagnostics and transport. The distribution of OOPE is semi-continuous, with many zero-spenders and a right-skewed distribution among spenders.

Five predictors were validated as key explanatory variables: ageing (household with member ≥60 years and age groups 60–69, 70–79, 80+); health status (chronic diseases, disability); and socioeconomic factors (health insurance: CNAM, AMG/AMEN, AG/Mutual, uncovered; and expenditure quintile Q1–Q5). These variables are widely identified as determinants of OOPE, CHE and impoverishment in Tunisia (Abu-Zaineh et al., 2014; Ismaïl & Arfa, 2022) and internationally. Households with elderly accounted for 15% of the sample (7.6% aged 60–69, 5.1% aged 70–79, 2.1% aged 80+). Overall, 47.4% reported chronic illness, 21.2% disability and 33.3% included at least one older adult (≥60), as shown in Table 7. Insurance coverage was dominated by social health insurance (63.9%), while 18% were uninsured. Households were evenly distributed across quintiles. Three binary SE indicators were constructed: teleconsultation use, assistive technology ownership and care-coordinator contact, with estimated rates of 5%, 19% and 7%.

Ethical considerations were fully respected, as the analysis relies on anonymized, publicly accessible microdata. No identifiable information was used, and all procedures adhered to national and international guidelines for household survey research.

Table 7. Descriptive statistics of selected variables

Variables		Number	Mean	SD
Ageing groups	60–69 yrs	1,328	7.6	26.5
	70–79 yrs	883	5.1	21.9
	80+ yrs	372	2.1	14.4
	No elderly in Households	14,811	85.2	35.5
Chronic disease	With ChrDis	8,240	47.37	49.93
	Without ChrDis	9,154	52.63	49.93
Disability	HH with disability	3,682	21.17	40.85
	HH without disability	13,712	78.83	40.85
Health insurance	Uncovered	1,390	7.99	27.11
	AMG	3,764	21.64	41.17
	CNAM	11,115	63.90	48.03
	AG	1,125	6.47	24.60
Expenditure quintile	Q1 (Poorest)	2,703	15.50	36.23
	Q2	3,341	19.20	39.39
	Q3	3,618	20.80	40.58
	Q4	3,773	21.70	41.21
	Q5 (Richest)	3,959	22.80	41.92
SE	Teleconsultation use	1,740	5.0	29.9
	Assistive technologies	3,300	19.0	39.3
	Care coordinator	1,200	6.9	25.3
Total		**17,394**		

The dataset provides the demographic, health, insurance, socioeconomic, and service-use variables required to analyze the determinants of OOPE and assesses the potential effects of age-responsive interventions. Given the semi-continuous nature of OOPE and its skewed distribution, the Marginalized Two-Part Model offers an appropriate analytical framework. It enables simultaneous estimation of the likelihood of incurring OOPE and the level of expenditure when costs occur, while supporting the simulation of teleconsultation, assistive technology, and care-coordination scenarios and their potential impact on CHE.

3.2. Results

3.2.1. OOPE Incidence and Intensity

MTP models were estimated under lognormal and gamma families. MTP-LN demonstrated superior fit (lower D, AIC, BIC) versus MTP-G (table 8). A Vuong non-nested test favoured the independent two-part specification over a Tobit (Z=21.7, p<0.001). Random intercepts by age group (60–69, 70–79, 80+) in both parts improved fit (LRT p<0.001).

Table 8. Goodness-of-fit comparison

Fitted model	Log-likelihood	D = −2LL	AIC	BIC	Converged
MTP-LN	−15,980	31,960	32,110	32,260	Yes
MTP-G	−16,610	33,220	33,370	33,520	Yes

Table 9 reports Part I (logit, incidence) and Part II (log-link GLM, intensity) estimates and indicates that ageing is a gradient effect on both the probability of incurring OOPE and the conditional level of OOPE. Compared with households with no elderly, households with members aged 60–69, 70–79, and especially 80+ have progressively higher odds of any OOPE and higher expected spending once OOPE occurs. The magnitude of the effect steepens sharply after age 70, in line with high chronic diseases and disabilities dependency. Chronic disease and disability were found strong predictors of both OOPE incidence and intensity. Insurance follows the expected profile: AMG does not significantly reduce spending; CNAM and AG/Mut slightly increase OOPE incidence through higher utilization but reduce conditional spending due to co-payment or coverage. As expected, richer quintiles show higher OOPE in both parts of the model. Silver-Economy variables demonstrate a dual pattern: Teleconsultation, assistive technology (AT), and care coordination slightly increase the probability of having OOPE. Age-group interaction terms (Age60–69×Teleconsult, Age70–79×Coordination, Age80+×AT) indicate that if such services placed into the SE could cost-moderating effects as age advances and confirm their potential for reducing financial hardships for the aged population.

Table 9. Marginalized two-part lognormal model: Tunisia 2021

Variables (references)	Zero-part (logit) (SE)*	Positive-part (log-link) (SE)
Ageing groups (ref: No elderly)		
60–69 yrs	0.14 (0.05) **	0.10 (0.04) **
70–79 yrs	0.22 (0.06) ***	0.14 (0.04) ***
80+ yrs	0.33 (0.08) ***	0.21 (0.05) ***
Chronic disease (without and with)	0.31 (0.04) ***	0.18 (0.03) ***
Disability (without and with)	0.27 (0.05) ***	0.22 (0.04) ***
Insurance (ref: Uncovered)		
AMG	0.09 (0.06)	−0.05 (0.04)
CNAM	0.21 (0.06) ***	−0.11 (0.04) **
AG/ MUT	0.28 (0.08) ***	−0.18 (0.05) ***
Expenditure quintile (ref: Q1)		
Q2	0.07 (0.05)	0.08 (0.03) **
Q3	0.13 (0.05) **	0.12 (0.03) ***
Q4	0.19 (0.05) ***	0.17 (0.03) ***
Q5	0.27 (0.06) ***	0.24 (0.04) ***
SE variables (ref: No)		
Teleconsultation (Yes)	0.10 (0.05) *	−0.09 (0.03) **
AT ownership (Yes)	0.06 (0.04)	−0.07 (0.03) *
Care-coordination (Yes)	0.14 (0.06) *	−0.12 (0.04) **
Interactions (ref: No elderly × No SE)		
60–69 × Teleconsultation	—	−0.05 (0.03) *
70–79 × Teleconsultation	—	−0.07 (0.03) **
80+ × Teleconsultation	—	−0.10 (0.04) **
60–69 × AT ownership	—	−0.04 (0.03)
70–79 × AT ownership	—	−0.06 (0.03) *
80+ × AT ownership	—	−0.09 (0.04) **
60–69 × Care-coordination	—	−0.06 (0.03) *
70–79 × Care-coordination	—	−0.09 (0.03) **
80+ × Care-coordination	—	−0.12 (0.04) ***
Random intercept variance (age-group level)	0.21 (0.06)	0.15 (0.05)

* Statistical significance: *p < 0.10, **p < 0.05, and ***p < 0.01

3.2.2. Scenario Analysis Based on MTP-LN estimates

To assess the financial impact of scaling up SE interventions in Tunisia, four scenarios were simulated using the MTP-LN model to evaluate how teleconsultation, assistive technology (AT), and care-coordination, separately and jointly, can modify the probability of OOPE, the conditional OOPE, and the exposure probability of CHE at threshold 10 (CHE10). The scenario was performed separately for three ageing groups (60–69, 70–79, 80+) to capture heterogeneity in needs, multimorbidity, and vulnerability to healthcare financing services.

Across all scenarios, SE interventions tend to slightly increase the probability of any OOPE, reflecting better access and more frequent contact with services. However, they significantly reduce conditional OOPE, particularly in households with members aged 70 or more. The intensity of reductions outweighs the small increases in incidence, generating net decreases in expected OOPE across all elderly groups, and reduction in CHE10. The magnitude of the financial risk protection gained intensifies with age: Aged 80+ benefit the most, followed by those aged 70–79.

Scenario A: Teleconsultation Scale-Up

Expanding teleconsultation coverage to 50% among older adults generates a clear and progressive reduction in financial burden across ageing groups. Because remote consultations lower barriers to accessing care particularly by reducing travel time, transport costs, and mobility constraints, the probability of incurring any OOPE increases slightly (table 9). However, this rise in incidence is more than offset by substantial reductions in conditional spending. Teleconsultation reduces the cost per episode of care by substituting in-person visits with remote follow-up, improving triage, and lowering reliance on costly face-to-face interactions. In practise, it should include activities such as remote primary care consultations, chronic disease follow-up, medication management and digital referral services. Teleconsultation can reduce geographic, mobility, and transportation barriers, particularly for vulnerable aging population.

In table 10, these efficiency gains translate directly into lower expected OOPE. Among households with members aged 60–69, expected OOPE falls by 6.5%. The effect becomes progressively stronger with age: households aged 70–79 experience a 6.6% decline, and those aged 80 and above see the largest reduction, at 6.7%. This gradient reflects higher baseline spending and a greater potential for teleconsultation to substitute in-person visits for the oldest adults. Improvements in financial protection follow the same pattern. Reduction in CHE10 range from −0.5% in the 60–69 group to −0.9% for the 80+ group, confirming that remote consultations disproportionately benefit households facing the greatest mobility limitations and chronic disease. Teleconsultation scaled to half of older households raises service contact only marginally but consistently reduces spending intensity. It delivers 6–7%

decreases in expected OOPE and meaningful reductions in CHE, with the largest gains concentrated in the oldest and most vulnerable groups. Teleconsultation therefore emerges as an age-responsive and cost-moderating intervention within Silver-Economy framework.

Table 10. Scenario A: Teleconsultation to 50% coverage among Aged 60+

Age group	Coverage	Δ Any-OOPE* (pp)	Δ Conditional OOPE (%)	Δ Expected OOPE (%)	Δ CHE10 (pp)
60–69	50%	+1.0	−7.9 (avg: 50% × −15.7)	−6.5	−0.5
70–79	50%	+1.0	−7.9	−6.6	−0.6
80+	50%	+1.0	−7.9	−6.7	−0.9

* Any-OOPE is a binary outcome indicating whether a household incurred any OOPE during the period (Yes = 1, No = 0). Any-OOPE = probability of having any positive OOPE.

Scenario B: Assistive Technology Scale-Up

For Scenario B (Expansion of Assistive Technologies), the target population should extend beyond persons with disabilities to include older adults, individuals with chronic conditions, persons with functional limitations, and other vulnerable groups who may benefit from assistive devices and digital support technologies. Such an inclusive approach is better aligned with the objectives of healthy ageing, financial protection, and UHC.

Scaling up assistive technologies (AT) to 40% among households with disability generates modest but meaningful improvements in financial protection, particularly for the oldest adults. Given that disability affects approximately one-fifth of all households and is more prevalent among the elderly (25% in the 60–69 group, 35% in the 70–79 group, and 50% in the 80+ group), the effective share of households benefiting from AT ranges from 10% in younger elderly groups to 20% among those aged 80 and above. Because AT is primarily functional in nature, supporting mobility, sensory adaptation, and fall prevention, it does not substantially change the likelihood of using health services. As a result, its effect on the incidence of OOPE remains very limited (table 11). However, AT meaningfully reduces conditional OOPE among those who adopt it. Combined effects from the main AT coefficient (−6.7%) and the age-specific interaction (−5.8%) yield an overall potential reduction of approximately −12.1% in conditional spending among older adults with disability. When weighted by the share of treated households, this translates into reductions in expected OOPE of −0.9% for those aged 60–69, −1.4% for those aged 70–79, and up to −2.0% for the 80+ group. Corresponding improvements in CHE10 remain modest but positive, ranging from −0.1 to −0.3% age points. Overall, AT acts as a complementary but not stand-alone financial-protection measure. Its benefits are concentrated among older adults with functional limitations, providing a small but targeted buffer against rising OOPE in the most vulnerable segments of the ageing population.

Table 11. Scenario B: Assistive technology to 40% coverage in HHs with disability

Age group	Treated share	Δ Any-OOPE (pp)	Δ Conditional OOPE (%)	Δ Expected OOPE (%)	Δ CHE10 (pp)
60–69	10%	+0.1	−1.2 (10% × −12.1%*)	−0.9	−0.1
70–79	14%	+0.1	−1.7	−1.4	−0.2
80+	20%	+0.2	−2.4	−2.0	−0.3

Scenario C: Care Coordination Scale-Up

Expanding care coordination to 30% of older adults living with at least one chronic condition generates stronger financial gains than those observed for assistive technologies. Because care coordination directly addresses fragmentation in service delivery by reducing unnecessary diagnostic tests, avoiding duplicated consultations, and guiding patients toward appropriate providers. It yields a clear reduction in spending intensity with only a small increase in service contact. If around 60% of older adults live with at least one NCD, the effective share of individuals benefiting from this intervention is approximately 18% of each age group.

In table 12, the combined effect of the care-coordination coefficient (−11.4%) and the age-specific interaction (–9.5%) produces a substantial potential reduction of nearly −19.8% in conditional OOPE for older adults. When weighted by the treated share, this translates into a –3.0% decline in expected OOPE among 70–79-year-olds and an even larger –3.1% decline among those aged 80 and above. The corresponding reductions in CHE10 are also meaningful, at –0.4% for the 70–79 group and –0.6% for the 80+ group. These results underscore the alignment between care-coordination benefits and the complex needs of older adults with multimorbidity. Even at modest coverage levels, care coordination lowers spending intensity and reduce CHE risk, with minimal induced utilization. It becomes a potential candidate for targeted expansion within CNAM and AMG survives packages, particularly for chronic disease for the elderly.

Table 12. Scenario C: Care coordination to 30% coverage among 70+ with ≥1 NCD

Age group	Treated share	Δ Any-OOPE (pp)	Δ Conditional OOPE (%)	Δ Expected OOPE (%)	Δ CHE10 (pp)
70–79	18%	+0.5	−3.6 (18% × (−19.9%))	−3.0	−0.4
80+	18%	+0.5	−3.6	−3.1	−0.6

Scenario D: Combined Integrated Silver-Economy Package

The integrated scenario, which combines teleconsultation, assistive technologies, and care coordination, delivers the strongest and most comprehensive improvements in financial protection among all simulated interventions. By simultaneously addressing mobility barriers, and the ineffective chronic disease management, the combined package produces reductions in OOPE that exceed the effect of any single component. These gains reflect the complementary mechanisms of the three services: teleconsultation lowers transport and visit-related costs; care coordination minimizes duplication and avoids unnecessary diagnostics; and assistive technologies sustain functional independence, reducing reliance on repeated in-person care.

When applied together, these interventions produce substantial reductions in conditional spending across all ageing groups, see table 13. Expected OOPE falls by 8.0% among adults aged 60–69, deepens to 9.5% in those aged 70–79, and reaches a maximum reduction of 10.3% among households with members aged 80 and above. This age gradient mirrors the increasing vulnerability and complexity of care needs in later life, showing that the oldest groups accrue the greatest benefit from integrated support. The impact on CHE10 follows the same pattern. The reductions range from −0.8% in the 60–69 group to −1.6% of the 80+ group demonstrate that the combined package meaningfully improves financial risk protection even at modest intervention coverage levels. These findings confirm the effective synergy of SE interventions: each component addresses a distinct source of cost burden, and together they create a multiplier effect that substantially reduces OOPE and protects vulnerable elderly households from CHE.

Table 13. Scenario integrated package (Teleconsultation 50% & AT 40% in disability & Care-coordination 30% in 70+ NCD)

Age group	Δ Any-OOPE (pp)	Δ Conditional OOPE (%)	Δ Expected OOPE (%)	Δ CHE10 (pp)
60–69	+1.1	−9.5	−8.0	−0.8
70–79	+1.4	−11.6	−9.5	−1.2
80+	+1.4	−12.6	−10.3	−1.6

SECTION 4. POLICY DIRECTIONS, AND SILVER ECONOMY PARTNERSHIPS

4.1 Policy Implications

Results confirm that population ageing is a major driver of the risk of health financial protection in Tunisia. OOPE rises steeply from ages 60–69 to 80+, and chronic disease and disability further increase both the likelihood and intensity of spending. Insurance schemes (CNAM and AMG/MUT) reduce conditional OOPE but remain insufficient to offset the higher costs associated with ageing and multimorbidity. Uninsured individuals, the oldest age groups, and poorer households remain exposed to financial risk protection. These findings point to several structural priorities:

- Strengthening risk pooling and solidarity-based financing
- Defining essential benefit packages for chronic and long-term care
- Expanding strategic purchasing
- Protecting low-income elderly through targeted subsidies and exemptions.

Digital-related variables (teleconsultation, assistive technologies, and care coordination) suggest a slight increase in OOPE by improving access, but a reduction in conditional and expected OOPE by lowering transport costs, enabling early detection and follow-up, and improving care coordination, with effects more significant at older ages. The simulation scenarios illustrate their potential effects. Expanding teleconsultation to 50% for older adults reduces expected OOPE by 6–7% and lowers CHE by up to 0.9%, with the greatest benefits among the 80+ group. Assistive technologies at 40% coverage yield modest but consistent reductions (1–2% in expected OOPE), particularly for disability-affected elderly. Care coordination at 30% coverage produces larger and more stable gains (3% reduction in expected OOPE), by reducing duplication and improving referral pathways. A combined scenario generates the largest effects, with expected OOPE declining by 8–10% and CHE falling by up to 1.6%, indicating complementarities between the interventions.

The results show also that while ageing increases exposure to CHE, Digital interventions moderate this risk when integrated into explicit benefit packages and delivered at scale. These interventions are constrained by regional disparities in term of digital infrastructure, workforce readiness, and governance. The digital capacity is still concentrated in coastal regions, while interior and southern areas lag. Additional barriers include cybersecurity concerns, interoperability limits, uneven digital literacy among health workers. Four priority interventions are needed and can be delivered through social and business partnerships:

- Integrate teleconsultation and care coordination into health insurance benefit packages.
- Subsidize assistive technologies for vulnerable older adults.
- Expand digital health infrastructure in underserved and remote regions.
- Establish digital stewardship through regulation and data governance standards.

In Tunisia, policy commitment to digital health and ageing is evident through pilots in tele-cardiology, tele-radiology, and tele-prenatal care, alongside progress toward digital hospital models. However, scaling and system-wide integration remain challenging. In this context, a more coordinated Silver Economy strategy could expand age-responsive services, create jobs in care sectors, and attract investment through structured partnerships, while strengthening linkages between primary care and social protection.

The policy relevance of these findings extends beyond Tunisia. MENA countries, such as Morocco, Egypt and Jordan, are experiencing similar demographic ageing, increasing prevalence of chronic diseases, and growing demand for long-term and integrated care services. At the same time, OOPE remain an important source of health financing in several countries of the region, exposing older adults to financial vulnerability. Within this context, the SE model proposed in this chapter "integrating teleconsultation, assistive technologies, and care coordination" offers a scalable framework for strengthening financial protection and supporting healthy ageing. Although implementation pathways may differ according to national contexts, the synergies observed between teleconsultation, assistive technologies, and care coordination indicate that the proposed SE model has broader applicability across MENA countries facing similar ageing, chronic diseases and financial protection challenges. These interventions align closely with regional priorities for healthy ageing, UHC, financial protection, and sustainable health system transformation.

4.2. Health-Focused Partnerships for the SE

Ageing in Tunisia should be viewed not only as a social challenge but as an investment opportunity. A SE approach allows demographic change to be harnessed to expand age-responsive services, stimulate innovation, and create jobs. Strategic partnerships, and regulatory stewardship can direct investments toward improving financial protection and access to care for older people. Properly aligned with UHC objectives, the SE can help Tunisia turn population ageing into a driver of equity, system sustainability, and inclusive growth. Demographic ageing creates opportunities across workplaces, markets, and firms, generating value for individuals, businesses, and society. When Tunisia looks at ageing through this lens, it becomes not just a challenge to manage but a driver of new markets, services and jobs.

Table 14. Silver economy: Markets, services, and jobs for age-friendly care

New Markets	New Services	New Jobs
Homecare and community care market	Home-based care and rehabilitation that prevent inpatient care and reduce OOPE	Home-care aides, geriatric assistants
Digital health and telehealth market (Scenario A)	Telemedicine and remote follow-up reducing travel costs and admissions	Telemedicine coordinators, digital health technicians
Assistive devices and medical aids market (Scenario B)	Provision and maintenance of autonomy-support tools that avoid costly complications	Assistive device technicians and suppliers
Chronic care services market (Scenario C)	Structured NCD management and caregiver support	Case managers, chronic care coordinators
Age-friendly health and care facilities market	Adapted care environments improving safety and preventing injury-related expenses	Accessibility and care-environment specialists

In Tunisia, population ageing is increasing demand for chronic and long-term care while creating opportunities for innovation and market development. With the right policies, it can foster startups and social enterprises in telehealth, assistive technologies, and coordinated care aligned with UHC. Silver entrepreneurship also enables older adults to act as founders, mentors, and co-creators. Unlocking this potential requires targeted SME support, blended financing, and preferential procurement, turning ageing into a driver of inclusive growth and resilient health financing. Partnerships with startups, social enterprises, and local innovators can help translate demographic change into practical and socially meaningful solutions.

Assistive technologies, home-based care, digital health, and age-friendly housing are not simply new service niches; they are enablers of dignity, autonomy, and continuity of care. When older Tunisians can live safely at home, manage chronic disease, and access care without excessive travel or cost, both financial and social vulnerability decline. For this transformation to occur, innovation must be embedded in a supportive ecosystem where public priorities and market initiatives reinforce each other. Pharmacies, telecom operators, insurers, and municipalities can serve as bridges between innovation and access, while CNAM and social protection programs can integrate successful models into mainstream financing and service delivery. Public–private partnerships are particularly relevant in Tunisia, where they can reduce risk for innovators while steering investments toward UHC goals. Nevertheless, PPPs implementation may also generate challenges related to affordability, equity of access, regulatory oversight, and alignment between commercial incentives and public health goals. An effective governance and regulation are therefore critical to ensure that PPPs support strengthen financial protection, and advance UHC while maximizing the benefits of the Silver Economy. Key SE actors in Tunisia include:

- Startups developing telehealth, remote monitoring, medication adherence tools, and home-based care platforms that extend services beyond hospitals.
- Social enterprises delivering affordable assistive devices, home adaptations, and community-based elderly support, particularly for vulnerable groups.
- SMEs and local manufacturers producing or assembling low-cost assistive technologies adapted to local needs.
- Telecom and digital firms enabling connectivity, telemedicine, and digital caregiver support.
- Financial actors (Microfinance Institutions, insurers, impact investors) facilitating affordability through instalment payments, micro-loans, and blended finance.
- Civil society and NGOs supporting caregiver training, outreach, and trust-building in communities.
- Public institutions (MoH, CNAM, local health authorities etc.) providing stewardship, regulation, and integration into PHC and social protection systems.

Ageing-related enterprises should be viewed not only as commercial activities but as social investments that can prevent complications, reduce avoidable hospital use, and lower CHE while improving system efficiency. As demographic ageing creates stable demand, the SE offers a practical avenue to align economic incentives with social protection goals. With clear policy direction, public stewardship, and strategic partnerships, Tunisia can use the SE to strengthen financial protection, support inclusive and age-responsive care, and advance progress toward UHC-SDG 3.8 and positioning ageing as a lever for innovation and sustainable development rather than a fiscal burden.

CONCLUSION

Tunisia's demographic transition is not only a challenge to manage but a policy opportunity to harness. As the population ages, rising demand for care and medicines exposes structural gaps and heightens financial vulnerability, particularly among older people with chronic disease and disability. MTP results confirm that ageing significantly increases both the likelihood and intensity of OOPE, raising risks of CHE and impoverishment. At the same time, simulations show that digital health, assistive technologies, and care coordination as core components of the SE, can moderate these risks when implemented together.

From a policy perspective, ageing-related services should be treated as social investments: preventing complications, reducing avoidable hospitalizations, and improving continuity of care can lower long-term costs and strengthen financial protection. Priority actions include integrating age-responsive services int explicit benefit packages, embedding them within PHC, and ensuring sustainable financing and strategic purchasing.

Moving forward, Tunisia would benefit from shifting from isolated pilots to a coherent SE strategy that links digital innovation, PHC, and financial protection. With robust and strategic stewardship and partnerships, the SE can help reposition ageing as a driver of resilience and progress toward UHC and SDG 3.8, rather than a fiscal burden.

REFERENCES

Abu-Zaineh, M., Arfa, C., Ventelou, B., Ben Romdhane, H., & Moatti, J.-P. (2014). Fairness in healthcare finance and delivery: What about Tunisia? *Health Policy and Planning*, *29*(4), 433–442. 10.1093/heapol/czt029. DOI: 10.1093/heapol/czt029

Adel Ben Youssef. (2024). *Accelerating the Progress of Tunisia Towards the Sustainable Development Goals* (Policy Research Report, Issue. https://www.arabdevelopmentportal.org/sites/default/files/2025-04/PRR%2053%20-%20Accelerating%20the%20Progress%20of%20Tunisia%20Towards%20the%20Sustainable%20Development%20Goals.pdf

Arfa, C., & Achouri, H. (2008). *Tunisia: good practice in expanding health care coverage. Lessons from reforms in a country in transition: Lessons from reforms in low-and middle-income countries.* (World Bank, Ed.) https://documents.worldbank.org/pt/publication/documents-reports/documentdetail/460481468150871322

Ayadi, I., & Zouari, S. (2017). Out-of-pocket health spending and equity implications in Tunisia. *Middle East Development Journal*, *9*(1), 1–21. DOI: 10.1080/17938120.2017.1293362

Bhatia, D., Mishra, S., Kirubarajan, A., Yanful, B., Allin, S., & Di Ruggiero, E. (2022). Identifying priorities for research on financial risk protection to achieve universal health coverage: A scoping overview of reviews. *BMJ Open*, *12*(3), e052041. DOI: 10.1136/bmjopen-2021-052041

Bieszk-Stolorz, B. Dmytrów, K. & Frąckiewicz, E. (2024). Multivariate Analysis of the Sustainable Development of the Silver Economy in the European Union Countries. *Journal of Sustainability, 16*(23), 10703. 10.3390/su162310703

Bisson, M., Palmieri, S., Ianniello, A., & Palomba, R. (2023). Academic research in between user needs and industry demands in the context of the silver economy. *Edulearn 23-15th International Conference on Education and New Learning Technologies* 1213-1220. https://re.public.polimi.it/handle/11311/1250739

Bousnina, A., & Souli, C. (2024). Le vieillissement de la population tunisienne: caractéristiques et perceptions. *Revue tunisienne de sciences sociales, 1*(150/151), pp. 39-72. ⟨halshs-04705203⟩

Bran, F. Popescu, Maria-Loredana, & Stanciu, P. (2016). Perspectives of silver economy in European Union. *Revista de Management Comparat International, 17*(2), 130. https://www.ceeol.com/search/article-detail?id=729831

Butt, S. A., Rava, K., Kangilaski, T., Pappel, I. & Draheim, D. (2021). Designing a digital collaborative platform for the silver economy: Inception and conceptualization. *2021 Eighth International Conference on eDemocracy & eGovernment (ICEDEG)*, 47-54. DOI: 10.1109/ICEDEG52154.2021.9530937

Butt, S. A. S. Shweta, P., Ingrid, S., Michael, K., Robert & Draheim, D. (2023). A digital collaborative platform for the silver economy: functionalities required by stakeholders in a multinational baltic sea region project. *Digital Government: Research Practise, 4*(2), 1-20. 10.1145/3592618

Chadha, N., & Gopal, K. S. Uplabdh, K., Oommen C, Kumar, S. & Singh, S.. (2025). *UHC for the Silver Dividend: Building Health Systems for an Ageing India*. https:// www.orfonline.org/

Daghaghele, E., Angali, K. A., Kamyari, N., & Seyedtabib, M. (2025). Marginalized two part model for analyzing multilevel semicontinuous medical costs in Iranian households. *Scientific Reports, 15*(1), 7491. DOI: 10.1038/s41598-025-91309-0

Das, T., Holland, P., Ahmed, M., & Husain, L. (2021). Sustainable Development Goal 3: Good Health and Well-being. In Das, T., & Nayar, P. D. (Eds.), *South-East Asia Eye Health: Systems, Practices, and Challenges* (pp. 61–78). Springer Singapore., DOI: 10.1007/978-981-16-3787-2_4

de Siqueira Silva, Í., de Araújo, A. J., Lopes, R. H., Silva, C. R. D. V., Xavier, P. B., de Figueirêdo, R. C., . . . de Araújo Nunes, V. M. (2024). Digital home care interventions and quality of primary care for older adults: a scoping. *PLOS ONE*. 10.1371/journal.pone.0316278

De Witte, J., and Regenmortel, T.V. (2023). *Silver empowerment: Fostering strengths and connections for an age-friendly society. Leuven University Press, 2023.* Leuven University Press. https://lup.be/book/silver-empowerment/

Elgazzar, H. A. Chokri, S., Nisreen, M., Mehdi, S.I., Djavad, R., Firas, C., Jad, F., Sanaz & Mataria, Awad (2013). Who pays? Out-of-pocket health spending and equity implications in the Middle East and North Africa. *Health, Nutrition Population discussion paper*. http://documents.worldbank.org/curated/en/464431468276384167

Eozenou, P. H.-V. Neelsen, Sven, Smitz, Marc-Francois. (2021). Financial protection in health among the elderly–a global stocktake. *Health Systems Reform, 7*(2), e1911067. 10.1080/23288604.2021.1911067

Fan, V. Sharma, J. and Hou, X. (Ed.). (2023). *Financing Primary Health Care for Older Adults: Framework and Applications*. World Bank Group. https://documents1.worldbank.org/curated/en/099025503072337503/pdf/P17583208782960a40bf6804d1758e50f1e.pdf

Felix, J. (2016). Silver economy: Opportunities and challenges to Brazil adopt the European Union's strategy. *Innovation (Abingdon), 29*(2), 115–133. 10.1080/13511610.2016.1166937. DOI: 10.1080/13511610.2016.1166937

Finland, F. (2025). *The Rise of the Silver Economy: Global Implications of Population Aging*. International Monetary Fund. 10.5089/9798400289583.081.CH002

Gabriel-Catalin, T.-T. Felicia-Cătălina Apetroi (Răcoare), Iuliana-Claudia Mihalache. (2023). The Silver Economy and its Importance to Society. *Journal EUFIRE*, 368. https://www.ceeol.com/search/chapter-detail?id=1237215

Gianfredi, V., Nucci, D., Pennisi, F., Maggi, S., Veronese, N., & Soysal, P. (2025). Aging, longevity, and healthy aging: The public health approach. *Aging Clinical and Experimental Research, 37*(1), 125. DOI: 10.1007/s40520-025-03021-8

Gilbert, N., & Brik, A. B. (2022). Family life and the demographic transition in MENA countries: Implications for social policy. *Journal of International and Comparative Social Policy, 38*(1), 15–35. DOI: 10.1017/ics.2021.17

Grinin, L., Grinin, A., & Korotayev, A. (2023). Global aging: An integral problem of the future. How to turn a problem into a development driver? In *Reconsidering the limits to growth: A report to the Russian association of the club of Rome* (pp. 117–135). Springer International Publishing. DOI: 10.1007/978-3-031-34999-7_7

Hajizadeh, A., Hafezi, R., Torabi, F., Sari, A. A., & Tajvar, M. (2025). Consequences of Population Ageing on Health Systems: A Conceptual Framework for Policy and Practice. *Ethiopian Journal of Health Sciences, 35*(1). Advance online publication. DOI: 10.4314/ejhs.v35i1.8

Hou, X. Sharma, J. and Zhao, F. (2023). *Silver Opportunity: Building Integrated Services for Older Adults Around Primary Health Care*. World Bank Publications. https://documents1.worldbank.org/curated/en/099025503072337503/pdf/P17583208782960a40bf6804d1758e50f1e.pdf

Hua, M. (2024). A Study on the Impact of the Aging Population-Driven Silver Economy on Social Development and Healthcare Systems in Russia. *SHS Web of Conferences, 207*, 04006. https://www.shs-conferences.org/articles/shsconf/abs/2024/27/shsconf_icdeba2024_04006/shsconf_icdeba2024_04006.html

Huegler, N., & Ruch, G. (2022). Risk, vulnerability and complexity: Transitional safeguarding as a reframing of binary perspectives. *Practice, 34*(1), 25–39. DOI: 10.1080/09503153.2021.1932787

Institut National de la Statistique. (2023). *Enquête Nationale sur le Budget, la consommation et le niveau de vie des ménages.* https://www.ins.tn/enquetes/enquete-nationale-sur-le-budget-la-consommation-et-le-niveau-de-vie-des-menages-2021

Institut National de la Statistique. (2024). *Recensement Général de la Population et de l'Habitat: Bilan Démographique* Tunisie Retrieved from https://www.ins.tn/sites/default/files-ftp3/files/2025-05/Bilan_D%C3%A9mographique.pdf

Ismaïl, S., & Arfa, C. (2022). Effects of out-of-pocket medicine's spending on catastrophic expenditure and impoverishment in Tunisia. *Value in Health Regional Issues, 30*, 109–118. 10.1016/j.vhri.2022.01.008. DOI: 10.1016/j.vhri.2022.01.008

Ismaïl, S., & Nejia. Z. (2022). Santé et assurance maladie en Tunisie: les enjeux de la réforme de 2004. *Eastern Mediterranean Health Journal, 28(6)*, 444 - 453. https://iris.who.int/handle/10665/359870

Jallouli, F. Yalouli, Tarek, Vyas, Sonali, and Gupta, Sunil. (2025). A prospective study of the determinants of economic growth in Tunisia 1990–2030. *International Journal of Critical Infrastructures, 21*(2), 105-127. 10.1504/IJCIS.2025.145207

Jane Osareme, O., Muonde, M., Maduka, C. P., Olorunsogo, T. O., & Omotayo, O. J. I. J. S. R. A. (2024). Demographic shifts and healthcare: A review of aging populations and systemic challenges. *International Journal of Science and Research Archive, 11*(1), 383–395. 10.30574/ijsra.2024.11.1.0067. DOI: 10.30574/ijsra.2024.11.1.0067

Jmaii, A. (2025). Remittance reinforcement and economic adaptation: Charting Tunisia's path towards climate resilience. *Mitigation and Adaptation Strategies for Global Change, 30*(2), 14. 10.1007/s11027-025-10201-4. DOI: 10.1007/s11027-025-10201-4

McGuirk, H. C. L. Aisling & Lenihan, N. (2022). Awareness and potential of the silver economy for enterprises: a European regional level study. *Small Enterprise Research, 29*(1), 6-19. 10.1080/13215906.2021.1919915

Merritt, G. (2025). *Timebomb: When Ageing Explodes*. Policy Press. https://books.google.ae/books?hl=en&lr=&id=z5IiEQAAQBAJ&oi=fnd&pg=PT10&dq=Merritt,+G.+(2025).+Timebomb:+When+Ageing+Explodes.+Policy+Press&ots=1vtfjiAB2W&sig=K8dCQ7g6Kb4ySbHU7ttBbUjoHMA&redir_esc=y#v=onepage&q=Merritt%2C%20G.%20(2025).%20Timebomb%3A%20When%20Ageing%20Explodes.%20Policy%20Press&f=false

Mingst, K. A., Karns, M. P., & Lyon, A. J. (2022). *The United Nations in the 21st century*. Routledge. 10.4324/9781003038269

Mohsin, K. F., Ahsan, M. N., & Haider, M. Z. (2024). Understanding variation in catastrophic health expenditure from socio-ecological aspect: A systematic review. *BMC Public Health*, *24*(1), 1504. 10.1186/s12889-024-18579-7. DOI: 10.1186/s12889-024-18579-7

Müller, D. M. (2021). *Classification of consumer goods into 5-digit COICOP 2018 codes* https://nva.sikt.no/registration/019909a810fc-691343f7-2ab7-4c94-a5f0-2dc785ca435d

O'Connell, T., Rasanathan, K., & Chopra, M. (2014). What does universal health coverage mean? *Lancet*, *383*(9913), 277–279. DOI: 10.1016/S0140-6736(13)60955-1

OECD. (2020). *Promoting an Age-Inclusive Workforce: Living*. Learning and Earning Longer.

OECD. (2024). Is care affordable for older people? In. Paris: OECD Health Policy Studies, OECD Publishing.

Oget, Q. (2021). When economic promises shape innovation and networks: A structural analysis of technological innovation in the silver economy. *Journal of Innovation Economics*, *35*(2), 55–80. 10.3917/e.jie.pr1.0096b

Park, Y., Kim, E. J., Park, S., & Lee, M. (2025). Digital health intervention effect on older adults with chronic diseases living alone: systematic review and meta-analysis of randomized controlled trials. Journal of Medical Internet Research, 27, e63168.

Patel, M. R., Jagsi, R., Resnicow, K., Smith, S. N., Hamel, L. M., Su, C., ... & Torby, M. (2021). A scoping review of behavioral interventions addressing medical financial hardship. Population Health Management, 24(6), 710-721.

Rahman, T., Gasbarro, D., & Alam, K. (2022). Financial risk protection from out-of-pocket health spending in low- and middle-income countries: A scoping review of the literature. *Health Research Policy and Systems*, *20*(1), 83. DOI: 10.1186/s12961-022-00886-3

Romdhane, H. B., Tlili, F., Skhiri, A., Zaman, S., & Phillimore, P. (2015). Health system challenges of NCDs in Tunisia. *International Journal of Public Health, 60*(S1, Suppl 1), 39–46. DOI: 10.1007/s00038-014-0616-0

Sanchini, V., Sala, R., & Gastmans, C. (2022). The concept of vulnerability in aged care: A systematic review of argument-based ethics literature. *BMC Medical Ethics, 23*(1), 84. DOI: 10.1186/s12910-022-00819-3

Tsega, Y. Tsega, G., Taddesse, G. & Getaneh, G. (2023). Leaving no one behind in health: financial hardship to access health care in Ethiopia. *PLOS ONE, 18*(3), e0282561. 10.1371/journal.pone.0282561

United Nation. (2024). *Asia-Pacific Report on Population Ageing 2022: Trends, policies and good practices regarding older persons and population ageing*. United Nationa. 10.18356/9789210021746

United Nations. (2025). *World Population Prospects: The 2015 Revision*. Key Findings and Advance Tables. [Online Edition UN DESA, New York]

Vera-Sanso, P. (2023). Will the SDGs and the UN decade of healthy ageing leave older people behind? *Progress in Development Studies*, *23*(4), 391–407. 10.1177/14649934231193808. DOI: 10.1177/14649934231193808

Wang, L., Tang, Y., Roshanmehr, F., Bai, X., Taghizadeh-Hesary, F., & Taghizadeh-Hesary, F. (2021). The Health Status Transition and Medical Expenditure Evaluation of Elderly Population in China. *International Journal of Environmental Research and Public Health, 18*(13), 6907. 10.3390/ijerph18136907. DOI: 10.3390/ijerph18136907

World Bank. (2025). *World Development Indicators*. Washington. Retrieved 20/02/2026 from World Health Organization. (2021a). *Decade of healthy ageing: baseline report*. World Health Organization. https://www.who.int/publications/i/item/9789240017900

World Health Organization. (2021b). *Monitoring progress on universal health coverage and the health-related Sustainable Development Goals in the WHO South-East Asia Region 2021 update*. World Health Organization, Regional Office for South-East Asia. https://www.who.int/publications/i/item/9789290228936

World Health Organization. (2025a). *Global Health Expenditure Database*. World Health Organization. Retrieved 1/11/2025 from https://apps.who.int/nha/database/Select/Indicators/en

World Health Organization. (2025b). *The Global Health Observatory: Explore a world of health data*.

Wu, W., Ying, S., & Wu, Y. (2025). Silver economy industry market consumption characteristics research. *Journal of Modern Social Sciences*, *2*(1), 94–98. 10.71113/JMSS.v2i1.187. DOI: 10.71113/JMSS.v2i1.187

Xu, K., Evans, D. B., Kawabata, K., Zeramdini, R., Klavus, J., & Murray, C. (2003). Household catastrophic health expenditure: A multicountry analysis. *Lancet*, *362*(9378), 111–117. DOI: 10.1016/S0140-6736(03)13861-5

Zeng, Y., Fu, J., Cao, W., Chen, Y., & Yang, Z. (2024). Research Hotspots and Knowledge Framework of Digital Healthcare Service Management from the Perspective of the Silver Economy. Sustainability, 16(22), 9735.

Zou, C., Harvard, A., Qian, J., & Fox, B. (2023). A systematic review of digital health technologies for the care of older adults during COVID-19 pandemic. *Gigital Health, 9*. 10.1177/20552076231191050

Chapter 7
Enhancing Silver Economies and Reviving Intangible Cultural Heritage:
The Business Opportunity for Intergenerational Collaboration

Zisheng Huang
Guangdong Polytechnic of Industry and Commerce, China

Weixi Zhang
Beijing Normal-Hong Kong Baptist University, China

Tianhao Zhi
http://orcid.org/0000-0001-6786-424X
Beijing Normal-Hong Kong Baptist University, China

ABSTRACT

This chapter investigates how effective intergenerational collaborations would contribute to the silver economy and the revival of intangible cultural heritage. Specifically, we strive to address three questions that represent three distinct social dimensions in ICH studies and practices, i.e. the culture, the instruments, and the people: i) What are the major obstacles in protecting intangible cultural heritage in terms of cultural preservation and sustainable commercialisation? (the cultural dimension) ii) What are the roles of technology and innovation in reviving intangible cultural heritage? (the instrumental dimension) iii) How would effective intergenerational collaboration play a role in safeguarding intangible cultural heritage? (the people

DOI: 10.4018/979-8-3373-9370-4.ch007

dimension). We further conduct two interview-based case studies to understand how the intergenerational transmission of ICH is achieved in real-world contexts, as well as its challenges and opportunities.

1 INTRODUCTION

1.1 Aims and Scope of this Chapter

This chapter strives to answer three fundamental questions on how intangible cultural heritage can best be protected and promoted in the process of intergenerational transmission via three distinctive perspectives:

1. What are the major obstacles to protecting intangible cultural heritage? Specifically, what are the practical challenges not only in cultural preservation but also in its sustainable commercialisation? (the culture)
2. What is the role of technology and innovation in reviving intangible cultural heritage? (the instruments)
3. What is the role of the silver-haired cultural practitioners in safeguarding intangible cultural heritage, and how would effective intergenerational collaboration play a role in cultural revival? (the people)

We continue to lay the background of our study in the following subsections. Section 2 continues to provide a comprehensive survey of the current literature from three aspects: *i)* the current challenges in the practice of ICH, with respect to three distinctive schools of thought, *ii)* the major innovative instruments in the current practices of ICH promotion, and *iii)* literature regarding intergenerational transmission and collaboration pertaining to ICH. Section 3 formulates an analogical theory, drawing on existing literature, that links intergenerational collaboration to ICH preservation and promotion, as well as its relevance to sustainable development. Section 4 further presents two case studies from distinct perspectives on transgenerational innovation and sustainable commercialisation. Section 5 concludes.

1.2 Digression: Following the Tradition or Aspiring to Innovate?

Classical music and fine arts can be regarded as two special and narrow forms of intangible cultural heritage within the European artistic tradition, which continue to inspire generations of pupils to learn from the past and envision the future. Despite the rise of pop music and post-modern contemporary art, classical music and fine arts are still carefully safeguarded by traditional academic institutions and promoted by well-established cultural industries.

There is a perennial debate in classical music whether the music performance ought to be historically informed, rendering the performer's role merely as musical acolytes of the centuries-old composers, or whether the performers ought to find their own re-interpretation in a modern world. This is particularly true for the performance of J.S. Bach's keyboard works, which is inspiring two dialectical styles of performance: one being the defender of historically informed performance, while the other strives to bring modern light to Bach's keyboard works beyond its instrumental limits, as they may argue that these works were written at the time for organs and harpsichords when the modern piano was yet to be invented (Butt, 2002). A similar dichotomy also exists in the history of fine arts, such as the battle between traditional academic art and the Impressionist revolution (White & White, 1965). The constant tug-of-war between the traditionalist and the *avant-garde* schools, however, continues to bring evolutionary forces to the arts that not only preserve important traditions but also render them timeless beauty beyond their forms, traditions, and cultural boundaries.

The perpetual evolution of art, as evidenced by a history of constant battles between conservatism and the avant-garde across eras, often reflects a fundamental transformation in aesthetics. The Renaissance was not simply about painting things to look realistic, but about the realisation of its core aesthetic principle, rooted in rationalism and humanism. Impressionism was not simply about loosening brushstrokes, but about an aesthetic shift that placed the perception of the moment and the experiences of light and colour above the academic conventions of its time. On the contrary, many radical artistic experiments have gained popularity nowadays, but if they still follow existing aesthetic standards, they ultimately remain just variations within the old system. Conservatism does not simply mean following tradition, nor does innovation mean creating superficial differences. Artistic innovation is only rendered possible when the aesthetic values that determine how the arts are viewed, understood, and valued are redefined and transformed.

The tension between preservation and innovation is not limited to classical music and fine arts. Many other forms of intangible cultural heritage, less institutionalised yet more down-to-earth, share similar traits but are less well-known to global audiences and receive less institutional support, as epitomised by the Cantonese tradition of Jiang-Gu (narration of history). For centuries, storytellers have performed classical tales and folklore in teahouses and temple courtyards across the Pearl River Delta. Jiang-Gu evolves with historical development and geographical location. Listening to a storyteller in a crowded teahouse, where the audience laughs and gasps together, is a fundamentally different experience from hearing the pre-recorded version on the air. Generations after generations, the storyteller strives to balance fidelity to traditional narratives with constant adaptation to contemporary audiences. The physical space, the live interaction between the narrator and the audience, and the spontaneity of the performance render it a true living heritage that transcends its mere textual content.

1.3 Natural Extinction or Revival through Re-creation?

While it constitutes purely a philosophical debate regarding the extent to which the arts should follow or break tradition, it is a life-or-death issue in the real world of safeguarding intangible cultural heritage. Many cultures cease to exist due to the relentless pursuit of economic growth and excessive globalisation, leading to cultural homogenisation (Hazaea et al., 2025; N. Li et al., 2025). Some remain, yet either in a highly preserved or frozen form, carefully kept as cultural relics in museums, or become overly gentrified in a superficial world of commerce that craves commodification, industrialisation and automation instead of handwork, high efficiency instead of slow formation, and constant psychological stimuli instead of timeless spiritual nuances. Some might argue that the world is changing; hence, old culture tends to, and ought to, die naturally. Yet one cannot deny the vital role of cultural heritage in preserving spiritual wisdom from our ancestors, fostering cultural identity, strengthening social cohesion, and, ultimately, unleashing hidden economic benefits. The death of culture, on the contrary, would lead to a myriad of sustainability issues, similar to the ramifications of biodiversity loss to our living environment (Gui et al., 2026; Niu et al., 2025).

Nostalgia alone, however, cannot solve the problem of cultural extinction. One ought to see cultural heritage not merely as memories of the past, but rather as a living heritage shared by living communities, as UNESCO defines cultural heritage:

> *"Traditions or living expressions inherited from our ancestors and passed on to our descendants, such as oral traditions, performing arts, social practices, rituals, festive events, knowledge and practices concerning nature and the universe or the knowledge and skills to produce traditional crafts."*
>
> *- UNESCO (n.d.)*

The living nature of cultural heritage implies a constant state of evolution. As cultural knowledge is passed from one generation to another, the cultural and spiritual essence remains, while its forms of expression constantly change. This is particularly relevant in the current aging society in many parts of the world, where the silver-haired generation is gradually withdrawing from the workforce yet wants to continue contributing to society, and intangible cultural heritage is an important area in which they can actively participate. In our current era of digital innovation, many emerging technologies have opened new channels for reviving cultural heritage, from the re-invention of crafts that have already gone extinct to the recent popularity of live-streaming e-commerce and the increasing adoption of virtual reality, which enables many local communities to disseminate and recreate their cultural products in the digital world. While the silver-haired practitioners gradually step out of their social roles, the black-haired practitioners continue to learn from the old and aspire to innovate, keeping their culture intact.

2 LITERATURE REVIEW

2.1 The Theory of Intergenerational Transmission: Kaplan, Jarrott, and Sánchez

Three scholars are central to the development of theories of intergenerational transmission: Matthew Kaplan, Shannon Jarrott, and Mariano Sánchez, who have collaboratively and individually shaped its conceptual foundations, yet each brings a distinct analytical lens. They reject a unidirectional service-delivery model in favour of mutual reciprocity, recognising the substantial mutual benefit from cross-generational exchange (Jarrott, 2011; Sánchez & Kaplan, 2014). All insist that theory must directly inform practice rather than remain an academic artefact. Jarrott (2011) raises the concern that many intergenerational studies lack theoretical underpinnings. Subsequently, Jarrott (2023) adopts Bronfenbrenner's ecological systems theory and Pettigrew's intergroup contact theory into a layered action framework, demonstrating how each environmental system, ranging from the micro-level of daily activity settings to the macro-level of cultural ideology, shapes who participates in intergenerational programmes and under what conditions. All three scholars caution against simplistic generational labelling, which obscures intra-group heterogeneity and the relational, context-dependent nature of generational identity (Kaplan et al., 2020).

The methodologies of the aforementioned research vary by speciality: Jarrott, trained as a gerontologist and social worker, foregrounds the methodological integrity of programme evaluation and the primacy of process quality over activity type, which leads to the development of the *Intergenerational Program Evaluation Tool* as a standardised instrument for the field (Jarrott, 2011; Jarrott et al., 2025). Sánchez, a sociologist, brings a relational and critically reflexive perspective to intergenerational learning. Sánchez challenges the presumption that cross-generational contact inherently produces positive outcomes, arguing that poorly designed programmes may reinforce stereotypes, obscure institutional power asymmetries, or generate concealed ambivalence rather than genuine understanding (Sánchez & Kaplan, 2014). The research reshaped the conceptualisation of age-diverse learning environments from the educator's perspective, emphasising generational awareness rather than mere age mixing. Kaplan, an environmental psychologist, takes a spatial and place-based approach through the concept of *Intergenerational Contact Zones* - physical and social settings intentionally designed to draw different generations into meaningful interaction (Sánchez, 2008). While Jarrott asks how programmes should be evaluated and Sánchez asks what generational dynamics unfold when generations meet, Kaplan asks where and in what kinds of spaces such encounters become possible. These three perspectives supply a robust conceptual apparatus for examining intergenerational ICH transmission. Jarrott's evaluative rigour offers criteria for assessing whether a transmission programme works; Sánchez's relational lens cautions against romanticising cross-generational contact and demands attention to power, conflict, and unspoken tension; Kaplan's spatial framework foregrounds the settings in which craft knowledge is physically passed from master to novice, such as workshops, studios, kiln sites, and apprenticeship venues. Their complementary insights provide the analytical architecture for the case studies that follow.

2.2 ICH as a Dying Art

We proceed from the theory of intergenerational transmission to the specific issue of ICH preservation and promotion through intergenerational collaboration. While the alarming rate of the extinction of cultural heritage and its adverse effects on cultural identity, social cohesion and creativity are well-documented, as discussed in the previous section, an equally pressing challenge exists regarding the means and scope of safeguarding intangible cultural heritage. Some have questioned whether it is economically and socially meaningful to preserve the dying culture at all costs, even if some cultures fade naturally. UNESCO (2023) warns of the potential *freezing risk*: the danger of "Museumification" – the overprotection through external intervention, which would detach ICH from its social context and turn living practices into frozen records, or even *zombie heritages* (Kirshenblatt-Gimblett, 2004; UNESCO, 2023). It contradicts UNESCO's vision of "safeguarding" (Kirshenblatt-Gimblett, 2004). Furthermore, the natural decline in practice and intergenerational transmission pose a threat to ICH globally (Falk & Hagsten, 2025; W. Li et al., 2025). When communities stop passing down their traditions, external intervention cannot revive their true living spirit. Instead, it may be more respectful to allow the practice to evolve or simply fade on its own terms (Poplawska, 2025). One must safeguard the living nature of ICH, empowering it to evolve naturally and remain socially relevant.

The second challenge lies in the conflicts between the community-based practice and public interventions. Although the public sector often comes with a benevolent will, its actions often conflict with the organic community's interests. The UNESCO listing of heritage often serves as national image-building rather than fulfilling local needs, thereby displacing the culture's original meaning (Gilman, 2022; Vera Zúñiga et al., 2026). Such an interventionist policy may add political and economic value, but may erode cultural intimacy and spiritual significance. Community members may be marginalised by a top-down approach that prioritises the public agenda of heritage diplomacy while undermining the ultimate purpose of safeguarding the community.

The third challenge lies in the conflicts between cultural entrepreneurship and community interests. While economic incentives are undeniable in cultural entrepreneurship, one cannot ignore the tension between economic development and maintaining cultural integrity. There are at least two risks of over-commercialisation and over-commodification of ICH, i.e. *standardisation* and *alienation*. *First*, the market may demand that cultural entrepreneurs simplify or even standardise diverse local variations, thereby undermining cultural authenticity. *Second*, cultural entrepreneurship may confer unfair benefits on entrepreneurs, while cultural practitioners are at risk of being reduced to mere performers for entertainment, corroding their importance as major players of cultural inheritance.

Table 1. Challenges of bringing intangible cultural heritage alive

Challenges	Core Tensions	Key Arguments	Reference
"Rescue" vs. "Natural Death" (Intervention Dilemma)	Active Salvage vs. Evolutionary Laissez-faire The debate over whether endangered elements must be "rescued" at all costs or allowed to fade if they lack community relevance.	• The "Freezing" Risk: Aggressive salvage can detach heritage from its social context, turning living practices into static "museum pieces" or "zombie heritage" solely for archiving. • Natural Evolution: ICH is defined by its living nature; protection should not impede natural change or disappearance if transmission ceases organically. • "Museumification": Treating ICH like tangible artifacts violates the Convention's spirit of "safeguarding without freezing."	(Kirshenblatt-Gimblett, 2004; Poplawska, 2025; UNESCO, 2023)
Safeguarding vs. Representation (Mechanism Critique)	Community Transmission vs. State Display The conflict between internal community-based practice (safeguarding) and external validation via lists/festivals (representation).	• Political Instrumentalisation: Listing often serves national image-building ("heritage diplomacy") rather than local needs. Communities may be marginalised in state-driven application processes. • Displacement of Meaning: The focus shifts from process (transmission) to product (performance), often distorting the practice to fit selection criteria. • "Value-Added" Paradox: Representation adds political/ economic value but may erode cultural intimacy and spiritual significance.	(Gilman, 2022; Vera Zúñiga et al., 2026)
Productive Protection vs. Authenticity (Commercialisation Paradox)	Economic Sustainability vs. Commodification The tension between using ICH for economic development (e.g., tourism, creative industries) and maintaining cultural integrity.	• Standardisation: Market demands force practitioners to simplify or standardise diverse local variations for tourist consumption (e.g., shortening rituals). • Alienation: "Productive protection" can lead to a loss of ownership where practitioners become performers for external gazes rather than community members. • Necessary Evil: Without economic incentives, transmission may be impossible in modernising societies, yet this reliance threatens "original" authenticity.	(Ma, 2022; Wang, 2022)

2.3 Living Heritage and Innovation in Cultural Industries

As discussed in previous section: unlike tangible cultural heritages, which is crystalised in historical relics and ruins, intangible cultural heritage is not meant to be in a past tense, but ought to be a living heritage, where descendants of the heritage learn from their old generations, while continue to practice such heritage in the form of cultural festivals, culinary arts, and important knowledge manifested in the timeless wisdoms, products, and communal ties. Numerous studies have documented the innovations of cultural entrepreneurship in ICH promotion (Borissova, 2018; Cicchiello et al., 2023; Zhi, 2025). By safeguarding, one ought to continuously infuse life into a timeless cultural identity that evolves and adapts to its time, transcending geographical constraints as it travels to other cultures and places and becomes accepted by a wider community. This raises a practical question: what tools and means are available to help ICH survive and adapt in contemporary society?

Skublewska-Paszkowska et al. (2022) conduct a systematic literature review examining 3D technologies and their applications for preserving intangible cultural heritage across major academic databases. They find a rapid increase in publications since 2015 and identify motion capture, 3D scanning, and virtual reality as the most used techniques for documenting the performing arts, craftsmanship, and ritual practices. Their review highlights that while these technologies are effective at capturing the physical dimensions of ICH (e.g., body movement in dance, hand gestures in craft-making), the intangible dimensions of meaning, context, and social function remain difficult to digitise. This observation echoes the broader concern raised by Kirshenblatt-Gimblett (2004) on the potential risk of "museumification" rather than genuine safeguarding.

Beyond documentation, digital technologies have also created new forms of ICH dissemination and engagement. Museums and cultural institutions have adopted VR and AR to create immersive experiences that bring heritage practices to audiences who would otherwise have no access to them (Borissova, 2018). Zheng et al. (2024) investigate user engagement with a digital museum of Beijing's Central Axis by using an integrated TTF-UTAUT model[1], and found that performance expectancy, design aesthetics, and perceived cultural value are significant predictors of continued use, while task-technology fit alone is not sufficient. Their findings suggest that the success of digital heritage tools depends not only on technical functionality but also on how well they convey cultural meaning and aesthetic experience. In a similar vein, Xu and Sun (Xu & Sun, 2017) apply the UTAUT model to ICH digital communication in China and find that performance expectancy, effort expectancy, social influence, and facilitating conditions positively influence public adoption of ICH digital technologies, with age and education acting as significant moderators.

The rise of online platforms and live-streaming commerce has opened additional channels for ICH practitioners. In China, platforms such as Douyin (TikTok) and *Kuaishou* have enabled artisans and performers to broadcast their craft in real time, reaching millions of viewers and converting cultural interest into commercial transactions (Wang, 2022). Live streaming transforms the relationship between practitioner and audience: unlike a museum display or a recorded video, it enables real-time interaction, allowing viewers to ask questions, request demonstrations, and place orders. This interactivity preserves something of the master-apprentice dynamic that characterises traditional ICH transmission. However, the commercial pressures of platform algorithms can also push practitioners to simplify or sensationalise their craft for visibility, raising concerns about authenticity (Ma, 2022).

Another strand of literature examines cultural entrepreneurship and IP-based innovation as tools for sustaining ICH. Cominelli and Greffe (2012) argue that ICH and creativity are mutually reinforcing: heritage provides the raw material for creative industries, while creative reinterpretation keeps heritage economically viable and socially relevant. This perspective connects ICH preservation to Schumpeterian theories of innovation, where the most durable forms of heritage are those that generate new economic value through reinterpretation rather than mere replication (Zhi, 2025). Examples include ICH-inspired fashion brands, restaurant franchises built on traditional culinary techniques, and tourism experiences centred on heritage practices. The challenge, as discussed in Section 2.1, lies in ensuring that commercial adaptation does not hollow out the cultural substance itself.

Finally, artificial intelligence is beginning to open a myriad of new possibilities for ICH documentation, dissemination, and creative reinterpretation. AI-powered tools have been applied to pattern recognition and automated classification of heritage artefacts (Shen et al., 2025), natural language processing for heritage knowledge retrieval and documentation (Yuan et al., 2025), and generative models that reconstruct or reimagine visual heritage materials informed by traditional aesthetics (Hu et al., 2024; Hwang et al., 2025). Li et al. (2025) systematically review digital technology applications in cultural heritage conservation from 2019 to 2024 and find that the field has progressed from basic digitisation and structural documentation toward increasingly integrated and AI-driven approaches, including multi-modal data fusion and cross-disciplinary knowledge systems. Alongside these developments, extended reality technologies have been explored as a means of recreating embodied and performative heritage experiences, including those involving dance, ritual, and craft, with reviews suggesting that while XR can enhance emotional engagement and spatial presence, the relational and affective dimensions of live transmission remain difficult to replicate (Lin et al., 2025). As evidence surveyed in this section indicates, the uptake of digital and AI tools among ICH practitioners is not self-evident. Xu and Sun (Xu & Sun, 2017) demonstrate that performance expectancy, effort expectancy, social influence, and facilitating conditions are all significant predictors of adoption, with age and education acting as moderators, suggesting that the fit between technological affordances and the specific requirements of particular heritage contexts continues to shape whether new tools are meaningfully integrated into living practice.

2.4 Intergenerational Collaborations in ICH Preservation and Promotion

The most essential aspect of cultural continuity lies in the people and in the ways cultural knowledge is passed from one generation to the next. In classical music, young protégés learn from their maestros, who themselves had studied under earlier generations of maestros. In fine arts, studio apprenticeships transmit tacit knowledge through hands-on learning that cannot be taught solely from textbooks. In the tradition of historical narration, the storyteller's craft is learned through years of observation and practice. Effective intergenerational collaboration plays a vital role not only in addressing the three challenges to ICH preservation discussed in Section 2.1, but also in promoting ICH by transferring skills, knowledge, and cultural meaning across age groups. Contemporary scholarship on intergenerational ICH transmission has moved from viewing transmission solely as a fragile, linear process to understanding it as a dynamic ecosystem of collaboration. Three distinct theoretical perspectives have emerged, as summarised in Table 2.

The first perspective, which we term the "crisis and safeguarding school, frames generational change primarily as a threat to continuity. Scholars in this camp emphasise the risk of knowledge disruption, arguing that the passing of elder practitioners often leads to an irreversible loss of embodied knowledge and cultural context (Kirshenblatt-Gimblett, 2004). This view draws on the UNESCO Convention's emphasis on the urgency of safeguarding (UNESCO, 2003) and the analysis of Blake (2008), which seeks to elaborate on the institutional mechanisms designed to protect transmission chains. The crisis school sees intergenerational relationships as fundamentally unidirectional: knowledge only flows from the old to the young, and when the chain is broken, the heritage is lost. From this standpoint, the priority is to ensure that tacit knowledge, including craft techniques, performative skills, and contextual understanding, is documented and transferred before it disappears. This perspective tends to favour interventionist approaches, such as archival documentation, government-sponsored apprenticeship programmes, and institutional preservation efforts.

The second perspective, the adaptation or the innovation school, argues that ICH must evolve to survive. Rather than treating heritage as a fixed body of knowledge to be passively received, this school sees it as something that must be actively reinterpreted in each generation. Lilley (2017) points out that the alienation of young people from traditional practices often stems from a lack of economic viability and perceived relevance, not from cultural indifference. Cominelli and Greffe (2012) argue that heritage and creativity are not opposed but mutually reinforcing: creative reinterpretation is what keeps heritage alive and economically sustainable. This school places emphasis on the agency of younger generations, who bring new tools, new audiences, and new aesthetic sensibilities to heritage practices. The rise of live-streaming, social media marketing, and digital content creation around ICH products are examples of how younger practitioners are redefining the context in which traditional arts are practised and consumed. From this perspective, the key to ICH survival is not preservation in its original form but continuous adaptation.

The third perspective, which has gained increasing support in recent years, is the integrative or the ecological school. This approach moves beyond the binary view of "preservation or innovation" and reframes intergenerational relations as a reciprocal cycle in which knowledge flows in both directions. Harris et al. (2010) argue that young people are not merely passive recipients of cultural knowledge but active agents who reshape it through their own experiences and social contexts. In this model, older practitioners contribute deep craft knowledge, historical understanding, and cultural authority, while younger participants bring technological fluency, market awareness, and fresh creative perspectives. The result is not a compromise between old and new, but a genuinely collaborative process that produces outcomes neither generation could achieve on its own. Gilman (Gilman, 2022) provides empirical support for this view, documenting cases where community-based intergenerational partnerships have proven more effective than top-down institutional interventions in sustaining living heritage practices.

Table 2. Intergenerational collaboration in safeguarding ICH: Three perspectives

Core Issue (Key Issue)	Crisis/Safeguarding Perspective ("Fragile Chains")	Adaptation/Innovation Perspective ("Necessary Renewal")	Integrative Perspective ("Virtuous Cycle")
Nature of Intergenerational Relations	Views intergenerational transmission as a unidirectional, fragile process of knowledge transfer. Emphasises that the passing of elders leads to irreversible knowledge loss.	Views intergenerational replacement as a mechanism for ICH evolution. Argues that each generation should redefine heritage in response to contemporary contexts, youth act as agents of transformation.	Views intergenerational relations as bidirectional and interactive. Stresses the mutual complementarity between the wisdom of elders and the vitality of youth within a "living system" of co-existence and co-prosperity.
Primary Challenges	Knowledge rupture and loss of authenticity.	Lack of relevance and economic disincentives.	Communication barriers and entrenched stereotypes.
The Role of Technology	Potential disruptor: Maintains a cautious or negative stance toward digitalisation, arguing that virtual experiences cannot substitute for embodied, bodily transmission, potentially resulting in superficialisation.	Key enabling tool: Digital technologies (VR, Web 3.0, live streaming) serve as core drivers for youth participation, revitalising traditional arts through new media without replacing them.	Bridging medium: Technology serves as a mediator for recording elders' memories while stimulating youth creativity and facilitating cross-generational collaboration rather than substitution.
Ideal Transmission Model	Archival preservation and strict master-apprentice system: Primary reliance on documentation (archiving) to preserve endangered knowledge, coupled with rigorous adherence to traditional apprenticeship structures.	Fusion of entrepreneurship and creativity: Advocates integrating ICH cultural capital into creative design, branding, and the digital economy to attract youth entrepreneurship.	Co-creation and bidirectional knowledge flow: Proposes "co-creation laboratories" in which elders provide cultural core content and youth contribute innovative forms, thereby achieving mutual knowledge circulation.
Representative Scholars / References	Blake (emphasises community participation and the central public role of intergenerational transmission). Kirshenblatt-Gimblett (2004) discusses the complexity of authenticity in the metacultural production of heritage.	Lilley (2017) : Highlight youth value divergence and alienation, calling for new incentives. Cominelli & St-Onge (2016): Argue for enhancing the economic value of ICH through innovation.	Harris et al. (2005): Explore youth participation in community-based models.

3 INTERGENERATIONAL PATHWAYS TOWARDS SUSTAINABILITY IN ICH DEVELOPMENT

Figure 1. Intergenerational collaboration in reviving ICH

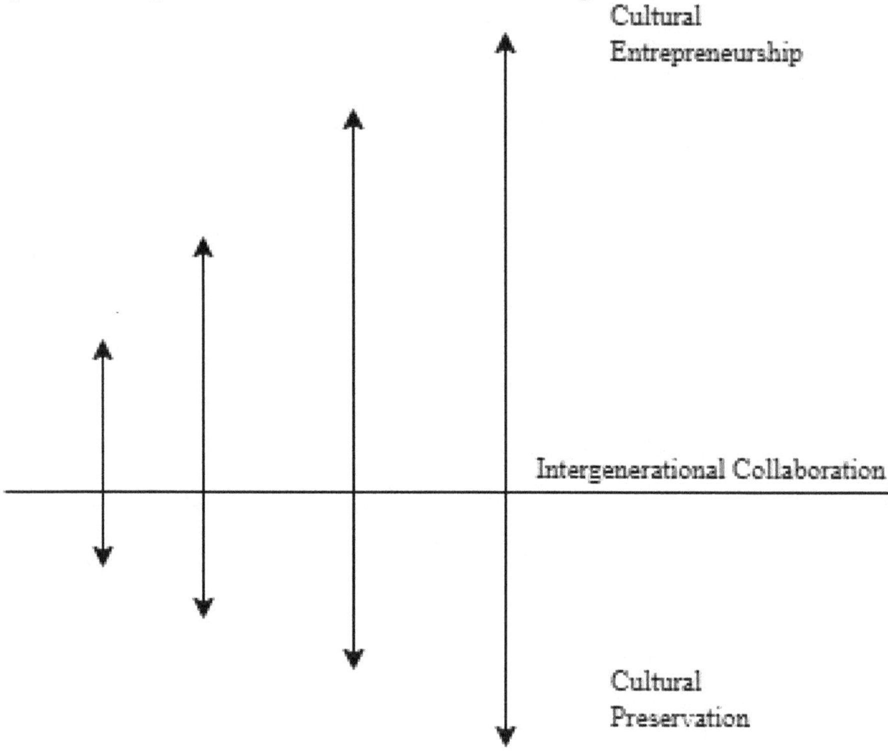

The aforementioned literature has revealed not only the evolutionary nature of intangible cultural heritage, but also the pivotal role of intergenerational collaboration in ensuring cultural authenticity and continuity in the progress of evolution, as well as in addressing the major challenges in the practice of cultural preservation and innovation: a resilient intercultural bond would ensure that authentic knowledge can be effectively transmitted from one generation to another without losing its spiritual and cultural substance, while generational individualism would ensure the perpetual growth of culture by innovating the forms of expression that reflects the contemporary taste and style. It is also inadequate to stereotype the intergenerational characters of cultural practitioners in a fragmented and isolated manner that the "silver-haired" ought to preserve, while the "black-haired" ought to innovate: it is undeniable that the silver-haired practitioners are endowed with first-hand experience of the ICH that was passed on directly from their earlier generations when traditions were still intact, while the younger generations are having a significant advantages in their creative and industrials pursuits and their quick adaptation to the latest technological tools such as live-streaming e-commerce and Web 3.0 entrepreneurship. Age alone, however, ought not to define their roles as preservers or innovators, since the intergenerational collaboration can take a bi-directional form: the black-haired can also be dedicated cultural preservers, while the silver-haired can also be great entrepreneurs. If the two generations can collaborate effectively, their comparative advantages can be leveraged to greater value, increasing the likelihood of preserving endangered cultural species while promoting some of them as successful cultural enterprises.

One may draw an analogy from a tree to depict the evolution of intangible cultural heritage, as illustrated in *Figure 1*: intergenerational collaboration ensures its continuity on a dimension of time, while the innovation and preservation of ICH resemble the extension of the tree's height, branches, and thickness, as well as its root that extends deeper and wider into the soil, enhancing its stability and access to water and nutrients. Photosynthesis supplies the energy and materials for all growth, as the culture needs to absorb external nutrients to continuously develop, while seeding and sowing enable its propagation across different geographical locations. The growth of its branches (innovation) is equally important to the growth of its roots (preservation): only a balanced growth would ensure the vitality and continuity from generation to generation.

Figure 2. Intergenerational collaboration in reviving ICH and sustainable development

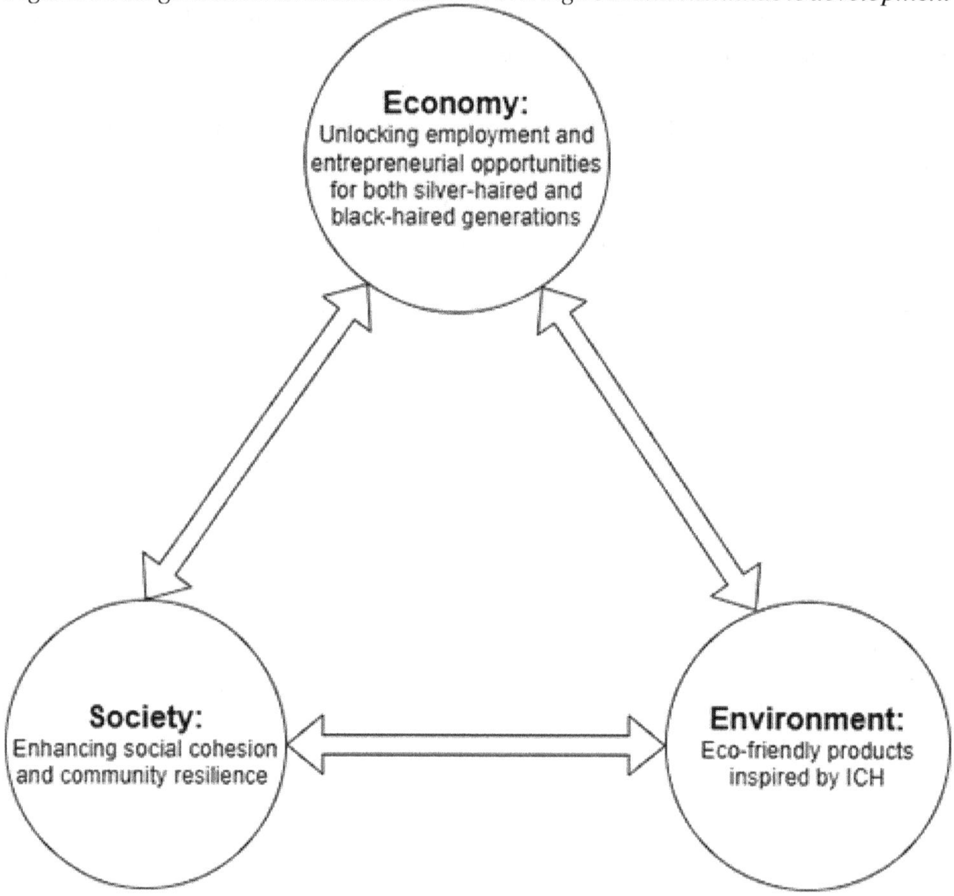

The process of reviving intangible cultural heritage through intergenerational collaboration also has broader relevance for promoting sustainability, which entails a balanced development of economic, social, and environmental dimensions (Purvis et al., 2019). Within the economic dimension, effective intergenerational collaboration would unlock hidden economic values through cultural innovations, as the silver-haired generation would continue to contribute to the economy. At the same time, the black-haired generation could also find entrepreneurial and employment opportunities through ICH practices inherited by the silver-haired practitioners, which would otherwise diminish amid urban gentrification and homogenisation. Furthermore, it would enhance social cohesion and community resilience in the social dimension, while also contributing to a better environment, as many heritage-inspired products rely on traditional handicrafts and are spiritually connected to a philosophy of human-nature harmony, making them more environmentally friendly.

4 CASE STUDIES

We conduct two case studies through interviews. The interview questions are based on the literature review from the previous section, which focuses on three dimensions: the background of the ICH the interviewee is currently practising, the technical, commercial, and institutional challenges of safeguarding ICH, and the role of intergenerational collaboration in preserving and promoting ICH. The generic questions are listed in the Appendix, while each interview has a slightly altered set of questions tailored to the case.

The choice of these two cases represents two distinct aspects of intergenerational collaborations that are crucial in the practice of ICH preservation and promotion: *i)* cross-generational re-invention and innovation, and *ii)* sustainable commercialisation of ICH-inspired cultural entrepreneurship. The first case highlights the importance of transgenerational innovation by examining the revival of a defunct colour glazing technique, leading to the birth of Nanshan Penta-coloured Ceramic Glaze, which Master Yingcai Yang reinvented and patented, while the second case looks at how a Hong Kong-based fashion house contributed to the revival of traditional textile and craftsmanship, which vindicates the vital role of sustainable commercialisation in ICH promotion. The set of case studies vindicates the vital role of silver-haired cultural practitioners in the continuing development and revival of intangible cultural heritage.

4.1 Living Heritage and Intergenerational Innovation: The Creation of the Nanshan Penta-coloured Ceramic Glaze

As discussed in previous sections, the revival of intangible cultural heritage requires not only preservation but also innovation: beyond mere replication of pre-existing techniques, it is more important to develop new forms of artistic expression and techniques that broaden traditional aesthetic experience, material knowledge, and craftsmanship relevant to contemporary culture. Thus, the key to intergenerational transmission of intangible cultural heritage lies in the continuing innovation inspired by the tradition. The Nanshan penta-coloured Glaze, created by Yingcai YANG, is a great example of Lingnan ceramic art. One defining feature of Yang's art lies in its cross-generational innovation: he did not inherit the specific formula and craftsmanship but learned only its historical characteristics from scant written records and oral accounts passed down by his predecessors. Since the traditional craftsmanship pedigree has not been fully inherited, and the relevant techniques have nearly been lost, his creation is not a direct restoration of ancient methods, but rather a distinct cross-generational innovation and reconstruction that reinvents and transforms the cultural heritage of making coloured ceramic glaze.

Figure 3. Inside Master Yang's workshop of penta-coloured ceramic glaze, photo taken by the author on 8 March 2026

The creation of Nanshan penta-coloured glaze is reminiscent of the creation of *Nigoshide* from the Kakiemon kiln in Arita, Japan. Both share an origin in the East Asian export porcelain system. *Nigoshide*, literally "cloudy hand," borrows the milky hue of rice-washing water to evoke the porcelain body's warm, lustrous quality, just as Yang mapped natural mineral glazes onto the imagery of sky, earth and landscape. Both are inspired by everyday experience, transforming the handicraft into a recognisable cultural symbol, and both utilise local materials, drawing artistic inspiration from their geographical origins. From the perspective of cross-generational transmission, both cases also share a similar path of reincarnation. The Nigoshide technique was lost for two centuries after the Meiji period (Agency for Cultural Affairs, Government of Japan, 2015; Nagatake, 2003). It is documented that the twelfth- and thirteenth-generation heirs relied on fragmentary family manuscripts and surviving antiques, spending thirty years reconstructing the lost recipe through laboratory analysis and continued experimentation before succeeding in 1953.

In terms of the institutional protection framework, the Kakiemon kiln has received multi-layered support, combining *i)* the traditional *Iemoto*[2] lineage, *ii)* formal state recognition since its 1971 designation as an Important Intangible Cultural Property of Japan, *iii)* local conservation subsidies from the government, *iv)* university partnerships through visiting professorships, and *v)* a high-end brand strategy that reinvests revenue into apprenticeship training (Agency for Cultural Affairs, Government of Japan, 2015; Goto, 2019). Comparable policies also exist in China, where ceramic masters collaborate with government cultural agencies, draw on regional material traditions, and engage with art academies to cultivate younger generations.

Below is the interview that the authors have conducted with Yingcai Yang at his workshop in Sanshui, Foshan, on 8 March 2026.

Q1: Can you share your story about the making of the penta-coloured ceramic glaze?

Yingcai Yang: In 1989, I was admitted to the Department of Fine Arts and Sculpture of Jingdezhen Ceramics College. My hometown was in Junyao, Henan. In my early years, I was taught by Teacher Yan Fu Li. He inspired my dream of leaving my hometown to pursue a university education. During my college years, I attended open classes taught by professors from Canada, the United States, and Japan. I realised from my studies that ceramics are not just a practical tool, but a great form of art.

After graduating, I came to Foshan to pursue a career in ceramic art and joined Mr Pan Bolin's ceramic company. In his early years, Master Pan allowed me to try my hand at the job for a month. Finally, he recognised my ability and hired me. Later, I met Master Liu Chuan (Shiwan pottery master). He said, "You are from Henan, you are the ancestor (of pottery art)," which encouraged me greatly. In 1996, I founded the "Tutian Pottery" brand. At first, I relied on art fairs to sell my work. In 2000, I bought a factory, and the products were sold to Harbin, Xinjiang and other places. To avoid frequent relocation, in 2005, I rented 40 acres of land in Nanshan Town (a 50-year lease) and began a journey in pottery. The combination of weeds and selenium-rich red clay here has created lightweight clay, and the mountains here, when viewed from a distance, are coloured, which inspired me to develop the "Nanshan Penta-coloured Glaze" - the five colours allude to our blue sky, white clouds, green mountains, green water and sunlight. They are the five elements that describe the beautiful countryside. They naturally fuse at high temperatures to form picturesque pottery. Every time I come out of the kiln, I see that the pottery exudes a mirror-like lustre, which reflects my own life in this environment.

In my pottery showroom, you can see the colourful pottery of Nanshan in various shapes, and the high-saturation colour blend often catches people at first sight. In the quiet showroom, these transparent glazed works: gentle white like moonlight, calm blue at night, bright green in the morning, warm yellow in the evening, and transparent cyan at dawn. All the unpredictable colours blend on the pottery, which is the state of "kiln change", reaching the climax of colour. Nanshan penta-coloured pottery is the art of mud, fire, and glaze. It is mainly composed of five colour glaze elements: blue, green, yellow, ochre, and gold crystal glaze. At a high temperature of 1220 °C to 1250 °C, after a series of physical and chemical reactions, an oil-painting-like colour palette forms in the kiln during firing. Hundreds of colours often appear, forming a sharp contrast due to differences in brightness, purity, and hue. I combined the enamel colour process described by Master Liu Chuan with the natural landscape of Nanshan and selenium-enriched clay and ultimately arrived at this unique glaze system.

Q2: Do you think it is useful and valuable to protect this intangible cultural heritage? Or is it protected too strictly, but it loses its original characteristics and authenticity, rendering it a "frozen decoration? To what extent should the public sector support it? What should individuals do? How should this boundary be drawn?

Yingcai Yang: In my early years, influenced by Western art education, I once looked down on intangible cultural heritage, regarding it as achievements of the past. But later I realised that intangible cultural heritage, as defined by UNESCO, is "living inheritance", not a static cultural relic in a museum.

The central role of the government is "licensing and endorsement" - through the identification of representative inheritors of ICH and the cultural inheritance system (such as the "five generations of inheritance" I declared: Master Liu Chuan Master Pan Bolin Myself Apprentice Qian Yongquan Other following inheritors), to give craftsmen identity recognition and brand support. Cultural promotion is also crucial: the inheritors are required to carry out activities such as campus, provincial, and municipal-level performances to expand the influence of their cultural heritage. But the government's competitive subsidy policy is problematic: for example, there are more than 50 ICH projects in Sanshui District, yet only 2-3 can receive effective subsidies, which can easily lead to craftsmen's distorted incentives driven solely by subsidies. It is recommended to adopt a "rotation system" instead, so that each inheritor can take turns to receive basic support from the subsidy.

It is important to keep in mind that intangible cultural heritage is a "craft of warmth", and spiritual values must be conveyed through creation (for example, I have integrated the blue sky, white clouds, green mountains, green water, and sunshine of Nanshan into five glazes to depict my hometown). It is apparent that protection cannot be "frozen", and ICH should evolve naturally in the living inheritance; the government can provide identity recognition and basic guarantee, while the ICH inheritors should devote themselves not only for profit but also for honour: once the title of "ICH Inheritor" is established, they can spontaneously and actively participate ICH education and teaching. The continuation of ICH should integrate lifestyle, innovation, and fun as core values, so that ICH can be integrated into everyday life.

Q3: Would the commercialisation/commodification of this ICH harness the authenticity of the ICH itself?

Yingcai Yang: The key to the commercialisation of intangible cultural heritage is to "keep the roots and be flexible in future innovation". The inheritors and practitioners rely on their arts to put the meals on the table: we all need income to continue working on our passion. Nonetheless, they cannot abandon the core technical characteristics for the myopic pursuit of profits. For example, in my own practice, I always retain the tacit understanding between local clay and mineral raw materials in my own practice, adhering to the glaze formula of blue, green, yellow, white and cyan for the Nanshan penta-coloured glaze, and the colour logic of kiln change also strictly follows the natural law of high temperature firing. As I said previously, I am against the practice of "creating for subsidies", but I am very supportive of the integration and "re-innovation" of different intangible cultural heritage projects: for example, I once wanted to use paper notation, woodblock New Year pictures, intangible cultural heritage projects and Nanshan penta-colour to create multi-coloured eggshell pottery, combined with lighting, AI voice, and home scenes, to develop ceramic products that "automatically light up in the middle of the night"; or we can cooperate with furniture companies to use gold crystal glaze as decorative panels to expand application scenarios. These innovations are "genetic mutation" - the roots are still in intangible cultural heritage (such as the traditional firing process of five glazes), but the form and function are adapted to modern needs and will not lose their authenticity. s demand for natural aesthetics. This is a continuation of this great cultural heritage.

Q4: How is this intangible heritage passed on from the older generation to the younger generation?

Yingcai Yang: Intergenerational discontinuity in ICH inheritance is a common phenomenon. The core of intangible cultural heritage inheritance is to "change from passive protection to active participation"that is important to plant the seeds to grow the young generation's interest (in ICH participation). The key is to make them actively want to learn rather than rely on coercion. Inheritance is not just about teaching skills by hand but also about transmitting the cultural core and its creative logic. For example, I once asked an apprentice to pinch 100 small heads, choose two usable ones from 100, and then destroy the others to train their mental capacity. From such training, they would develop their sense of shaping through practical experience. Then I would gradually guide them in matching the five glazes. It is also important to encourage the young people to be "down-to-earth". For example, my son grew up in a kiln factory, got along with the workers, which has planted a seed in his heart, and he will naturally be willing to inherit this great art in future.

Q5: How can current technological means (such as the Internet, live broadcast, virtual reality, etc.) help in the development of this intangible cultural heritage?

Yingcai Yang: Technology is an efficient tool that can enhance creative efficiency and communication. For example, my son and I use a 3D scanner to scan works, which can be enlarged or reduced without reshaping and printed quickly. A live broadcast allows more people to see the kiln-transformed works in five glazes, attracting potential apprentices and customers. Virtual reality allows young people to "immerse" themselves in the experience of the connection between the natural environment of Nanshan and glaze and stimulate interest. The bottom line is that technology ought not to be a destructor, but an empowering agent - the key is to use technology to serve the living inheritance of ICH, not to replace manual creation (for example, the blending of five glazes still needs to be controlled by hand, and technology only plays a role in assisting production and commercial dissemination).

Q6: What is the role of intergenerational collaboration in preserving and promoting this ICH?

Yingcai Yang: The core of intergenerational cooperation is the integration of experience and vitality: Experience transfer empowers and increases efficiency: the older generation teaches practical skills (for example, I teach apprentices heat control for five glazes and the laws of kiln change) to avoid detours for young people. I believe in the younger generation's vitality and innovation, and it is important to follow an "interest first, diploma second" principle: young people use technology (such as live broadcast, 3D scanning) and new innovations (such as using gold crystal glaze with animation images) to expand the application scenarios of this ICH. It is also important to maintain a mentor-apprentice alliance and to share resources across generations. For example, I am willing to share client resources with apprentices to ensure their income. On the other hand, the apprentices would promote a wider range of multicoloured glaze products through their learned skills, using new media in new contexts. Furthermore, it is also important to establish new awards to strengthen the role-model effect; for example, my 70-year-old apprentice (a Shanghai polymer engineer) won the 2025 New Pottery Award. After learning pottery on his own through Douyin, he studied with me for a year, rain or shine. The work "City Light", created with yellow and ochre glazes, won a bronze award at the Shenzhen-Hong Kong Intangible Cultural Heritage Exhibition. His case has shown more people that, regardless of age, you can be successful in inheriting the art, as long as you have a genuine passion. Intergenerational cooperation should break down the "age label", focus on interests and abilities, and combine the roots of the older generation (the traditional crafts of the five glazes) with the new (modern design and technology) from the younger generation, so that intangible cultural heritage can truly come alive.

4.2 From Cultural Heritage to Oriental Fashion

Beyond innovation in ICH handicraft techniques, the intergenerational transmission of ICH increasingly depends on sustainable commercialisation, which provides economic incentives for practitioners while disseminating culture to a wider community. In the second case study, we have conducted an interview with Ms Jiawen XIONG, who established an independent brand in Hong Kong in 2025 as an entrepreneurial attempt to revitalise heritage fabrics, most prominently, Cantonese silk (Xiang-Yun-Sha), through the fashion industry. Her efforts to translate this cultural vision into a viable international business have been continually tested by significant challenges, yet have also uncovered the immense potential of cultural entrepreneurship in the fashion industry. The Cantonese silk, just like many other ICH-inspired products being developed over the recent years, has ventured beyond its cultural origin and gained increasing popularity in the overseas market.

Ms Xiong encountered two major obstacles from her experience, both of which reveal the vulnerability of the cultural heritage when translated into commercial practice. The first concerns the production of Cantonese silk itself. The traditional manufacturing process, which requires repeated immersion, sun-drying, and mud-coating over an extended period, is highly labour-intensive, ecologically contingent, and resistant to industrial scaling. As a result, high costs of time and manual labour, and low short-term returns, deter younger practitioners from entering the trade, while limited supply and elevated prices pose significant disadvantages when they enter the market and compete with mass-produced fashion products. The second challenge is intergenerational: the older generation of cultural practitioners is less willing to promote their handicrafts to other markets due to cultural and translational barriers they encounter, especially to the overseas markets, despite the immense opportunities outside their comfort zone. This requires collaboration between the older and younger generations of cultural practitioners, not only to preserve the handicraft in its slow formation, but also to ensure its opportunities to "go overseas" and reach a broader global audience.

Q1: Can you introduce your intangible cultural heritage business?

Jiawen Xiong: The core of Isabelle.C, the brand that I founded in 2025, is to commercialise Chinese intangible cultural heritage fabrics and crafts (such as Cantonese silk, Song-Jin, Ke-Si, etc.) into ready-to-wear or products through original designs. Our customer base has high-quality requirements and demands meticulous standards in artistic, aesthetic, and design sensibilities, pursues uniqueness, and dislikes popular products. There are several reasons for doing this: first, I hope to let more people understand the value of intangible cultural heritage through commercial promotion; second, out of personal feelings, I liked to draw when I was a child but lacked creative cultivation, and now I want to convey my love for traditional culture through brand stories; third, I see that many intangible cultural heritage fabrics (such as fragrant cloud yarn) are misunderstood as "old-fashioned", hoping to make them younger through innovative design. Our products have several characteristics: first, scarcity, many fabrics cannot be mass-produced, and each product is unique; second, innovation, such as dyeing my daughter's paintings on fragrant cloud yarn, through "front spray" (dyeing from white cloth) and "post spray" (plant dyeing on the basis of red cloud yarn) two processes, so that traditional fabrics show colourful effects; third, integration and diversity, in addition to fragrant cloud yarn, we also have silk, silk old materials, Song brocade and other products. For example, we will use intangible cultural heritage processes, such as Kesi silk, to integrate master works into the design and to retain as much of their artistic value as possible.

Q2: Do you think it is really useful and valuable to protect this intangible cultural heritage? Or is it protected too strictly, but it loses its original characteristics and authenticity, rendering it a "frozen decoration? To what extent should the public sector support it? What should individuals do? How should this boundary be drawn?

Jiawen Xiong: I think the protection of intangible cultural heritage is very valuable, but the key is not to turn it into a decoration in a museum. When it comes to government support, this is, of course, very important. The government hopes to attract tourists through a combination of culture and tourism and to play a role in education and promotion, yet the event's quality still has room for improvement. Besides, the government's support for the ecology of intangible cultural heritage should be fairer, not just for ICH inheritors. Companies and workers like us, who are non-inheritors, but who do intangible cultural promotion, also need resource support. At the same time, I believe that individuals and civil society organisations should take the initiative to assume responsibility for education and promotion. For example, I organise activities to popularise knowledge of fragrant cloud yarn among the public, so that everyone can understand the value of the craftsmanship behind it.

Q3: In the process of commercialisation of Cantonese silk into fashion products, will it change its original appearance? Will it lose the most authentic feeling?

Jiawen Xiong: Commercialisation itself will not change the essence of intangible cultural heritage. The key is to maintain the core production process. For example, although our Cantonese silk products have made innovative designs, they have always retained the traditional dyeing and finishing process. However, the phenomenon of "bad money drives out good money" (adverse selection) does exist in the market: some cheap products use lower-quality fabrics, and machine processing shortens the traditional "three steams and nine boils" process - these actions will affect the true value of intangible cultural heritage and mislead consumers. Hence, we should enhance the cultural added value of our products so that consumers are willing to pay for the true intangible cultural heritage process, rather than simplifying the process to reduce costs.

Q4: How is this intangible heritage passed on from the older generation to the younger generation?

Jiawen Xiong: Intangible cultural heritage inheritance faces great challenges. For example, the drying and dyeing process of Cantonese silk takes seven or eight years to become a mature master, and most young people are unwilling to engage in this kind of manual work. Moreover, Cantonese silk is mainly passed down through families, but many young people lack interest in traditional crafts, posing a risk of a generation gap.

Q5: How can current technological means (such as the Internet, live broadcast, virtual reality, etc.) help in the development of this intangible cultural heritage?

Jiawen Xiong: Technology is a great tool. For example, AI can help us design patterns quickly and provide more creative inspiration. The most important thing is to "reduce costs and increase efficiency" - for example, product display images on the official website can be generated with AI models, which saves the time and money spent on hiring models to shoot. But technology also has negative effects. For example, big data push will bring anxiety and make people feel "over-comparison".

Q6: What is the role of intergenerational collaboration in preserving and promoting this ICH?

Jiawen Xiong: I think the heart of it is this "experience + vitality" dynamic. The older generation has decades of craft knowledge that you just can't replicate quickly. And my generation, we're better at picking up new tools, using social media, and thinking about how to reach new audiences. For Cantonese silk, it works out naturally: they hold the craft, I handle the outreach.

But it's not always smooth, especially when it comes to taking the craft international. That's where the generational gap really shows up. The older generation, the master craftspeople, are deeply protective of the traditions. They worry that going too commercial, or adapting too much for foreign tastes, will dilute what Cantonese silk actually is. And I get that. For them, the "three steamings, nine boilings, eighteen sunnings" process isn't just a technique. It's the soul of the craft. You don't mess with that.

My perspective is a bit different. I think we can keep that core process completely intact and still find room to innovate around it. Things like botanical dyeing, pattern design, and colour palettes that speak to international fashion markets. The craft doesn't have to look the same to be authentic. But convincing the older generation of that takes time and a lot of mutual trust. So, it's not really a conflict. It's more of a complementary tension. Their insistence on doing things properly is what keeps the craft real. My job is to take that realness and figure out how to make it land in a global context. The way I see it, successful "ICH going overseas" genuinely needs both of us: the older generation provides technical backbone and cultural credibility, and my generation handles brand-building. International fashion weeks, social media, and finding the right channels to show the world what this craft actually is. The real threat isn't commercialisation itself. It's the copycats who shortcut the process, use cheaper materials, and sell them as authentic products. Consumers can't tell the difference, which ends up crowding out good products. That's exactly why IP protection matters so much. The answer isn't to race to the bottom on price. It's to make people value real craftsmanship. And that's something both generations are actually aligned with.

4.3 Discussions

4.3.1 The Vital Role of Intergenerational Innovation in the Evolution of ICH

The two case studies reveal two distinct perspectives from two ICH practitioners with hands-on experience. Both cases highlight the importance of innovation in their pursuits and the need to recognise the rich experience of the older generation and the vitality of the younger generation, thereby revealing the crucial role of intergenerational collaboration in unleashing the comparative advantages of both generations. There are, however, unique challenges in preserving ICH techniques and commercialising ICH.

In the process of ICH inheritance, if a single skill remains within a small local practice, it is often difficult to endure. Therefore, it is crucial to embed local cultural heritage within a larger cultural system that not only retains its regional characteristics but also contributes to broader cultural dissemination. The development of *Nanshan penta-coloured glaze* reflects this path. Although it was born in the small area of Nanshan Town, Sanshui, Foshan, it was not isolated as a separate local heritage in the process of ICH recognition and cultural dissemination but was incorporated into the larger traditional system- the Shiwan Art Glaze System. In 2017, Nanshan Penta-coloured Pottery Glaze was included in the list of intangible cultural heritage and renamed "Shiwan Art Glaze", forming a "local style + regional brand" structure. This structure not only retains Nanshan's regional characteristics but also enables it to enter the long-standing cultural system of "Shiwan Pottery", thereby gaining a broader cultural identity and a wider dissemination space. From an intergenerational perspective, the development of Lingnan ceramics has often taken on a "branching" structure. For example, Yuan Huji in the Guangzhou export ceramics system of the Qing Dynasty was actually a workshop brand. In the production and trade network of the time, ceramic products from workshops across the region often entered the international market through the Guangzhou trade system and gradually became integrated into the overall Guangcai Porcelain system. Through intergenerational innovation, the new crafts or styles do not exist in isolation but gradually become branches of a larger system.

Similarly, in the second case, the commercialisation of existing ICH highlights a divergence in intergenerational perspectives, particularly regarding international outreach. While the older generation is often deeply rooted in domestic preservation and may be unaware of the need to expand overseas, younger practitioners demonstrate a strong inclination to export ICH to global audiences. To effectively commercialise and export these traditions, it is essential to build and consolidate regional ICH brands. By integrating local resources and unifying promotional narratives, practitioners can forge highly recognisable regional brands that significantly enhance market competitiveness and cultural visibility on the global stage. Furthermore, bridging this intergenerational gap requires systematic initiatives such as youth incubator programmes. Establishing a hybrid model that combines traditional master-apprentice mentorship with modern education can foster a new generation of practitioners, thereby addressing the chronic shortage of successors while injecting modern entrepreneurial visions into traditional crafts.

4.3.2 Fostering Creativity in a Market of Efficiency and Free Competition

The economic value of ICH-inspired products and services lies not only in their functional value, but also in their artistic value: while the functional value is relatively tangible and easy to measure, the aesthetic value is intangible and harder to gauge. The market practice often demands fast-paced efficiency, automation, and constant sensual stimulation through ever-changing fashion trends and the redesign of existing products, in stark contrast to the slow, manual, high-cost and nostalgic nature of ICH-related products. While mass production enables homogeneous, functional products to be produced at significantly lower costs, when applied to the production of cultural goods, it often undermines aesthetic value and poses a threat to handmade, creativity-intensive cultural products, especially when such products compete in the same marketplace with merely functional products. The true challenge of promoting ICH-inspired products, therefore, is how to fully realise its intangible value aesthetics through strategic positioning. It is crucial to avoid direct competition with the fast-growing fashion industry and to seek a market for art that attracts consumer segments seeking beauty beyond functionality.

The introduction of expert think tanks is invaluable for addressing the information asymmetry in the ICH artisan market. Inviting scholars, master artisans, and design experts for on-site guidance can facilitate the modern adaptation of traditional techniques. This ensures that ICH products retain their traditional roots while aligning with contemporary aesthetics and market demands, elevating them from mere commodities to culturally resonant artworks. Intergenerational transmission of aesthetic knowledge, therefore, is vital to maintaining the aesthetic standards of the ICH market on the consumer side, thereby ensuring fair transactions, which is similar to the commercial ecology of classical music and the fine arts industry.

Additionally, fostering cross-disciplinary collaboration is imperative to compete in a diverse market. Encouraging the intersection of ICH with modern design, digital technology, animation, and new media can transcend the limitations of traditional forms, leading to scenario-based, lifestyle-oriented products that appeal to younger demographics. Furthermore, merging ICH with the cultural tourism industry by introducing traditional crafts into scenic areas, heritage blocks, and rural revitalisation projects transforms intangible heritage into experiential and consumable cultural assets.

4.3.3 The Importance of Institutional Protection and Learning-by-Doing

As mentioned in the introduction, classical music and fine arts are two distinct forms of intangible cultural heritage that are carefully safeguarded by traditional academic institutions and promoted by a well-established artistic industry. Many other ICHs, however, receive less institutional protection and are at significantly higher extinction risks. It is therefore important to introduce institutional protections as a social guarantee in cultural preservation.

The current certification system for ICH inheritors in China, for instance, provides formal recognition but must be expanded to support not only master artisans but also cultural entrepreneurs and frontline workers who facilitate the market operations of these crafts. To achieve this, governments should streamline administrative processes and establish dedicated funding mechanisms. Optimising the application and subsidy procedures will significantly lower the institutional costs associated with the creation, production, and commercialisation of ICH, providing a stable financial guarantee for continuous innovation. At the local level, the establishment of innovation pilot platforms can effectively integrate ICH with regional culture. These platforms would encourage local practitioners and designers to utilise indigenous materials and cultural intellectual properties, achieving a synergistic effect that roots innovation deeply within the community. Moreover, institutional support must extend to the digital preservation of cultural assets. Systematically archiving techniques, oral histories, and classic works into comprehensive digital databases ensures their permanent preservation and provides a robust foundation for future academic research and creative adaptation.

The way ICH are taught at tertiary institutions also deserves further discussion. Traditional university curricula often emphasise theoretical knowledge, which can lack practical experience. Therefore, integrating ICH education into higher education through embedded curricula and guest lectures by master artisans is crucial. Some ICH practitioners call for a learning-by-doing approach that incorporates a significant component of mentorship directly with ICH inheritors as a compulsory requirement, in addition to the theoretical component offered by university curricula. Institutional protection, along with hands-on experience, would ensure that cultural heritage is not only preserved passively but also reinvigorated through mentorship and continuous practice.

5 CONCLUSION

The death of intangible cultural heritage due to the relentless pursuit of economic growth has been alarming. Cultural diversity, as reflected in the rich and diverse intangible cultural heritage worldwide, not only enhances cultural identity and social cohesion but also fosters creativity – the lifeblood of cultural and creative industries. The challenge is more alarming in the context of today's silver-haired economy: as the older generation gradually retreats from its social roles, the culture is at tremendous risk of extinction if the younger generation fails to inherit the intangible treasure that carries tremendous economic and social value.

To further investigate the issues of reviving intangible cultural heritage in this challenging world, this chapter examines the perspectives of culture, instruments, and people as three distinct angles in the study and practice of intangible cultural heritage. First, from a cultural perspective, the main challenge of cultural continuity lies not only in preventing extinction, but also in understanding the organic growth of culture and the degree of intervention needed for effective preservation and promotion. It is important to emphasise UNESCO's definition of cultural heritage as a living heritage, thereby warning of *"freezing risks"* – turning living practices into static "museum pieces" or "zombie heritage" solely for archiving. Unlike investment in fixed capital, which is tangible and controllable, cultural capital is intangible; high investment inputs do not always lead to high cultural outputs. Over-intervention by the public sector could distort the fundamental goal of cultural preservation, leading to wasteful investment and undermining the natural evolution of ICH. On the other hand, excessive commercialisation and gentrification of cultural heritage would threaten cultural authenticity and potentially cause social and economic tensions between cultural inheritors and cultural entrepreneurs, due to the uneven distribution of income from the cultural industry to the community. While the natural decline of certain cultural heritages is inevitable and common, one ought to respect the natural growth in the course of its evolution, eventually aligning the interests of the community, the cultural entrepreneurs, and the public sector.

Second, from an instrumental perspective, transgenerational innovation is the vital means for cultural revival. This is particularly true in our current era, where the widespread adoption of digital technology, from live-streaming to 3D scanning to AI-assisted creativity, has created abundant opportunities for both cultural preservation and promotion, benefiting both younger and older generations of cultural practitioners. It may be overly stereotypical to assume that the older generation possesses authentic cultural knowledge, while the younger generation is energetic and innovative. One cannot deny that innovation is the fundamental tool that propels cultural evolution, benefiting both black-haired and silver-haired cultural practitioners. Transgenerational innovation not only inspires cultural entrepreneurship across generations but also provides a means to rescue and recreate lost cultural heritage.

Third, people are the ultimate contributors to intangible cultural heritage. We ought to recognise the indispensable role of the silver-haired generation and the cultural knowledge that they possess, as well as the critical role of intergenerational collaboration in ensuring that cultural knowledge can be effectively passed down from one generation to another, despite the fragility of intergenerational transmission as society evolves. The individualism of each generation would foster cultural entrepreneurship that reflects its specific cultural context. As people and culture constantly renew themselves across generations, the cultural tree grows thicker and taller, while its roots stretch deeper into the soil. Intergenerational collaboration ought to be mutually beneficial: the younger and older generations learn from and co-create with each other, ensuring cultural renewal and fostering a virtuous cycle of sustainable cultural evolution that continuously yields economic and social benefits across generations.

From a policy-setting perspective, it is crucial to find the balance between *bottom-up* cultural entrepreneurship and *top-down* institutional protection. Imbalanced policies would lead to a loss of cultural authenticity: either through over-commercialisation and cultural gentrification arising from the incessant pursuit of profits over cultural missions, or through a freezing of risk due to the *museumification* of cultural heritage. Therefore, a successful private-public partnership is necessary to address this issue, as Zhi (2025) has discussed. In addition, it is crucial to integrate ICH knowledge and practices into school curricula, particularly in tertiary education institutions, to incentivise both younger and older generations to continue their cultural pursuits through formal studies and mentorship.

Due to the limited time and scope of this research, many unexplored areas remain, which would serve as landmarks for future research. For example, the two case studies in this chapter are mainly focused on Chinese cultural contexts. We may extend our investigation to a broader comparative analysis of global perspectives, incorporating more regions, such as Africa, the Americas, and Europe, as well as using more complex methodologies in both qualitative and quantitative terms, to develop a systemic theory of intangible cultural heritage and sustainable development. We will further examine these unexplored areas in future research.

AUTHOR CONTRIBUTIONS

The authors are listed in alphabetical order, and all the authors have made equal contributions to this work. Zisheng Huang elaborated on the development of fine arts in relation to the changing artistic taste and contributed to the first case study; Weixi Zhang contributed to the discussion of the Cantonese narration of history (Jiang-Gu), conducted a substantial literature review and assisted with the development of both case studies; Tianhao Zhi initiated the project, contributed to the writing and theorising parts, as well as participated in both case studies. The remaining errors are ours.

ACKNOWLEDGEMENT

The authors would like to thank a number of experienced ICH practitioners for valuable feedback and suggestions.

REFERENCES

Agency for Cultural Affairs, Government of Japan. (2015). *Handbook for facilities and management of cultural properties*. https://www.bunka.go.jp/seisaku/bunkazai/hokoku/pdf/setchi_kanri_handbook.pdf

Blake, J. (2008). Chapter UNESCO's 2003 Convention on Intangible Cultural Heritage: The implications of community involvement in 'safeguarding. In *Intangible Heritage* (1st ed.). Routledge., https://doi.org/https://doi.org/10.4324/9780203884973

Borissova, V. (2018). Cultural heritage digitization and related intellectual property issues. *Journal of Cultural Heritage, 34*, 145–150. DOI: 10.1016/j.culher.2018.04.023

Butt, J. (2002). *Playing with history: The historical approach to musical performance*. (Original work published Cambridge University Press)

Cang, V. (2008). Preserving Intangible Heritage in Japan: The Role of the Iemoto System. *International Journal of Intangible Heritage, 3*, 53–63.

Cicchiello, A. F., Gallo, S., & Monferrà, S. (2023). Financing the cultural and creative industries through crowdfunding: The role of national cultural dimensions and policies. *Journal of Cultural Economics, 47*(1), 133–175. DOI: 10.1007/s10824-022-09452-9 PMID: 38625194

Cominelli, F., & Greffe, X. (2012). Intangible cultural heritage: Safeguarding for creativity. *City, Culture and Society*, *3*(4), 245–250. DOI: 10.1016/j.ccs.2012.10.003

Falk, M. T., & Hagsten, E. (2025). Intangible Cultural Heritage differently exposed across continents. *NPJ Heritage Science*, *13*(1), 600. DOI: 10.1038/s40494-025-02169-w

Gilman, L. (2022). 'Our Culture is dying': Safeguarding versus representation in the implementation of the UNESCO ICH Convention. *International Journal of Intangible Heritage*, *17*, 40–52.

Goto, K. (2019). Crafts Policies in Japan. In Mignosa, A., & Kotipalli, P. (Eds.), *A Cultural Economic Analysis of Craft* (pp. 115–127). Springer International Publishing., DOI: 10.1007/978-3-030-02164-1_10

Gui, Y., Ma, Y., Chen, Y., Zhou, C., & Xiao, T. (2026). Ecosystem services in UNESCO World Heritage sites: A review of research trends and future directions. *NPJ Heritage Science*, *14*(1), 115. DOI: 10.1038/s40494-026-02380-3

Harris, A., Wyn, J., & Younes, S. (2010). Beyond apathetic or activist youth: 'Ordinary' young people and contemporary forms of participation. *Young*, *18*(1), 9–32. DOI: 10.1177/110330880901800103

Hazaea, A. N., Bin-Hady, W. R. A., & Metwally, A. A. (2025). Globalization, multiculturalism, and national identity in Najran's linguistic landscape: A study of English and Arabic in coffee shop signage. *Humanities & Social Sciences Communications*, *12*(1), 1616. DOI: 10.1057/s41599-025-05957-8

Hu, W., Li, M., Chi, X., Wang, X., & Khan, A. U. (2024). Intangible cultural heritage research in China from the perspective of intellectual property rights based on bibliometrics and knowledge mapping. *Humanities & Social Sciences Communications*, *11*(1), 825. DOI: 10.1057/s41599-024-03314-9

Hwang, H., Park, C.-W., Kim, H.-K., & Lee, J.-H. (2025). CATS: Cultural-heritage classification using LLMs and distribute model. *NPJ Heritage Science*, *13*(1), 76. DOI: 10.1038/s40494-025-01621-1

Jarrott, S. E. (2011). Where Have We Been and Where are We Going? Content Analysis of Evaluation Research of Intergenerational Programs. *Journal of Intergenerational Relationships*, *9*(1), 37–52. DOI: 10.1080/15350770.2011.544594

Jarrott, S. E. (2023). Intergenerational Theory as a Tool to Diversify Practice and Policy. *Generations Journal, 47*(4), 1–10. ProQuest One Academic (3053147423).

Jarrott, S. E., Juris, J. J., & Turner, S. G. (2025). The Intergenerational Program Evaluation Tool: Results of a Delphi Study. *Journal of Intergenerational Relationships, 23*(3), 280–296. DOI: 10.1080/15350770.2024.2349927

Kaplan, M., Thang, L. L., Sánchez, M., & Hoffman, J. (2020). *Intergenerational Contact Zones: Place-based Strategies for Promoting Social Inclusion and Belonging* (Kaplan, M., Thang, L. L., Sánchez, M., & Hoffman, J., Eds.; 1st ed.). Routledge., DOI: 10.4324/9780429199097

Kirshenblatt-Gimblett, B. (2004). Intangible Heritage as Metacultural Production1. *Museum International, 56*(1–2), 52–65. DOI: 10.1111/j.1350-0775.2004.00458.x

Li, N., Li, X., & Xiao, W. (2025). Intangible cultural heritage threatened-level categories and criteria. *Humanities & Social Sciences Communications, 12*(1), 271. DOI: 10.1057/s41599-025-04595-4

Li, W., Xie, Q., Ao, J., Lin, H., Ji, S., Yang, M., & Sun, J. (2025). Systematic review: A scientometric analysis of the status, trends and challenges in the application of digital technology to cultural heritage conservation (2019–2024). *NPJ Heritage Science, 13*(1), 90. DOI: 10.1038/s40494-025-01636-8

Lilley, I. (2017). Review of Victor T. King (ed.), UNESCO in Southeast Asia: World Heritage Sites in Comparative Perspective. Studies in Asian Topics no. 55. xv + 463 pp. Copenhagen: Nordic Institute of Asian Studies, 2016. *International Journal of Cultural Property, 24*(2), 239–241. DOI: 10.1017/S0940739117000066

Lin, C., Xia, G., Nickpour, F., & Chen, Y. (2025). A review of emotional design in extended reality for the preservation of culture heritage. *NPJ Heritage Science, 13*(1), 86. DOI: 10.1038/s40494-025-01625-x

Ma, H. (2022). The Missing Intangible Cultural Heritage in Shanghai Cultural and Creative Industries. *International Journal of Heritage Studies, 28*(5), 597–608. DOI: 10.1080/13527258.2022.2042717

Nagatake, T. (Ed.). (2003). *Classic Japanese porcelain: Imari and Kakiemon*. Kodansha International.

Niu, X., Wang, X., & Bi, X. (2025). Mapping the nexus of sustainability and cultural heritage: A systematic review and empirical analysis. *NPJ Heritage Science, 13*(1), 471. DOI: 10.1038/s40494-025-02006-0

Poplawska, M. (2025). Intangible heritage system: Challenges of culture preservation in a cross-cultural perspective. *Ethnomusicology Forum, 34*(1), 91–119. DOI: 10.1080/17411912.2025.2484707

Purvis, B., Mao, Y., & Robinson, D. (2019). Three pillars of sustainability: In search of conceptual origins. *Sustainability Science, 14*(3), 681–695. https://doi.org/https://doi.org/10.1007/s11625-018-0627-5. DOI: 10.1007/s11625-018-0627-5

Sánchez, M. (2008). Intergenerational Programmes: Towards a Society for All Ages: By Mariano Sanchez (Ed.) *Barcelona: Obra Social, Social Studies Collection No. 23 "la Caixa" Foundation, 2007. 228 pages. Journal of Intergenerational Relationships, 6*(4), 485–487. DOI: 10.1080/15350770802466286

Sánchez, M., & Kaplan, M. (2014). Intergenerational Learning in Higher Education: Making the Case for Multigenerational Classrooms. *Educational Gerontology, 40*(7), 473–485. DOI: 10.1080/03601277.2013.844039

Shen, J., Liu, N., Sun, H., Li, D., Zhang, Y., & Han, L. (2025). An algorithm based on lightweight semantic features for ancient mural element object detection. *NPJ Heritage Science, 13*(1), 70. DOI: 10.1038/s40494-025-01565-6

Skublewska-Paszkowska, M., Milosz, M., Powroznik, P., & Lukasik, E. (2022). 3D technologies for intangible cultural heritage preservation—Literature review for selected databases. *Heritage Science, 10*(1), 3. DOI: 10.1186/s40494-021-00633-x PMID: 35003750

UNESCO. (2003). *Basic Texts of the 2003 Convention for the Safeguarding of the Intangible Cultural Heritage*. https://ich.unesco.org/doc/src/2003_Convention_Basic_Texts_2024_version_EN.pdf

UNESCO. (2023). *Living heritage: Safeguarding without freezing* (Programme and Meeting Document CPE-2023/WS/10). https://unesdoc.unesco.org/ark:/48223/pf0000387872_eng

UNESCO. (n.d.). *What is Intangible Cultural Heritage?* UNESCO Intangible Cultural Heritage. Retrieved https://ich.unesco.org/en/what-is-intangible-heritage-00003

Vera Zúñiga, J., Urbina Parada, F., & Cornejo Meza, D. (2026). Mapping semantic bias in UNESCO intangible heritage metadata through community detection in South America. *NPJ Heritage Science, 14*(1), 133. DOI: 10.1038/s40494-026-02400-2

Wang, Q. (2022). The Digitisation of Intangible Cultural Heritage Oriented to Inheritance and Dissemination under the Threshold of Neural Network Vision. *Mobile Information Systems, 2022*, 1–10. DOI: 10.1155/2022/6323811

White, H. C., & White, C. A. (1965). *Canvases and careers: Institutional change in the French painting world*. John Wiley & Sons.

Xu, X., & Sun, Y. (2017). Study on the adoption of information technology in digital transmission of intangible cultural heritage (CN). *Library and Information Service, 61*(6), 68–75. https://doi.org/https://doi.org/10.11968/tsyqb.1003-6938.2017124

Yuan, H., Li, Y., Wang, B., Liu, K., & Zhang, J. (2025). Knowledge graph-based intelligent question answering system for ancient Chinese costume heritage. *NPJ Heritage Science, 13*(1), 198. DOI: 10.1038/s40494-025-01776-x

Zheng, F., Wu, S., Liu, R., & Bai, Y. (2024). What influences user continuous intention of digital museum: Integrating task-technology fit (TTF) and unified theory of acceptance and usage of technology (UTAUT) models. *Heritage Science, 12*(1), 253. DOI: 10.1186/s40494-024-01365-4

Zhi, T. (2025). Safeguarding Intangible Cultural Heritage in a Knowledge Economy: Envisioning a Paradigm Shift of Chinese Economic Development. In Wong, J. H.-C., & Yu, P. (Eds.), *Driving Community Change Through Social Service and Business Partnerships* (pp. 59–96). IGI Global Scientific Publishing., DOI: 10.4018/979-8-3373-1852-3.ch003

ENDNOTES

1. TTF-UTAUT stands for Task Technology Fit - Unified Theory of Acceptance and Use of Technology.

2. **Iemoto system:** A traditional Japanese mode of artistic transmission in which a designated head of a lineage, the *Iemoto*, holds authority over the standards, repertoire, and certification of practitioners within a school of craft or performance (Cang, 2008).

Chapter 8

Elderly Care Services in Türkiye From a Silver Economy and Gerontology Perspective:

An Integrated Social Service and Care Economy Model

Berra Cansız Kösesoy
http://orcid.org/0000-0003-1043-4139
Faculty of Economics and Administrative Sciences, Department of Social Work, Firat University, Turkey

Merve Nur Oktar
http://orcid.org/0000-0001-8149-2809
Burdur Mehmet Akif Ersoy Üniversitesi, Turkey

ABSTRACT

This study examines elderly care services in Türkiye from a silver economy and gerontology perspective. Türkiye's rapidly aging population is increasing the need for care services. However, the fragmented structure of existing services, inter-institutional coordination problems, and inequalities in access make the provision of care services difficult. Therefore, in this study, elderly care services are considered a sector and a component of the silver economy. Firstly, the dynamics of aging in Turkey and the conceptual framework of the silver economy are explained. The institutional structure of elderly care services is then analyzed, and the service models offered in Turkey are examined. The strengths and weaknesses of the care system are discussed. The study reveals that the care system in Turkey, involving the

DOI: 10.4018/979-8-3373-9370-4.ch008

public, private, and non-governmental sectors, has a multi-actor but not integrated character. Within the scope of the study, an "Integrated Social Service and Care Economy Model" is developed for this non-integrated, multi-actor care system.

INTRODUCTION

In Türkiye, elderly care is provided by various actors through different models, including home care, home health services, institutional care, and community-based support services. Today, due to the impact of demographic transformation, elderly care has ceased to be merely an area of individual need. It has become a priority area on a global scale across social policy, health systems, and economic sustainability (World Health Organization [WHO], 2020; Organization for Economic Co-operation and Development [OECD], 2025). The increase in average life expectancy, the decrease in fertility rates, and transformations in family structures are increasing the need for long-term care services. In this context, the need for care is not only related to the aging process but also to the individual's capacity to perform daily living activities independently. As the individual's level of functionality decreases, the need for care, care costs, and the need for caregiver support increase. Türkiye is one of the OECD countries where the dynamics of an aging population are becoming increasingly evident. According to the OECD, the need for long-term care is particularly concentrated among older age groups, where physical or mental impairments are more common (OECD, 2005). Therefore, the organization and financing of elderly care services are directly related to countries' welfare regimes, care policies, and social protection systems. Care models differ across public care services, social insurance systems, private insurance, and individual financing mechanisms (Yıldırım, 2012; Jayawardhana et al., 2023). However, the aging population is rapidly increasing demand for care services and calling into question the sustainability of existing financing models (Colombo et al., 2011; Wang et al., 2023; OECD, 2025).

In Türkiye, elderly care services are provided within a multi-actor structure by public institutions, local governments, the private sector, non-governmental organizations, and family members. However, the fragmented structure of the current system, the lack of inter-institutional coordination, regional inequalities, and differences in service standards make it difficult to provide holistic care services (Atasü Topcuoğlu, 2021; İzdeş Terkoğlu & Memiş, 2022). In particular, the fact that care services largely rely on family-based and informal care labor means the care burden is mostly borne by women, creating significant problems for the system's sustainability. According to International Labour Organization (ILO) data, a significant portion of elderly individuals worldwide who require long-term care are supported by family members and volunteers (ILO, 2022). This situation makes the care gap visible on a global scale and underscores the need to develop professional care services.

This transformation in elderly care services makes the role of social workers more visible. Social workers are in a crisis in addressing needs, conducting psychosocial support processes, coordinating services, providing case management, and ensuring cooperation. Given that care needs encompass not only medical but also social and psychological dimensions, social work interventions are seen as a fundamental component of the care system (Karahan & Güven, 2002; Özmete & Hussein, 2017). However, the fact that elderly care services in Türkiye are mostly organized in a health-focused manner limits the holistic approach to addressing psychosocial needs.

In recent years, elderly care services have become increasingly visible in discussions of the silver and care economies. The silver economy approach views services for older individuals not only as an area of social spending but also as a strategic sector with potential for economic growth, job creation, and service innovation (European Commission, 2018; Eager, Maritz, & Millemann, 2022). In this context, care services create new areas of cooperation between social work systems and economic actors. In Türkiye, however, the fragmented structure and coordination problems in care services make it difficult for them to transform into a sustainable, integrated system. This section examines the current structure of elderly care services in Türkiye from the perspectives of the silver economy, gerontology, and social works. The study evaluates the institutional structure of elderly care services, the psychosocial dimensions of care services, and the development of the care economy, and presents a critical analysis of the current system's fragmented structure. Furthermore, the study proposes an "Integrated Social Work and Care Economy Model" to strengthen coordination among social works, health services, and economic actors. In this respect, the chapter aims to provide an interdisciplinary and policy-oriented framework for the restructuring of elderly care services in Türkiye.

1. THEORETICAL FRAMEWORK

This study examines elderly care services within an interdisciplinary theoretical framework that integrates perspectives from the silver economy, care economics, gerontology, and social work. With the aging of the population, care services have become an important area of discussion not only in social policy but also in terms of economic sustainability, social welfare, and health systems. In this context, the silver economy approach emphasizes that services for the elderly are a strategic sector for economic growth, job creation, and social innovation (European Commission,

2018). In particular, elderly care services are becoming a fundamental component of the care economy as long-term care systems expand.

The care economics approach draws attention to the role of care labor in social reproduction and critically examines the view that care services are merely an invisible responsibility carried out within the family (Razavi, 2007; Costa Font et al., 2022). This perspective makes visible the relationships among care services, gender inequalities, social protection mechanisms, and welfare policies. In Türkiye, the fact that elderly care services are largely delivered through family-based, informal care models makes the care economics approach particularly important.

Another theoretical basis of the study is gerontology and the gerontological social work approach. Gerontology is an interdisciplinary field that addresses the aging process across its biological, psychological, social, and environmental dimensions (Hooyman & Kiyak, 2011). Gerontological social work, on the other hand, focuses on improving the quality of life of elderly individuals, meeting their psychosocial needs, supporting social participation, and strengthening access to care services (Sanders et al., 2019). This approach not only focuses on physical health needs in elderly care services but also highlights psychosocial dimensions, including social isolation, loneliness, caregiver burden, and social support mechanisms.

This study also uses an integrated care approach. The integrated care approach is considered a person-centered service model that aims to strengthen coordination among health, social, and care services (WHO, 2020; Costa Font et al., 2022). In line with this approach, it is argued that elderly care services should be organized within a holistic framework based on interdisciplinary and inter-institutional cooperation, rather than delivered in a fragmented manner across different institutions and actors. Within this context, the "Integrated Social Work and Care Economy Model" developed in this study offers a conceptual framework that combines the silver economy, care economy, gerontology, and integrated care approaches from a social work perspective.

2. METHODOLOGY

This study uses document analysis, policy review, and narrative-based literature review methods within a qualitative research framework. Qualitative research approaches allow for the contextual and multidimensional examination of social phenomena (Creswell & Creswell, 2018). In this context, elderly care services in Türkiye are examined from the perspectives of the silver economy, gerontology, and social work. This context is examined through national and international academic literature, policy documents, institutional reports, and secondary data sources. Document analysis is an important qualitative research method that allows systematic evaluation of written materials (Bowen, 2009). Accordingly, reports from international organizations such as the OECD, the WHO, and the European Commission, as well as policy documents published by public institutions on elderly care services in Türkiye, and relevant academic literature have been evaluated. Within the scope of the study, the fragmented structure of elderly care services, inter-institutional coordination mechanisms, psychosocial support needs, and the roles of social workers in the care system have been examined within a conceptual and analytical framework. Narrative-based literature review methods were used in this examination process. Narrative-based literature review is considered an important method that allows for a holistic assessment of the existing knowledge on a particular subject, the comparison of different research findings, and the creation of a theoretical framework (Baumeister & Leary, 1997). Based on the findings from the literature review and policy analysis, an "Integrated Social Work and Care Economics Model" has been developed in Türkiye, aiming to support integrated, person-centered, and sustainable long-term care services. This study, which aims to generate primary empirical data, seeks to provide a theoretical and policy-oriented analysis to understand, evaluate, and restructure the current structure of elderly care services in Türkiye.

3. SILVER ECONOMY AND AGING DYNAMICS IN TÜRKIYE

In Türkiye, the silver economy is not merely a field limited to social assistance and care services. It should be considered a developing, multidimensional service sector that is generating new collaborations among public institutions, the private sector, local governments, and community-based organizations. The increasing need for care, health, social support, and quality of life due to an aging population makes the relationship between social policy systems and economic structures more visible. This situation creates new economic and social opportunities in areas such as long-term care services, age-friendly technologies, digital health applications, and community-based care models. According to projections by the Turkish Statistical Institute (TUIK), the share of the population aged 65 and over in Türkiye is expected to increase significantly in the coming years (TUIK, 2026). This demographic shift not only creates new pressures on social work systems but also directly affects labor markets, health systems, the care economy, and local development processes. Therefore, the aging population is becoming a strategic area of discussion in Türkiye regarding the sustainability and reorganization of care services. The silver economy approach views older individuals not merely as passive service recipients in need of social support, but as active components of the economic system and key actors in new service markets (European Commission, 2018). In line with this approach, the silver economy encompasses a broad economic sector involving the production, distribution, and consumption of products, services, and technologies responsive to the needs of the elderly population. Institutional healthcare services, long-term care systems, home care services, age-friendly housing, digital health technologies, and social care applications are among the key components of the silver economy sector (OECD, 2025). Care services, in particular, are among the fastest-growing areas of the silver economy. This is because, as the population ages, the need for long-term care increases, and care services become not only a social protection area but also a job-creating sector (Colombo et al., 2011; OECD, 2025). This situation underscores the strategic importance of the care economy for both social welfare and economic sustainability. An examination of the current structure of care services in Türkiye reveals that the system is largely based on family-based and informal care mechanisms. While this structure helps meet care needs in the short term, it largely concentrates the care burden on family members, especially women (Atasü Topcuoğlu, 2021).

The dominance of family-based care structures impedes the development of professional care services and makes institutionalization difficult. In addition, the fact that care services are largely provided through informal relationships creates significant problems in terms of care quality, service standardization, and caregiver burnout (Gok Metin et al., 2019). Especially in a society where the elderly population is rapidly increasing, the sustainability of a system based solely on family-based care models is becoming increasingly debatable. In this context, re-evaluating care services from a silver economy perspective emerges as an important necessity both economically and socially. The silver economy approach does not view care services solely as a social assistance-oriented field. Care services are considered a strategic sector that creates employment, promotes social innovation, and supports local economic development. However, the fragmented structure of elderly care services in Türkiye, the lack of inter-institutional coordination, and the limited professional care infrastructure make it difficult to fully leverage the potential of the silver economy. Therefore, a more integrated care model involving public institutions, the private sector, local governments, and social work systems is needed to sustain care services. In particular, the role of social workers in care coordination, psychosocial support, and service planning processes is critically important for addressing elderly care services not only from a medical perspective but also from social, economic, and societal dimensions.

4. INSTITUTIONAL STRUCTURE OF ELDERLY CARE SERVICES IN TÜRKIYE

The development of aged care services is closely linked to the transformation of welfare-state practices. While in traditional welfare state models care services were largely provided by the state as a public responsibility, in recent years the role of the private sector and civil society organizations in care services has been increasing (Evers, 2005; Thurston, 2015). This transformation has led to care services being considered not only within the field of social policy but also as a sector that generates economic value (European Commission, 2018). The silver economy approach, in particular, positions aged care services as a strategic area for employment, service innovation, and local economic development. However, strengthening the multi-actor structure in care services underscores the importance of inter-institutional coordination and service standards. Indeed, in systems where the division of labor among actors is poorly defined, care services are delivered in a fragmented manner, leading to significant differences in service quality (Eriksson & Hellström, 2021; OECD, 2025). In the case of Türkiye, the multi-actor, yet weakly integrated, structure of elderly care services creates significant problems in terms of access to care services, service continuity, and psychosocial support processes.

The economic sustainability of elderly care services is one of the fundamental policy debates that has become more visible with the aging population. The limited nature of public resources necessitates the development of alternative care financing models. In this regard, public-private partnerships, social enterprises, digital care platforms, and community-based care practices offer significant opportunities for the sustainability of care services. However, evaluating care services within market mechanisms also raises questions of access inequalities and social justice (OECD, 2025). In particular, the proliferation of care services through high-cost private models can limit low-income elderly individuals' access to professional care services (Çakmur, 2015; Greenfield et al., 2018). This situation shows that care services should not only be considered from the perspective of economic sustainability, but also in line with the principles of social protection, rights-based service delivery, and equality. At this point, the social work discipline, with its ethical principles and holistic assessment approach, plays a critical role in coordinating care services (Sanders et al., 2019).

In Türkiye, elderly care services are provided within a multi-layered structure by public institutions, local governments, the private sector, non-governmental organizations, and family members. However, this multi-actor structure does not mean that care services are organized in an integrated manner. On the contrary, in the current system, care services are often provided in a fragmented manner within the institutions' service boundaries (Aydın, 2024). While local governments focus more on social support and day care services, the Ministry of Family and Social Works plays a decisive role in organizing long-term social care services, and the Ministry of Health plays a decisive role in medical care processes. This fragmented structure makes it difficult to holistically assess the health, care, and psychosocial support needs of elderly individuals. In addition, the limited institutionalization of private-sector and non-governmental, society-based elderly care services leads to differences in service standards and uncertainties about the sustainability of care services. Therefore, one of the fundamental problems of the elderly care system in Türkiye is the inability to support the multi-actor structure with an effective coordination mechanism.

4.1. Local government-based elderly care services

In Türkiye, local governments are considered key actors in supporting the independent living and social participation of elderly individuals. Elderly care services provided by municipalities are mostly carried out free of charge or at low cost within the framework of social municipalism. These services encompass a wide range, including home care support, day care, hot meals, cleaning, personal care, social support, and active living practices. These services offered by local governments play an important role in delaying the need for institutional care for elderly individuals and in helping them continue living in their own environments. Considering that elderly individuals often prefer to live in their own homes despite their care needs, community-based care services offered by local governments are of strategic importance for the well-being of the elderly (Oktar, 2025).

However, in Türkiye, the scope, quality, and accessibility of local government-based elderly care services vary significantly across municipalities, depending on institutional capacity, financial resources, and local social policy priorities. This situation creates regional inequalities in access to care services and makes standardization of care services difficult. In small-scale municipalities in particular, the limited capacity of professional care staff, social workers, and multidisciplinary teams often leads to care services remaining at the level of social assistance (Akyol Güner & Ulama, 2025). This situation demonstrates that elderly care services need to be restructured not only with an aid-based approach but also with a rights-based, sustainable, and professional care perspective. The role of local governments in elderly care services is also important from a silver economy perspective. Because in-home care services that support the independent living of elderly individuals, daytime support mechanisms, digital care technologies, and active aging practices contribute to the development of new service areas at the local level. This situation transforms care services from merely a social support area into an important sector for local economic development, care employment, and social innovation (European

Commission, 2018). However, in Türkiye, local governments' practices regarding elderly care services are often shaped by short-term social assistance policies.

Nevertheless, the impact of local government practices on elderly individuals has been examined at a relatively limited level (Koru Uzkurt, 2023). Therefore, in terms of the sustainability and effectiveness of care services, local governments need to restructure their care policies in line with the perspectives of active aging, community-based care, and the silver economy. Social workers play a significant role in coordinating local government-based care services. Social workers undertake critical functions, including assessing the care needs of elderly individuals, referring them to appropriate services, providing psychosocial support, and ensuring inter-institutional coordination (Nazlı, 2025). In this respect, social workers can be considered not only service providers but also coordinating actors who support the social participation, independent living, and access to rights-based services of elderly individuals. Therefore, local governments' shift towards social work-oriented integrated care models in elderly care services can make significant contributions to both social sustainability and service quality.

4.2. Elderly care services provided by the Ministry of Family and Social Works

The Ministry of Family and Social Works is the primary public institution responsible for planning, regulating, and coordinating elderly welfare and long-term care services in Türkiye. Within the Ministry, elderly care services are administered by the General Directorate of Services for Persons with Disabilities and the Elderly; the aim is to meet the care needs of elderly individuals through institutional residential care, home care support, economic assistance, and day care services (Özmete & Hussein, 2017; Republic of Türkiye Ministry of Family and Social Services - General Directorate of Services for Persons with Disabilities and the Elderly, 2023). While these services constitute an important public guarantee mechanism for the protection and care needs of elderly individuals, the current system is largely shaped around institutional care and social assistance. Especially considering the rapidly aging population, the sustainability of the current service structure in meeting long-term care needs has become a significant area of debate. One of the most common service models offered by the Ministry in Türkiye is institutional residential care services. Practices such as nursing homes, elderly care and rehabilitation centers, and elderly living facilities aim to protect elderly individuals with high care needs. However, the proliferation of institutional care services can also bring the risk of older individuals becoming isolated from social life and of care processes being limited to a medical framework. Given that the vast majority of older individuals prefer to age in their own homes, policies focused solely on institutional care are insufficient.

Therefore, the development of community-based alternative care models, such as elderly care homes, in recent years can be considered a significant transformation in terms of social inclusion and independent living. Home care support and economic assistance provided by the Ministry aim to help older individuals age in their own homes. However, the fact that this support in Türkiye is primarily delivered through cash assistance mechanisms has, in practice, limited the development of professional care services. Although the original intent of this policy was to encourage families to purchase professional care services from the market-thereby alleviating family burdens and stimulating the professional care sector-the reality often diverges from this goal. Due to insufficient supply of professional services, limited availability of care centers, long waiting lists, or high out-of-pocket costs that remain even with the subsidy, many families are unable to access formal care. Consequently, the cash assistance effectively functions as a substitute for, rather than a facilitator of, professional care, often serving as a meager compensation for the unpaid labor undertaken by family members (predominantly women). This dynamic not only fails to alleviate the actual care burden but also institutionalizes the invisibility of care work and exacerbates caregiver burnout. Furthermore, by failing to generate effective demand for formal services, this approach hinders the growth and professionalization of the broader care economy. This situation shows that care services should be addressed holistically, not only through economic support but also with professional care personnel, psychosocial support mechanisms, and social work interventions. Indeed, as the population ages, the sustainability of family-based care models is increasingly debated. The social support services provided by the Ministry through day care and elderly care centers have significant potential for active aging policies. These centers play important roles in reducing the social isolation of elderly individuals, increasing their social participation, and supporting their psychosocial well-being. However, the prevalence and accessibility of these services are still limited in Türkiye. The inadequacy of day care services, particularly in rural areas and small towns, exacerbates regional inequalities in access to care services for elderly individuals. Therefore, elderly care services need to be restructured not only through a preventative social assistance approach but also around active aging, social participation, and care coordination. In this process, social workers play a central role in assessing care needs, planning services, providing psychosocial support, and coordinating between institutions.

4.3. Elderly care services offered by the Ministry of Health

In Türkiye, elderly care services provided by the Ministry of Health are primarily structured around health and medical care. Home health care services, palliative care applications, geriatric services, and healthy aging centers aim to protect the health of elderly individuals, manage their chronic diseases, and improve their quality of life. The main goal of these services is to facilitate elderly individuals' access to the healthcare system, reduce hospitalizations, and make care processes sustainable in their home environment. Home health care services, in particular, are considered an important service model because they provide support to elderly individuals in their own homes rather than in institutional settings (Solmaz & Altay, 2019).

However, it is observed that home health care services in Türkiye are largely structured around medical care. Although social workers, psychologists, and other social care professionals may be included in the teams formed by the Ministry of Health, in practice services are often shaped around medical care processes (Doğusan, 2019). This situation can lead to the elderly individuals' needs for loneliness, social isolation, caregiver burden, and psychosocial support being relegated to secondary importance. However, the gerontology literature emphasizes that elderly care services should be provided holistically, encompassing not only health-focused but also psychological, social, and environmental dimensions (Ossenfort, 1965; Mohd Tohit & Haque, 2024).

Healthy Aging Centers and tele-medicine applications can be considered among the important innovations in Türkiye in terms of the digitalization of elderly care services and the development of community-based care models. These applications, which facilitate access to health services for individuals in the elderly age group, support the continuity of care services. However, the widespread adoption of digital care services also raises new discussions about digital inequalities and the technology-use skills of elderly individuals (Republic of Türkiye Ministry of Health - General Directorate of Public Hospitals, 2023). The inability of elderly individuals living in rural areas or with limited access to digital technologies to benefit sufficiently from these services can create new areas of inequality in care services.

Palliative care and geriatric services constitute important components that strengthen the medical specialization dimension of the elderly care system in Türkiye. However, the limited coordination between health and social care services within the current system contributes to the fragmentation of care processes; moreover, the insufficient visibility of social workers' roles within interdisciplinary teams often results in the psychosocial dimension of care remaining underdeveloped in practice. In this respect, strengthening the integration between healthcare systems and social work practices has become a critical requirement for the provision of comprehensive and person-centered elderly care services. Indeed, the coordination mechanisms developed between the Ministry of Health and the Ministry of Family and Social Services, together with the introduction of social workers into primary healthcare settings, represent significant developments in terms of advancing an integrated care approach. Within this framework, the protocol signed in 2026 initiated the integration of services provided by the Ministry of Health and the Ministry of

Family and Social Services within Healthy Life Centers. Through the employment of social workers in primary healthcare institutions, the initiative aims to enhance comprehensive care support for older adults by integrating medical, rehabilitative, and psychosocial dimensions of care. Accordingly, this service structure may be considered an important transformation toward the development of a more holistic elderly care system in Türkiye (Republic of Türkiye Ministry of Health, 2026).

4.4. Private-sector and civil-society-based elderly care services

In Türkiye, private-sector and civil-society-based elderly care services are becoming increasingly visible with the rise of the aging population, but remain under-institutionalized. Private nursing homes, private care centers, home care companies, and various civil society initiatives provide care services for elderly individuals. While these services contribute to the diversification of the care system, they differ significantly in terms of financing structures, service standards, and accessibility. In particular, the provision of care services within market mechanisms directly links elderly individuals' access to care services with their economic means (Zaidi et al., 2023; Nazlı, 2025).

Private-sector elderly care services have significant economic potential from a silver-economy perspective. This is because, as the aging population increases, care services create new employment opportunities, encourage the adoption of digital care technologies, and contribute to the growth of the care economy. In particular, private nursing homes, home care companies, and initiatives operating in the field of care technologies make the economic dimension of elderly care services visible. However, the market-oriented development of care services also reveals the tension between the social right nature of care services and the production of economic value. High-cost private care services limit access to professional care for low-income elderly individuals and can shift the care burden back onto family members (Poudel et al., 2024).

The role of NGOs in elderly care services is still in its developmental stage in Türkiye. NGOs primarily provide social support, volunteer opportunities, and initiatives to increase social participation among elderly individuals. However, limited financial resources and insufficiently developed institutional capacity for care services limit the impact of these organizations on the care system. This situation leads to care services in Türkiye being largely provided in a public and family-based manner. Therefore, to more effectively involve the private sector and civil society in the elderly care system, it is necessary to strengthen service standards, improve monitoring mechanisms, and support social work-oriented care coordination. From a gerontology and social work perspective, private-sector and civil-society-based elderly care services should be evaluated not only for economic sustainability but also for social justice, accessibility, and the quality of care. Therefore, while the market-based expansion of elderly care services is important, it is equally crucial that these services are provided in a rights-based, accessible, and integrated manner. Social workers play a critical role in this regard, coordinating care services, protecting the rights of elderly individuals, supporting access to services, and assessing psychosocial needs.

5. PROBLEMS OF THE CARE SYSTEM IN TÜRKIYE FROM A SILVER ECONOMIC PERSPECTIVE

The aging population is increasing demand for care services worldwide and necessitating the restructuring of existing care systems to improve quality, accessibility, and sustainability (Wang et al., 2023; OECD, 2025). The increasing prevalence of chronic diseases, functional losses, and long-term care needs, particularly in older age groups, makes the pressure on health and social work systems more visible. The gerontology literature emphasizes that the care needs of older individuals are not limited to biomedical issues; they should be considered alongside multidimensional factors such as social support, psychological well-being, environmental adaptation, and community participation. However, in Türkiye, the insufficient integration of elderly care services across the health and social work systems limits the development of a person-centered, holistic approach to care (Atasü Topcuoğlu, 2021; İzdeş Terkoğlu & Memiş, 2022). This situation can lead to only the medical needs of older individuals being prioritized in care processes, while psychosocial support mechanisms remain secondary. Therefore, the current system is insufficient to meet the complex care needs of elderly individuals holistically.

The silver economy approach views elderly care services not merely as an area of social assistance or public spending, but as a strategic sector that generates economic value, creates employment, and supports social innovation (European Commission, 2018). However, structural problems in Türkiye's current care system limit the effective use of the potential offered by the silver economy. One of the most prominent problems in elderly care services in Türkiye is that the inadequacy of formal care systems forces care processes to rely largely on informal, family-based structures. Although gerontological approaches emphasize the principle of "aging in place," which supports elderly individuals in their own living environments, the sustainability of this approach depends on the availability of robust formal care systems (Wang et al., 2023). As in many countries around the world, the inadequacy of formal care systems in meeting total care needs in Türkiye results in the transfer of the care burden largely to family members (Gok Metin et al., 2019; OECD, 2025). This situation particularly increases women's unpaid care work and deepens gender inequalities. It also limits the professionalization of care services and the development of the care sector as a sustainable economic area.

In Türkiye, the fact that care services are largely family-centered leads to limited demand and investment in professional care services. This makes it difficult to institutionalize care services and creates significant problems with care quality and service standardization. In particular, the relatively limited participation of the private sector in elderly care services and the fact that existing services are mostly provided at high costs increase income-based inequalities in access to professional care services (WHO, 2020). The fact that private sector-based care services mainly cater to high-income groups makes it difficult for low-income elderly individuals to access care services. It again concentrates the care burden on family members. Therefore, expanding care services in Türkiye solely through market mechanisms can create problems of social justice and accessibility. All these structural characteristics can be considered among the main problem areas that limit the social inclusion and sustainable growth potential of the silver economy.

From an economic sustainability perspective, long-term care expenditures are expected to increase rapidly in Türkiye due to an aging population (Oğlak, 2023; OECD, 2025). This situation creates significant financial pressure on public budgets and underscores the need for new policies to finance care services. The silver economy approach considers the care sector a strategic sector for new employment opportunities, care technologies, service innovation, and local economic development (European Commission, 2018). However, the literature indicates that the main factors limiting the development of the care sector include the shortage of a care workforce, low wages, worsening working conditions, limited public investment, and the continuous increase in the cost of care services (Iwański, 2024). In the Turkish context, the coexistence of these problems makes it difficult for elderly care services to establish a sustainable social and economic structure. In particular, the lack of coordination among social work, health, and care systems leads to fragmented care services and limits the development of the care economy. Therefore, for the sustainability of elderly care services in Türkiye, the development of social work-oriented, integrated, and multi-actor care models is an important necessity.

6. PROPOSAL FOR AN INTEGRATED SOCIAL WORK AND CARE ECONOMY MODEL

The "Integrated Social Work and Care Economy Model" proposed in this study aims to overcome the current fragmented structure of elderly care services in Türkiye and to transform care services into a holistic, sustainable, and coordinated system. The model proposes a multi-actor care system based on cooperation among public institutions, the private sector, local governments, and civil society organizations (Figure 1). The fact that care services in Türkiye are currently provided independently by different institutions creates significant problems with service continuity, coordination, and accessibility. Therefore, the model's fundamental starting point is the creation of a central coordination mechanism that integrates the health, social work, and economic dimensions of elderly care services. Such a coordination structure is of strategic importance for ensuring standardized care services, reducing service duplication, and using resources more efficiently.

Figure 1. Integrated social work and care economy model

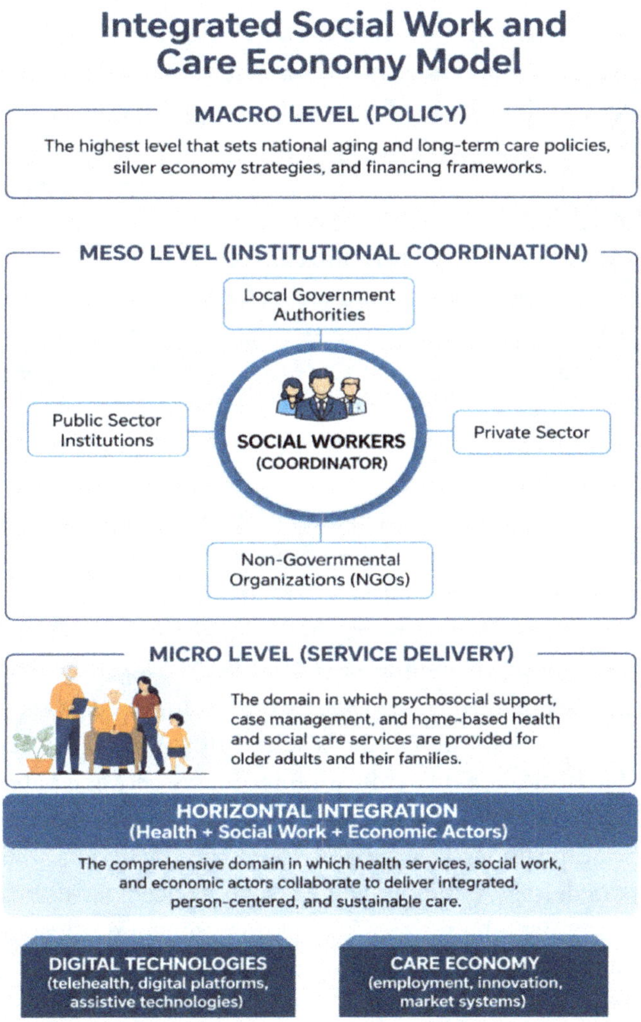

The model's core components are service integration, psychosocial support mechanisms, the use of digital technologies, and principles of economic sustainability. In particular, the coordinated delivery of care services by different actors enables a more effective meeting of the multifaceted needs of elderly individuals. This approach recognizes that elderly care is not solely medical; it is a biopsychosocial process encompassing social support, psychological well-being, social participation, and environmental adaptation. Therefore, within the model, psychosocial support services are considered an integral component of standard care processes. The aim is to systematically address issues frequently highlighted in gerontological literature, such as loneliness, social isolation, caregiver burden, and the risk of depression (Koosha & Lalegani, 2024; Shao et al., 2022). In this respect, the model aims to transform care services from a structure that only meets physical needs into a holistic social care system that supports quality of life. Economic sustainability constitutes another fundamental dimension of the model. In Türkiye, the rapidly increasing demand for care services driven by an aging population suggests that existing public resources may be insufficient in the long term. Therefore, the model encourages public-private partnerships, social entrepreneurship practices, and mechanisms that support the local care economy to sustain care services.

In line with the silver economy approach, care services are considered not only as a social assistance area but also as a strategic sector that creates employment, promotes service innovation, and contributes to local economic development. Areas such as care technologies, digital health applications, and community-based care services offer significant opportunities for developing the care economy. However, the fragmented structure of care services and the limited professional care infrastructure in Türkiye make it difficult to leverage this economic potential effectively. Therefore, the model proposes the development of multi-source and sustainable mechanisms for financing care services. The model is structured within a multilayered framework consisting of macro, mezzo, and micro levels. The macro level encompasses aging policies, long-term care strategies, legal regulations related to care services, and financing mechanisms. At this level, the goal is to create national policy frameworks that will support the sustainability of care services. The mezzo-level refers to the institutional coordination processes between public institutions, local governments, the private sector, and civil society organizations. In the model, social workers are positioned as the key coordinating actors at the mezzo-level. Social workers undertake critical functions such as needs assessment, referral to appropriate services, facilitating inter-institutional communication, monitoring care plans, and administering psychosocial support processes. In this respect, social workers are considered not only service providers but also coordinating actors who ensure the integrated functioning of the system. The micro-level encompasses older individuals, family members, and caregivers, focusing directly on service delivery processes. The model's micro-level approach is consistent with the principle of "aging in place," supporting older individuals in maintaining their independence and continuing to live in their own homes.

One of the most critical components of the model is the service flow and coordination mechanism. This process consists of four basic stages: (i) needs assessment, (ii) service planning, (iii) referral to appropriate service providers, and (iv) monitoring and evaluation. In the first stage of the process, social workers comprehensively assess the elderly individual's health status, economic conditions, social support networks, care needs, and psychosocial risks. The individual care plan created based on this assessment is implemented through coordination between different institutions and service providers. Regular monitoring and feedback mechanisms support the continuity and quality of care services. Thus, the model aims to create an integrated, person-centered service flow rather than fragmented care practices. The model also aims to build an interdisciplinary bridge between the literature of social work, gerontology, and the silver economy. While current discussions on elderly care services in Türkiye are mostly conducted within the framework of health services or social assistance, the economic dimension of care services is addressed only to a limited extent. However, with the aging population, care services are becoming a fundamental agenda area for both social welfare systems and economic structures. In this context, the model proposed in this study has the potential to contribute to the creation of new employment opportunities in the care sector, the development of service diversity, the support of local economic development, and the more sustainable organization of care services. Furthermore, by centering on the coordination role of social workers in care services, the model proposes that care processes be evaluated not only from a medical perspective but also from social, psychological, and economic dimensions. In this respect, the model can be considered a unique approach that aims to both address the interdisciplinary gap in the academic literature and develop a concrete, applicable care coordination framework for practitioners.

CONCLUSION AND RECOMMENDATIONS

This study analyzes the current structure of elderly care services in Türkiye from the perspectives of the silver economy, gerontology, and social work, discussing the fundamental structural problems and the system's transformation potential. The evaluations conducted within the scope of the study reveal that although elderly care services in Türkiye are provided within a multi-actor structure by public institutions, local governments, the private sector, NGOs, and family members, the services are largely fragmented. Lack of inter-institutional coordination, differences in service standards, regional inequalities, and the reliance of care services on mostly informal care mechanisms are among the main problems limiting the effectiveness of the current system. In particular, the fact that family members largely bear the care burden, including women, makes both the professionalization of care services and the sustainable development of the care economy difficult. In addition, the rapidly increasing demand for care services due to an aging population raises significant questions about the long-term sustainability of existing care models. The study also emphasizes that the silver economy approach offers significant opportunities for restructuring elderly care services in Türkiye. The silver economy perspective views elderly care services not only as an area of social assistance or public spending, but also as a strategic sector that creates employment, supports service innovation, and contributes to local economic development. However, the current fragmented structure of care services in Türkiye, the limited professional care infrastructure, and the lack of intersectoral coordination make it difficult to utilize this economic and social potential effectively. This situation shows that elderly care services should be re-evaluated not only within the framework of health-focused approaches but also through a multidimensional lens that integrates social work, care economics, local development, and gerontological perspectives. In this context, the "Integrated Social Work and Care Economics Model" developed within the scope of this study offers a holistic framework for the restructuring of elderly care services in Türkiye. The model proposes a coordination-based cooperation mechanism among health services, social work systems, local governments, the private sector, and civil society organizations. In particular, the positioning of social workers as coordinating actors enables them to address care services not only from a medical perspective but also from psychosocial, economic, and societal perspectives. The model also supports public-private partnerships, digital care technologies, community-based care practices, and innovative care models to enhance the sustainability of care services. In this respect, the proposed model is based on a person-centered, integrated care approach that supports elderly individuals in maintaining their independence and continuing to live in their own homes. At the macro level, Türkiye primarily needs to develop integrated, long-term care policies and strengthen coordination between the health and social work systems. Updating legal regulations regarding elderly care services, standardizing care services, and creating sustainable financing models should be among the key priorities of this process. In addition, strengthening the role of local governments in elderly care services and planning care services that are sensitive to local needs can facilitate access to services and help reduce regional inequalities. Furthermore, encouraging private-sector participation in care services offers significant opportunities for developing the care economy, including creating care-related employment, enhancing the professionalization of care services, and contributing tax revenue to local economies, which aligns with the silver economy's theoretical positioning of care services as a strategic sector. However, because developing care services solely through market mechanisms can lead to inequalities in access to quality care (where high-income groups can afford premium professional care services while low-income groups struggle to access them), private-sector practices need to be supported by strong oversight and regulatory mechanisms aligned with the principles of social justice to ensure equitable access to care services.

At the micro and mezzo levels, strengthening social workers' coordination role within the care system is a crucial necessity. Social workers taking a more active role in needs assessment, case management, care planning, psychosocial support, and inter-institutional referral processes will support the delivery of person-centered and holistic care services. In particular, integrating psychosocial issues that directly affect the quality of life of elderly individuals, such as loneliness, social isolation, caregiver burden, and depression, into the care system is critically important. Accordingly, the concept of social care needs to become a fundamental component of the elderly care system. In conclusion, the future of elderly care services in Türkiye is closely linked not only to the expansion of health services but also to the development of integrated policies that bring together the perspectives of social work, gerontology, care economics, and the silver economy. This study contributes to the re-evaluation of elderly care services in Türkiye within the framework of the silver economy, while also creating an interdisciplinary discussion platform to transform care services into a human-centered, accessible, sustainable, and coordinated structure. The study also suggests new research agendas for future research in areas such as the economic impact of care services, access to services in rural areas, the adoption of digital care practices, and the effectiveness of cross-sector collaborations.

REFERENCES

Akyol Güner, T., & Ulama, G. (2025). Avrupa ve Türkiye'de yaşlı bakım modellerinin karşılaştırmalı analizi: Türkiye için bir model önerisi [Comparative Analysis of Elderly Care Models in Europe and Türkiye: A Model Proposal for Türkiye]. *Yaşlı Sorunları Araştırma Dergisi (YSAD)* [EIRJ]. *Elderly Issues Research Journal, 18*(2), 130–146. DOI: 10.46414/yasad.1711656

Atasü Topcuoğlu, R. (2021). Gender inequality, the welfare state, disability, and distorted commodification of care in Türkiye. *New Perspectives on Turkey, 66*, 61–87. DOI: 10.1017/npt.2020.35

Aydın, A. (2024). Türkiye ve seçilmiş Avrupa ülkelerinde evde bakım hizmetlerinin organizasyonu, kapsamı ve içeriği [Organization, Scope and Content of Home Care Services in Türkiye and Selected European Countries]. *Gümüşhane Üniversitesi Sağlık Bilimleri Dergisi, 13*(3), 1408–1421. DOI: 10.37989/gumussagbil.1410883

Baumeister, R. F., & Leary, M. R. (1997). Writing narrative literature reviews. *Review of General Psychology, 1*(3), 311–320. DOI: 10.1037/1089-2680.1.3.311

Bowen, G. A. (2009). Document analysis as a qualitative research method. *Qualitative Research Journal, 9*(2), 27–40. DOI: 10.3316/QRJ0902027

Çakmur, H. (2015). Frailty among elderly adults in a rural area of Türkiye. *Medical Science Monitor, 21*, 1232–1242. DOI: 10.12659/MSM.893400 PMID: 25925800

Colombo, F., Llena Nozal, A., Mercier, J., & Tjadens, F. (2011). *Help wanted? Providing and paying for long-term care*. OECD Publishing., DOI: 10.1787/9789264097759-en

Costa Font, J., Jiménez Martín, S., & Vilaplana Prieto, C. (2022). Do public caregiving subsidies and supports affect the provision of care and transfers? *Journal of Health Economics, 84*, 102639. Advance online publication. DOI: 10.1016/j.jhealeco.2022.102639 PMID: 35671607

Creswell, J. W., & Creswell, J. D. (2018). *Research design: Qualitative, quantitative, and mixed methods approaches* (5th ed.). Sage.

Doğusan, A. R. (2019). Türkiye'de evde sağlık hizmetleri ile ilgili mevzuat ve gelişimi [Legislation and Development of Home Health Services in Türkiye]. *Ankara Medical Journal, 19*(3), 684–693. DOI: 10.17098/amj.624563

Eager, B., Maritz, A., & Millemann, J. (2022). The silver economy on wheels: A narrative review of the mature-aged, hypermobile gig worker phenomena. *Small Enterprise Research*, *29*(1), 68–85. DOI: 10.1080/13215906.2022.2032295

Eriksson, E., & Hellström, A. (2021). Multi-actor resource integration: A service approach in public management. *British Journal of Management*, *32*(2), 456–472. DOI: 10.1111/1467-8551.12414

European Commission. (2018). *The silver economy: Final report.* https://doi.org/ DOI: 10.2759/685036

Evers, A. (2005). Mixed welfare systems and hybrid organizations: Changes in the governance and provision of social services. *International Journal of Public Administration*, *28*(9-10), 737–748. DOI: 10.1081/PAD-200067318

Gok Metin, Z., Karadas, C., Balci, C., & Cankurtaran, M. (2019). The perceived caregiver burden among Turkish family caregivers providing care for frail older adults. *Journal of Transcultural Nursing : Official Journal of the Transcultural Nursing Society*, *30*(3), 222–230. DOI: 10.1177/1043659618790041 PMID: 30040049

Greenfield, E. A., Black, K., Buffel, T., & Yeh, J. (2018). Community gerontology: A framework for research, policy, and practice on communities and aging. *The Gerontologist*, *59*(5), 803–810. DOI: 10.1093/geront/gny089 PMID: 30124872

Hooyman, N. R., & Kiyak, H. A. (2011). *Social gerontology: A multidisciplinary perspective* (9th ed.). Pearson.

International Labour Organization. (2022). *Care at work: Investing in care leave and services for a more gender equal world of work* (L. Addati, U. Cattaneo, & E. Pozzan, Eds.). International Labour Office. https://www.ilo.org/sites/default/files/wcmsp5/groups/public/@dgreports/@dcomm/documents/publication/wcms_838653.pdf

Iwański, R. (2024). Growth prospects for the silver economy in the market segment of residential care services provided to dependent elderly people. *Economics and Business Review*, *10*(2), 165–186. DOI: 10.18559/ebr.2024.2.1255

Jayawardhana, T., Jayathilaka, R., Nimnadi, T., Anuththara, S., Karadanaarachchi, R., Galappaththi, K., & Dharmasena, T. (2023). The cost of aging: Economic growth perspectives for Europe. *PLoS One*, *18*(6), e0287207. Advance online publication. DOI: 10.1371/journal.pone.0287207 PMID: 37352177

Karahan, A., & Güven, S. (2002). Yaşlılıkta evde bakım [Homecare for elderly]. *Türk Geriatri Dergisi*, *5*(4), 155–159.

Koosha, M., & Lalegani, A. (2024). Assessing the social health of the elderly in Tehran: Challenges and strategic solutions. *Archives of Gerontology and Geriatrics Plus, 1*(4), 100091. Advance online publication. DOI: 10.1016/j.aggp.2024.100091

Koru Uzkurt, B. (2023). Toplumsal ve ekonomik bir dönüşüm olarak gümüş ekonomi modeli [The silver economy model as a social and economic transformation]. *Tüketici ve Tüketim Araştırmaları Dergisi, 15*(1), 299–324. DOI: 10.15659/ttad.15.1.171

Mohd Tohit, N. F., & Haque, M. (2024). Gerontology in public health: A scoping review of current perspectives and interventions. *Cureus, 16*(7), e65896. Advance online publication. DOI: 10.7759/cureus.65896 PMID: 39092340

Nazlı, E. (2025). Türkiye'de yaşlılara yönelik sosyal hizmetlerin tarihsel gelişimi [Historical development of social services for the elderly in Türkiye]. *International Journal of Social and Humanities Sciences Research, 112*(115), 171–182. DOI: 10.5281/zenodo.14787691

Oğlak, S. (2023). Bakım yoksulluğu ve uzun süreli bakım politikaları ilişkisi [The relationship between care poverty and long-term care policies]. *İktisat ve Toplum, 149*, 74-84.

Oktar, M. N. (2025). Evde yalnız yaşayan yaşlı bireylerin deneyimleri: Sosyal hizmet bağlamında bir değerlendirme [Experiences of Elderly Individuals Living Alone at Home: An Assessment in the Context of Social Work]. *Sosyal Politika Çalışmaları Dergisi, 25*(67), 310–344. DOI: 10.21560/spcd.vi.1563712

Organization for Economic Co-operation and Development. (2005). *Long-term care for older people*. OECD Publishing., DOI: 10.1787/9789264015852-

Organization for Economic Co-operation and Development. (2025). *The economic benefit of promoting healthy ageing and community care*. OECD Publishing., DOI: 10.1787/0f7bc62b-

Ossenfort, W. (1965). Handbook of social gerontology. *Archives of Internal Medicine, 116*(5), 804–805. DOI: 10.1001/archinte.1965.03870050158041

Özmete, E., & Hussein, S. (2017). *Türkiye'de yaşlı bakım hizmetleri raporu: Avrupa'dan en iyi uygulama örnekleri ve Türkiye için bir model tasarımı [Report on elderly care services in Türkiye: Best practice examples from Europe and a model design for Türkiye]. Republic of Türkiye Ministry of Family and Social Policies.* https://www.aile.gov.tr/media/26767 1/tuerkiye-de-yas-li-bakim-hizmetleri-avrupa-dan -en-iyi-uygulama-oernekleri-ve-tuerkiye-ic-in-bir-model-tasarimi-proje-kitabi.pdf

Poudel, K., Malla, D. K., & Thapa, K. (2024). Health care service utilization among elderly in rural setting of Gandaki province, Nepal: A mixed method study. *Frontiers in Health Services, 4*, 1321020. Advance online publication. DOI: 10.3389/frhs.2024.1321020 PMID: 39386356

Razavi, S. (2007). *The political and social economy of care in a development context: Conceptual issues, research questions and policy options* (Gender and Development Programme Paper No. 3). UNRISD.

Republic of Türkiye Ministry of Family and Social Services - General Directorate of Services for Persons with Disabilities and the Elderly. (2023). *Yaşlı bireyler için bilgilendirme rehberi-IV* [Information guide for elderly individuals-IV]. https://www.aile.gov.tr/media/143153/yasli_bireyler_i-cin_bilgilendirme_rehberi_2023.pdf

Republic of Türkiye Ministry of Health. (2026, April 2). *Sağlık Bakanlığı ile Aile ve Sosyal Hizmetler Bakanlığı arasında iş birliği protokolü imzalandı* [A cooperation protocol was signed between the Ministry of Health and the Ministry of Family and Social Services]. https://www.saglik.gov.tr/TR-117252/saglik-bakanligi-ile-aile-ve-sosyal-hizmetler-bakanligi-arasinda-is-birligi-protokolu-imzalandi.html

Republic of Türkiye Ministry of Health - General Directorate of Public Hospitals. (2023, April 10). *Sağlıklı yaş alma merkezlerinin kurulmasına dair genelge yayımlandı* [Circular on the establishment of healthy aging centers has been published]. https://khgmsaglikhizmetleridb.saglik.gov.tr/TR-96308/saglikli-yas-alma-merkezlerinin-kurulmasina-dair-genelge-yayimlandi.html

Sanders, S., Kolomer, S. R., Spellman, C. W., & Rizzo, V. M. (Eds.). (2019). *Gerontological social work and the grand challenges: Focusing on policy and practice*. Springer., DOI: 10.1007/978-3-030-26334-8

Shao, M., Chen, J., & Ma, C. (2022). Research on the relationship between Chinese elderly health status, social security, and depression. *International Journal of Environmental Research and Public Health, 19*(12), 7496. Advance online publication. DOI: 10.3390/ijerph19127496 PMID: 35742744

Solmaz, T., & Altay, B. (2019). Yaşlılara yönelik evde bakım hizmetleri [Home care services for elder people]. *Sağlık Akademisyenleri Dergisi, 6*(2), 150-157. https://izlik.org/JA66FE63WK

Thurston, C. N. (2015). Policy feedback in the public-private welfare state: Advocacy groups and access to government homeownership programs, 1934-1954. *Studies in American Political Development, 29*(2), 250–267. DOI: 10.1017/S0898588X15000097

Turkish Statistical Institute. (2026). *İstatistiklerle yaşlılar, 2025* [Elderly statistics, 2025]. https://veriportali.tuik.gov.tr/tr/press/58231

Wang, H., Coyte, P. C., Shi, W., Zong, X., & Zhong, R. (2023). Social governance and sustainable development in elderly services: Innovative models, strategies, and stakeholder perspectives. *Sustainability (Basel), 15*(21), 15414. Advance online publication. DOI: 10.3390/su152115414

World Health Organization. (2020). *Decade of healthy ageing: Baseline report.* https://www.who.int/publications/i/item/9789240017900

Yıldırım, H. H. (2012). *Sağlık sigortacılığı* [Health insurance]. Anadolu Üniversitesi Yayınları.

Zaidi, I., Sharma, T., Chaudhary, S., Alam, A., Anjum, S., & Vardha, J. (2023). Barriers to access healthcare among the elderly population in rural regions of India. *International Journal of Community Medicine and Public Health, 10*(11), 4480–4484. DOI: 10.18203/2394-6040.ijcmph20233498

Chapter 9
Health-Oriented Residential Care Models Within the Silver Economy Ecosystem: Policy and Practice Analysis in Da Nang, Vietnam

Lam Thi Le
http://orcid.org/0009-0007-2301-8026
University of Science and Education, The University Da Nang, Vietnam

ABSTRACT

In the context of rapid population aging and the emergence of the silver economy in Vietnam, developing health-oriented residential care models for older adults has become increasingly urgent. This chapter examines such models in Da Nang City, focusing on policy frameworks, service organization, and the integration of health-care, social work, and rehabilitation. Using a case study design, the study draws on policy analysis and qualitative data from documents and semi-structured interviews with key stakeholders. The findings indicate a shift toward a multi-actor system involving the state, private sector, and community, alongside the early development of integrated care models. However, key challenges persist, including institutional fragmentation, workforce shortages, weak intersectoral coordination, and limited private sector participation. Policy directions are proposed to strengthen integrated care and advance the silver economy ecosystem in Vietnam.

DOI: 10.4018/979-8-3373-9370-4.ch009

1. INTRODUCTION

1.1. Global Population Aging and the Restructuring of Long-Term Care Systems

Population aging has emerged as a global and irreversible demographic trend. According to projections by the United Nations, the number of individuals aged 60 and over is expected to increase rapidly in the coming decades, particularly in developing countries. This demographic shift not only alters population structures but also places significant pressure on social protection systems, healthcare services, and long-term care provision.

In this context, traditional family-based care systems are increasingly revealing their limitations, especially in rapidly urbanizing settings. Declining household sizes, rising labor migration, and broader social transformations have reduced the capacity for informal care for older adults.

As a result, many countries are transitioning from informal care models toward institutionalized long-term care systems, encompassing home-based care, community-based services, and, notably, residential care. This transition represents a critical restructuring aimed at ensuring the sustainability of care systems in the context of accelerated population aging.

1.2. The Silver Economy as an Emerging Socioeconomic Development Paradigm

The silver economy refers to the aggregate of economic activities, services, products, and policies designed to meet the needs of older adults while simultaneously harnessing the economic potential of this population group.

Unlike traditional approaches that primarily view older adults as beneficiaries of social welfare, the silver economy reframes them as active socioeconomic agents both as consumers of care services and as contributors to society.

Within this framework, healthcare, long-term care, and particularly residential care services constitute key components of the silver economy. These are not only social services but also high value-added service sectors that intersect with healthcare, social work, rehabilitation, care technologies, and service management.

Accordingly, the development of the silver economy necessitates a restructuring of care models toward greater integration across social welfare systems, healthcare systems, and market-based mechanisms.

1.3. The Increasing Importance of Residential Care in Aging Societies

Residential care is a form of long-term care designed for older adults who are no longer able to live independently or who require continuous support in daily living. Within this model, older adults reside in care facilities where they receive a combination of healthcare services, personal care, psychosocial support, and rehabilitation.

In the context of population aging, the role of residential care is becoming increasingly significant for three main reasons. First, the demand for complex care is rising, particularly in relation to chronic conditions, dementia, and functional decline. Second, the family is no longer the sole provider of care due to shifting social structures and economic pressures. Third, the need to enhance quality of life and preserve the dignity of older adults calls for professional, organized, and interdisciplinary care models.

However, in practice, residential care models in many developing countries remain fragmented, with limited integration across healthcare, social, and rehabilitation services, resulting in suboptimal care outcomes.

1.4. Research Gap: Limited Evidence from Middle-Income Countries

Although a growing body of international research has examined the silver economy and long-term care systems, most existing evidence is concentrated in high-income countries with well-developed welfare systems, such as Japan, South Korea, and European nations.

In contrast, middle-income countries particularly in Southeast Asia still lack systematic research on several key aspects: the development and operation of residential care models; the degree of integration across healthcare, social work, and rehabilitation services; the role of the private sector in care provision; and the regulatory policy frameworks in the transition toward a silver economy.

In this context, Vietnam represents a critical case study, where rapid population aging is occurring alongside a long-term care system that remains in its early stages of development. Da Nang City, as a dynamic urban center with notable social welfare initiatives, provides a representative setting to examine the emergence and functioning of residential care models in practice.

This study therefore contributes to addressing the existing scholarly gap by providing empirical evidence from a developing country undergoing the formation of a silver economy ecosystem.

1.5. Research Objectives and Questions

This chapter aims to analyze the development of health-oriented residential care models within the silver economy ecosystem in Da Nang City, Vietnam. The analysis focuses on four key dimensions: the relevant policy framework, the organization and delivery of services, the level of integration across care sectors, and the challenges and policy implications in the context of the silver economy.

The chapter is guided by the following research questions:

(i) How are residential care models in Da Nang developed and operated within the context of the silver economy?

(ii) To what extent are healthcare, social work, and rehabilitation services integrated within these models?

(iii) Which policy and institutional factors facilitate or hinder the development of residential care models?

(iv) What policy implications can be drawn to promote a more sustainable silver economy ecosystem in Vietnam?

2. RESIDENTIAL CARE WITHIN THE SILVER ECONOMY ECOSYSTEM

2.1. Long-Term Care Systems and Organizational Models

Long-term care (LTC) refers to a system of health, social, and personal support services for individuals experiencing prolonged functional limitations, particularly older adults (World Health Organization [WHO], 2015). LTC encompasses not only medical care but also assistance with daily living activities, rehabilitation, and social support aimed at maintaining quality of life and individual independence.

In international contexts, LTC systems are typically organized into three main models: home-based care, community-based care, and residential care (OECD, 2020). The Nordic model emphasizes the role of the state in providing universal services, whereas East Asian models, such as those in Japan and South Korea, have developed comprehensive long-term care insurance systems that combine state provision with market mechanisms (Campbell et al., 2010).

In many developing countries, LTC systems remain insufficiently institutionalized, resulting in a heavy reliance on family-based and informal care (UNESCAP, 2017). This situation creates significant service gaps in the context of rapidly accelerating population aging.

2.2. The Concept of Healthcare-Oriented Residential Care

In the context of rapid population aging and changing family structures, long-term care models have undergone significant transformations, with residential care playing an increasingly important role. Residential care is commonly understood as a model in which older adults transition from family-based living arrangements to long-term residence in specialized care facilities, where they receive comprehensive support services. These services extend beyond medical care to include assistance with daily living, psychosocial support, and rehabilitation aimed at maintaining independence and enhancing quality of life (Sancho et al., 2017).

However, the growing prevalence of chronic conditions, functional decline, and complex care needs among older adults has led to a notable shift in the approach to residential care. Rather than focusing solely on custodial care, contemporary models increasingly adopt a healthcare-oriented perspective. This approach emphasizes integrated service delivery, in which three core components, namely healthcare, social work, and rehabilitation, are closely coordinated within a unified system.

Specifically, healthcare services are responsible for managing chronic diseases, monitoring health conditions, and providing clinical interventions when necessary. Social work focuses on psychosocial support, social connectivity, the maintenance of family and community relationships, and the protection of older adults' rights throughout the care process. Rehabilitation plays a critical role in maintaining and improving physical mobility, cognitive functioning, and overall autonomy. The integration of these components shifts the focus of care from meeting basic needs to optimizing overall health and functional capacity.

This orientation is also consistent with the recommendations of the World Health Organization, which emphasizes that modern long-term care systems should be structured around integrated care models that ensure continuity of services across different levels, from hospitals and community settings to residential facilities (World Health Organization, 2021). This is particularly important given that older adults often require continuous and multidimensional care, necessitating close coordination among service providers.

In rapidly aging contexts, especially in developing countries, healthcare-oriented residential care is increasingly seen as a critical intermediary solution. It occupies a position between family-based care, which is declining due to social changes, and hospital-based care, which is often costly and not suited for long-term needs. According to OECD (2020), the development of integrated residential care models can reduce pressure on hospital systems while enhancing the efficiency and sustainability of long-term care systems as a whole.

In sum, healthcare-oriented residential care can be understood as an integrated care model in which health, social, and rehabilitation services are systematically coordinated to meet the comprehensive needs of older adults. This model not only reflects a shift in care paradigms but also represents a key component of the silver economy ecosystem, where elder care functions both as a pillar of social welfare and as a service sector with significant development potential.

2.3. The Silver Economy as an Ecosystem

In the context of accelerating global population aging, the concept of the silver economy has emerged as a new approach to redefining the role of older adults in socioeconomic development. According to the European Commission, the silver economy encompasses all economic activities related to the needs, consumption capacity, and contributions of individuals aged 50 and over, spanning sectors such as healthcare, long-term care, financial services, housing, assistive technologies, and services aimed at enhancing quality of life (European Commission, 2018).

Recent approaches increasingly conceptualize the silver economy as an ecosystem involving interconnected actors, services, and policy institutions rather than as a single market sector. This perspective highlights the interactions among the state, private sector, families, and social organizations in shaping care services and support systems for older adults.

Within this ecosystem, care services, particularly long-term care and residential care, occupy a central role, as they are directly linked to the essential needs of older adults and are closely connected with other sectors such as healthcare, insurance, technology, and social services. Consequently, the development of care models cannot be understood in isolation from the broader context of the silver economy ecosystem.

2.3.1. Market Actors

A core characteristic of the silver economy ecosystem is the participation of multiple groups of actors, each performing distinct roles while maintaining close interactions with one another.

The state plays a central role in establishing policy frameworks, regulating the market, and ensuring social equity. Through social protection policies, insurance schemes, service standards, and financial mechanisms, the state not only shapes the development of care systems but also enables the participation of other actors. In the context of the silver economy, the role of the state is particularly important in balancing welfare objectives with economic efficiency (World Health Organization, 2015).

The private sector is increasingly becoming a key actor in the provision of care services for older adults. Private enterprises are involved in a wide range of activities, including the operation of residential care facilities, the provision of healthcare services, the development of long-term care insurance, and investment in assistive technologies. Their participation contributes to service diversification, quality improvement, and innovation. At the same time, it raises the need for effective regulatory mechanisms to ensure equitable access and to prevent inequalities in service provision.

In addition, social organizations and non-governmental organizations play a complementary role, particularly in delivering community-based services, supporting vulnerable groups, and promoting social innovation. These organizations often operate with greater flexibility, maintain close connections with local communities, and help address gaps that are not fully covered by the state or the market.

Family members and informal caregivers constitute another indispensable component of the silver economy ecosystem. In many Asian countries, including Vietnam, families remain the primary providers of care for older adults. According to WHO (2015), informal care accounts for a substantial share of total long-term care provision, although it is often underrecognized in formal economic systems. The role of the family is not only culturally significant but also directly influences the demand for and organization of formal care services.

The interaction among these groups of actors forms the operational structure of the silver economy ecosystem. As noted by Maresova et al. (2019), the development of this ecosystem depends on the effectiveness of coordination among the state, the market, and society. When these actors are connected through appropriate policy mechanisms and service networks, the silver economy can function as both a driver of economic growth and a means of improving the quality of life of older adults (Maresova et al, 2019).

2.3.2. Care Services within the Silver Economy Ecosystem

Within the silver economy ecosystem, care services occupy a central position, as they directly reflect the diverse and increasingly complex needs of older adults. Unlike conventional consumer markets, care services for older adults combine medical, social, and functional support elements, requiring integrated and interdisciplinary approaches in both organization and delivery.

Healthcare and long-term care services constitute the core pillars of the care system. These services include chronic disease management, clinical care, nursing care, and assistance with daily living for older adults experiencing functional decline. According to the Organisation for Economic Co-operation and Development, demand for long-term care services is rising rapidly across most countries due to increased life expectancy and the growing prevalence of non-communicable diseases (OECD, 2020). As a result, long-term care has become one of the fastest-growing sectors within the silver economy.

Housing and residential care services also play a crucial role in ensuring safe, stable, and supported living environments for older adults. These include nursing homes, assisted living facilities, and age-friendly housing models. Beyond providing accommodation, such models integrate personal care, basic healthcare, and social support, thereby creating comprehensive living environments. In the context of urbanization and shrinking family size, these services are increasingly necessary as alternatives or complements to traditional family-based care.

Rehabilitation services are increasingly recognized as an essential component of elder care. Rather than focusing solely on treatment, rehabilitation aims to maintain and improve physical mobility, cognitive function, and autonomy. This not only enhances quality of life but also helps reduce the long-term care burden. According to WHO (2021), integrating rehabilitation into long-term care systems is a key element in developing person-centered care models (World Health Organization, 2021).

Another notable trend is the growing role of care technologies, including assistive technologies and digital health solutions. Innovations such as remote health monitoring, emergency response systems, artificial intelligence in care support, and smart home environments are transforming service delivery. These technologies improve care efficiency and enable older adults to maintain independence for longer periods within familiar settings.

Despite the increasing diversity of care services, their organization and delivery are strongly shaped by institutional structures and levels of national development. According to OECD (2020), countries with more developed long-term care systems tend to adopt hybrid models, where certain services are market-based to enhance flexibility and efficiency, while the state maintains a strong regulatory role to ensure equity and access. Balancing market mechanisms with social welfare objectives is therefore critical to the sustainable development of care service ecosystems. (OECD, 2020).

From an ecosystem perspective, care services do not operate in isolation but are interconnected through flows of demand, financing, and information. Effective development of these services requires not only expanding supply but also strengthening integration across service types, thereby creating a continuous, flexible care system that better responds to the multidimensional needs of older adults within the silver economy.

Recent developments in digital health and artificial intelligence (AI) are increasingly transforming long-term care systems and residential care services for older adults. Technologies such as telehealth, remote monitoring systems, AI-assisted care management, and smart-home environments are improving service efficiency while supporting independent living and personalized care. In ageing societies, these technologies are becoming important components of integrated care systems, particularly in contexts facing workforce shortages and rising care demands (World

Health Organization, 2022; Marston et al., 2022). However, unequal access to digital technologies and limited digital literacy among older adults remain important challenges for implementation.

2.4. Intersectoral Integration: Healthcare, Social Work, and Rehabilitation

A defining feature of contemporary residential care models is interdisciplinarity, reflecting a shift from fragmented approaches toward integrated, comprehensive, and person-centered care. As care needs become increasingly complex, encompassing biomedical, psychosocial, and functional dimensions, organizing services along isolated sectoral lines is no longer effective. Instead, modern care systems require close coordination across multiple professional domains.

According to the World Health Organization, effective care for older adults should be developed under the framework of integrated people-centered care, in which services are designed around individual needs rather than administrative structures (World Health Organization, 2021). Within this model, three core pillars, healthcare, social work, and rehabilitation, are interconnected within a continuous care pathway.

Healthcare provides the foundation for managing the physical health of older adults, including diagnosis and treatment, chronic disease management, nursing care, and clinical interventions. However, a solely medical focus is insufficient to address the broader and more complex needs of older adults, particularly those related to psychological well-being, social relationships, and overall quality of life.

Social work extends the scope of care to non-medical dimensions, including psychosocial support, strengthening social connections, maintaining family and community relationships, and safeguarding the rights and interests of older adults. Social workers often act as key coordinators, facilitating access to appropriate services and supporting individualized care planning.

Rehabilitation is an essential component in maintaining and improving functional capacity. Through physical therapy, occupational therapy, and cognitive interventions, rehabilitation helps reduce dependency, prolong independent living, and enhance quality of life. As emphasized by WHO (2021), integrating rehabilitation into long-term care systems is critical for shifting from passive care toward capacity-enhancing approaches.

Despite widespread recognition of its importance, intersectoral integration remains limited in many long-term care systems, which continue to exhibit sectoral fragmentation. According to OECD (2020), the separation between healthcare, social services, and rehabilitation leads to service duplication, discontinuities in care, and increased costs. Older adults in such systems are often required to navigate multiple services independently, reducing both efficiency and equity in access.

In this context, social work is increasingly recognized as a system integrator, capable of coordinating and linking different components of the care system. As Ungerson and Yeandle (2007) suggest, the role of social work extends beyond direct service provision to include case management, service coordination, and the promotion of person-centered approaches (Ungerson & Yeandle, 2007).

From the perspective of the silver economy ecosystem, intersectoral integration is not merely a technical requirement but a fundamental condition for ensuring the effectiveness, sustainability, and equity of care systems. The development of healthcare-oriented residential care models therefore needs to be situated within an integrated framework in which healthcare, social work, and rehabilitation are connected through appropriate governance and coordination mechanisms.

2.5. Analytical Framework

This chapter employs a multi-layered analytical framework to examine the development of healthcare-oriented residential care models within the silver economy. The framework captures the phenomenon across interconnected levels, linking service delivery with broader socioeconomic dynamics and governance structures.

At the care system level, the analysis focuses on the organization and operation of long-term care services, particularly residential care. Key dimensions include the structure of care provision across home-based, community-based, and residential services; the organizational characteristics of residential care models; and the degree of integration among healthcare, social work, and rehabilitation. This level highlights how services are designed and implemented to address the multidimensional needs of older adults.

At the silver economy ecosystem level, the framework situates care systems within a broader socioeconomic context. It examines the roles of key actors, including the state, private sector, social organizations, and families, as well as the flows of resources such as finance, workforce, and information. It also considers the role of technological and social innovation in shaping service delivery. This level underscores that elder care is both a social welfare domain and an emerging economic sector.

At the multi-level governance level, the analysis addresses the institutional and policy environment shaping care systems. This includes national policies, local government implementation, and service providers as frontline actors. This level reveals how policy intentions are translated into practice and where coordination challenges may arise.

The framework emphasizes the interconnections among these levels. Care provision reflects not only service design but also ecosystem dynamics and governance arrangements. By integrating these dimensions, the study conceptualizes residential care as part of a broader silver economy ecosystem shaped by policy, market forces, and social structures.

3. METHODOLOGY

3.1. Research Design

This study employs a qualitative case study approach combined with policy analysis to examine the development of healthcare-oriented residential care models within the silver economy ecosystem in Da Nang, Vietnam. A case study design is appropriate for investigating complex social phenomena embedded within real-life institutional and policy contexts (Yin, 2018). Da Nang was selected as an illustrative urban case due to its relatively advanced social welfare initiatives, emerging care service market, and ongoing experimentation with integrated elderly care models.

The study also adopts a policy analysis perspective to examine how national and local policy frameworks shape the organization, governance, and implementation of residential care services. Combining case study and policy analysis enables a multi-level understanding of interactions among governance structures, service delivery systems, and market actors.

3.2. Data Sources and Collection

The study applies data triangulation to improve analytical validity and reliability (Flick, 2014). Data were collected from three primary sources: (1) policy and legal documents, (2) institutional and program reports, and (3) semi-structured interviews with key stakeholders.

Policy documents included national legislation, local government policies, and official reports related to ageing, long-term care, social protection, and healthcare services. Institutional reports and service documents were used to examine operational practices and organizational structures of residential care facilities.

In addition, semi-structured interviews were conducted with 12 stakeholders between March and June 2024. Participants included local policymakers, residential care managers, healthcare professionals, social workers, and rehabilitation staff. Interviews focused on service organization, intersectoral coordination, institutional challenges, workforce issues, and policy implementation.

3.3. Data Analysis

Data were analyzed using qualitative content analysis and thematic analysis approaches (Mayring, 2014). Documentary and interview data were coded manually through an iterative process combining inductive and theory-informed coding strategies.

Initial coding focused on identifying recurring themes related to residential care models, integrated care practices, governance structures, workforce capacity, and stakeholder interactions. These codes were subsequently grouped into broader analytical categories linked to the study's conceptual framework, including care integration, institutional fragmentation, policy coordination, and silver economy dynamics.

Triangulation across multiple data sources was used to strengthen interpretive consistency and analytical credibility.

3.4. Ethical Considerations

The study followed established ethical principles for social research, including informed consent, confidentiality, voluntary participation, and secure data handling (Israel & Hay, 2006). All interview participants were informed about the purpose of the study and their right to withdraw at any stage of the research process.

4. POLICY CONTEXT OF ELDER CARE AND THE SILVER ECONOMY IN VIETNAM

4.1. National Policies on Aging and Long-Term Care

Vietnam is undergoing a rapid demographic transition, with one of the fastest rates of population aging globally. The country officially entered the aging phase in 2011 and is projected to become an aged society by around 2036 (United Nations, 2019). This shift places increasing pressure on social protection systems, particularly long-term care for older adults.

The national policy framework has gradually evolved, with the Law on Older Persons (2009) serving as a key legal foundation. Together with national programs and social protection policies, it reflects the state's commitment to improving the well-being of older adults. Current policies primarily focus on supporting vulnerable groups through social assistance, expanding access to primary healthcare, and promoting the role of families and communities in care provision (Vietnam National Assembly, 2009).

However, significant limitations remain. Vietnam lacks a comprehensive and integrated policy framework for long-term care. Existing services are fragmented across healthcare, social services, and functional support, with limited coordination mechanisms (World Health Organization, 2021). As a result, service delivery is often discontinuous and inefficient. Moreover, care provision remains heavily dependent on family-based models, which are increasingly strained by urbanization, labor migration, and shrinking household size. Formal care services, both public and private, remain underdeveloped in scale and quality, creating substantial gaps in long-term care provision (Help Age International, 2015).

Overall, Vietnam is in a transitional phase where basic policy foundations exist but are insufficient to support an integrated and sustainable long-term care system.

4.2. Emerging Directions in the Silver Economy

In recent years, the concept of the silver economy has gained attention in Vietnam's policy discourse, linked to broader shifts toward service-oriented growth, innovation, and the development of new markets. While not yet formalized in a dedicated national strategy, elements of the silver economy are increasingly embedded in existing policies.

Key policy directions include strengthening healthcare and care services for older adults, expanding primary healthcare, and gradually developing long-term care systems. There is also growing emphasis on encouraging private sector participation to diversify resources and improve service quality. Private actors are beginning to engage not only in service provision but also in insurance, investment, and assistive technologies.

Another emerging trend is the development of integrated care models, particularly in urban areas. These models aim to link healthcare, social services, and rehabilitation within a unified system to better address complex care needs. However, such initiatives remain at a pilot stage and have not yet been scaled up systematically.

Despite these developments, Vietnam still lacks a coherent and comprehensive policy framework for the silver economy. Policies related to aging and care remain dispersed across sectors, limiting the ability to fully harness the economic potential of population aging and to develop a sustainable care market (World Bank, 2016). The silver economy in Vietnam can therefore be characterized as being in an early stage of policy emergence.

4.3. Institutional Structure and Fragmentation

A key feature of Vietnam's elder care system is institutional fragmentation, with responsibilities distributed across multiple ministries and levels of governance.

Healthcare services are managed by the health sector, while social protection falls under labor and social affairs authorities. Local governments are responsible for implementation and service management, while private and non-state actors provide supplementary services.

This sector-based structure reflects a traditional vertical governance model, but it has become increasingly inadequate in addressing complex and multidimensional care needs. Fragmentation leads to overlapping responsibilities, weak coordination, and inefficient resource use (OECD, 2020). As a result, care systems lack continuity, and older adults often must navigate multiple disconnected services.

International evidence highlights the need to shift toward integrated governance models, where services are coordinated based on user needs rather than administrative boundaries (World Health Organization, 2021). In Vietnam, addressing institutional fragmentation is essential for improving care quality and system efficiency.

4.4. Policy Gaps in Integrated Residential Care

Although elder care services have expanded in recent years, particularly in major cities such as Hanoi, Ho Chi Minh City, and Da Nang, integrated residential care models remain underdeveloped and insufficiently institutionalized. Current developments are largely fragmented and lack a coherent regulatory framework.

A major gap is the absence of a dedicated legal framework for long-term care. Existing services operate under dispersed regulations across healthcare and social protection sectors, limiting system coherence and development (World Bank, 2016). In addition, there are no unified national standards for residential care, leading to variations in service quality and difficulties in monitoring and evaluation.

Financial mechanisms also remain underdeveloped. Long-term care costs are largely borne by individuals and families, while insurance systems provide limited coverage. The absence of risk-sharing mechanisms, such as long-term care insurance, restricts access and increases the financial burden on households (OECD, 2020).

Furthermore, the care service market remains small and lacks strong policy incentives for private investment. This constrains resource mobilization and service diversification (UNESCAP, 2017). At the same time, limited integration across healthcare, social work, and rehabilitation continues to hinder effective service delivery.

Overall, these policy gaps indicate that integrated residential care in Vietnam is still at an early stage of development. Addressing these challenges requires a comprehensive approach that aligns public policy, market mechanisms, and social needs within the broader framework of the silver economy ecosystem.

5. CASE STUDY: DEVELOPMENT OF RESIDENTIAL CARE MODELS IN DA NANG

5.1. Rationale for Selecting Da Nang: A Pioneer in Social Welfare and Service Innovation

The selection of Da Nang as a case study is not merely based on its geographic location or urban scale, but primarily on its prominent role as a pioneer in advancing social welfare policies, urban governance reform, and innovation in public service delivery in Vietnam. In the context of rapid population aging, major urban centers are increasingly becoming important testing grounds for new care models, particularly in elderly care and the development of integrated social services.

From a theoretical perspective, studies on urban development and social policy suggest that highly urbanized localities often function as "policy laboratories," where new initiatives are developed, tested, and refined before being scaled up nationally. As noted by the World Bank (2016), it is within such urban settings that multi-actor and market-oriented long-term care models tend to emerge earlier, driven by the convergence of economic resources, governance capacity, and increasingly diverse service demands.

Within this context, Da Nang stands out as a representative case due to a combination of enabling factors. The city has established a relatively strong social welfare foundation, reflected in its network of social protection institutions and proactive support programs. At the same time, local authorities demonstrate a flexible and innovative approach to policymaking and implementation, creating favorable conditions for experimenting with new service delivery models. Furthermore, although still at an early stage, the growing participation of the private sector in care services has contributed to diversifying supply and improving service quality.

Another important factor is Da Nang's strategic vision of becoming a "livable city," where quality of life is placed at the center of urban development. This approach extends beyond economic infrastructure to include social domains such as healthcare, social services, and welfare for vulnerable populations, including older adults. Such a vision provides a conducive environment for the emergence and development of residential care models linked to health and well-being.

Taken together, these characteristics position Da Nang as a valuable illustrative case for understanding the transformation of elderly care systems within the emerging silver economy ecosystem in Vietnam. As emphasized by Yin (2018), the selection of a representative case is not only intended to describe a specific context but also to illuminate broader mechanisms and dynamics that may be present in similar settings (Yin, 2018). Therefore, analyzing the case of Da Nang offers not only insights into local practices but also meaningful implications for policy development and care models in other urban areas across the country.

5.2. Current Types of Residential Care

The residential care system for older adults in Da Nang is increasingly diversifying, reflecting a shift from a traditional welfare-based model toward a multi-actor service structure within the emerging silver economy. The coexistence of public, private, and hybrid models indicates a system in transition, where social welfare principles are gradually complemented by market mechanisms and cross-sector collaboration.

Public residential care facilities continue to play a foundational role, particularly for vulnerable older adults who lack financial resources or family support. These facilities primarily provide basic care services, daily living assistance, and social support, thereby fulfilling the state's social protection function. However, due to reliance on public funding and institutional constraints, public models often face limitations in scaling up and improving service quality, especially in delivering specialized or integrated care services. This restricts their capacity to meet the increasingly diverse needs of an aging population.

Alongside the public sector, the growth of private care facilities reflects the marketization of elderly care services, a key feature of the silver economy. These facilities typically target higher-income groups and are therefore able to offer higher-quality services, more personalized living environments, and partial integration of healthcare services. Their managerial flexibility and investment capacity enable service innovation and contribute to raising care standards. Nevertheless, the high cost of these services creates significant barriers to access for middle- and low-income older adults, increasing the risk of inequality in care provision.

In this context, public–private partnership models are emerging as a promising approach to balancing social welfare objectives with economic efficiency. Although still at an early stage in Da Nang, these models demonstrate the potential to leverage the strengths of both sectors: the state provides policy support, infrastructure, or land, while the private sector undertakes investment, management, and service delivery. This approach not only expands service capacity but also enhances quality through competition and innovation.

Overall, the coexistence of these three types of residential care reflects an ongoing restructuring process in which public and private elements interact. However, linkages between these models remain limited, and a fully integrated care system has yet to emerge. This highlights the urgent need for a coherent policy framework and more effective coordination mechanisms to ensure balanced development across sectors and improved access to care services.

5.3. Service Organization and Delivery Mechanisms

The organization and delivery of residential care services in Da Nang reflect a multi-layered system involving multiple functional actors. At the governance level, state agencies establish the regulatory framework, licensing, and oversight of service providers. Meanwhile, residential care facilities are responsible for delivering day-to-day services, including basic care, daily living support, and, to some extent, healthcare services.

Beyond direct service provision, the system is supported by specialized service networks. The healthcare sector including hospitals and primary care facilities provides diagnosis, treatment, and management of complex health conditions. At the same time, social work services and community support networks address psychosocial needs, strengthen family connections, and assist older adults in adapting to residential environments.

Despite this theoretically comprehensive structure, weak coordination across service layers results in system fragmentation. Services often operate in isolation, lacking effective communication channels and unified coordination mechanisms. Consequently, healthcare, social care, and functional support are not integrated into a continuous care pathway, requiring older adults to navigate multiple disconnected systems.

This fragmentation reduces service efficiency while increasing costs and burdens for both users and providers. From a silver economy perspective, improving service delivery requires not only expanding service capacity but also restructuring relationships among stakeholders. Strengthening coordination between government, service providers, and health–social support networks is essential to developing an integrated, continuous, and person-centered care system.

5.4. Level of Service Integration: Health – Social Care – Rehabilitation

A key indicator of modern residential care development is the degree of integration across service domains, particularly healthcare, social care, and rehabilitation. According to the World Health Organization, effective elderly care should follow an integrated care model in which services are continuously coordinated and centered on individual needs. This approach ensures that medical, psychosocial, and functional needs are addressed in a unified system (World Health Organization, 2022; World Health Organization, 2023)

In practice, however, the level of integration in Da Nang remains uneven. Healthcare services continue to dominate, reflecting a traditional focus on clinical treatment and disease management. Residential care facilities especially those linked to medical providers prioritize chronic disease management and acute care, ensuring physical health and safety for older adults.

In contrast, social work remains underdeveloped and insufficiently professionalized. Psychosocial support and social engagement activities are often treated as supplementary rather than core components of care, partly due to workforce limitations and the still-emerging status of the profession within institutional settings.

Similarly, rehabilitation services essential for maintaining independence and functional capacity are not yet systematically integrated. Constraints in specialized personnel, infrastructure, and financing mean that such services are either basic or outsourced to external healthcare providers. This limits the transition from passive care models to capacity-enhancing approaches that are central to contemporary long-term care systems.

Overall, a significant gap persists between policy aspirations for integrated care and actual implementation. Institutional fragmentation, resource constraints, and weak coordination mechanisms continue to hinder progress. From a silver economy perspective, limited integration not only affects care quality but also reduces system efficiency and constrains the sustainable development of residential care models.

5.5. Stakeholder Ecosystem

The residential care ecosystem in Da Nang reflects an emerging multi-actor structure within the transition toward a silver economy. Moving beyond the traditional reliance on the state and family, the system increasingly involves a diverse set of public, private, and social actors, forming a complex network of service provision and governance. This shift signals a broader transformation from welfare-based care to a mixed model incorporating market mechanisms and social innovation.

Within this structure, the state remains central as a regulator and system architect, responsible for setting legal frameworks, licensing, and oversight. However, its role is gradually shifting from direct provider to coordinator and enabler, focusing on creating conditions for other actors to participate and expand services.

The private sector is becoming an important driver of service expansion and diversification, particularly in middle and high-end market segments. While it enhances innovation and quality through competition, its growth also raises concerns about equity, as access to services becomes increasingly tied to individuals' ability to pay.

Professional care workers including healthcare providers, social workers, and rehabilitation specialists are critical to service quality and integration. Yet workforce shortages and the lack of standardized training remain significant constraints, limiting the development of integrated care models.

At the same time, families and communities continue to play a foundational role, especially within the cultural context of intergenerational care. However, social changes such as urbanization and migration are weakening informal care capacity, placing greater pressure on formal services.

Overall, while the stakeholder ecosystem is increasingly diverse and dynamic, coordination among actors remains limited. Strengthening governance mechanisms and cross-sector collaboration is essential to building an integrated, efficient, and person-centered care system within the silver economy.

6. DISCUSSION

The findings from the Da Nang case indicate that the development of healthcare-oriented residential care models in Vietnam is occurring within a context characterized by rapid population ageing, institutional transition, and emerging marketization of care services. While the system shows initial signs of diversification and service integration, significant structural and governance challenges continue to constrain its development. Recent regional analyses also suggest that ageing societies in Asia are likely to experience rapidly growing demand for integrated long-term care services and age-friendly technologies in the coming decades (McKinsey & Company, 2023).

A major contradiction within Vietnam's emerging long-term care system lies in the coexistence of rapidly growing ageing-related care demands and limited institutional preparedness. Although multiple ministries and sectors are involved in elderly care provision, coordination mechanisms remain weak and fragmented. This suggests that policy expansion has progressed more rapidly than governance capacity building, limiting the development of integrated and continuous care pathways. As a result, healthcare, social work, and rehabilitation services continue to operate in relatively separate institutional structures despite policy recognition of integrated care principles.Recent evidence increasingly emphasizes that integrated care systems are essential for improving service continuity and addressing the complex health and social needs of older adults (Briggs et al., 2021; World Health Organization, 2023).

The findings also reveal important tensions between traditional welfare-based approaches and the increasing marketization of elder care services within the silver economy. The expansion of private residential care facilities reflects growing demand for higher-quality and diversified care services. However, this trend also raises concerns regarding equity and accessibility, as access to better-quality services increasingly depends on financial capacity. In this sense, the development of the silver economy may simultaneously improve service diversity while deepening inequalities in access to care among older adults, particularly for lower-income groups. This reflects broader international debates regarding the balance between market efficiency and social equity within ageing societies and silver economy development (European Commission, 2021).

Another important tension concerns the transition from family-based care toward formalized residential care systems. In the Vietnamese sociocultural context, family caregiving remains a dominant norm shaped by intergenerational responsibility and filial expectations. However, demographic ageing, declining household size, urbanization, and labor migration are gradually weakening the capacity of families to provide long-term care. This creates a structural gap between increasing care needs and declining informal care resources. Consequently, the expansion of residential care services is constrained not only by institutional and financial limitations but also by cultural attitudes toward institutional care.

Workforce shortages represent another systemic barrier to the development of integrated care models. The lack of adequately trained professionals in geriatrics, social work, rehabilitation, and long-term care management affects both service quality and continuity of care. This challenge is particularly significant because integrated care systems depend heavily on interdisciplinary collaboration and coordinated service delivery. Without sufficient human resource capacity, policy ambitions for integrated and person-centered care may remain largely symbolic rather than operational. Recent OECD reports further indicate that ageing societies are facing growing shortages of long-term care workers due to rising service demand and insufficient workforce supply (OECD, 2023).

According to the ILO (2022), strengthening care workforce systems is increasingly critical for ensuring sustainable and equitable long-term care provision.(ILO, 2022).

The findings further suggest that Vietnam's long-term care system remains heavily influenced by sector-based governance structures. Despite increasing recognition of integrated care approaches in international policy discourse, coordination across healthcare, social protection, and rehabilitation sectors remains limited in practice. This institutional fragmentation not only reduces service efficiency but also increases burdens on older adults and families, who must navigate multiple disconnected service systems. From a governance perspective, this highlights the need to shift from administrative fragmentation toward more integrated and user-centered models of service coordination.

At the same time, emerging digital technologies and AI-assisted care systems present important opportunities for improving long-term care delivery within the silver economy ecosystem. Technologies such as telemedicine, remote monitoring, digital care coordination, and smart residential environments have the potential to improve service efficiency and support independent living among older adults. Recent studies suggest that digital technologies are increasingly transforming long-term care systems through telehealth, AI-assisted care, and smart-home support systems (Marston et al., 2022; World Health Organization, 2022).

These technologies may become particularly important in ageing societies facing workforce shortages and rising care demands (Czaja et al., 2021; Sixsmith & Gutman,

2023). However, unequal access to digital technologies and limited digital literacy among older populations may also create new forms of inequality if not adequately addressed through policy and service design.

More broadly, the Vietnamese case reflects a fundamental tension commonly observed in transitional welfare systems: the balance between social protection objectives and market-oriented reforms. On the one hand, the state seeks to expand long-term care services in response to rapid population ageing. On the other hand, limited public resources increasingly encourage market participation and private investment in elder care services. This creates a hybrid system in which welfare goals, service accessibility, and market efficiency do not always align. The sustainability of the silver economy in Vietnam will therefore depend not only on expanding care services, but also on the state's ability to regulate inequalities, strengthen governance capacity, and ensure equitable access to integrated care.

From a policy perspective, this suggests that the future development of the silver economy in Vietnam will require stronger governance coordination, workforce investment, and digitally supported integrated care systems

7. CONCLUSION AND POLICY IMPLICATIONS

7.1. Conclusion

This study examined the development of healthcare-oriented residential care models within the emerging silver economy ecosystem in Da Nang, Vietnam. The findings indicate that the care system is gradually transitioning toward a multi-actor structure and shows initial signs of service integration. However, significant challenges remain, including institutional fragmentation, workforce shortages, and a relatively low level of integration across care sectors.

From a theoretical perspective, the study contributes to expanding the analytical framework of the silver economy in the context of middle-income countries. It highlights the role of residential care models as a key component of an integrated service ecosystem. The multi-layered analytical approach also helps clarify the dynamic interactions between policy frameworks, market forces, and service delivery practices.

From a practical standpoint, the study provides empirical evidence to inform the reform of long-term care systems in Vietnam. It offers insights into pathways for developing integrated models that connect healthcare, social work, and market mechanisms. These findings are particularly relevant for policymakers seeking to design strategies for silver economy development and to improve the quality of elderly care services.

Nevertheless, the study has certain limitations. Its focus on a single urban case restricts the generalizability of findings. Future research should expand comparative analysis across different localities and incorporate quantitative methods to assess the effectiveness of care models. Further investigation into the operational mechanisms and impacts of integrated care models is essential to support evidence-based policymaking in the context of rapid population aging.

7.2. Policy Implications: Toward Integrated Care Models in the Silver Economy

Based on the identified challenges, several policy directions are proposed to promote the development of integrated and sustainable residential care models within the silver economy.

First, establishing a dedicated legal framework for long-term care is essential. A national law or strategy on long-term care would provide a foundation for coordinating services, clarifying stakeholder roles, and setting standardized regulations, in line with experiences from OECD countries.

Second, developing an interdisciplinary workforce should be prioritized. This requires integrated training programs that combine healthcare, social work, and rehabilitation, enabling professionals to deliver comprehensive and coordinated care services.

Third, strengthening intersectoral governance is crucial. Establishing effective coordination mechanisms across ministries, sectors, and levels of government would help reduce institutional fragmentation and ensure continuity of care.

In addition, promoting private sector participation is key to expanding service capacity. Policy instruments such as tax incentives, land access support, and the development of long-term care insurance schemes can attract investment and diversify service provision.

In the context of digital transformation, leveraging innovation in care delivery also presents important opportunities. Solutions such as digital care, AI-assisted services, and smart housing can enhance efficiency and reduce pressure on traditional care systems.

In addition, digital transformation should be incorporated into long-term care strategies. AI-assisted care systems, telemedicine, digital monitoring technologies, and smart residential environments can improve service coordination, reduce workforce pressures, and enhance care efficiency. However, policies should also address digital inequality and ensure that technological innovations remain accessible and user-friendly for older adults.

Finally, the experience of Da Nang suggests the potential for scaling up integrated residential care models to other urban areas in Vietnam and across ASEAN.

However, such scaling should be adapted to local socio-economic conditions and institutional capacities, rather than applied uniformly.

REFERENCES

Briggs, A. M., Valentijn, P. P., Thiyagarajan, J. A., & de Carvalho, I. A. (2021). Integrated care for older people and the role of health systems. *The Lancet. Healthy Longevity*, *2*(9), e581–e592. DOI: 10.1016/S2666-7568(21)00143-0

Campbell, J. C., Ikegami, N., & Gibson, M. J. (2010). Lessons from public long-term care insurance in Germany and Japan. *Health Affairs (Project Hope)*, *29*(1), 87–95. DOI: 10.1377/hlthaff.2009.0548

Czaja, S. J., Boot, W. R., Charness, N., & Rogers, W. A. (2021). Designing for older adults in the digital age. *Human-Computer Interaction*, *36*(5–6), 371–402. DOI: 10.1080/07370024.2021.1884627

European Commission. (2018). *The silver economy*. Publications Office of the European Union.

European Commission. (2021). The silver economy and ageing societies. *European Union.*

Flick, U. (2014). *An introduction to qualitative research* (5th ed.). Sage.

Help Age International. (2015). *Ageing population in Vietnam: Policy and practice*. HelpAge International.

International Labour Organization. (2022). *Care at work: Investing in care leave and services for a more gender equal world*. ILO.

Israel, M., & Hay, I. (2006). Research ethics for social scientists. *Sage (Atlanta, Ga.).*

Maresova, P., Mohelska, H., & Kuca, K. (2019). Social and economic aspects of ageing population. *Current Gerontology and Geriatrics Research*, *2019*, 8501258.

Marston, H. R., Ivan, L., & Fernández-Ardèvol, M. (2022). Digital technologies and the ageing population: A systematic review. *International Journal of Environmental Research and Public Health*, *19*(4), 2325. DOI: 10.3390/ijerph19042325

Mayring, P. (2014). *Qualitative content analysis: Theoretical foundation, basic procedures and software solution*. Klagenfurt.

McKinsey & Company. (2023). *The future of aging in Asia: Trends, challenges, and opportunities*. McKinsey Global Institute.

Organisation for Economic Co-operation and Development (OECD). (2020). *Who cares? Attracting and retaining care workers for the elderly*. OECD Publishing.

Organisation for Economic Co-operation and Development (OECD). (2023). *Ready for the future? Long-term care and ageing societies*. OECD Publishing.

Sancho, M.. (2017). Residential care and quality of life in older adults. *Journal of Aging Studies*, *42*, 1–10.

Sixsmith, A., & Gutman, G. (2023). Technologies for active and assisted living in ageing societies. *Gerontechnology (Valkenswaard)*, *22*(1), 1–14. DOI: 10.4017/gt.2023.22.2.six.08

Ungerson, C., & Yeandle, S. (2007). *Cash for care systems in developed welfare states*. Palgrave Macmillan.

United Nations. (2019). *World population ageing 2019: Highlights*. United Nations Department of Economic and Social Affairs.

United Nations Economic and Social Commission for Asia and the Pacific (UNESCAP). (2017). *Ageing in Asia and the Pacific: Overview*. United Nations.

Vietnam National Assembly. (2009). *Law on the Elderly (Law No. 39/2009/QH12)*. Hanoi, Vietnam. Link < https://m.thuvienphapluat.vn/van-ban/van-hoa-xa-hoi/Law-No-39-2009-QH12-on-the-elderly-106095.aspx>

World Bank. (2016). *Live long and prosper: Aging in East Asia and Pacific*. World Bank.

World Health Organization. (2015). *World report on ageing and health*. WHO.

World Health Organization. (2020). *Decade of healthy ageing 2020–2030*. WHO.

World Health Organization. (2021). *Integrated care for older people (ICOPE): Guidelines on community-level interventions to manage declines in intrinsic capacity*. WHO.

World Health Organization. (2022). *Global strategy on digital health 2020–2025*. WHO.

World Health Organization. (2023). *Framework for integrated people-centred long-term care*. WHO.

Yin, R. K. (2018). *Case study research and applications: Design and methods* (6th ed.). Sage.

Chapter 10
Powering the Silver Economy Vitality Through Collaborative Partnerships, Intergenerational Strategies, and Quantifiable Benchmarks in Older Adult Care

Alan Lai
http://orcid.org/0009-0002-1399-1301
Beijing Normal-Hong Kong Baptist University, China

ABSTRACT

This chapter presents a novel approach to examining how social service and business partnerships sustain the Silver Economy through intergenerational strategies. It defines Silver Economy Vitality (SEV), presents collaborative frameworks, and assesses their benefits and challenges. Using database sources to seek credible, real-world cases (n=7) that have generated impactful outcomes through intergenerational strategies, it outlines how the SEV Scale—a tool of evaluation with a rubric designed to measure innovation, adaptability, intergenerational impact, quality of life, and community resilience in Silver Economy initiatives—is developed. The findings highlight that growth leverages innovative, intergenerational strengths

DOI: 10.4018/979-8-3373-9370-4.ch010

and actionable, evidence-based assessments. Policy implications emphasize using the SEV Scale — as a means to advancing the Silver Economy — by benchmarking progress, guiding improvements, and expanding strategic, data-driven investments in older adult care.

INTRODUCTION

The Silver Economy refers to the system of production, distribution, and consumption of goods and services that primarily benefit people aged 50 and older (European Commission, 2018). It is rooted in the recognition that older adults represent a dynamic market segment whose needs extend beyond healthcare to housing, transportation, leisure, and financial services, as demonstrated world-widely by their leadership in community initiatives, advocacy for age-friendly policies, and active participation in intergenerational programs that foster innovation and social cohesion (Kaplan, Sanchez & Hoffman, 2017; Lai, Qi & Luo, 2025).

According to WHO (2015), the Silver Economy is closely linked to active aging and the empowerment of older people as contributors to society or drivers of change rather than passive recipients of care:

> *"Older people are not passive in their relationship with their environments. Rather, this interaction is shaped to varying degrees by the choices they make to respond to, or change, their situation. Retaining the ability and right to choose is closely linked to notions of agency and autonomy..., which have been shown to have a powerful influence on an older person's dignity, integrity, freedom and independence.... This is true whether they live in the community, in an assisted living facility or in an institution" (p.35).*

Building upon the active-aging foundation of the Silver Economy, the concept of Silver Economy Vitality (SEV) represents a dynamic system of production, distribution, and consumption of goods and services that not merely benefit but also benefit from older adults. It is also characterized by continuous innovation, adaptability, and the active involvement of older adults in economic and social spheres. SEV thus extends the Silver Economy concept to emphasize vitality — by not only empowering older adults but also in ways powering involved stakeholders or their sectors' capability to respond to evolving needs, foster collaboration, and generate sustainable growth.

By focusing on vitality, SEV underscores the importance of resilience, cross-generational engagement, and creative partnerships in driving social and economic development, particularly in the context of older people care. The importance of sustaining SEV lies in its potential to improve quality of life for older adults while driving innovation and growth in related industries — especially those with collaborative models such as public-private partnerships, social enterprises or cross-sector alliances that leverage the strengths of each sector (Klimczuk, 2015). These models aim to facilitate resource sharing, joint innovation, and the scaling of impactful solutions for older people care.

Furthermore, when social service and business partnerships harness intergenerational programs to bridge generational gaps, they foster ongoing innovation, efficient services, and age-friendly environments (Lai, Qi & Luo, 2025). These efforts often involve combining cross-sector strengths for accessible, actionable, and impactful solutions. This chapter contends that successful outcomes frequently go unnoticed, resulting in diminished lasting impact that could otherwise extend to benefit a broader population. The challenge of sustaining success persists, largely due to cross-sector complexities and the absence of qualifiable benchmarks and rubrics applicable across sectors.

To address to the challenge, this chapter outlines how a rubric is developed from successful cases to support the creation of the Silver Economy Vitality (SEV) Scale, which is designed to transform qualitative achievements into measurable and actionable results. It is presented as a tool for preserving success, proposed to allow practitioners to track progress, replicate and expand demonstrated impacts, thereby serving as a method for advancing the Silver Economy. In other words, it advocates enhancing the scope of program impacts by systematically measuring SEV through a benchmarking or rating process. To set a foundational stage for this proposed scale, this chapter conceptually situates the framework of SEV within the context of demographic aging, emphasizing the need for cross-sector partnerships and intergenerational strategies to address emerging challenges and opportunities.

BENEFITS AND COMPLEXITIES OF SOCIAL SERVICE AND BUSINESS PARTNERSHIPS

Effective partnerships between social service organizations and businesses are fundamental to the sustainability of the Silver Economy. As partnerships encompass a vast, intricate or cross-sector scope such as healthcare, housing, transportation, ICT, leisure, finance, and beyond, they are matched by each sector's complexities (e.g., demographic variability, rapid technological advancements, diverse stakeholder interests, and the substantial heterogeneity within the older adult population) (Liu, 2025). Furthermore, the interplay between public, private, and third-sector actors creates a dynamic landscape where needs and solutions are constantly evolving (Rijken et al., 2018). To better understand the practical implications of these collaborations, it is essential to examine both the benefits and issues they entail.

First of all, the benefits are multifaceted (European Commission, 2018). For example, Wang, Coyte, Shi, Zong & Zhong (2023) emphasize that such alliances create platforms for continuous innovation, service delivery, increased efficiency, and the creation of age-friendly environments, enabling rapid adaptation to emerging needs and technologies in older adult care. By integrating social expertise with business-driven research and development, partnerships can accelerate the delivery of personalized solutions—such as digital health services, assistive devices, and community-based care models—while ensuring their accessibility and affordability (Sorrentino, et al., 2024). Moreover, partnerships have been shown to improve health outcomes and promote well-being. According to Matos, Nascimento, Campos Fernandes & Matos, 2025), integrated care models developed through cross-sector collaboration yield improvements in physical health, mental health, and social engagement. This is achieved by coordinating services across clinical, community, and economic domains, addressing the holistic needs of older adults and their families. Likewise, collaboration also drives economic sustainability. Buffel (2025) reports that joint ventures and co-created programs expand the market for age-friendly goods and services, spurring entrepreneurship and employment while ensuring that economic growth aligns with societal goals and demographic trends.

However, complexities that persist give rise to issues. First, as the Silver Economy encompasses a wide range of sectors beyond healthcare such as housing, transport, ICT, leisure, finance, and education for older adults, it is challenged inevitably by differing organizational cultures, regulatory barriers, governance requirements (WHO, 2015) as well as regional demographic variations (Galeotti et al., 2024). In addition, adapting to shifting consumer demands, the rise of tele-health and smart home technologies, evolving care models, and advancements in AI and robotics—combined with the growing diverse needs of older people and the intricate interdependencies created by the collaboration of public, private, and non-profit sectors, each with distinct goals and constraints—further complicates service delivery and management (Liu, 2025). Addressing all these challenges requires ongoing dialogue and adaptive leadership.

Given the complexities, recent research highlights the critical need for systematic, evidence-based tools that can help policymakers, service providers, and investors support more adaptive leadership and make informed decisions (Liu, 2025; Rijken et al., 2018). These informed decisions are many in the Silver Economy context such as determining how to allocate resources efficiently to best support the diverse needs of older adults, deciding which policy interventions or regulatory frameworks will foster innovation while ensuring accessibility and equity, identifying which programs or services yield greater impact on quality of life and well-being for older adults, adapting to rapidly changing technologies and consumer preferences, requiring clear data to evaluate the potential return and societal value of investing in age-friendly products, services, or infrastructure, etc.

The SEV Scale approach is to address this need by offering a structured rubric for assessing the dynamic and sustained vitality of Silver Economy initiatives. Its use of objective criteria—spanning innovation, adaptability, intergenerational engagement, and impact—aim to help stakeholders benchmark progress, identify best practices, and prioritize resources effectively. In this context, the remainder of this chapter will focus on the possibility of equipping sectoral initiatives with reliable, evidence-based tools and skills for meaningful evaluation and guidance. As a natural progression though, there is a need to illustrate how vitality and adaptability manifest within the Silver Economy — that is, by spotlighting intergenerational strategies or purposeful approaches that bring together different age groups for mutual support, learning, and collaboration. These strategies lie at the heart of social cohesion and innovation, making them potent drivers for driving progress in older people care and industries.

INTERGENERATIONAL STRATEGIES

Conceptually, intergenerational strategies involve purposeful interactions between groups that are significantly older and younger than each other, fostering mutual support, learning, and collaboration. These purposeful interactions between generations drive social cohesion, reduce ageism, and enhance the quality and effectiveness of care for older adults (Kaplan, 2002).

This chapter expands on intergenerational strategies, highlighting the broader context of the Silver Economy in which they aim to fuel innovation and adaptability by actively engaging older adults as both recipients and contributors. This involvement is key to the concept of SEV, which emphasizes the dynamic and resilient nature of economic and social systems serving people aged 50 and older. By integrating intergenerational approaches—such as mentorship programs, shared housing models, and co-designed community services—SEV initiatives are offered diverse perspectives and experiences as more creative solutions are required to address ever-evolving needs and generate sustainable growth (Kaplan, Sanchez & Hoffman, 2017).

Furthermore, it is not difficult to see social service and business partnerships strengthened through intergenerational strategies when collaboration between them manages to benefit from the unique capacity of intergenerational programs to bridge generational divides, creation of platforms for continuous innovation, efficient service delivery, and the development of age-friendly environments. For example, intergenerational learning centers bring together children and older adults for joint educational and recreational activities, fostering reciprocal benefits and building social capital (Kaplan, 2002). However, such initiatives often require cross-sector collaboration between social service organizations and businesses, leveraging each sector's strengths to deliver more accessible, actionable, and impactful solutions.

While intergenerational strategies are widely recognized, the core challenge extends beyond simply the scarcity of case studies demonstrating positive outcomes. The critical issue lies in the absence of systematic approaches to documenting, benchmarking, and replicating or expanding the success of these strategies. Without clear mechanisms for learning from exemplary cases—where intergenerational initiatives have demonstrably advanced health, economic participation, and community resilience—the valuable lessons and successful models risk being overlooked, underutilized, or lost altogether. This underscores the central argument and purpose of this chapter: by leveraging robust case studies as credible contexts, it becomes possible to develop evidence-based scales and benchmarks that not only validate impacts but also guide the replication and scaling of effective intergenerational practices. Such a systematic approach is thus proposed to ensure that the Silver Economy can advance in a more sustainable, recognizable, and actionable manner, ultimately preserving and amplifying the benefits of intergenerational collaboration for future generations. Due to the limited availability of case studies demonstrating the positive impacts of intergenerational strategies, our comprehension of their full potential remains constrained. Accordingly, this chapter initiates an inquiry to search and identify exemplary instances in the field.

CASE SEARCHES, SELECTION CRITERIA, AND RATIONALE

Recent case searches in credible global databases and repositories provide a gateway into the prevalence of intergenerational initiatives that align with a set of case selection criteria outlined for this chapter. First, the Stanford Center on Longevity's "Intergenerational Programs Database" lists over 200 initiatives worldwide that purposefully integrate intergenerational strategies and cross-sector collaboration, many of which report measurable outcomes and have received formal recognition (Gan, 2021; Stanford Center on Longevity: https://vicpcp.org.au/). Similarly, the Generations United's "Programs of Distinction" directory highlights more than 100 exemplary U.S.-based programs that meet standards for evidence-based impact and replicability (Generations United: https://www.gu.org/ig-program-database). Similarly, Social Innovative Match (SIM: https://socialinnovationplus.eu/social-innovation-match-sim/) is another database that includes 400 cases. Additionally, a filtered search of the European Commission's "European Social Innovation Database (ESID) including 11,468 projects from 159 countries" using terms such as "intergenerational," "social enterprise," and "cross-sector partnership" yields over 200 projects (Gök et al., 2022).

This chapter presents seven real-world cases that exemplify intergenerational strategies within the Silver Economy. They are selected due to their proven collaboration between social service and business sectors as well as intergenerational strategies involved. Additionally, each case was chosen for its strong reputation, measurable impact, ability to illustrate core mechanisms that foster intergenerational collaboration, demonstrated replicability, and wide recognition. To ensure methodological rigor and meaningful comparison, the selection criteria for these cases were defined. First, each initiative had to demonstrate active partnership between social service organizations and business entities, reflecting the cross-sector collaboration that is central to the Silver Economy. Second, the cases were required to integrate purposeful intergenerational strategies—such as mentorship, shared spaces, co-designed services, or reciprocal support—enabling mutual engagement between older and younger participants. Third, only cases with clear, documented outcomes and measurable impacts were considered, allowing for objective assessment using evidence-based tools like the SEV Scale. Fourth, the selected cases needed to provide insight into replicable mechanisms and practical models that could inform policy or practice in diverse contexts. Finally, wide recognition and reputation—whether through academic literature, policy endorsements, or community uptake—were essential, ensuring that each example has demonstrated credibility and influence beyond its immediate setting. These criteria collectively support the systematic, comparative analysis of intergenerational collaboration in the Silver Economy, providing a robust foundation for evaluating effectiveness, adaptability, and innovation across varied cultural and socioeconomic environments. Through this selection process, seven cases—that is, community-based intergenerational care centers in Japan, business-led urban infrastructure partnerships in Germany, mentorship programs like the United States' Experience Corps, Singapore's integrated multigenerational developments, Spain's Intergenerational Housing Program, China's transparent, intergenerational program driven by blockchain technologies, and South Africa's GABA led by grandmothers— were selected precisely due to these inclusion criteria matched best, thereby setting the stage of relevance and reliability for comparative analysis.

The primary rationale for systematically analyzing or comparing these cases is to extract actionable insights and identify common ingredients that underpin the success of intergenerational Silver Economy initiatives. By closely examining exemplary cases, it becomes possible to discern recurring patterns and mechanisms—such as shared spaces, mentorship, and mutual assistance—that consistently contribute to positive outcomes. These identified elements are then synthesized and transformed into key dimensions, forming the conceptual basis for developing a robust assessment tool: the SEV Scale. The scale approach is thus not simply an evaluative proposal to follow, but an organic product of evidence-based benchmarking that emerges directly from the comparative study of proven models — and it should keep evolving when more data access is available.

This approach supports the argument that a deep understanding of high-performing cases is essential for insights to learn, thereby constructing more reliable benchmarks and scalable dimensions, which, in turn, enables systematic measurement, adaptation, and replication of effective strategies across diverse contexts. Scholarly literature underscores the value of rubric-oriented and comparative analysis in generating meaningful benchmarks and guiding the evolution of best practices in complex social systems (Thang, Yui, Wakabayashi & Miyazawa, 2023). Therefore, the systematic review of exemplary cases serves not only to highlight their unique features but, more importantly, to inform the development of standardized scales and benchmarks that can drive innovation and sustained vitality within the Silver Economy worldwide.

CASE STUDIES AND INSIGHTS LEARNED

The comparative analysis of the seven cases aims to highlight the shared features and distinctive elements of the presented cases by examining their approaches, results, and adaptability across varied cultural and socioeconomic contexts. In other words, such comparative examination yields profound insights into five dimensions that to a certain extent underpin the vitality of Silver Economy initiatives. For an overview, Table 1 and Diagram 1 summarize them as distinctive results rooted in each initiative and insights learned. These dimensions are: (1) Social Integration, (2) Economic Engagement, (3) Health and Well-being, (4) Reciprocal Support, and (5) Community Resilience.

Social Integration reflects the capacity of programs to foster meaningful connections and reduce isolation across generations. Economic Engagement captures how intergenerational strategies stimulate active participation and value creation within local economies. Health and Well-being addresses the multifaceted benefits to both older and younger participants, while Reciprocal Support highlights the mechanisms of mutual aid and shared learning that strengthen individual and collective outcomes. Finally, Community Resilience encompasses the adaptability and sustained cohesiveness of communities facing demographic and social change. The emergence of these five dimensions from cross-case analysis provided the conceptual foundation for developing a structured rubric, which in turn inspired the creation of the Silver Economy Vitality Scale—that is, a framework proposed in the following section to systematically assess, interpret vitality, and benchmark the effectiveness of intergenerational strategies across a range of contexts within the Silver Economy.

It is important to acknowledge that the interpretations of the five dimensions are initial, meaning that they are openly shaped or influenced by the depth of insight learned and each cases's availability of information. The extent to which these dimensions is thus determined by the richness, scope, and detail present. As such, further evaluations and comparative analyses will demonstrate further refine or expand the understanding of these dimensions later in the section after next.

1. Japan: Nagayama Model

The Nagayama Model in Tama New Town, Tokyo, is a community-based intergenerational care system created through a collaborative workshop in 2016. Stakeholders—including local government, non-profit organizations, businesses, and residents—jointly developed shared facilities and programs involving older adults, children, college student interns, and families. The model aims to enable aging in place, foster intergenerational interaction, and reinforce community integration. Outcomes include improved well-being, reduced isolation, enhanced social participation, and stronger neighborhood bonds. The model is recognized for its replicability and as a successful example of neighborhood regeneration, with implications for healthy aging policy. (Thang et al., 2023).

Features/Highlights: Key initiatives include shared facilities and activities, such as community cafes, support centers, and programs that bring together seniors, children, college student interns, and younger families. These efforts have improved social participation, reduced isolation, and strengthened neighborhood bonds, creating a sustainable and age-friendly environment. The model is recognized as a successful example of neighborhood regeneration and intergenerational care, with significant implications for healthy aging policies and practices.

Insights learned: The Nagayama Model in Tama New Town, Tokyo, offers valuable insights into the five key dimensions underpinning the vitality of Silver Economy initiatives. First, Social Integration is evident through shared facilities—such as community cafes and support centers—where seniors, children, college student interns, and families regularly interact, fostering meaningful connections and reducing isolation. For Health and Well-being, the model's programs have enabled older adults to age in place with enhanced social participation, positively impacting their physical and mental health. Reciprocal Support emerges from collaborative activities, where mutual assistance between generations strengthens neighborhood bonds and encourages shared learning. Finally, Community Resilience is demonstrated by the successful regeneration of the neighborhood; the model's replicability and sustained engagement across diverse groups have created a robust, age-friendly environment adaptable to demographic changes. These outcomes show how the Nagayama Model serves as practical evidence for the effectiveness of intergenerational strategies in cultivating integrated, resilient, and healthy communities.

2. Germany: Urban Development Support Programme

Germany's Urban Development Support Programme (since 1971) is a business-led initiative in partnership with local governments, addressing social, ecological, demographic, and economic challenges. It features integrated planning, participatory approaches, and flexible, needs-oriented measures. Examples include Bremerhaven's Vario-Wohnungen (Flexible Homes), which provide adaptable housing for both older and younger residents, and Frankfurt am Main's Quäkerplatz Neighbourhood Pavilion, a district meeting point fostering intergenerational connections through cultural events, play areas, and food services. With €19.3 billion in funding for over 9,300 projects across 3,900 municipalities, the program has achieved sustainable urban renewal, strengthened ties across generations, and supported long-term care. (Federal Ministry of the Interior, Building and Community, 2020).

Features/Highlights: Key features include integrated planning, participatory approaches, and flexible, needs-oriented measures. For example, the Bremerhaven - Vario-Wohnungen (Flexible Homes) model developed accessible housing designed to serve both older and younger residents, with the adaptability to be repurposed as retirement housing or for other community needs as demographics shift. Similarly, the Frankfurt am Main - Quäkerplatz Neighbourhood Pavilion was established as a district meeting point that encourages intergenerational connections by providing cultural events, play areas, and food services that attract people of all ages. For more than 50 years, the program has not only provided long-term, structured older adult care but also demonstrated how built environments focus on flexibility for diverse populations while strengthening ties across generations.

Insights learned: Germany's Urban Development Support Programme demonstrates the emergence of all five key dimensions that underpin the vitality of Silver Economy initiatives. Social Integration is evident through district meeting points like Frankfurt am Main's Quäkerplatz Neighbourhood Pavilion, which hosts cultural events, play areas, and food services that foster meaningful connections across generations. Economic Engagement is supported by business-led partnerships and flexible, needs-oriented measures, such as adaptable housing models in Bremerhaven (Vario-Wohnungen), which stimulate local economies by addressing shifting demographic needs and creating opportunities for both older and younger residents. Health and Well-being emerges from integrated urban planning and accessible housing, enabling older adults to live comfortably while promoting active participation and long-term care. Reciprocal Support is seen in participatory approaches and community spaces where residents of all ages engage in shared activities, reinforcing mutual assistance and collective learning. Finally, Community Resilience is demonstrated by the program's sustained impact—over 50 years and thousands of projects—showing adaptability to ecological, demographic, and economic challenges while strengthening intergenerational bonds and supporting sustainable urban renewal. These examples illustrate how Germany's approach provides practical evidence for the effectiveness of intergenerational strategies in cultivating cohesive, economically active, and resilient communities.

3. The United States: Experience Corps

Experience Corps is an intergenerational health promotion initiative recruiting, training, and deploying older adult volunteers in underserved elementary schools. Volunteers commit 15+ hours per week, participating as teams to maximize school-wide impact and generativity. Features include structured training, ongoing support, and expense reimbursement. Outcomes documented include 80% volunteer retention, proven cost-effectiveness, improved physical, mental, and cognitive health for older adults, enhanced academic performance and school climate, higher teacher retention, and increased community engagement. (Glass et al., 2004).

Features/Highlights: Grounded in the concept of generativity and social capital, key features of the program include generative roles, time commitment (15+ hours per week), deployment of volunteers in critical mass to maximize school-wide impact, and a team-based approach to foster collaboration. Volunteers receive training, ongoing support, and expense reimbursements to encourage participation. The program has demonstrated significant outcomes, including 80% volunteer retention rates, proven cost-effectiveness, improved physical, mental, and cognitive health for older adults, enhanced academic performance and school climate, higher teacher retention, and increased community involvement (2004).

Insights learned: The Experience Corps initiative in the United States exemplifies the emergence of all five key dimensions underpinning the vitality of Silver Economy projects. Social Integration is fostered through the deployment of older adult volunteers in underserved elementary schools, where their regular participation as teams promotes meaningful intergenerational relationships and strengthens community ties. Economic Engagement is demonstrated by the program's cost-effectiveness and expense reimbursement for volunteers, making participation accessible and incentivizing ongoing involvement. Health and Well-being is evident in documented outcomes such as improved physical, mental, and cognitive health among older adults, as well as enhanced academic performance and school climate for children and teachers. Reciprocal Support arises from the generative roles played by volunteers, who provide tutoring and mentorship to students while benefiting themselves from structured training, ongoing support, and a sense of purpose. Finally, Community Resilience is reflected in the program's high volunteer retention rate, increased community engagement, and positive impact on teacher retention, collectively contributing to a more cohesive, supportive, and adaptable school environment. These examples from Experience Corps provide practical evidence for the effectiveness of intergenerational strategies in cultivating integrated, economically active, healthy, mutually supportive, and resilient communities.

4. Singapore: Kampung Admiralty

Kampung Admiralty is Singapore's first integrated public housing development, combining residential, healthcare, and community spaces for seniors and families. Located near a train station on a compact 0.9-hectare site with 4,730 m^2 of green spaces, it features senior housing, a medical center, food court, retail spaces, childcare center, active aging hub, and community plaza. The rooftop includes cascading terraces, a park, and a farm, creating a "vertical village" that encourages active aging, sustainable living, and improved access to services. This integrated planning approach enhances quality of life and provides a supportive multigenerational environment. (Urban Land Institute Asia Pacific, 2023; Loh et al., 2025).

Features/Highlights: A highlight of Kampung Admiralty is its intergenerational contact zone, which fosters connections (e.g., gardening in the rooftop community farm and participating in workshops and health programs) between the childcare center and the active aging hub on the sixth floor, complemented by a community park with a children's playground and exercise equipment for older people (Lim, Teo, Tan & Ong, 2022).

Insights learned: The Kampung Admiralty development in Singapore provides compelling insights into all five key dimensions that underpin successful intergenerational initiatives. Social Integration is promoted through the intergenerational contact zone, where seniors and children interact via activities like gardening in the rooftop community farm, participating in workshops, and health programs, fostering meaningful relationships across age groups. Economic Engagement emerges from the mix of retail spaces, food courts, and a community plaza, which not only generate economic activity but also provide affordable access to essential goods and services for residents of all ages. Health and Well-being is addressed through the inclusion of a medical center, active aging hub, and exercise equipment tailored to older adults, as well as a children's playground, ensuring that both physical and mental health needs are met within an integrated environment. Reciprocal Support is evident in the design that encourages mutual assistance; for example, the proximity of the childcare center and active aging hub allows opportunities for seniors to support families and vice versa, strengthening community bonds. Finally, Community Resilience is embodied in the sustainable, compact "vertical village" model with green spaces and cascading terraces, which enhances quality of life, supports multigenerational living, and adapts to changing demographic needs, making Kampung Admiralty a robust and adaptable urban community.

5. Spain: Intergenerational Home-Sharing Program

Spain's Intergenerational Home-Sharing Program matches older homeowners with university students or young people seeking accommodation. The arrangement fosters mutual support: young participants provide companionship and light assistance in exchange for affordable housing, usually sharing utility costs without extra compensation. The program addresses loneliness among older adults, supports affordable housing needs of youth, and promotes social inclusion and community ties. (Martinez et al., 2020; Sánchez et al., 2011).

Features/Highlights: Key initiatives include "Convive" in Madrid and "Vive y Convive" in Barcelona. In "Convive," students spend at least two hours daily with elders, engaging in activities like chatting, eating together, or walking and are expected to return home before 10:30 PM except for one day a week, while "Vive y Convive" similarly follows a mutual aid model with shared utility costs (Costa, 2020). This program model has undergone multiple reviews world-wide since 2011, consistently demonstrating positive outcomes in promoting active aging, reducing social isolation, and encouraging intergenerational learning by building trust and dispelling stereotypes (Sánchez, et al., 2011; Labit & Dubost, 2016; Costa, 2020; Martinez et al., 2020).

Insights learned: The Intergenerational Home-Sharing Program in Spain exemplifies several key dimensions of successful intergenerational initiatives. Social Integration is fostered by matching older homeowners with university students or young people, creating daily opportunities for companionship through shared activities such as chatting, eating together, or walking—helping to reduce loneliness and promote social inclusion. Economic Engagement is achieved by offering affordable housing to young participants who share utility costs, making the arrangement financially accessible for both parties. Health and Well-being is addressed as the program promotes active aging for seniors, providing emotional support and reducing isolation, which can have positive effects on mental health. Reciprocal Support is central to the model: young residents offer light assistance and companionship in exchange for accommodation, building trust and dispelling stereotypes between generations. Finally, Community Resilience is strengthened by encouraging intergenerational learning and mutual aid, as seen in initiatives like "Convive" and "Vive y Convive," which have consistently demonstrated positive outcomes in reviews, helping to create a more cohesive and supportive community environment.

6. China: Sunflower Hut Program

Originating in Guangzhou, the Sunflower Hut Program is an intergenerational initiative organized by the Guangdong Family Planning Association and managed by the Wenchong Sub-district Office. It facilitates engagement between grandparents, parents, and children, targeting childcare burdens and caregiving stress for dual-working families. The model integrates nursing and nursery services in shared facilities, with co-shared grandparents as core participants. The program is distinguished by its replicability and innovative approach to intergenerational caregiving in urban communities. (Southern Daily, 2022; Lai, Qi & Luo, 2025).

Features/Highlights: Operating daily from 3 PM to 5 PM, the program offers interactive activities for grandparents and parents on weekdays and parent-child courses on weekends, utilizing advanced technologies such as blockchain for secure, timestamped information sharing, as well as smart screens and cameras for remote monitoring to ensure safety and convenience (Southern Daily, 2022). Additionally, the program has demonstrated significant impact and scalability, serving 126 families, facilitating 750 service instances, and involving 120 senior volunteers within three months. Its wide adoption across multiple cities (n=8) China's Greater Bay Area highlights its replicability and potential for broader implementation (Lai, Qi & Luo, 2025).

Insights learned: The Sunflower Hut Program in Guangzhou offers valuable insights across several key dimensions of successful intergenerational initiatives. Social Integration is promoted through daily interactive activities that engage grandparents, parents, and children, fostering meaningful connections across generations within a shared space. The program enhances Health and Well-being by alleviating childcare burdens and caregiving stress for dual-working families, providing a safe and supportive environment where both children and caregivers benefit emotionally and physically. Reciprocal Support is evident in the model's structure, which relies on co-shared grandparents as core participants, encouraging mutual assistance between seniors and families, and empowering older adults to contribute actively as volunteers—demonstrated by the involvement of 120 senior volunteers. The program also strengthens Community Resilience through its innovative integration of technology (such as blockchain for secure information sharing and smart screens for remote monitoring), ensuring safety, convenience, and adaptability to urban community needs. Its successful replication in eight cities within the Greater Bay Area and its rapid scalability—serving 126 families and facilitating 750 service instances in just three months—demonstrate its capacity to support and adapt to changing demographic and social needs at a broader scale.

7. South Africa: Grandmothers Against Poverty and AIDS (GAPA)

GAPA, founded in Cape Town in 2001, empowers grandmothers—particularly those caring for children orphaned by public health crises—as community anchors and key agents of the Silver Economy. Program activities include group meetings, skills training, health education workshops, peer support, and micro-finance. GAPA strengthens intergenerational ties and community resilience, highlighting the role of older adults in crisis response and sustainable development. (Gianturco, 2012; Brodrick & Mafuya, 2005).

Features/Highlights: GAPA's grandmothers —often called "The Nevergiveups" — and GAPA as the "place of healing" focus on a model of self-help, leverage the collaboration of grandmothers to bridging generational gaps, combating ageism, and providing emotional and practical support in the face of social and familial disruption caused by public health crisis epidemic (Gianturco, 2012). According to GABA's website (www.gapa.org.za/), the initiative's income-generation projects (such as crafts and gardening) aim to enable grandmothers to support their families and contribute to local economic vitality, and it highlights demonstrated outcomes in terms of stronger intergenerational ties with children experiencing increased emotional security and educational support, along with measurable results, such as, GAPA's after-school, everyday program providing meals, homework help, and a safe environment for over 100 vulnerable children since 2008.

Insights learned: The Grandmothers Against Poverty and AIDS (GAPA) initiative in South Africa demonstrates the importance of all five dimensions of successful intergenerational programming. Social Integration is fostered through group meetings and peer support, where grandmothers serve as community anchors, bridging generational gaps and combating ageism. Economic Engagement is achieved by empowering grandmothers with income-generation projects such as crafts and gardening, enabling them to support their families and contribute to local economic vitality. Health and Well-being is addressed through health education workshops and the provision of a "place of healing," supporting grandmothers and children emotionally and practically in the aftermath of public health crises. Reciprocal Support is evident as grandmothers provide daily meals, homework help, and a safe environment to over 100 vulnerable children through GAPA's after-school program, while also gaining emotional support and empowerment from their peers. Finally, Community Resilience is strengthened by positioning older adults as key agents of crisis response and sustainable development, with GAPA's model of self-help and collaboration illustrating how communities can adapt and thrive in the face of social disruption.

Table 1. Cases of intergenerational and age-friendly community initiatives

Cases	Dimensions Highlighted in Insights Learned as Results
(1) Japan's "Nagayama model"	Social Integration, Health and Well-being, Reciprocal Support, and Community Resilience.
(2) Germany's Urban Development Support Programme	Social Integration, Economic Engagement, Health and Well-being, Reciprocal Support, and Community Resilience.
(3) US's Experience Corps	Social Integration, Economic Engagement, Health and Well-being, Reciprocal Support, and Community Resilience.
(4) Singapore's Kampung Admiralty	Social Integration, Economic Engagement, Health and Well-being, Reciprocal Support, and Community Resilience.
(5) Spain's Home-Sharing Program	Social Integration, Economic Engagement, Health and Well-being, Reciprocal Support, and Community Resilience.
(6) China's Sunflower Hut	Social Integration, Health and Well-being, Reciprocal Support, and Community Resilience.
(7) South Africa's GAPA	Social Integration, Economic Engagement, Health and Well-being, Reciprocal Support, and Community Resilience.

Figure 1. The five dimensions rooted in the insights learned from seven cases

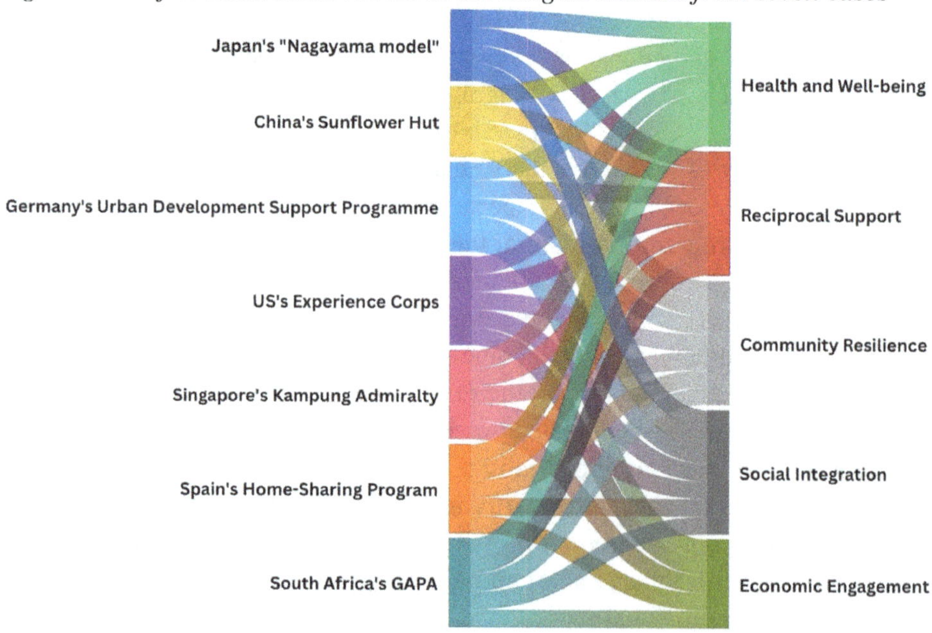

Comparison and Contrast

Across all seven cases, a unifying theme is the strategic use of intergenerational engagement to strengthen and sustain the Silver Economy. The Nagayama model and Sunflower Hut, for example, demonstrate how organizing activities for various age groups, from health classes to collaborative workshops, helps reactivate mutual support between generations and builds a network of care. These grassroots efforts create environments where knowledge, skills, and social support are shared among young and old alike.

Similarly, Germany's Urban Development Support Programme and Singapore's Kampung Admiralty leverage intergenerational strategies in their urban planning and policy initiatives, designing inclusive spaces and integrated services that encourage daily interaction and shared experiences among multiple generations. The US's Experience Corps offers a compelling example of older adults serving as mentors to youth, turning volunteerism into a powerful tool for both social cohesion and lifelong contribution. Spain's Home-Sharing Program matches older adults with younger residents, directly addressing isolation and housing challenges for both groups while promoting mutual assistance. Meanwhile, South Africa's GAPA stands out for empowering older women to lead and advocate for community well-being, particularly strengthening intergenerational ties in contexts affected by poverty and public health epidemic.

While the specific methods and cultural contexts differ, Table 1 also illustrates that successful age-friendly and intergenerational community initiatives consistently address multiple dimensions—such as social integration, reciprocal support, and community resilience—regardless of geography. Notably, programs that incorporate economic engagement and health and well-being outcomes, like Germany's Urban Development Support Programme or South Africa's GAPA, tend to produce broader societal benefits. This underscores the importance of designing interventions that holistically engage older and younger generations, adapt to local needs, and leverage both formal policy frameworks and grassroots action for sustainable community impact.

Together, these cases reveal that intergenerational strategies are not only effective for fostering solidarity and resilience, but are also key to unlocking the creative, social, and economic potential of aging populations. By intentionally bridging generational divides, each initiative highlights new possibilities for innovation, adaptability, and shared prosperity within the Silver Economy.

TOWARDS THE SILVER ECONOMY VITALITY SCALE

Building on findings learned within a comparative framework, there is a compelling opportunity to develop a systematic scale for measuring SEV. Such a scale aims to facilitate consistent assessment of intergenerational strategies across varied contexts while providing researchers and policymakers with actionable metrics for evaluating impact. Additionally, systematically measuring SEV holds significant importance for the broader Social Economy, as it enables stakeholders to amplify the social and economic contributions of older adults within communities.

A proposed SEV scale could incorporate the five dimensions reflected in the cases, and initial interpretations have been presented before. With greater access and deeper understanding to data and viewpoints, the dimensions are refined and broadened to better reflect how service and business collaboration advances the Silver Economy as follows:

- **Social Integration**: Degree of participation and engagement among different generations, measured by participation rates in shared activities and perceived community cohesion.
- **Economic Engagement**: Involvement of older and younger populations in productive activities, employment, or entrepreneurship, tracked through employment statistics, volunteerism, or business partnerships.
- **Health and Well-being**: Outcomes related to physical and mental health, well-being, and quality of life, assessed through health indicators and self-reported well-being.
- **Reciprocal Support**: Extent of mentorship, mutual assistance, and knowledge exchange between generations, captured by the frequency and depth of intergenerational interactions.
- **Community Resilience**: Capacity of communities to adapt, innovate, and respond to demographic change, as indicated by measures of local collaboration and perceived resilience.

The following section explains the necessity of incorporating qualitative dimensions to translate them into actionable benchmarks. To support practical implementation, Table 2 will provide a 1-to-5 rubric for each dimension, including benchmarks and illustrative examples at every level.

TRANSFORMING QUALITATIVE DIMENSIONS INTO ACTIONABLE BENCHMARKS

Accurately measuring SEV is essential for policymakers and researchers seeking to assess and enhance the social and economic contributions of older adults within communities. While refined qualitative dimensions—such as those describing social integration, economic engagement, and reciprocal support—provide contextualized understanding, relying solely on qualitative interpretations is arguably problematic. This section aims to present the necessity of translating qualitative insights into quantifiable rubrics, outline the process for developing benchmarks, and provide illustrative examples for this transformation.

Limitations of Qualitative Dimensions

Qualitative dimensions offer nuanced perspectives, capturing the lived experiences and contextual realities of diverse populations. However, they present notable limitations for systematic assessment and policy application since they are inherently subjective and can be interpreted differently by various evaluators, leading to inconsistencies in assessment. Without quantifiable benchmarks, it is challenging to compare results across programs, settings, or time periods. Furthermore, qualitative data alone often lack the precision required for policy formulation, resource allocation, and outcome monitoring. The absence of standardized measurement impedes the ability to scale successful interventions and to demonstrate impact in a manner that is both credible and actionable.

Need for Quantifiable Rubrics

Transforming qualitative interpretations into quantifiable rubrics addresses these challenges by establishing clear, consistent criteria for evaluating SEV dimensions. Rubrics enable the systematic translation of descriptive insights into measurable indicators, allowing for comparative analysis and longitudinal tracking. Quantifiable rubrics enhance the reliability of assessments, facilitate aggregation of results, and support evidence-based decision-making. Importantly, they bridge the gap between rich qualitative understanding and the requirements of rigorous program evaluation and policy development.

Transformation Process: From Qualitative Insights to Rubric Benchmarks

The process of converting qualitative insights into rubric benchmarks involves several steps. First, qualitative data—such as case study descriptions, comparative interpretations, reported findings, and observational data—are analyzed to identify themes, recurring insights learned or critical indicators of success as dimensions within each SEV case. These dimensions are then — proposed — as benchmarks representing distinct levels of performance, typically ranging from minimal to exemplary (e.g., a 1-to-5 scale). Each benchmark is defined with clear, observable criteria and supported by illustrative examples drawn from empirical evidence.

For instance, in the Social Integration dimension, qualitative evidence of frequent intergenerational activities and strong community participation may be mapped to a higher benchmark (e.g., "Advanced" or "Exemplary"), whereas sporadic engagement or limited shared spaces would correspond to lower ratings. This transformation ensures that qualitative richness informs, rather than supplants, standardized assessment.

Determining Rubric Descriptions and Ratings

From a scholarly perspective, developing rubric descriptions and ratings is grounded in established qualitative research methodologies and psychometric principles. This approach aims to ensure that rubric benchmarks are both theoretically sound and empirically grounded, enhancing the credibility and utility of SEV measurement. The process involves:

- Systematic Analysis: Systematic coding of qualitative data to extract key patterns and indicators relevant to each dimension.
- Operationalization: Defining abstract concepts (e.g., "community resilience") as concrete, observable behaviors or outcomes.
- Benchmark Calibration: Assigning performance levels based on the frequency, consistency, and depth of observed behaviors, supported by empirical examples.
- Validation: Engaging subject matter experts to review and refine rubric descriptions, ensuring content validity and practical relevance.

Illustrative Examples: Developing and Interpreting Ratings

Considering the dimensions as articulated in the SEV framework, the following illustrates how qualitative findings are systematically converted into rubric ratings:

- Minimal (1): Qualitative data reveal infrequent or isolated intergenerational activities. Benchmark: "Limited opportunities for interaction; participation is rare and largely unstructured."
- Developing (3): Evidence shows regular but not widespread engagement. Benchmark: "Some shared activities and spaces; participation is growing but not yet consistent across the community."
- Exemplary (5): Qualitative accounts describe seamless, daily intergenerational integration and high levels of belonging. Benchmark: "Intergenerational interaction is embedded in daily life; shared spaces and collaborative activities are the norm."

Each level is substantiated with concrete examples or direct quotations from case studies, providing both clarity and transparency. This approach ensures that ratings are not arbitrary but are instead anchored in observable reality and scholarly consensus.

With both quantitative and qualitative data to inform the SEV scale in place, enabling a nuanced understanding of impact becomes more possible. Take the Japanese model as an example. The benchmark ratings of the Social Integration dimension span from "advanced=4" to "exemplary=5," with each level supported by qualitative findings extracted directly from a published journal article. For example, the "Advanced=4" rating (indicating frequent collaborative activities, shared spaces, and strong participation) is substantiated by evidence such as:"*To prevent social isolation: encouraging seniors to get out of the home and socialize by getting university students from nearby universities to form groups and knock on doors. It also calls for creating more community spaces for gathering*" (p. 3). Likewise, the "Exemplary=5" rating (reflecting seamless integration into daily life and a high sense of belonging across generations) is demonstrated by the following excerpt: "*To promote multigenerational interaction: this includes to engage seniors as volunteers for children; and finding community spaces for residents to hold gathering. This can be done through transforming the vacant classrooms in schools for community usage and providing multi-generational housing for new residents*" (p. 3). Other similar findings and dimensions of the case can be referred to Table 3.

SEV Scorecard and Radar Chart

Additionally, Appendix A (SEV Benchmark Assessment) includes the SEV Scorecard, which is designed to visualize the measurement of SEV performance and provide performance metrics aligned with the scale. The appendix also presents the radar chart—a filled polygon that visually emphasizes areas of strength—depicting a case's Silver Economy Vitality profile across the five SEV dimensions. Leveraging both the scorecard and radar chart, GAPA is incorporated as a case study in the benchmark assessment, illustrating how grandmother-led initiatives can drive Silver Economy Vitality by:

- Benchmarking intergenerational reciprocity and resilience at exemplary levels,
- Demonstrating that older adults are economic and social agents, not dependents,
- Providing a scalable reference point for policy investment in community embedded, intergenerational care models.

By establishing clear benchmarks and outcome measures within these domains, the SEV scale would guide program design, support comparative analysis, and inform policy adaptation.

Table 2. SEV scale rubric: Dimensions and stages of intergenerational integration in the silver economy

Dimension	Minimal=1	Emerging=2	Developing=3	Advanced=4	Exemplary=5	Examples
Social Integration	Limited or no interaction between generations; high social isolation	Occasional organized intergenerational activities; low awareness	Regular scheduled intergenerational events; moderate participation	Frequent collaborative activities and shared spaces; strong participation	Seamless integration in daily life; high sense of belonging across ages	Japan's community-based care centers (4–5): Daily shared activities and facilities.
Economic Engagement	Few opportunities for productive engagement; age-segregated employment	Some targeted initiatives for older/younger workers; limited impact	Collaborative or mentorship programs linking generations in work/volunteering	Cross-generational entrepreneurship and business partnerships	Integrated economic roles and ongoing innovation driven by all age groups	Germany's age-friendly urban partnerships (3–4): Business and government cooperation
Health and Well-being	High prevalence of loneliness, low access to services, or poor reported well-being	Basic health promotions, limited preventative or social supports	Structured wellness programs and periodic health screenings	Integrated physical/mental health supports accessible to all ages	Holistic well-being with reported improvements across all generations	Singapore's Kampung Admiralty (4–5): Integrated housing, health, and social spaces; China's Sunflower Hut (4): Reduces caregiving stress and fosters meaningful intergenerational connections in a supportive environment.

continued on following page

Table 2. Continued

Dimension	Minimal=1	Emerging=2	Developing=3	Advanced=4	Exemplary=5	Examples
Reciprocal Support	Minimal or one-way assistance between age groups	Occasional mentorship or support, but not systematic	Organized mentoring/tutoring, mutual support programs	Reciprocal, ongoing exchange of skills, knowledge, and assistance	Embedded culture of mutual aid and learning across generations	US Experience Corps (3–4): Older adults as regular school mentors/tutors; Spain's Intergenerational Housing (4–5): Mutual support and co-living
Community Resilience	Fragmented community, limited capacity to address demographic shifts	Emerging networks, ad hoc collaborations in crisis	Regularized partnerships with social and business sectors	Proactive planning, innovation, and adaptation for demographic challenges	Robust, adaptable community systems with cross-sector resilience	Germany's infrastructure partnerships (4); Singapore's Kampung Admiralty (5): Multi-sector collaboration; China's Sunflower Hut (4-5): a model for sustainable and impactful intergenerational programming and urban community development.

Table 3. Using Japan's "Nagayama model" case to demonstrate mapping of qualitative findings to SEV dimensions

Dimension	Advanced=4	Exemplary=5	Case Example
Social Integration	*"To provide 'Chokotto service' (Daily life support): creating the role of a life support coordinator in the community, ensuring the provision of services to support daily life at a reasonable rate; and to achieve more aims by providing lunch services for seniors in the nursery so as to promote exchanges between the seniors and children*" (p. 3).	*"To promote 'Choibora' (lit. to volunteer through paying some attention to the surrounding): setting up of a casual watch group to watch out for one another, focusing on relationship development and raise awareness on the need to help those requiring help around us*" (p. 3).	Japan's community-based care centers (Thang, Yui, Wakabayashi & Miyazawa, 2023)
Economic Engagement	*"Nekosapo provides services for all ages, including working couples who may need similar housework and cleaning support services"* (p. 5).	*"The community seems to be based on local networks united by a commonality of interest (i.e.12 tackling depopulation in Nagayama) with outcomes for community more aimed at positive local development"* (p. 6).	
Health and Well-being	*"It organizes classes such as health check, painting class for adults, cooking class for mothers, parent and child yoga, handicraft classes and so on... For health promotion, it organizes free walking activity during the weekends for the residents*" (P. 5).	*"Having in existence for close to two decades, Fukushi-tei has essentially formed a care node that provides comfort and build reliable network support among the residents in the neighbourhood. It has developed a strong reputation for its community roles and achievements, and are widely featured in publications and national media as a successful community project in depopulated bed-towns"* (p. 5)	
Reciprocal Support	*"The system suggests a 'reactivation of the mutual help that may still exist within families or among residents of a same community"* (p. 3).	*"The first 'Nagayama district workshop' set the momentum for subsequent regular workshops among the stakeholders as they co-created concrete measures for the ideas proposed, with the administration playing a supporting role"* (p. 3).	
Community Resilience	[Yet detected]	*"The involvement of community-minded private entities could inject new ideas to strengthen community-based support... Furthermore, it may enable local municipalities to leverage on the nature of courier business in accessing private homes and connecting with residents in need of community support, such as those who are living alone or turning frail*" (p. 5).	

IMPLICATIONS

Recent literature affirms that data-driven evaluation frameworks are vital for but often hampered by the attempts of navigating complexities, ensuring accountability, and fostering innovation (European Commission, 2018; Galeotti et al., 2024; Liu, 2025). The SEV Scale is in this light a direct response to these challenges, providing a standardized means of measuring progress, supporting strategic investment, and enhancing cross-sector collaboration. The inclusion of concrete examples from international cases grounds the scale in real-world application, offering guidance for future research and policy innovation.

One implication is that given the diverse health, mobility, digital literacy, and socioeconomic backgrounds among older adults (WHO, 2015; Rijken et al., 2018), the SEV scale can be considered as a practice/policy-oriented tool for benchmarking efforts made, setting goals for improvement, and evaluating the effectiveness of intergenerational strategies in enhancing the Silver Economy.

In illustrating the potential of data-driven evaluation for the Silver Economy, this chapter presents how diverse cases exemplifies the transformative impact of initiatives when assessed with the SEV Scale. By applying the SEV rubric, stakeholders can rigorously appraise contributions, efforts, and outcomes across dimensions such as economic engagement, intergenerational interaction, and community cohesion.

The integration of evaluative mechanisms—such as the SEV Scorecard, radar charts, and detailed profiles—suggests that policymakers are likely to gain more nuanced and actionable insights, a development that focuses on more precise decision-making regarding resource allocation and program development. This implication underscores the potential for these tools not only to enhance analytical rigor but also to advance evidence-based policy formulation within the evolving landscape of the Silver Economy.

With the SEV Scale rubric, policymakers could also draw up pipelines prioritizing the development of frameworks that support cross-sector partnerships and intergenerational strategies for sustaining the Silver Economy.

In doing so, recommendations include incentivizing collaborative innovation, investing in intergenerational programming, and fostering inclusive governance models. In these fronts, the scale aims to promote dialogue and enhance adaptability.

FINAL REMARKS

This chapter relates Silver Economy frameworks to encompassing the broad spectrum of economic activities, products, and services that cater to the needs and preferences of older adults, with an emphasis on ongoing dynamism, adaptability, and innovative capacity. Notably, the database sources suggest that while numerous initiatives exist globally, only a subset fully meets the comprehensive criteria regarding intergenerational involvement, partnership, impact, replicability, and recognition, as applied in the comparative analysis of this chapter.

All in all, intergenerational strategies are highlighted as a viable method for the Silver Economy mainly due to the economic value generated by the aging population and the potential for growth by actively engaging older adults as contributors and innovators. The challenge perhaps is to understand how to relate its viability to how the exchange of knowledge and resources is encouraged, and how inclusive, sustainable models for older people care are created and sustained. There is also a need in practice to relate progress to related industries, thereby facilitating resource sharing, and scaling impactful solutions that benefit both older adults and society as a whole. This interconnectedness underscores the importance of developing evidence-based tools, such as the scale and benchmark approach presented in this chapter, to assess and inform the effectiveness of intergenerational strategies, thereby supporting ongoing innovation, social cohesion, and adaptive leadership. The SEV Scale is introduced in this advancement to facilitate the transition from theoretical potential to practical implementation or dissemination within the Silver Economy.

While the SEV rubric and scale approach may offer a replicable framework for benchmarking similar programs, it is important to note that the tool's introduction draws from a small size of case examples, and additional studies are required to assess its effectiveness, validity, and reliability. A key limitation of this chapter is that it remains unsure on how to fully address the long-term implementation and institutionalization of the SEV Scale and its reporting instruments within policy formulation for the Silver Economy. Future research should focus on evaluating the sustained integration of these tools in diverse policy contexts, exploring their effectiveness over time, and identifying best practices for widespread adoption. This gap highlights the need for ongoing investigation to ensure that the SEV Scale can serve as a robust foundation for policy innovation and practical impact in the Silver Economy.

It is also crucial to note that sustaining the vitality of the Silver Economy requires a multifaceted approach that integrates social service and business partnerships with intergenerational strategies and expect/evaluation supports for benchmarking how much has been accomplished. By leveraging the strengths of diverse age groups, organizational sectors, and relevant expertise, stakeholders can create resilient, innovative systems of older people care. Considering the reality that tailoring effective and adaptable initiatives is particularly challenging, future research should explore new models of collaboration while investigating the evolving needs of aging populations more effectively.

In summary, while qualitative dimensions are indispensable for capturing the complexity of Silver Economy initiatives, their practical value is significantly enhanced when systematically transformed into quantifiable rubrics. This process offers a consistent and actionable approach for SEV measurement that can inform policy development and program evaluation across contexts; however, its true value in promoting inclusive policies, equitable opportunities, and sustainable community development within the Silver Economy remains to be fully demonstrated through further research. Ultimately, the ongoing challenge of advancing innovation and resilience in the Silver Economy lies in equipping stakeholders with the capacity to identify, implement, and expand successful intergenerational strategies through quantifiable, rubric-based assessment.

REFERENCES

Brodrick, K., & Mafuya, M. (2005). Effectiveness of the non-profit organisation,'Grandmothers Against Poverty and AIDS'-a study. *Southern African Journal of HIV Medicine*, *2005*(19), 37–41. DOI: 10.4102/sajhivmed.v6i2.588

Buffel, T. (2025). Co-creating Age-Friendly Futures. *Generations Journal*, *49*(1), 1–8.

Costa, G. (2020). Intergenerational homesharing programmes: A piece of the'ageing in place'puzzle?. Interações: Sociedade e as novas modernidades, (38), 11-42.

European Commission. (2018). The Silver Economy Study: How to Stimulate the Economy by Hundreds of Millions of Euros per Year. Publications Office of the European Union. Retrieved from https://digital-strategy.ec.europa.eu/en/library/silver-economy-study-how-stimulate-economy-hundreds-millions-euros-year

Federal Ministry of the Interior. Building and Community. (2020). Holistic, Sustainable, Collaborative 50 Years of the Urban Development Support Programme in Germany. Berlin, Germany: Federal Ministry of the Interior, Building and Community. Retrieved from https://www.staedtebaufoerderung.info/EN/home/home_node.html

Galeotti, M., D'Andrassi, E., Savio, R., & Ventimiglia, F. (2024). The intersection of governmental policies and corporate strategies: Population aging and the silver economy. *Corporate Ownership & Control*, *21*(4), 117–128. DOI: 10.22495/cocv21i4art10

Gan, L. (2021). *Building Communities for All Ages: Good Intergenerational Practice*. Inner East Primary Care Partnership. Retrived from https://vicpcp.org.au/wp-content/uploads/2022/06/IEPCP-Building-Communities-for-All-Ages-Good-Intergenerational-Practice.pdf

Gianturco, P. (2012). *Grandmother power: A global phenomenon*. PowerHouse Books.

Glass, T. A., Freedman, M., Carlson, M. C., Hill, J., Frick, K. D., Ialongo, N., & Fried, L. P. (2004). Experience Corps: Design of an intergenerational program to boost social capital and promote the health of an aging society. *Journal of Urban Health : Bulletin of the New York Academy of Medicine*, *81*(1), 94–105. DOI: 10.1093/jurban/jth096 PMID: 15047788

Gök, A., Antai, R., Milošević, N., & Al-Nabki, W. (2022). Building the European Social Innovation Database with Natural Language Processing and Machine Learning. *Scientific Data*, *9*(1), 697. DOI: 10.1038/s41597-022-01818-0 PMID: 36371515

Kaplan, M., Sanchez, M., & Hoffman, J. (2017). *Intergenerational pathways to a sustainable society*. Springer International Publishing. DOI: 10.1007/978-3-319-47019-1

Kaplan, M. S. (2002). International programs in schools: Considerations of form and function. *International Review of Education, 48*(5), 305–334. DOI: 10.1023/A:1021231713392

Klimczuk, A. (2015). Economic Foundations for Creative Ageing Policy: Volume I Context and Considerations. Springer.

Labit, A., & Dubost, N. (2016). Housing and ageing in France and Germany: The intergenerational solution. Housing. *Care and Support, 19*(2), 45–54. DOI: 10.1108/HCS-08-2016-0007

Lai, A., Qi, J., & Luo, T. (2025). *Intergenerational Silk Route: The Greater Bay "WIN-WIN" Area*. China Culture Publishing House.

Lim, Y. W., Teo, K., Tan, C., & Ong, J. (2022). Promoting Healthy Longevity–The Role of Social Innovation. Future Urban Habitation: Transdisciplinary Perspectives, Conceptions, and Designs, 287-300.

Liu, Y. (2025). Research on the Silver Economy from the Perspective of Human Resource Development. In *2025 International Conference on Financial Innovation and Marketing Management (FIMM 2025)* (pp. 1300-1308). Atlantis Press. DOI: 10.2991/978-94-6463-874-5_147

Loh, W. Y., Nasir, M. H. A., Hassan, A. S., Nordin, J., & Fachrudin, H. T. (2025). Analysis of the level of Permeability and Wayfinding of a Retirement Village: The Case of Kampung Admiralty, Singapore. *International Journal of Built Environment and Sustainability, 12*(1), 135–155. DOI: 10.11113/ijbes.v12.n1.1341

Martinez, L., Mirza, R. M., Austen, A., Hsieh, J., Klinger, C. A., Kuah, M., Liu, A., McDonald, L., Mohsin, R., Pang, C., Rajewski, J., Salomons, T., & Sheikh, I. (2020). More than just a room: A scoping review of the impact of homesharing for older adults. *Innovation in Aging, 4*(2), igaa011. DOI: 10.1093/geroni/igaa011 PMID: 32382662

Matos, R. C. D., Nascimento, G. D., Campos Fernandes, A., & Matos, C. (2025). Health and social care integration: insights from international implementation cases. *Journal of Market Access & Health Policy, 13*(2), 28. DOI: 10.3390/jmahp13020028 PMID: 40568385

Rijken, M., Hujala, A., van Ginneken, E., Melchiorre, M. G., Groenewegen, P., & Schellevis, F. (2018). Managing multimorbidity: Profiles of integrated care approaches targeting people with multiple chronic conditions in Europe. *Health Policy (Amsterdam), 122*(1), 44–52. DOI: 10.1016/j.healthpol.2017.10.002 PMID: 29102089

Sánchez, M., García, J. M., Díaz, P., & Duaigües, M. (2011). Much more than accommodation in exchange for company: Dimensions of solidarity in an Intergenerational Homeshare Program in Spain. *Journal of Intergenerational Relationships, 9*(4), 374–388. DOI: 10.1080/15350770.2011.619410

Sorrentino, M., Fiorilla, C., Mercogliano, M., Esposito, F., Stilo, I., Affinito, G., Moccia, M., Lavorgna, L., Salvatore, E., Maida, E., Barbi, E., Triassi, M., & Palladino, R. (2024). Technological interventions in European dementia care: a systematic review of acceptance and attitudes among people living with dementia, caregivers, and healthcare workers. *Frontiers in Neurology, 15*, 1474336. Sorrentino, M., Fiorilla, C., Mercogliano, M., Esposito, F., Stilo, I., Affinito, G., ... & Palladino, R. (2024). Technological interventions in European dementia care: a systematic review of acceptance and attitudes among people living with dementia, caregivers, and healthcare workers. *Frontiers in Neurology, 15*, 1474336. DOI: 10.3389/fneur.2024.1474336 PMID: 39416661

Southern Daily. (2022, September 5). The first in Guangzhou! Huangpu District to create a "sunflower parent-child hut," explore the community "mutual care childcare services" ! " ", " ". .

Thang, L. L., Yui, Y., Wakabayashi, Y., & Miyazawa, H. (2023). Promoting age-friendly community of support and care in Japan's aging neighborhood: The Nagayama model. *Aging and Health Research, 3*(1), 100111. DOI: 10.1016/j.ahr.2022.100111

Urban Land Institute Asia Pacific. (2023). Kampung Admiralty Case Study, Singapore. Retrieved from https://knowledge.uli.org/-/media/files/case-studies/2023/kampung-admiralty-case-study.pdf

Wang, H., Coyte, P. C., Shi, W., Zong, X., & Zhong, R. (2023). Social governance and sustainable development in elderly services: Innovative models, strategies, and stakeholder perspectives. *Sustainability (Basel), 15*(21), 15414. DOI: 10.3390/su152115414

World Health Organization (WHO). (2015). World Report on Ageing and Health. Geneva: WHO. Retrieved from https://www.who.int/publications/i/item/9789241565042

APPENDIX A

Table 4. SEV Benchmark Assessment: GABA **Scorecard**

SEV Dimension	Benchmark Score (1–5)	Justification (Evidence-Based)
Social Integration	**4 – Advanced**	GAPA operates group meetings, after-school programs, and community spaces that deliberately bring grandmothers and children together, strengthening intergenerational ties and reducing isolation. The organization is described as a "place of healing" and a community anchor, indicating strong, sustained participation rather than occasional interaction.
Economic Engagement	**3 – Developing**	GAPA supports income-generation activities (crafts, gardening) that enable grandmothers to contribute economically and support families. However, the evidence does not show fully integrated, cross-generational entrepreneurship or broader business partnerships, placing it below "advanced."
Health and Well-being	**4 – Advanced**	The program provides health education workshops, peer support, emotional support, meals, and safe environments for children, with measurable outcomes such as improved emotional security and caregiving stability. These indicate integrated psychosocial and health-related benefits, though not a fully holistic system across all ages.
Reciprocal Support	**5 – Exemplary**	GAPA is explicitly built on reciprocal intergenerational support: grandmothers care for and mentor children, while peer collaboration among grandmothers strengthens resilience. Mutual aid is embedded as a cultural norm rather than a program add-on.
Community Resilience	**5 – Exemplary**	GAPA demonstrates long-term adaptability and crisis response (HIV/AIDS context), sustained since 2001, with community-level impacts such as education support, food provision, micro-finance, and collective coping mechanisms. This aligns with "robust, adaptable community systems."

Dimension-by-Dimension Interpretation

1. Social Integration – Advanced (4)

GAPA fosters **frequent and meaningful intergenerational interaction** through structured programs (after-school care, group meetings, shared activities). The evidence supports strong participation and reduced isolation but does not explicitly indicate *seamless daily integration across all community systems*, which would warrant a 5.

2. Economic Engagement – Developing (3)

Income-generation projects empower grandmothers economically and contribute to local vitality. However, the document does not show **systemic cross-generational**

business partnerships or innovation ecosystems, positioning GAPA at a solid but not advanced level.

3. Health and Well-being – Advanced (4)

Health education, peer support, emotional security for children, and caregiving stability demonstrate **integrated mental and social health benefits**. The absence of evidence on fully integrated, multi-age clinical or preventive health systems limits the score to 4.

4. Reciprocal Support – Exemplary (5)

Reciprocity is the **core operating logic** of GAPA. Knowledge exchange, caregiving, emotional labor, and peer collaboration are continuous and culturally embedded, meeting the rubric's highest benchmark.

5. Community Resilience – Exemplary (5)

GAPA's longevity, adaptability to public-health crises, and capacity to mobilize older women as community anchors reflect **high systemic resilience and cross-sector sustainability**, fully aligned with the "exemplary" criterion.

SEV Radar Chart for GAPA

Figure 2.

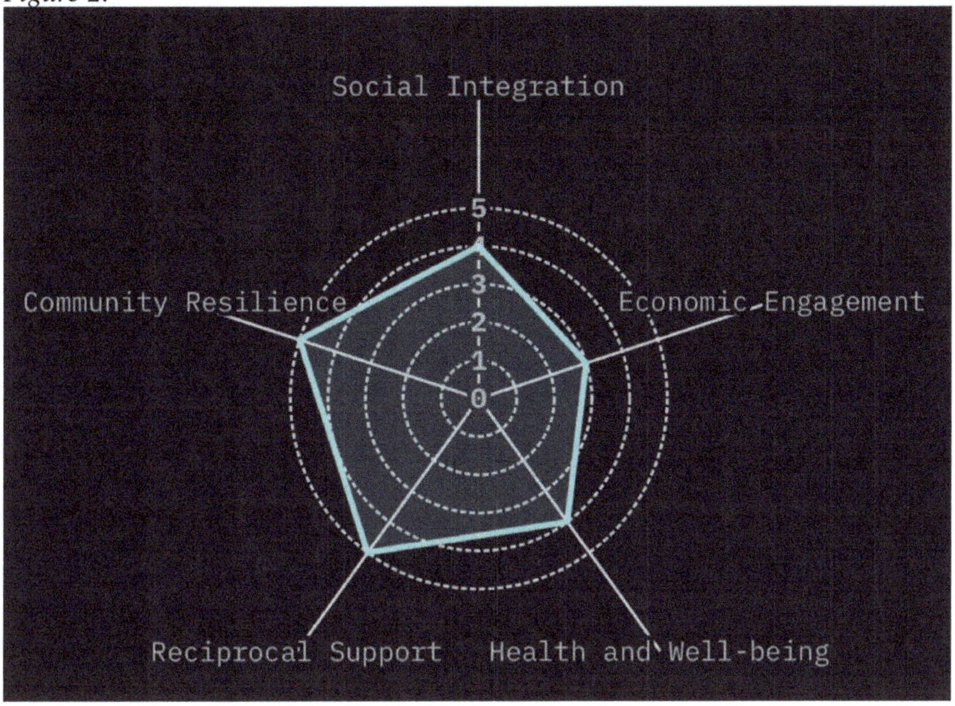

Overall SEV Profile for GABA

GABA Pattern:

- **Strengths:** Reciprocal Support, Community Resilience
- **Solid Performance:** Social Integration, Health & Well-being
- **Growth Opportunity:** Economic Engagement (scaling toward intergenerational entrepreneurship and business partnerships)

Indicative SEV Position:

— **High-Vitality, Community-Anchored Intergenerational Model**

Chapter 11
Expanding Market of Silver Health and Wellness Tourism in China:
The Golden Opportunities for Business and Social Service Partnership

Allen Hu
http://orcid.org/0009-0008-1128-0964
Beijing Normal-Hong Kong Baptist University, China

Johnston H. C. Wong
Beijing Normal-Hong Kong Baptist University, China

Sam Poshan Yu
http://orcid.org/0000-0003-1069-3675
Australian Studies Centre, Shanghai University, China & European Business Institute of Luxembourg, Luxembourg

ABSTRACT

Silver tourism constitutes a major segment of the silver economy, as older adults are healthy and financially independent after retirement. This sector can be broadly divided into two categories namely traditional sightseeing, particularly related to cultural heritage, and health and wellness-oriented activities such as hot spring bathing and physical relaxation. With the expansion of middle-income groups in China, tourism enterprises specifically designed for older adults are emerging and

DOI: 10.4018/979-8-3373-9370-4.ch011

growing rapidly. This development presents a significant opportunity for collaboration between private enterprises and social services, as they bring complementary expertise in business models and understanding the needs of older adults, respectively. This study examines selected cases of such ventures to identify key success factors and examine sustainable collaboration models. Findings suggest that most cases have yet to sharpen their marketing mix however, companies background, professional management, well-defined business plans, and financial strengths are essential factors of commercial viability. As the silver tourism market continues to expand, this study shows that involvement of state-owned enterprises, a distinctive feature of the Chinese economy, can be a contributive partner to social services organizations. The Model of Public Services with Contracted Operators allows medium sized private enterprises to enter the market partnering with both social services and local governments. Finally, integrating care and attention services for older people with disgenerating abilities with the expading businesses of silver tourism, allow the society to rely less on social assistances and income transfers.

INTRODUCTION

Kang (Health) and Yang (Wellness) Tourism

Kang tourism primarily addresses physical or mental health deficiencies and corresponds to the English term medical tourism. Yang tourism, by contrast, focuses on maintaining or enhancing individuals' health and well-being, can be referred as wellness tourism. Health and wellness tourism encompasses all tourism activities that employ various means—such as beauty and fitness regimens, nutritional diets, mental and spiritual cultivation, and engagement with natural environments—to help individuals achieve a state of natural harmony across body, mind, and spirit. This sector is characterized by four key features: a health-oriented focus, extended length of stay, a high degree of specialization, and counter-cyclical travel patterns (DTZ Research, 2023).

In China, the primary consumer group for health and wellness tourism has historically engaged in outbound kang tourism (i.e., medical tourism) to access more advanced medical technologies. Meanwhile, the yang tourism industry, centred on elderly care and recuperation, is flourishing domestically. Currently, as China is rich in geographic and cultural attractions, different regions exhibit special appeals to silver toruism. For example the Chengdu-Chongqing region is rich in its natural environment resources, yet a comprehensive health and wellness industry system has not been formed. The strengths of Shandong region are its high-quality ecological and coastal attractions, but it lacks marketing promotion targetted at the senior traveller. Similarly, Yunnan regions are advantaged by abundant natural and ethnic resources, but there is a disconnect between vacationing and daily life, and the integration of health and wellness elements with tourism is relatively low. Hainan perhaps is most famous among all regions as a special attraction to senior travellers because of its year round warm weather and abundant tourism facilities.

Policy Support for Health and Wellness Tourism

The General Office of the State Council (2021) explicitly proposed to "promote the integrated development of elderly care and tourism," requiring tourist attractions and resorts to strengthen age-friendly renovations and develop health and wellness tourism bases. It also encouraged the creation of tourism products tailored for older adults and supported social forces in building tourism service facilities for residency-based elderly care, thereby fostering this market.

In 2022, the General Office of the State Council, under the section "Optimizing and Strengthening the Health Industry" in its 14th Five-Year Plan, proposed promoting the integrated development of health with elderly care and tourism, supporting the deep integration of residency-based elderly care formats, advancing health tourism, and accelerating the construction of health tourism bases (General Office of the State Council of PRC, 2022). The General Office of the State Council further in 2024 proposed to "expand tourism service formats," requiring the establishment of a nationwide cooperative platform for the residency-based elderly care industry, cultivating residency-based elderly care destinations, and carrying out promotional activities. This marked the first national-level policy document titled after the "silver-haired economy".

Seven departments—including the China Meteorological Administration, the Ministry of Civil Affairs, the Ministry of Culture and Tourism, the National Healthcare Security Administration, the National Forestry and Grassland Administration, the National Administration of Traditional Chinese Medicine, and the National Disease Control and Prevention Administration (2026), jointly issued a document aimed at promoting the deep integration of meteorology and the health and wellness industry. It proposed surveying and assessing climatic wellness resources, creating a unified national map of such resources, enriching "meteorology + culture and tourism" service scenarios, developing climate livability services, transforming climatic resources into health and wellness advantages, and providing scientific support for residency-based health and wellness.

Current Development of Silver Tourism in China

China's ageing population, among which people aged 60 and above will account for 23% and reach approximately 3.23 billion in 2025, has laid a massive market foundation (National Bureau of Statistics of China, 2026). Meanwhile, statistics released by the General Administration of Sport of China in 2025 indicate that the physical fitness qualification rate of the elderly has reached 86.1%, with active elderly groups constituting the majority (China News Service, 2025). According to the Tongcheng Travel, over 80% of surveyed senior citizens stated that they are willing to engage in travelling as long as their physical health and financial conditions permit (CNR.cn., 2016).

A survey conducted among 1,464 respondents aged 60 to 75 reveals that 25.7% of them tend to opt for elderly care via residence tourism (Huatai Life Insurance & AgeClub, 2024). Regarding the monetary value of silver residence tourism, CCTV.com indicated that China's elderly care residence tourism market exceeded 200 billion yuan in 2025 (CCTV.com, 2026). The Blue Book of Silver Economy: Report on the Development of China's Silver Economy, published by the China Federation of Welfare & Senior Service, & Institute of Contemporary Social Service (2024), even forecasts that by 2035, the scale of China's wellness residence tourism featuring in-depth integration of cultural tourism and healthcare wellness, will amount to 5 trillion yuan, and account for 16.7% of the total output value of the silver economy

In terms of regional developments, the Research Report on Development Trends and Competitive Strategies of China's Tourism Industry points out that a complementary spatial pattern has been formed among eastern, central and western China at present (Zero Power Intelligence Group, 2025). Eastern regions develop resort-oriented products relying on high-end medical resources (such as Boao, Hainan), while central and western regions undertake the demand for elderly care residence tourism by virtue of their ecological advantages (such as Guizhou and Sichuan). Simultaneously, the optimisation of transportation networks underpins cross-regional cooperation.

Silver tourism is certainly fueled by the widespread applications of latest technologies. The extensive coverage of high-speed railway networks and the expansion of feeder airports have rendered the trend of migrating southward to escape cold weather and northward to escape summer heat a common phenomenon. Digital technologies further empower the silver tourism growth. Applications including artificial intelligence health monitoring and intelligent healing spaces improve service efficiency, and drive the evolution of wellness tourism towards all-region integration and regularised operation.

Market Dilemmas, Barriers and Failures of Silver Tourism in China

Despite its rapid expansion, the silver tourism market in China faces several challenges that could hinder its maturation. One of the most pressing barriers is the lack of services knowledge in organizing silver tourism. This is a service industry and requires complicated expertise in health and social care. For traditional social service workers and providers, they lack business magament concepts, skills and capital. Meanwhile for private enterprises that intend to enter the silver tourism market, how to design relevant service products while ensuring quality, safety and legal standards, are beyond their realms. This is a golden opportunity for the partnership of private enterprises and social service organizations, if they know how to collaborate. However, such collaborations have difficulties in finding partners, developing business models and sustaining commercial viability. The aim of this chapter is to identify the success factors and workable business models oin the collaborations of Private Enterprises and Social Services, sometimes even involving public policy supports and local government assistance.

LITERATURE REVIEW

The European Commission (EU) published a Report titled "The Silver Economy" in 2018. The report reviewed relevant policy initiatives across EU Member States and have identified a total of 78 policies that are related to the Silver Economy. Their Silver Economy data targeted at EU residents of age 50+. Specific Sectoral Policies of Silver Economy discussed in the Report include Health and Care, Connectivity & Social participation, Entertainment, Culture & Tourism, Living & Building, Mobility & Transport, Physical & Cognitive Abilities, Work & Training, Food and nutrition, and Financial services. (EU, 2018, pg 48-62)

The Report provided case studies on specific industries including Silver Tourism. (EU, 2018. pg 83-90). It is recognized that the industry has diffiuclties in adapting to the interests, needs and expectations of the consumers. The 50+ tourism covers a broad market segment that combines people that are fit, healthy and active with people that are frailer and require more support to overcome mobility and accessability. Subsegments of silver consumers also have different prioirities in health and wellness concerns.

When segmentatization arises as an issue there is a need to refer to the classical theory of marketing mix. Elaborated by Neil Borden of the Harvard Business School as early as 1948, his Marketing Mix theory identified eight variables in the marketing strategy, namely: marketing research, product development, pricing, packaging, distribution, advertising and sales promotion, selling and merchandising, and after-sales services. (Borden, 1959) Subsequently, in 1971, E. Jerome McCarthyl produced the 4Ps version of the marketing mix, placing various components of the mix under Product, Price, Place and Promotion. (McCarthyl, 1960)

As Silver Economy presents a virgin market for private enterprises and social services to collaborate, the parties even interested are not ready. Daniele and Quezada (2017) in their study of business models for tourism social enterprises, suggested that the key components of successful and sustainable operations should include identification of value propositions, key resources, key networks, revenue streams, cost structures, legal structures and marketing channels. The issue becomes more complicated when the social service organization is not only transforming itself into a social enterprise, but to collaborate closely with one or more private enterprises.

Collaboratives of private enterprises and social service organizations, which may or may not be transformed into social enterprises, are not simple business alliances. A strategic alliance involves at least two partner firms that remain legally independent but share benefits and managerial control over the performance of assigned tasks that make continuing commercial contributions in one or more strategic areas. (Yoshino & Rangan, 1995) When social service organization or social enterprises enter into collaborations with private enterprises, a better model to describe the operational models is better provided by Alter (2006). Alter identified seven types of these models that include Entrepreneur Support, Market Intermediary, Employment, Fee for Service, Market Linkage, Service Subsidization and Organizational Support.

The Alter operational types unfortuantely focused mainly from the angle of social enterprises. It does not provide discussions on the success factors for full collaborations between private enterprises and social services organizations which must guarantee social values as well as economic values. Weppen & Cochrane (2012) took the investigation further by collecting data from 11 social tourism projects. They proposed the concepts integrative drivers for success that include leadership, strategy and organisational culture, strategic planning with mission and vision, good internal communications and training, and necessary implementing mechanisms. For successful social enterprises in tourism, implementation mechanisms can be divided further into areas of (1) processes and structure, (2) human resources, (3) financing, (4) governance, (5) performance measurement and (6) market awareness.

Austin et al. (2006) stressed that strong values related to social and environmental mission such as “solidarity, ethics, trust, and mobilisation for action, will help to enhance internal morale. Nevertheless the collaboratives need to balance social values with economic values by creating an income generating culture.

The unfold of literature shows, to make silver tourism business successful we have to design not only the product mix, but archetect a comprehensive business plan. Such business plans should cover company mission and vision, organizational structure, marketing, production and sales operations, training and staff development, finance and evaluation of performances. In terms of performances both economic and social values are at stake. Social impact assessments and reports on Environmental, Social and Governance (ESG) should be considered. Particularly the Integrative Drivers framework can help us to predict whether an operation on silver health and wellness tourism can be successful and sustainable.

METHODLOGY

Since Silver Health and Wellness Tourism is still an emerging market, it is beneficial to adopt a case analysis approach to reveal how pioneers in the field are trying to enter and develop the market. Purposive sampling method is adopted to include different modes of Social Service and Business partnerships available. There are three mjaor modes of operation which can be described as (1) Commercial Social Services, mainly for profit commercial companies eyeing on the Silver consumption power, (2) China state enterprises assisting the city or rural government to provide social services to older people which are supposed to balance their books; and (3) Private and Social Service Partnership which is for profit but enjoy government tangible or intangible financial support such that services to older people can be provided at a lower than market cost.

The three cases selected are the Taikang Community (operated by Private enterprise), the Silver Tourism projects provided by the Wuchan Zhongda Jinshi Group Co., Ltd. (a State Enterprise) and the Koayoung Group Qujing Liaokuo Street Comprehensive Elderly Care Service Center, Yunnan (a Communal social service operated by a private enterprise the Koayoung Group.

It is important to note that all these facilities and services are cater for both local and tourist customers. In China, as in other parts of the world, residents may wish to own an additional property for seasonal living, to avoid either the extreme hot or cold weather. Seasonal properties have led many developers to build vacational flats nearby the tourist spots. However, these types of facilities is outside the realm of silver tourism defined for this chapter. However, elderly services operators also find these type of seasonal customers as a source of income. Therefore the three operators selected also offer short term rental stays from one month, to one season, or even half a year. Often such rental facilities will also provide daily living, health maintainence and even medical services. This type of short term stay is considered as part of silver tourism.

The basic framework of description of these cases will be presented according to the concepts of marketing strategies, namely (1) market segmentation; (2) product design; (3) pricing strategies; (4) channels of deliveries; and (5) service promotion.

Then operations of the three cases will also be analyzed according to the theory of Integrative Drivers Framework for Suceess. In particular, the aspects of (1) Clear Mission and Vision Statements, (2) Governance and Leadership, (3) Financial Sustanability, (4) Social Impacts Assessments, will be examined.

To evaluate marketing mix, demographic characteristics in age and income will be adopted to classify market segments, since gender, education and geographical location data are either not available or irrelevant. For pricing, it will be coded in two dimensions. First it will be classified as high, medium and low price and second as narrow range and wide range of prices. For products, the nature of products will be classified as health, wellness or both (health+wellness). The types of products will be classified as facilities, services, or both (facilities+ services). The levels of products will be divided into medical, health maintainence, and personal care. The duration of products is broadly divided into one time, short term and long term. Delivery channels vary significantly but for this study the characteristics of in person and online or both (in person + online) will be indicated. The aspect of promotion, finally, will be discussed in terms of advertising, words of mouth, or both (advertising+social network) oriented.

CASE DESCRIPTIONS

Case One: The Taikang Community

Taikang Insurance Group's travel-integrated wellness and senior care business in Hainan centers around the Taikang Community Resort Sanya, a Tribute Portfolio Hotel, located in Haitang Bay, Sanya. It is based on the nationwide network of Taikang Community Senior Living Facilities to construct a "insurance + healthcare & senior care + travel living" business model (Taikang Life, 2025). The following provides a detailed analysis of its marketing plan.

Market Segmentation: targeting all-age and high-net-worth clients, and focusing on the "migratory" travel-living population. Taikang Community's travel-living wellness services are not exclusively for the elderly but adopt an "all-age client" coverage strategy, with precise segmentation achieved through product design.

1. Core Customer Base (Primary Payers): Affluent families and Taikang's high-net-worth (HNW) insurance clients. These individuals strategically pre-purchase future senior care and "nationwide travel living" entitlements through specific insurance products, most notably the "Happiness Appointment" series.
2. Core Users: Active "Migratory Bird" Seniors: Mr. Qiu Jianwei highlighted that migratory travel-living seniors have several key characteristics: first, they are

relatively younger in age; second, they do not prefer staying in one place year-round but wish to experience different landscapes; third, they desire a homely feel rather than a hotel stay; fourth, they require access to healthcare and senior care security; and fifth, they have social needs (Chunzuo.com, 2025).

3. Family Vacation Clients: They utilize the hotel's family-friendly facilities (e.g., children's playground, swimming pools) and all-age services to meet family travel demands.
4. Experience and Potential Clients: Non-insurance clients can access the offerings through short-term experience packages (e.g., 3-day, 2-night stays) and may convert into long-term residents or insurance clients.

Product Design: Deep Integration of "Hotel + Wellness," Creating Three Travel-Living Lifestyle Paradigms. The product breaks the boundaries of traditional hotels or senior living communities, achieving an organic fusion of "high-end vacation experience" and "professional wellness services" (China Financial News, 2022).

1. Sanya Taikang Community Resort Hotel, Tribute Portfolio: Operated by Marriott International, its design blends the Eastern "walled city" concept with Hainan's local culture. It features 343 guest rooms, including 39 specially designed elderly-care rooms that fully incorporate senior-friendly design (anti-glare lighting, rounded furniture, etc.).
2. Supporting Wellness Facilities: The hotel houses a "Wellness Experience Center" providing services like smart healthcare, telemedicine, fitness guidance, traditional Chinese medicine therapies, and health recovery. It also includes an adult pool, gym, and over 4,000 square meters of indoor/outdoor children's playgrounds.
3. Service Core: Anchored by Taikang's proprietary "one community, one hospital" integrated care model, we bridge the gap between hospitality and healthcare. While the facility itself is not a hospital, it ensures seamless access to elite medical resources—such as the 301 Hospital Hainan Branch—providing guests with 24/7 emergency response channels and proactive daily health management.
4. Product Systematization: In 2025, Taikang Community upgraded its travel-living products into three paradigms: "Coastal Living, Mountain and Water Living, and Original Realm Living", and launched the nationwide "Enjoy Travel Living" pass product (e.g., 7/14/30-night packages). This product covers operating communities and partner homestays in 28 cities across the country, enabling "all-inclusive travel and multi-destination combinations" (Taikang Community, 2025).

Pricing Strategies: Centered on "Insurance-Based Lock-in," supplemented by Flexible Short-Stay Options. Pricing is deeply linked with residency eligibility, forming a structure combining high-threshold long-term value and flexible mid-to-short-term choices.

1. Long-Term Rights Lock-in (Primary Channel): Clients purchase the "Happiness Appointment" pension plan (the associated insurance products typically require reaching a certain total premium threshold, e.g., 3 million RMB) to obtain "Guaranteed Residency Rights" and "Priority Residency Rights" for Taikang Community senior living facilities. This essentially converts future travel-living and long-stay rights into current sales of insurance/financial products (Li, 2026).
2. Existing Residents: When traveling within the national Taikang Community network, fees are paid according to the monthly standard of the destination community. If the resident leaves their original community for more than 15 days while retaining their original room, the monthly fee for the original room enjoys a 40% discount (Taikang Home, 2026).
3. Short Stays for Non-Residents: Non-residents can stay by paying a deposit and signing a short-stay agreement, with a single stay not exceeding 3 months. Short-stay fees are typically higher than the average monthly fees for long-term residents and do not qualify for long-stay discounts.
4. Experience Packages: Short-duration experience packages are offered for new clients, with separately determined pricing, serving as a market lead-generation tool.

Channels of Delivery: The Nationwide Chain Network is the Core Delivery Platform. The realization of travel-living services heavily depends on Taikang Community's established extensive physical network and integrated online platforms.

1. Core Delivery Channel: The Taikang Community network serves as our primary platform. By the end of 2025, we have established 47 projects across 37 major cities nationwide, with 27 communities already operational in 24 cities. This infrastructure solidifies the foundation for our "One Home Base, Nationwide Travel Living" model, guaranteeing consistent service standards and seamless medical-security support for our clients wherever they reside.
2. Online Integration Platform: Through the "Taixianggou" platform for senior products, it integrates the "Taixianggou, Taixiangwan, Taixiangzhu" system, building an online-offline one-stop solution for "supplies – services - culture" (Urban Evening News, 2025).

3. Collaborative Channel: Partnership with Marriott International leverages its global hotel management expertise and membership system to enhance operational quality and brand appeal.

Promotion: Integrating Brand Building and Sales Conversion, Multi-Layered Target Reach. The promotion strategy balances brand image building and sales lead conversion.

1. Industry Showcase: Active participation in industry events like the "2025 Hainan International Elderly Care, Wellness & Travel Living Industry Conference" to comprehensively display full-industry-chain service capabilities and establish an industry benchmark image.
2. Membership Products and Cross-Industry Partnerships: Launch of the "Enjoy Membership" system, introducing the "Enjoy Card" containing rights for health, courses, travel living, air tickets, etc., and co-branding a senior card with Air China to directly stimulate consumption and enhance customer stickiness (Xinhua Net, 2026).
3. Content and Experience Marketing: Dissemination of the "enjoying aging" philosophy and client travel-living stories via the official website, press releases, and authoritative media reports. Design of short-term experience packages to lower the barrier for initial trial.
4. Core Sales Drive: The most fundamental promotion lies in its "insurance + healthcare & senior care" business model itself. Through its vast team of insurance agents selling the "Happiness Appointment" policies to high-net-worth clients, it directly secures long-term clients, constituting the most core and stable customer source guarantee for its travel-living business.

Summary: Taikang Community's travel-living wellness business in Hainan is an extension of its "payment + service" closed-loop business model in both space and time. It locks in the consumption of high-net-worth clients for decades to come through insurance products, then delivers high-quality services through its nationwide heavy-asset layout of medical-care community networks and professional hotel-style operational capabilities, ultimately achieving concentrated value realization and an experience in the "travel living" consumption scenario.

Case Two: Wuchan Zhongda Jinshi Group Co., Ltd.

According to public information, the wellness residence tourism business of Wuchan Zhongda Jinshi Group Co., Ltd. (core subsidiary of the Wuchan Zhongda Group, a Fortune Global 500 enterprise) stands as a key practice for the company to implement its Common Prosperity Elderly Care Strategy and explore the development of silver economy. Wuchan Zhongda Jinshi upholds "Seniors First, Exceed Expectations" as its core value, "Wholehearted Companionship" and "Sincere Care" as its service tenet, and the seven dimensions of "Clothing, Food, Housing, Care, Learning, Recreation and Affection" as its service connotation. It adopts a Six-in-One Integrated Service Model for elderly care supply chain as its business model, and has been listed as a recommended Benchmark Service by the National Working Commission on Ageing of the People's Republic of China (Wuchan Zhongda Jinshi Group Co., Ltd., 2026). In 2021, Wuchan Zhongda Jinshi was awarded the title of China's Top Ten Elderly Care Brands, and its subsidiary Langhe International Medical and Elderly Care Center was awarded the title of China's Top Ten Brands for Integrated Medical and Elderly Care. Its marketing plan is described as follows:

Market Segmentation: Focus on "Active Seniors", with coverage extended to full-age families and corporate clients. The wellness residence tourism services of Wuchan Zhongda Jinshi are precisely positioned to serve active seniors with spending power and leisure demand, with a gradual expansion into the broader market. A large proportion of its clients are from Hangzhou, Wenzhou, Shanghai, Jiangsu, and even Beijing, among other regions (Zhe Shang Magazine & Healthy Aging China, 2026).

1. Core target group: Active retirees aged 65 and above who are in good physical health and pursue high quality of life. Dissatisfied with traditional sightseeing tours, they aspire to an in-depth, experiential residence tourism lifestyle featuring a relaxed pace, comfortable accommodation, and integrated health management as well as cultural and social activities.

Product Design: The "Yi · He · Yuan" Brand Matrix. The company is committed to the development and operation of five-star elderly care institutions and community elderly care service institutions. It leverages its brand strengths featuring high-end elderly care and integrated medical and elderly care to implement brand output (Wuchan Zhongda Jinshi Group, 2026).

1. Business positioning: To meet the rigid elderly care needs of urban advanced-age seniors.
2. Service content: Covering medical care, food, houing, nursing, learning, recreation and affection.
3. Service objective: To ensure comfort for seniors, peace of mind for their children, and reduced administrative burden for the government.
4. The company has established a well-defined product brand system and in-depth service core to meet the needs of diverse scenarios.

5. Three major product lines (the "Yi · He · Yuan" brand matrix):
    a. Langhe Series (Care and Attention Homes): With Langhe (Yintai) International Medical and Elderly Care Center as its benchmark project, which has a total gross floor area of approximately 22,000 square meters and a total investment of 400 million yuan. The center is a council member of the China National Association of Geriatric Care, with its core target group being semi-disabled or disabled seniors aged 80 and above, and focuses on the integrated provision of medical treatment, nursing and elderly care. Another distinctive project is Langhe (Yinhu) International Medical and Elderly Care Center, which specializes in the care of seniors living with dementia, stroke, Parkinson's disease, diabetes, heart disease and other medical conditions, and is equipped with functional rehabilitation rooms, hydrotherapy rooms, barber shops, sensory awakening cinemas and other facilities fitted with world-class equipment.
    b. Langyi Series (Elderly Homes): Home-based elderly care service centers, which are elderly care complexes integrating the five core functions of medical care, elderly support, nursing, day care, and home-based services.
    c. Langyuan Series (Elderly Community Centers): Positioned as elderly care communities, represented by the Zhongda Langyuan (Yunhe) Elderly Care Community, which is designed with more than 700 beds. Relying on local natural resources including its reputation as a *Town of Longevity*and hot spring resources, the project has built a large-scale new wellness service park featuring *care-oriented services with integrated medical care and wellness support*, and strives to become a demonstration project for the integrated development of elderly care services in the Yangtze River Delta region.

Pricing Strategies: Member Card-based Customer Acquisition + Flexible Package Combinations. The company adopts a flexible pricing mechanism designed to lower the threshold for trial experiences and drive long-term consumption.

1. Wellness Residence Tourism All-in-One Card member product: This serves as the company's core tool for sales promotion and customer retention. Launched during the 2025 Spring Festival, the all-in-one card is priced at 4,999 yuan, granting access to 20 high-quality wellness residence tourism sites under the company. It comes with a complimentary 1,000-yuan consumption voucher and free access to activities including health check-ups and interest courses, delivering exceptional value for money and strong gifting attributes.
2. Pay-per-visit / short-term residence tourism packages: For individual customers, the company provides daily-rated residence tourism packages, with prices

fluctuating based on room type (single room, standard room, suite), season, and project location (urban area or scenic spot).

3. Long-term residence / migratory elderly care packages: For customers opting for long-term stays (monthly / quarterly), the company provides more competitive all-inclusive services.

Channels of Delivery: Nationwide Self-operated Network + Government-Enterprise Cooperation + Online Platform. The company's delivery capacity is built on physical networks, cooperative resources and digital tools.

1. Core delivery network: As of the end of 2025, the company has deployed 48 elderly care projects nationwide, forming a physical service network covering Zhejiang Province and extending to Ganzhou in Jiangxi Province, Rongcheng in Shandong Province, Kunming in Yunnan Province and other regions, realizing the strategic layout of *stringing beads into a chain*to form an interconnected service network.
2. Alliance Development Model: The company actively cooperates with local governments and local state-owned enterprises (such as Shandong Chengshan Group), adopts an asset-light operation model, and exports its brand, management and service systems to rapidly expand its market coverage.
3. Online direct sales platform: Through online channels such as its proprietary mini-program, the company directly sells the *Wellness Residence Tourism All-in-One Card*and various packages, shortening the transaction chain.
4. Bundled tourism products (China News Network, Zhejiang Branch, 2024): Through cooperation with travel agencies, the company has established a *residence tourism and wellness*service system centered on four core components: cultural, recreational and social travel services (travel), home care butler services (residence), traditional Chinese medicine physiotherapy and health services (wellness), and nutritional diet conditioning services (care).
5. Offline channel cooperation: The company has established in-depth cooperation with major travel agencies, leveraging their extensive customer reach and sales networks for distribution.

Promotion: Brand Endorsement + Experiential Marketing + Word-of-Mouth Communication. The promotion strategy combines the credibility of a state-owned enterprise with market-oriented dynamism.

1. Authority certification and brand building: Three of the company's institutions, namely Langhe (Yinhu No.1), Zhongda Langyuan (Duniao) and Zhongda Langyuan (Quzhou), were included in the Top 10 List of 2025 Excellent Wellness

Residence Tourism Venues in Zhejiang Province. The company leverages such awards to establish industry authority and trust. Meanwhile, it actively promotes its mission as a state-owned enterprise to explore the Common Prosperity Elderly Caremodel, so as to enhance brand reputation.

2.. Holiday experiential marketing: During golden weeks such as the May Day Holiday and the National Day Holiday, the company launches themed events to attract customer traffic, and generates market momentum through media coverage of the popular events.

3. Word-of-mouth and content marketing: The company encourages and disseminates positive feedback from customers, such as songs spontaneously created by customers to praise its services, and touches potential customers through real stories. Meanwhile, it elaborates on its residence tourism philosophy of poetry and distant landscapes through exclusive media interviews.

4. Innovative member product promotion: The company packages the Wellness Residence Tourism All-in-One Cardas a premium New Year gift for elders, tapping into the gift market and creating new consumption scenarios.

Summary: In essence, the wellness residence tourism model of Wuchan Zhongda Jinshi relies on the resource integration capacity and nationwide chain layout of the state-owned enterprise to integrate high-quality ecological landscape and cultural resources with professional age-friendly services and medical care security, providing active seniors with a mobile homethat is safe, comfortable, enriching and heart-warming. Its strategic approach featuring brand-oriented product development, systematic service provision, membership-based sales model, and nationwide network layouthas formed distinctive characteristics and strong replicability in the wellness residence tourism sector.

Case Three: the Koayoung Group Qujing Liaokuo Street Comprehensive Elderly Care Service Center, Yunnan

The predecessor of the Liaokuo Street Comprehensive Elderly Care Service Center was the idle asset of the former Kunqu Grand Hotel. It was invested in and constructed by the sub-district office, innovatively adopting a "Public Service with Contracted Operator" model. It is an urban embedded elderly care complex integrating institutional, community, home-based, and sojourn services (Dehong Prefecture Government, 2025). The project involved a 4.6 million RMB investment from the community for renovation and a 2 million RMB investment from the operating enterprise for equipment procurement, with an annual rent of 580,000

RMB. It focuses on providing care, accommodation, and home-based services for seniors with disabilities or dementia, sojourning seniors, and community-dwelling seniors, comprehensively meeting the diverse needs of medical care, rehabilitation, nourishment, fitness, culture, and entertainment, thereby achieving full-cycle, all-scenario elderly service coverage.

The Liaokuo Street Office, an administrative unit of the local government of the Qujing City, is responsible for infrastructure and supervision to safeguard public welfare attributes. The Koayoung Investment Group, a nation wide private enterprise specializes in elderly services, is recruited as the operator of edlerly services center, to offer comprehensive services with management efficiency. Currently, the center has 113 beds. Since 2024, the center has been striving to establish a new benchmark for comprehensive elderly care services through professional practices. Its marketing plan is described in the following:

Market Segmentation: It serves local seniors with disabilities or dementia and community-dwelling seniors, while simultaneously leveraging Qujing's climatic advantage as a “summer retreat” to attract sojourning seniors from across the country. It is a key carrier for Qilin District in cultivating the “silver-haired sojourn” core format.

Product Design: Among the four core service formats, wellness and recuperation form the fundamental core that attracts people and supports development. The Liaokuo Street Comprehensive Elderly Care Service Center constructs an integrated service system encompassing “medical care, rehabilitation, nourishment, fitness, culture, and entertainment” around the all-scenario needs of seniors. The facility separately houses a care zone for seniors with disabilities or dementia (floors 5-6) and apartments for sojourning seniors. The center has a total of 113 beds, comprising 58 sojourn beds and 55 care beds, enabling the flexible provision of services such as short-term care, long-term care, and summer retreat wellness. For the sojourning population, the center has planned 26 rooms of various types on the third and fourth floors, equipped with a 24-hour call system and professional butler service. It also connects diverse scenarios such as cultural and creative displays, book café socialization, and recreational activities. The care zone on the fifth and sixth floors focuses on individuals with disabilities or dementia. Senior-friendly bathrooms are paired with pre-bathing temperature/humidity control and physical assessment, ensuring safety down to the details. More crucially, the center is equipped with professional medical care facilities and achieves comprehensive chronic disease management through linkage with the Traditional Chinese Medicine Hospital located just next door (Qujing Daily, 2025).

Pricing Strategies: As a “Public Service with Contracted Operator” project, with the government investing in infrastructure and enterprises responsible for operation, it aims to ensure public welfare attributes while achieving sustainable development through market-oriented operation. The per person daily cost for sojourn is only RMB 70-80 (Culture and Tourism Headlines, 2025).

*Distribution:*Since this comprehensive elderly care service is center based, its targets are confined to the residents of the area of Liukao Street. Its distribution channels therefore are self referrals or referrals by residents committees and local leaders. Street public services and other public officers will also refer residents to the center when they come across seniors in need.

Promotion: As a provincial Gold Medal Elderly Care Institution and an innovative model for "public construction, private operation," it has received extensive coverage from official media at provincial and municipal levels (e.g., Qujing News Network, Yunling Window), forming powerful brand endorsement. Simultaneously, the community actively breaks down industry barriers. Since the beginning of this year, it has increased promotional efforts and established a cooperative platform covering surrounding hotels and guesthouses. Businesses that were once competitors have now formed a community. Once a particular hotel is fully booked, it shares new orders within the platform group, recommending other hotels with available rooms. This achieves mutual benefit through helping one another, fostering a positive culture of industry cooperation.

INTEGRATIVE DRIVERS TO SUCCESS OF THE SAMPLE OPERATORS

Significant Integrative Drivers of Operators

In the final analysis, this chapter will examine the three cases, namely the Taikang Community, the Wuchan Zhongda Jinshi Elderly Service, and the Koayoung Group - Qujing Liaokuo Street Comprehensive Elderly Care Service Center, in the light of the following Integrative Drivers: Clear Mission and Vision Statements, Governance and Leadership, Financial Sustanability, and Social Impacts Assessments. Data of these three case projects are derived from their official web sites. The performances of the three case projects in terms of the four integrative drivers are summarized in Table 1.

Table 1. Case analysis of Integrative Drivers

Integrative Drivers of the three cases	Taikang Community[1]	Wuchan Zhongda Jinshi Elderly Service[2]	Koayoung Group - Qujing Liaokuo Street Comprehensive Elderly Care Service Center[3]
Mission and Vision Statements	Enjoy Life: High Quality and Rich Spirituality	Elderly First, Beyond Expectations	Mission: To serve the rich and facinating senior years.
Governance and Leadership	It is a subsidiary of Taikang Insurance Group which was established in 1996 as a Private Enterprise. It is led by professional managers.	This is a State Enterprise established in 1996 and governed by the Board of Directors. In parallel there is the Committee of Communist Party. The Legal Person and Head of the Group is Chairman of the Board.	This is a private enterprise registered in 2004. It is led by the Chairman of the Board of Directors.
Financial Sustanability	Taikang Insurance Group is ranked as Fortune 500 since 2018. Taikang Community operates 30 facilities in 24 cities with over 22k senior residents in June 2026.	The Group Elderly Service Sector operates 50 facilities of more than 16000 beds. It is ranked as Fortune 500.	The Group by 2024 has built and manage 6 elderly homes with 1050 beds.
Social Impacts Assessments	No systematic social values and impact assessment.	No systematic social values and impact assessment.	No systematic social values and impact assessment.

Note: Source of data.

[1]Taikang Community (2026). *The Taikang Service System.* Accessed on 2026-07-07. https://www.taikangzhijia.com/index.html

[2]Wuchan Zhongda Jinshi Elderly Service (2026). *The Pension Industry.* Accessed on 2026-07-07. https://www.zhongdajinshi.com/block_pension.html

[3]Koayoung Group (2026). *Elderly Services.* Accessed on 2026-07-07. http://www.koayoung.com/product/cp2/

Discussion on Integrative Drivers

One observation from the above data is that all these projects are intitiated or operated by financially strong operators. From the angle of financial sustainability, they can provide sufficient cash flow even the breakeven time may be longer than forecasted. It shows that at this early stage of market development of silver health and wellness business it requires heavy capital investments. Small and medium size companies cannot enter the market because of high risks in financial loss. Proper financing mechanisms need to be encouraged by the government to give the market growth a push.

Going back to the intergratie driver of Mission and Vision, all three operators have well designed and appealing Mission Statements. Matching their mission statements with their marketing mix strategies reported earlier, these companies show very neat and strong management professionalism. Similarly, these companies have very strong leadership as the Taikang and the Wuchan Zhongda Jinshi are listed on Fortune 500, and the Koayoung, though much smaller in size, is managing more than one thousand senior resident beds and contiuing to grow. This indicates though indirectly that these three companies have strong management and effective leadership.

None of the three companies are listed, except Wuchan Zhongda Jinshi Elderly Service is owned by the Wuchan Zhongda Group Co. Ltd. which has been listed on Shanghai Stock Exchange since 1996. As the three are not listed companies, they do not have to report on the areas of Environmental, Social and Governance affairs. From the official websites of these three operators, information on social gains, such as the satisfaction of the senior customers and the benefits in terms of health and wellness, are not available. It is likely that all the three companies which are equipped with professional business management experts, must have collected customers and local government satisfaction data. Such information should be available to the public.

To summarize, as demonstrated by their integrative drivers these three operations are likely to be sustainable. Their success, therefore depends on the maturity of the fine tuning in their business models and particular their refined marketing strategies.

MARKETING MIX MATURATION

After reviewing the strategic plans and company strengths of the three operators the analyis on marketing mix which is crucial to business success will be evaluated. Please refer to Table 2.

Table 2. Marketing Mix of the Operators

Marketing Mix of the three cases	Taikang Community[1]	Wuchan Zhongda Jinshi Elderly Service[2]	Koayoung Group - Qujing Liaokuo Street Comprehensive Elderly Care Service Center[3]
Segments	All-age and high-net-worth insurance (HNW) clients, focusing on the travel-and-living population (migratory bird seniors, family vacationers).	Active retirees aged 65 and above, in good physical health and pursue high quality of life, seeking experiential residence tourism.	Local seniors with disabilities and dementia. Summer senior vacationers from other cities and regions.
Product	Community resort + medical and health management services, in coastal, mountain and water living areas. Provide experientia (very short), short term, and long term stay.	Three levels of care facilities: care and attention homes, general homes and community centers. Providing residential, health, and wellness facilities and services.	Sojourn and care beds, enabling short and long term care, and summer wellness retreat. Nature of services include nourishment, entertainment, fitness, culture, medical and rehabilitation.
Price	High. Paid out of pocket or as insurance benefits. Different levels of "Enjoy Travel Living" Membership Cards.	Prepaid cards (roughly RMB250/visit), pay on site short term visits with seasonal/locational pricing, and long term residential rate.	Low. For sojourn stay is only RMB70-80 per person per night. Services for disabled and dementia seniors are either covered by social security fund, pyblic assistance or family supporters.
Place (Delivery Channel)	Tied to the "insurance + healthcare & senior care", or insurance-led business model.	Alliance with local governemnt and state enterprises, bundled with travel packages, and online direct sales.	Through self referrals and local social and public networks.
Promotion	Industry show case, Marriot Hotel Alliance, and Online Digital Platform.	Award winning and governemnt endorsement. Word of mouth and content marketing. Gift branding.	Publicity on city and provincial public platforms. Words of mouth promotion for sojourn stays.

Note: Source of data.

[1]Taikang Community (2026). *The Taikang Service System*. Accessed on 2026-07-07. https://www.taikangzhijia.com/index.html

[2]Wuchan Zhongda Jinshi Elderly Service (2026). *The Pension Industry*. Accessed on 2026-07-07. https://www.zhongdajinshi.com/block_pension.html

[3]Koayoung Group (2026). *Elderly Services*. Accessed on 2026-07-07. http://www.koayoung.com/product/cp2/

Discussion on Marketing Mix

One obvious observation is the segmentations for price. There are two dimensions and probably two clusters reflected by the marketing strategies of the three operators. On one hand there is the need for providing care and attention facilities and services to seniors with physical and mental difficulties, however most of them cannot afford the basic costs of professional services. On the other hand, there is the niche market of silver tourism demnaded by middle to high income groups who are enjoying their active aging. Figure 1 helps to illustrate this point.

Figure 1. Marketing Segmentation of Elderly Care and Positioning of the Operators

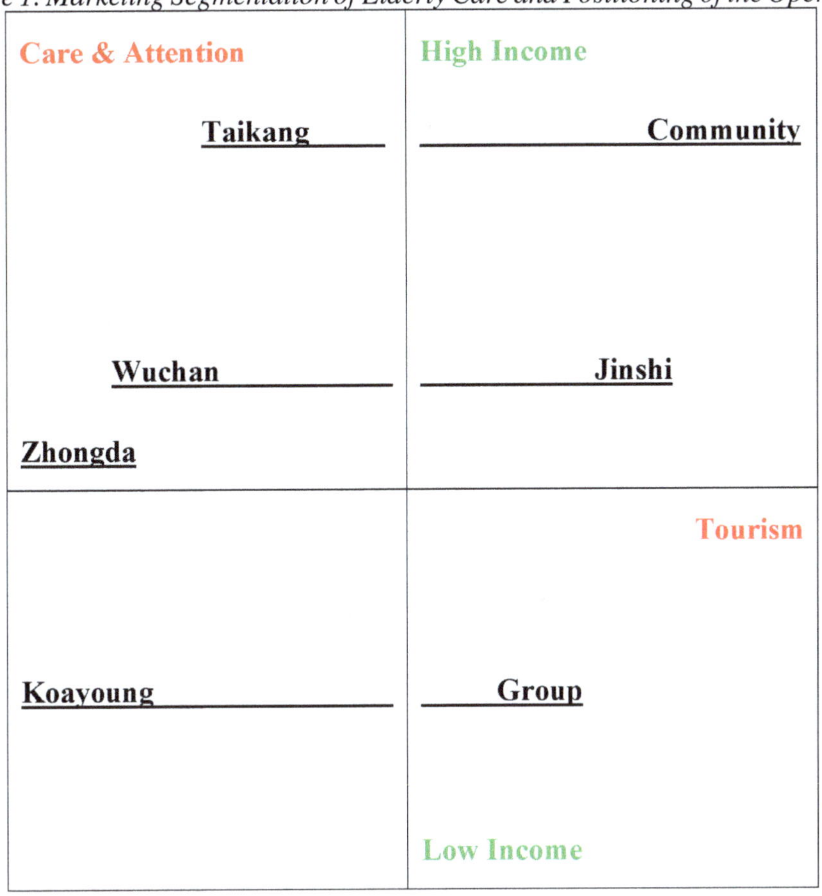

Note: Figure created by authors.

SUMMARY OF FINDINGS

The Case Studies provide us a very important insight on the financing of elderly care. Traditionally, support for older people of the society in the western developed countried rely on (1) direct income transfer via taxation system and social assistance, (2) compulsory savings in forms of contributory social security contributions or provident funds, (3) prolonged employment by extending retirement age, (4) personal savings which is not enforcable, and (5) family support which is not reliable.

Experiementation of the three sample operators suggest that it is possible to recover the deficits in residential care services with income generated by silver and cross-generational tourism business. The sampled operations represent 3 types of ownership, namely private ownership (the Taikang's), state ownership (The Wuchan Zhongda Jinxin's) and the public service with contracted operator (the Koayoung's). Our findings show that all three operators are fianancially sustainable, efficiently manageable, and organizationally accountable. Given time, better adjustment in market mix will allow these projects to replicate in a larger scale to tap the opportunities of the expanding silver economy.

Theoretically speaking, Integrative Drivers including Company Background, Strategic Plan, Leadership and Governance, Financial Strengths, and Professional Management can be considered as the Necessary and Foundational Drivers for financial sustainability of the Business and Social Services Partnerships in Silver Tourism and other projects. However, Integrative Drivers in Marketing Mix of Products, Price, Place (Distribution) and Promotion should be the Sufficient and Additional Drivers for financial profitability. In this study, unfortunately, there is no data on social impact assessments. This is a crucial factor deserving further investigations.

FUTURE CHALLENGES AND RECOMMENDATIONS

Expansion of Silver Tourism

In the coming decade, the elderly population in China is projected to exceed 400 million by 2035, indicating sustained market demand for wellness and residence tourism services. Rising life expectancy, which is expected to reach 79 years by 2030, will further expand the market scale. Some optimistic forecasts predict that the total scale of silver tourism will reach RMB 3.39 trillion in 2035, registering a year-on-year growth of 38.2%. Silver wellness residence tourism market centred on active seniors will contribute RMB1.42 trillion, surpassing parent-child educational tourism and become the largest pillar in tourism. This robust market foundation is supported by a total elderly population of 321 million, with approximately 146 million active seniors who possess sufficient consumption power and travelling willingness.

Market expansion is reflected not only in overall scale, but also in extensions of consumer demands. The industry will move away from the one-fits-all model, and shift towards customised solutions for consumer groups with different health conditions, and lifestyle preferences.

Product Customization and Innovations

In the post-pandemic era, health safety, social distancing and spiritual comfort have become critical consumer considerations, giving rise to new industrial forms. Air-based wellness, respiratory purification, small-group private tours, and off-peak travel, become popular. Traditional sightseeing can no longer meet market demands. Integrating natural ecology, regional humanistic resources and professional wellness elements to create immersive and healing residence tourism experiences has become a core development priority.

The Wuyi Mountain Tourism Agency in Fujian Province, relying on local ecological and cultural resources, develops stress-relief products such as forest yoga and sound healing. Also available are aesthetic education courses including nature study tours and rock painting experiences. The Yixian County of Anhui Province adds medicinal dietary therapy, Hui Ink craftsmanship, forest healing experiences, ancient villages residency to their wellness and cultural services (Yixian County People's Government, 2025). Successful wellness residence tourism projects must accurately identify and satisfy diversified demands.

Suichang in the Zhejiang Province fully leverages its ecological advantages to develop an integrated travel route consisting of Baima Mountain forest healing, medicinal cuisine services at the King of Medicine Valley, and hot spring medical care at Hongxingping, enabling tourists to achieve lung purification, eye nourishment and physical fitness improvement during travel (Lishui Daily, 2025). In only three months after opening, the Baima Mountain Langyuan Hotel attracted over 10,000 person-times of visitors for residence medical and wellness services.

The Swan Lake Forest Wellness Base in Chishui, Guizhou Province has achieved further breakthroughs (Department of Civil Affairs of Guizhou Province, 2020). In addition to green activities including forest hiking, yoga and camping, the base built an independent hospital and established cooperation with Grade A tertiary care hospitals to provide professional medical support covering health management, family physician services and emergency care, realising seamless integration of wellness preservation and medical services.

Rising Health Awareness and Cross Genrational Innovations

Statistics show that consumers aged 26 to 35 have become the primary group of health service consumers, accounting for 57% of total orders (Yi, 2026). People born in the 1980s and 1990s generally face heavy occupational pressure and sub-health conditions. Their health concerns have shifted from conventional disease treatment to preventive and quality-improving domains such as balanced diet, sufficient sleep, mental vitality and physical posture management.

On one hand, products targeting young consumer groups need to emphasise fashionables, social attributes and lightweight wellness experiences. The "New Youth Wellness Sessions" in Sanya and the Artistic Wellness Scenarios constructed for young makers in Yixian County are good examples. On the other hand, family-oriented consumption has evolved into a mainstream pattern. According to the Report on Consumption Trends of China's Wellness Industry, 2025, as many as 76% of consumers choose to participate in wellness activities together with their parents (People's Tribune, 2026). This indicates that products are required to feature full-age friendliness, simultaneously satisfying medical care needs of the elderly generation, stress relief demands of the middle-aged generation, and study tour entertainment needs of children.

Future product innovations will inevitably rely on precise insight into cross generations demands including high-quality elderly care for the post-1960s generation, anti-ageing wellness for the post-1980s generation, casual wellness maintenance for the post-1990s generation, and health fashion pursuits of the post-2000s generation.

Technology and Reshaping of the Wellness Service Ecosystem

As the above report on marketing channels indicates that all operators have to deliver their products via online platforms, it shows that the entire industry is standing at a critical stage of digital transformation. Leading practical cases demonstrate that intelligent wellness services have moved from conceptual design to comprehensive on-site implementation.

On the service side, the "Anyi Elderly Care" platform promoted across Yunnan Province integrates resources from governmental authorities, communities and medical institutions through Internet of Things and artificial intelligence technologies to construct a 15-minute elderly care service circle. Through the use of intelligent wristbands, one-click alarm devices and other terminals, the elderly can achieve real-time monitoring of health data and abnormal early warning, as well as one-click reservation of home-based services through mini-programs. In terms of residential experience, chips are embedded in mattresses and bed linens in guest rooms of the Xidi Residence Tourism Capacity Sharing Centre in Yixian County, Anhui Province, enabling contactless monitoring of occupants' heart rate, respiratory rate and sleep quality, with corresponding data synchronised to mobile mini-programs for personal review (Anhui Daily, 2025).

The Fanghuali Family Elderly Care Community in Beijing has deployed Xiaoli, an accompanying robot equipped with a domain-specific large model adapted for elderly care scenarios. Capable of understanding daily conversational language of the elderly, the robot provides daily companionship, health reminders and fall detection, acting as an efficient auxiliary for nursing staff (Fengtai Times, 2025). These practices clearly outline a future vision of wellness residence tourism which will be developed into a data-driven and artificial intelligently interconnected ecosystem. Technologies will be seamlessly integrated into all links including medical treatment, healthcare, wellness preservation, nursing and entertainment, achieving more precise services, more reassuring care, and higher-quality residence tourism experiences.

Silver Tourism focusing on health, care and wellnes is a dynamic and reapidly growing sector. Driven by policy support, demographic changes, and increasing health awareness, silver tourism is witnessing the explosion of more personalized, technology-integrated, innovative and diversified business entrepreunerships.

REFERENCES

Alter, S.K. (2006). Social enterprise models and their mission and money relationships. In Nicholls, A. (Ed.), *Social entrepreneurship: New models of sustainable change*, (pp. 205–232). Oxford University Press.

Anhui Daily. (2025, October 21). *Technology integrates wellness: Experience new sojourn care*. Anhui Daily. https://szb.ahnews.com.cn/szb/content/202510/21/c1109419.html

CCTV.com. (2026, February 6). *China's Health and Wellness Market Size reached 9.8 trillion yuan in 2025*. Retrieved from https://jingji.cctv.cn/2026/02/06/ARTIsR0oidemKmT9HqXWW4Ud260206.shtml

China Federation of Welfare & Senior Service, & Institute of Contemporary Social Service. (2024). *Annual report on the development of silver economy in China (2024)*. Social Sciences Academic Press.

China Financial News. (2022, July 18). *Taikang extends its full life-cycle industry chain: Taikang Community Resort Hotel Sanya opens as a new product line*. https://www.financialnews.com.cn/bx/jg/202207/t20220718_251429.html

China Meteorological Administration. Ministry of Civil Affairs, Ministry of Culture and Tourism, National Healthcare Security Administration, National Forestry and Grassland Administration, National Administration of Traditional Chinese Medicine, & National Disease Control and Prevention Administration. (2025, December 30). *Guidelines on strengthening collaborative linkage to promote high-quality development of health and wellness meteorological services*. Retrieved from https://www.cma.gov.cn/ztbd/2023zt/20230524/2023052401/202601/t20260116_7547994.html

China Mobile Smart Family. (2026, April 3). Digital intelligence empowers "wellness destinations" to make "sojourn care" more caring. China Mobile Smart Family. https://mp.weixin.qq.com/s?__biz=MzAwNzA0MjIwNg==&mid=2652664531&idx=1&sn=620b479789295ac70b5106f2e239f3bb&chksm=819d0ad22a2d0aca815fdb68fd73c75faaac2d47119aa41e0991fd3a54fa9e3ee5bdf49e055c#rd

China News Network. Zhejiang Branch. (2024, August 29). *Silver economy and county tourism: Zhongda Jinshi expands co-op elderly care model*. https://www.zj.chinanews.com.cn/jzkzj/2024-08-29/detail-ihefqtew4677494.shtml

China News Service. (2025, December 29). *Official bulletin: China's national physical fitness qualification rate and excellent rate hit new highs*. Phoenix News. Retrieved from https://news.ifeng.com/c/8pTn5zATKDh

Chunzuo.com. (2025, November 9). *From elderly care to enjoyable aging: Taikang Community creates a "China model" for residential aging and travel.* https://chunzuo.com/article_detail/a-6893.html

CNR.cn. (2016, September 19). *Research report on travel consumption behavior of middle-aged and older adults in China (2016).* Retrieved from https://tech.cnr.cn/techgd/20160919/t20160919_523146510.shtml

Culture and Tourism Headlines. (2025, September 15). *Public construction and private operation creates a "happy harbor": Qujing adds new model of traveling and wellness care.* http://www.wenlvnews.com/p/747069.html

Daniele, R. & Quezada, I. (2017). Business Models for Social Entrepreneurship in Tourism. In: Sheldon, P. & Daniele, R. (eds) *Social Entrepreneurship and Tourism.* Springer. https://doi.org/10.1007/978-3-319-46518-0_5

Dehong Prefecture Government. (2025, August 31). *Idle assets transformed into a silver-haired home: Qujing explores a new "public construction and private operation" elderly care model.* http://www.dhms.gov.cn/sfpz/Web/_F0_0_6B3ROUQSEF558FB9C3BD40BCB7.htm

Department of Civil Affairs of Guizhou Province. (2020, November 20). *Guizhou builds demonstration elderly care institutions: Chishui Tian'e Fort Forest Wellness Base integrates medical care and recreation.* Guizhou Provincial Department of Civil Affairs. https://mzt.guizhou.gov.cn/ztzl/rdzt/ylfw/gzdt_69738/202011/t20201120_65322964.html

DTZ Research. (2023). *Development and trends of wellness tourism in China*[Report].

European Commission, 2018. *The Silver Economy.* doi:10.2759/338976.

Fengtai Times. (2025, December 8). *Technology empowers elderly care: Robots become companions in Fengtai's family pension community.* Fengtai Times. https://www.bjft.gov.cn/fengtaishibao/html/2025-12/08/content_9504_19112068.htm

General Office State Council of the People's Republic of China. (2021). *The 14th Five-Year Plan for the development of national aging undertakings and the elderly care service system.* Retrieved from http://www.gov.cn/zhengce/content/2022-02/21/content_5674844.htm

General Office of the State Council of the People's Republic of China. (2022, April 27). *Notice of the General Office of the State Council on printing and distributing the "14th Five-Year Plan for National Health"*(Guobanfa [2022] No. 11). Central People's Government of the People's Republic of China. https://www.gov.cn/zhengce/content/2022-05/20/content_5691424.htm

General Office of the State Council of the People's Republic of China. (2024, January 11). *Opinions on developing the silver economy to improve the well-being of the elderly*(Guo Ban Fa [2024] No. 1). Retrieved from https://www.gov.cn/zhengce/content/202401/content_6926087.htm

General Office of the State Council of the People's Republic of China. (2025, January 9). *Notice on issuing the "Several measures for further cultivating new growth points and prospering cultural and tourism consumption"*(Guo Ban Fa [2025] No. 2). Retrieved from http://big5.www.gov.cn/gate/big5/www.gov.cn/govweb/zhengce/content/202501/content_6998238.htm

Huatai Life Insurance & AgeClub. (2024). *2024 New Health And Wellness Demand Insight White Paper.* Huatai Life Insurance Co., Ltd.

Li, X. (2026, February 21). *Is a 2 million yuan threshold a big misunderstanding? Securing a high-quality spot in Taikang Community: Which is more reliable, buying an insurance policy or paying a deposit?* https://mp.weixin.qq.com/s?src=11&timestamp=1776525117&ver=6668&signature=eBIwhddDt068zKydHMyu0WnX27m241u0s-vn9rtNAFSsPuuwfIfNy2GSoI6qekV-NqzNQWQErl1rnO0Le2SKRVnm90jK-siu4VhD77lCGQH7AFAVq*yT4B0yElIrLqUm&new=1

Lishui Daily. (2025, October 11). *Transformation from traditional tourism to deep living destination: "Check-in" remains popular while "long-stay living" gains traction.* Lishui News. https://www.lsnews.com.cn/assets/detail.html?id=68e99c3e805e29728ff278d5

McCarthy, E. J. (1960). *Basic marketing: A managerial approach.* Homewood, IL: Irwin.

National Bureau of Statistics of China. (2026, January 19). *Statistical communiqué of the People's Republic of China on the 2025 national economic and social development.* Retrieved from https://www.stats.gov.cn/sj/zxfbhjd/202601/t20260119_1962330.html

People's Tribune. (2026, April 6). *"Pre-retirement wellness" becomes a new trend: How to promote high-quality development of wellness services?*People's Tribune. https://news.qq.com/rain/a/20260406A02NRZ00

Qujing Daily (2025, November 12). *Qilin District explores new path for silver economy: Medical-nursing integration builds foundation, health-preserving summer retreat boosts traveling care.* Qujing News. https://www.qjrb.cn/2025-11/12/content_738373.html

Taikang Community (2025, March 17). The golden age of migratory bird-style retirement is here! How Taikang Community helps parents "live across the country". https://www.taikangzhijia.com/news/2025/11308.html

Taikang Home (2026, March 7). *A complete explanation of Taikang Care Community residency policies.* WeChat Official Account. https://mp.weixin.qq.com/s?src=11&timestamp=1776525129&ver=6668&signature=BnYaK36rgIr4y2Gca-Fnkoj3e*3shthZz30VZnINL5pXryb5Zph2GfGyT4bKxmOBwWeUoQIj7pB94y0I1kh2o9gDdcrpoocCH0cZaCpUYMOg2f*XBZWYxrSrnuc3NRz8&new=1

Taikang Life. (2025, March 17). *The golden age of migratory bird-style retirement is here! How Taikang Community helps parents "live across the country"*. Taikang Community Official Website. https://www.taikangzhijia.com/news/2025/mob_11308.html

Urban Evening News. (2025, December 25). *Taikang Community debuts at 2025 Hainan International Elderly Care and Wellness Travel Industry Conference, leading the new journey of the silver economy with leading strength*[News article]. Urban Evening News. https://so.html5.qq.com/page/real/search_news?docid=70000021_753694cacd289352

Weppen, Von der J. & Cochrane, J. (2012) Social enterprises in tourism: an exploratory study of operational models and success factors, *Journal of Sustainable Tourism*, 20:3, 497-511, DOI: 10.1080/09669582.2012.663377

Wuchan Zhongda Jinshi Group Co., Ltd. (2026a). *Company profile: Real estate finance + senior care services*. Wuchan Zhongda Group. Retrieved April 19, 2026, from https://www.wzgroup.cn/business/company_info/43.html?plate=22

Wuchan Zhongda Jinshi Group Co., Ltd. (2026b). Pension business: Project portfolio. Retrieved April 19, 2026, from https://www.zhongdajinshi.com/block_pension.html

Xinhua Net (2026, April 10). Service extension and ecological co-construction: Taikang Community partners with Air China, Qunar, Guokai Beihe, and ZEISS China to launch a new silver life. https://www.xinhuanet.com/money/20260410/2e9868c91ecb4a27ac7bcbc4a0ec33f0f3/c.html

Yi, S. (2026, April 6). *Consumption characteristics and development path of wellness services*. People's Tribune. https://so.html5.qq.com/page/real/search_news?docid=70000021_97369d308d282552

Yixian County People's Government. (2025, September 29). *"Painting-like countryside" Yixian: Innovation engine drives cultural tourism integration, focusing on homestays, wellness, and film industries.* https://www.yixian.gov.cn/zwzx/mtyx/9303225.html

Yoshino, M. Y. & Rangan, U. S. (1995). *Strategic Alliances: An Entrepreneurial Approach to Globalization*. Cambridge, MA: Harvard University Press.

Zero Power Intelligence Group (2025). Research report on the development trends and competition strategies of China's tourism industry (2025–2030). China Report Hall. https://m.chinabgao.com/report/17431094.html

Zhe Shang Magazine & Healthy Aging China (2026, January 27). *Zheng Guangliang: Silver economy enters a new stage led by brand influence*[Interview]. World Zhe Shang Network. http://www.wzs.org.cn/sjzs/news?id=23419

Chapter 12
Community-Based Models in Vietnam:
Lessons Learned From Social Innovations for Silver Economy in Emerging Markets

Lan Huong
http://orcid.org/0009-0009-9180-295X
Independent Researcher, Vietnam

ABSTRACT

This chapter examines the role of social innovation in the development of the silver economy in emerging markets, with a focus on community-based models in Vietnam. The purpose of the chapter is to develop an integrated analytical framework that combines social innovation theory, the silver economy, and community-based approaches to explain how care systems for older persons can emerge under resource constraints. Through a case study of the Intergenerational Self-Help Club model, the chapter elucidates operational mechanisms based on co-production, social capital, and community participation, while assessing economic, social, and institutional impacts. The findings indicate that community-based models can serve as a foundational pathway for inclusive silver economy development. The chapter also provides policy implications for Vietnam and other emerging economies, emphasizing the need for hybrid models that integrate community, state, and market actors.

DOI: 10.4018/979-8-3373-9370-4.ch012

1. INTRODUCTION

Population ageing has become one of the most profound demographic transformations of the twenty-first century, particularly in emerging economies where the pace of demographic transition often outstrips the capacity of economic systems and social welfare institutions to adapt. According to the United Nations, the global population aged 60 and above is projected to exceed 2 billion by 2050, with the majority of this increase occurring in developing countries (United Nations, 2020). This trend not only intensifies demand for healthcare, social protection, and long-term care services, but also calls for a fundamental restructuring of socio-economic systems to accommodate a rapidly ageing population (Bloom et al., 2015).

In this context, the concept of the silver economy has gained increasing attention as a framework for capturing the economic and social opportunities associated with ageing. The silver economy encompasses not only consumption patterns of older adults but also their participation in economic activities, social engagement, and contributions to development processes (European Commission, 2018). However, much of the existing literature and policy practice on the silver economy is grounded in experiences from developed countries, where welfare systems are well-established and markets for ageing-related services are relatively mature. This creates a significant research gap: how can the silver economy be developed in emerging markets where financial resources are constrained, welfare systems are incomplete, and service markets for older populations remain underdeveloped (Klimczuk, 2016).

Against this backdrop, social innovation, particularly in the form of community-based models, has emerged as a critical alternative approach. Unlike state-led or market-driven solutions, social innovation emphasizes bottom-up initiatives, community participation, and the mobilization of endogenous resources to address complex social challenges (Moulaert et al., 2013). In the context of ageing, this perspective is especially relevant, as the needs of older persons extend beyond healthcare and income security to include social participation, community engagement, and quality of life.

In the case of Vietnam, the relevance of such an integrated framework becomes particularly evident. The United Nations Population Fund (UNFPA) highlights that Vietnam is entering a phase of rapid population ageing, with a growing demand for social services, care provision, and social protection for older persons (United Nations Population Fund, 2019). At the same time, empirical studies indicate that care provision remains heavily dependent on families and communities, while formal long-term care systems are still in the process of development (Nguyen et al., 2022). In this context, models such as the *Intergenerational Self-Help Clubs* (ISHC) are of particular theoretical significance. They provide a clear illustration of community-based social innovation grounded in co-production, the mobilization of existing social assets, and the integration of multiple functions, including livelihood support, healthcare services, regular health monitoring, home-based care provided by volunteers, lifelong learning, rights protection, and local resource mobilization (HelpAge International, 2022). Evidence from HelpAge shows that this model has been scaled nationwide and has been recognized by the government as a cost-effective and efficient solution for addressing population ageing (HelpAge International, 2022). From a theoretical perspective, ISHC represents a compelling example supporting the argument that in emerging markets, the silver economy often develops first through social and community-based forms before gradually expanding into more formalized service markets (Moulaert et al., 2013; Klimczuk, 2016).

Building on these considerations, this chapter aims to examine the role of community-based social innovation in the development of the silver economy in Vietnam, using the ISHC model as a central case study. Specifically, the chapter seeks to address three key research questions. First, what contextual factors have driven the emergence of social innovation models in the field of ageing and care in Vietnam? Second, how do the operational mechanisms of the ISHC model reflect the characteristics of social innovation and the silver economy in emerging markets? Third, what theoretical and policy insights can be drawn from the Vietnamese experience for other countries undergoing similar demographic transitions?

Methodologically, the chapter adopts a case study approach, combining secondary data analysis with theoretical synthesis to construct an integrated analytical framework linking social innovation and the silver economy. This approach allows not only for a detailed description of the ISHC model but also for an in-depth explanation of its underlying mechanisms and its broader applicability.

The contribution of this chapter is twofold. Theoretically, it extends the concept of the silver economy beyond a market-oriented perspective by incorporating a social innovation framework in which communities play a central role. Practically, it provides empirical evidence from Vietnam demonstrating that community-based models can serve as a foundational pathway for inclusive and sustainable silver economy development, particularly in resource-constrained settings.

In conclusion, by analyzing the Vietnamese case, this chapter contributes to a deeper understanding of the relationship between social innovation and the silver economy, while also offering an alternative development pathway for emerging economies. Rather than relying solely on market expansion or large-scale public investment, the development of the silver economy can be rooted in community-based initiatives, endogenous resources, and socially embedded innovation processes, enabling societies to adapt more effectively to the profound demographic transformations of the twenty-first century.

2. THEORETICAL AND ANALYTICAL FRAMEWORK

From a theoretical perspective, research on social innovation has developed from the recognition that many contemporary social challenges particularly population ageing, inequalities in access to care services, and the weakening of traditional support networks cannot be effectively addressed solely through market mechanisms or unilateral state interventions. In this context, social innovation is understood as an analytical concept that transcends the boundaries of technological and business innovation, as it emphasizes the creation of new ways to meet social needs, restructure social relations, and expand the agency of communities. Phills, Deiglmeier, and Miller (2008) are among the most influential scholars who argue that social innovation should be understood as a novel solution to a social problem, in which the value created is primarily captured by society rather than by individual actors. A key aspect of their argument is that social innovation is not confined to the nonprofit sector but often emerges at the intersection of government, business, and civil society. This perspective is particularly relevant to the study of the silver economy, as services for older persons are typically formed within the overlapping domains of social welfare, healthcare, consumer markets, and community initiatives (Phills et al., 2008).

However, while the definition proposed by Phills et al. has been widely influential, it tends to focus more on outcomes than on explaining the mechanisms through which social innovation emerges. A significant theoretical advancement in this regard comes from Moulaert and his colleagues, who argue that social innovation is not merely a "new solution" but a relational and political process. This process must be understood through three interrelated dimensions: satisfying human needs that are neglected by the market or the state, reconfiguring social relations and institutions, and enhancing the capacities and participation of marginalized groups in community life (Moulaert & Nussbaumer, 2005; Moulaert, MacCallum, & Hillier, 2013). This approach is particularly useful for studying older populations in emerging markets, as older persons often face not only a lack of services but also limited voice, restricted access to resources, and marginal positions in policy design. Therefore, conceptualizing the silver economy merely as a market for goods and services targeted at older people risks overlooking the deeper issue of restructuring the relationships between ageing, welfare, social citizenship, and community development.

Another important theoretical contribution is provided by Cajaiba-Santana (2014), who critiques the polarization in social innovation research between agency-centered and structure-centered approaches. Drawing on institutional theory and structuration theory, Cajaiba-Santana argues that social innovation should be understood as a driver of social transformation, constructed through socially embedded actions that are legitimized within existing norms, rules, and values that both constrain and enable innovation. This perspective is particularly relevant for analyzing community-based models within the silver economy, as initiatives supporting older persons rarely emerge from a complete institutional vacuum. Instead, they are shaped through the renegotiation of existing norms regarding family roles, state responsibilities, cultural values such as filial piety, and gendered divisions of care work. In other words, social innovation in the silver economy is not simply about introducing new services, but about redefining who provides care, who bears the costs, and who has the authority to design care ecosystems (Cajaiba-Santana, 2014).

When situated within the context of population ageing, these theoretical debates suggest that social innovation should be understood as an alternative development logic to passive welfare models. This is directly linked to the concept of the silver economy. In European policy discourse, the silver economy is described as the totality of economic activities associated with the needs and capabilities of older persons, including healthcare, long-term care, housing, mobility, assistive technologies, finance, consumption, and quality-of-life services (European Commission, 2018). However, Klimczuk (2016) argues that the concept of the silver economy is still evolving and should not be reduced to a consumer market for older adults. Rather, social innovations, gerontechnology, welfare models, and state structures collectively shape different forms of silver economies. This perspective is particularly valuable as it allows the silver economy in Vietnam to be conceptualized not merely as a market for ageing-related services, but as an emerging socio-economic and institutional architecture.

A critical point to emphasize is that emerging economies approach the silver economy under very different structural conditions compared to developed countries. In Europe or Japan, the silver economy is often associated with technological innovation, mature care service markets, and relatively high purchasing power among older populations. In contrast, in countries such as Vietnam, population ageing is occurring rapidly while average income levels, social protection coverage, and long-term care infrastructure remain limited. According to UNFPA, Vietnam is among the fastest ageing countries in the world, with people aged 60 and above accounting for 11.9% of the population in 2019 and projected to exceed 25% by 2050; by 2036, Vietnam will transition from an "ageing society" to an "aged society." At the same time, empirical studies indicate that care for older persons remains largely dependent on families and informal networks, while formal care systems remain underdeveloped (United Nations Population Fund, 2019; Giang et al., 2023; Nguyen et al., 2022). Under these conditions, theories of the silver economy must be adapted: rather than being market-centered, they should emphasize the mobilization of community resources, the integration of formal and informal care systems, and the recognition of older persons as active participants in socio-economic life rather than passive recipients.

A key theoretical foundation for this adjustment is the *active ageing* framework developed by WHO. Since the early 2000s, WHO has proposed that ageing should be understood not merely as biological decline, but as a process of optimizing opportunities for health, participation, and security in order to enhance quality of life in later years (World Health Organization, 2002). The strength of this framework lies in challenging the perception of older persons as dependent burdens. Instead, older individuals are seen as capable actors who can continue contributing to economic, social, cultural, and civic life if appropriate institutional and community environments are established. This framework has been further developed into the concept of *healthy ageing*, which focuses on maintaining *intrinsic capacity* and *functional ability*, emphasizing that communities, living environments, and service systems should be redesigned to support "ageing in place," allowing older persons to live safely, independently, and meaningfully within their own communities for as long as possible (World Health Organization, 2015; World Health Organization, 2017). Thus, from a theoretical perspective, the silver economy should not be understood simply as an economy that "serves the elderly," but as one that reorganizes environments, services, and social relations to sustain functional capacity and participation.

From this perspective, community-based models emerge as a central analytical pillar. Their foundation lies in social capital theory. Putnam (1993) defines social capital as networks, norms, and trust that facilitate coordination and cooperation for mutual benefit. For older persons, social capital is not merely a matter of social connections, but a tangible resource that enables access to care, emotional support, information, trust, and opportunities for participation. In rapidly ageing societies, the sustainability of support systems for older persons depends heavily on the strength of intergenerational ties, the cohesion of local communities, and the ability to transform social relationships into practical support mechanisms. This is particularly relevant in Vietnam, where formal care systems have not yet replaced the role of families, community organizations, and local networks. From this perspective, social innovation in the silver economy can be understood as a process of reorganizing social capital to adapt to demographic ageing .

However, social capital alone is insufficient to fully explain how community-based models operate. Another important theoretical layer is *co-production.* In public administration theory, co-production emphasizes that public service outcomes are not produced solely by service providers but are co-created by users, families, and communities. Bovaird and colleagues demonstrate that co-production is not a peripheral phenomenon but a core logic of many contemporary public services, particularly in care and welfare sectors, where citizen contributions significantly influence service quality (Bovaird et al., 2015). Applied to the silver economy, this perspective implies that older persons should not be positioned merely as service recipients, but as co-creators who participate in designing, delivering, and evaluating services. This is consistent with intergenerational clubs, volunteer-based home care, and self-help groups, where the boundaries between caregivers and care recipients become increasingly fluid.

Complementing co-production is the *asset-based community development* approach developed by Kretzmann and McKnight, which critiques deficit-based models of community development. This approach emphasizes identifying what communities possess rather than what they lack, including individual skills, local associations, informal networks, social reputation, community spaces, organizational experience, and local linkages. When applied to the silver economy, this perspective is particularly important because it shifts the perception of older persons from "dependent burdens" to "underutilized social resources." Older individuals can contribute professional knowledge, life experience, intergenerational mediation, part-time labor, volunteer work, and community leadership. Theoretically, this helps avoid reducing the silver economy to a mere consumer market, and instead frames it as an ecosystem that enables older persons to continue creating value.

Another relevant theoretical approach is the concept of *age-friendly communities*. According to WHO, an age-friendly community is one in which policies, services, institutions, and physical and social environments are designed to enable older persons to live safely, stay healthy, remain connected, and continue participating in society. From this perspective, ageing is not merely a health or income issue, but also a matter of social design. Empirical studies, such as those by Nieboer and Cramm, demonstrate a strong relationship between age-friendly environments and overall well-being among older persons. This expands the understanding of social innovation: innovation may not only involve new products or organizations, but also the transformation of entire community environments to support independence, social connection, and dignity in later life. In emerging market contexts, this is particularly important because institutional care is often costly, whereas community-based "ageing in place" strategies can achieve greater social impact at lower cost when well designed.

Bringing these theoretical strands together, it becomes clear that the analytical framework for this chapter should not rely on a single theoretical lens. Instead, an integrated framework is required. At the first level, social innovation theory explains why solutions for ageing must address unmet needs, empower individuals, and transform institutions. At the second level, silver economy and active ageing theories shift the focus from ageing as a burden to ageing as a domain of capability, consumption, care, and contribution. At the third level, community-based theories encompassing social capital, co-production, and asset-based development explain how such solutions operate in practice under resource constraints. The integration of these three layers allows for a deeper analysis of community-based models in Vietnam, moving beyond questions of service provision to examine whether such models transform social relations, enhance the agency of older persons, and contribute to the development of an inclusive and contextually appropriate silver economy.

When synthesizing the aforementioned theoretical strands, it becomes evident that the analytical framework appropriate for this chapter should not be confined to a linear or single-dimensional model. Rather, it necessitates an integrated, multi-layered framework. At the first level, social innovation theory provides the foundation for understanding why solutions addressing the needs of older populations must be examined through the lenses of unmet needs, empowerment, and institutional transformation. At the second level, the theoretical perspectives of the silver economy and active ageing reorient the analytical focus from ageing as a societal burden to ageing as a domain of capability, consumption, care, and social contribution. At the third level, community-based theories including social capital, co-production, and asset-based community development offer critical insights into the operational mechanisms through which community-based models function under conditions of resource constraints.

The integration of these three analytical layers enables a more nuanced and comprehensive examination of community-based models in Vietnam. It moves beyond the conventional question of whether such models merely provide services, and instead interrogates whether they contribute to the restructuring of social relations, enhance the agency and voice of older persons, and foster the emergence of an inclusive form of the silver economy that is contextually aligned with the structural conditions of emerging markets (as illustrated in Figure 1).

To synthesize the theoretical strands discussed above and guide the empirical investigation in the subsequent chapters, this study constructs a multi-layered integrated analytical framework, as illustrated in Figure 1. The framework operates through three interconnected levels that collectively reframe the silver economy within the structural realities of emerging markets.

Figure 1. The multi-layered integrated analytical framework

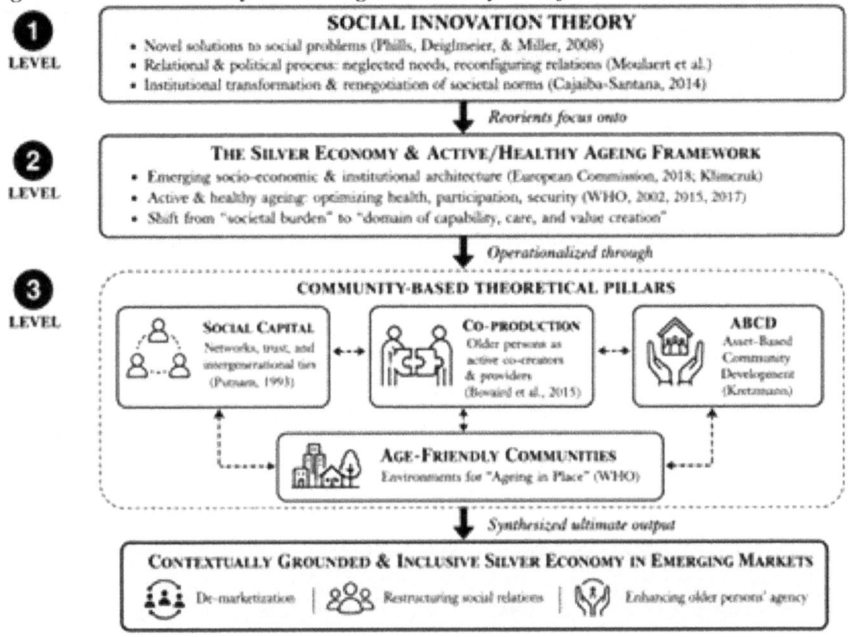

At the first level of the framework, Social Innovation Theory provides the foundational logic of transformation. Rather than treating elderly care as a static service market, this level captures how unmet social needs trigger the reconfiguration of social relations, the institutional renegotiation of filial norms, and the enhancement of community agency (Moulaert et al., 2013; Cajaiba-Santana, 2014). At the second level, the Silver Economy and Active/Healthy Ageing Frameworks define the macro objective. This layer shifts the analytical lens from perceiving population ageing as a societal burden or passive welfare dependency to recognizing older adults as active agents possessing intrinsic capacities for participation, consumption, and social contribution (World Health Organization, 2015; Klimczuk, 2016). At the third level, Community-Based Theories supply the concrete operational mechanisms under severe resource constraints. Here, Social Capital (Putnam, 1993) mobilizes local networks and trust; Co-production (Bovaird et al., 2015) reconfigures older persons from passive recipients into active co-creators of welfare; and Asset-Based Community Development (ABCD) unlocks underutilized local resources. These pillars are geographically and socially anchored by the concept of Age-Friendly Communities, which fosters cost-effective "ageing in place" strategies (World Health Organization, 2007).

Ultimately, the convergence of these three layers yields a contextually grounded, inclusive model of the silver economy. This framework allows the study to move beyond conventional metrics of service volume to rigorously interrogate whether community-based initiatives in Vietnam can successfully restructure social relations, empower marginalized older populations, and pioneer a viable pathway for rapid demographic transitions in emerging economies.

From the foregoing analysis, a theoretical stance for this chapter can be articulated as follows. First, social innovation within the silver economy should be understood as a multi-actor process of social transformation, rather than merely the introduction of new service initiatives. Second, in the context of emerging markets, the silver economy framework requires a degree of de-marketization; that is, it must explicitly incorporate the roles of communities, families, civil society organizations, and semi-formal institutions. Third, community-based models should not be regarded as temporary solutions arising from resource constraints, but rather as an intrinsic component of an inclusive silver economy, as they contribute to maintaining functional ability, supporting ageing in place, reducing social costs, and expanding opportunities for participation among older persons. Finally, the Vietnamese case points to an important theoretical pathway for emerging economies: instead of directly importing consumptionand technology-driven silver economy models from developed countries, there is a need to develop a contextually grounded model rooted in social innovation, community linkages, and the co-production of welfare.

3. RESEARCH DESIGN AND METHODOLOGY

This chapter adopts a qualitative comparative case study design combining secondary data analysis, theoretical synthesis, and illustrative case analysis. The objective is not to statistically test causal relationships but to identify common patterns and contextual mechanisms through which community-based social innovation contributes to the development of the silver economy in emerging markets.

The research relies exclusively on secondary sources collected from international organizations (United Nations, UNFPA, WHO, OECD, European Commission), academic publications indexed in Scopus and Web of Science, national policy documents, and reports published by governmental and non-governmental organizations. The reviewed materials were published primarily during the period 2015–2025, while statistical and demographic data cover the period 2010–2025, depending on data availability in each country.

To enhance analytical rigor, the study employs a purposive comparative case selection strategy. Five emerging economies, Thailand, China, Brazil, India, and South Africa were selected based on four criteria:

(1) experiencing rapid population ageing and increasing demand for long-term care services;
(2) belonging to the Global South or emerging market context characterized by resource constraints and incomplete welfare systems;
(3) possessing documented community-based or social innovation initiatives addressing ageing-related challenges;
(4) representing different geographical regions (Southeast Asia, East Asia, South Asia, Latin America, and Africa), thereby allowing broader analytical comparison.

The comparative analysis focuses on five analytical dimensions:

(i) demographic ageing context;
(ii) dominant community-based care model;
(iii) governance and stakeholder arrangements;
(iv) mechanisms of social innovation and community participation;
(v) implications for silver economy development.

The Vietnamese Intergenerational Self-Help Club (ISHC) model is subsequently examined as the focal case to illustrate how community-based social innovation can contribute to an inclusive silver economy under conditions of limited resources.

4. COMMUNITY-BASED SOCIAL INNOVATION MODELS IN THE SILVER ECONOMY: EVIDENCE FROM EMERGING MARKETS

In emerging economies, social innovation models within the silver economy often take the form of community-based initiatives that compensate for the limitations of formal welfare systems while leveraging social capital and informal networks. A prominent example is the *Intergenerational Self-Help Clubs* (ISHC) model in Vietnam, developed with the support of HelpAge International. This model integrates multiple functions, including livelihood support, healthcare provision, microfinance, home-based care, and social activities, thereby creating a comprehensive support ecosystem for older persons at the community level (HelpAge International, 2020). Empirical studies indicate that ISHC not only improves the living conditions of older persons but also strengthens social cohesion and the self-organizing capacity of local communities (Knodel et al., 2017). This provides strong evidence for the argument that social innovation in the silver economy in developing countries tends to be more integrated and community-based rather than market-driven (Moulaert et al., 2013).

In Thailand, the *Community-Based Long-Term Care* (CBLTC) model has been widely implemented as part of the national strategy for elderly care, in which local governments collaborate with community volunteers to provide home-based services (Suwanrada & Sukontamarn, 2023). Research shows that this system is significantly more cost-effective than institutional care models, while also aligning with the family-oriented and community-based cultural context of Thai society (Suwanrada & Sukontamarn, 2023). Notably, volunteers play not only a service delivery role but also act as social connectors, helping to reduce social isolation among older persons (World Health Organization, 2015). This case reinforces the co-production perspective, in which care services are generated through direct community participation rather than being solely state-driven (Bovaird et al., 2015).

In China, the "home-based and community-supported care" model has become a central pillar in addressing rapid population ageing. According to Feng et al. (2020), this system combines family support, community services, and state intervention to create a flexible care network for older persons. Community service centers play a crucial role in providing day care, basic healthcare services, and social activities, enabling older individuals to maintain independent living (Feng et al., 2020). At the same time, the development of this model reflects a broader institutional transition from traditional family-based care to a multi-actor governance structure, consistent with Cajaiba-Santana's view of social innovation as a process of institutional reconfiguration (Cajaiba-Santana, 2014).

In Brazil, programs such as the *Family Health Strategy* and various community-based care initiatives demonstrate the role of primary healthcare networks in supporting an ageing population. These systems rely on multidisciplinary community health teams, including doctors, nurses, and social workers, who operate directly within local neighborhoods (Macinko & Harris, 2015). Empirical evidence suggests that this approach not only improves health outcomes among older persons but also reduces healthcare costs and enhances community participation in health governance (Macinko & Harris, 2015). The Brazilian case illustrates how social innovation can be institutionalized at scale while maintaining its community-based and inclusive characteristics.

In India, initiatives such as the *Self-Employed Women's Association* (SEWA) have expanded their activities to support older persons, particularly women in the informal sector. SEWA provides microfinance services, health insurance, and livelihood support, enabling older individuals to maintain economic independence (Chen et al., 2015). Studies indicate that such models not only address economic vulnerabilities but also enhance the social empowerment of older persons, aligning with the social innovation perspective that emphasizes empowerment as a core dimension (Moulaert & Nussbaumer, 2005).

Similarly, in South Africa, community-based care models for older persons have developed in the context of the HIV/AIDS epidemic, where older individuals often act as primary caregivers for younger generations (Schatz & Ogunmefun, 2007).

This highlights the dual role of older persons within community ecosystems and reinforces the argument that the silver economy should be understood not merely as a domain of consumption but also as a space of social contribution (World Health Organization, 2015).

Taken together, these empirical examples reveal several common characteristics of social innovation in the silver economy across emerging markets. First, such models are typically highly integrated, combining healthcare, livelihood support, and social engagement to address the multidimensional needs of older persons (HelpAge International, 2020). Second, communities play a central role in designing and implementing solutions, consistent with theories of social capital and co-production (Putnam, 1993; Bovaird et al., 2015). Third, these models tend to be cost-effective due to their reliance on endogenous resources and informal networks (World Health Organization, 2015). Finally, these initiatives not only address care needs but also contribute to the restructuring of social relations and the enhancement of the social status of older persons, in line with the view of social innovation as a process of social transformation (Cajaiba-Santana, 2014).

Table 1. Innovation models in silver economy development

Country	Community-Based Model	Core Operating Mechanism	Role of State and Market	Key Resources Mobilized
Thailand	Community-Based Long-Term Care (CBLTC)	Community health volunteers provide home-based care, health monitoring, and social support for older persons	Government provides policy framework, training, and healthcare integration; limited private-sector involvement	Community volunteers, local health networks, public health resources
China	Home and Community-Based Elderly Care System	Integration of family care, community services, digital platforms, and local elderly service centers	Strong state leadership; increasing participation of private service providers and digital technology firms	Community service centres, digital platforms, public funding, family support
India	SEWA and Community Elder Support Initiatives	Self-help groups and community organizations support livelihoods, social protection, and elderly empowerment	Civil society plays a major role; government programs provide complementary support	Social networks, women's groups, collective action, community participation
Brazil	Family Health Strategy and Community Health Networks	Community health workers provide preventive care and household-level support	Strong public health system support; limited market role in community care delivery	Public healthcare resources, community health agents, local participation
South Africa	Community Care Networks for Older Persons	Community caregivers and local organizations provide home-based support and social services	Government provides social grants; NGOs and community organizations play important implementation roles	Volunteer caregivers, social grants, NGO support, community solidarity

Source: Compiled by the author based on UN, WHO, OECD and relevant literature.

These findings strongly support the argument that in emerging economies, the silver economy cannot be effectively developed through purely market-based approaches. Instead, it must rely on social innovation particularly community-based models to ensure inclusiveness, sustainaility, and alignment with specific institutional and cultural contexts.

5. COMMUNITY-BASED SOCIAL INNOVATION MODELS IN THE SILVER ECONOMY: THE CASE OF VIETNAM

5.1. Vietnam's Context and the Emergence of the Silver Economy

5.1.1. Overview

Vietnam is undergoing a rapid demographic transition in which population ageing is no longer a distant trend but has become a structural variable shaping socio-economic development. The country officially entered the ageing phase in 2011, and according to analyses by the United Nations Population Fund (UNFPA) and the General Statistics Office (GSO), it is expected to transition into an aged society within the next decade significantly faster than the trajectory experienced by many developed countries (United Nations Population Fund, 2019; GSO & UNFPA, 2022). Recent estimates indicate that the proportion of people aged 60 and above reached approximately 12.6% of the population in 2024, equivalent to around 14.2 million individuals, an increase of more than 2.8 million compared to 2019. By 2038, this age group is projected to account for nearly 20% of the total population (Pham, 2025).

A notable feature of population ageing in Vietnam is that it is occurring in a context where average income levels, social protection coverage, and long-term care systems remain underdeveloped. This condition reflects the phenomenon of "ageing before becoming rich," in which demographic ageing outpaces the accumulation of economic and institutional resources needed to support older populations (Bloom et al., 2015; United Nations Population Fund, 2019). Consequently, while in developed countries the silver economy is often driven by high-value consumer markets, advanced care technologies, and professional long-term care services, in Vietnam it must initially be conceptualized as a hybrid structure integrating social protection, care provision, community-based support, appropriate technologies, and flexible social organizational models (Klimczuk, 2016; Pham, 2025).

Another defining characteristic of Vietnam's context is that care for older persons remains heavily dependent on families and informal networks. Analyses by GSO and UNFPA show that although care needs are increasing significantly, the dominant care model continues to rely on households, even as household size declines, labor migration intensifies, and intra-family care resources become increasingly dispersed (GSO & UNFPA, 2022; United Nations Population Fund, 2019). This creates a paradox: people are living longer, yet not necessarily experiencing better health, improved care, or greater opportunities for social participation. In this context, the silver economy in Vietnam cannot be reduced to a "market for goods for older persons," but must instead be situated within the broader framework of the care economy, which involves not only service provision but also the restructuring of social relations and institutional arrangements supporting ageing (United Nations Population Fund, 2025).

5.1.2. Policy Foundations and the Absence of a Comprehensive Silver Economy Strategy

Vietnam has made notable progress in establishing policy frameworks related to ageing and older persons. Key instruments such as the Law on the Elderly (2009), the Vietnam Population Strategy to 2030 (Decision No. 1679/QĐ-TTg), and the National Action Program for Older Persons (2021–2030, Decision No. 2156/QĐ-TTg) demonstrate that ageing has been recognized as a critical policy issue (Prime Minister, 2019, 2021). The Population Strategy sets out concrete targets, including achieving age-friendly environments in 50% of communes and wards by 2030, ensuring universal health insurance coverage for older persons, and expanding access to healthcare and care services at home, in communities, or in institutional settings (Prime Minister, 2019).

However, existing policies remain primarily oriented toward social protection and care provision rather than framing ageing as a driver of a broader silver economy. As noted in recent policy analyses, Vietnam has yet to fully conceptualize the silver economy as a new domain of socio-economic development linked to innovation, technology, service markets, and the active role of older persons (Pham, 2025). In other words, while Vietnam has policies for older persons, it has not yet developed a comprehensive silver economy strategy that systematically integrates healthcare, social protection, digital transformation, lifelong learning, tourism, finance, housing, flexible employment, and innovation-driven enterprises serving ageing populations (Pham, 2025).

This highlights a clear distinction between "ageing response policies" and a "silver economy development strategy." The former focuses on mitigating risks and protecting vulnerable groups, whereas the latter requires a paradigm shift in which older persons are viewed not only as care recipients but also as consumers, contributors of knowledge and experience, participants in the labor force, and drivers of new market opportunities (European Commission, 2018; World Health Organization, 2002). In Vietnam, this gap remains pronounced, explaining why the concept of the silver economy, although increasingly present in policy discourse, is still relatively new in governance practice and market development (Pham, 2025).

5.1.3. Strengths: Community Foundations, Social Capital, and Integrated Care Models

From a social innovation perspective, Vietnam possesses several notable advantages. First, social capital and community cohesion remain relatively strong, particularly at the local level, including villages, communes, neighborhoods, and mass organizations. This creates favorable conditions for the development of community-based care models, intergenerational support systems, and co-produced services for older persons. Such social cohesion is increasingly rare in contexts characterized by rapid urbanization and individualization (Putnam, 1993; World Health Organization, 2015).

In addition, the development of the silver economy in Vietnam increasingly requires stronger engagement from private enterprises and social enterprises. While community-based models provide social embeddedness and local legitimacy, business actors can contribute technological innovation, investment resources, assistive devices, digital platforms, and age-friendly services. From this perspective, the future development of the silver economy is likely to depend on collaborative arrangements among communities, public institutions, and market actors rather than on any single sector operating independently.

Second, Vietnam has developed relatively successful pilot models, such as the Intergenerational Self-Help Clubs (ISHC), which are widely recognized as exemplary cases of community-based social innovation. These models integrate livelihood support, healthcare, social interaction, home-based care, and local resource mobilization, thereby improving quality of life for older persons while reducing pressure on formal care systems (HelpAge International, 2020). From an academic perspective, this represents a clear illustration of the argument that in emerging markets, the silver economy often develops initially through integrated community-based models rather than through high-end service markets (Moulaert et al., 2013; World Health Organization, 2015).

Third, Vietnam stands at a critical juncture in its digital transformation. Policy discussions emphasize that in the digital era, the silver economy extends beyond healthcare and welfare to include digital platforms for health monitoring, lifelong learning, flexible employment, smart consumption, age-friendly devices, and applications of artificial intelligence, robotics, and smart home technologies (Pham, 2025). This suggests that the development of the silver economy can be closely aligned with Vietnam's broader digital economy and digital society strategies, provided that appropriate institutional frameworks and incentives are established.

5.1.4. Weaknesses and Barriers: Institutional Fragmentation, Data Gaps, and Underdeveloped Markets

Despite these advantages, Vietnam faces several structural constraints. First, there is a lack of an integrated, cross-sectoral institutional framework for the silver economy. Policies related to ageing remain fragmented across sectors such as healthcare, population, labor and social affairs, culture, social protection, and digital transformation, without being consolidated into a unified development strategy with clear socio-economic objectives (Pham, 2025). As a result, many initiatives remain at the level of isolated projects rather than forming part of a cohesive national strategy.

Second, there is a lack of specialized data infrastructure for ageing populations. As highlighted in policy analyses, Vietnam does not yet have a sufficiently robust national database dedicated to older persons to support evidence-based policymaking (Pham, 2025). Although the Population Strategy aims to achieve universal population registration and improve data utilization, there remains a significant gap between policy objectives and the actual capacity to integrate and use data specifically for silver economy development (Prime Minister, 2019).

Third, the market for ageing-related services remains underdeveloped. Income levels among many older persons, particularly in rural areas and the informal sector, are not yet sufficient to support the rapid emergence of high-value consumer markets. Consequently, private sector investment in products and services targeting older populations remains limited, further constrained by the absence of strong policy incentives such as tax benefits, credit support, or innovation funding (Pham, 2025).

Fourth, digital inequality poses an emerging risk. As the silver economy becomes increasingly linked to digital transformation, a significant proportion of older persons may be excluded due to limited digital skills, lack of access to devices, or insufficient support environments. Without appropriate policy interventions, digitalization may exacerbate inequalities rather than reduce them. Therefore, the development of a digital silver economy in Vietnam must be accompanied by efforts to enhance digital literacy among older persons and to design technologies that are accessible, affordable, and user-friendly (Pham, 2025).

5.1.5. Comparative Assessment: Strengths and Limitations of Vietnam's Approach

Compared to many emerging economies, Vietnam's key advantage lies in its ability to develop a community-based, cost-effective silver economy model. Strong local networks, community organizations, and experience in intergenerational care provide a solid foundation for "ageing in place" strategies, enabling older persons to live safely, healthily, and meaningfully within their communities (World Health Organization, 2015).

However, the country's main limitation lies in the relatively low level of institutional integration. While successful models exist, they lack comprehensive support in terms of strategy, financing, data infrastructure, human resources, and private sector engagement needed to scale up from pilot initiatives to nationwide systems (United Nations Population Fund, 2019; Pham, 2025).

In summary, Vietnam's strengths are rooted in its social and community structures, while its weaknesses lie in market development and institutional integration. The country demonstrates strong capacity to develop inclusive, culturally embedded, and socially adaptive models, but remains less advanced in selective commercialization, service standardization, technological innovation, and private sector mobilization. Consequently, the most appropriate development pathway is not to replicate the silver economy models of Japan or Europe, but to pursue a hybrid silver economy model, in which community-based social innovation serves as the foundation, while digital technologies, innovative enterprises, and policy frameworks function as enabling layers for scaling and sustainability.

Looking ahead, this hybrid pathway will become increasingly important as Vietnam approaches the transition to an aged society by 2036 and faces a rapidly growing older population by 2050. Strategic foresight therefore requires policymakers to consider whether existing community-based models possess sufficient organizational capacity, financing mechanisms, and technological support to remain effective under future demographic pressures. The challenge is not only to expand current initiatives but also to ensure their long-term scalability and resilience.

5.2. The Intergenerational Self-Help Club Model as a Form of Community-Based Social Innovation in the Development of the Silver Economy in Vietnam

In the context of rapid population ageing in Vietnam, coupled with the underdevelopment of welfare systems and long-term care services, the *Intergenerational Self-Help Club* (ISHC) model has emerged as a socio-institutional adaptive response to the gap between the growing demand for care and the limited capacity of both the state and the market. According to UNFPA, Vietnam is among the fastest ageing countries in the world; the population aged 60 and above accounted for 11.9% in 2019 and is projected to exceed 25% by 2050, with the country expected to transition from an "ageing society" to an "aged society" by 2036. Under such conditions, traditional family-based care models are increasingly under strain, making the need for community-based support mechanisms more urgent. The World Health Organization (WHO) also emphasizes that in low- and middle-income countries, rapid ageing requires health and social systems to be restructured in ways that maintain functional ability, enhance social participation, and support older persons in remaining within their communities for as long as possible.

Within this context, the ISHC model can be understood as a form of community-based social innovation. Rather than merely providing additional services for older persons, the model reorganizes how communities mobilize resources, distribute care responsibilities, and create opportunities for older individuals to remain active participants in socio-economic life. According to HelpAge International, ISHC was first introduced in Vietnam in 2006, expanding from approximately 60 clubs to 980 by 2016, and was subsequently recognized in national policy as a cost-effective solution for addressing population ageing. The fact that the model originated from community needs and was later institutionalized demonstrates that ISHC is not simply a social support program, but a bottom-up innovation process in which local initiatives inform policy design at broader scales.

In terms of organizational structure, ISHC represents a multi-functional integrated model. Each club typically operates at the village or commune level on a voluntary basis, with around 50–70 members and a democratically elected management board. The clubs implement eight core areas of activity, including social and cultural engagement, food security and livelihoods, promotion of healthy ageing, volunteer-based home care, self-help and community development, lifelong learning, support for accessing rights and policies, and local resource mobilization. This structure reflects a holistic approach in which the needs of older persons are not treated as isolated issues but are understood as interconnected dimensions encompassing health, income, social relationships, civic voice, and access to services. This integrative design makes ISHC particularly consistent with the logic of an inclusive silver economy, where older persons are recognized not only as beneficiaries of welfare but also as individuals with both specific needs and productive capacities, requiring comprehensive support ecosystems rather than fragmented interventions.

A defining feature of the ISHC model is its reliance on co-production at the community level. In this model, older persons are not passive recipients but active participants in designing activities, managing club operations, supporting other members, and mobilizing local resources. HelpAge emphasizes that club activities are based on needs identified by members themselves, and that implementation remains flexible to local conditions and aligned with the priorities of grassroots authorities. This distinguishes ISHC from conventional top-down service delivery models, where communities primarily receive externally designed interventions. Here, the value of the model lies in the fact that communities are not merely recipients of policy but co-creators of solutions. This co-production mechanism reduces transaction costs, enhances social acceptance, and ensures adaptability across diverse local contexts.

At a deeper level, the functioning of ISHC is grounded in social capital and endogenous community assets. Rotating funds resembling microfinance schemes, livelihood training activities such as livestock raising or small-scale agriculture, regular health check-ups, physical exercise programs, home visits, legal support, and policy dialogue with local authorities all rely more on trust, social cohesion, and coordination capacity than on large-scale external financial investment. This is particularly suited to the Vietnamese context, where public resources for elderly care remain limited, but community networks remain relatively strong. In this sense, the ISHC model demonstrates that the development of the silver economy in emerging markets does not necessarily need to originate from high-tech solutions or expensive commercial services; rather, it can begin with the reorganization of communities, enabling them to function as localized providers of welfare in a cost-effective manner.

Importantly, the impact of ISHC extends beyond individual-level support. According to HelpAge, these clubs are structured as intergenerational organizations, involving older persons, middle-aged individuals, and women, thereby providing direct support to older populations while simultaneously strengthening social cohesion and collective action capacity within communities. When older persons actively participate in cultural, educational, and livelihood activities, support one another, and engage in monitoring policy implementation, they are no longer positioned as dependent groups but emerge as socially active agents. This approach aligns closely with WHO's concept of healthy ageing, which emphasizes not merely longevity but the ability to live meaningful lives, remain socially engaged, and maintain dignity in later years.

From the perspective of silver economy development, ISHC is particularly significant because it illustrates an inclusive development pathway. While dominant discourses on the silver economy often focus on consumer markets, technological solutions, or commercial care services, the Vietnamese case demonstrates that in emerging markets, the silver economy can be built upon community-based initiatives in which economic activities, healthcare, and social participation are integrated within a single organizational structure. HelpAge reports that the model has been implemented nationwide, recognized internationally for innovation in healthy ageing, and considered for replication in other low- and middle-income countries. This suggests that ISHC holds relevance beyond Vietnam, providing empirical evidence that community-based models can generate meaningful outcomes in terms of livelihoods, care provision, social connectivity, and empowerment core components of an inclusive silver economy.

While the ISHC model has been primarily developed through community participation and public support mechanisms, its long-term sustainability may increasingly depend on partnerships with social enterprises and private-sector actors. Community organizations possess local trust, social capital, and direct knowledge of older persons' needs, whereas businesses can contribute technological innovation, investment resources, age-friendly products, and service delivery expertise. From this perspective, the future development of community-based silver economy models should not be understood as a choice between community and market approaches, but rather as a process of building complementary relationships between them.

In emerging economies such as Vietnam, social enterprises may play a particularly important intermediary role by linking social objectives with financial sustainability. Through services such as telecare, assistive technologies, digital literacy training, community health support, and age-friendly livelihood initiatives, social enterprises can help scale community-based innovations while maintaining their inclusive and socially embedded character. This suggests that effective silver economy development requires collaborative governance arrangements involving communities, public institutions, and market actors.

5.3. Structural Bottlenecks and Vulnerabilities of the ISHC Model in Vietnam

Although the ISHC model has been widely recognized as an innovative community-based approach to addressing population ageing in Vietnam, a balanced assessment requires acknowledging several structural bottlenecks and vulnerabilities that may affect its long-term sustainability and scalability. Understanding these limitations is essential not only for evaluating the Vietnamese experience objectively but also for drawing lessons for other emerging economies seeking to develop community-based silver economy models.

5.3.1. Financial Sustainability Beyond Donor Support

One of the most significant challenges facing the ISHC model concerns long-term financial sustainability. The establishment and expansion of ISHCs have benefited substantially from technical and financial support provided by international organizations, particularly HelpAge International and its development partners. External support has played a critical role in developing operational guidelines, training facilitators, strengthening organizational capacity, and supporting pilot implementation.

However, as international development assistance gradually declines and donor priorities shift, questions emerge regarding the long-term financial viability of the model. While many clubs have developed small revolving funds and local resource mobilization mechanisms, these resources may not be sufficient to sustain all activities, particularly those related to home-based care, health promotion, training, and livelihood support.

The challenge therefore lies in moving from donor-supported innovation to institutionally embedded and financially sustainable community systems. This requires a diversified financing structure combining local government support, community contributions, social enterprises, public–private partnerships, and integration into broader ageing and social protection programs.

5.3.2. Uneven Implementation Across Localities

A second vulnerability concerns significant variations in implementation quality across different localities. Although the ISHC model follows common principles, actual performance often depends on local leadership capacity, volunteer engagement, availability of resources, and support from grassroots authorities.

In localities where commune authorities actively support club activities and community organizations remain strong, ISHCs often evolve into multifunctional platforms that effectively combine healthcare support, livelihood activities, social participation, and community development. Conversely, in areas with weaker institutional commitment or limited resources, some clubs may struggle to maintain regular activities or achieve their intended outcomes.

This unevenness suggests that replication alone does not guarantee success. The effectiveness of community-based social innovation remains highly dependent on local governance conditions and contextual factors.

5.3.3. Institutional Fragmentation and Coordination Challenges

The ISHC model operates at the intersection of multiple policy domains, including ageing policy, healthcare, social protection, community development, and local governance. However, these domains are often managed by different agencies with separate mandates, funding mechanisms, and administrative procedures.

As a result, coordination challenges may arise in areas such as service delivery, monitoring, resource allocation, and policy implementation. Without stronger institutional integration, the model risks remaining a community initiative operating alongside formal systems rather than becoming an integral component of Vietnam's ageing and silver economy strategy.

Strengthening horizontal and vertical coordination among government agencies, community organizations, healthcare providers, and social protection institutions therefore remains a critical requirement.

5.3.4. Dependence on Volunteerism and Community Capacity

Another challenge concerns the model's reliance on volunteer-based support systems. Volunteers play a central role in home visits, health monitoring, social support, and community mobilization. While this approach significantly reduces costs and strengthens local ownership, it also creates vulnerabilities associated with volunteer turnover, varying skill levels, and limited professional capacity.

As Vietnam's population continues to age and care needs become increasingly complex, community volunteers may face growing difficulties in addressing issues such as dementia, chronic diseases, disability, and mental health challenges. Without systematic training, supervision, and referral mechanisms, the capacity of volunteer networks may become a limiting factor for future expansion.

5.3.5. Social Change and the Limits of Community-Based Care

The sustainability of ISHC also depends on broader social and demographic trends. Traditionally, Vietnam has relied heavily on family-based care and strong community networks. However, urbanization, labour migration, declining household size, and changing family structures are gradually weakening these traditional support mechanisms.

Consequently, community-based models cannot be assumed to have unlimited social resources. While they can complement formal welfare systems, they may not be able to fully compensate for growing care demands in rapidly ageing societies. Future silver economy strategies will therefore need to combine community-based initiatives with professional care services, digital technologies, and strengthened public welfare institutions.

5.3.6. Critical Reflection

The Vietnamese experience demonstrates both the strengths and limitations of community-based social innovation in responding to population ageing. The ISHC model has shown considerable potential in mobilizing social capital, promoting active ageing, strengthening community resilience, and supporting older persons in resource-constrained settings.

Nevertheless, its long-term effectiveness depends on several enabling conditions, including stable financing mechanisms, institutional coordination, capacity building, supportive public policies, and adaptive local governance. Without these conditions, the model may encounter difficulties in sustaining impact and scaling effectively.

Importantly, the Vietnamese experience suggests that community-based social innovation should not be viewed as a substitute for formal welfare institutions.

Rather, it functions as a complementary governance mechanism that strengthens the resilience, inclusiveness, and sustainability of silver economy development. The value of the ISHC model therefore lies not only in the services it provides but also in its ability to connect community resources with broader public policy objectives in an ageing society.

6. POLICY RECOMMENDATIONS AND IMPLICATIONS FOR EMERGING ECONOMIES

From the foregoing analysis, it is evident that the development of the silver economy in Vietnam cannot remain confined to fragmented community-based initiatives, but must transition toward an integrated and systemic framework. First and foremost, Vietnam needs to establish a national silver economy strategy based on an intersectoral approach that connects healthcare, social protection, labor, population, and digital transformation. Within this framework, the silver economy should be recognized not merely as a domain of social protection, but as a new space for socio-economic development (European Commission, 2018). Community-based social innovation models, such as the Intergenerational Self-Help Clubs, should therefore be formally acknowledged as core pillars of the care system, rather than being treated as supplementary or ad hoc solutions (HelpAge International, 2022). However, to ensure effectiveness, the expansion of such models should go beyond quantitative replication and be accompanied by the standardization of operational processes, capacity building for human resources, the establishment of monitoring and evaluation mechanisms, and the development of sustainable financing models, including public funding, social impact investment, and public private community partnerships (Moulaert et al., 2013; United Nations Population Fund, 2019).

In addition, a key strategic direction is to further strengthen co-production mechanisms and empower older persons. This requires the design of governance structures that enable meaningful participation of older persons, as well as the promotion of intergenerational programs, lifelong learning, and flexible employment opportunities. Such measures would facilitate the transition of older persons from passive beneficiaries to active contributors in socio-economic life (World Health Organization, 2002; Bovaird et al., 2015). At the same time, digital transformation should be leveraged as a critical driver for the development of the silver economy, while ensuring inclusiveness through policies aimed at enhancing digital literacy among older persons, developing user-friendly platforms, and promoting assistive technologies such as telecare, smart homes, and supportive devices (World Health Organization, 2015; Pham, 2025). Moreover, to ensure sustainability and scalability, it is essential to encourage the participation of the private sector and social enterprises in developing products and services for older persons through appropriate incentive mechanisms, including tax incentives, innovation support, and the development of entrepreneurial ecosystems in this sector (Klimczuk, 2016). Simultaneously, the establishment of integrated and interoperable data systems on ageing populations, supported by advanced data analytics, is a prerequisite for improving policy design and service delivery (United Nations Population Fund, 2019).

From a broader perspective, the Vietnamese experience also offers important implications for emerging economies seeking to develop inclusive and sustainable silver economies. First, the silver economy should not be approached solely as a consumer market or a service sector targeting older persons, but rather as part of a broader framework of social innovation and care system development (Phills et al., 2008; Moulaert et al., 2013). Under conditions of limited resources, emerging economies are unlikely to replicate the technology-intensive and service-oriented models of developed countries. Instead, priority should be given to community-based models, where social capital, networks, and citizen participation play central roles in service provision and co-production (Putnam, 1993; Bovaird et al., 2015).

Second, the development of the silver economy should begin at the grassroots level, through locally driven initiatives that are adaptable to specific socio-cultural contexts. These models not only help to bridge institutional gaps but also provide the foundation for building flexible care ecosystems that can gradually be scaled up and institutionalized over time (Cajaiba-Santana, 2014). Therefore, developing countries should design policy frameworks that enable experimentation, learning, and scaling of social innovation, rather than imposing top-down models from the outset (Moulaert et al., 2013).

Third, a fundamental shift is needed in the perception of older persons from beneficiaries to development resources. Promoting co-production and enabling older persons to participate actively in economic, social, and community activities can enhance the effectiveness of care systems, strengthen social cohesion, and reduce fiscal pressure on public budgets (World Health Organization, 2002; Knodel et al., 2017).

Fourth, emerging economies should pursue a hybrid development model in which community-based social innovation serves as the foundation, while the state and the market act as enabling and scaling mechanisms. The state should provide the institutional framework, initial investment, and safeguards for equity, whereas the private sector and civil society organizations can contribute to the development of innovative services and solutions (Carayannis & Campbell, 2012). At the same time, digital transformation should be harnessed as a supportive tool, ensuring accessibility and avoiding the exacerbation of inequalities (World Health Organization, 2015). Finally, an important lesson is that the development of the silver economy in emerging markets should not follow a "leapfrogging" approach directly toward highly marketized models, but rather an evolutionary pathway: starting with community-based initiatives, gradually integrating them into policy systems, and eventually expanding into service markets (Klimczuk, 2016; United Nations Population Fund, 2019).

In this sense, the greatest value of the Vietnamese case does not lie in offering a complete or fully developed model, but in demonstrating a feasible and adaptive pathway a silver economy framework grounded in social innovation, community embeddedness, and the co-production of welfare which can serve as a valuable reference for countries facing rapid population ageing under conditions of constrained resources (Moulaert et al., 2013; World Health Organization, 2015).

More broadly, the Vietnamese experience suggests that silver economy development in emerging economies may follow a different trajectory from that observed in high-income countries. Rather than being driven primarily by technology-intensive markets and commercial service expansion, development may emerge through social innovation, community participation, and co-production mechanisms. This perspective contributes to broadening existing conceptualizations of the silver economy by highlighting the role of community capacity as a foundational resource for ageing societies.

7. FUTURE RESEARCH DIRECTIONS

Although this chapter has provided an integrated analytical framework and empirical evidence from the Vietnamese case, significant research gaps remain that warrant further exploration in order to deepen the understanding of the silver economy in the context of emerging economies.

First, there is a need for more rigorous empirical research, particularly quantitative and mixed-method studies, to systematically assess the impacts of community-based social innovation models especially initiatives such as the Intergenerational Self-Help Clubs on key outcomes, including quality of life, health status, income, levels of social participation, and the ability of older persons to maintain independence. The development of context-sensitive measurement indicators tailored to developing countries would help address the current lack of evidence and support data-driven policymaking.

Second, future research should expand toward comparative international studies across emerging economies in order to identify different pathways of silver economy development, as well as the institutional, cultural, and economic conditions that determine the success or failure of these models. Comparative analyses involving countries such as Vietnam, Thailand, China, India, and selected Latin American economies would be particularly valuable in assessing whether community-based approaches can be generalized into a broader theoretical framework for the Global South, or whether they remain context-specific.

Third, an important research direction lies in examining the role of digital transformation in the development of the silver economy, particularly the interaction between technological innovation and community-based models. It is necessary to investigate whether technologies such as artificial intelligence, telecare, digital platforms, and smart devices can be effectively integrated into community ecosystems, and under what conditions they can enhance rather than undermine inclusiveness and the participation of older persons.

Fourth, further research is needed on financing models and investment mechanisms for the silver economy under conditions of resource constraints. This includes evaluating the roles of social impact investment, blended finance, community development funds, and public–private–community partnerships in ensuring the sustainability and scalability of social innovation initiatives.

Fifth, deeper analysis is required on institutional and governance dimensions, particularly how community-based models can be integrated into national policy systems without compromising their flexibility and adaptive capacity. This entails studying multi-level coordination mechanisms, the role of local governments, and hybrid governance arrangements that involve the state, the market, and communities.

Finally, an important theoretical direction for future research is the continued development of the concept of the silver economy in emerging market contexts. Rather than merely adopting frameworks derived from developed countries, there is a need to construct a new theoretical approach in which the silver economy is conceptualized as a hybrid ecosystem combining social innovation, community structures, and market dynamics. Such an approach would not only enrich existing theory but also provide a more appropriate foundation for designing policies that align with the socio-economic conditions of developing countries.

8. CONCLUSION

This chapter has examined the role of social innovation in the development of the silver economy in emerging markets, with a particular focus on community-based models in the Vietnamese context. By integrating theoretical perspectives on social innovation, the silver economy, and community-based development, the chapter demonstrates that, under conditions of resource constraints, community-driven initiatives are not merely complementary but can constitute a foundational component of care systems for older persons.

Through the analysis of the Intergenerational Self-Help Club model, the chapter elucidates operational mechanisms grounded in co-production, social capital, and community participation. The findings highlight the capacity of such models to generate simultaneous economic, social, and institutional value. In particular, community-based approaches contribute to maintaining the functional independence of older persons, alleviating pressure on formal welfare systems, and strengthening social cohesion in the context of rapid population ageing.

From a comparative perspective, the chapter further suggests that the development of the silver economy in emerging markets may follow a pathway distinct from that observed in many developed economies. While silver economy development in high-income countries is often driven by market expansion, technological innovation, and commercial service systems, the Vietnamese experience indicates that an alternative trajectory may emerge under conditions of resource constraints. In such contexts, community-based social innovation, social capital, and co-production mechanisms can serve as the initial foundations of silver economy development, while public institutions, business partnerships, and technological innovations function as enabling and scaling mechanisms. Rather than representing competing approaches, community, state, and market actors operate as complementary components within a hybrid ecosystem that supports both social well-being and economic sustainability.

Operational Framework for a Hybrid Model of Silver Economy Development

To move beyond general calls for collaboration among communities, the state, and the market, the hybrid model for silver economy development should be translated into a practical implementation framework. In this framework, community-based organizations such as Intergenerational Self-Help Clubs (ISHCs) serve as the social foundation of elderly support systems; the state acts as an institutional enabler through policy, regulation, financing, and coordination; while the private sector contributes innovation, investment, technologies, and scalable service solutions. Rather than operating independently, these three actors interact within a collaborative governance system aimed at generating economic, social, and welfare outcomes for older persons.

The first principle of the framework is that communities should serve as the primary arena for identifying needs and co-creating solutions. Community organizations, elderly associations, volunteer networks, and local support groups are best positioned to understand the lived experiences and priorities of older persons. In this model, older adults are not viewed merely as beneficiaries of services but as active participants in designing, implementing, and evaluating programs that affect their well-being. Community participation therefore becomes a central mechanism for ensuring relevance, legitimacy, and responsiveness.

The second principle is that the state should create an enabling institutional environment and safeguard social equity. Governments at national and local levels should establish policy frameworks, quality standards, financing mechanisms, and regulatory safeguards that support the development of the silver economy. In addition, public authorities should facilitate coordination across sectors such as healthcare, social protection, community development, and digital transformation to ensure that services for older persons are delivered through an integrated ecosystem rather than fragmented interventions.

The third principle is that the private sector should function as a provider of innovation, technology, and investment. Businesses can contribute to the silver economy through age-friendly healthcare technologies, telemedicine services, assistive devices, financial products, adapted housing solutions, and leisure or tourism services tailored to older populations. However, market participation should be guided by ethical principles, including affordability, transparency, accessibility, data protection, and social responsibility. The objective is not to commercialize ageing, but to leverage private-sector capabilities in ways that enhance the quality of life of older persons.

The fourth principle is the establishment of mechanisms for co-creation and collaborative governance among communities, public institutions, and private actors. Programs and services should be co-designed, co-delivered, and co-evaluated by multiple stakeholders. Such arrangements help ensure that solutions reflect local needs, mobilize diverse resources, and remain aligned with broader public policy goals. Universities, research institutions, civil society organizations, and professional associations may also play important intermediary roles by providing evidence, training, evaluation, and knowledge exchange.

The fifth principle is that economic value generated within the silver economy should be partially reinvested in strengthening community capacity and social infrastructure. Financial instruments such as social impact investment, blended finance mechanisms, community development funds, and public–private partnerships can help channel resources back into local care systems, volunteer networks, training programs, and social innovation initiatives. This reinvestment approach helps ensure that economic growth contributes directly to social well-being and community resilience.

From this perspective, the hybrid model should not be understood simply as a division of responsibilities among the state, the market, and the community. Rather, it represents a collaborative governance framework in which community organizations provide social embeddedness and trust, the state ensures institutional support and equity, and the market contributes innovation, investment, and scalable service solutions. The sustainability of the silver economy therefore depends not on the dominance of any single actor, but on the capacity to create mutually reinforcing relationships among all three sectors while preserving the social capital that underpins community resilience.

The Vietnamese experience suggests that an inclusive silver economy in emerging markets cannot be built solely through welfare provision or market expansion. Instead, it requires a carefully designed hybrid ecosystem in which community-based social innovation forms the foundation, public policy provides legitimacy and protection, and private enterprises contribute technology, finance, and scalable services under ethical and socially accountable conditions.

The main contribution of this chapter lies in proposing an integrated theoretical framework that connects social innovation, community-based development, and the silver economy, while providing empirical evidence from Vietnam to illustrate an alternative pathway for silver economy development in emerging contexts. The chapter demonstrates that community-based social innovation can function not only as a complementary welfare mechanism but also as a foundational component of inclusive silver economy development under conditions of resource constraints. In doing so, it advances the argument that silver economy development in emerging markets may originate from community-based innovation and collective action before being expanded through supportive public policies, business partnerships, and technological innovation.

By critically examining both the strengths and limitations of the Vietnamese experience and by proposing a hybrid governance framework involving communities, the state, and the market, the chapter extends existing scholarship beyond predominantly market-oriented perspectives on the silver economy. In doing so, it offers relevant theoretical insights, policy implications, and practical lessons for countries facing similar challenges of rapid population ageing and limited welfare resources.

ACKNOWLEDGMENT

This reaearch is funded by University of Finance-Marketing, Viet Nam.

REFERENCES

Bloom, D. E., Canning, D., & Fink, G. (2015). Implications of population ageing for economic growth. *Oxford Review of Economic Policy, 26*(4), 583–612. DOI: 10.1093/oxrep/grq038

Bovaird, T., Van Ryzin, G. G., Loeffler, E., & Parrado, S. (2015). Activating citizens to participate in collective co-production of public services. *Journal of Social Policy, 44*(1), 1–23. DOI: 10.1017/S0047279414000567

Cajaiba-Santana, G. (2014). Social innovation: Moving the field forward. *Technological Forecasting and Social Change, 82*, 42–51. DOI: 10.1016/j.techfore.2013.05.008

Chen, M. A., Jhabvala, R., & Kanbur, R. (2015). *Informal economy and development*. Routledge.

European Commission. (2018). *The silver economy*. Publications Office of the European Union., DOI: 10.2759/338976

General Statistics Office of Viet Nam, & United Nations Population Fund. (2022). *Older persons in Viet Nam: An analysis of the Population Change and Family Planning Survey 2021*.

Giang, L. T., Nguyen, N. T., Pham, T. T. H., & Phi, P. M. (2023). Factors associated with receipt of informal care among the Vietnamese older persons: Evidence from a national survey. *Frontiers in Public Health, 11*, 1065851. Advance online publication. DOI: 10.3389/fpubh.2023.1065851 PMID: 36969636

HelpAge International. (2022). *Global ageing report*.

Klimczuk, A. (2016). Comparative analysis of national and regional models of the silver economy in the European Union. *International Journal of Ageing and Later Life, 10*(2), 31–59. DOI: 10.3384/ijal.1652-8670.15286

Knodel, J., Teerawichitchainan, B., Prachuabmoh, V., & Pothisiri, W. (2017). *The situation of Thailand's older population*. College of Population Studies, Chulalongkorn University.

Kretzmann, J. P., & McKnight, J. L. (1993). *Building communities from the inside out: A path toward finding and mobilizing a community's assets.* ACTA Publications.

Macinko, J., & Harris, M. J. (2015). Brazil's Family Health Strategy. *The New England Journal of Medicine, 372*(23), 2177–2181. DOI: 10.1056/NEJMp1501140 PMID: 26039598

Moulaert, F., MacCallum, D., Mehmood, A., & Hamdouch, A. (Eds.). (2013). *The international handbook on social innovation: Collective action, social learning and transdisciplinary research.* Edward Elgar Publishing., DOI: 10.4337/9781849809993

Moulaert, F., & Nussbaumer, J. (2005). The social region: Beyond the territorial dynamics of the learning economy. *European Urban and Regional Studies, 12*(1), 45–64. DOI: 10.1177/0969776405048500

Nguyen, L. T., Nantharath, P., & Kang, E. (2022). The sustainable care model for an ageing population in Vietnam: Evidence from a systematic review. *Sustainability (Basel), 14*(5), 2518. Advance online publication. DOI: 10.3390/su14052518

Pham, T. (2025). Ethical and legal considerations in healthcare AI: Innovation and policy for safe and fair use. *Royal Society Open Science, 12*(5), 241873. DOI: 10.1098/rsos.241873 PMID: 40370601

Phills, J. A.Jr, Deiglmeier, K., & Miller, D. T. (2008). Rediscovering social innovation. *Stanford Social Innovation Review, 6*(4), 34–43.

Prime Minister of Vietnam. (2019). *Decision No. 1679/QĐ-TTg dated November 22, 2019 approving the Vietnam Population Strategy to 2030.*

Prime Minister of Vietnam. (2021). *Decision No. 2156/QĐ-TTg dated December 21, 2021 approving the National Action Program for Older Persons for the period 2021–2030.*

Putnam, R. D. (1993). *Making democracy work: Civic traditions in modern Italy.* Princeton University Press.

Schatz, E., & Ogunmefun, C. (2007). Caring and contributing: The role of older women in rural South African households. *World Development, 35*(8), 1390–1403. DOI: 10.1016/j.worlddev.2007.04.004

Suwanrada, W., & Sukontamarn, P. (2023). Should social pensions be universal or targeted? OLder persons' preferences over the old-age allowance system in thailand. *Journal of Aging & Social Policy, 35*(1), 52–69. DOI: 10.1080/08959420.2022.2029267 PMID: 35067211

United Nations Population Fund. (2019). *Ageing in Viet Nam.*

United Nations Population Fund. (2025). *Applying foresight to curate a care economy for older persons in Viet Nam.*

World Health Organization. (2002). *Active ageing: A policy framework.*

World Health Organization. (2007). *Global age-friendly cities: A guide.*

World Health Organization. (2015). *World report on ageing and health.*

World Health Organization. (2017). *Integrated care for older people: Guidelines on community-level interventions to manage declines in intrinsic capacity.*

Chapter 13
Repositioning the Role of the Elderly in Vietnam:
Social Capital in the Longevity Economy

Hai Trung Nguyen
http://orcid.org/0009-0007-6095-0867
Independent Researcher, Vietnam

Tuan Dinh Nguyen
http://orcid.org/0000-0002-2079-6750
Independent Researcher, Vietnam

ABSTRACT

Against the backdrop of rapid population aging in Vietnam, this chapter proposes a shift from viewing older adults as a medical "burden" to recognizing them as a "strategic asset" within the Longevity Economy framework. Drawing on human capital and social capital theories, it argues that older adults represent a multidimensional form of capital contributing to national development. The chapter highlights three key pillars. First, economic value is reflected in "silver brainpower," including risk management, preservation of traditional crafts, and indirect support to the workforce, contributing an estimated 2–3% of GDP. Second, social capital emphasizes their role in community cohesion, intergenerational education, and volunteerism. Third, structural barriers such as ageism, the digital divide, and rigid retirement policies limit their potential. The chapter concludes with policy recommendations to promote active aging, including flexible retirement, lifelong learning, and age-responsive business models.

DOI: 10.4018/979-8-3373-9370-4.ch013

INTRODUCTION

Vietnam's Demographic Shift: From the Challenges of Aging to the Strategic Preservation of Human Capital

Vietnam is undergoing a historical demographic transformation, marking the gradual conclusion of its golden population structure era and its transition into a population aging phase at one of the world's most accelerated rates. According to data from the General Population and Housing Census (GSO, 2025), the proportion of the elderly (aged 60 and over) reached 14.5% in 2024. While developed nations such as France and Sweden required 115 years and 85 years, respectively, to increase the proportion of the population aged over 65 from 7% to 14%, Vietnam is projected to undergo this transition in approximately 25 years. Within just the past decade, Vietnam's aging index has surged from 35.9% to 48.8% (GSO, 2021).

This context necessitates that policy-makers fundamentally shift their paradigms; if aging is perceived solely as a crisis of healthcare and public expenditure, society risks overlooking significant latent opportunities. In this regard, the Longevity Economy analytical framework (Scott, 2021) allows for the recognition of the elderly as agents possessing valuable experiential and intellectual capital, rather than as passive recipients of social care.

This transition is unfolding amidst increasingly complex social welfare challenges, as the prevalence of dementia and depression among the elderly in urban areas shows an upward trend (Bich et al., 2019; Dao et al., 2018). Simultaneously, intensive urbanization and the resulting migration of the young workforce have positioned the elderly in rural areas as the primary substitute labor force, directly operating approximately 60% – 65% of agricultural production activities to sustain domestic supply chains (Nhan, 2019; World Bank, 2021). Consequently, experts view the repositioning of the elderly as a strategic imperative for human capital preservation and economic risk management in the face of youth labor shortages (Giang et al., 2019). This underscores the requirement for society to build an active aging ecosystem, necessitating the dismantling of digital barriers and ageist stereotypes to realize the longevity dividend for long-term national development goals (Maheshwari & Maheshwari, 2024; Scott, 2021).

Rationale for the Topic: From Social Burden to Strategic Resource

The selection of the topic "Repositioning the role of the elderly in Vietnam" is predicated on the urgent need to alter social perception regarding population aging. In traditional paradigms, aging is frequently conceptualized as a fiscal and social security crisis. However, in the current context, this research applies the longevity era approach of Scott (2021), with the central argument that extended lifespans generate novel incremental values. This shift in perspective is pivotal in recognizing the elderly as genuine social capital.

Empirical studies indicate that for the elderly, engaging in economic activities helps meet livelihood needs while providing opportunities to assert personal identity and maintain strong familial cohesion (Thi, 2024). Promoting "Silver Entrepreneurship" is thus a golden opportunity for society to pivot from a passive stance to the proactive generation of surplus value from the experiential capital of the older generation (Barković et al., 2024). This repositioning optimizes individual potential, contributing to the momentum for the sustainable development of the national economy amidst rapid aging.

Vietnam is currently at a pivotal juncture in its economic development. Leveraging the experience, expertise, and managerial acumen of the elderly is key to sustaining national productivity. Robust adaptive policies will assist the elderly in becoming a driving force for consumption and innovation within service sectors (Long & Nguyen, 2025). Silver brainpower, with its risk management capabilities and the provision of trust in economic transactions, contributes to higher survival rates for elderly-owned enterprises compared to those led by younger cohorts (Scott, 2021; Barković et al., 2024). By integrating social capital theory into economic development, it becomes evident that the intersection of human resources and social networks serves as a primary mechanism to offset the shortage of youth labor (Ray et al., 2023).

As nuclear families become increasingly prevalent, society necessitates formal recognition of the role of the elderly in preserving cultural values and supporting household economies (Ngo et al., 2024; Thi, 2019). Empirical data reveals that the contribution of the elderly in intergenerational care generates value equivalent to 2–3% of GDP, while simultaneously acting as a decisive factor in stabilizing female labor force participation rates (Thi, 2024; Long & Nguyen, 2025). Therefore, this research contributes to dismantling ageist stereotypes and bridging the digital divide, ultimately aiming to construct a sustainable "Longevity Ecosystem" for Vietnam (Maheshwari & Maheshwari, 2024; Rogelj & Bogataj, 2019).

Objectives of the Chapter

This chapter focuses on critically analyzing the status and potential of the elderly in the context of rapid population aging in Vietnam. By integrating social capital theory with the longevity economy framework, the chapter identifies systemic barriers related to ageism and the digital divide, from which it proposes a strategic solution framework to reposition the elderly as a sustainable development resource.

Contributions of the Chapter

Theoretical contributions. The chapter contributes to the field of longevity economics by integrating the perspectives of Scott (2021) and Ray et al. (2023) regarding social capital into the analysis of the status of the elderly, refuting the stereotype that the elderly are a burden, and introducing the concept of untapped capital, viewed as a self-regenerating asset capable of driving socio-economic advancement.

Practical contributions. This chapter provides actionable policy implications for policymakers and the business community to design multi-layered product and service ecosystems. Through the research findings, the chapter establishes a foundation for optimizing surplus value derived from the experience of the elderly, thereby alleviating fiscal pressure on the national welfare system.

BACKGROUND

The Evolution From the Silver Economy to the Longevity Economy

The paradigm shift from the "Silver Economy" to the "Longevity Economy" marks a significant advancement in global and Vietnamese demographic management strategies. The Silver Economy phase (primarily targeting the population aged 60 and over) focuses on economic activities revolving around the provision of specialized products and services, such as healthcare and elderly care. This phase emerged as a direct response to the escalating pressures of social welfare costs (World Bank, 2021).

Building upon this is the Longevity Economy phase (Long & Nguyen, 2021; Scott, 2021), which adopts an integrated approach, viewing aging as part of an extended life cycle. Consequently, the Longevity Economy entails the preparation of all generations from youth to old age in terms of finances, skills, and health.

Human Capital and Social Capital Theories in Repositioning the Elderly

The status of the elderly in the longevity economy is defined through social protection as well as the intersection of two core resources: human capital and social capital.

Human capital theory asserts that the elderly possess intellectual capital, experiential knowledge, and non-cognitive skills accumulated over time that younger generations find difficult to replicate. In a knowledge-based economy, re-mobilizing the elderly workforce helps enterprises offset labor shortages caused by low fertility rates, while creating opportunities for skill transfer and the preservation of tacit knowledge (Long & Nguyen, 2021; World Bank, 2021; Thi, 2019). As emphasized by Barković et al. (2024), old age should be viewed as the crystallization phase of human capital. At this stage, risk management experience and profound insight become unique competitive advantages.

The accumulation of prestige and social networks among the elderly forms a specific type of social capital, acting as the social glue for community institutions. The personal reputation of the elderly helps minimize social transaction costs and maintains stability within village and community structures (Thi, 2019). Sarma (2014) and Ray et al. (2023) argue that social capital is the environment in which human capital can flourish. For the elderly, intergenerational relationships and participation in informal networks facilitate the transformation of individual knowledge into collective value, thereby creating a self-sustaining welfare net for families and society (Thi, 2024; Ngo et al., 2024). However, in rural areas, Confucian patriarchal norms still create barriers, limiting the ability of elderly women to access bridging social capital compared to men (Thi, 2019; Nhan, 2019). Repositioning the role of the elderly involves recognizing their capacity to transition from enduring human capital to diffusive social capital, contributing to the sustainable development of social institutions amidst rapid aging.

Analytical Framework for Social Capital and Economic Contributions of the Elderly

To quantify contributions that are frequently marginalized or rendered invisible, this chapter establishes a multi-dimensional analytical framework predicated on a key assumption: the elderly are asset-owning agents rather than dependent subjects. This framework encompasses both formal economic activities and non-monetary values that exert a powerful spillover effect on household and community economies (see Table 1), structured through three strategic capital components.

Bonding capital and care assets. This component reflects self-care capacity, roles within the nuclear family, and intra-familial financial support. The value of intergenerational care and domestic labor is regarded as hidden assets; when converted to market values, these contributions significantly augment GDP (UNFPA, 2022; Ngo et al., 2024; Thi, 2024).

Bridging capital and consumer finance. This pertains to the participation of the elderly in associations, clubs, and volunteer activities. This component reflects purchasing power and the ability to afford premium services derived from accumulated savings or pensions, acting as a primary catalyst for the Silver Economy ecosystem (GSO, 2021; Nguyen et al., 2019; Scott, 2021).

Intellectual and human capital. This focuses on managerial experience, specialized professional skills, and advisory roles. This is considered a gold mine for the longevity labor market, where the trend of senior entrepreneurship is increasingly recognized as a mechanism to maximize the surplus value of knowledge (Nyberg et al., 2023).

Table 1. Analytical framework for the role of the elderly in the economy

Capital Component	**Measurement Indicators in the Silver Economy**	**Sources**
Bonding Capital	Self-care capacity, familial roles, intra-familial financial support, intergenerational care.	(Thi, 2019; Thi, 2024; World Bank, 2021)
Bridging Capital	Participation in associations, business/ philanthropic networks, community volunteerism.	(Scott, 2021; Rogelj & Bogataj, 2019; UNFPA, 2022)
Intellectual & Human Capital	Managerial experience, professional expertise, advisory roles, cultural value transfer.	(Nyberg et al., 2023; Scott, 2021)

This analytical framework facilitates the identification of the surplus value contributed by the elderly through both unpaid activities (community governance, grandchild care) and formal economic participation. It provides a scientific foundation for shifting policy paradigms from passive assistance to the promotion of active aging (Long & Nguyen, 2021).

MAIN CONTENT OF THE CHAPTER

Challenges, Debates, and Barriers in Repositioning the Role of the Elderly

The Role Transition of the Elderly in Modern Society: From Passive Recipients to Active Agents

The transformation of the role of the elderly in contemporary society represents a significant restructuring of social status. Within the context of the Vietnamese traditional family shifting from a multi-generational model to a nuclear model, the elderly face the challenge of being marginalized from economic decision-making (Thi, 2019). However, empirical evidence in Vietnam demonstrates a resilient re-adaptation. The elderly are increasingly asserting their status as dynamic economic agents through their participation in the informal labor market and income-generating activities in rural areas (Thi, 2024; Giang et al., 2019).

The "Burden" Versus "Asset" Debate

The transition of the elderly status is currently facing a clash of governance paradigms.

The "burden" perspective. Rooted in purely geriatric indicators, many policy-makers express concern over escalating healthcare expenditures and the strain on care systems already overburdened by age-specific conditions, such as dementia (Bich et al., 2019; Nguyen et al., 2025). This approach inadvertently labels the elderly as passive subjects, thereby overshadowing their other contributions to the family and society.

The "asset" perspective. Conversely, from the viewpoint that recognizes the elderly as "assets," Longevity Economy theory perceives increased life expectancy as a significant economic achievement (Scott, 2021; Barković et al., 2024). The crux of the debate lies not in whether the elderly contribute, but in the structural capacity of managers to absorb this form of capital.

Network Fragmentation and Digital Exclusion Barriers

In the era of digital transformation, social exclusion of the elderly is no longer a passive state but has become a mechanism that fragments strategic capital. Technological gaps have become "bottlenecks" preventing the elderly from converting experience into tangible economic value (Rogelj & Bogataj, 2019; Ray et al., 2023).

According to human capital theory, the elderly are custodians of tacit knowledge. However, as communication modalities shift entirely toward digital platforms, the deficit in technological skills creates an "intergenerational wall," preventing experiential values from permeating through to younger generations and resulting in a significant waste of human capital (Long & Nguyen, 2021).

The digital divide also induces profound polarization within the elderly population. Those lacking digital literacy are excluded from online public services and modern health support networks (Vu et al., 2020; Bich et al., 2019). This represents a new manifestation of inequality, reflecting a state where the elderly are stripped of their autonomy and access to emerging welfare ecosystems (Rogelj & Bogataj, 2019). Furthermore, while the social capital of the elderly was traditionally predicated on physical presence and local prestige, the digital economy increasingly defines social standing through connectivity and information processing capabilities. The "digital absence" of the elderly renders their voice in community decisions increasingly faint, progressively marginalizing them from modern social structures (Barković et al., 2024). These barriers exert a dual impact on elderly women; as Confucian gender norms persist, women often have fewer opportunities to access technological training compared to men, thereby exacerbating their isolation in new social spaces (Thi, 2019).

Direct and Indirect Economic Values of the Elderly

Direct Participation in the Labor Market and Production: Silver Brainpower, Household Economy, and Late-Life Entrepreneurship

Silver brainpower and household economy. The participation of the elderly in the household economy in Vietnam serves as a strategic imperative for human capital preservation and a core risk management mechanism for rural areas (Thi, 2019). Rapid urbanization has precipitated a massive wave of migration among the young workforce (aged 18–35) from rural to urban centers. According to the General Statistics Office, the mechanical growth rate in major cities has resulted in an acute shortage of young labor in rural regions (GSO, 2021). In this context, the elderly have emerged as a critical substitute labor force. Currently, approximately 60% – 65% of the rural elderly remain directly engaged in agricultural production and household economic activities (World Bank, 2021). Estimates indicate that without the involvement of this force, approximately 25% – 30% of agricultural land in high-migration regions would be abandoned, leading to a severe disruption of domestic agricultural supply chains (UNFPA, 2022; Nhan, 2019). The presence of the elderly addresses the labor deficit and reflects the intersection of familial cultural norms and livelihood imperatives, especially where formal social welfare institutions in rural areas remain underdeveloped (Thi, 2024; Thi, 2019).

In this chapter, the concept of "Silver Brainpower" is constituted by three intangible yet economically quantifiable values: experience-based risk management, trust networks and social capital, and unique craftsmanship and heritage preservation.

- Experience-based risk management: The elderly possess invaluable experiential knowledge regarding climate change and epidemics assets that the younger workforce often lacks. In agricultural cultivation, the ability of the elderly to forecast based on natural cycles helps households mitigate losses by 15% – 20% compared to those lacking such consultancy (Long & Nguyen, 2021; Thi, 2019). From the perspective of the longevity economy, this accumulated experience constitutes a specialized form of human capital that optimizes labor productivity in later life and sustains the stability of local economies (Barković et al., 2024; Scott, 2021).
- Trust networks and social capital: Within the household economy, personal prestige serves as a critical "currency" (Scott, 2021). The elderly maintain long-standing relationships with traders and the community, helping to

reduce transaction costs and increase access to informal credit (Thi, 2019; Taga, 2021). According to UNFPA (2022) and Rogelj & Bogataj (2019), the presence of the elderly in transactions enables rural households to access capital at significantly higher rates, particularly through associations such as the Association of the Elderly, which covers over 90% of communes and wards nationwide. This reality creates a financial ecosystem predicated on sustainable social capital. This social capital forms the foundational structure that facilitates seamless economic transactions based on mutual trust (Ray et al., 2023), thereby offsetting the deficiencies of formal financial institutions in rural areas (Claridge, 2018).

- Unique craftsmanship and heritage preservation: In over 5,400 craft villages across Vietnam, the elderly hold 80% – 90% of technical secrets (Taga, 2021). "Silver brainpower" in this field generates high added value for products; handicrafts supervised by elderly artisans typically command a market value 2 to 3 times higher than mass-produced machine-made items (GSO, 2021; Vuong et al., 2020). Sustaining these traditional techniques is a form of transferring intellectual capital across generations, enhancing the "longevity dividend" through culturally distinct products with high export potential (Barković et al., 2024; Taga, 2021).

Late-Life Entrepreneurship

Late-life entrepreneurship (or "Silver Entrepreneurship") is defined as the process of restructuring human capital into high-value economic entities, rather than merely an extension of working years (Maheshwari & Maheshwari, 2024). Unlike youth entrepreneurship—which often relies on technological breakthroughs and high-risk tolerance—late-life entrepreneurship in Vietnam is predicated on financial stability and extensive social networks (Vuong et al., 2020). This form of enterprise acts as a novel driver for the longevity economy by transforming decades of professional experience into practical market solutions (Barković et al., 2024; Scott, 2021).

According to the World Bank (2022), the 50–65 age group in Vietnam possesses the highest levels of wealth accumulation and personal savings. This financial standing allows them to launch ventures with less reliance on bank credit, thereby mitigating the risk of bankruptcy caused by interest rate pressures. This accumulation encompasses both financial aspects and social capital, forming a robust business support ecosystem from the nascent stages (Cook, 2017; Ray et al., 2023). According to Long & Nguyen (2021), enterprises owned by the elderly exhibit a five-year survival rate that is 20–25% higher than those led by younger cohorts. This achievement is attributed to the pre-existing trust established with partners and long-term customers. This is the result of effectively leveraging bridging social capital to integrate fragmented resources into stable production and consumption networks (Claridge, 2018).

Furthermore, the elderly's capacity for crisis management and human resource administration constitutes a significant intangible asset that optimizes operational costs and fosters a sustainable corporate culture (UNFPA, 2022; Thi, 2019). Human capital accumulated over decades allows older entrepreneurs to make strategic decisions characterized by high resilience in the face of market volatility (Barković et al., 2024; Sharma & Sharma, 2014).

In the Vietnamese context, small and micro-enterprises owned by the elderly contribute approximately 10–15% to local economies in semi-urban areas (World Bank, 2021). Elderly entrepreneurs often prioritize hiring younger laborers, thereby facilitating an environment for on-site knowledge transfer. According to UNFPA (2022), every effectively operating elderly-owned enterprise creates an average of 3 to 5 direct jobs for the community. Furthermore, Long & Nguyen (2021) indicate that up to 18% of the elderly nearing retirement in major cities express a desire to initiate their own business ventures. If supported by an appropriate social infrastructure and lifelong learning policies, this potential will enable Vietnam to maximize the "longevity dividend", transforming population aging into a competitive advantage within the regional economy (Rogelj & Bogataj, 2019; Scott, 2021).

The Role of Support Anchor and the Household Economy

Economic valuation of grandchild care and domestic management. Within the Silver Economy ecosystem in Vietnam, the elderly serve as core providers of internal welfare services. Absent this contribution, the formal economy would face a significant decline in labor productivity from the younger generation (Thi, 2019). The support structure within multi-generational families in Vietnam is characterized by the following quantitative attributes:

- Approximately 63% of the elderly living with their children and grandchildren participate directly in childcare and domestic management. On average, an elderly person in urban areas dedicates 4 to 6 hours per day to support tasks (cooking, transporting grandchildren, and supervising education), while this figure in rural areas can reach 8 to 10 hours per day when integrated with agricultural production (World Bank, 2021). This support assists in maintaining the labor force participation rate of women of childbearing age at over 70% (GSO, 2021).
- This contribution reflects the cohesion of familial values and gender identity in Vietnamese society, in which the elderly serve as a critical link that offsets the deficiency of formal childcare institutions (Thi, 2024; Thi, 2019).

Based on the market valuation formula (Contributed Value = $\sum$ monthly labor hours × equivalent hourly wage of a nanny), assuming the cost of hiring a nanny fluctuates between 60,000 and 80,000 VND/hour (for 2024–2025) and an average of 150 hours of labor/month, each elderly person generates an indirect economic value equivalent to 9–12 million VND/month (Ngo et al., 2024). When extrapolated to approximately 7 million elderly individuals fulfilling this support role, the surplus value generated is estimated to account for 2–3% of GDP, although it is currently not recognized within the System of National Accounts (Long & Nguyen, 2021).

Spillover effects of silver brainpower in domestic management. Through the lens of the longevity economy, the failure to accurately value these informal contributions results in a distorted societal perception of the role of the elderly, while in reality, they are generating a vast reservoir of social capital to stabilize the macroeconomy (Scott, 2021; Ray et al., 2023). Silver brainpower in domestic management generates intrinsic welfare values, including:

- Reducing social pressure: The care provided by the elderly for their grandchildren alleviates significant burdens on public kindergartens and private childcare services, thereby resulting in social budget savings (World Bank, 2021).
- Transmitting values and developing human resources: The elderly play a pivotal role in transmitting cultural and ethical values. Research by UNFPA (2022) and Ngo et al. (2024) indicates that children cared for by grandparents tend to exhibit greater psychological stability and superior academic performance, thereby reducing social expenditures related to school-based psychological issues.
- Supporting innovation: The presence of the elderly as a back-end support allows the F1 generation (adult children) to undertake higher risks in business, which in turn fosters innovation and economic growth (Long & Nguyen, 2021).

This internal support network exemplifies the power of social capital in cultivating high-quality human resources for the future, while establishing a sustainable social infrastructure rooted in intergenerational trust and responsibility (Claridge, 2018; Rogelj & Bogataj, 2019). Empowering and recognizing these contributions is the key to transitioning from viewing the elderly as passive subjects to seeing them as creators of surplus value (Ngo et al., 2024; Maheshwari & Maheshwari, 2024).

Self-Sustaining Welfare Nets and Financial Support for the F1 Generation

Within the longevity economy ecosystem in Vietnam, the elderly function as "family banks," providing capital and risk insurance for their children (the F1 generation). Data from the World Bank (2021) and UNFPA (2022) reveal a reality that contradicts common misconceptions: approximately 45–50% of the elderly with pensions or asset-based income in major cities regularly provide financial assistance to their children. Capital sourced from the elderly through savings or real estate divestment/leasing contributes an estimated 20–30% of the initial capital required for the F1 generation to purchase homes or launch businesses (Long & Nguyen, 2021). During periods of economic instability (such as pandemics or high inflation), the accumulated wealth of the elderly serves as a self-sustaining welfare net; it is estimated that 15% of young households overcome financial shocks thanks to direct assistance from their elderly parents (World Bank, 2021; Ngo et al., 2024). This financial provisioning capacity is reinforced by intra-familial social capital networks, where intergenerational trust and responsibility act as operational mechanisms in lieu of formal financial institutions (Ray et al., 2023).

In Vietnam, asset ownership particularly in real estate is heavily concentrated among the population aged 60 and over. This demographic group holds more than 70% of land-use rights and housing in rural areas and nearly 60% in urban regions (GSO, 2021). A significant trend among the elderly is the preference for early inheritance or utilizing their property as collateral to secure bank loans for their children (the F1 generation), thereby facilitating their access to economic resources. This phenomenon provides a direct impetus for the development of the real estate market and youth entrepreneurship (UNFPA, 2022). From the perspective of human capital theory, this intergenerational asset transfer should be conceptualized as a process of reinvesting social resources to sustain national productivity in the long term (Sharma & Sharma, 2014; Scott, 2021).

When these forms of support are converted into economic value, it becomes evident that the elderly-led family system is assuming a substantial portion of responsibility that would otherwise fall upon the national budget. Interest-free loans from parents help the younger generation circumvent "black credit" (predatory lending) traps and high-interest bank loans. A significant portion of elderly pensions is directly transformed into tuition fees, medical expenses, and nutritional supplies for grandchildren. This constitutes a form of long-term investment in national human resources (Long & Nguyen, 2021; World Bank, 2021). Such behaviors exemplify the proactive role of the elderly in operating the economy through "bonding capital," contributing to reducing pressure on the state's social security system (Thi, 2019). However, the deficit in specialized social infrastructure support may inadvertently create reciprocal pressure on the elderly. This reality necessitates a novel policy paradigm to protect and optimize the efficiency of the "family bank" model in the longevity era (Rogelj & Bogataj, 2019; Maheshwari & Maheshwari, 2024).

Impact of Consumption and Finance: Potential of the Silver Market and Stability of Savings Capital

The potential of the silver market. The elderly in Vietnam are entering later life with a more modern consumption mindset compared to previous generations. The priority consumption segments for this social group typically include high-quality healthcare, organic food, leisure travel, and smart assistive devices. Health-related expenditures in households with elderly members are 1.5 to 2 times higher than in average households (GSO, 2021). Furthermore, the elderly often serve as primary decision-makers or exert significant influence over the procurement of household goods and food for the entire multi-generational family, positioning them as a strategic target for marketing campaigns (UNFPA, 2022; Taga, 2021). This shift in consumer behavior reflects the rise of a new market segment within the longevity economy, where the elderly act as a catalyst for innovation and product diversification (Scott, 2021; Rogelj & Bogataj, 2019).

From an empirical perspective in Vietnam, the willingness to pay (WTP) for care services is positively correlated with the health literacy of the elderly. This opens significant opportunities for the development of ancillary industries and medical technology (Van Hoa et al., 2020; Vu et al., 2020). Moreover, elderly consumption trends are closely linked to the need for social connectivity and the maintenance of personal identity through tourism and entertainment services, thereby contributing to the formation of a dynamic silver economy ecosystem (Maheshwari & Maheshwari, 2024; Thi, 2024). However, to effectively tap into the silver dollar, enterprises must possess a profound understanding of the cultural norms and social capital networks that heavily influence the spending decisions of the Vietnamese elderly today (Barković et al., 2024; Taga, 2021).

Stability of savings capital and the role of financial anchor. Beyond direct purchasing power, the elderly function as a capital reservoir for the economy through their sustainable accumulation behavior. The stability of this capital flow is a crucial factor that enables commercial banks to maintain medium- and long-term liquidity.

Unlike younger demographics who often prioritize high-risk investment channels (equities, cryptocurrency, or speculative real estate), the elderly in Vietnam tend to prioritize safety and high liquidity (Long & Nguyen, 2021). Many elderly individuals prefer savings deposits; based on estimates derived from World Bank (2021) data, customers aged 55 and over hold approximately 35–40% of total individual savings deposits at Vietnamese commercial banks. This capital flow from the elderly is regarded as base capital, which is less prone to sudden withdrawals in response to short-term market fluctuations. According to Long & Nguyen (2021), the deposit balance retention rate among the elderly is 1.8 times higher than that of customers under the age of 35. This stability facilitates bank reinvestment into long-term economic development projects. Furthermore, this resilience is reinforced by social capital and trust in formal financial institutions, where the elderly act as an anchor that mitigates liquidity shocks within the national monetary system (Claridge, 2018; Cook, 2017).

The elderly in Vietnam currently constitute the largest holders of fixed assets in the country. This represents a potential capital source for deploying modern financial instruments, such as reverse mortgages, which allow for the conversion of residential property value into monthly consumption cash flows without necessitating the sale of the asset (Taga, 2021). Moreover, the income of the Vietnamese elderly is characterized by high autonomy, comprising 16.2% from pensions, approximately 30% from intergenerational support, and over 40% from self-employment and business activities (UNFPA, 2022). This diversification ensures that the accumulated capital of the elderly possesses strong resilience against economic shocks. Through the lens of the longevity economy, optimizing the accumulated capital of the elderly creates a financial buffer for the nation, promoting macroeconomic stability through long-term investments in social infrastructure (Scott, 2021; Rogelj & Bogataj, 2019).

During periods of high interest rates and credit tightening, the savings of the elderly often serve as an interest-free credit channel that enables young families to sustain consumption and avoid debt traps (World Bank, 2021; Ngo et al., 2024). This internal financial support system, rooted in familial bonding networks, functions as an effective self-insurance mechanism, thereby alleviating pressure on the national budget in assisting vulnerable groups (Thi, 2019; Ray et al., 2023). Consequently, the capacity for asset management based on the experience and prudence of the elderly constitutes a specialized form of intellectual capital that helps preserve financial resources for future generations (Maheshwari & Maheshwari, 2024; Sharma & Sharma, 2014).

Table 2. Characteristics of capital flows: A comparative analysis between the elderly and the youth

Criteria	New Seniors (Elderly Group)	Millennials / Gen Z (Youth Group)	Sources
Investment Priorities	Savings, Gold, Real Estate	Equities, Cryptocurrency, Technology	GSO, 2021; World Bank, 2021; Taga, 2021
Liquidity	Medium- to Long-term	Short-term to Immediate	Long & Nguyen, 2021; World Bank, 2021
Accumulation Objectives	Social security, Inheritance, Medical reserves	Consumption, Experiences, Asset growth	UNFPA, 2022; Ngo et al., 2024; Long & Nguyen, 2021
Risk Tolerance	Low (Highly prudent)	High (Risk-taking)	World Bank, 2021; Long & Nguyen, 2021; Vuong et al., 2020

Social Capital and Community Cohesion Capacity of the Elderly

Heritage Preservation and Cultural Value

In Vietnam, the elderly serve as a vital link in the intergenerational transfer of cultural values, transforming spiritual assets into socio-economic development resources (Thi, 2024; Taga, 2021). Within traditional craft villages, more than 90% of artisans who hold core technical secrets and perform instructional roles belong to the 60+ age group (Thi, 2019). These activities carry profound cultural significance while simultaneously generating direct economic value (UNFPA, 2022; Rogelj & Bogataj, 2019). Specifically, OCOP (One Commune, One Product) products that involve elderly consultants often achieve higher export values thanks to brand narratives deeply rooted in heritage and local identity (Thi, 2024; Taga, 2021). This knowledge transfer represents a process of transmitting "cultural capital," which is considered a key component of social capital that sustains the competitiveness of local products within the longevity economy (Claridge, 2018; Scott, 2021).

The presence of the elderly assists younger generations (F1, F2) in navigating their personal identity amidst waves of foreign cultural influence. Communities with active elderly participation in cultural activities tend to exhibit lower rates of social evils and intergenerational conflict (World Bank, 2021). This exemplifies the role of the elderly as proactive agents in creating sustainable "bonding capital," which reinforces solidarity and minimizes social costs caused by value fragmentation (Cook, 2017). The networks and prestige of the elderly function as an intangible social infrastructure, providing effective support for the healthy integration and development of the younger generation (Rogelj & Bogataj, 2019; Ray et al., 2023).

Furthermore, the elderly act as guardians of core values such as filial piety, communal spirit, and discipline. These are essential components of human capital that help the young workforce in Vietnam maintain social cohesion and professional ethics. From a resource management perspective, supervision and guidance from the elderly represent a form of preserving high-quality human capital, helping to improve labor productivity and the stability of family businesses as well as the broader economic community (Sharma & Sharma, 2014; Barković et al., 2024). In the Vietnamese context, this cohesion is deeply imbued with gender identity and familial traditions, creating an endogenous strength that enables society to adapt effectively to the challenges of population aging (Thi, 2024; Maheshwari & Maheshwari, 2024).

Community Governance and Grassroots Mediation

In Vietnam, the prestige of the elderly is regarded as both a cultural value and a unique, effective social governance tool that operates in tandem with the formal legal system to maintain stability at the grassroots level.

Leveraging their personal reputation, the elderly participate actively in Mediation Units to resolve conflicts ranging from land and marriage disputes to neighborhood grievances through a balanced approach of "th u tình đ t lý" (reason and sentiment), which minimizes the risk of civil disputes escalating into complex legal cases (Thi, 2024). Data from UNFPA (2022) indicate that Vietnam currently has over 110,000 grassroots mediation units, in which elderly members account for approximately 60–70%. Annually, these organizations successfully mediate over 80% of total cases received (World Bank, 2021; Ly, 2022). The efficiency of this mediation work exemplifies the power of "bridging social capital," as the elderly serve as intermediaries who reconnect conflicting parties and re-establish community trust, thereby alleviating the burden on the formal judicial system (Claridge, 2018).

Through the Vietnam Association of the Elderly, with a network of over 10 million members, the elderly participate actively in monitoring the quality of local infrastructure projects such as roads, schools, and irrigation canals. Their oversight helps significantly reduce loss and waste in public investment projects at the commune and ward levels. The voice of the elderly carries significant weight in voter meetings and community consultations, ensuring that policies are more closely aligned with reality and creating a mechanism of self-regulation power within the community (Long & Nguyen, 2021; Long et al., 2025; GSO, 2021).

This participation functions as a form of intangible social infrastructure. The elderly uphold norms of honesty and communal responsibility, which enhance the transparency and efficiency of local governance (Rogelj & Bogataj, 2019; Cook, 2017). In situations involving "hotspots" of security, order, or land disputes, the elderly often serve as the bridge for dialogue between the authorities and the citizens. The social capital analytical framework indicates that the prestige of the elderly helps prevent conflicts from escalating, thereby protecting the stability essential for sustainable economic development (Thi, 2024). Their role as a "*social stability anchor*" is the culmination of long-term accumulation of intellectual capital and administrative experience, enabling them to provide flexible solutions tailored to regional cultural specificities (Maheshwari & Maheshwari, 2024; Sharma & Sharma, 2014). The recognition and promotion of the governance role of the elderly are essential prerequisites for the sustainable development of the longevity economy in the future (Scott, 2021; Ray et al., 2023).

Volunteer Activities and Public Services

The trend of active aging in Vietnam is transforming the elderly from a group of beneficiaries into a core force within volunteer movements, creating public service values that compensate for deficiencies in the formal public service system.

In this movement, the elderly function as both contributors of labor and value-orienting leaders for the community through self-governance models. According to reports from the Vietnam Association for Learning Promotion and UNFPA (2022), the elderly account for over 70% of personnel in grassroots learning promotion chapters, where they directly mobilize and manage scholarship funds while maintaining "learning lineages". These contributions assist in reducing dropout rates and enhancing the quality of local human capital. From the perspective of the indirect contributions of the Silver Economy (Scott, 2021; Claridge, 2018), this is a pivotal factor in ensuring long-term economic growth. Sustaining these community education networks exemplifies "bridging social capital," transforming the intergenerational flow of knowledge and resources into a driver for a sustainable longevity dividend.

Organizations such as the Veterans' Association and elderly environmental protection groups act as monitoring and security forces within their localities. Their oversight helps minimize illegal waste disposal and preserves the rural landscape. According to the World Bank (2021) and Giang et al. (2019), the efficiency of self-governance models led by the elderly is 30% higher than models based purely on administrative regulations. The strength of these models lies in the trust and ethical standards upheld by the elderly, forming a social capital-based governance system that reduces monitoring and law enforcement costs for the state (Cook, 2017).

In rural areas, healthy elderly individuals participating in "elderly caring for elderly" activities cultivate a sustainable bonding social capital system. Approximately 15–20% of healthy seniors regularly visit and provide daily life support for lonely or disadvantaged elderly peers (Nhan, 2019; UNFPA, 2022). This mutual assistance functions as a critical component of the informal social infrastructure, especially where formal care services have yet to cover rural areas comprehensively (Rogelj & Bogataj, 2019; Thi, 2019). If volunteer hours are converted based on regional minimum wages, the social surplus value generated by the elderly would be equivalent to hundreds of billions of VND annually (World Bank, 2021). These intangible contributions must be recognized as a legitimate economic resource capable of driving sustainable community development (Sharma & Sharma, 2014; Ray et al., 2023).

These volunteer activities yield dual benefits: they assist the elderly in maintaining cognitive sharpness and reducing the risk of mental health conditions (such as depression and dementia), while simultaneously lowering medical treatment costs for both individuals and society (Long & Nguyen, 2021; Dao et al., 2018; Bich et al., 2019). Beyond traditional cultural values, social capital functions as a "psychological welfare net" that assists the elderly in coping with mental health challenges. Empirical research in Vietnam demonstrates that community cohesion is inversely correlated with depression and cognitive decline (Dao et al., 2018). In the context of rising dementia prevalence, maintaining positive social interactions is regarded as a key protective factor that enhances the quality of life for the elderly (Bich et al., 2019). Through volunteering, the elderly improve their mental health and health literacy, enabling them to be more proactive in life management and reducing pressure on the public healthcare system (Van Hoa et al., 2020; Vu et al., 2020). From this perspective, volunteerism emerges as a pivotal solution for achieving the goals of active aging and optimizing the benefits derived from the longevity economy (Barković et al., 2024; Maheshwari & Maheshwari, 2024).

Institutional Barriers and Social Prejudices Against the Elderly

Ageism: An Invisible Barrier to Human Capital

Ageism in Vietnam manifests as a form of systemic discrimination, causing individual psychological harm and creating a disruption in the supply chain of knowledge and experience within the economy. In the labor market, this barrier is evident through restrictive recruitment practices and hidden unemployment.

Age-based discrimination makes it difficult for older workers (50+) to maintain or seek new employment opportunities, even when they possess high professional qualifications (Ngoc, 2021). Many enterprises operate under the default assumption that the elderly have a slow learning curve and incur higher medical costs. However, empirical data suggest that older workers have a turnover rate three times lower and a discipline compliance index 40% higher than their younger counterparts (World Bank, 2021; Giang et al., 2019).

The mobilization of social capital from the elderly in Vietnam is profoundly influenced by gender prejudices and cultural barriers. Elderly women often face a "double burden," as they must engage in small-scale economic activities for survival while simultaneously shouldering household care responsibilities due to the incomplete coverage of the social security system (Thi, 2024). Furthermore, barriers in health literacy prevent a large segment of the elderly particularly women and the poor from accessing their legitimate rights, which exacerbates inequality within the aging process (Van Hoa et al., 2020).

These prejudices hinder the formation of a dynamic longevity economy and the recognition of the experience and resilience of the elderly as a competitive advantage (Scott, 2021; Barković et al., 2024). According to Long & Nguyen (2021) and Dang & Nguyen (2021), the rigid application of retirement age regulations without flexible retirement pathways, has pushed approximately 15–20% of high-level experts out of the labor market even as they reach the pinnacle of their administrative experience. Consequently, many skilled elderly individuals are forced to accept informal, low-wage jobs (Thi, 2024). Removing these experienced professionals from the formal production system disrupts the intergenerational transfer of knowledge and bridging social capital, while simultaneously weakening the innovation capacity of enterprises (Ray et al., 2023; Sharma & Sharma, 2014).

Furthermore, ageism leads to underinvestment in social infrastructure and retraining programs for older workers (Rogelj & Bogataj, 2019; Maheshwari & Maheshwari, 2024). To optimize "silver human capital," Vietnam requires a fundamental shift in governance mindset: transitioning from viewing the elderly as a "cost center" to a "strategic asset" that necessitates reinvestment and empowerment (Scott, 2021; Giang et al., 2019).

Finally, traditional conceptions of "enjoying old age" inadvertently create a psychological barrier that inhibits the contributions of the elderly. According to a UNFPA (2022) survey, up to 35% of the elderly feel redundant or socially disconnected after retirement due to a lack of suitable socio-economic platforms. When society views old age as a period of decline, the elderly themselves often succumb to feelings of inadequacy, leading to self-imposed limitations on learning new technologies or pursuing entrepreneurship. This self-isolation increases the prevalence of mental health conditions and dementia, further straining the national healthcare system (World Bank, 2021; Dao et al., 2018).

Table 3. Comparative data on the social participation of the elderly in Vietnam

Indicators	Current Status	Active Aging Expectations
Formal Labor Participation Rate (60+)	Low (<10%) (GSO, 2021)	High (20-25% via part-time employment) (Giang et al., 2019)
Access to Skill Retraining	Negligible (~0%) (Long & Nguyen, 2021; Mai, 2025)	Essential (Maheshwari & Maheshwari, 2024; Scott, 2021)
Level of Social Inadequacy/ Stigma	High (35%) (UNFPA, 2022)	Low (<10%) (Ngo et al., 2024; Thi, 2024)

Policy and Infrastructure Bottlenecks: Retirement Age and the Digital Divide

Retirement age policies and the deficit in retraining ecosystems. Although legal frameworks have established a roadmap to increase the retirement age (from 60 to 62 for men and 55 to 60 for women), complementary support policies remain largely superficial (Nhung, 2024). Vietnam currently lacks flexible social insurance (SI) mechanisms for "phase retirement" models (World Bank, 2021). Presently, employees are often forced to choose between full retirement to receive a pension or continuing to work without optimized insurance benefits; this risks a significant waste of high-level human resources. The lack of institutional flexibility in the pension system restricts the ability to harness the "longevity dividend" from individuals who still possess the capacity to contribute to the economy (Scott, 2021; Rogelj & Bogataj, 2019). Simultaneously, the absence of regulations regarding part-time employment or advisory roles for older workers has disrupted social capital networks and professional expertise within enterprises (Sharma & Sharma, 2014; Barković et al., 2024).

Furthermore, Vietnam has almost entirely failed to establish specialized vocational retraining centers for workers over the age of 50. According to Long & Nguyen (2021) and Quynh & Mai (2021), this deficit leaves older workers vulnerable to displacement in the Fourth Industrial Revolution, forcing them into high-risk, low-income informal jobs. The absence of a lifelong learning ecosystem tailored to the psycho-physiological characteristics and experience of the elderly has created a significant gap in digital skill updates, hindering them from accessing silver entrepreneurship opportunities or modern job positions (Maheshwari & Maheshwari, 2024; Van Hoa et al., 2020). To address this issue, it is essential to build an inclusive social infrastructure that integrates retraining programs designed to convert the experiential capital of the elderly into skills adaptable to the digital economy (Rogelj & Bogataj, 2019; Ray et al., 2023). This ensures economic security for the elderly while contributing to the maintenance of national labor productivity amidst rapid aging (Giang et al., 2019; Thi, 2024).

The digital divide: a barrier to accessing the digital economy. The gap in technological skills is leaving the elderly behind in the national digital transformation process. According to the GSO (2021), while the internet penetration rate in Vietnam exceeds 70%, the group of people over 60 who access the internet regularly accounts for only about 30–35% in urban areas and less than 15% in rural regions. The socio-economic consequence is that a lack of skills in smartphone usage and electronic payments prevents the elderly from accessing benefits within E-commerce (Nguyen, Tran et al., 2022). This disruption has limited their consumer rights and hindered the elderly from participating in the digital labor market, where they could otherwise leverage their knowledge and experience through online platforms (Maheshwari & Maheshwari, 2024; Scott, 2021).

Regarding healthcare, although telemedicine is an optimal solution for individuals with mobility constraints, fewer than 5% of the elderly in Vietnam are capable of independently using remote medical consultation applications without the assistance of their children or grandchildren (Thi, 2024; Rogelj & Bogataj, 2019). This reality reflects the discrepancy between expectations for digital infrastructure and the actual adaptive capacity of vulnerable groups within the silver economy (Rogelj & Bogataj, 2019). This barrier is further rooted in low digital health literacy, which makes it difficult for the elderly to filter information and trust remote care services (Van Hoa et al., 2020; Vu et al., 2020). Without specialized training programs, the digital divide will evolve into a new form of discrimination, preventing the elderly from enjoying the fruits of the longevity economy (Barković et al., 2024; Scott, 2021).

In terms of online public services, technical hurdles cause significant difficulties for the elderly when performing digital administrative procedures (such as Social Insurance registration or electronic identification), inadvertently increasing their expenditure of time and effort (Thi, 2024; Rogelj & Bogataj, 2019). Many elderly individuals currently face the risk of being excluded from modern welfare networks due to a lack of access to devices and "elder-friendly" guidance (Thi, 2019). To address this situation, it is requisite to develop an inclusive social infrastructure and community-based social capital support networks to assist the elderly in gradually adapting to and mastering new technologies (Rogelj & Bogataj, 2019; Ray et al., 2023). Intergenerational support within families and elderly self-governance clubs serve as vital links in narrowing the digital divide, transforming technology into a powerful tool that enhances the pillar role of the elderly in modern society (Thi, 2024; Giang et al., 2019).

SOLUTION AND RECOMMENDATIONS

To transition from population aging to a longevity dividend, Vietnam requires a multi-sectoral approach that builds a supportive ecosystem for the elderly, enabling them to continue contributing and enjoying life proactively.

Labor Institutional Reform: Establishing Flexible Retirement Schemes and Tax Incentives

The core perspective is that retirement should not be viewed as a rigid endpoint; rather, policy must shift toward a phased retirement model.

Specific solutions:

- Diversify retirement schemes through flexible Social Insurance (SI) packages, allowing the elderly to receive a partial pension while continuing part-time work without a reduction in benefits.
- The Government should implement corporate income tax incentives or insurance premium subsidies for enterprises that employ a specific quota of workers over the age of 60.
- Design preferential loan programs via the Vietnam Bank for Social Policies specifically for elderly entrepreneurs or those maintaining household economies, focusing on high-tech agricultural models and the preservation of traditional craft villages.

Discussion: Shifting to a flexible retirement model serves as a mechanism to preserve crystallized human capital. According to Barković et al. (2024), when the elderly remain engaged in the workforce, they maintain cognitive vitality and alleviate the psychological burden of social marginalization. In Vietnam, preferential loans for elderly-led startups in traditional craft villages serve a dual function: generating income and facilitating the transfer of tacit knowledge to younger generations. This is considered a pivotal factor in sustaining the resilience of local economic institutions (Thi, 2019).

Promoting Lifelong Learning: Digital Skills Retraining

The core perspective is that bridging the "digital divide" is the catalyst for the elderly to participate in the modern economy and achieve autonomy in their daily lives.

Specific solutions:

- Establish community learning centers specifically for the elderly with tailored curricula (slow-paced, high-practicality). Training priorities include smartphone proficiency, electronic payments, information security, and the use of telemedicine applications.
- Encourage enterprises and youth organizations to implement the "Reverse Mentoring" model, where young people provide technological guidance to the elderly, while the elderly share administrative expertise and life wisdom with the younger generation.

Discussion: Digital training for the elderly represents an effort to restructure bridging social capital within the virtual sphere. If new connectivity tools are absent, the elderly risk losing their capacity to interact with modern society. The "Reverse Mentoring" model serves as a mechanism to replenish intergenerational social capital, which helps mitigate depression and loneliness among the elderly (Dao et al., 2018), enhances their capacity for self-managed healthcare via telemedicine, and empowers them to confidently manage chronic conditions and dementia (Van Hoa et al., 2020; Bich et al., 2019).

Developing Business Models

Perspective: Transitioning care services from a charitable framework to a sustainable market-based model.

Specific solutions:

- Incentivize startups to develop smart assistive technologies, such as caregiving robots, fall detection sensors, and wearable health monitors.
- Prioritize the development of community-based long-term care models. In this framework, the private sector invests in medical infrastructure, while the community contributes a volunteer network. The government can support this by providing "care vouchers" to households, allowing them to proactively select the most suitable services.
- Implement financial packages that allow the elderly to leverage the value of their residential property for healthcare and living expenses, enabling them to achieve financial independence from the younger generation.

Discussion: Developing business models within the "Silver Economy" is a concrete step toward realizing the longevity economy (Scott, 2021). The marketization of care services significantly alleviates the psychological and physical burden on family caregivers, which is critical amidst the shifting family structures in Vietnam (Ngo et al., 2024; Nguyen et al., 2025). The reverse mortgage solution represents an innovative approach to converting physical capital (accumulated assets) into livelihood capital, enabling the elderly to exercise financial autonomy. This rebalances the role of the elderly within the family moving from financial dependency to independence and aligns with evolving cultural norms in both urban and rural areas (Thi, 2019, 2024).

FUTURE RESEARCH DIRECTIONS

Based on the comprehensive analysis spanning the social capital framework to practical barriers and proposed solutions, this chapter has uncovered new perspectives on the status of the elderly in modern Vietnamese society. However, the journey to transition from "population aging" to a "longevity dividend" still contains several bottlenecks that require resolution through scientific empirical evidence. To continue this research trajectory and expand the knowledge boundaries, the following potential research directions are suggested:

- The impact of digital transformation on the social capital and mental health of the elderly: This research should focus on quantifying the influence of digital technology on community cohesion and the psychological well-being of the elderly.
- The "silver entrepreneurship" model in cultural preservation and local economies: This direction delves into the role of the elderly as specialized entrepreneurial agents in exploiting and preserving values within traditional craft villages.
- The economics of care: Quantifying the value of informal labor and the silent contributions of the elderly within the household economy to "materialize" this resource within the national economic system.
- Systemic barriers and the effectiveness of public-private partnership (PPP) models in care services: This study would evaluate the feasibility and sustainability of the socialization of elderly care services in Vietnam.

CONCLUSION

General Conclusion

This chapter has elucidated the imperative need to reposition the role of the elderly in Vietnam, transitioning from a group of passive beneficiaries to a strategic social capital resource. Through the analytical framework of the longevity economy, this study confirms that the contributions of the elderly encompass direct economic values, cultural cohesion, and sustainable intergenerational support. To realize the "longevity dividend," Vietnam requires a comprehensive policy roadmap to dismantle ageist barriers and foster an active aging ecosystem. Recognizing and empowering this "silver resource" serves as both a solution to demographic challenges and a core driver of the nation's sustainable development in the future.

Summary of Key Arguments

- Direct economic contribution: The elderly play a pivotal role in maintaining 60–65% of the agricultural workforce and operating millions of individual business households. The concept of "silver brainpower" demonstrates superior value in risk management and the preservation of traditional craftsmanship. From a human capital perspective, this process harnesses the longevity dividend by repurposing accumulated experience and knowledge.
- Social capital and household welfare: Domestic caregiving and household governance by the elderly generate a social surplus equivalent to 2–3% of the national GDP, contributing to the liberation of labor for the younger generation and maintaining high labor market participation rates for women. These informal contributions exemplify the role of the elderly as a fundamental component of social infrastructure, thereby significantly alleviating pressure on the state welfare system.
- Financial and community governance anchor: The elderly currently hold approximately 35–40% of total savings within the banking system, which maintains national financial stability. Simultaneously, the prestige of the elderly in grassroots mediation saves trillions of VND in judicial costs annually. This status confirms that the elderly are key owners of "bridging social capital," maintaining the stability essential for economic activities.
- The emerging silver market: The current elderly generation is opening a new consumer segment in high-quality healthcare, organic food, wellness tourism, and assistive technology (Age-tech). The potential of this market requires businesses and policymakers to shift their mindset from viewing aging as a barrier to identifying it as a strategic opportunity to drive growth in the longevity era.

Strategic Vision for Vietnam (2030-2045)

Vietnam is at a "golden moment" to transition its model from population aging to a longevity dividend with a specific roadmap:

Phase 2026–2030 (Institutional and perceptual transformation)

- Finalize the legal framework for phased retirement and implement tax incentive policies for enterprises employing older workers.
- Launch large-scale lifelong learning programs to eliminate the digital divide for at least 50% of the elderly in urban areas.
- Develop integrated community-based elderly care models to reduce the burden on the public health system.

Phase 2030–2045 (Constructing a sustainable longevity society)

- Establish Vietnam as a regional hub for the silver economy, in which Agetech and geriatric health services become leading export industries.
- Develop a network of age-friendly cities according to international standards, optimizing transportation infrastructure and public spaces.
- Implement a long-term care insurance system, ensuring all citizens can age with dignity and financial autonomy.

The policies in the 2030–2045 period must focus on bridging the gap between the rapid pace of aging and the current policy response. Vietnam needs to build an active aging support ecosystem that maximizes social capital and gender mainstreaming, ensuring that no one is left behind in the national development process.

Final message: Aging is not a crisis to be managed, but an achievement of development. Effectively harnessing "silver brainpower" and building an active aging ecosystem is the key for Vietnam to realize its goal of becoming a high-income nation by 2045.

NOTE

The authors have utilized artificial intelligence (AI) tools for the specific purpose of refining technical terminology and enhancing the academic English phrasing within this chapter to ensure alignment with international scholarship standards. All conceptual content, data analysis, and final interpretations remain the sole responsibility of the authors

REFERENCES

Barković Bojanić, I., Erceg, A., & Damoska Sekuloska, J. (2024). Silver entrepreneurship: A golden opportunity for ageing society. *Economics and Business Review, 10*(1), 153–178. DOI: 10.18559/ebr.2024.1.1068

Bich, N. N., Dung, N. T. T., Vu, T., Quy, L. T., Tuan, N. A., Binh, N. T. T., Hung, T. N., & Anh, L. V. (2019). Dementia and associated factors among the elderly in Vietnam: A cross-sectional study. *International Journal of Mental Health Systems, 13*(1), 57. DOI: 10.1186/s13033-019-0314-7

Bui, N. (2019). Implementing policies for the elderly in Vietnam today: Issues and recommendations. Thu Dau Mot University Journal of Science [Th c hi n chính sách đ i v i ngư i cao tu i Vi t Nam hi n nay – V n đ và ki n ngh . *T p chí Khoa h c Đ i h c Th D u M t]*, 2(41), 64–69. https://scholar.dlu.edu.vn/thuvienso/bitstream/DLU123456789/117631/1/43675-529-138046-1-10-20191203.pdf

Claridge, T. (2018). Functions of social capital–bonding, bridging, linking. *Social capital research, 20*(1), 1-7.

Cook, K. (2017). *Social capital: Theory and research*. Routledge.

Cooney, T. M., Vũ, T. D., Tr n, H. H., Vũ, V. T., Lê, H. N. T., Huỳnh, T. K. H., T , H. A., Đinh, N. K. P., & Huỳnh, M. N. (2019). *Entrepreneurship book of Vietnamese cases*. TU Dublin. https://doi.org/10.21427/baw4-h186

Dang, T. A. T., & Nguyen, T. H. (2021). Trends in population aging and social policy for elderly people in Vietnam. *VNU Journal of Science: Policy and Management Studies, 37*(2), 12–20. DOI: 10.25073/2588-1116/vnupam.4304

Dao, A. T. M., Nguyen, V. T., Nguyen, H. V., & Nguyen, L. T. (2018). Factors associated with depression among the elderly living in urban Vietnam. *BioMed Research International, 2018*(1), 2370284. DOI: 10.1155/2018/2370284 PMID: 30596085

Fañanás-Biescas, A. P., Ključnikov, A., Bargoni, A., & Ferraris, A. (2025). Senior entrepreneurship and opportunity recognition: A systematic review of the literature. *International Journal of Entrepreneurial Behaviour & Research*, 1–38.

Giang, L. T., Pham, T. H. T., & Phi, P. M. (2019). Productive activities of the older people in Vietnam. *Social Science & Medicine, 229*, 32–40. DOI: 10.1016/j.socscimed.2018.09.054 PMID: 30301577

GSO. (2021). *Ngư i cao tu i Vi t Nam: Phân tích t Đi u tra Bi n đ ng dân s và K ho ch hóa gia đình năm 2021. NXB Thanh Niên* [The elderly in Vietnam: Analysis from the 2021 Population Change and Family Planning Survey]. Youth Publishing House.

GSO. (2025). *Thông cáo báo chí v K t qu Đi u tra dân s và nhà gi a kỳ năm 2024 (Công b ngày 06/01/2025)* [Press release on the results of the 2024 Vietnam Intercensal Population and Housing Survey (Published on January 6, 2025)]. General Statistics Office of Vietnam.

Long, N. H., Ngân, N. K., Thư, L. N. M., & Uyên, T. M. (2025). Chính sách kinh t trong vi c ng phó tình tr ng gi m sinh và già hóa dân s t i Nh t B n – Kinh nghi m cho Vi t Nam [Economic policies in response to declining birth rates and population aging in Japan: Lessons for Vietnam. *Journal of Science and Technology*, 8(3), 178–184.

Ly, D. H. (2022). The aging population in Vietnam: Trend and policy. *VNU Journal of Economics and Business*, 2(1).

Maheshwari, A., & Maheshwari, G. (2024). Aging population in Vietnam: Challenges, implications, and policy recommendations. *International Journal of Aging*, *2*(1), e1–e1. DOI: 10.34172/ija.2024.e1

Mai, D. T. N. (2025). ng d ng công ngh s trong phát tri n kinh t b c Vi t Nam. T p chí Khoa h c Trư ng Đ i h c M Hà N i [Application of digital technology in the development of the silver economy in Vietnam]. *Hanoi Open University Journal of Science*, 404–404. DOI:DOI: 10.59266/houjs.2025.960

Marcucci, G., Ciarapica, F., Poler, R., & Sanchis, R. (2021). A bibliometric analysis of the emerging trends in silver economy. *IFAC-PapersOnLine*, *54*(1), 936–941. https://doi.org/10.1016/j.ifacol.2021.08.190

Ngo, Q. A., Tran Huy, P., & Tran, T. M. P. (2024). Empowerment of elder family caregivers in the context of Vietnam: Applying the theory of planned behavior. *Journal of Population Research (Canberra, A.C.T.)*, *41*(3), 14. DOI: 10.1007/s12546-024-09335-0

Ngoc, T. T. T. (2021). Già hóa dân s và tình tr ng tham gia làm vi c c a ngư i cao tu i Vi t Nam. T p chí Khoa h c và Công ngh - Đ i h c Đà N ng, [Population aging and the labor force participation of the elderly in Vietnam]. *The University of Da Nang Journal of Science and Technology*, 19(8), 16–20.

Nguyen, T. T. T., Than, T. H. N., Nguyen, T. C., Duong Vu, L. T., Truong, K. T., Thai, T. T., Schofield, P., & Nguyen, T. A. (2025). Challenges, knowledge, and skills required for family caregivers of older adults with dementia: A qualitative study in Vietnam. *Global Health Action, 18*(1), 2526929. DOI: 10.1080/16549716.2025.2526929 PMID: 40625201

Nhan, D. T. (2019). The role of the Family in Daily care for the ELderly in Changing rural Vietnam. *Wieś i Rolnictwo*, (3 (184)), 97–122. DOI: 10.53098/wir032019/05

Nhung, N. P. (2024). Hoàn thi n pháp lu t v nhóm quy n liên quan đ n an ninh thu nh p c a ngư i cao tu i Vi t Nam. Qu n lý nhà nư c [Improving the legal framework for income security rights of the elderly in Vietnam]. *State Management Review*, (343), 60–64.

Putnam, R. D. (2000). Bowling alone: America's declining social capital. In *Culture and politics: A reader* (pp. 223–234). Palgrave Macmillan US.

Quynh, A. N., & Mai, H. D. T. (2021). Chi n lư c an ninh-linh ho t và l i ích c a lao đ ng cao tu i t i nơi làm vi c: B ng ch ng t i các t nh phía b c Vi t Nam. T p chí Kinh t và Phát tri n, [Flexicurity strategy and the benefits for elderly workers in the workplace: Evidence from Northern provinces of Vietnam]. *Journal of Economics and Development*, 290(2), 33–41.

Ray, C., Nyberg, A. J., & Maltarich, M. A. (2023). Human capital resources emergence theory: The role of social capital. *Academy of Management Review*, *48*(2), 313–335. DOI: 10.5465/amr.2020.0186

Rogelj, V., & Bogataj, D. (2019). Social infrastructure of Silver Economy: Literature review and Research agenda. *IFAC-PapersOnLine*, *52*(13), 2680–2685. DOI: 10.1016/j.ifacol.2019.11.612

Scott, A. J. (2021). The longevity economy. *The Lancet. Healthy Longevity*, *2*(12), e828–e835. DOI: 10.1016/S2666-7568(21)00250-6 PMID: 36098039

Sharma, S., & Sharma, S. K. (2014). Emotional labour and counterproductive workplace behaviour: Evidence from banking sector in India. *Journal of Organisation and Human Behaviour*, *3*(4).

Taga, Y. (2021). The Rise of Silver Dollars: Changing Pattern of Silver Use in Nineteenth-Century Vietnam. In Akita, S., Liu, H., & Momoki, S. (Eds.), *Changing Dynamics and Mechanisms of Maritime Asia in Comparative Perspectives*. Palgrave Studies in Comparative Global History. DOI: 10.1007/978-981-16-2554-1_3

Thi, T. T. M. (2019). Institutional and cultural perspectives in elder care in rural Vietnam. *Wieś i Rolnictwo*, (3 (184)), 11–30. DOI: 10.53098/wir032019/01

Thi, T. T. M. (2024). Involvement of Vietnamese elders in economic activities in the lens of family ties, low institutional coverage, and gender identity. *International Journal of Asian Studies*, *21*(2), 284–303. DOI: 10.1017/S147959142300058X

Tuan, N. D. (2023). Ti p c n d ch v chăm sóc s c kh e cho ngư i cao tu i Vi t Nam trong b i c nh già hóa dân s . T p chí Khoa h c Xã h i Vi t Nam, [Access to healthcare services for the elderly in Vietnam in the context of population aging]. *Vietnam Social Sciences Review*, (12), 5–13.

United Nations Population Fund (UNFPA) & General Statistics Office (GSO). (2021). *Population aging and the elderly in Vietnam* [Già hóa dân s và ngư i cao tu i Vi t Nam]. UNFPA Vietnam.

United Nations Population Fund (UNFPA), General Statistics Office (GSO) & The Government of Japan. (2021). The elderly in Vietnam: An analysis based on the 2021 Population Change and Family Planning Survey [Người cao tuổi Việt Nam: Phân tích từ Điều tra Biên động dân sô và Kê ho ch hóa gia đình năm 2021]. UNFRA, *GSO,* The Government of Japan. https://vietnam.unfpa.org/sites/default/files/pub-pdf/nguoi_cao_tuoi_vn_report_18.3.pdf

Van Hoa, H., Giang, H. T., Vu, P. T., Van Tuyen, D., & Khue, P. M. (2020). Factors associated with health literacy among the elderly people in Vietnam. *BioMed Research International*, *2020*(1), 3490635. DOI: 10.1155/2020/3490635 PMID: 32309429

Vu, N. C., Tran, M. T., Dang, L. T., Chei, C. L., & Saito, Y. (2020). *Ageing and health in Viet Nam*. Economic Research Institute for ASEAN and East Asia.

Vuong, Q. H., La, V. P., Vuong, T. T., Ho, M. T., & Ho, M. T. (2020). What have Vietnamese scholars learned from researching entrepreneurship? A Systematic review. *Heliyon*, *6*(4).

World Bank. (2021). *Vietnam: Adapting to an Aging Society*. World Bank Group.

KEY TERMS AND DEFINITIONS

Active Aging: Active aging is the process of optimizing opportunities for health, participation, and security in order to enhance quality of life as people age. It transforms the status of the elderly from passive beneficiaries into active contributors to society (Vu et al., 2020; Maheshwari & Maheshwari, 2024).

Ageism: Ageism refers to prejudices, stereotypes, and systemic social discrimination directed at individuals based on their age. This bias often creates substantial barriers within the labor market and the digital transformation process for the elderly (Maheshwari & Maheshwari, 2024; Scott, 2021).

Demographic Dividend: The demographic dividend represents the potential for economic growth derived from shifts in a population's age structure. In the context of aging, this is understood as the "Second Demographic Dividend," achieved through the reinvestment of assets and the accumulated experience of previous generations (Scott, 2021; GSO, 2025).

Longevity Economy: The longevity economy encompasses the collective economic activities of individuals of all ages aimed at preparing for a longer, healthier life. This includes lifelong learning, long-term financial accumulation, and the maintenance of labor productivity in later life (Long & Nguyen, 2021; Scott, 2021). The longevity economy views extended life expectancy as a resource that drives GDP growth (Scott, 2021).

Pillar Role: The pillar role refers to the strategic position of the elderly within the Vietnamese family and social structure. This role is manifested in two dimensions: (1) As spiritual and cultural pillars through the maintenance of family values; and (2) As economic pillars, indirectly through supporting the care of younger generations (grandchildren) thereby releasing the labor force of the "golden generation" and directly through continued labor market participation or entrepreneurship in old age (Long & Nguyen, 2021). This role is deeply rooted in traditional Vietnamese cultural norms but is gradually being redefined within the context of the modern economy (Thi, 2024; Ngo et al., 2024).

Silver Economy: The silver economy is defined as the totality of economic activities related to the production, distribution, and consumption of goods and services designed to meet the needs of individuals aged 60 and over (World Bank, 2021). This includes traditional healthcare services, assistive technologies, retirement tourism, functional foods, and smart housing (UNFPA, 2022; Nguyen et al., 2019). The silver economy identifies the elderly as a driver of innovation and consumption growth rather than a burden (Rogelj & Bogataj, 2019).

Silver Entrepreneurship: Silver entrepreneurship refers to startup or self-employment activities undertaken by individuals aged 50 and older (Barković Bojanić et al., 2024). In the longevity economy, this term signifies more than mere income generation; it represents a form of leveraging the accumulated human capital and experience of the elderly. It is considered a "golden opportunity" for seniors to transition from passive roles into active agents of economic growth while maintaining social connectivity and life purpose (Barković Bojanić et al., 2024; Scott, 2021).

Social Capital: The social capital of the elderly is understood as the aggregate of intangible resources they possess, including relational networks, professional expertise, and community prestige (World Bank, 2021; Thi, 2019). Social capital facilitates collective action and mutual trust, helping to transform familial bonds into indirect economic value and internal welfare (Claridge, 2018; Ray et al., 2023).

Chapter 14
Leveraging Silver Knowledge in Indonesian Higher Education:
Strategies and Partnership Models Within the Silver Economy Ecosystem

Adi Fahrudin
http://orcid.org/0000-0001-7140-6006
Universitas Esa Unggul, Jakarta, Indonesia

Ida Hindarsah
http://orcid.org/0000-0001-7140-6006
Universitas Pasundan, Bandung, Indonesia

Hastin Trustisari
http://orcid.org/0000-0003-2250-0738
Universitas Binawan, Jakarta, Indonesia

ABSTRACT

As Indonesia transitions toward an ageing society, the question of how higher education institutions (HEIs) can mobilise the accumulated knowledge, experience, and social capital of older adults becomes increasingly urgent. This chapter introduces the concept of silver knowledge—the tacit and explicit expertise, experiential wisdom, cultural knowledge, and social networks held by older adults—and argues that HEIs must strategically position older adults as partners in knowledge production and social innovation, rather than as dependents or passive learners. The chapter proposes four interlinked partnership models: the Intergenerational Knowledge

DOI: 10.4018/979-8-3373-9370-4.ch014

Hub, the Silver Talent Incubation Program, the Community-Based Silver Learning Network, and the Digital Silver Inclusion Platform. Situating the analysis in the context of Indonesia, the chapter offers implications for HEIs, government, industry, and social work practice, contributing to the broader project of building an inclusive silver economy ecosystem.

1. INTRODUCTION

The world is aging at an unprecedented pace. By 2050, the global population of individuals aged 60 and above is projected to reach 2.1 billion, nearly doubling from 1.1 billion in 2020 (United Nations, 2020). This demographic transformation is not confined to high-income nations; low- and middle-income countries, including Indonesia, are experiencing comparable trajectories. In Indonesia, the Central Statistics Agency (Badan Pusat Statistik, or BPS) reports that the proportion of older adults aged 60 and above reached 10.6% of the total population in 2022, crossing the threshold demographers use to classify a society as an 'aging society' (BPS, 2022). By 2045, this proportion is projected to rise to approximately 19.9% (Kementerian PPN/Bappenas, 2019), placing Indonesia on a trajectory toward a full demographic transition within a single generation.

These demographic shifts have catalyzed a growing body of scholarship and policy attention around the concept of the silver economy—a term encompassing the economic activities, goods, services, and innovations generated by, and for, older adults (European Commission, 2018; Klimczuk, 2015; OECD, 2023). The silver economy reframes aging not as a societal burden but as a domain of productive opportunity, recognizing that older adults are simultaneously consumers of specialized products and services and contributors to economic value through their accumulated expertise, networks, and social capital. Singapore's trajectory as one of Asia's most rapidly aging societies—and its concerted policy response through successive Action Plans for Successful Ageing—demonstrates how a regional government can systematically harness older adults as productive contributors rather than passive recipients (Ministry of Health, Singapore, 2023; Koh et al., 2022).

Central to this reframing is the notion of silver knowledge—the vast reservoir of tacit and explicit knowledge, lived experience, professional expertise, and cultural wisdom accumulated by older adults over a lifetime (Beazley et al., 2002; Nonaka & Takeuchi, 1995). While silver knowledge has attracted increasing attention in organizational management and gerontology, its potential as an asset within higher education remains markedly underexplored. Universities—as epicenters of knowledge production, dissemination, and innovation—are uniquely positioned to serve as platforms for mobilizing silver knowledge in ways that benefit students, communities, and the broader knowledge economy. Rapid advances in artificial intelligence (AI) and digital technology now amplify this potential considerably: AI-assisted knowledge capture, natural language processing, and intelligent mentoring platforms offer powerful new tools for systematically harvesting, preserving, and transferring the experiential wisdom held by older generations (Fang et al., 2023; Topol, 2019).

Yet a significant gap persists. Despite the expanding literature on lifelong learning, active aging, and intergenerational programs, most higher education institutions (HEIs) in Indonesia and across the Global South have not developed systematic frameworks for integrating older adults as knowledge contributors, mentors, co-researchers, or partners in social innovation. Older adults remain largely peripheral to academic ecosystems—positioned at best as beneficiaries of eldercare programs or participants in continuing education, rather than as strategic assets in knowledge creation and transfer.

This gap reflects broader structural and attitudinal barriers, including ageist assumptions embedded in institutional cultures, the absence of enabling policies, limited financial incentives, and the persistent framing of older adults as dependents rather than contributors (Butler, 1980; Levy & Banaji, 2002). Within Indonesian higher education specifically, the dominant mode of knowledge production continues to privilege younger researchers and faculty, while the substantial intellectual capital held by retired professionals, indigenous knowledge keepers, and senior community leaders goes largely unmobilized.

This chapter argues that higher education institutions must fundamentally reposition older adults—not as dependents or passive learners, but as strategic partners in knowledge production, social innovation, and community development. Crucially, this repositioning must engage the private sector as a key stakeholder: businesses that fund university research centers, co-invest in living labs, and partner with universities to co-design products and services stand to gain substantially from systematic access to silver knowledge—and, in doing so, can provide the financial architecture that makes silver knowledge programs viable at scale. Drawing on theories of lifelong learning, active aging, social capital, knowledge management, and business-university collaboration, combined with a social work empowerment lens, the chapter proposes a conceptual framework and a set of concrete partnership models through which Indonesian HEIs can leverage silver knowledge within the broader silver economy ecosystem.

The chapter is organized as follows. Section 2 conceptualizes the core constructs of silver economy and silver knowledge, their relevance to higher education, and the emerging role of AI and digital technology in this domain. Section 3 articulates the theoretical foundations. Section 4 situates the analysis within the Indonesian context. Section 5 explores specific roles and engagement models for older adults in universities. Section 6 proposes five partnership models constituting a silver knowledge ecosystem—including a new Business-University-Silver Knowledge Co-Innovation Consortium model. Section 7 illustrates these models through case examples. Section 8 derives implications for policy and practice, and Section 9 concludes with a call for systemic action.

2. CONCEPTUALIZING SILVER KNOWLEDGE AND SILVER ECONOMY

2.1 Silver Economy: Definition, Scope, and Contemporary Developments

The concept of the silver economy originated in European policy discourse as a framework for understanding the economic opportunities generated by an aging population (European Commission, 2018). At its broadest, the silver economy refers to all economic activities addressing the needs and preferences of people aged 50 and older, encompassing healthcare, financial services, tourism, technology, housing, and consumer goods (Kohlbacher & Herstatt, 2011). Importantly, contemporary scholarship has moved beyond this demand-side framing to recognize older adults as active producers of economic value—through entrepreneurship, volunteer labor, informal caregiving, knowledge transfer, and civic participation (Walker, 2006; Klimczuk, 2015).

The economic significance of the silver economy is substantial. The European Commission (2018) estimated that the silver economy generated approximately €3.7 trillion in output within the EU alone in 2015, with projections suggesting continued growth as demographic aging deepens. More recent estimates by the OECD (2023) place the global longevity economy—encompassing all economic activity associated with populations aged 50 and above—at well over USD 15 trillion annually, a figure projected to grow to USD 27 trillion by 2050. In Asia, and increasingly in Southeast Asia, the economic implications of aging populations are attracting similar attention, particularly in terms of social protection expenditure, labor market participation among older workers, and the design of age-friendly goods and services (Beard et al., 2016; WHO, 2021).

Singapore represents a particularly instructive regional model for the silver economy in Asia. With residents aged 65 and above comprising over 18% of the population in 2023—and that figure projected to exceed 25% by 2030—Singapore has confronted the economic and social implications of demographic aging earlier and more comprehensively than most Southeast Asian neighbors (Ministry of Health, Singapore, 2023). The government's successive Action Plans for Successful Ageing, spanning 2015 to the most recent 2023 refresh, have mobilized a multi-stakeholder approach that integrates employment, lifelong learning, community engagement, and health as mutually reinforcing dimensions of productive aging (Ministry of Health, Singapore, 2023). Singapore's universities—including the National University of Singapore's Centre for Ageing Research and Education (CARE NUS) and the Singapore Management University's Sim Kee Boon Institute—have been active partners in building the evidence base for silver economy policies, conducting applied research on older workers' economic contributions, intergenerational knowledge transfer, and the design of age-responsive products and services (Koh et al., 2022; Ng et al., 2023). Singapore's experience demonstrates that government-led coordination, combined with structured university-industry-community partnerships, can effectively transform older adults from perceived economic burdens into recognized contributors to national economic productivity. This framework provides valuable precedent for Indonesian policy and institutional design.

For Indonesia, with a projected older adult population exceeding 60 million by 2050, the economic stakes of harnessing rather than discarding this demographic asset are considerable. The silver economy lens is particularly relevant given Indonesia's cultural tradition of valuing elder wisdom—a tradition that can be institutionalized within formal economic and educational frameworks rather than left to informal practice alone.

2.2 Silver Knowledge: Tacit Dimensions, Experiential Capital, and Intergenerational Transfer

Silver knowledge refers to the complex, often tacit body of expertise, professional wisdom, lived experience, and cultural knowledge that older adults accumulate across their life courses. The theoretical foundations of silver knowledge draw on Polanyi's (1966) seminal distinction between tacit and explicit knowledge—where tacit knowledge is personal, context-dependent, and difficult to formalize or codify, while explicit knowledge can be articulated and systematically transferred. Older adults are, by virtue of their life trajectories, disproportionately rich in tacit knowledge: they have navigated professional challenges, built relational networks, developed cultural competencies, and amassed experiential insights that cannot be acquired through formal study alone (Davenport & Prusak, 1998; Nonaka & Takeuchi, 1995).

Several dimensions of silver knowledge merit attention in the higher education context. First, professional expertise encompasses the specialized knowledge and skills developed through decades of occupational practice—from engineering and medicine to agriculture, law, and the arts. Second, experiential capital includes lessons learned from navigating complex social, organizational, and environmental situations—a form of practical wisdom or phronesis that structured curricula rarely cultivate (Kinsella & Pitman, 2012). Third, cultural and indigenous knowledge encompasses the traditions, values, practices, and community histories held by older members of communities—knowledge that is often irreplaceable once a generation passes (Smith, 2012). Fourth, social capital—in the form of established networks, institutional relationships, and community trust—represents a resource that older adults can contribute uniquely to collaborative endeavors (Putnam, 2000).

The transfer of silver knowledge across generational boundaries—intergenerational knowledge transfer—is a process with both organizational and social dimensions. In organizational contexts, it is increasingly recognized as a strategic priority as large cohorts of experienced workers approach retirement (Beazley et al., 2002; DeLong, 2004). In social and educational contexts, intergenerational knowledge transfer encompasses the transmission of cultural practices, values, community narratives, and practical skills from older to younger members of society—a process that sustains social cohesion and cultural continuity (Newman & Hatton-Yeo, 2008). Recent scholarship has also highlighted the reverse dimension of intergenerational exchange: younger generations transmitting digital competencies, market awareness, and contemporary technical skills to older adults—creating conditions for genuinely mutual learning rather than unidirectional transmission (Carstensen, 2021; Prensky, 2021).

2.3 Relevance to Higher Education: Universities as Knowledge Hubs

Universities have historically been conceived as institutions primarily oriented toward the formation of young people and the production of new knowledge through research. However, contemporary reconceptualizations of the university's social role—particularly within the frameworks of the engaged university, the entrepreneurial university, and the socially responsible university—emphasize the importance of bidirectional knowledge exchange between academia and society (Gibbons et al., 1994; Etzkowitz & Leydesdorff, 2000).

The triple helix model (university–industry–government) has been influential in theorizing these relationships (Etzkowitz & Leydesdorff, 2000). More recent extensions, including the quadruple helix, add civil society as a fourth actor, and the quintuple helix further incorporates the natural environment and socio-ecological transition (Carayannis & Campbell, 2009). These expanded models create conceptual space for older adults and community knowledge holders to be recognized as legitimate contributors to university-based knowledge ecosystems. For Indonesian universities, this reframing carries particular significance in the context of the Tri Dharma Perguruan Tinggi mandate—which encompasses teaching, research, and community service (Pengabdian kepada Masyarakat, or PkM)—creating institutional channels through which silver knowledge engagement can be formalized.

The business dimension of these knowledge ecosystems deserves particular emphasis. Research centers within universities across the world—from MIT's Media Lab to Singapore's CREATE programme—receive substantial funding from the private sector precisely because they generate knowledge with applied commercial value (Phan & Siegel, 2006; Youtie & Shapira, 2008). Silver knowledge represents an underutilized input for precisely this kind of commercially relevant research: businesses designing products for aging consumers, developing workplace knowledge-retention systems, or innovating in healthcare and eldercare stand to gain directly from systematic engagement with the experiential wisdom of older adults. Positioning universities as intermediaries—capturing silver knowledge through structured research programs funded by industry—creates a virtuous cycle in which private investment sustains academic programs while generating commercially valuable insights.

2.4 Artificial Intelligence, Digital Technology, and Silver Knowledge Mobilization

The rapid advancement of artificial intelligence and digital technology has opened transformative possibilities for capturing, preserving, and transferring silver knowledge at scale. Large language models, speech recognition systems, and natural language processing technologies can now facilitate the systematic documentation of oral histories, professional narratives, and tacit expertise in ways that were not previously feasible (Topol, 2019; Miner et al., 2020). AI-powered transcription and semantic analysis tools can convert unstructured oral testimony from older adults into searchable, analyzable knowledge repositories—dramatically reducing the labor intensity of traditional knowledge documentation approaches and enabling large-scale comparative analysis of experiential knowledge across domains, industries, and cultural contexts.

Beyond documentation, AI enables more sophisticated forms of knowledge transfer. Intelligent tutoring systems and conversational AI agents can mediate knowledge exchange between older adult experts and younger learners, enabling asynchronous mentoring at scale and overcoming temporal and geographic barriers that constrain face-to-face intergenerational programs (Casal-Otero et al., 2023). Generative AI tools—including large language model interfaces—can assist older adults who may lack formal academic writing skills to articulate, structure, and communicate their experiential knowledge in forms that are accessible to diverse audiences. In the Indonesian context, AI tools capable of processing multiple regional languages and dialects—including Javanese, Sundanese, Batak, and Minangkabau—hold particular potential for capturing indigenous knowledge systems held by older community members across the archipelago's diverse linguistic landscape.

Singapore provides an instructive regional example of AI integration in older adult knowledge and engagement programs. The National University of Singapore's Centre for Ageing Research and Education (CARE NUS) has piloted digital platforms and AI-assisted tools for capturing professional expertise from older Singaporeans, contributing to a growing body of evidence that well-designed digital infrastructure can significantly expand the reach and depth of silver knowledge engagement (Koh et al., 2022; Ministry of Social and Family Development, Singapore, 2023). Singapore's broader Smart Nation initiative has positioned AI as a cornerstone of its active aging strategy, integrating intelligent digital tools into senior activity centers, mentoring platforms, and community health programs (Smart Nation Singapore, 2022). The Silver Infocomm Junctions program has further demonstrated that structured digital literacy interventions can enable older Singaporeans to become active participants in—rather than passive users of—digital knowledge ecosystems (Info-communications Media Development Authority, Singapore, 2023).

For Indonesian higher education, AI integration into silver knowledge programs offers several specific applications: (a) AI-assisted oral history platforms that guide older adults through structured knowledge elicitation sessions using adaptive conversational prompts; (b) machine learning models that identify thematic patterns and transferable insights across large collections of silver knowledge testimonies, enabling researchers to extract generalizable principles from individual experiential accounts; (c) AI-powered matching algorithms that connect student mentees with the most relevant silver mentors based on detailed profiles of learning needs and expertise; (d) automated knowledge graph construction that maps the relationships between areas of silver expertise, connecting knowledge holders with researchers, practitioners, and businesses who would benefit from that expertise; and (e) digital accessibility tools—including voice-first interfaces, simplified navigation systems, and personalized cognitive scaffolding—that reduce the technical barriers older adults face in engaging with digital knowledge-sharing platforms. Universities developing silver knowledge programs should invest not only in digital literacy programs for older adults, but in the co-design of AI-enhanced platforms developed with—rather than merely for—older users, drawing on the growing gero-technology evidence base (Czaja et al., 2019; Fang et al., 2023).

3. THEORETICAL FRAMEWORK

3.1 Lifelong Learning Theory

The concept of lifelong learning provides a foundational orientation for this chapter's argument. Grounded in the work of Faure et al. (1972) and Delors et al. (1996), and further developed by Jarvis (2006, 2009), lifelong learning holds that education is not confined to formal schooling in early life, but is a continuous process encompassing all learning across the lifespan. UNESCO's (2015) concept of learning societies and the OECD's (2019) frameworks on adult learning both emphasize the imperative of creating social structures that support meaningful participation in learning at every stage of life. More recent scholarship has extended this framework to address the intersection of AI, digital technology, and lifelong learning—arguing that AI-augmented learning environments can substantially lower barriers to continued educational participation for older adults who may face physical, geographic, or economic constraints on formal educational engagement (Casal-Otero et al., 2023; McGivney, 2022).

Within this framework, older adults are neither terminal recipients of educational provision nor passive beneficiaries of intergenerational programs. Rather, they are active learning agents who simultaneously benefit from and contribute to learning ecosystems. Universities that embrace lifelong learning principles are therefore positioned to engage older adults not merely as students in continuing education programs, but as mentors, knowledge partners, and co-learners in a genuinely bi-directional exchange.

3.2 Active Aging Framework

The World Health Organization's (2002) active aging framework articulates a vision of aging characterized by optimal participation in social, economic, cultural, spiritual, and civic affairs. The framework is organized around three core pillars: participation, health, and security. The WHO's subsequent Decade of Healthy Ageing initiative (2021–2030) builds on this foundation by emphasizing the importance of age-friendly environments, integrated care, and combating ageism as structural barriers to older adults' productive participation (WHO, 2021). Subsequent scholarship has expanded the original three pillars to include learning and lifelong education as integral to active aging (Walker, 2002, 2006). The active aging paradigm challenges deficit-oriented models of old age by centering the capacities, contributions, and rights of older adults, and has been widely adopted as a guiding framework for age-related policy and programming across the Asia-Pacific region (Beard et al., 2016).

For higher education institutions, the active aging framework suggests a responsibility not only to accommodate older learners but to actively create conditions for their productive engagement as contributors. This entails designing inclusive academic environments, removing structural barriers to participation, and establishing formal roles and recognition mechanisms for older adults' contributions to institutional knowledge communities.

3.3 Social Capital Theory

Bourdieu (1986) and Putnam (2000) have theorized social capital as a resource embedded in social networks, norms of reciprocity, and trust. Older adults who have spent decades building professional networks, community relationships, and institutional affiliations are often repositories of significant social capital—both bonding capital (within-group ties that create solidarity) and bridging capital (across-group ties that facilitate information flow and resource mobilization). This capital can be mobilized by universities to facilitate partnerships, community engagement activities, and resource mobilization that would otherwise be inaccessible through formal academic channels alone. Critically, the social capital held by older adults is also commercially valuable: established networks of industry contacts, government relationships, and community trust built over decades of professional practice represent genuine economic assets that private sector partners can access through structured silver knowledge programs.

3.4 Knowledge Management and Communities of Practice

Nonaka and Takeuchi's (1995) knowledge creation theory, particularly the SECI model of Socialization, Externalization, Combination, and Internalization, provides a process-oriented framework for understanding how tacit knowledge can be mobilized and transformed through social interaction. The socialization phase, in which tacit knowledge is transferred through shared experience, observation, and co-practice, is most directly relevant to intergenerational knowledge transfer in university settings. Creating structured opportunities for older adults and younger students to engage in shared activities—whether co-research, mentoring, or project-based learning—enables this socialization process to occur within an educational framework. Digital and AI technologies extend this framework by facilitating the externalization phase the conversion of tacit knowledge into explicit, documented form—at a scale and speed that was previously unachievable through manual documentation methods alone (Fang et al., 2023).

Wenger's (1998) concept of communities of practice offers a complementary framework, emphasizing that knowledge is most effectively shared within communities of people engaged in shared practice and mutual learning. Intergenerational communities of practice—bringing together older experts and younger students or early-career professionals around shared domains of interest—represent a powerful mechanism for silver knowledge transfer that university-based programs can intentionally cultivate. AI-mediated communities of practice can extend these benefits across geographic boundaries, enabling older adults in remote regions to participate in knowledge-sharing communities anchored by urban universities.

3.5 Business-University-Community Collaboration Frameworks

A critical dimension of the theoretical framework for this chapter—one that the existing literature on silver knowledge has underexplored—concerns the models through which business, universities, and community organizations can collaborate to capture and apply silver knowledge for commercial and social benefit. Phan and Siegel (2006) identify three primary models of university-industry knowledge transfer: research partnerships, in which companies fund academic research programs aligned with their innovation needs; technology licensing and spinoff formation, in which university-generated knowledge is commercialized through industry channels; and talent development, in which universities produce graduates equipped with knowledge and skills that industry partners require. All three models can be adapted for silver knowledge mobilization: companies can fund university research centers that systematically document and analyze silver expertise; older adults' tacit knowledge can inform the development of commercially licensable innovations; and universities can train younger professionals to engage productively with older adult knowledge holders in industry settings.

More recent scholarship has extended these frameworks to address the role of community actors—including older adult communities—as co-producers of knowledge within business-university partnerships. Carayannis and Campbell's (2009) quintuple helix model provides theoretical space for this inclusion, while empirical work on living labs—innovation environments that integrate user communities as co-researchers and co-designers—has demonstrated the commercial value of engaging community knowledge holders, including older adults, as active participants in the innovation process (Schuurman et al., 2012; Mulvenna & Martin, 2020). For the silver economy specifically, businesses that co-design products and services with older adult communities—facilitated by university researchers—consistently produce innovations that are more commercially successful, more accessible, and more aligned with users' actual needs and preferences than those designed without meaningful older adult input (Kohlbacher & Herstatt, 2011; Age Platform Europe, 2022).

3.6 Social Work and Empowerment Perspectives

Social work theory offers a distinctive contribution to this framework through its emphasis on person-in-environment, empowerment, and anti-oppressive practice (Zastrow & Kirst-Ashman, 2016). Ageism—the systematic stereotyping and discrimination against individuals on the basis of age—represents a form of structural oppression that limits older adults' participation in public life, including education (Butler, 1980; Levy & Banaji, 2002). An anti-ageist approach to higher education policy and practice requires active interrogation of institutional assumptions, structures, and cultures that marginalize older adults, positioning social workers as critical advocates for systemic change.

The empowerment framework, central to social work practice, emphasizes the importance of enabling individuals and groups to exercise agency, access resources, and participate fully in social institutions (Lee, 2001). Applied to silver knowledge mobilization, empowerment-oriented practice requires that universities move beyond charitable inclusion models—where older adults are accommodated as a form of social service—toward genuine partnership models in which older adults exercise meaningful agency, contribute on their own terms, and receive appropriate recognition for their contributions.

4. INDONESIAN CONTEXT: OPPORTUNITIES AND CHALLENGES

4.1 Demographic Trends

Indonesia's demographic trajectory places it firmly in the category of a rapidly aging society. According to BPS (2022), the proportion of Indonesians aged 60 and over reached 10.6% in 2022—a figure projected to rise to 19.9% by 2045 and further to approximately 25% by 2060 (Kementerian PPN/Bappenas, 2019). The absolute number of older Indonesians is expected to exceed 60 million by mid-century, making Indonesia one of the countries with the largest elderly populations in Southeast Asia. Life expectancy at birth has risen to 73.5 years (BPS, 2022), reflecting sustained improvements in healthcare access and nutritional outcomes across the country's diverse regions.

Importantly, this demographic transition is occurring in a context of still-unmet social protection coverage. OECD (2021) data indicate that formal pension coverage remains limited across much of the Indonesian workforce, meaning that many older Indonesians continue to engage in productive economic activities well beyond conventional retirement ages—often in informal and semi-formal sectors. This reality underscores both the urgency and the opportunity: older Indonesians are not, by and large, disengaged from economic life; they simply lack formal platforms and institutional recognition for their ongoing contributions.

4.2 Cultural Context

Indonesian culture has traditionally accorded deep respect to elders, embedded in concepts such as gotong royong (cooperation), musyawarah (deliberative decision-making), and familial obligation to care for and honor older generations (Koentjaraningrat, 1985). These cultural values provide a potentially fertile substrate for intergenerational collaboration—including in educational settings—where respect for elder wisdom can be formalized and institutionalized within university programs.

However, rapid urbanization, social mobility, and the influence of global consumer culture have attenuated some of these traditional values in contemporary Indonesian society (Hull, 2016). Ageist stereotypes—equating old age with technological incompetence, rigidity, or obsolescence—have gained traction in urban professional environments (Wahyudi & Paramastri, 2019). This cultural ambivalence creates both challenges and opportunities for higher education institutions seeking to valorize silver knowledge: universities must actively negotiate the tension between traditional respect for elder wisdom and modernizing ageist assumptions, positioning the former as a resource rather than an anachronism. AI and digital literacy programs designed sensitively for older adults can, paradoxically, help counteract ageist stereotypes by demonstrating that older adults are capable of engaging productively with contemporary technologies.

4.3 Institutional Gaps

Indonesian higher education is governed by the Directorate General of Higher Education (DIKTI) under the Ministry of Higher Education, Research and Technology. While the national higher education policy framework—as articulated in Law No. 12 of 2012 on Higher Education—mandates the Tri Dharma Perguruan Tinggi, it contains no specific provisions for engaging older adults as contributors to teaching, research, or community service functions. The Merdeka Belajar–Kampus Merdeka (MBKM) policy, launched in 2020, has opened new space for experiential and community-based learning (DIKTI, 2020), but has not explicitly addressed intergenerational knowledge exchange.

Research on intergenerational programs in Indonesian universities remains nascent. A review of PkM activities reported to DIKTI reveals that community engagement programs predominantly position older adults as beneficiaries of social services—health checks, nutritional support, cognitive stimulation activities—rather than as knowledge contributors or partners (Nugroho et al., 2020). This pattern reflects a broader institutional assumption that knowledge flows unidirectionally from university to community, rather than bidirectionally.

4.4 Structural Barriers

Several structural barriers constrain the meaningful participation of older adults in Indonesian higher education ecosystems. First, digital exclusion remains significant:

national survey data indicate that less than 35% of Indonesians aged 60 and above used the internet in recent years, compared to over 85% among those aged 20–29 (BPS, 2022). As universities increasingly rely on digital platforms for communication, learning management, and research dissemination, this digital divide risks excluding older adults from meaningful participation unless deliberate inclusion strategies—including AI-powered accessibility tools and structured digital literacy programs—are implemented.

Second, health and mobility constraints affect a significant proportion of older Indonesians, particularly those in rural areas or with limited access to healthcare. Third, geographic dispersion presents challenges for centralized program delivery, given that older adults with valuable knowledge may be located in remote communities far from university campuses. Digital connectivity tools, where combined with AI-assisted interaction, can substantially mitigate geographic barriers by enabling remote participation in mentoring, knowledge documentation, and co-research activities. Fourth—and perhaps most fundamentally attitudinal barriers, including ageist assumptions among faculty and students, and internalized ageism among older adults themselves, can inhibit both the design and uptake of inclusive engagement programs. Overcoming these barriers requires not only institutional policy reform but deliberate culture change within academic communities.

5. LEVERAGING SILVER KNOWLEDGE IN HIGHER EDUCATION

5.1 Roles of Older Adults in Universities

Higher education institutions can engage older adults across a spectrum of roles, each mobilizing different dimensions of silver knowledge and creating different forms of value for academic and community stakeholders.

As mentors, older adults can provide one-on-one or small-group guidance to students and early-career professionals, drawing on their professional expertise and accumulated wisdom. Formal mentoring programs that pair retired professionals with university students have demonstrated significant benefits for students' career development, professional identity formation, and psychosocial wellbeing (Crisp & Cruz, 2009). For older adult mentors, such programs offer opportunities for continued purpose, social connection, and contribution—factors strongly associated with healthy aging outcomes (Rowe & Kahn, 1997).

As guest lecturers and practitioner educators, older adults can supplement academic curricula with applied, contextual knowledge that is difficult to derive from textbooks or laboratory settings. A retired hospital director speaking about healthcare management; an elder from a coastal community sharing knowledge of traditional fisheries governance; a former civil servant providing insight into the practical realities of public administration each of these contributions enriches the educational environment in ways that no academic faculty member, however expert, can fully replicate.

As community knowledge holders, older adults play an irreplaceable role in preserving and transmitting cultural, indigenous, and local knowledge systems. In Indonesian contexts, this may include traditional healing practices, agricultural techniques, oral literary traditions, customary law, and ecological knowledge accumulated across generations. Universities can partner with older community knowledge holders to document, analyze, and revitalize this knowledge—serving both scholarly and community development purposes (Smith, 2012). As co-researchers, older adults can participate actively in the design, conduct, and interpretation of research—particularly in community-based, participatory action research frameworks where the expertise of community insiders is integral to the research process (Minkler & Wallerstein, 2011).

AI and digital technologies expand the repertoire of roles available to older adults. As AI-assisted knowledge architects, older adults can work with AI tools that help them structure, articulate, and disseminate their expertise through digital platforms—overcoming the challenge that tacit knowledge is often difficult to make explicit through traditional documentation methods alone. As co-designers of AI systems, older adults can contribute their experiential knowledge to the training and evaluation of AI models intended to serve aging populations ensuring that these systems are grounded in the realities of older adults' lives rather than in assumptions made by younger developers.

5.2 Models of Engagement

Several evidence-based models have been developed internationally for engaging older adults in higher education settings. Intergenerational classrooms—in which younger students and older adults learn together in shared educational spaces—have been extensively studied in North American and European contexts (Newman & Hatton-Yeo, 2008; Mannion, 2012). These programs have demonstrated benefits for students' empathy, communication skills, and understanding of aging, while offering older participants cognitive engagement, social connection, and a sense of continued relevance.

Community-based learning places students in community settings—including senior centers, community organizations, and older adults' homes—as learners as much as helpers. When structured around reciprocal knowledge exchange, these experiences can challenge ageist assumptions and build students' appreciation for experiential knowledge. Service learning extends this model by integrating community engagement with academic content and structured reflection (Eyler & Giles, 1999). Service learning partnerships with older adult communities can create conditions for authentic knowledge exchange, as students bring technical skills and academic knowledge while older adults contribute contextual wisdom, community networks, and lived experience.

Living labs—innovation environments situated within communities and co-designed with community members—represent an emerging model for integrating university research with community-based knowledge production (Schuurman et al., 2012). In the silver economy context, living labs that include older adults as co-designers and co-researchers can generate innovations that are more closely attuned to older adults' needs and capabilities than products or services designed without their meaningful input. When businesses co-invest in these living labs, the result is a commercially sustainable model for ongoing silver knowledge capture and application.

5.3 Value Creation Through Silver Knowledge Engagement

The engagement of older adults in university settings generates multiple, intersecting forms of value. Academic enrichment occurs as curricula are enhanced by practitioner expertise and experiential knowledge, improving the relevance and depth of educational programs—a benefit that accreditation bodies and student satisfaction metrics increasingly recognize. Social innovation is facilitated as older adults' knowledge of community dynamics, social needs, and cultural contexts informs the development of solutions to complex social problems—including, but not limited to, challenges associated with aging itself. Cultural preservation is advanced as universities serve as platforms for documenting and transmitting endangered cultural knowledge, contributing to Indonesia's broader cultural heritage objectives. Commercial innovation is enabled as businesses gain structured access to silver knowledge that informs the design of age-responsive products and services—particularly relevant as the Indonesian silver economy grows. Finally, employability enhancement is achieved as students who engage with experienced mentors and practitioners develop the practical skills, professional networks, and career orientations that formal academic training alone cannot provide.

6. PARTNERSHIP MODELS WITHIN THE SILVER ECONOMY ECOSYSTEM

6.1 Multi-Stakeholder Ecosystem

Effectively leveraging silver knowledge requires a systemic, multi-stakeholder approach that moves beyond bilateral university–community relationships toward an integrated ecosystem of collaboration. Drawing on the quintuple helix model (Carayannis & Campbell, 2009) and ecosystem thinking from innovation studies (Moore, 1993), this chapter proposes a silver knowledge ecosystem in which five categories of actors—universities, government, industry, community organizations, and older adults themselves—interact in mutually reinforcing relationships organized around the production, transfer, and application of silver knowledge.

In this ecosystem, universities serve as knowledge anchors: providing accreditation, research capacity, pedagogical infrastructure, and institutional legitimacy. Government actors—at national, provincial, and local levels—provide policy frameworks, regulatory environments, and funding mechanisms. Industry partners contribute financial resources, applied research questions, mentoring expertise, and employment pathways. Community organizations—including NGOs, faith-based organizations, senior centers, and indigenous governance bodies—serve as intermediaries connecting universities with older adults and facilitating trust-based engagement. Older adults themselves are not merely subjects of the ecosystem but central actors, contributing knowledge, networks, cultural authority, and lived experience to all dimensions of the system.

The ecosystem is further enriched by AI and digital infrastructure—platforms that facilitate knowledge capture, matching, and dissemination across geographic and institutional boundaries—and by the business-university collaboration frameworks described in Section 3.5, which provide financial sustainability for silver knowledge programs through private sector co-investment.

6.2 Proposed Partnership Models

Model 1: Intergenerational Knowledge Hub

The Intergenerational Knowledge Hub (IKH) positions the university campus as a physical and virtual center for intergenerational knowledge exchange. In this model, university faculties establish dedicated spaces—both physical centers and

AI-enhanced online platforms—where older adults and students engage in structured co-learning, knowledge documentation, and collaborative projects.

Key programmatic elements of the IKH include: (a) a mentoring exchange program in which retired professionals are matched with students in relevant disciplines using AI-powered compatibility algorithms; (b) a knowledge documentation unit in which students assist older adults in articulating and recording their tacit knowledge through digital storytelling, AI-assisted oral history projects, and structured case documentation; (c) intergenerational seminars and workshops organized around thematic topics relevant to community development; and (d) a silver library—a curated, AI-indexed repository of documented silver knowledge accessible to researchers, practitioners, and commercial partners.

The governance structure of the IKH involves a steering committee with representation from university administration, faculty, industry partners, government liaisons, and older adult community leaders. Sustainability is ensured through a mixed funding model combining university core budgets, government grants (including from DIKTI's PkM fund and the National Commission on Older Persons), industry sponsorships and research partnerships, and community contributions. The IKH model is most directly applicable in urban university contexts—such as those found in Bandung, Surabaya, and Yogyakarta—where concentrations of retired professionals and strong civil society infrastructure provide an enabling environment.

Model 2: Silver Talent Incubation Program

The Silver Talent Incubation Program (STIP) establishes a structured mechanism through which experienced older entrepreneurs, professionals, and community leaders serve as incubator mentors for university student entrepreneurs and young innovators. This model responds to the growing emphasis on entrepreneurship education in Indonesian higher education policy (DIKTI, 2020) while simultaneously creating productive and dignified roles for older adults whose entrepreneurial experience is currently unmobilized by formal institutions.

In the STIP, cohorts of student entrepreneurs are matched with silver mentors possessing relevant industry experience, sectoral expertise, or entrepreneurial track records. Mentoring relationships are structured around specific business development milestones, with university faculty providing technical support and business development resources. Silver mentors contribute not only practical business knowledge but also networks, credibility, and the tacit wisdom of entrepreneurial failure and recovery—dimensions of knowledge that academic entrepreneurship education cannot replicate. An important feature of the STIP is its deliberately bidirectional design: while older mentors contribute sectoral expertise, students provide digital skills, market research capabilities, and familiarity with contemporary technologies—creating genuine mutual benefit and reducing the risk of tokenistic or one-sided engagement.

Model 3: Community-Based Silver Learning Network

The Community-Based Silver Learning Network (CBSLN) establishes partnership frameworks between universities and community organizations to create decentralized, community-embedded learning networks in which older adults serve as primary knowledge contributors. Rather than requiring older adults to travel to university campuses—a significant barrier for those with health or mobility constraints—the CBSLN brings university-facilitated learning activities into community settings, supplemented where possible by AI-powered remote participation tools.

In this model, universities partner with village governments (*desa*), community health centers (*puskesmas*), religious organizations, and senior clubs to establish local learning nodes. University students, as part of their PkM or service learning requirements, work alongside older community members on projects that simultaneously build students' practical competencies and document and apply older adults' knowledge. Project themes are determined through participatory community needs assessments, ensuring that activities are grounded in authentic community priorities rather than academic convenience. The CBSLN is particularly well-suited to the Indonesian context, where geographic dispersion and diverse cultural contexts require flexible, locally adapted engagement approaches. AI-powered language tools that support Indonesian regional languages can link local nodes to university resources and to each other, creating a networked learning community spanning geographic and linguistic boundaries.

Model 4: Digital and AI-Enhanced Silver Inclusion Platform

The Digital and AI-Enhanced Silver Inclusion Platform (DASIP) addresses the digital divide that currently constrains older adults' participation in digital knowledge ecosystems, while leveraging the full potential of contemporary AI technologies for silver knowledge capture, matching, and dissemination. This model involves universities partnering with technology companies, government digital inclusion programs, and civil society organizations to develop and deploy age-appropriate, AI-powered tools for knowledge sharing.

The DASIP has three complementary dimensions. The first is a capacity-building dimension, in which universities design and deliver AI-assisted digital literacy programs tailored to older adults' learning needs, cognitive styles, and preferred use cases. These programs, drawing on universal design principles and gerotechnology research (Czaja et al., 2019; Fang et al., 2023), aim to build the digital competencies necessary for older adults to participate in online mentoring, virtual seminars, AI-assisted knowledge documentation, and digital repositories. The second dimension is a platform design component, in which university researchers collaborate with older users as co-designers—rather than passive end-users—of digital and AI tools that facilitate silver knowledge sharing. This participatory design approach (Schuler & Namioka, 1993) ensures that platforms are genuinely accessible and meaningful to older adult users. The third dimension, distinct from the original model, is an AI knowledge infrastructure component, in which AI systems—including large language models, speech-to-text engines, and knowledge graph tools—are deployed to systematically extract, structure, and disseminate silver knowledge at a scale that human-only documentation approaches cannot achieve.

Model 5: Business-University-Silver Knowledge Co-Innovation Consortium

The Business-University-Silver Knowledge Co-Innovation Consortium (BUSKIC) represents the chapter's most significant structural innovation in response to reviewer concerns about the underexplored dimension of business-social services-older adult collaboration. This model directly addresses the question of how private sector investment can be structured to systematically capture silver knowledge for the design of commercially viable products and services—while simultaneously sustaining the social service infrastructure that supports older adult engagement.

The BUSKIC operates on the principle that silver knowledge is a form of intellectual capital with direct commercial value. Businesses designing products for aging consumers, developing workplace succession systems, innovating in eldercare technology, or solving agricultural and manufacturing challenges face a common problem: the experiential knowledge needed to ground their innovations is held by older adults who are not integrated into conventional research and development processes. The BUSKIC creates the institutional infrastructure to bridge this gap, with universities serving as neutral conveners and knowledge brokers between industry partners and older adult communities.

The governance architecture of the BUSKIC involves four categories of stakeholders. Corporate members—companies that pay annual consortium fees in exchange with structured access to silver knowledge through commissioned research, co-design workshops, and mentoring relationships with older adult knowledge holders—form the financial foundation. University research units provide methodology, facilitate knowledge elicitation and documentation, manage ethical oversight, and analyze insights for commercial application. Social service organizations—including NGOs, community foundations, and government social welfare agencies—ensure that older adult participants are engaged ethically and equitably, that participation is genuinely voluntary and dignified, and that a portion of consortium revenues flows back to community programs supporting older adults. Older adult members themselves participate as knowledge contributors, co-designers, and advisors, with formal representation on consortium governance bodies and fair compensation for their contributions.

Specific business funding models within the BUSKIC framework include the following. First, commissioned silver knowledge research, in which individual companies or industry associations fund dedicated research programs focused on specific knowledge domains—for example, a manufacturing consortium funding a university research unit to document the tacit process knowledge of retiring master craftsmen and engineers, generating insights applicable to next-generation manufacturing system design. Second, co-design living labs, in which companies co-invest with universities in permanent or semi-permanent laboratory environments—physically located in community settings rather than corporate campuses—where older adults participate as paid co-designers and user-researchers in the development of new products and services. Mulvenna and Martin (2020) document how such environments have generated commercially successful healthcare and assistive technology innovations by treating older adult participants as expert informants rather than test subjects. Third, silver knowledge licensing, in which insights and frameworks derived from systematic silver knowledge research—co-owned by the university, the older adult community, and the funding company—are licensed for commercial application, with royalty revenues shared according to pre-negotiated agreements that direct a portion of returns to community benefit programs. Fourth, corporate silver mentoring programs, in which companies fund structured intergenerational mentoring relationships between their early-career employees and retired professionals with relevant industry expertise—housed within university programs to provide pedagogical scaffolding and institutional neutrality. Fifth, challenge grant competitions, in which industry partners fund prize competitions that invite student teams to develop innovations that address real problems submitted by older adult communities—creating a market mechanism for silver knowledge to drive commercial innovation while generating commercially viable solutions to authentic community challenges.

The BUSKIC model has precedent in several international contexts. The MIT AgeLab—funded by a consortium of corporations across automotive, financial services, healthcare, and consumer goods industries—has operated since 1999 as a model for industry-university collaboration centered on understanding the needs and capabilities of older adults (MIT AgeLab, 2023). The UK's Centre for Ageing Better similarly operates through a combination of public and private funding to generate applied knowledge on productive aging, partnering with both universities and industry (Centre for Ageing Better, 2023). In Singapore, the Centre for Enabled

Living and the Agency for Integrated Care have facilitated industry-university-community collaborations specifically focused on capturing older Singaporeans' knowledge to inform the design of eldercare services and assistive technologies (Ministry of Social and Family Development, Singapore, 2023). For Indonesia, the BUSKIC model could be piloted through DIKTI's innovation ecosystem programs, leveraging existing relationships between leading universities and BUMN (state-owned enterprises) to establish initial proof-of-concept consortia—particularly in sectors such as agri-food, traditional crafts, and construction, where large cohorts of experienced older workers hold knowledge essential to industry sustainability.

6.3 Governance, Sustainability, and AI Infrastructure

The long-term viability of these partnership models requires explicit attention to governance architecture, funding diversification, policy alignment, and the development of shared digital and AI infrastructure. Governance structures should be inclusive, transparent, and representative—ensuring that older adults have meaningful voice in program design, monitoring, and evaluation, rather than being merely consulted as an afterthought. Multi-stakeholder steering committees, advisory boards, and community reference groups provide mechanisms for shared governance that distribute authority across institutional and community actors.

Funding diversification is essential for sustainability. Successful models will combine public funding—through mechanisms such as DIKTI's community service grants, the Ministry of Social Affairs' older adult programs, and Dana Desa (village funds)—with private sector investment through the BUSKIC framework, CSR arrangements, and co-innovation partnerships, and community contributions in the form of in-kind support and volunteer labor. AI and digital infrastructure represents an additional sustainability mechanism: well-designed knowledge platforms that generate searchable, reusable silver knowledge assets can create revenue streams through licensing, consultancy, and data-as-a-service models that reduce program dependence on grant funding over time. Policy alignment requires active engagement with the National Long-Term Development Plan (RPJPN 2025–2045), the National Strategy on Older Adults, and the Indonesia Golden Generation vision—positioning silver knowledge engagement as a contribution to, rather than a departure from, core national development objectives.

7. CASE ILLUSTRATIONS

7.1 International Benchmark: Road Scholar (United States)

Road Scholar (formerly Elderhostel), established in 1975, represents one of the longest-running institutional models of older adult engagement with educational institutions. The program offers experiential learning programs at universities, cultural institutions, and natural sites across the United States and internationally, engaging older adults simultaneously as learners and as contributors of life experience to shared educational environments (Road Scholar, 2023). The Road Scholar model demonstrates that older adults—given appropriate institutional support and programming—are enthusiastic and capable educational participants, and that their engagement enriches the experience of co-participants across generations. While primarily a continuing education model, Road Scholar's sustained success across five decades offers important lessons for HEIs in Indonesia about the organizational infrastructure, marketing approaches, and program design elements that enable older adult engagement to flourish.

7.2 Regional Benchmark: Singapore's Integrated Approach to Silver Knowledge

Singapore's acute demographic aging has prompted universities, government agencies, and private sector actors to develop an integrated ecosystem for engaging older adults as mentors, advisors, researchers, and community co-designers. The Silver Generation Office—a government program operating in partnership with universities and community organizations—trains older adults as ambassadors and community educators, leveraging their networks and credibility to facilitate health promotion and community development activities (Ministry of Social and Family Development, Singapore, 2023). This model illustrates the potential of government-university-community triangulation in mobilizing silver knowledge for community benefit, and the importance of government leadership in creating enabling policy and funding environments.

Critically, Singapore's approach has also engaged the private sector as a structural partner in silver knowledge programs. The Agency for Integrated Care's industry engagement program funds companies—including pharmaceutical firms, assistive technology developers, and eldercare service providers—to collaborate with universities and older adult communities in co-designing services and products (Ministry of Social and Family Development, Singapore, 2023). The National University of Singapore's CARE NUS has partnered with multinational corporations operating in Singapore to document the tacit professional knowledge of retiring senior executives—generating both commercially valuable insights for corporate succession planning and publicly accessible research on professional expertise in aging workforces (Koh et al., 2022). Singapore's Smart Nation initiative has further deployed AI tools—including conversational agents, speech recognition, and automated knowledge structuring platforms—to accelerate the capture and dissemination of silver knowledge at national scale (Smart Nation Singapore, 2022). For Indonesia, Singapore's experience highlights the value of national-level coordination frameworks that create consistent incentives for universities, industry, and community organizations to participate in silver knowledge ecosystems, and demonstrates that AI infrastructure is not a luxury but a structural enabler of silver knowledge programs at scale.

7.3 International Business-University Model: MIT AgeLab

The MIT AgeLab, established at the Massachusetts Institute of Technology in 1999, provides the most developed international example of the BUSKIC model in practice. Funded by a consortium of more than 50 corporate partners spanning automotive, insurance, consumer goods, financial services, and healthcare industries, the AgeLab conducts applied research on the experiences, needs, and capabilities of older adults—generating knowledge that directly informs corporate product development, service design, and marketing strategy (MIT AgeLab, 2023). The laboratory's approach systematically engages older adults as research co-participants and expert informants, treating their experiential knowledge as a valuable input to innovation rather than a variable to be controlled. Corporate partners pay consortium fees and may commission additional targeted research projects, creating a financially sustainable model that does not depend on grant funding. For Indonesian higher education, the MIT AgeLab demonstrates that business-funded silver knowledge research is commercially viable, academically rigorous, and genuinely beneficial to older adult communities—and that the BUSKIC model proposed in this chapter has robust international precedent on which to draw.

7.4 Indonesian Grassroots Example: Posyandu Lansia and PkM Collaboration

At the grassroots level, Indonesia's network of Posyandu Lansia—community-based health posts for older adults—provides an existing infrastructure that universities have begun to engage through PkM activities. Several state universities, including Universitas Gadjah Mada and Universitas Airlangga, have implemented PkM programs that move beyond conventional health service provision to engage older participants as knowledge contributors—for example, documenting traditional medicinal plant knowledge, traditional food processing techniques, and local ecological knowledge (Nugroho et al., 2020; Santoso & Harimurti, 2021).

These emerging examples, while not yet systematically scaled or institutionalized, demonstrate the feasibility and community resonance of silver knowledge engagement in the Indonesian context. They also reveal persistent gaps: program sustainability typically does not extend beyond the academic year in which it is funded; AI and digital tools for knowledge documentation and dissemination are rarely deployed; business partners are not engaged as co-funders or co-designers; and documentation and replication of successful approaches remain limited. These gaps define the agenda for institutional reform that the partnership models proposed in Section 6—and particularly the BUSKIC model—are designed to address.

7.5 Proposed Pilot: Bandung Intergenerational Knowledge Hub and BUSKIC

The city of Bandung, West Java—home to major universities including Institut Teknologi Bandung (ITB) and Universitas Padjadjaran (UNPAD)—presents a promising site for piloting both the Intergenerational Knowledge Hub model and the Business-University-Silver Knowledge Co-Innovation Consortium. Bandung's older adult population includes a high concentration of retired professionals, academics, engineers, and skilled artisans from the city's strong industrial and creative heritage—including the textile, garment, and creative industries for which the city is internationally known. Existing community organizations, including Karang Taruna networks and local adat institutions, provide potential partnership infrastructure.

A Bandung BUSKIC pilot could engage the city's established textile and fashion industries—which face acute knowledge loss as master craftspeople and experienced designers approach retirement—as founding corporate members. University research units at ITB's Faculty of Art and Design and UNPAD's social science faculties could document and analyze the tacit knowledge of older textile artisans and industry veterans, generating both commercially licensable design knowledge and academic publications. AI-powered oral history and pattern recognition tools could be deployed to capture the visual and tacit dimensions of textile knowledge that verbal documentation alone cannot preserve. Community benefit provisions—directing a portion of consortium revenues to the community organizations supporting older artisans' wellbeing—would ensure that the model meets social service as well as commercial objectives. A Bandung pilot, developed through a consortium of universities, city government, creative industry associations, and community organizations—aligned with Bandung's Smart City agenda—could serve as a proof-of-concept for national replication, generating evidence on program design, cost-effectiveness, and impact that would inform scaled implementation.

8. IMPLICATIONS FOR POLICY AND PRACTICE

8.1 Higher Education Institutions

Universities in Indonesia must undertake a fundamental reimagining of their relationship with older adults. At the curricular level, this requires integrating gerontology, aging studies, intergenerational learning competencies, and AI ethics into professional education programs—including social work, public health, business, education, and engineering—equipping graduates to engage productively with aging communities throughout their careers. At the programmatic level, universities should establish formal mechanisms for older adult engagement, including visiting practitioner programs, intergenerational research units, AI-assisted knowledge documentation centers, and silver mentorship schemes, with appropriate institutional recognition and compensation for older adults' contributions.

Institutional culture change is equally important. University leadership must actively challenge ageist assumptions within academic communities, developing awareness-raising programs for faculty, students, and administrative staff. Research and teaching evaluation frameworks should be updated to recognize intergenerational engagement activities and business-university silver knowledge partnerships as legitimate forms of scholarly and pedagogical contribution, ensuring that faculty who invest time in developing these partnerships are not disadvantaged in promotion and performance review processes.

8.2 Government

National government policy must create enabling environments for silver knowledge mobilization in higher education. This requires, first, the development of a national framework on aging and higher education that explicitly recognizes older adults as knowledge contributors, not only as beneficiaries of social services or adult learners. Second, funding mechanisms—through DIKTI, the Ministry of Social Affairs, and the National Commission on Older Persons—should be aligned to support university–community–industry partnerships centered on silver knowledge. Third, data infrastructure must be strengthened: Indonesia currently lacks systematic data on older adults' educational participation, mentoring activities, and knowledge contributions, making evidence-based policy development difficult (BPS, 2022). A national registry of silver knowledge programs and standardized outcome metrics—supported by AI-powered data aggregation tools—would create a foundation for evidence-informed scaling.

8.3 Industry: Business Funding Models for Silver Knowledge

Private sector actors have a strong stake in the silver knowledge ecosystem, and the development of diverse, sustainable business funding models is essential for the long-term viability of the partnership approaches proposed in this chapter. Access to experienced mentors, industry networks, and tacit professional knowledge can accelerate the development of student entrepreneurs and early-career workers—generating returns for industry partners through a more capable and connected talent pipeline. More strategically, businesses that systematically engage with silver knowledge through structured university partnerships can gain competitive advantages in product design, service innovation, and market insight.

Several distinct business funding models merit specific attention. First, consortium-based research funding, modeled on the MIT AgeLab approach, allows multiple companies within an industry sector to share the cost of systematic silver knowledge research conducted by university research centers—reducing individual firm investment while generating industry-wide knowledge goods that benefit all members. This model is particularly suitable for sectors such as Indonesian agri-food, batik and textile manufacturing, traditional herbal medicine (jamu), and civil infrastructure, where large cohorts of experienced older workers hold tacit knowledge that is commercially valuable to the entire sector. Second, co-investment in living labs positions companies and universities as joint developers of community-embedded innovation environments where older adults serve as paid co-researchers and co-designers. The commercial return on this investment lies in the superior quality of innovations developed with authentic older adult input—products and services that better meet market needs because they reflect genuine lived experience rather than design assumptions. Age Platform Europe (2022) documents numerous cases in which co-design with older adults substantially improved commercial performance relative to conventionally designed alternatives.

Third, sponsored chairs and fellows programs—in which companies fund named professorial chairs or senior research fellowship positions at universities, focused on silver knowledge domains relevant to their business—create sustained, deep research partnerships that generate both academic and commercial knowledge. Fourth, challenge grant competitions, in which companies publish specific knowledge capture or innovation challenges and fund prize competitions for student and researcher teams, create a market mechanism for silver knowledge mobilization without requiring ongoing corporate management of program delivery. Fifth, corporate silver mentoring programs, funded by companies seeking to address internal knowledge succession challenges, position universities as providers of structured intergenerational mentoring services that serve the company's talent development needs while creating dignified, productive roles for older mentors. Sixth, data and analytics partnerships, in which companies gain access to anonymized, ethically governed silver knowledge databases maintained by university research units, can generate subscription revenues that partially self-fund ongoing program delivery.

For social services organizations and community partners within these business-funded models, key structural safeguards are required. Contracts between universities, companies, and community partners should specify the proportion of commercial revenues directed to community benefit programs—ensuring that older adult participants receive fair compensation, that community organizations are remunerated for facilitation, and that social protection provisions (including health support and travel reimbursement for older participants) are funded as non-negotiable program components. Independent ethical oversight—provided by university ethics boards with community representation—should govern all silver knowledge research and ensure that older adult participants' rights, dignity, and data privacy are protected. Social work professionals, given their expertise in community engagement, empowerment practice, and ethical facilitation, are uniquely positioned to serve as program coordinators within the BUSKIC framework—bridging the interests of business, university, and community partners.

8.4 Social Work and Community Development

Social work practitioners are positioned as critical facilitators and advocates within the silver knowledge ecosystem. Through direct practice, social workers can support older adults in articulating and sharing their knowledge, navigating institutional systems, and overcoming internalized ageism. Through community development, social workers can build the organizational infrastructure—community groups, intergenerational networks, advocacy coalitions—through which silver knowledge ecosystems are sustained. Through policy practice, social workers can advocate for the rights of older adults to meaningful participation in educational and civic life, contributing to the broader agenda of anti-ageist social transformation (Levy & Banaji, 2002; Lee, 2001). Social work education programs should incorporate silver knowledge mobilization, AI ethics in older adult programs, and business-community partnership facilitation as core competencies, preparing graduates to play active roles in designing and implementing the partnership models proposed in this chapter.

9. CONCLUSION

This chapter has argued that Indonesian higher education institutions stand at a critical juncture in relation to the nation's accelerating demographic transformation. The rapid growth of the older adult population is not merely a challenge to be managed through expanded social protection and healthcare provision; it is an opportunity to be seized through the strategic mobilization of the accumulated knowledge, experience, and social capital held by older Indonesians—their silver knowledge. Advances in AI and digital technology provide powerful new instruments for this mobilization, enabling the capture, structuring, and dissemination of tacit expertise at scales that were previously impossible. Business investment in structured silver knowledge programs—channeled through the Business-University-Silver Knowledge Co-Innovation Consortium model—offers a financially sustainable pathway that aligns commercial incentives with social benefit.

Five interconnected propositions have been advanced throughout this analysis. First, silver knowledge—encompassing the tacit and explicit expertise, experiential capital, cultural wisdom, and social networks of older adults—represents a significant and currently underutilized asset for Indonesian higher education and the broader knowledge economy. Second, higher education institutions are uniquely positioned to serve as anchors for silver knowledge ecosystems by virtue of their Tri Dharma mandate, their research capacity, and their convening authority. Third, AI and digital technology represent transformative enablers of silver knowledge mobilization—not merely as accessibility tools but as infrastructure for systematic knowledge capture, analysis, and dissemination at scale. Fourth, realizing this potential requires purposeful partnership models—the Intergenerational Knowledge Hub, Silver Talent Incubation Program, Community-Based Silver Learning Network, Digital and AI-Enhanced Silver Inclusion Platform, and Business-University-Silver Knowledge Co-Innovation Consortium—that engage multiple stakeholders in a coordinated ecosystem. Fifth, this agenda demands systemic change across institutional, policy, and commercial dimensions: the active dismantling of ageist assumptions, the development of business funding models that align commercial and social objectives, and the positioning of older adults as central actors—not peripheral recipients—in the university knowledge ecosystem.

Regional comparators—particularly Singapore's integrated approach to silver economy development, its AI-enabled knowledge programs, and its structured engagement of private sector funding—demonstrate that this agenda is achievable and commercially viable in the Asian context. International models—particularly the MIT AgeLab's consortium-funded approach to silver knowledge research—provide proof of concept for the BUSKIC model at institutional scale. Indonesian grassroots examples demonstrate community resonance and cultural feasibility.

Future research should empirically test these models through rigorous program evaluations, longitudinal assessments of participant outcomes, and comparative studies across different regional and institutional contexts. Particular attention should be paid to the design of ethical AI systems for silver knowledge capture; the distribution of commercial benefits between corporate, university, and community partners within BUSKIC consortia; and the specific cultural adaptations required for silver knowledge programs to function effectively across Indonesia's extraordinary regional and linguistic diversity.

The stakes are high. As Indonesia advances toward its 2045 Golden Generation vision, the question of how to productively engage an increasingly large older population in national development—and how to create commercially sustainable institutional structures for doing so—is not merely academic. Higher education institutions have both the opportunity and the responsibility to lead in answering this question: by repositioning the university as a multigenerational institution, a true knowledge commons in which the wisdom of age, the energy of youth, and the innovation resources of business are brought into generative dialogue for the benefit of individuals, communities, and Indonesian society as a whole. The silver economy needs silver knowledge. Silver knowledge needs AI-powered infrastructure. And both need the university as their institutional home.

REFERENCES

Age Platform Europe. (2022). *Silver economy and ageing well: Report on co-design approaches for older adult inclusion in product and service development.* Age Platform Europe.

Badan Pusat Statistik (BPS). (2022). *Statistik penduduk lanjut usia 2022.* Badan Pusat Statistik.

Beard, J. R., Officer, A., de Carvalho, I. A., Sadana, R., Pot, A. M., Michel, J.-P., Lloyd-Sherlock, P., Epping-Jordan, J. E., Peeters, G., Mahanani, W. R., Thiyagarajan, J. A., & Chatterji, S. (2016). The World Report on Ageing and Health: A policy framework for healthy ageing. *Lancet, 387*(10033), 2145–2154. DOI: 10.1016/S0140-6736(15)00516-4 PMID: 26520231

Beazley, H., Boenisch, J., & Harden, D. (2002). *Continuity management: Preserving corporate knowledge and productivity when employees leave.* John Wiley & Sons.

Bourdieu, P. (1986). The forms of capital. In Richardson, J. G. (Ed.), *Handbook of theory and research for the sociology of education* (pp. 241–258). Greenwood.

Butler, R. N. (1980). Ageism: A foreword. *The Journal of Social Issues, 36*(2), 8–11. DOI: 10.1111/j.1540-4560.1980.tb02018.x

Carayannis, E. G., & Campbell, D. F. J. (2009). 'Mode 3' and 'quadruple helix': Toward a 21st century fractal innovation ecosystem. *International Journal of Technology Management, 46*(3–4), 201–234. DOI: 10.1504/IJTM.2009.023374

Carstensen, L. L. (2021). Integrating cognitive and emotional processing in late life: The case for older adults as resources in an age of uncertainty. *Annual Review of Psychology, 72*, 45–70. DOI: 10.1146/annurev-psych-092220-093702

Casal-Otero, L., Catala, A., Fernández-Morante, C., Taboada, M., Cebreiro, B., & Mato-Abad, V. (2023). AI literacy in K-12 and implications for adult education: A systematic review. *Computers and Education: Artificial Intelligence, 4*, 100130. DOI: 10.1016/j.caeai.2023.100130

Centre for Ageing Better. (2023). *Annual review 2022–23: Creating a society where everyone can age well.* Centre for Ageing Better.

Crisp, G., & Cruz, I. (2009). Mentoring college students: A critical review of the literature between 1990 and 2007. *Research in Higher Education, 50*(6), 525–545. DOI: 10.1007/s11162-009-9130-2

Czaja, S. J., Boot, W. R., Charness, N., & Rogers, W. A. (2019). *Designing for older adults: Principles and creative human factors approaches* (3rd ed.). CRC Press. DOI: 10.1201/b22189

Davenport, T. H., & Prusak, L. (1998). *Working knowledge: How organizations manage what they know*. Harvard Business School Press.

DeLong, D. W. (2004). *Lost knowledge: Confronting the threat of an aging workforce*. Oxford University Press. DOI: 10.1093/acprof:oso/9780195170979.001.0001

Delors, J., Al Mufti, I., Amagi, I., Carneiro, R., Chung, F., Geremek, B., Gorham, W., Kornhauser, A., Manley, M., Quero, M. P., Savane, M. A., Singh, K., Stavenhagen, R., Suhr, M. W., & Nanzhao, Z. (1996). *Learning: The treasure within. Report to UNESCO of the International Commission on Education for the Twenty-first Century*. UNESCO.

Direktorat Jenderal Pendidikan Tinggi (DIKTI). (2020). Buku panduan Merdeka Belajar – Kampus Merdeka. Kementerian Pendidikan dan Kebudayaan.

Etzkowitz, H., & Leydesdorff, L. (2000). The dynamics of innovation: From national systems and 'Mode 2' to a triple helix of university–industry–government relations. *Research Policy*, *29*(2), 109–123. DOI: 10.1016/S0048-7333(99)00055-4

European Commission. (2018). The silver economy: Final report. Publications Office of the European Union. https://doi.org/DOI: 10.2759/33378

Eyler, J., & Giles, D. E. (1999). *Where's the learning in service-learning?* Jossey-Bass.

Fang, M. L., Canham, S. L., Battersby, L., Sixsmith, J., Wada, M., & Sixsmith, A. (2023). Exploring privilege in the digital divide during the COVID-19 pandemic: Implications for digital health equity in older adults. *The Gerontologist*, *63*(1), 14–24. DOI: 10.1093/geront/gnab154

Faure, E., Herrera, F., Kaddoura, A.-R., Lopes, H., Petrovsky, A. V., Rahnema, M., & Champion Ward, F. (1972). Learning to be: The world of education today and tomorrow. UNESCO/Harrap.

Gibbons, M., Limoges, C., Nowotny, H., Schwartzman, S., Scott, P., & Trow, M. (1994). The new production of knowledge: The dynamics of science and research in contemporary societies. *Sage (Atlanta, Ga.)*.

Hull, T. H. (2016). Demographic perspectives on Indonesia's future. In Hill, H. (Ed.), *Indonesia rising: The repositioning of Asia's third giant* (pp. 29–56). Institute of Southeast Asian Studies.

Info-communications Media Development Authority, Singapore. (2023). Silver Infocomm Initiative: Annual report 2022–23. IMDA Singapore.

Jarvis, P. (2006). *Towards a comprehensive theory of human learning*. Routledge.

Jarvis, P. (2009). *Learning to be a person in society*. Routledge.

Kementerian PPN/Bappenas. (2019). *Proyeksi penduduk Indonesia 2015–2045: Hasil SUPAS 2015*. Badan Perencanaan Pembangunan Nasional.

Kinsella, E. A., & Pitman, A. (Eds.). (2012). *Phronesis as professional knowledge: Practical wisdom in the professions*. Sense Publishers. DOI: 10.1007/978-94-6091-731-8

Klimczuk, A. (2015). Economic foundations for creative ageing policy, volume I: Context and considerations. Palgrave Macmillan. https://doi.org/DOI: 10.1057/9781137465467

Koentjaraningrat. (1985). Javanese culture. Oxford University Press.

Koh, G., Yeo, E. Y., & Tang, C. S. (2022). Productive aging and knowledge transfer in Singapore: Evidence from the Senior Academy programme. *Journal of Aging & Social Policy, 34*(4), 578–597. DOI: 10.1080/08959420.2021.1955724

Kohlbacher, F., & Herstatt, C. (Eds.). (2011). *The silver market phenomenon: Marketing and innovation in the aging society* (2nd ed.). Springer. DOI: 10.1007/978-3-642-14338-0

Lee, J. A. B. (2001). *The empowerment approach to social work practice: Building the beloved community* (2nd ed.). Columbia University Press.

Levy, B. R., & Banaji, M. R. (2002). Implicit ageism. In Nelson, T. D. (Ed.), *Ageism: Stereotyping and prejudice against older persons* (pp. 49–75). MIT Press. DOI: 10.7551/mitpress/1157.003.0006

Mannion, G. (2012). Intergenerational education: The significance of reciprocity and place. *Journal of Intergenerational Relationships, 10*(4), 386–399. DOI: 10.1080/15350770.2012.726601

McGivney, V. (2022). Lifelong learning in the digital age: Challenges and opportunities for older adults. *International Journal of Lifelong Education, 41*(3), 215–230. DOI: 10.1080/02601370.2022.2055432

Miner, A. S., Haque, A., Fries, J. A., Ross, S., Shah, N. H., & Milstein, A. (2020). Assessing the accuracy of automatic speech recognition for psychotherapy. *NPJ Digital Medicine*, *3*(82), 82. Advance online publication. DOI: 10.1038/s41746-020-0285-8 PMID: 32550644

Ministry of Health. Singapore. (2023). Action plan for successful ageing: 2023 refresh. Government of Singapore. https://www.moh.gov.sg/news-highlights/details/action-plan-for-successful-ageing

Ministry of Social and Family Development. Singapore. (2021). Action plan for successful ageing: 2021 refresh. Government of Singapore.

Minkler, M., & Wallerstein, N. (Eds.). (2011). *Community-based participatory research for health: From process to outcomes* (2nd ed.). Jossey-Bass.

MIT AgeLab. (2023). About the MIT AgeLab: Mission and sponsors. Massachusetts Institute of Technology. https://agelab.mit.edu

Moore, J. F. (1993). Predators and prey: A new ecology of competition. *Harvard Business Review, 71*(3), 75–86. PMID: 10126156

Mulvenna, M., & Martin, S. (2020). Living labs for co-designing digital solutions with older adults: Methods and outcomes from AgeTech consortia. *The Gerontologist*, *60*(3), 567–578. DOI: 10.1093/geront/gnz137

Newman, S., & Hatton-Yeo, A. (2008). Intergenerational learning and the contributions of older people. *Ageing Horizons*, *8*, 31–39.

Ng, T. P., Feng, L., Nyunt, M. S. Z., & Yap, K. B. (2023). Productive aging and health outcomes in older Singaporeans: Evidence from longitudinal cohort studies. *Annals of the Academy of Medicine, Singapore*, *52*(1), 14–26. DOI: 10.47102/annals-acadmedsg.2022337

Nonaka, I., & Takeuchi, H. (1995). *The knowledge-creating company: How Japanese companies create the dynamics of innovation*. Oxford University Press. DOI: 10.1093/oso/9780195092691.001.0001

Nugroho, P., Setiawan, D., & Dewi, R. (2020). Community-based programs for older adults in Indonesian universities: A scoping review of PkM reports 2015–2020. Jurnal Gerontologi dan Geriatri, 5(2), 45–62.

OECD. (2019). *OECD skills outlook 2019: Thriving in a digital world*. OECD Publishing., DOI: 10.1787/df80bc12-

OECD. (2021). *Pensions at a glance: Asia/Pacific 2021*. OECD Publishing., DOI: 10.1787/9789264099401-

OECD. (2023). *Ageing and employment policies: Working better with age 2023.* OECD Publishing., DOI: 10.1787/59752153-

Phan, P. H.I, & Siegel, D. S. (2006). The effectiveness of university technology transfer: Lessons learned from qualitative and quantitative research in the US and the UK. *Foundations and Trends in Entrepreneurship, 2*(2), 65–144. DOI: 10.1561/0300000006

Polanyi, M. (1966). *The tacit dimension.* Doubleday.

Prensky, M. (2021). Digital wisdom: Empowering older adults in the AI era. *Journal of Intergenerational Relationships, 19*(2), 134–150. DOI: 10.1080/15350770.2020.1844571

Putnam, R. D. (2000). *Bowling alone: The collapse and revival of American community.* Simon & Schuster.

Rowe, J. W., & Kahn, R. L. (1997). Successful aging. *The Gerontologist, 37*(4), 433–440. DOI: 10.1093/geront/37.4.433 PMID: 9279031

Santoso, B., & Harimurti, P. (2021). Documenting traditional knowledge in rural Java: A university-community partnership model. Masyarakat, Kebudayaan dan Politik, 34(1), 56–71. https://doi.org/DOI: 10.20473/mkp.V34I12021.56-71

Scholar, R. (2023). About Road Scholar: Mission and history. https://www.roadscholar.org/about/

Schuler, D., & Namioka, A. (Eds.). (1993). *Participatory design: Principles and practices.* Lawrence Erlbaum Associates.

Schuurman, D., De Moor, K., De Marez, L., & Evens, T. (2012). A living lab research approach for mobile TV. *Telematics and Informatics, 29*(2), 207–220. DOI: 10.1016/j.tele.2011.06.001

Singapore, S. N. (2022). *Digital government blueprint 2020: Progress update 2022.* Smart Nation and Digital Government Office., https://www.smartnation.gov.sg

Smith, L. T. (2012). *Decolonizing methodologies: Research and indigenous peoples* (2nd ed.). Zed Books.

Topol, E. J. (2019). High-performance medicine: The convergence of human and artificial intelligence. *Nature Medicine, 25*(1), 44–56. DOI: 10.1038/s41591-018-0300-7 PMID: 30617339

UNESCO. (2015). *Rethinking education: Towards a global common good?* UNESCO.

United Nations. (2020). World population ageing 2020: Highlights. Department of Economic and Social Affairs, Population Division. https://www.un.org/development/desa/pd/

Wahyudi, A., & Paramastri, I. (2019). Ageism attitudes among young adults in urban Indonesia. *Jurnal Psikologi, 46*(3), 189–201. DOI: 10.22146/jpsi.37561

Walker, A. (2002). A strategy for active ageing. *International Social Security Review, 55*(1), 121–139. DOI: 10.1111/1468-246X.00118

Walker, A. (2006). Active ageing in employment: Its meaning and potential. *Asia-Pacific Review, 13*(1), 78–93. DOI: 10.1080/13439000600697621

Wenger, E. (1998). *Communities of practice: Learning, meaning, and identity.* Cambridge University Press. DOI: 10.1017/CBO9780511803932

World Health Organization. (2002). Active ageing: A policy framework. WHO. https://apps.who.int/iris/handle/10665/67215

World Health Organization. (2021). Decade of Healthy Ageing: Baseline report. WHO. https://www.who.int/publications/i/item/9789240017900

Youtie, J., & Shapira, P. (2008). Building an innovation hub: A case study of the transformation of university roles in regional technological and economic development. *Research Policy, 37*(8), 1188–1204. DOI: 10.1016/j.respol.2008.04.012

Zastrow, C., & Kirst-Ashman, K. K. (2016). *Understanding human behavior and the social environment* (10th ed.). Cengage Learning.

Chapter 15
Institutionalizing Silver Knowledge in Education:
A Multi-Level Policy Analysis From the Vietnamese Context

Minh Van Vo
University of Science and Education, The University of Da Nang, Vietnam

Lam Thi Le
http://orcid.org/0009-0007-2301-8026
University of Science and Education, The University of Da Nang, Vietnam

Kien The Pham
http://orcid.org/0009-0001-0246-9254
University of Science and Education, The University of Da Nang, Vietnam

ABSTRACT

This chapter examines the institutionalization of "silver knowledge", defined as the accumulated expertise of senior educators, in Vietnam's education system. Using policy analysis and qualitative content analysis of legal documents, draft policies, and consultation materials, the study explores how this knowledge resource is recognized and utilized. The findings show that, while Vietnam has begun to establish a legal framework for engaging retired teachers, policy remains largely grounded in a labor management approach. Key aspects of knowledge governance, such as mentoring, knowledge transfer, and organizational knowledge accumulation, are not yet fully institutionalized. A multi level analysis reveals interactions across macro, meso, and micro levels, alongside an imbalance between top down policy processes and bottom up knowledge flows. The chapter argues for a shift toward an intergenerational knowledge governance model as a more sustainable approach.

DOI: 10.4018/979-8-3373-9370-4.ch015

1. INTRODUCTION

In the context of population ageing and the transformation of education systems toward greater flexibility and lifelong learning, the effective utilization of knowledge resources from senior educators has become an issue of growing global concern. Beyond being a workforce that has completed the formal stage of their professional life cycle, retired teachers represent "living repositories of knowledge", having accumulated professional experience, practical insights, and academic capital through many years of teaching and research. In this study, this resource is conceptualized as "silver knowledge", a distinctive form of intellectual asset with the potential to make strategic contributions to education systems.

In Vietnam, ongoing educational reforms and institutional development have created new opportunities to engage senior educators through various roles, including adjunct teaching, consultancy, and participation in training and research activities. Recent legal documents and draft policies indicate a gradual recognition of the role of this group within the education system. However, current policy approaches continue to focus primarily on expanding human resources, while the core dimensions of knowledge governance, such as the transmission of experience, the accumulation of organizational knowledge, and the development of academic mentoring roles, have not yet been fully and systematically institutionalized.

This gap raises a central research question: whether "silver knowledge" is being utilized merely as an extension of labor, or whether it is recognized as a form of intellectual asset that requires strategic governance. Addressing this question is crucial not only for improving the efficiency of human resource utilization, but also for strengthening the long term knowledge development capacity of the education system.

To address this issue, this chapter analyzes the institutionalization of "silver knowledge" in Vietnam's education system through a multi level policy analysis approach, drawing on data from legal documents, draft policies, and consultation processes at the institutional level.

Specifically, the study pursues four main objectives:

(i) to clarify how existing policies shape the use of senior educators;
(ii) to examine the gap between knowledge utilization goals and policy implementation instruments;
(iii) to propose a multi level analytical framework for understanding the institutionalization of "silver knowledge"; and
(iv) to provide policy implications aimed at shifting from a model of "utilizing ageing human resources" to a model of "intergenerational knowledge governance".

From an academic perspective, the study contributes by integrating a knowledge governance approach into the analysis of education policy, while also proposing a multi level framework to illuminate interactions across institutional levels. From a practical perspective, it offers evidence and policy recommendations in the Vietnamese context, a country currently adapting to population ageing while pursuing education system reform. The following section presents the literature review and analytical framework, followed by the research methodology, findings, and discussion.

2. LITERATURE REVIEW

2.1. Silver Knowledge and Ageing in the Educational Workforce

In the context of global population ageing, extending the participation of older workers in the labor market has become a significant trend across multiple sectors, including education. Studies on active ageing emphasize that older adults should not be viewed solely as a group in need of support, but also as a valuable resource for society (World Health Organization, 2002; OECD, 2019).

Within the field of education, retired teachers often possess substantial experiential knowledge and accumulated academic capital developed over the course of their careers (Eraut, 2000; Polanyi, 1966). These forms of knowledge, particularly tacit knowledge, play a critical role in teaching practices, academic mentoring, and curriculum development (Nonaka and Takeuchi, 1995).

Building on this foundation, the concept of "silver knowledge" in this study is approached as an extension of theories of experiential knowledge and human capital (Becker, 1993), emphasizing the value of knowledge accumulated in the later stages of the professional life course.

2.2. Knowledge Governance in Educational Organizations

Knowledge governance has emerged as a central approach in organizational and educational research, emphasizing the transformation of individual knowledge into organizational knowledge through mechanisms of sharing, storage, and continuous learning (Nonaka and Takeuchi, 1995; Davenport and Prusak, 1998).

In the context of higher education, knowledge governance is particularly significant due to the sector's strong reliance on specialized and academic knowledge (Rowley, 2000). Mechanisms such as mentoring, communities of practice, and knowledge repositories are considered essential tools for facilitating knowledge transfer across generations (Wenger, 1998).

However, a growing body of research indicates that educational institutions continue to face challenges in effectively leveraging tacit knowledge from senior experts, particularly in the absence of formal institutional arrangements that support such processes (Eraut, 2000).

2.3. Policies on the Utilization of Senior Educators and Adjunct Faculty

In many countries, the engagement of senior educators has been institutionalized through models such as adjunct faculty and emeritus professors. In the United States, these groups play an important role in supplementing teaching capacity while contributing valuable practical experience (Kezar & Sam, 2010).

In Japan, reemployment systems allow workers to continue their professional engagement beyond the statutory retirement age, thereby supporting the retention and utilization of accumulated knowledge within organizations (OECD, 2018). In Europe, policies on lifelong learning and active ageing are integrated across both the education system and the labor market (European Commission, 2012).

However, several studies suggest that the use of senior educators is often confined primarily to teaching roles, without fully leveraging their potential contributions to research, academic mentoring, and strategic development (Altbach et al., 2009).

2.4. Policy Analysis and Multi Level Approaches

Traditional approaches to education policy analysis have primarily focused on policy design and implementation at the central level. However, more recent studies emphasize the importance of multi level governance, in which policies are shaped and enacted through interactions across different levels of the system (Hill and Hupe, 2002).

This approach enables not only the examination of gaps between policy intentions and implementation practices, but also a clearer understanding of the roles of actors at the institutional level and the feedback flows from practice into policy making processes. In the field of education, multi level approaches are particularly useful for analyzing reforms related to university autonomy and human resource governance (Marginson and Rhoades, 2002).

2.5. Research Gaps and Analytical Framework Orientation

Although previous studies have provided important foundations on workforce ageing, knowledge governance, and education policy, several notable gaps remain. First, research on senior educators has largely approached the issue from labor or demographic perspectives, without fully considering their role as a strategic knowledge resource. Second, studies on knowledge governance tend to focus at the organizational level and are rarely integrated into education policy analysis, resulting in a separation between these two domains. Third, in the context of developing countries such as Vietnam, there is a lack of empirical research on the institutionalization of "silver knowledge" within education systems.

These gaps highlight the need for an integrated analytical framework capable of linking institutional levels with knowledge flows in the education system. In particular, within a multi level institutional context, a purely top down approach is insufficient to fully explain the process of institutionalizing "silver knowledge".

Therefore, this study proposes a multi level analytical framework to examine how "silver knowledge" is institutionalized through the interaction between policy levels and knowledge flows. This framework is presented in the following section and serves as the theoretical foundation for the empirical analysis of this chapter.

3. ANALYTICAL FRAMEWORK

3.1. Positioning the Framework

Building on the identified research gaps, this chapter proposes a multi level analytical framework to explain the process of institutionalizing "silver knowledge" in education. The framework integrates two main approaches: (i) knowledge governance, which emphasizes the role of knowledge as a strategic asset; and (ii) multi level governance, which highlights the interactions among institutional levels in policy making and implementation.

By combining these approaches, the framework addresses the limitations of previous studies that have often treated policy analysis and knowledge governance as separate domains. It also provides an integrated perspective on the role of "silver knowledge" within the education system (see Figure 1).

Figure 1. Multi level analytical framework for the institutionalization of "silver knowledge" in education

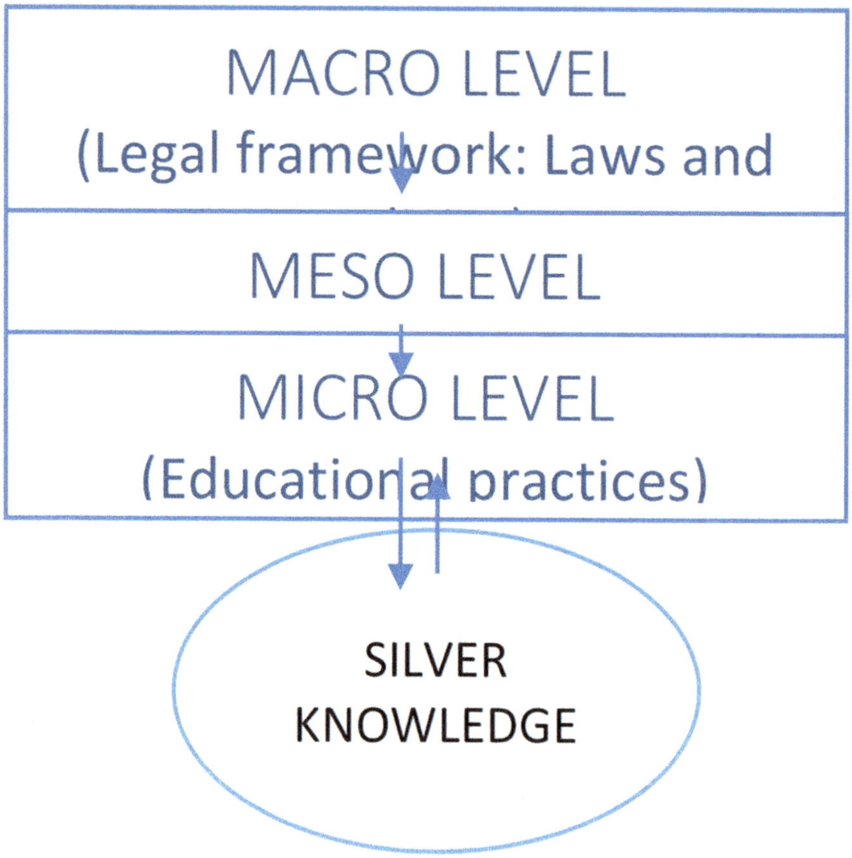

3.2. Multi Level Structure of Policy

The analytical framework identifies three principal levels in the process of institutionalization. The macro level includes legal documents such as the Law on Education, the Law on Teachers, and related decrees, which establish the legal foundation and define overall policy directions. This level provides the basis of legitimacy for mobilizing and engaging senior educators.

The meso level comprises draft policies, circulars, and specific regulatory mechanisms, where legal principles are translated into operational instruments. Policy consultation processes at this level reflect the interactions among stakeholders within the education system.

The micro level refers to implementation practices within educational institutions, where policies are enacted through internal regulations, teaching activities, and academic practices. These three levels are not independent but are closely interconnected within a dynamic institutional structure, in which policies are shaped, adjusted, and reconfigured through continuous interactions across levels.

3.3. Dual Flows of Policy and Knowledge

A key contribution of the framework lies in identifying two parallel flows. The first is a top down policy flow, representing the process through which legal regulations are specified and implemented from the macro level to the micro level. The second is a bottom up knowledge flow, reflecting the accumulation, sharing, and feedback of experiential knowledge from practice, which in turn influences policy adjustment.

The interaction between these two flows is critical for transforming individual knowledge into organizational and system level knowledge. However, in many cases, bottom up knowledge flows remain limited, resulting in weak linkages between practice and policy design.

In practice, these two flows do not operate independently but continuously interact with and reshape one another. While the top-down policy flow establishes the institutional framework for mobilizing senior educators, the bottom-up knowledge flow reflects practical experiences, organizational needs, and forms of knowledge transfer occurring within educational institutions. When this knowledge flow is not effectively integrated back into the policymaking process, institutional disconnections may emerge between policy objectives and implementation capacity.

3.4. The Central Role of "Silver Knowledge"

In this study, "silver knowledge" is not simply understood as experiential knowledge or the tacit knowledge of older workers. This concept is used to refer to a form of knowledge accumulated in the later stage of a professional career, characterized by three key features: (i) long-term accumulation of professional expertise and institutional experience; (ii) the capacity to mentor, guide, and facilitate intergenerational knowledge transfer; and (iii) its strategic value for ensuring the continuity of organizational knowledge. Therefore, silver knowledge is not merely individual knowledge, but also a resource capable of connecting organizational knowledge, institutional memory, and intergenerational learning capacity.

Within this framework, "silver knowledge" occupies a central position, functioning both as an object of policy and as a factor shaping policy making and implementation processes. This body of knowledge encompasses professional experience, specialized expertise, and accumulated academic capital held by senior educators.

In contrast to traditional approaches that view this group primarily as a supplementary labor resource, the framework emphasizes "silver knowledge" as a strategic intellectual asset capable of linking policy levels and fostering organizational learning processes.

3.5. Analytical Implications of the Framework

The multi level analytical framework suggests that the institutionalization of "silver knowledge" is not a linear process, but rather unfolds within a complex institutional ecosystem. The effectiveness of policy depends on the degree of alignment across levels and the balance between policy flows and knowledge flows.

From this perspective, one of the key challenges lies not only in policy design, but also in the development of intermediary mechanisms that enable the transformation of individual knowledge into organizational and system level knowledge. This is a critical condition for shifting from a model of utilizing ageing human resources to one of intergenerational knowledge governance.

The framework serves not only as a theoretical foundation, but also as a guiding tool for data collection and analysis. Specifically, the levels of analysis and the policy and knowledge flows are operationalized as key analytical dimensions in the following methodology section.

4. RESEARCH METHODOLOGY

4.1. Research Design

This study adopts a policy analysis approach combined with qualitative content analysis to examine how Vietnam's education system approaches and institutionalizes "silver knowledge" through legal and regulatory instruments.

This approach enables not only the description of policy content, but also the analysis of underlying policy logics embedded in the processes of design and consultation. It thereby facilitates the identification of patterns and orientations in the utilization of knowledge resources from senior educators.

4.2. Data Sources

The study draws on multi level policy data in order to capture the institutional context of the research problem. Data were collected from three primary levels.

At the macro level, the analysis includes current legal documents related to education and the teaching workforce, such as the Law on Teachers (June 16, 2025), the Law on Higher Education (December 10, 2025), Decree No. 32/CP (April 4, 1994), and Decision No. 1559/QĐ-BGDĐT (June 4, 2024) issued by the Ministry of Education and Training regarding professional title promotion, appointment, salary classification, retirement, and extension of working duration for public employees under the Ministry.

At the meso level, the study examines ministerial draft policies, particularly the Draft Circular on full time contracted teachers after retirement and adjunct faculty (March 23, 2026).

At the micro level, the data include consultation materials and feedback from educational institutions and relevant stakeholders.

More specifically, the dataset consists of three main groups of documents:

(i) the Draft Circular on full time contracted teachers after retirement and adjunct faculty (March 23, 2026), publicly released for consultation;
(ii) the consolidated report summarizing and responding to feedback from 98 agencies, organizations, and educational institutions on the draft circular; and
(iii) related institutional documents from selected universities in Vietnam, including regulations on retirement and extension of employment at the University of Da Nang, official conclusions from the Rector of the University of Sciences, Hue University regarding labor contracts for retired professors, associate professors, and doctoral degree holders, and regulations on employment contracts with older workers at the University of Medicine and Pharmacy, Hue University.

These documents not only reflect proposed policy content but also provide insights into diverse perspectives, levels of consensus, and policy debates emerging during the consultation process.

4.3. Data Analysis Methods

The study employs qualitative content analysis using a combination of inductive and deductive approaches. The analysis proceeds in three main steps.

First, the data were read and initially coded using an inductive approach to identify emerging themes in stakeholder feedback, including key concerns, proposed revisions, and critical perspectives on the policy.

Secondly, the codes were systematized and categorized into major analytical themes based on the proposed multi-level analytical framework. This process combined deductive coding, derived from the theoretical components of the study, with inductive coding to capture emerging themes from the empirical data. The primary code groups include: (i) labor governance; (ii) knowledge governance; (iii) institutional autonomy; (iv) quality control; (v) intergenerational knowledge transfer; and (vi) institutional gaps. Table 1 below illustrates some of the primary code categories utilized during the data analysis process.

Table 1. Primary code categories in data analysis

Code category	Analytical content
Labor governance	Employment contracts, retirement age, working hours, insurance
Knowledge governance	Mentoring, experience transmission, knowledge retention
Institutional autonomy	Institutional autonomy of educational establishments in policy implementation
Quality control	Academic standards, quality assessment, age limits
Intergenerational transfer	Knowledge transfer across generations of faculty members
Institutional gaps	The mismatch between policy design and implementation capacity

Thirdly, these themes are interpreted at the level of policy logic, aiming to clarify how policy approaches "silver knowledge" either as a prolonged labor supply or as a strategic knowledge asset. Concurrently, the study employs a multi-level analytical framework to trace the interaction between two primary streams: (i) a top-down policy flow; and (ii) a bottom-up knowledge flow.

Cross-referencing these data levels enables the identification of institutional gaps, disruptions in the knowledge transfer process, and the degree of alignment between policy design and empirical implementation.

To enhance the reliability of the study, the coding process was iteratively conducted across multiple rounds to ensure consistency between thematic groups and analytical levels. Furthermore, the study utilizes a data triangulation strategy by combining legal texts, consultation documents, and internal institutional regulations to bolster both the reliability and analytical validity of the findings.

However, this study relies primarily on the analysis of policy documents and institutional texts; consequently, the findings reflect policy logic and institutional discourse rather than the direct experiences of the stakeholders involved. Future research could expand upon this by conducting interviews with retired educators, institutional leaders, and policymakers to more deeply validate the implementation dynamics and the actual transformation of "silver knowledge" in practice.

4.4. Application of the Analytical Framework

The multi level analytical framework is applied as a guiding tool throughout the data analysis process. Data sources are categorized and coded according to the three corresponding levels: macro, meso, and micro. The coding process combines deductive coding, based on predefined components of the framework, with inductive coding to capture themes emerging from empirical data.

In addition, the framework is used to trace two principal flows. The top down policy flow is examined through the degree of consistency across policy documents at different levels. The bottom up knowledge flow is analyzed through the extent to which practical experience is reflected in policy content.

By comparing across levels and flows, the analysis identifies gaps, disconnections, and degrees of alignment in the institutionalization of "silver knowledge". In this way, the framework functions not only as a theoretical lens but also as an analytical tool for structuring data and revealing policy patterns.

4.5. Reliability and Research Validity

To ensure the reliability of the findings, the study employs several strategies. First, it utilizes multiple data sources across different levels to enhance the consistency of the analysis. Second, it ensures transparency by clearly describing the coding and analytical procedures. To enhance analytical rigor and reliability, themes were iteratively cross-examined across different data levels. Third, it maintains consistency by applying the analytical framework throughout the entire research process.

These measures contribute to strengthening the reliability and scientific rigor of the study within the context of qualitative policy analysis.

5. FINDINGS

The analysis reveals that, despite a relatively high level of consensus on the necessity of the policy, stakeholder feedback and policy responses converge around four core issue clusters. These clusters reflect clear policy patterns and policy tensions in the process of institutionalizing "silver knowledge" in Vietnam. More importantly, the findings indicate that current policy is operating in a transitional state, shifting from a labor management model toward a knowledge governance model, although this transition remains incomplete.

To elucidate the operationalization of the multi-level analysis framework, Table 2 below synthesizes the interactions among institutional levels, policy streams, and knowledge streams within the process of institutionalizing "silver knowledge".

Policy and Knowledge Streams Matrix

Table 2. Operationalization of the multi-level framework for the institutionalization of "silver knowledge"

Analytical Level	Top-down Policy Stream	Bottom-up Knowledge Stream	Gaps/Challenges
Macro	Education Law, Law on Teachers, regulations on working age extension	Absence of feedback mechanisms for practice-based knowledge	Policies remain limited to resource expansion
Meso	Draft Circulars and implementation guidelines	Feedback and consultations from educational institutions	Limited absorption of knowledge management principles
Micro	Implementation at the university level	Experiential insight from mentoring and knowledge transfer	Lack of institutionalization and knowledge retention mechanisms

5.1. Institutional Continuity and Limitations of the Legal Framework

At the macro level, the analysis shows that the draft policy does not emerge in isolation but is grounded in the existing legal system, including the Law on Education, the Law on Teachers, the Law on Higher Education, and related regulations. This reflects a strong degree of institutional continuity in policy development.

However, while the current legal framework enables the engagement of retired educators, it primarily provides general principles rather than specific mechanisms for knowledge governance. In other words, the macro level creates legal openness but does not yet define how knowledge can be strategically utilized as an intellectual asset. This finding highlights an important limitation, namely the gap between the enabling capacity of the legal framework and the level of operational specification in policy design.

5.2. Tension between Quality Control and Resource Mobilization

At the meso level, a key policy tension emerges between the need for quality control and the objective of expanding resource mobilization. Many stakeholders proposed additional control measures, such as age limits and requirements related to academic qualifications and research experience. However, most of these proposals were not adopted. Instead, the policy drafters opted to maintain an open approach, without imposing maximum age limits or rigid qualification criteria.

This reflects a deliberate policy choice to prioritize flexibility and the mobilization of "silver knowledge" over stricter input control. At the same time, this choice creates a gap in quality assurance mechanisms, particularly in the absence of evaluation tools based on competencies and knowledge contributions.

5.3. Increasing Autonomy without Supporting Institutional Mechanisms

Another important finding is the growing level of institutional autonomy granted to educational institutions in policy implementation. Key aspects such as teaching workload, remuneration, incentives, and professional evaluation are delegated to institutions rather than regulated in detail at the central level. This reflects a shift from centralized management toward decentralized governance.

However, the analysis indicates that this transfer of authority is not accompanied by the development of corresponding institutional mechanisms, particularly in the domain of knowledge governance. The absence of intermediary structures such as mentoring systems, knowledge repositories, and formal processes for knowledge transfer limits the ability of institutions to translate autonomy into effective implementation capacity.

As a result, educational institutions may face several systemic challenges. These include uneven policy implementation across institutions, reflecting differences in organizational capacity and contextual conditions; the risk of formalistic adjunct teaching practices, where the roles of senior educators are not aligned with their strengths in knowledge and experience; and limitations in transforming individual knowledge into organizational knowledge, thereby constraining the sustainable utilization of "silver knowledge".

These patterns point to the existence of an institutional gap, understood as the discrepancy between the level of autonomy granted and the actual implementation capacity of educational institutions. This gap represents a major barrier to the transition from a model of utilizing ageing human resources to one of intergenerational knowledge governance.

5.4. Dominance of Labor Management Logic

The content analysis of stakeholder feedback reveals a consistent pattern in which most policy discussions focus on labor management issues, including contract types, working time, social insurance, and administrative procedures.

In contrast, aspects related to knowledge governance, such as mentoring, experience transfer, the development of organizational knowledge, and strategic academic roles, are largely absent from both feedback and policy responses. This finding suggests that, although the policy aims to leverage "silver knowledge", its practical orientation remains dominated by traditional labor management logic. This results in a significant gap between policy objectives and implementation instruments.

5.5. Emerging Systemic Risks and the Need for Multi Level Coordination

Beyond issues of policy design, the data also reveal increasing awareness of systemic risks in implementation. Identified risks include difficulties in monitoring total working time, excessive adjunct teaching beyond standard limits, potential conflicts of interest, and uneven teaching quality. Some proposals, such as the development of a national database and strengthened monitoring mechanisms, have been partially incorporated.

However, these risks do not only reflect challenges at the micro level. They also point to weak coordination across policy levels. In particular, the lack of mechanisms for coordination and information sharing across levels constrains the system's capacity to effectively manage and optimize resources.

5.6. Imbalance between Policy Flow and Knowledge Flow

Taken together, the findings reveal a systemic characteristic, namely the imbalance between top down policy flow and bottom up knowledge flow. While the policy flow is relatively well established through the legal framework, the knowledge flow, including the accumulation, sharing, and feedback of practical experience, remains insufficiently institutionalized.

As a result, individual knowledge is not effectively transformed into organizational or system level knowledge. This imbalance constitutes one of the core factors limiting the effectiveness of policies aimed at leveraging "silver knowledge".

Overall, the findings suggest that current policy is in a transitional phase, moving from a model of utilizing ageing human resources toward a model of intergenerational knowledge governance. However, this transition is largely confined to the level of policy orientation, while implementation instruments continue to reflect the characteristics of traditional labor management models. This creates a gap between the potential of "silver knowledge" and its actual utilization within the education system.

5.7. Micro Level Illustration: Diversity in Implementation Practices

The analysis of internal documents from selected educational institutions, including the University of Da Nang, the University of Medicine and Pharmacy under Hue University, and the University of Sciences under Hue University, reveals significant diversity in the implementation of policies related to retired educators.

At this level, institutions not only implement policies but also actively interpret and adapt them to their organizational contexts. However, these practices remain largely focused on administrative aspects such as contracts, teaching workload, and remuneration. Mechanisms for knowledge utilization, including mentoring, experience transfer, and the development of organizational knowledge, have not yet been clearly institutionalized.

The variation across institutions also reflects uneven implementation capacity, particularly in the absence of detailed guidance from the central level on knowledge governance. From the perspective of the analytical framework, these cases illustrate the role of the micro level as a space of policy interpretation, while also highlighting the limitations of bottom up knowledge flows, as practical experiences are not systematically fed back into policy making processes.

During the policy consultation process on extending the working age for Professors, Associate Professors, and doctoral degree holders at a higher education institution in Vietnam, feedback from the institutional level provided important insights into how such policies operate in practice.

These perspectives emerge from the broader context of the higher education system, including the ageing academic workforce, increasing pressure to enhance teaching quality, and the need to strengthen research capacity. Within this context, policies on extending working age are viewed as a mechanism to retain and utilize the accumulated academic knowledge of senior faculty members.

However, the feedback also indicates that if such policies merely extend the duration of employment without clear guidance on implementation, several limitations may arise. First, extended faculty members may continue to perform the full range of traditional responsibilities, including teaching, administrative duties, and research, despite their comparative advantage lying in experiential knowledge and mentoring capacity. Second, evaluation based primarily on quantitative indicators, such as teaching hours or publication output, may fail to capture the full value of activities such as mentoring, academic review, and policy advisory roles. Third, without appropriate role differentiation, the policy may inadvertently slow down generational transition within the academic workforce.

From these observations, an important policy principle is proposed: rather than mechanically extending professional titles or positions, it is necessary to redesign roles in ways that align with the strengths of senior faculty. Accordingly, instead of maintaining all traditional responsibilities, senior educators could take on more specialized roles, such as academic advisors, mentors for early career faculty, research reviewers, or contributors to policy advisory and community engagement activities.

In addition, the feedback highlights the need to reform evaluation mechanisms toward greater flexibility, shifting from rigid performance metrics to approaches that recognize the value and impact of contributions. The establishment of intergenerational mentoring programs and coordination mechanisms at the institutional level is also identified as a critical condition for effective policy implementation.

This case illustrates that even when the policy framework at the central level expands opportunities to engage senior faculty, the actual effectiveness of the policy depends significantly on how roles are redesigned and how knowledge governance mechanisms are developed at the institutional level. It thus reinforces the central argument of this chapter that the institutionalization of "silver knowledge" is not merely about expanding human resources, but about transitioning toward a model of intergenerational knowledge governance.

6. DISCUSSION

The findings indicate that current policies have taken initial steps toward re engaging senior educators and social experts within the education system. However, the analysis also shows that the prevailing policy approach remains largely focused on expanding the labor supply, rather than being fully transformed into a knowledge governance strategy. In this sense, "silver knowledge" continues to operate as a form of extended labor, rather than being positioned as a strategic intellectual asset to be systematically leveraged, accumulated, and transferred. The following discussion elaborates on the theoretical and policy implications of these findings.

6.1. Multi Level Policy Structure and Limits of Institutional Alignment

The findings reinforce the argument that policies concerning retired educators in Vietnam are shaped within a multi level institutional structure, including the macro level of legal frameworks, the meso level of policy design, and the micro level of implementation practices.

However, contrary to the expectations of multi level governance models, the alignment across these levels remains relatively weak. While macro level legal documents create an enabling policy space, the processes of specification at the meso level and implementation at the micro level have not developed sufficiently robust mechanisms to transform individual knowledge into organizational knowledge.

This finding contributes to existing literature by highlighting that, in developing country contexts, policy challenges are not limited to design issues but also involve the capacity to connect institutional levels effectively.

6.2. The Gap between Knowledge Objectives and Policy Instruments

A key finding of the study is the existence of a structural gap between policy objectives and implementation instruments. Although policies aim to leverage "silver knowledge", the instruments employed are primarily administrative, focusing on contracts, working time, and remuneration. This reflects a common tendency in policy systems, where abstract objectives such as knowledge are difficult to translate into concrete instruments.

From a knowledge governance perspective, this suggests that experiential knowledge has not yet been adequately codified, resulting in reliance on individuals and limiting sustainability at the organizational level. Evidence from institutional level feedback further illustrates this gap.

Several stakeholders noted that if extending the working age is limited to prolonging employment duration without redesigning roles, senior educators may continue to perform all traditional responsibilities, including teaching, administration, and research targets. This not only reduces the effectiveness of leveraging experiential knowledge but also imposes unnecessary burdens and fails to reflect the true value of "silver knowledge". These observations reinforce the argument that current policies remain oriented toward labor extension rather than knowledge governance.

6.3. Dominance of Administrative Logic in Policy Thinking

The analysis of stakeholder feedback reveals a consistent pattern in which policy discussions are predominantly framed through a labor management perspective. This reflects the dominance of administrative logic in policy making processes.

As a consequence, strategic knowledge related dimensions, such as mentoring, experience transfer, and the development of organizational knowledge, are largely absent from policy debates. This suggests that "silver knowledge" has not yet been established as an independent policy category but is instead subsumed within traditional labor management frameworks. This finding highlights a theoretical gap, namely the limited integration of knowledge governance perspectives into education policy analysis.

6.4. Educational Autonomy and the Need for Institutional Capacity

The expansion of institutional autonomy is a notable feature of current policy. However, the findings indicate that this increased autonomy is not accompanied by a corresponding development of institutional capacity, particularly in the area of knowledge governance. This creates a policy paradox: educational institutions are granted greater decision making authority, yet lack the tools and institutional arrangements necessary to effectively utilize "silver knowledge".

Evidence from practice suggests that in the absence of clear guidance on role redesign, increased autonomy may lead to uneven implementation across institutions. For example, without explicit role differentiation, senior educators may continue to engage heavily in teaching and administrative tasks, while strategically valuable roles such as mentoring, academic advising, and policy consultation remain underutilized. This indicates that institutional autonomy, without accompanying knowledge governance capacity, may reduce policy effectiveness.

6.5. Positioning Vietnam in the International Context

A comparison with international models reveals that Vietnam is currently in the initial stage of institutionalizing "silver knowledge" within its education system. While many nations have developed relatively comprehensive mechanisms to sustain, retain, and transfer knowledge from their senior scholar workforce, policies in Vietnam currently focus primarily on extending the labor market participation of this demographic rather than fostering an intergenerational knowledge management ecosystem. In the United States, numerous universities have established Emeritus Professor programs as formal academic institutions dedicated to retired faculty. Within these models, the role of senior faculty is not confined to teaching but extends to research mentoring, academic advising, peer review, and supporting the maintenance of the institution's academic networks (Kezar & Sam, 2010). Recent studies also indicate that emeritus faculty are increasingly recognized as a vital source of institutional memory, contributing to the preservation of academic continuity and facilitating knowledge transfer in an era where universities confront workforce volatility and generational shifts in academia (McMurray et al., 2022). This underscores an approach that conceptualizes "silver knowledge" as a strategic knowledge asset rather than merely a supplementary post-retirement labor supply. In Japan, policies regarding the re-employment of older workers and the senior expert system are relatively well-integrated into the national human resource management strategy against a backdrop of rapid population aging (OECD, 2018). Far from just prolonging labor market participation, these mechanisms target the maintenance of knowledge continuity and mitigate the risk of institutional knowledge loss when senior experts exit the system. Within higher education, the mobilization of retired faculty is often coupled with roles in mentoring, research support, and academic advising for the younger generation. Compared to Japan, policy in Vietnam remains skewed toward administrative logic and labor management, while mechanisms for intergenerational knowledge transfer have yet to be fully institutionalized. Meanwhile, in many European countries, communities of practice, lifelong learning models, and knowledge management systems in higher education are utilized as intermediary institutions to catalyze knowledge-sharing processes across generations of faculty (Wenger, 1998; European Commission, 2012). These models emphasize that the retention of institutional knowledge depends not only on labor policies but also requires the development of knowledge management infrastructure, a culture of knowledge sharing, and intergenerational collaboration mechanisms within academic organizations. This indicates that "silver knowledge" is not merely a human resource issue but a matter of knowledge management and institutional capacity building. These disparities suggest that Vietnam is currently transitioning from an "elderly labor utilization" model toward an "intergenerational knowledge management" model. However, this transitional state also opens up opportunities for Vietnam to construct models tailored to its unique institutional and educational culture, rather than blindly replicating existing international frameworks. In the context of university reform and an increasingly visible aging academic workforce, developing mentoring mechanisms, institutional knowledge retention, and intergenerational communities of practice could form a vital foundation for the future institutionalization of "silver knowledge".

6.6. Theoretical Contribution

This study contributes to the field of education policy analysis by proposing an integrated approach in which policy is understood as a dynamic process of interaction across institutional levels rather than a static product. Specifically, the study advances a multi level analytical framework while incorporating a knowledge governance perspective that shifts the focus from human resources to intellectual assets through the conceptualization of “silver knowledge” as a strategic resource within the education system.

The study also clarifies the existence of two parallel flows in the institutionalization process, namely top down policy flow and bottom up knowledge flow, and demonstrates that policy effectiveness depends on the degree of alignment and balance between these flows. Another important conceptual contribution lies in the initial positioning of “silver knowledge” as an independent policy category, opening new avenues for analysis in the context of population ageing. Furthermore, by providing empirical evidence from Vietnam, the study contributes to diversifying the academic discourse, which has been largely dominated by developed country contexts. Furthermore, by providing empirical evidence from Vietnam, the study contributes to diversifying the academic context, which is currently dominated by developed nations. “Silver knowledge” is not merely personal expertise; it represents a form of institutional memory that helps sustain academic continuity, organizational culture, and the adaptive capacity of the education system amid demographic transition

The findings indicate that the institutionalization of “silver knowledge” in Vietnam is occurring within a transitional state characterized by the coexistence of two logics: labor management and knowledge governance. However, the dominance of administrative logic, together with limitations in institutional capacity, has constrained the completion of this transition.

This situation underscores the need for deeper policy reforms aimed at moving from a model of expanding human resources toward one of building an intergenerational knowledge ecosystem. More importantly, the study highlights that the core challenge lies not in the absence of policy, but in the capacity to transform knowledge into an object that can be systematically recognized, accumulated, and governed within institutional structures.

6.7. Research Limitations

As this study relies primarily on the analysis of policy documents, the findings reflect policy logic and institutional discourse rather than the direct experiences of relevant stakeholders. Subsequent studies could be expanded by conducting interviews with retired educators, institutional leaders, and policymakers to gain a deeper verification of the implementation dynamics.

7. CONCLUSION AND POLICY IMPLICATIONS

7.1. Conclusion

This chapter has examined the institutionalization of "silver knowledge" in Vietnam's education system through a multi level policy analysis approach, drawing on legal documents, draft policies, and consultation processes.

The findings indicate that Vietnam has made an important step in recognizing and mobilizing senior educators as a valuable resource within the education system. However, the analysis also shows that current policy approaches continue to operate primarily within a labor management framework and have not yet transformed knowledge into a strategic asset. In other words, existing policies have largely focused on enabling participation, rather than designing a knowledge ecosystem. This gap reflects a broader institutional challenge, namely the absence of mechanisms through which knowledge can be systematically accumulated, shared, and reproduced.

From a broader perspective, the study suggests that Vietnam is currently in a critical transitional phase, characterized by the coexistence and interaction of two logics: labor management and knowledge governance. Advancing this transition is not only essential for improving the efficiency of human resource utilization, but also plays a key role in building a flexible, lifelong learning oriented, and sustainable education system.

More importantly, the Vietnamese case demonstrates that the central challenge in institutionalizing "silver knowledge" does not lie in the absence of policy, but in the capacity to transform knowledge into an object that can be governed within institutional structures. This represents a key direction for future research and policy reform.

7.2. Policy Implications

The findings suggest that effectively leveraging "silver knowledge" requires not merely technical adjustments in policy, but a systemic shift from a labor management approach toward intergenerational knowledge governance. Based on this perspective, several key policy directions are proposed.

7.2.1. Redesigning Roles Rather than Extending Positions

A key policy implication is the need to move from extending working duration to redesigning roles of contribution. International experience suggests that policy effectiveness depends on the ability to assign roles that align with the strengths of senior educators, rather than maintaining all traditional responsibilities.

Accordingly, policies should allow senior educators to take on specialized roles such as academic advisors, mentors, research reviewers, or policy consultants. This approach not only enhances the effective use of "silver knowledge" but also facilitates generational transition within the academic workforce.

7.2.2. Shifting from Labor Management to Knowledge Governance

Policy should shift its focus from labor management, which emphasizes working conditions and administrative obligations, to knowledge governance, where knowledge is treated as a strategic asset to be systematically leveraged, accumulated, and disseminated.

This involves formally establishing academic mentoring roles for senior educators and developing intergenerational knowledge transfer programs that facilitate the sharing of expertise across generations. In addition, expanding the involvement of senior educators in research, curriculum development, and quality enhancement activities can broaden their contributions beyond traditional teaching roles.

These measures not only enhance the utilization of "silver knowledge" but also support the transformation of individual knowledge into organizational knowledge, thereby strengthening the learning and innovation capacity of the education system.

7.2.3. Developing Intermediary Knowledge Institutions

An important finding of the study is the absence of intermediary structures. Therefore, policy should prioritize the development of such mechanisms to connect individual knowledge with organizational knowledge.

This includes establishing knowledge repositories to store teaching materials, professional experience, and academic resources, as well as fostering communities of practice that facilitate interaction between senior and early career educators. The development of formal mentoring programs within educational institutions is also essential to support systematic knowledge transfer.

These intermediary structures not only serve as bridges but also strengthen bottom up knowledge flows within the policy system.

7.2.4. Designing Incentive Mechanisms Aligned with Knowledge Value

In addition to existing remuneration schemes, policy should develop recognition mechanisms that reflect the intellectual and academic contributions of senior educators.

This may include honorary titles such as emeritus professor or senior advisor, as well as formal recognition systems that acknowledge contributions in mentoring, academic review, and policy engagement. Creating opportunities for continued participation in research, publication, and training activities is also important for sustaining and enhancing accumulated knowledge.

Such mechanisms not only provide motivation but also contribute to positioning "silver knowledge" as a valued asset within the education system.

7.2.5. Strengthening Governance Infrastructure and Multi Level Coordination

To address the identified systemic risks, it is necessary to develop a coherent and effective governance infrastructure. This includes establishing data systems to monitor teaching and adjunct activities, thereby ensuring transparency and accountability.

At the same time, evaluation criteria should be redesigned to focus on quality and knowledge contribution rather than relying solely on traditional quantitative indicators. In addition, multi dimensional feedback mechanisms involving students, colleagues, and institutions should be developed to enhance evaluation processes and inform policy adjustments.

More importantly, strengthening coordination across policy levels is essential to ensure consistency and effectiveness in implementation within a multi level institutional context.

7.2.6. Linking "Silver Knowledge" with Digital Transformation in Education

In the context of rapid digital transformation in education, "silver knowledge" can be more effectively leveraged through technological platforms. In this regard, it is important to develop digital learning materials and open educational resources to store and disseminate knowledge. Encouraging senior educators to engage in online teaching and distance education can also extend their influence beyond traditional physical settings.

Moreover, promoting the documentation and digitization of experiential knowledge can contribute to the preservation and sustainable transfer of knowledge across the education system.

7.2.7. The Need to Build an Intergenerational Knowledge Ecosystem

Taken together, these policy directions suggest that policy interventions should not remain fragmented but should instead move toward the development of an intergenerational knowledge ecosystem. Within such a system, knowledge is systematically accumulated, shared, and reproduced; actors across different levels are connected through intermediary structures; and knowledge generated from practice is reintegrated into policy making processes.

This represents a fundamental condition for transforming "silver knowledge" from a latent resource into a strategic asset within the education system.

Note

AI tools were used to refine terminology and improve academic English. All content, analysis, and interpretations remain the responsibility of the authors.

REFERENCES

Altbach, P. G., Reisberg, L., & Rumbley, L. E. (2009). *Trends in global higher education: Tracking an academic revolution.* UNESCO.

Becker, G. S. (1993). *Human capital: A theoretical and empirical analysis, with special reference to education* (3rd ed.). University of Chicago Press. DOI: 10.7208/chicago/9780226041223.001.0001

B Giáo d c và Đào t o. (2024). *Quy t đ nh s 1559/QĐ-BGDĐT ngày 04 tháng 6 năm 2024 v vi c xét thăng h ng ch c danh ngh nghi p, b nhi m ch c danh ngh nghi p, x p lương, nâng b c lương, ngh hưu, kéo dài th i gian công tác đ i v i viên ch c đơn v s nghi p công l p tr c thu c B Giáo d c và Đào t o.* [Decision No. 1559/QĐ-BGDĐT on professional title promotion, appointment, salary arrangement, retirement, and extension of working duration for public employees under the Ministry of Education and Training].

B Giáo d c và Đào t o. (2026). *Báo cáo t ng h p, gi i trình ti p thu ý ki n góp ý đ i v i D th o Thông tư quy đ nh v nhà giáo h p đ ng toàn th i gian sau khi ngh hưu và nhà giáo th nh gi ng.* [Report on synthesis and response to stakeholder feedback on the Draft Circular on post-retirement contracted teachers and visiting lecturers].

B Giáo d c và Đào t o. (2026). *D th o Thông tư quy đ nh v nhà giáo h p đ ng toàn th i gian sau khi ngh hưu và nhà giáo th nh gi ng (ngày 23 tháng 3 năm 2026).* [Draft Circular on full-time contracted teachers after retirement and adjunct/visiting lecturers].

Chính ph Vi t Nam. (1994). *Ngh đ nh s 32-CP ngày 04 tháng 4 năm 1994 c a Chính ph v ch đ đ i v i cán b , công ch c ngh hưu.* [Decree No. 32-CP on policies for retired public officials and employees].

Đ i h c Đà N ng. (n.d.). *Quy t đ nh s a đ i, b sung m t s đi u quy đ nh v ngh hưu, kéo dài th i gian công tác đ i v i viên ch c và ngư i lao đ ng.* [Decision on amendments to regulations on retirement and extension of working duration for employees at the University of Da Nang].

Davenport, T. H., & Prusak, L. (1998). *Working knowledge: How organizations manage what they know.* Harvard Business School Press.

Eraut, M. (2000). Non-formal learning and tacit knowledge in professional work. *The British Journal of Educational Psychology, 70*(1), 113–136. DOI: 10.1348/000709900158001 PMID: 10765570

European Commission. (2012). Rethinking education: Investing in skills for better socio-economic outcomes. *European Union.*

European Commission. (2012). *Rethinking education: Investing in skills for better socio-economic outcomes.* European Commission. https://eur-lex.europa.eu/legal-content/EN/TXT/?uri=CELEX:52012DC0669

Hill, M., & Hupe, P. (2002). Implementing public policy: Governance in theory and practice. *Sage (Atlanta, Ga.).*

Kezar, A., & Sam, C. (2010). Understanding the new majority of non-tenure-track faculty in higher education. *ASHE Higher Education Report, 36*(4), 1–133. DOI: 10.1002/aehe.3604

Marginson, S., & Rhoades, G. (2002). Beyond national states, markets, and systems of higher education: A glonacal agency heuristic. *Higher Education, 43*(3), 281–309. DOI: 10.1023/A:1014699605875

McMurray, A. J., Islam, M. M., Sarros, J. C., & Pirola-Merlo, A. (2022). Knowledge retention and transfer in ageing academic workforces: Challenges and opportunities for universities. *Journal of Higher Education Policy and Management, 44*(5), 543–558. DOI: 10.1080/1360080X.2022.2057104

Nonaka, I., & Takeuchi, H. (1995). *The knowledge-creating company: How Japanese companies create the dynamics of innovation.* Oxford University Press. DOI: 10.1093/oso/9780195092691.001.0001

OECD. (2018). *Working better with age.* OECD Publishing., DOI: 10.1787/9789264201996-

OECD. (2019). *Working better with age.* OECD Publishing., DOI: 10.1787/c4d4f66a-

Organisation for Economic Co-operation and Development (OECD). (2018). *Working better with age.* OECD Publishing., DOI: 10.1787/9789264201996-

Polanyi, M. (1966). *The tacit dimension.* University of Chicago Press.

Qu c h i Vi t Nam. (2018). *Lu t Giáo d c đ i h c (s a đ i, b sung).* [Law on Higher Education (amended)].

Qu c h i Vi t Nam. (2025). *Lu t Nhà giáo ngày 16 tháng 6 năm 2025.* [Law on Teachers].

Rowley, J. (2000). Is higher education ready for knowledge management? *International Journal of Educational Management, 14*(7), 325–333. DOI: 10.1108/09513540010378978

Trư ng Đ i h c Khoa h c – Đ i h c Hu . (n.d.). *Thông báo s 10330/TB-ĐHKH v k t lu n c a Hi u trư ng t i cu c h p xét ký h p đ ng lao đ ng đ i v i cán b có h c hàm Giáo sư, Phó Giáo sư, trình đ Ti n sĩ đ tu i ngh hưu*. [Notice No. 10330/TB-ĐHKH on conclusions regarding labor contract signing for retired professors, associate professors, and PhD holders].

Trư ng Đ i h c Y Dư c – Đ i h c Hu . (n.d.). *Quy t đ nh ban hành quy đ nh v h p đ ng lao đ ng v i ngư i lao đ ng cao tu i t i Trư ng Đ i h c Y Dư c, Đ i h c Hu* . [Decision on regulations for labor contracts with senior employees at the University of Medicine and Pharmacy, Hue University].

Wenger, E. (1998). *Communities of practice: Learning, meaning, and identity*. Cambridge University Press. DOI: 10.1017/CBO9780511803932

Wenger, E. (1998). *Communities of practice: Learning, meaning, and identity*. Cambridge University Press., DOI: 10.1017/CBO9780511803932

World Health Organization. (2002). *Active ageing: A policy framework*. WHO.

Compilation of References

Aayog, N. (2021). *CSR and Voluntary Sector Partnerships: Assessment Report 2020–21*. Government of India.

Abu-Zaineh, M., Arfa, C., Ventelou, B., Ben Romdhane, H., & Moatti, J.-P. (2014). Fairness in healthcare finance and delivery: What about Tunisia? *Health Policy and Planning*, *29*(4), 433–442. 10.1093/heapol/czt029. DOI: 10.1093/heapol/czt029

Actuarial Standards Board. (2014). *Actuarial Standard of Practice No. 48: Life settlements mortality* (Effective April 30, 2014).

ADB. (2023). *Asian Development Outlook 2023: Toward Inclusive Aging*. Asian Development Bank.

Adel Ben Youssef. (2024). *Accelerating the Progress of Tunisia Towards the Sustainable Development Goals* (Policy Research Report, Issue. https://www.arabdevelopmentportal.org/sites/default/files/2025-04/PRR%2053%20-%20Accelerating%20the%20Progress%20of%20Tunisia%20Towards%20the%20Sustainable%20Development%20Goals.pdf

Age Platform Europe. (2022). *Silver economy and ageing well: Report on co-design approaches for older adult inclusion in product and service development*. Age Platform Europe.

Agency for Cultural Affairs, Government of Japan. (2015). *Handbook for facilities and management of cultural properties*. https://www.bunka.go.jp/seisaku/bunkazai/hokoku/pdf/setchi_kanri_handbook.pdf

Akyol Güner, T., & Ulama, G. (2025). Avrupa ve Türkiye'de yaşlı bakım modellerinin karşılaştırmalı analizi: Türkiye için bir model önerisi [Comparative Analysis of Elderly Care Models in Europe and Türkiye: A Model Proposal for Türkiye]. *Yaşlı Sorunları Araştırma Dergisi (YSAD)* [EIRJ]. *Elderly Issues Research Journal*, *18*(2), 130–146. DOI: 10.46414/yasad.1711656

Al Ali, A. S. (2025). Exploring the interplay of creativity, innovation, exploration, and artificial intelligence: A conceptual analysis. *International Journal of Technology Innovation and Management, 5*(2), 40–57.

Altbach, P. G., Reisberg, L., & Rumbley, L. E. (2009). *Trends in global higher education: Tracking an academic revolution*. UNESCO.

Amin, C., Sigit, A. A., Saputra, A., Samson, M. G. M., & Sattar, F. (2026). Beyond access: Understanding digital platform adoption in Indonesia's informal economy. *Digital Geography and Society, 10*, 100162. DOI: 10.1016/j.diggeo.2026.100162

Anderson, S. J., Ghys, P. D., Ombam, R., & Hallett, T. B. (2018). Frontloading HIV financing maximizes the achievable impact of HIV prevention. *Journal of the International AIDS Society, 21*(3), e25087. DOI: 10.1002/jia2.25087 PMID: 29498234

Arfa, C., & Achouri, H. (2008). *Tunisia: good practice in expanding health care coverage. Lessons from reforms in a country in transition: Lessons from reforms in low-and middle-income countries.* (World Bank, Ed.) https://documents.worldbank.org/pt/publication/documents-reports/documentdetail/460481468150871322

Armendáriz, B., & Morduch, J. (2010). *The economics of microfinance* (2nd ed.). MIT Press.

Askari, M., Ray, S., & Suri, S. (2026). Behavioral barriers to blue economy reform: A policy synthesis on ESG, emissions, and governance. *Marine Policy, 184*, 106938. DOI: 10.1016/j.marpol.2025.106938

Atasü Topcuoğlu, R. (2021). Gender inequality, the welfare state, disability, and distorted commodification of care in Türkiye. *New Perspectives on Turkey, 66*, 61–87. DOI: 10.1017/npt.2020.35

Austin, J. E., & Seitanidi, M. M. (2012). Collaborative value creation: A review of partnering between nonprofits and businesses. *Nonprofit and Voluntary Sector Quarterly, 41*(5), 726–758. DOI: 10.1177/0899764012450777

Australian Securities Exchange. (2024). Investing in A-REITs. https://www.asx.com.au/investors/learn-about-our-investment-solutions/a-reits

Avdic, D., Kunz, J. S., Méndez, S. J., & Wiśniewska, M. (2026). Does telemedicine technology affect prescribing quality in primary care? The case of antibiotics. *Journal of Health Economics, 105*, 103096. DOI: 10.1016/j.jhealeco.2025.103096 PMID: 41411812

Ayadi, I., & Zouari, S. (2017). Out-of-pocket health spending and equity implications in Tunisia. *Middle East Development Journal, 9*(1), 1–21. DOI: 10.1080/17938120.2017.1293362

Aydın, A. (2024). Türkiye ve seçilmiş Avrupa ülkelerinde evde bakım hizmetlerinin organizasyonu, kapsamı ve içeriği [Organization, Scope and Content of Home Care Services in Türkiye and Selected European Countries]. *Gümüşhane Üniversitesi Sağlık Bilimleri Dergisi, 13*(3), 1408–1421. DOI: 10.37989/gumussagbil.1410883

Badan Pusat Statistik (BPS). (2022). *Statistik penduduk lanjut usia 2022*. Badan Pusat Statistik.

Bansal, N.. (2023). Capitalizing on Conservation: The Synergy Between Financial Gains and Environmental Goals in Impact Investing. In *Green Management*. Nova Science Publishers.

Barković Bojanić, I., Erceg, A., & Damoska Sekuloska, J. (2024). Silver entrepreneurship: A golden opportunity for ageing society. *Economics and Business Review, 10*(1), 153–178. DOI: 10.18559/ebr.2024.1.1068

Basque Government Department of Economic Development. (2023). *Cooperative banking and the silver economy: The Mondragon experience*. Basque Institute of Competition and Cooperation.

Bauer, D., Russ, J., & Zhu, N. (2020). Asymmetric information in secondary insurance markets: Evidence from the life settlements market. *Quantitative Economics, 11*(3), 1143–1175. DOI: 10.3982/QE1333

Baumeister, R. F., & Leary, M. R. (1997). Writing narrative literature reviews. *Review of General Psychology, 1*(3), 311–320. DOI: 10.1037/1089-2680.1.3.311

BAZNAS. (2023). *Annual Report on Social Programs for the Elderly in Indonesia*. National Zakat Agency of Indonesia.

Beard, J. R., Officer, A., de Carvalho, I. A., Sadana, R., Pot, A. M., Michel, J.-P., Lloyd-Sherlock, P., Epping-Jordan, J. E., Peeters, G., Mahanani, W. R., Thiyagarajan, J. A., & Chatterji, S. (2016). The World Report on Ageing and Health: A policy framework for healthy ageing. *Lancet, 387*(10033), 2145–2154. DOI: 10.1016/S0140-6736(15)00516-4 PMID: 26520231

Beazley, H., Boenisch, J., & Harden, D. (2002). *Continuity management: Preserving corporate knowledge and productivity when employees leave*. John Wiley & Sons.

Becker, G. S. (1993). *Human capital: A theoretical and empirical analysis, with special reference to education* (3rd ed.). University of Chicago Press. DOI: 10.7208/chicago/9780226041223.001.0001

Bernard, C., Kolkiewicz, A., & Tang, J. (2024). Optimal surrender policy for reverse mortgage loans. *ASTIN Bulletin, 54*(3), 600–625. DOI: 10.1017/asb.2024.21

Bhatia, D., Mishra, S., Kirubarajan, A., Yanful, B., Allin, S., & Di Ruggiero, E. (2022). Identifying priorities for research on financial risk protection to achieve universal health coverage: A scoping overview of reviews. *BMJ Open, 12*(3), e052041. DOI: 10.1136/bmjopen-2021-052041

Bich, N. N., Dung, N. T. T., Vu, T., Quy, L. T., Tuan, N. A., Binh, N. T. T., Hung, T. N., & Anh, L. V. (2019). Dementia and associated factors among the elderly in Vietnam: A cross-sectional study. *International Journal of Mental Health Systems, 13*(1), 57. DOI: 10.1186/s13033-019-0314-7

Bieszk-Stolorz, B. Dmytrów, K. & Frąckiewicz, E. (2024). Multivariate Analysis of the Sustainable Development of the Silver Economy in the European Union Countries. *Journal of Sustainability, 16*(23), 10703. 10.3390/su162310703

Bieszk-Stolorz, B., Dmytrów, K., & Frąckiewicz, E. (2024). Multivariate analysis of the sustainable development of the silver economy in the European Union countries. *Sustainability (Basel), 16*(23), 10703. DOI: 10.3390/su162310703

Binsar, F., Arief, M., Tjhin, V. U., & Susilowati, I. (2025). Exploring consumer sentiments in telemedicine and telehealth services: Towards an integrated framework for innovation. *Journal of Open Innovation, 11*(1), 100453. DOI: 10.1016/j.joitmc.2024.100453

Birchall, J. (2013a). *Finance in an age of austerity*. Edward Elgar Publishing. DOI: 10.4337/9781781951842

Birchall, J. (2013b). *Resilience in a downturn: The power of financial cooperatives*. International Labour Office.

Bisetti, E., Favero, C. A., Nocera, G., & Tebaldi, C. (2017). A multivariate model of strategic asset allocation with longevity risk. *Journal of Financial and Quantitative Analysis, 52*(5), 2251–2275. DOI: 10.1017/S0022109017000692

Bisson, M., Palmieri, S., Ianniello, A., & Palomba, R. (2023). Academic research in between user needs and industry demands in the context of the silver economy. *Edulearn 23-15th International Conference on Education and New Learning Technologies* 1213-1220. https://re.public.polimi.it/handle/11311/1250739

Blake, D. (2006). *Pension economics*. John Wiley & Sons.

Blake, J. (2008). Chapter UNESCO's 2003 Convention on Intangible Cultural Heritage: The implications of community involvement in 'safeguarding. In *Intangible Heritage* (1st ed.). Routledge., https://doi.org/https://doi.org/10.4324/9780203884973

Bloom, D. E., Canning, D., & Fink, G. (2015). Implications of population ageing for economic growth. *Oxford Review of Economic Policy*, *26*(4), 583–612. DOI: 10.1093/oxrep/grq038

B Giáo d c và Đào t o. (2024). *Quy t đ nh s 1559/QĐ-BGDĐT ngày 04 tháng 6 năm 2024 v vi c xét thăng h ng ch c danh ngh nghi p, b nhi m ch c danh ngh nghi p, x p lương, nâng b c lương, ngh hưu, kéo dài th i gian công tác đ i v i viên ch c đơn v s nghi p công l p tr c thu c B Giáo d c và Đào t o*. [Decision No. 1559/QĐ-BGDĐT on professional title promotion, appointment, salary arrangement, retirement, and extension of working duration for public employees under the Ministry of Education and Training].

B Giáo d c và Đào t o. (2026). *Báo cáo t ng h p, gi i trình ti p thu ý ki n góp ý đ i v i D th o Thông tư quy đ nh v nhà giáo h p đ ng toàn th i gian sau khi ngh hưu và nhà giáo th nh gi ng*. [Report on synthesis and response to stakeholder feedback on the Draft Circular on post-retirement contracted teachers and visiting lecturers].

B Giáo d c và Đào t o. (2026). *D th o Thông tư quy đ nh v nhà giáo h p đ ng toàn th i gian sau khi ngh hưu và nhà giáo th nh gi ng (ngày 23 tháng 3 năm 2026)*. [Draft Circular on full-time contracted teachers after retirement and adjunct/visiting lecturers].

Borissova, V. (2018). Cultural heritage digitization and related intellectual property issues. *Journal of Cultural Heritage*, *34*, 145–150. DOI: 10.1016/j.culher.2018.04.023

Bourdieu, P. (1986). The forms of capital. In Richardson, J. G. (Ed.), *Handbook of theory and research for the sociology of education* (pp. 241–258). Greenwood.

Bousnina, A., & Souli, C. (2024). Le vieillissement de la population tunisienne: caractéristiques et perceptions. *Revue tunisienne de sciences sociales, 1*(150/151), pp. 39-72. ⟨halshs-04705203⟩

Bovaird, T., Van Ryzin, G. G., Loeffler, E., & Parrado, S. (2015). Activating citizens to participate in collective co-production of public services. *Journal of Social Policy*, *44*(1), 1–23. DOI: 10.1017/S0047279414000567

Bowen, G. A. (2009). Document analysis as a qualitative research method. *Qualitative Research Journal*, *9*(2), 27–40. DOI: 10.3316/QRJ0902027

BPS. (2023). *Statistik Penduduk Lanjut Usia Indonesia 2023*. Badan Pusat Statistik.

Bran, F. Popescu, Maria-Loredana, & Stanciu, P. (2016). Perspectives of silver economy in European Union. *Revista de Management Comparat International, 17*(2), 130. https://www.ceeol.com/search/article-detail?id=729831

Briegas, J. J. M., et al. (2021). Silver Economy: A Development Opportunity. Confinia Cephalalgica, 31(2).

Briggs, A. M., Valentijn, P. P., Thiyagarajan, J. A., & de Carvalho, I. A. (2021). Integrated care for older people and the role of health systems. *The Lancet. Healthy Longevity, 2*(9), e581–e592. DOI: 10.1016/S2666-7568(21)00143-0

Brodrick, K., & Mafuya, M. (2005). Effectiveness of the non-profit organisation,'Grandmothers Against Poverty and AIDS'-a study. *Southern African Journal of HIV Medicine, 2005*(19), 37–41. DOI: 10.4102/sajhivmed.v6i2.588

Bromage, M., Foth, M., Osman, K., & Hearn, G. (2025). From innovation theatre to systemic change: The role of intermediaries in design thinking. *Design Studies, 101*, 101360. DOI: 10.1016/j.destud.2025.101360

Buffel, T. (2025). Co-creating Age-Friendly Futures. *Generations Journal, 49*(1), 1–8.

Bui, N. (2019). Implementing policies for the elderly in Vietnam today: Issues and recommendations. Thu Dau Mot University Journal of Science [Th c hi n chính sách đ i v i ngư i cao tu i Vi t Nam hi n nay – V n đ và ki n ngh . *T p chí Khoa h c Đ i h c Th D u M t]*, 2(41), 64–69. https://scholar.dlu.edu.vn/thuvienso/bitstream/DLU123456789/117631/1/43675-529-138046-1-10-20191203.pdf

Butler, R. N. (1980). Ageism: A foreword. *The Journal of Social Issues, 36*(2), 8–11. DOI: 10.1111/j.1540-4560.1980.tb02018.x

Butt, J. (2002). *Playing with history: The historical approach to musical performance*. (Original work published Cambridge University Press)

Butt, S. A. S. Shweta, P., Ingrid, S., Michael, K., Robert & Draheim, D. (2023). A digital collaborative platform for the silver economy: functionalities required by stakeholders in a multinational baltic sea region project. *Digital Government: Research Practise, 4*(2), 1-20. 10.1145/3592618

Butt, S. A., Rava, K., Kangilaski, T., Pappel, I. & Draheim, D. (2021). Designing a digital collaborative platform for the silver economy: Inception and conceptualization. *2021 Eighth International Conference on eDemocracy & eGovernment (ICEDEG)*, 47-54. DOI: 10.1109/ICEDEG52154.2021.9530937

Cajaiba-Santana, G. (2014). Social innovation: Moving the field forward. *Technological Forecasting and Social Change*, *82*, 42–51. DOI: 10.1016/j.techfore.2013.05.008

Çakmur, H. (2015). Frailty among elderly adults in a rural area of Türkiye. *Medical Science Monitor*, *21*, 1232–1242. DOI: 10.12659/MSM.893400 PMID: 25925800

Câmara, S. F., Buarque, B., Pinto, G. P., Ribeiro, T. V., & Soares, J. B. (2024). Innovation policy and public funding to stimulate innovation in knowledge intensive companies: The influence of human and social capital. *Journal of Science and Technology Policy Management*, *15*(2), 418–442. DOI: 10.1108/JSTPM-09-2021-0135

Campbell, J. C., Ikegami, N., & Gibson, M. J. (2010). Lessons from public long-term care insurance in Germany and Japan. *Health Affairs (Project Hope)*, *29*(1), 87–95. DOI: 10.1377/hlthaff.2009.0548

Cang, V. (2008). Preserving Intangible Heritage in Japan: The Role of the Iemoto System. *International Journal of Intangible Heritage*, *3*, 53–63.

Carayannis, E. G., & Campbell, D. F. J. (2009). 'Mode 3' and 'quadruple helix': Toward a 21st century fractal innovation ecosystem. *International Journal of Technology Management*, *46*(3–4), 201–234. DOI: 10.1504/IJTM.2009.023374

Carstensen, L. L. (2021). Integrating cognitive and emotional processing in late life: The case for older adults as resources in an age of uncertainty. *Annual Review of Psychology*, *72*, 45–70. DOI: 10.1146/annurev-psych-092220-093702

Carvalho, J. V. F., & Araújo, G. G. (2024). A feasibility analysis of reverse mortgages in Brazil. *Journal of Urban Management*, *13*(1), 74–87. DOI: 10.1016/j.jum.2023.11.003

Casal-Otero, L., Catala, A., Fernández-Morante, C., Taboada, M., Cebreiro, B., & Mato-Abad, V. (2023). AI literacy in K-12 and implications for adult education: A systematic review. *Computers and Education: Artificial Intelligence*, *4*, 100130. DOI: 10.1016/j.caeai.2023.100130

Cassell, H. M., Rose, E. S., Moon, T. D., Bello-Manga, H., Aliyu, M. H., & Mutale, W. (2022). Strengthening research capacity through an intensive training program for biomedical investigators from low-and middle-income countries: The Vanderbilt Institute for Research Development and Ethics (VIRDE). *BMC Medical Education*, *22*(1), 97. DOI: 10.1186/s12909-022-03162-8 PMID: 35164739

CBRE Research. (2024). Australian Seniors Housing. CBRE Australia. https://www.cbre.com.au/insights/reports/australian-seniors-housing

Centre for Ageing Better. (2023). *Annual review 2022–23: Creating a society where everyone can age well.* Centre for Ageing Better.

Chadha, N., & Gopal, K. S. Uplabdh, K., Oommen C, Kumar, S. & Singh, S.. (2025). *UHC for the Silver Dividend: Building Health Systems for an Ageing India.* https://www.orfonline.org/

Chen, M. A., Jhabvala, R., & Kanbur, R. (2015). *Informal economy and development.* Routledge.

Chhillar, I., Sandhu, S., Parida, S., & Majewski, P. (2025). Certification for solar panel reuse: A systematic review of cross-sector practices and gaps. *Sustainability (Basel), 17*(13), 5995. DOI: 10.3390/su17135995

China National Committee on Ageing. (2022). *Report on the Fifth National Survey on Living Conditions of Urban and Rural Older Adults.*

Chính ph Vi t Nam. (1994). *Ngh đ nh s 32-CP ngày 04 tháng 4 năm 1994 c a Chính ph v ch đ đ i v i cán b , công ch c ngh hưu.* [Decree No. 32-CP on policies for retired public officials and employees].

Christiansen, B., & Branch, J. D. (2025). Critical economic implications of global demographic changes.

Cicchiello, A. F., Gallo, S., & Monferrà, S. (2023). Financing the cultural and creative industries through crowdfunding: The role of national cultural dimensions and policies. *Journal of Cultural Economics, 47*(1), 133–175. DOI: 10.1007/s10824-022-09452-9 PMID: 38625194

Claridge, T. (2018). Functions of social capital–bonding, bridging, linking. *Social capital research, 20*(1), 1-7.

Colombo, F., Llena Nozal, A., Mercier, J., & Tjadens, F. (2011). *Help wanted? Providing and paying for long-term care.* OECD Publishing., DOI: 10.1787/9789264097759-en

Cominelli, F., & Greffe, X. (2012). Intangible cultural heritage: Safeguarding for creativity. *City, Culture and Society, 3*(4), 245–250. DOI: 10.1016/j.ccs.2012.10.003

Commission, E. (2021). *Silver Economy: Opportunities for Older People and the Economy.* Publications Office of the European Union.

Consumer Action Law Centre. (2017, July 10). How retirement villages can swallow your nest egg. The New Daily. https://www.thenewdaily.com.au/finance/retirement/2017/07/10/retirement-village-costs

Consumer Financial Protection Bureau. (2023). *§ 1026.33 Requirements for reverse mortgages*. https://www.consumerfinance.gov/rules-policy/regulations/1026/33/

Cook, K. (2017). *Social capital: Theory and research*. Routledge.

Cooney, T. M., Vũ, T. D., Tr n, H. H., Vũ, V. T., Lê, H. N. T., Huỳnh, T. K. H., T , H. A., Đinh, N. K. P., & Huỳnh, M. N. (2019). *Entrepreneurship book of Vietnamese cases*. TU Dublin. https://doi.org/10.21427/baw4-h186

Corporation, N. S. D. (2022). *Silver Skills Initiative: Annual Evaluation Report 2021–22*. NSDC.

Costa Font, J., Jiménez Martín, S., & Vilaplana Prieto, C. (2022). Do public caregiving subsidies and supports affect the provision of care and transfers? *Journal of Health Economics*, *84*, 102639. Advance online publication. DOI: 10.1016/j.jhealeco.2022.102639 PMID: 35671607

Costa, G. (2020). Intergenerational homesharing programmes: A piece of the'ageing in place'puzzle?. Interações: Sociedade e as novas modernidades, (38), 11-42.

Coughlin, J. F. (2017). *The Longevity Economy: Unlocking the World's Fastest-Growing, Most Misunderstood Market*. PublicAffairs.

Crane, A., Palazzo, G., Spence, L. J., & Matten, D. (2014). Contesting the value of creating shared value. *California Management Review*, *56*(2), 130–153. DOI: 10.1525/cmr.2014.56.2.130

Creswell, J. W., & Creswell, J. D. (2018). *Research design: Qualitative, quantitative, and mixed methods approaches* (5th ed.). Sage.

Crisp, G., & Cruz, I. (2009). Mentoring college students: A critical review of the literature between 1990 and 2007. *Research in Higher Education*, *50*(6), 525–545. DOI: 10.1007/s11162-009-9130-2

Czaja, S. J., Boot, W. R., Charness, N., & Rogers, W. A. (2019). *Designing for older adults: Principles and creative human factors approaches* (3rd ed.). CRC Press. DOI: 10.1201/b22189

Czaja, S. J., Boot, W. R., Charness, N., & Rogers, W. A. (2021). Designing for older adults in the digital age. *Human-Computer Interaction*, *36*(5–6), 371–402. DOI: 10.1080/07370024.2021.1884627

Dabare, S., Rajapaksha, S., & Munaweera, I. (2025). Lifecycle analysis of nanotechnology-enhanced soft materials in the circular economy. *Molecular Systems Design & Engineering*, *10*(10), 799–816. DOI: 10.1039/D5ME00067J

Daghaghele, E., Angali, K. A., Kamyari, N., & Seyedtabib, M. (2025). Marginalized two part model for analyzing multilevel semicontinuous medical costs in Iranian households. *Scientific Reports, 15*(1), 7491. DOI: 10.1038/s41598-025-91309-0

Đ i h c Đà N ng. (n.d.). *Quy t đ nh s a đ i, b sung m t s đi u quy đ nh v ngh hưu, kéo dài th i gian công tác đ i v i viên ch c và ngư i lao đ ng*. [Decision on amendments to regulations on retirement and extension of working duration for employees at the University of Da Nang].

Dang, T. A. T., & Nguyen, T. H. (2021). Trends in population aging and social policy for elderly people in Vietnam. *VNU Journal of Science: Policy and Management Studies, 37*(2), 12–20. DOI: 10.25073/2588-1116/vnupam.4304

Dao, A. T. M., Nguyen, V. T., Nguyen, H. V., & Nguyen, L. T. (2018). Factors associated with depression among the elderly living in urban Vietnam. *BioMed Research International, 2018*(1), 2370284. DOI: 10.1155/2018/2370284 PMID: 30596085

Das, T., Holland, P., Ahmed, M., & Husain, L. (2021). Sustainable Development Goal 3: Good Health and Well-being. In Das, T., & Nayar, P. D. (Eds.), *South-East Asia Eye Health: Systems, Practices, and Challenges* (pp. 61–78). Springer Singapore., DOI: 10.1007/978-981-16-3787-2_4

Davenport, T. H., & Prusak, L. (1998). *Working knowledge: How organizations manage what they know*. Harvard Business School Press.

Davidoff, T., Gerhard, P., & Post, T. (2023). Reverse mortgage usage and racial disparities in the United States. *Journal of Urban Economics, 135*, 103542. Advance online publication. DOI: 10.1016/j.jue.2023.103542

de Siqueira Silva, Í., de Araújo, A. J., Lopes, R. H., Silva, C. R. D. V., Xavier, P. B., de Figueirêdo, R. C., . . . de Araújo Nunes, V. M. (2024). Digital home care interventions and quality of primary care for older adults: a scoping. *PLOS ONE*. 10.1371/journal.pone.0316278

De Witte, J., and Regenmortel, T.V. (2023). *Silver empowerment: Fostering strengths and connections for an age-friendly society. Leuven University Press, 2023.* Leuven University Press. https://lup.be/book/silver-empowerment/

DeLong, D. W. (2004). *Lost knowledge: Confronting the threat of an aging workforce*. Oxford University Press. DOI: 10.1093/acprof:oso/9780195170979.001.0001

Delors, J., Al Mufti, I., Amagi, I., Carneiro, R., Chung, F., Geremek, B., Gorham, W., Kornhauser, A., Manley, M., Quero, M. P., Savane, M. A., Singh, K., Stavenhagen, R., Suhr, M. W., & Nanzhao, Z. (1996). *Learning: The treasure within. Report to UNESCO of the International Commission on Education for the Twenty-first Century*. UNESCO.

Direktorat Jenderal Pendidikan Tinggi (DIKTI). (2020). Buku panduan Merdeka Belajar – Kampus Merdeka. Kementerian Pendidikan dan Kebudayaan.

Doğusan, A. R. (2019). Türkiye'de evde sağlık hizmetleri ile ilgili mevzuat ve gelişimi [Legislation and Development of Home Health Services in Türkiye]. *Ankara Medical Journal, 19*(3), 684–693. DOI: 10.17098/amj.624563

Eager, B., Maritz, A., & Millemann, J. (2022). The silver economy on wheels: A narrative review of the mature-aged, hypermobile gig worker phenomena. *Small Enterprise Research, 29*(1), 68–85. DOI: 10.1080/13215906.2022.2032295

Edmiston, D., & Nicholls, A. (2018). Social Impact Bonds: The role of private capital in outcome-based commissioning. *Journal of Social Policy, 47*(1), 57–76. DOI: 10.1017/S0047279417000125

Egeland, T., Heinonen, K., & Stensaker, I. G. (2026). The silver economy: A business perspective on the ageing society. *Journal of Service Research*. Advance online publication. DOI: 10.1177/10946705251397563

Elgazzar, H. A. Chokri, S., Nisreen, M., Mehdi, S.I., Djavad, R., Firas, C., Jad, F., Sanaz & Mataria, Awad (2013). Who pays? Out-of-pocket health spending and equity implications in the Middle East and North Africa. *Health, Nutrition Population discussion paper*. http://documents.worldbank.org/curated/en/464431468276384167

Emerson, J. (2003). The blended value proposition: Integrating social and financial returns. *California Management Review, 45*(4), 35–51. DOI: 10.2307/41166187

Empowerment, M. of S. J. and. (2020). *Inspection Report: Registered Old-Age Homes Compliance 2019–20*. Government of India.

Eozenou, P. H.-V. Neelsen, Sven, Smitz, Marc-Francois. (2021). Financial protection in health among the elderly–a global stocktake. *Health Systems Reform, 7*(2), e1911067. 10.1080/23288604.2021.1911067

Eraut, M. (2000). Non-formal learning and tacit knowledge in professional work. *The British Journal of Educational Psychology, 70*(1), 113–136. DOI: 10.1348/000709900158001 PMID: 10765570

Eriksson, E., & Hellström, A. (2021). Multi-actor resource integration: A service approach in public management. *British Journal of Management, 32*(2), 456–472. DOI: 10.1111/1467-8551.12414

Eriksson, S. (2025). *Impact investing. In the Elgar Encyclopedia of Innovation Management.* Edward Elgar.

Estrada, S., Cabrera-Flores, M., León-Pozo, A., & Cota-Cota, C. (2025). Reflecting on challenges and opportunities: Examining the colour economy of innovation and entrepreneurship. In *SHS Web of Conferences* (Vol. 211, Article 07001). EDP Sciences.

Etzkowitz, H., & Leydesdorff, L. (2000). The dynamics of innovation: From national systems and 'Mode 2' to a triple helix of university–industry–government relations. *Research Policy, 29*(2), 109–123. DOI: 10.1016/S0048-7333(99)00055-4

European Commission. (2012). *Rethinking education: Investing in skills for better socio-economic outcomes.* European Commission. https://eur-lex.europa.eu/legal-content/EN/TXT/?uri=CELEX:52012DC0669

European Commission. (2012). Rethinking education: Investing in skills for better socio-economic outcomes. *European Union.*

European Commission. (2018). The Silver Economy Study: How to Stimulate the Economy by Hundreds of Millions of Euros per Year. Publications Office of the European Union. Retrieved from https://digital-strategy.ec.europa.eu/en/library/silver-economy-study-how-stimulate-economy-hundreds-millions-euros-year

European Commission. (2018). *The silver economy.* Publications Office of the European Union.

European Commission. (2018). *The silver economy: Final report.* https://doi.org/ DOI: 10.2759/685036

European Commission. (2018). The silver economy: Final report. Publications Office of the European Union. https://doi.org/DOI: 10.2759/33378

European Commission. (2021). The silver economy and ageing societies. *European Union.*

European Investment Bank. (2025). *Blended finance for active aging: Lessons from EU structural funds.* European Investment Bank.

Evangelene, A. D. C., Siripalli, D. K., & Pothumani, S. (2025). Crowdfunding application using blockchain. DOI: 10.1063/5.0265037

Evers, A. (2005). Mixed welfare systems and hybrid organizations: Changes in the governance and provision of social services. *International Journal of Public Administration, 28*(9-10), 737–748. DOI: 10.1081/PAD-200067318

Eyler, J., & Giles, D. E. (1999). *Where's the learning in service-learning?* Jossey-Bass.

Falk, M. T., & Hagsten, E. (2025). Intangible Cultural Heritage differently exposed across continents. *NPJ Heritage Science, 13*(1), 600. DOI: 10.1038/s40494-025-02169-w

Fan, V. Sharma, J. and Hou, X. (Ed.). (2023). *Financing Primary Health Care for Older Adults: Framework and Applications*. World Bank Group. https://documents1.worldbank.org/curated/en/099025503072337503/pdf/P17583208782960a40bf6804d1758e50f1e.pdf

Fañanás-Biescas, A. P., Ključnikov, A., Bargoni, A., & Ferraris, A. (2025). Senior entrepreneurship and opportunity recognition: A systematic review of the literature. *International Journal of Entrepreneurial Behaviour & Research*, •••, 1–38.

Fandrejewska-Nowakowska, A. (2025). The role of digital competence and trust in technology in inclusive and sustainable e-health development for seniors. *Ekonomia, 31*(3), 43–57. DOI: 10.19195/2658-1310.31.3.3

Fang, M. L., Canham, S. L., Battersby, L., Sixsmith, J., Wada, M., & Sixsmith, A. (2023). Exploring privilege in the digital divide during the COVID-19 pandemic: Implications for digital health equity in older adults. *The Gerontologist, 63*(1), 14–24. DOI: 10.1093/geront/gnab154

Faure, E., Herrera, F., Kaddoura, A.-R., Lopes, H., Petrovsky, A. V., Rahnema, M., & Champion Ward, F. (1972). Learning to be: The world of education today and tomorrow. UNESCO/Harrap.

Federal Ministry of the Interior. Building and Community. (2020). Holistic, Sustainable, Collaborative 50 Years of the Urban Development Support Programme in Germany. Berlin, Germany: Federal Ministry of the Interior, Building and Community. Retrieved from https://www.staedtebaufoerderung.info/EN/home/home_node.html

Fedorko, R., & Mondal, S. R. (2025). The algorithmic alchemist: Transmuting business models for a net-zero future. In *Generative AI for a net-zero economy: Managing climate change and business innovation in the digital era* (pp. 37–55). Springer Nature Singapore. DOI: 10.1007/978-981-96-8015-3_3

Felix, J. (2016). Silver economy: Opportunities and challenges to Brazil adopt the European Union's strategy. *Innovation (Abingdon), 29*(2), 115–133. 10.1080/13511610.2016.1166937. DOI: 10.1080/13511610.2016.1166937

Finland, F. (2025). *The Rise of the Silver Economy: Global Implications of Population Aging*. International Monetary Fund. 10.5089/9798400289583.081.CH002

Fiordelisi, F., Grimaldi, S., Lopez, J. S., Mazzilis, M. C., & Ricci, O. (2022). The beauty of being involved: The case of cooperative banks. *British Journal of Management, 34*(4), 2290–2311. DOI: 10.1111/1467-8551.12698

Flick, U. (2014). *An introduction to qualitative research* (5th ed.). Sage.

Flyvbjerg, B. (2006). Five misunderstandings about case-study research. *Qualitative Inquiry, 12*(2), 219–245. DOI: 10.1177/1077800405284363

Forsyth, P. A., Vetzal, K. R., & Westmacott, G. (2024). Optimal performance of a tontine overlay subject to withdrawal constraints. *ASTIN Bulletin, 54*(1), 94–128. DOI: 10.1017/asb.2023.35

Freeman, R. E. (1984). *Strategic Management: A Stakeholder Approach*. Pitman.

French, M., Kimmitt, J., Wilson, R., Jamieson, D., & Lowe, T. (2023). Social impact bonds and public service reform: Back to the future of New Public Management? *International Public Management Journal, 26*(3), 376–395. DOI: 10.1080/10967494.2022.2050859

Frumence, G., Nyamhanga, T., Mwangu, M., & Hurtig, A. K. (2014). The dependency on central government funding of decentralised health systems: Experiences of the challenges and coping strategies in the Kongwa District, Tanzania. *BMC Health Services Research, 14*(1), 39. DOI: 10.1186/1472-6963-14-39 PMID: 24460781

Fu, K., Zhao, H., & Wang, N. (2023). Optimal investment problem for a hybrid pension with intergenerational risk-sharing and longevity trend under model uncertainty. arXiv. https://doi.org//arXiv.2302.02351DOI: 10.48550

Gabriel-Catalin, T.-T. Felicia-Cătălina Apetroi (Răcoare), Iuliana-Claudia Mihalache. (2023). The Silver Economy and its Importance to Society. *Journal EUFIRE*, 368. https://www.ceeol.com/search/chapter-detail?id=1237215

Galeotti, M., D'Andrassi, E., Savio, R., & Ventimiglia, F. (2024). The intersection of governmental policies and corporate strategies: Population aging and the silver economy. *Corporate Ownership & Control, 21*(4), 117–128. DOI: 10.22495/cocv21i4art10

Gan, L. (2021). *Building Communities for All Ages: Good Intergenerational Practice*. Inner East Primary Care Partnership. Retrived from https://vicpcp.org.au/wp-content/uploads/2022/06/IEPCP-Building-Communities-for-All-Ages-Good-Intergenerational-Practice.pdf

General Statistics Office of Viet Nam, & United Nations Population Fund. (2022). *Older persons in Viet Nam: An analysis of the Population Change and Family Planning Survey 2021*.

Gianfredi, V., Nucci, D., Pennisi, F., Maggi, S., Veronese, N., & Soysal, P. (2025). Aging, longevity, and healthy aging: The public health approach. *Aging Clinical and Experimental Research, 37*(1), 125. DOI: 10.1007/s40520-025-03021-8

Giang, L. T., Nguyen, N. T., Pham, T. T. H., & Phi, P. M. (2023). Factors associated with receipt of informal care among the Vietnamese older persons: Evidence from a national survey. *Frontiers in Public Health, 11*, 1065851. Advance online publication. DOI: 10.3389/fpubh.2023.1065851 PMID: 36969636

Giang, L. T., Pham, T. H. T., & Phi, P. M. (2019). Productive activities of the older people in Vietnam. *Social Science & Medicine, 229*, 32–40. DOI: 10.1016/j.socscimed.2018.09.054 PMID: 30301577

Gianturco, P. (2012). *Grandmother power: A global phenomenon*. PowerHouse Books.

Gibbons, M., Limoges, C., Nowotny, H., Schwartzman, S., Scott, P., & Trow, M. (1994). The new production of knowledge: The dynamics of science and research in contemporary societies. *Sage (Atlanta, Ga.)*.

Gilbert, N., & Brik, A. B. (2022). Family life and the demographic transition in MENA countries: Implications for social policy. *Journal of International and Comparative Social Policy, 38*(1), 15–35. DOI: 10.1017/ics.2021.17

Gilman, L. (2022). 'Our Culture is dying': Safeguarding versus representation in the implementation of the UNESCO ICH Convention. *International Journal of Intangible Heritage, 17*, 40–52.

Glass, T. A., Freedman, M., Carlson, M. C., Hill, J., Frick, K. D., Ialongo, N., & Fried, L. P. (2004). Experience Corps: Design of an intergenerational program to boost social capital and promote the health of an aging society. *Journal of Urban Health : Bulletin of the New York Academy of Medicine, 81*(1), 94–105. DOI: 10.1093/jurban/jth096 PMID: 15047788

Gok Metin, Z., Karadas, C., Balci, C., & Cankurtaran, M. (2019). The perceived caregiver burden among Turkish family caregivers providing care for frail older adults. *Journal of Transcultural Nursing : Official Journal of the Transcultural Nursing Society, 30*(3), 222–230. DOI: 10.1177/1043659618790041 PMID: 30040049

Gök, A., Antai, R., Milošević, N., & Al-Nabki, W. (2022). Building the European Social Innovation Database with Natural Language Processing and Machine Learning. *Scientific Data, 9*(1), 697. DOI: 10.1038/s41597-022-01818-0 PMID: 36371515

Gölçek, A. G. (2024). *Perspectives on the Economics of Aging*. IGI Global. DOI: 10.4018/979-8-3693-7753-6

Gonzales, E., Matz-Costa, C., & Morrow-Howell, N. (2015). Increasing opportunities for the productive engagement of older adults: A response to population aging. *The Gerontologist*, *55*(2), 252–261. DOI: 10.1093/geront/gnu176 PMID: 26035601

Goodkind, D. (2025). *Business opportunities in China's aging society*. CKGSB Knowledge.

Goto, K. (2019). Crafts Policies in Japan. In Mignosa, A., & Kotipalli, P. (Eds.), *A Cultural Economic Analysis of Craft* (pp. 115–127). Springer International Publishing., DOI: 10.1007/978-3-030-02164-1_10

Government Pension Investment Fund. Japan. (2022). *GPIF annual report 2022*. Government Pension Investment Fund.

Grabenwarter, U. (2017). Measuring Impact: A Debate About the Concepts of Profit and Value. In *Principles and Practice of Impact Investing*. Routledge. DOI: 10.4324/9781351284769-5

Greenfield, E. A., Black, K., Buffel, T., & Yeh, J. (2018). Community gerontology: A framework for research, policy, and practice on communities and aging. *The Gerontologist*, *59*(5), 803–810. DOI: 10.1093/geront/gny089 PMID: 30124872

Grigsby v. Russell, 222 U.S. 149 (1911).

Grimsey, D., & Lewis, M. (2007). Public private partnerships and public procurement. *Agenda: A Journal of Policy Analysis and Reform, 14*(2), 171–188. http://doi.org/DOI: 10.22459/AG.14.02.2007

Grinin, L., Grinin, A., & Korotayev, A. (2023). Global aging: An integral problem of the future. How to turn a problem into a development driver? In *Reconsidering the limits to growth: A report to the Russian association of the club of Rome* (pp. 117–135). Springer International Publishing. DOI: 10.1007/978-3-031-34999-7_7

GSO. (2021). *Ngư i cao tu i Vi t Nam: Phân tích t Đi u tra Bi n đ ng dân s và K ho ch hóa gia đình năm 2021. NXB Thanh Niên* [The elderly in Vietnam: Analysis from the 2021 Population Change and Family Planning Survey]. Youth Publishing House.

GSO. (2025). *Thông cáo báo chí v K t qu Đi u tra dân s và nhà gi a kỳ năm 2024 (Công b ngày 06/01/2025)* [Press release on the results of the 2024 Vietnam Intercensal Population and Housing Survey (Published on January 6, 2025)]. General Statistics Office of Vietnam.

Gui, Y., Ma, Y., Chen, Y., Zhou, C., & Xiao, T. (2026). Ecosystem services in UNESCO World Heritage sites: A review of research trends and future directions. *NPJ Heritage Science*, *14*(1), 115. DOI: 10.1038/s40494-026-02380-3

Guo, Q., Zeng, X., & Yuan, L. (2026). How population aging and digital transformation reshape labor income share? Mechanisms of firm-level substitution and urban job expansion. *Economic Modelling*, *158*, 107517. DOI: 10.1016/j.econmod.2026.107517

Gustafsson-Wright, E., Boggild-Jones, I., Segell, D., & Durland, J. (2020). *Impact bonds in developing countries: Early learnings from the field.* Brookings Institution.

Gustafsson-Wright, E., Gardiner, S., & Putcha, V. (2015). *The potential and limitations of impact bonds: Lessons from the first five years of experience worldwide.* Brookings Institution.

Hajizadeh, A., Hafezi, R., Torabi, F., Sari, A. A., & Tajvar, M. (2025). Consequences of Population Ageing on Health Systems: A Conceptual Framework for Policy and Practice. *Ethiopian Journal of Health Sciences*, *35*(1). Advance online publication. DOI: 10.4314/ejhs.v35i1.8

Harper, S. (2014). Economic and social implications of aging societies. *Science*, *346*(6209), 587–591. DOI: 10.1126/science.1254405 PMID: 25359967

Harris, A., Wyn, J., & Younes, S. (2010). Beyond apathetic or activist youth: 'Ordinary' young people and contemporary forms of participation. *Young*, *18*(1), 9–32. DOI: 10.1177/110330880901800103

Hazaea, A. N., Bin-Hady, W. R. A., & Metwally, A. A. (2025). Globalization, multiculturalism, and national identity in Najran's linguistic landscape: A study of English and Arabic in coffee shop signage. *Humanities & Social Sciences Communications*, *12*(1), 1616. DOI: 10.1057/s41599-025-05957-8

Help Age International. (2015). *Ageing population in Vietnam: Policy and practice.* HelpAge International.

HelpAge International. (2022). *Global ageing report.*

HelpAge International. (2023). *Global AgeWatch Insight Report: Southeast Asia.* HelpAge International.

Hevenstone, D., Fraser, A., Hobi, L., & Geuke, G. (2023). Why is impact measurement abandoned in practice? Evidence use in evaluation and contracting for five European Social Impact Bonds. *Evaluation*, *29*(1), 91–109. DOI: 10.1177/13563890221136890

Hill, M., & Hupe, P. (2002). Implementing public policy: Governance in theory and practice. *Sage (Atlanta, Ga.).*

Hodgkin, D., Horgan, C. M., Brown, S. J., Bart, G., & Stewart, M. T. (2023). Financial sustainability of novel delivery models in behavioral health treatment. *The Journal of Mental Health Policy and Economics, 26*(4), 149. PMID: 38113385

HomeEquity Bank. (2025). *CHIP Reverse Mortgage.* https://www.homeequitybank.ca/products/chip-reverse-mortgage/

Hooyman, N. R., & Kiyak, H. A. (2011). *Social gerontology: A multidisciplinary perspective* (9th ed.). Pearson.

Hou, X. Sharma, J. and Zhao, F. (2023). *Silver Opportunity: Building Integrated Services for Older Adults Around Primary Health Care.* World Bank Publications. https://documents1.worldbank.org/curated/en/099025503072337503/pdf/P17583208782960a40bf6804d1758e50f1e.pdf

Hou, X., Sharma, J., & Zhao, F. (2023). *Silver Opportunity: Building Integrated Services for Older Adults Around Primary Health Care.* World Bank. DOI: 10.1596/978-1-4648-1958-2

Household Capital. (2024). *HHC 2024-1 RMBS Trust transaction summary.* Household Capital Australia.

Hua, M. (2024). A Study on the Impact of the Aging Population-Driven Silver Economy on Social Development and Healthcare Systems in Russia. *SHS Web of Conferences, 207*, 04006. https://www.shs-conferences.org/articles/shsconf/abs/2024/27/shsconf_icdeba2024_04006/shsconf_icdeba2024_04006.html

Huegler, N., & Ruch, G. (2022). Risk, vulnerability and complexity: Transitional safeguarding as a reframing of binary perspectives. *Practice, 34*(1), 25–39. DOI: 10.1080/09503153.2021.1932787

Hull, T. H. (2016). Demographic perspectives on Indonesia's future. In Hill, H. (Ed.), *Indonesia rising: The repositioning of Asia's third giant* (pp. 29–56). Institute of Southeast Asian Studies.

Hussain, S., Zardari, S., & Ullah, M. (2025). Systematic Analysis of Blockchain Based Trust Management Frameworks in Crowdfunding. *IEEE Access : Practical Innovations, Open Solutions.*

Hu, W., Li, M., Chi, X., Wang, X., & Khan, A. U. (2024). Intangible cultural heritage research in China from the perspective of intellectual property rights based on bibliometrics and knowledge mapping. *Humanities & Social Sciences Communications, 11*(1), 825. DOI: 10.1057/s41599-024-03314-9

Hwang, B. N., Puntha, P., & Jitanugoon, S. (2025). AI-driven circular transformation: Unlocking sustainable startup success through co-creation dynamics in circular economy ecosystems. *Sustainable Development (Bradford)*, *33*(S1), 245–274. DOI: 10.1002/sd.70001

Hwang, H., Park, C.-W., Kim, H.-K., & Lee, J.-H. (2025). CATS: Cultural-heritage classification using LLMs and distribute model. *NPJ Heritage Science*, *13*(1), 76. DOI: 10.1038/s40494-025-01621-1

IFC. (2024). *IFC Silver Economy Initiative: Southeast Asia Strategy*. International Finance Corporation.

ILO. (2022). *Global employment trends for women: Building back fairer*. International Labor Organization.

IMF. (2023). *Navigating demographic headwinds*. International Monetary Fund.

India, G. of. (2025). *Silver Economy: Status and Opportunities in India*. Ministry of Social Justice.

India, S. and E. B. of. (2021). *Business Responsibility and Sustainability Reporting (BRSR)*. SEBI.

India, T. R. A. of. (2022). *Annual Report on Telecom Services 2021–22*. TRAI.

India, H. (2021). *State of Elderly in India Report 2021: Annual Impact Assessment*. HelpAge India.

India, U. (2017). *Caring for Our Elders: Early Responses—India Ageing Report 2017*. UNFPA.

India, U. (2025). *UHC for the Silver Dividend: Building Health Systems for an Ageing India*. UNFPA India.

Info-communications Media Development Authority, Singapore. (2023). Silver Infocomm Initiative: Annual report 2022–23. IMDA Singapore.

Institut National de la Statistique. (2023). *Enquête Nationale sur le Budget, la consommation et le niveau de vie des ménages*. https://www.ins.tn/enquetes/enquete-nationale-sur-le-budget-la-consommation-et-le-niveau-de-vie-des-menages-2021

Institut National de la Statistique. (2024). *Recensement Général de la Population et de l'Habitat: Bilan Démographique* Tunisie Retrieved from https://www.ins.tn/sites/default/files-ftp3/files/2025-05/Bilan_D%C3%A9mographique.pdf

Inter-American Development Bank. (2025). *FACIL program: Financial inclusion for the silver economy in the Dominican Republic*. Inter-American Development Bank.

International Finance Corporation. (2024a). *IFC provides US$45 million financing and advisory services to Caja 18 to support retirees and low-income women workers.* https://www.ifc.org/en/pressroom/2024/ifc-provides-us-45-million-financing-and-advisory-services-to-caja-18-to-support-retirees-and-low-income-women-workers

International Finance Corporation. (2024b). *IFC invests in Consubanco's historic silver economy bond issuance in Mexico.* International Finance Corporation.

International Finance Corporation. (2024c). *IFC launches Silver Economy Initiative to address growing underserved population in Latin America & the Caribbean.* https://www.ifc.org/en/pressroom/2024/ifc-launches-silver-economy-initiative-to-address-growing-underserved-population-in-latin-america-the-caribbean

International Labour Organization. (2022). *Care at work: Investing in care leave and services for a more gender equal world of work* (L. Addati, U. Cattaneo, & E. Pozzan, Eds.). International Labour Office. https://www.ilo.org/sites/default/files/wcmsp5/groups/public/@dgreports/@dcomm/documents/publication/wcms_838653.pdf

International Labour Organization. (2022). *Care at work: Investing in care leave and services for a more gender equal world.* ILO.

Invest, I. D. B. (2022). *IDB Invest launches its first silver economy social bond to support financial inclusion of seniors in Latin America and the Caribbean.* https://idbinvest.org/en/news-media/idb-invest-launches-its-first-silver-economy-social-bond-support-financial-inclusion

Ismaïl, S., & Nejia. Z. (2022). Santé et assurance maladie en Tunisie: les enjeux de la réforme de 2004. *Eastern Mediterranean Health Journal, 28(6)*, 444 - 453. https://iris.who.int/handle/10665/359870

Ismaïl, S., & Arfa, C. (2022). Effects of out-of-pocket medicine's spending on catastrophic expenditure and impoverishment in Tunisia. *Value in Health Regional Issues, 30*, 109–118. 10.1016/j.vhri.2022.01.008. DOI: 10.1016/j.vhri.2022.01.008

Israel, M., & Hay, I. (2006). Research ethics for social scientists. *Sage (Atlanta, Ga.).*

Iwański, R. (2024). Growth prospects for the silver economy in the market segment of residential care services provided to dependent elderly people. *Economics and Business Review, 10*(2), 165–186. DOI: 10.18559/ebr.2024.2.1255

Jallouli, F. Yalouli, Tarek, Vyas, Sonali, and Gupta, Sunil. (2025). A prospective study of the determinants of economic growth in Tunisia 1990–2030. *International Journal of Critical Infrastructures, 21*(2), 105-127. 10.1504/IJCIS.2025.145207

Jane Osareme, O., Muonde, M., Maduka, C. P., Olorunsogo, T. O., & Omotayo, O. J. I. J. S. R. A. (2024). Demographic shifts and healthcare: A review of aging populations and systemic challenges. *International Journal of Science and Research Archive, 11*(1), 383–395. 10.30574/ijsra.2024.11.1.0067. DOI: 10.30574/ijsra.2024.11.1.0067

Jarrott, S. E. (2023). Intergenerational Theory as a Tool to Diversify Practice and Policy. *Generations Journal, 47*(4), 1–10. ProQuest One Academic (3053147423).

Jarrott, S. E. (2011). Where Have We Been and Where are We Going? Content Analysis of Evaluation Research of Intergenerational Programs. *Journal of Intergenerational Relationships*, *9*(1), 37–52. DOI: 10.1080/15350770.2011.544594

Jarrott, S. E., Juris, J. J., & Turner, S. G. (2025). The Intergenerational Program Evaluation Tool: Results of a Delphi Study. *Journal of Intergenerational Relationships*, *23*(3), 280–296. DOI: 10.1080/15350770.2024.2349927

Jarvis, P. (2006). *Towards a comprehensive theory of human learning*. Routledge.

Jarvis, P. (2009). *Learning to be a person in society*. Routledge.

Jayawardhana, T., Jayathilaka, R., Nimnadi, T., Anuththara, S., Karadanaarachchi, R., Galappaththi, K., & Dharmasena, T. (2023). The cost of aging: Economic growth perspectives for Europe. *PLoS One*, *18*(6), e0287207. Advance online publication. DOI: 10.1371/journal.pone.0287207 PMID: 37352177

Ji, Y., & Li, J. (2025). Population aging, digital economy and family tourism consumption. *Finance Research Letters*, *82*, 107634. DOI: 10.1016/j.frl.2025.107634

JKM. (2023). *Kasih Sejahtera Program Annual Report*. Department of Social Welfare Malaysia.

Jmaii, A. (2025). Remittance reinforcement and economic adaptation: Charting Tunisia's path towards climate resilience. *Mitigation and Adaptation Strategies for Global Change*, *30*(2), 14. 10.1007/s11027-025-10201-4. DOI: 10.1007/s11027-025-10201-4

Kang, S., Li, K., & Wang, R. (2025). A survey on pareto front learning for multiobjective optimization. *Journal of Membrane Computing*, *7*(2), 128–134. DOI: 10.1007/s41965-024-00170-z

Kaplan, M. S. (2002). International programs in schools: Considerations of form and function. *International Review of Education*, *48*(5), 305–334. DOI: 10.1023/A:1021231713392

Kaplan, M., Sanchez, M., & Hoffman, J. (2017). *Intergenerational pathways to a sustainable society*. Springer International Publishing. DOI: 10.1007/978-3-319-47019-1

Kaplan, M., Thang, L. L., & Heydon, M. (2017). Intergenerational contact zones: Place-based strategies for promoting social inclusion and belonging. *Journal of Intergenerational Relationships*, *15*(1), 1–9. DOI: 10.1080/15350770.2017.1404428

Kaplan, M., Thang, L. L., Sánchez, M., & Hoffman, J. (2020). *Intergenerational Contact Zones: Place-based Strategies for Promoting Social Inclusion and Belonging* (Kaplan, M., Thang, L. L., Sánchez, M., & Hoffman, J., Eds.; 1st ed.). Routledge., DOI: 10.4324/9780429199097

Karahan, A., & Güven, S. (2002). Yaşlılıkta evde bakım [Homecare for elderly]. *Türk Geriatri Dergisi*, *5*(4), 155–159.

Kato, A. I. (2024). Building resilience and sustainability in small business enterprises. *Cogent Economics & Finance*, *12*(1). Advance online publication. DOI: 10.1080/23322039.2024.2399760

Kementerian PPN/Bappenas. (2019). *Proyeksi penduduk Indonesia 2015–2045: Hasil SUPAS 2015*. Badan Perencanaan Pembangunan Nasional.

Kerala State Planning Board. (2022). *Elderly care cooperatives in Kerala: A model for inclusive aging*. Government of Kerala.

Kezar, A., & Sam, C. (2010). Understanding the new majority of non-tenure-track faculty in higher education. *ASHE Higher Education Report*, *36*(4), 1–133. DOI: 10.1002/aehe.3604

Khattak, W. A., Anas, M., Hakki, E. E., Iqbal, J., Abbasi, B. A., & Munir, A. (2026). Economical and societal debut on sustainable environment and industry using bioenergy and nanotechnology. In *Sustainable nanostrategies for biorefineries: Environmental, economic, and social perspectives* (pp. 191–219). Springer Nature Singapore. DOI: 10.1007/978-981-95-5875-9_10

Kilaru, A. S., Mondal, A., Jesteen, S., Geng, Z., Isenberg, D., Zikry, H. E., & Meisel, Z. F. (2026). Telemedicine use and outcomes following discharge from the emergency department, 2020–2022. *Annals of Emergency Medicine*, *87*(6), 697–708. Advance online publication. DOI: 10.1016/j.annemergmed.2026.01.024 PMID: 41817487

Kılıç, M., & Uyar, A. (2014). The Impact of Corporate Characteristics on Social Responsibility Disclosures. In *Corporate Governance*. Springer. DOI: 10.1007/978-3-642-45167-6_14

King, S. (2014). *Social Impact Bonds: A new tool for social financing*.

Kinsella, E. A., & Pitman, A. (Eds.). (2012). *Phronesis as professional knowledge: Practical wisdom in the professions*. Sense Publishers. DOI: 10.1007/978-94-6091-731-8

Kirshenblatt-Gimblett, B. (2004). Intangible Heritage as Metacultural Production1. *Museum International*, *56*(1–2), 52–65. DOI: 10.1111/j.1350-0775.2004.00458.x

Klimczuk, A. (2015). Economic foundations for creative ageing policy, volume I: Context and considerations. Palgrave Macmillan. https://doi.org/DOI: 10.1057/9781137465467

Klimczuk, A. (2015). Economic Foundations for Creative Ageing Policy: Volume I Context and Considerations. Springer.

Klimczuk, A. (2016). Comparative analysis of national and regional models of the silver economy in the European Union. *International Journal of Ageing and Later Life*, *10*(2), 31–59. DOI: 10.3384/ijal.1652-8670.15286

Knodel, J., Teerawichitchainan, B., Prachuabmoh, V., & Pothisiri, W. (2017). *The situation of Thailand's older population*. College of Population Studies, Chulalongkorn University.

Koentjaraningrat. (1985). Javanese culture. Oxford University Press.

Koh, G., Yeo, E. Y., & Tang, C. S. (2022). Productive aging and knowledge transfer in Singapore: Evidence from the Senior Academy programme. *Journal of Aging & Social Policy*, *34*(4), 578–597. DOI: 10.1080/08959420.2021.1955724

Kohlbacher, F., & Herstatt, C. (Eds.). (2011). *The silver market phenomenon: Marketing and innovation in the aging society* (2nd ed.). Springer. DOI: 10.1007/978-3-642-14338-0

Kongmalai, T., Yodmalai, C., Luerithiphong, S., Sitasuwan, T., & Thongtang, N. (2026). Hybrid vs in-person diabetes care: Outcomes and barriers to telemedicine utilization in a post-pandemic setting. *Primary Care Diabetes*, *20*(3), 313–319. Advance online publication. DOI: 10.1016/j.pcd.2026.03.004 PMID: 41794635

Koosha, M., & Lalegani, A. (2024). Assessing the social health of the elderly in Tehran: Challenges and strategic solutions. *Archives of Gerontology and Geriatrics Plus*, *1*(4), 100091. Advance online publication. DOI: 10.1016/j.aggp.2024.100091

Koru Uzkurt, B. (2023). Toplumsal ve ekonomik bir dönüşüm olarak gümüş ekonomi modeli [The silver economy model as a social and economic transformation]. *Tüketici ve Tüketim Araştırmaları Dergisi*, *15*(1), 299–324. DOI: 10.15659/ttad.15.1.171

Kretzmann, J. P., & McKnight, J. L. (1993). *Building communities from the inside out: A path toward finding and mobilizing a community's assets*. ACTA Publications.

Lab, I. D. B. (2025, October 31). *Silver economy: Three pillars for a more productive longevity*. https://bidlab.org/en/blog/silver-economy-three-pillars-more-productive-longevity

Labit, A., & Dubost, N. (2016). Housing and ageing in France and Germany: The intergenerational solution. Housing. *Care and Support, 19*(2), 45–54. DOI: 10.1108/HCS-08-2016-0007

Lai, A., Qi, J., & Luo, T. (2025). *Intergenerational Silk Route: The Greater Bay "WIN-WIN" Area*. China Culture Publishing House.

Lankide, T. U. (2023). *MONDRAGON surpassed the 11 billion sales barrier in 2023*. https://www.tulankide.com/en/mondragon-surpassed-the-11-billion-sales-barrier-in-2023

Lanzavecchia, A., & Bavado, L. (2018). A Triple Bottom Line Return: Impact Investing. In *Asset Management*. Nova Science Publishers.

Laureola Advisors & Lee, A. (2021). Life settlements can become fixed income alternative for investors. *SMSF Adviser*.

Lee, J. A. B. (2001). *The empowerment approach to social work practice: Building the beloved community* (2nd ed.). Columbia University Press.

Lee, R., & Mason, A. (2011). *Population aging and the generational economy: A global perspective*. Edward Elgar. DOI: 10.4337/9780857930583

Lee, R., & Mason, A. (2022). *The generational economy and population aging*. Edward Elgar.

Levy, B. R., & Banaji, M. R. (2002). Implicit ageism. In Nelson, T. D. (Ed.), *Ageism: Stereotyping and prejudice against older persons* (pp. 49–75). MIT Press. DOI: 10.7551/mitpress/1157.003.0006

Lewis, M. K. (2021). *Rethinking public private partnerships*. Edward Elgar Publishing., DOI: 10.4337/9781789906400

Lilley, I. (2017). Review of Victor T. King (ed.), UNESCO in Southeast Asia: World Heritage Sites in Comparative Perspective. Studies in Asian Topics no. 55. xv + 463 pp. Copenhagen: Nordic Institute of Asian Studies, 2016. *International Journal of Cultural Property, 24*(2), 239–241. DOI: 10.1017/S0940739117000066

Lim, Y. W., Teo, K., Tan, C., & Ong, J. (2022). Promoting Healthy Longevity–The Role of Social Innovation. Future Urban Habitation: Transdisciplinary Perspectives, Conceptions, and Designs, 287-300.

Li, N., Li, X., & Xiao, W. (2025). Intangible cultural heritage threatened-level categories and criteria. *Humanities & Social Sciences Communications*, *12*(1), 271. DOI: 10.1057/s41599-025-04595-4

Lin, C., Dai, G., Liu, Y., Ye, G., & Fu, X. (2026). Exploring the future of sustainable ocean economies: Marine trade's role in advancing inclusive green growth. *Ocean and Coastal Management*, *272*, 108003. DOI: 10.1016/j.ocecoaman.2025.108003

Lin, C., Xia, G., Nickpour, F., & Chen, Y. (2025). A review of emotional design in extended reality for the preservation of culture heritage. *NPJ Heritage Science*, *13*(1), 86. DOI: 10.1038/s40494-025-01625-x

Li, R., Yang, Z., Zhang, Y., Bai, W., Du, Y., Sun, R., Tang, J., Wang, N., & Liu, H. (2022). Cost-effectiveness and cost-utility of traditional and telemedicine combined population-based age-related macular degeneration and diabetic retinopathy screening in rural and urban China. *The Lancet Regional Health. Western Pacific*, *23*, 100435. DOI: 10.1016/j.lanwpc.2022.100435 PMID: 35355615

Liu, K., Yang, Y., Song, Z., Li, H., Lyu, Y., Zhang, K., Wu, X., Hou, Z., & Wang, Y. (2026, January 21). Using the Theoretical Domains Framework to identify barriers to and enablers of patient telemedicine services use in China: Qualitative study. *JMIR Human Factors*, *13*, e78457. DOI: 10.2196/78457 PMID: 41564349

Liu, Y. (2025). Research on the Silver Economy from the Perspective of Human Resource Development. In *2025 International Conference on Financial Innovation and Marketing Management (FIMM 2025)* (pp. 1300-1308). Atlantis Press. DOI: 10.2991/978-94-6463-874-5_147

Livingston, G., Huntley, J., Sommerlad, A., Ames, D., Ballard, C., Banerjee, S., & Mukadam, N. (2020). Dementia prevention, intervention, and care: 2020 report of the Lancet Commission. *Lancet*, *396*(10248), 413–446. DOI: 10.1016/S0140-6736(20)30367-6 PMID: 32738937

Li, W., Xie, Q., Ao, J., Lin, H., Ji, S., Yang, M., & Sun, J. (2025). Systematic review: A scientometric analysis of the status, trends and challenges in the application of digital technology to cultural heritage conservation (2019–2024). *NPJ Heritage Science*, *13*(1), 90. DOI: 10.1038/s40494-025-01636-8

Li, X., Wang, Q., & Chen, J. (2025). Activating the longevity economy: Digital literacy among older residents and household consumption structure upgrading. *Humanities & Social Sciences Communications*, *12*(1), 1–14. DOI: 10.1057/s41599-025-06175-y

Li, X., Xie, J., Luo, J., & Yang, A. (2025). The silver-hair economy in the new era: Political economy perspectives on its dilemmas and solutions. *Sustainability (Basel)*, *17*(15), 6760. DOI: 10.3390/su17156760

Loh, W. Y., Nasir, M. H. A., Hassan, A. S., Nordin, J., & Fachrudin, H. T. (2025). Analysis of the level of Permeability and Wayfinding of a Retirement Village: The Case of Kampung Admiralty, Singapore. *International Journal of Built Environment and Sustainability*, *12*(1), 135–155. DOI: 10.11113/ijbes.v12.n1.1341

Long, N. H., Ngân, N. K., Thư, L. N. M., & Uyên, T. M. (2025). Chính sách kinh t trong vi c ng phó tình tr ng gi m sinh và già hóa dân s t i Nh t B n – Kinh nghi m cho Vi t Nam [Economic policies in response to declining birth rates and population aging in Japan: Lessons for Vietnam. *Journal of Science and Technology*, 8(3), 178–184.

Longevity & Mortality Investor. (2024). Volume 3 Issue 4.

Longevity & Mortality Investor. (2025). Society of Actuaries considers switch from general to insured population mortality data.

Lopane, F. (2025). *Silver Economy for Innovation and Inclusivity*. Springer Briefs in Applied Sciences and Technology.

Ly, D. H. (2022). The aging population in Vietnam: Trend and policy. *VNU Journal of Economics and Business*, 2(1).

Ly, R., & Ly, B. (2024). Digital payment systems in an emerging economy. *Computers in Human Behavior Reports*, *16*, 100517. DOI: 10.1016/j.chbr.2024.100517

Macdonald, D. (2019, January 10). Social impact bonds: Everyone's profiting, except at-risk Indigenous women. *Canadian Centre for Policy Alternatives.* https://www.policyalternatives.ca/news-research/social-impact-bonds-everyones-profiting-except-at-risk-indigenous-women/

Macinko, J., & Harris, M. J. (2015). Brazil's Family Health Strategy. *The New England Journal of Medicine*, *372*(23), 2177–2181. DOI: 10.1056/NEJMp1501140 PMID: 26039598

Ma, H. (2022). The Missing Intangible Cultural Heritage in Shanghai Cultural and Creative Industries. *International Journal of Heritage Studies*, *28*(5), 597–608. DOI: 10.1080/13527258.2022.2042717

Maheshwari, A., & Maheshwari, G. (2024). Aging population in Vietnam: Challenges, implications, and policy recommendations. *International Journal of Aging, 2*(1), e1–e1. DOI: 10.34172/ija.2024.e1

Mai, D. T. N. (2025). ng d ng công ngh s trong phát tri n kinh t b c Vi t Nam. T p chí Khoa h c Trư ng Đ i h c M Hà N i [Application of digital technology in the development of the silver economy in Vietnam]. *Hanoi Open University Journal of Science*, 404–404. DOI:DOI: 10.59266/houjs.2025.960

Maltby, J. (2005). Showing a Strong Front: Corporate Social Reporting and the Business Case in Britain, 1914–1919. *The Accounting Historians Journal, 32*(2), 145–171. DOI: 10.2308/0148-4184.32.2.145

Mannion, G. (2012). Intergenerational education: The significance of reciprocity and place. *Journal of Intergenerational Relationships, 10*(4), 386–399. DOI: 10.1080/15350770.2012.726601

Manolache, M., Manolache, A. I., & Andrei, G. (2025). Floating solar energy systems: A review of economic feasibility and cross-sector integration with marine renewable energy, aquaculture and hydrogen. *Journal of Marine Science and Engineering, 13*(8), 1404. DOI: 10.3390/jmse13081404

Manzano, F. A. (2025). Silver economy: Structural challenges and strategies for inclusive development. *Ateliê Geográfico, 19*(1), 35–57. DOI: 10.5216/ag.v19i1.80921

Marcucci, G., Ciarapica, F., Poler, R., & Sanchis, R. (2021). A bibliometric analysis of the emerging trends in silver economy. *IFAC-PapersOnLine, 54*(1), 936–941. https://doi.org/10.1016/j.ifacol.2021.08.190

Maresova, P., Mohelska, H., & Kuca, K. (2019). Social and economic aspects of ageing population. *Current Gerontology and Geriatrics Research, 2019*, 8501258.

Marginson, S., & Rhoades, G. (2002). Beyond national states, markets, and systems of higher education: A glonacal agency heuristic. *Higher Education, 43*(3), 281–309. DOI: 10.1023/A:1014699605875

Marston, H. R., Ivan, L., & Fernández-Ardèvol, M. (2022). Digital technologies and the ageing population: A systematic review. *International Journal of Environmental Research and Public Health, 19*(4), 2325. DOI: 10.3390/ijerph19042325

Martinez, C., & Weyman, T. (2017). *Demographic change in a complex world.* Advances in Spatial Science. DOI: 10.1007/978-3-319-63197-4_1

Martinez, L., Mirza, R. M., Austen, A., Hsieh, J., Klinger, C. A., Kuah, M., Liu, A., McDonald, L., Mohsin, R., Pang, C., Rajewski, J., Salomons, T., & Sheikh, I. (2020). More than just a room: A scoping review of the impact of homesharing for older adults. *Innovation in Aging*, *4*(2), igaa011. DOI: 10.1093/geroni/igaa011 PMID: 32382662

Matos, R. C. D., Nascimento, G. D., Campos Fernandes, A., & Matos, C. (2025). Health and social care integration: insights from international implementation cases. *Journal of Market Access & Health Policy*, *13*(2), 28. DOI: 10.3390/jmahp13020028 PMID: 40568385

Matsumoto, K., Tsukamoto, K., Ishikawa, S., Oishi, M., & Okamoto, N. (2000). Reconstruction of cities through the utilization of reverse mortgage system: Lesson from the Hanshin-Awaji Great Earthquake and its universality. *Studies in Regional Science*, *30*(1), 197–212. https://www.jstage.jst.go.jp/article/srs1970/30/1/30_1_197/_article

Mawdsley, E., & Hughes-McLure, S. (2024). Blended finance. In *Handbook of Aid and Development*. Edward Elgar. DOI: 10.4337/9781800886810.00028

Mayring, P. (2014). *Qualitative content analysis: Theoretical foundation, basic procedures and software solution*. Klagenfurt.

McGivney, V. (2022). Lifelong learning in the digital age: Challenges and opportunities for older adults. *International Journal of Lifelong Education*, *41*(3), 215–230. DOI: 10.1080/02601370.2022.2055432

McGuirk, H. C. L. Aisling & Lenihan, N. (2022). Awareness and potential of the silver economy for enterprises: a European regional level study. *Small Enterprise Research, 29*(1), 6-19. 10.1080/13215906.2021.1919915

McGurk, P. (1998). Traded endowments. *British Actuarial Journal*, *4*(2), 391–428. DOI: 10.1017/S1357321700003013

McKinsey & Company. (2023). *The future of aging in Asia: Trends, challenges, and opportunities*. McKinsey Global Institute.

McMurray, A. J., Islam, M. M., Sarros, J. C., & Pirola-Merlo, A. (2022). Knowledge retention and transfer in ageing academic workforces: Challenges and opportunities for universities. *Journal of Higher Education Policy and Management*, *44*(5), 543–558. DOI: 10.1080/1360080X.2022.2057104

Mele, C., Pels, J., & Polese, F. (2022). Silver economy innovation: A bibliometric analysis of the service ecosystem perspective. *Sinergie – Italian. Journal of Management*, *40*(3), 1–24. DOI: 10.7433/s118.2022.01

Merritt, G. (2025). *Timebomb: When Ageing Explodes*. Policy Press. https://books.google.ae/books?hl=en&lr=&id=z5IiEQAAQBAJ&oi=fnd&pg=PT10&dq=Merritt,+G.+(2025).+Timebomb:+When+Ageing+Explodes.+Policy+Press&ots=1vtfjiAB2W&sig=K8dCQ7g6Kb4ySbHU7ttBbUjoHMA&redir_esc=y#v=onepage&q=Merritt%2C%20G.%20(2025).%20Timebomb%3A%20When%20Ageing%20Explodes.%20Policy%20Press&f=false

Miner, A. S., Haque, A., Fries, J. A., Ross, S., Shah, N. H., & Milstein, A. (2020). Assessing the accuracy of automatic speech recognition for psychotherapy. *NPJ Digital Medicine, 3*(82), 82. Advance online publication. DOI: 10.1038/s41746-020-0285-8 PMID: 32550644

Mingst, K. A., Karns, M. P., & Lyon, A. J. (2022). *The United Nations in the 21st century*. Routledge. 10.4324/9781003038269

Ministry of Foreign Affairs of Japan. (1996). *Social security in Japan: Case I social welfare services in Musashino City*. National Diet Library. https://warp.ndl.go.jp/info:ndljp/pid/11383817/www.mofa.go.jp/j_info/japan/socsec/maruo/maruo_10.html

Ministry of Health and Family Welfare. G. of I. (2019). *NPHCE Evaluation Report: PPP Pilot States*. Government of India.

Ministry of Health. S. (2022). *Community Networks for Seniors: Annual Evaluation Report 2021–22*. Ministry of Health.

Ministry of Health. Singapore. (2023). Action plan for successful ageing: 2023 refresh. Government of Singapore. https://www.moh.gov.sg/news-highlights/details/action-plan-for-successful-ageing

Ministry of Social and Family Development. Singapore. (2021). Action plan for successful ageing: 2021 refresh. Government of Singapore.

Minkler, M., & Wallerstein, N. (Eds.). (2011). *Community-based participatory research for health: From process to outcomes* (2nd ed.). Jossey-Bass.

MIT AgeLab. (2023). About the MIT AgeLab: Mission and sponsors. Massachusetts Institute of Technology. https://agelab.mit.edu

Mohd Tohit, N. F., & Haque, M. (2024). Gerontology in public health: A scoping review of current perspectives and interventions. *Cureus, 16*(7), e65896. Advance online publication. DOI: 10.7759/cureus.65896 PMID: 39092340

Mohsin, K. F., Ahsan, M. N., & Haider, M. Z. (2024). Understanding variation in catastrophic health expenditure from socio-ecological aspect: A systematic review. *BMC Public Health*, *24*(1), 1504. 10.1186/s12889-024-18579-7. DOI: 10.1186/s12889-024-18579-7

Mokhele, M. O. (2026). Assessment of the effectiveness of public-private partnerships in collaborative projects in South Africa: Building back better in post-disaster recovery. *Progress in Disaster Science*, *30*, 100553. DOI: 10.1016/j.pdisas.2026.100553

MOLISA. (2022). Report on National Program for Elderly Care 2021–2022 Ministry of Labor, Invalids and Social Affairs, Vietnam.

Mondragon Corporation. (2023). *Annual report 2022: Cooperative banking and social innovation*. Mondragon Corporation.

Moore, J. F. (1993). Predators and prey: A new ecology of competition. *Harvard Business Review*, *71*(3), 75–86. PMID: 10126156

Moulaei, K., & Kazemi-Arpanahi, H. (2026). Telemedicine-based geriatric assessment (tele-GA): A scoping review on applications, benefits and challenges. *Health Policy and Technology*, *15*(3), 101157. DOI: 10.1016/j.hlpt.2026.101157

Moulaert, F., MacCallum, D., Mehmood, A., & Hamdouch, A. (Eds.). (2013). *The international handbook on social innovation: Collective action, social learning and transdisciplinary research*. Edward Elgar Publishing., DOI: 10.4337/9781849809993

Moulaert, F., & Nussbaumer, J. (2005). The social region: Beyond the territorial dynamics of the learning economy. *European Urban and Regional Studies*, *12*(1), 45–64. DOI: 10.1177/0969776405048500

Mufarokhah, L., Putra, A. R. S., & Nurhadi, N. (2025). Optimizing government procurement through social procurement policy innovation: Insights from cross-sector collaboration at the Ministry of Health, Indonesia. *Journal of Public Procurement*, 1–28.

Müller, D. M. (2021). *Classification of consumer goods into 5-digit COICOP 2018 codes* https://nva.sikt.no/registration/019909a810fc-691343f7-2ab7-4c94-a5f0-2dc785ca435d

Mulvenna, M., & Martin, S. (2020). Living labs for co-designing digital solutions with older adults: Methods and outcomes from AgeTech consortia. *The Gerontologist*, *60*(3), 567–578. DOI: 10.1093/geront/gnz137

Nagatake, T. (Ed.). (2003). *Classic Japanese porcelain: Imari and Kakiemon*. Kodansha International.

Nakajima, M. (2018). The structure and issues of housing reverse mortgage trust in Japan. *Trusts & Trustees, 24*(6), 548–556. DOI: 10.1093/tandt/cty082

Nasaj, M. (2025). Intercultural stressors and team innovative behaviour: The role of coping strategies in multicultural workplaces. *Global Knowledge, Memory and Communication*. Advance online publication. DOI: 10.1108/GKMC-10-2024-0680

Nasaj, M., Badi, S., Murtagh, N., & Ding, L. (2025). *Collective AI anxiety and team innovative behaviour: The role of coping strategies*. Construction Innovation: Information, Process. *Management*. Advance online publication. DOI: 10.1108/CI-08-2024-0222

Nasional, K. (2023). Khazanah [Khazanah Nasional Berhad.]. *Sustainability Report*, •••, 2023.

National Bureau of Statistics of China. (2024). *Population data by age range*. https://data.stats.gov.cn

Nations, U. (2022). *World Population Prospects 2022: Summary of Results*. United Nations. DOI: 10.18356/9789210014380

Nazlı, E. (2025). Türkiye'de yaşlılara yönelik sosyal hizmetlerin tarihsel gelişimi [Historical development of social services for the elderly in Türkiye]. *International Journal of Social and Humanities Sciences Research, 112*(115), 171–182. DOI: 10.5281/zenodo.14787691

Neumann, A., König, H.-H., & Hajek, A. (2024). Determinants of telemedicine service use among middle-aged and older adults in Germany during the COVID-19 pandemic: Cross-sectional survey study. *JMIR Aging, 7*, e50938. DOI: 10.2196/50938 PMID: 38654578

Newman, S., & Hatton-Yeo, A. (2008). Intergenerational learning and the contributions of older people. *Ageing Horizons, 8*, 31–39.

Ngoc, T. T. T. (2021). Già hóa dân s và tình tr ng tham gia làm vi c c a ngư i cao tu i Vi t Nam. T p chí Khoa h c và Công ngh - Đ i h c Đà N ng, [Population aging and the labor force participation of the elderly in Vietnam]. *The University of Da Nang Journal of Science and Technology*, 19(8), 16–20.

Ngo, Q. A., Tran Huy, P., & Tran, T. M. P. (2024). Empowerment of elder family caregivers in the context of Vietnam: Applying the theory of planned behavior. *Journal of Population Research (Canberra, A.C.T.), 41*(3), 14. DOI: 10.1007/s12546-024-09335-0

Ng, T. P., Feng, L., Nyunt, M. S. Z., & Yap, K. B. (2023). Productive aging and health outcomes in older Singaporeans: Evidence from longitudinal cohort studies. *Annals of the Academy of Medicine, Singapore, 52*(1), 14–26. DOI: 10.47102/annals-acadmedsg.2022337

Nguyen, L. T., Nantharath, P., & Kang, E. (2022). The sustainable care model for an ageing population in Vietnam: Evidence from a systematic review. *Sustainability (Basel), 14*(5), 2518. Advance online publication. DOI: 10.3390/su14052518

Nguyen, T. T. T., Than, T. H. N., Nguyen, T. C., Duong Vu, L. T., Truong, K. T., Thai, T. T., Schofield, P., & Nguyen, T. A. (2025). Challenges, knowledge, and skills required for family caregivers of older adults with dementia: A qualitative study in Vietnam. *Global Health Action, 18*(1), 2526929. DOI: 10.1080/16549716.2025.2526929 PMID: 40625201

Nhan, D. T. (2019). The role of the Family in Daily care for the ELderly in Changing rural Vietnam. *Wieś i Rolnictwo*, (3 (184)), 97–122. DOI: 10.53098/wir032019/05

NHSO. (2023). *Long-Term Care for Dependent Elderly: Annual Report 2023*. National Health Security Office.

Nhung, N. P. (2024). Hoàn thi n pháp lu t v nhóm quy n liên quan đ n an ninh thu nh p c a ngư i cao tu i Vi t Nam. Qu n lý nhà nư c [Improving the legal framework for income security rights of the elderly in Vietnam]. *State Management Review*, (343), 60–64.

Nicholls, A., & Tomkinson, E. (2015). *The Peterborough Pilot Social Impact Bond*. Oxford University Press. DOI: 10.1093/acprof:oso/9780198703761.003.0013

Nieto-Vieites, A., Gaspar, P., Victor, J., Pérez-Blanco, L., Felpete-López, A., & Facal, D. (2022). Technological development in preventing cognitive frailty, promoting active aging, and the economics of aging. In *Marketing and Smart Technologies: Proceedings of ICMarkTech 2021* (Vol. 2, pp. 213–223). Springer Nature Singapore. DOI: 10.1007/978-981-16-9272-7_18

Niu, X., Wang, X., & Bi, X. (2025). Mapping the nexus of sustainability and cultural heritage: A systematic review and empirical analysis. *NPJ Heritage Science, 13*(1), 471. DOI: 10.1038/s40494-025-02006-0

Nonaka, I., & Takeuchi, H. (1995). *The knowledge-creating company: How Japanese companies create the dynamics of innovation*. Oxford University Press. DOI: 10.1093/oso/9780195092691.001.0001

Norges Bank Investment Management. (2024). *Government Pension Fund Global responsible investment 2024*. Norges Bank Investment Management.

Nugroho, P., Setiawan, D., & Dewi, R. (2020). Community-based programs for older adults in Indonesian universities: A scoping review of PkM reports 2015–2020. Jurnal Gerontologi dan Geriatri, 5(2), 45–62.

O'Connell, T., Rasanathan, K., & Chopra, M. (2014). What does universal health coverage mean? *Lancet, 383*(9913), 277–279. DOI: 10.1016/S0140-6736(13)60955-1

OECD. (2018). *Working better with age*. OECD Publishing., DOI: 10.1787/9789264201996-

OECD. (2019). *OECD skills outlook 2019: Thriving in a digital world*. OECD Publishing., DOI: 10.1787/df80bc12-

OECD. (2020). *Promoting an Age-Inclusive Workforce: Living*. Learning and Earning Longer.

OECD. (2021). *Ageing and Long-Term Care: Country Notes*. OECD Publishing.

OECD. (2021). *Pensions at a glance: Asia/Pacific 2021*. OECD Publishing., DOI: 10.1787/9789264099401-

OECD. (2022). *Fiscal challenges and inclusive growth in aging societies*. OECD Publishing.

OECD. (2023). [OECD indicators. OECD Publishing.]. *Health at a Glance*, •••, 2023.

OECD. (2023). *Ageing and employment policies: Working better with age 2023*. OECD Publishing., DOI: 10.1787/59752153-

OECD. (2024). Is care affordable for older people? In. Paris: OECD Health Policy Studies, OECD Publishing.

OECD. (2025a). *The economic benefit of promoting healthy ageing and community care (OECD Health Policy Studies)*. OECD Publishing., DOI: 10.1787/0f7bc62b-

OECD. (2025b). *Pensions at a glance 2025: OECD and G20 indicators*. OECD Publishing., DOI: 10.1787/e40274c1-

Oget, Q. (2021). When economic promises shape innovation and networks: A structural analysis of technological innovation in the silver economy. *Journal of Innovation Economics, 35*(2), 55–80. 10.3917/e.jie.pr1.0096b

Oğlak, S. (2023). Bakım yoksulluğu ve uzun süreli bakım politikaları ilişkisi [The relationship between care poverty and long-term care policies]. *İktisat ve Toplum, 149*, 74-84.

Okayama City SIB Study. (2024). Validating weight optimization's impact on participants via Social Impact Bonds. *European Journal of Public Health*, 34(Supplement_3), ckae144.1743. https://doi.org/DOI: 10.1093/eurpub/ckae144.1743

Oktar, M. N. (2025). Evde yalnız yaşayan yaşlı bireylerin deneyimleri: Sosyal hizmet bağlamında bir değerlendirme [Experiences of Elderly Individuals Living Alone at Home: An Assessment in the Context of Social Work]. *Sosyal Politika Çalışmaları Dergisi*, *25*(67), 310–344. DOI: 10.21560/spcd.vi.1563712

Organisation for Economic Co-operation and Development (OECD). (2020). *Who cares? Attracting and retaining care workers for the elderly*. OECD Publishing.

Organisation for Economic Co-operation and Development (OECD). (2023). *Ready for the future? Long-term care and ageing societies*. OECD Publishing.

Organisation for Economic Co-operation and Development. (2024). *Ageing and long-term care: Financing challenges and innovative solutions.*

Organization for Economic Co-operation and Development. (2005). *Long-term care for older people*. OECD Publishing., DOI: 10.1787/9789264015852-

Ossenfort, W. (1965). Handbook of social gerontology. *Archives of Internal Medicine*, *116*(5), 804–805. DOI: 10.1001/archinte.1965.03870050158041

Özmete, E., & Hussein, S. (2017). *Türkiye'de yaşlı bakım hizmetleri raporu: Avrupa'dan en iyi uygulama örnekleri ve Türkiye için bir model tasarımı [Report on elderly care services in Türkiye: Best practice examples from Europe and a model design for Türkiye]. Republic of Türkiye Ministry of Family and Social Policies.* https://www.aile.gov.tr/media/267671/tuerkiye-de-yas-li-bakim-hizmetleri-avrupa-dan-en-iyi-uygulama-oernekleri-ve-tuerkiye-ic-in-bir-model-tasarimi-proje-kitabi.pdf

Page, M. J., McKenzie, J. E., Bossuyt, P. M., Boutron, I., Hoffmann, T. C., Mulrow, C. D., Shamseer, L., Tetzlaff, J. M., Akl, E. A., Brennan, S. E., Chou, R., Glanville, J., Grimshaw, J. M., Hróbjartsson, A., Lalu, M. M., Li, T., Loder, E. W., Mayo-Wilson, E., McDonald, S., & Moher, D. (2021). The PRISMA 2020 statement: An updated guideline for reporting systematic reviews. *BMJ (Clinical Research Ed.)*, *372*, n71. Advance online publication. DOI: 10.1136/bmj.n71 PMID: 33782057

Park, Y., Kim, E. J., Park, S., & Lee, M. (2025). Digital health intervention effect on older adults with chronic diseases living alone: systematic review and meta-analysis of randomized controlled trials. Journal of Medical Internet Research, 27, e63168.

Patel, M. R., Jagsi, R., Resnicow, K., Smith, S. N., Hamel, L. M., Su, C., ... & Torby, M. (2021). A scoping review of behavioral interventions addressing medical financial hardship. Population Health Management, 24(6), 710-721.

People's Bank of China, & Eight Other Departments. (2024, December). *Guiding opinions on financial support for the high-quality development of Chinese-style pension services and the silver economy*. People's Bank of China.

Pham, T. (2025). Ethical and legal considerations in healthcare AI: Innovation and policy for safe and fair use. *Royal Society Open Science*, *12*(5), 241873. DOI: 10.1098/rsos.241873 PMID: 40370601

Phan, P. H.I, & Siegel, D. S. (2006). The effectiveness of university technology transfer: Lessons learned from qualitative and quantitative research in the US and the UK. *Foundations and Trends in Entrepreneurship*, *2*(2), 65–144. DOI: 10.1561/0300000006

Phills, J. A.Jr, Deiglmeier, K., & Miller, D. T. (2008). Rediscovering social innovation. *Stanford Social Innovation Review*, *6*(4), 34–43.

Piskorska, B., & Adamczyk, M. D. (2025). The challenge of social security in an aging European Union. Online Journal Modeling the New Europe.

Polanyi, M. (1966). *The tacit dimension*. Doubleday.

Poplawska, M. (2025). Intangible heritage system: Challenges of culture preservation in a cross-cultural perspective. *Ethnomusicology Forum, 34*(1), 91–119. DOI: 10.1080/17411912.2025.2484707

Poudel, K., Malla, D. K., & Thapa, K. (2024). Health care service utilization among elderly in rural setting of Gandaki province, Nepal: A mixed method study. *Frontiers in Health Services*, *4*, 1321020. Advance online publication. DOI: 10.3389/frhs.2024.1321020 PMID: 39386356

Pradeep, K. G. M., Palvadi, S. K., & Rammurthy, D. (2026). Conclusion: Toward a sustainable future with block chain. In Kumar, A., Batta, P., Rathore, P. S., Kumar, T. A., & Ramírez, J. R. J. (Eds.), *Blockchain innovations for a sustainable circular economy* (Vol. 180). Springer., DOI: 10.1007/978-3-032-02428-2_19

Prasad, N. D., & Lal, R. (2024). Silver linings for the silver economy: Institutional and entrepreneurial responses to healthy ageing and long-term care in India. *Journal of Social and Economic Development*, *26*(1), 1–24. DOI: 10.1007/s40847-024-00411-y

Pratama, C. G., Nurlianti, R., Herstatt, C., & Goeldner, M. (2026). Telemedicine adoption for managing chronic and rare diseases in Indonesia during and beyond the COVID-19 era: Qualitative study. *Journal of Medical Internet Research*, *28*, e83462. DOI: 10.2196/83462 PMID: 41855417

Prensky, M. (2021). Digital wisdom: Empowering older adults in the AI era. *Journal of Intergenerational Relationships, 19*(2), 134–150. DOI: 10.1080/15350770.2020.1844571

Prete, D., Zito, A., Napoli, M., De Pascalis, A., & Elia, G. (2026). Experimenting innovation in telemedicine: The case of home haemodialysis. *European Journal of Innovation Management, 29*(1), 207–232. DOI: 10.1108/EJIM-03-2025-0365

Prime Minister of Vietnam. (2019). *Decision No. 1679/QĐ-TTg dated November 22, 2019 approving the Vietnam Population Strategy to 2030.*

Prime Minister of Vietnam. (2021). *Decision No. 2156/QĐ-TTg dated December 21, 2021 approving the National Action Program for Older Persons for the period 2021–2030.*

PSA. (2023). *2023 Philippine Statistics Authority Report on Senior Citizens*. Philippine Statistics Authority.

Purvis, B., Mao, Y., & Robinson, D. (2019). Three pillars of sustainability: In search of conceptual origins. *Sustainability Science, 14*(3), 681–695. https://doi.org/https://doi.org/10.1007/s11625-018-0627-5. DOI: 10.1007/s11625-018-0627-5

Putnam, R. D. (1993). *Making democracy work: Civic traditions in modern Italy.* Princeton University Press.

Putnam, R. D. (2000). Bowling alone: America's declining social capital. In *Culture and politics: A reader* (pp. 223–234). Palgrave Macmillan US.

Putnam, R. D. (2000). *Bowling alone: The collapse and revival of American community.* Simon & Schuster.

Qu c h i Vi t Nam. (2018). *Lu t Giáo d c đ i h c (s a đ i, b sung).* [Law on Higher Education (amended)].

Qu c h i Vi t Nam. (2025). *Lu t Nhà giáo ngày 16 tháng 6 năm 2025.* [Law on Teachers].

Quynh, A. N., & Mai, H. D. T. (2021). Chi n lư c an ninh-linh ho t và l i ích c a lao đ ng cao tu i t i nơi làm vi c: B ng ch ng t i các t nh phía b c Vi t Nam. T p chí Kinh t và Phát tri n, [Flexicurity strategy and the benefits for elderly workers in the workplace: Evidence from Northern provinces of Vietnam]. *Journal of Economics and Development*, 290(2), 33–41.

Rahman, T., Gasbarro, D., & Alam, K. (2022). Financial risk protection from out-of-pocket health spending in low- and middle-income countries: A scoping review of the literature. *Health Research Policy and Systems*, *20*(1), 83. DOI: 10.1186/s12961-022-00886-3

Rania, F. (2025). Reverse Mortgages and Pension Sustainability: An Agent-Based and Actuarial Approach. *Risks*, *13*(8), 147. DOI: 10.3390/risks13080147

Rauner, Y., & Stummer, H. (2025). The socio-technical adoption and diffusion of digital health innovations: The development of the STAD-HC model based on telemedicine in Germany. *Digital Business*, *5*(2), 100135. DOI: 10.1016/j.digbus.2025.100135

Ray, C., Nyberg, A. J., & Maltarich, M. A. (2023). Human capital resources emergence theory: The role of social capital. *Academy of Management Review*, *48*(2), 313–335. DOI: 10.5465/amr.2020.0186

Razavi, S. (2007). *The political and social economy of care in a development context: Conceptual issues, research questions and policy options* (Gender and Development Programme Paper No. 3). UNRISD.

Republic of Türkiye Ministry of Family and Social Services - General Directorate of Services for Persons with Disabilities and the Elderly. (2023). *Yaşlı bireyler için bilgilendirme rehberi-IV* [Information guide for elderly individuals-IV]. https://www.aile.gov.tr/media/143153/yasli_bireyler_i-cin_bilgilendirme_rehberi_2023.pdf

Republic of Türkiye Ministry of Health - General Directorate of Public Hospitals. (2023, April 10). *Sağlıklı yaş alma merkezlerinin kurulmasına dair genelge yayımlandı* [Circular on the establishment of healthy aging centers has been published]. https://khgmsaglikhizmetleridb.saglik.gov.tr/TR-96308/saglikli-yas-alma-merkezlerinin-kurulmasina-dair-genelge-yayimlandi.html

Republic of Türkiye Ministry of Health. (2026, April 2). *Sağlık Bakanlığı ile Aile ve Sosyal Hizmetler Bakanlığı arasında iş birliği protokolü imzalandı* [A cooperation protocol was signed between the Ministry of Health and the Ministry of Family and Social Services]. https://www.saglik.gov.tr/TR-117252/saglik-bakanligi-ile-aile-ve-sosyal-hizmetler-bakanligi-arasinda-is-birligi-protokolu-imzalandi.html

Reshetnikova, L., Boldyreva, N., Perevalova, M., Kalayda, S., & Pisarenko, Z. (2021). Conditions for the growth of the "silver economy" in the context of sustainable development goals: Peculiarities of Russia. *Journal of Risk and Financial Management*, *14*(9), 401. DOI: 10.3390/jrfm14090401

Resonanz Capital. (2025). *Life settlements as an investment asset class.*

Retirement Living Online. (2022, June 20). *What are departure fees in a retirement village?* https://www.retirementlivingonline.com.au/news/26/60/What-are-Departure-Fees-in-a-Retirement-Village/retirement/retirement/facilities/retirement/retirement/retirement/retirement/retirement/south-australia

Reverse Mortgage, C. H. I. P. (2023). *CHIP Reverse Mortgage program overview: Home equity for retirement security*. HomeEquity Bank.

Rijken, M., Hujala, A., van Ginneken, E., Melchiorre, M. G., Groenewegen, P., & Schellevis, F. (2018). Managing multimorbidity: Profiles of integrated care approaches targeting people with multiple chronic conditions in Europe. *Health Policy (Amsterdam), 122*(1), 44–52. DOI: 10.1016/j.healthpol.2017.10.002 PMID: 29102089

Rogelj, V., & Bogataj, D. (2019). Social infrastructure of Silver Economy: Literature review and Research agenda. *IFAC-PapersOnLine, 52*(13), 2680–2685. DOI: 10.1016/j.ifacol.2019.11.612

Romdhane, H. B., Tlili, F., Skhiri, A., Zaman, S., & Phillimore, P. (2015). Health system challenges of NCDs in Tunisia. *International Journal of Public Health, 60*(S1, Suppl 1), 39–46. DOI: 10.1007/s00038-014-0616-0

Rowe, J. W., & Kahn, R. L. (1997). Successful aging. *The Gerontologist, 37*(4), 433–440. DOI: 10.1093/geront/37.4.433 PMID: 9279031

Rowley, J. (2000). Is higher education ready for knowledge management? *International Journal of Educational Management, 14*(7), 325–333. DOI: 10.1108/09513540010378978

Sahut, J., & Bouheni, F. B. (2019). Profitability and Risk-Taking Among Cooperative Banks in the Eurozone. *Economic Bulletin, 39*, 1103–1117.

Sánchez, M. (2008). Intergenerational Programmes: Towards a Society for All Ages: By Mariano Sanchez (Ed.) *Barcelona: Obra Social, Social Studies Collection No. 23 "la Caixa" Foundation, 2007. 228 pages. Journal of Intergenerational Relationships, 6*(4), 485–487. DOI: 10.1080/15350770802466286

Sánchez, M., García, J. M., Díaz, P., & Duaigües, M. (2011). Much more than accommodation in exchange for company: Dimensions of solidarity in an Intergenerational Homeshare Program in Spain. *Journal of Intergenerational Relationships, 9*(4), 374–388. DOI: 10.1080/15350770.2011.619410

Sánchez, M., & Kaplan, M. (2014). Intergenerational Learning in Higher Education: Making the Case for Multigenerational Classrooms. *Educational Gerontology, 40*(7), 473–485. DOI: 10.1080/03601277.2013.844039

Sanchini, V., Sala, R., & Gastmans, C. (2022). The concept of vulnerability in aged care: A systematic review of argument-based ethics literature. *BMC Medical Ethics*, *23*(1), 84. DOI: 10.1186/s12910-022-00819-3

Sancho, M.. (2017). Residential care and quality of life in older adults. *Journal of Aging Studies*, *42*, 1–10.

Sanders, S., Kolomer, S. R., Spellman, C. W., & Rizzo, V. M. (Eds.). (2019). *Gerontological social work and the grand challenges: Focusing on policy and practice*. Springer., DOI: 10.1007/978-3-030-26334-8

Santoso, B., & Harimurti, P. (2021). Documenting traditional knowledge in rural Java: A university-community partnership model. Masyarakat, Kebudayaan dan Politik, 34(1), 56–71. https://doi.org/DOI: 10.20473/mkp.V34I12021.56-71

SCG. (2022). SCG [Siam Cement Group.]. *Sustainability Report*, •••, 2022.

Schatz, E., & Ogunmefun, C. (2007). Caring and contributing: The role of older women in rural South African households. *World Development*, *35*(8), 1390–1403. DOI: 10.1016/j.worlddev.2007.04.004

Scholar, R. (2023). About Road Scholar: Mission and history. https://www.roadscholar.org/about/

Schuler, D., & Namioka, A. (Eds.). (1993). *Participatory design: Principles and practices*. Lawrence Erlbaum Associates.

Schuurman, D., De Moor, K., De Marez, L., & Evens, T. (2012). A living lab research approach for mobile TV. *Telematics and Informatics*, *29*(2), 207–220. DOI: 10.1016/j.tele.2011.06.001

Scott, A. J. (2021). The longevity economy. *The Lancet. Healthy Longevity*, *2*(12), e828–e835. DOI: 10.1016/S2666-7568(21)00250-6 PMID: 36098039

Selsky, J. W., & Parker, B. (2005). Cross-sector partnerships to address social issues: Challenges to theory and practice. *Journal of Management*, *31*(6), 849–873. DOI: 10.1177/0149206305279601

Shaikh, A., Patel, D., & Sakhuja, A. (2026). Innovation, technology, and telemedicine in critical care. *Critical Care Clinics*, *42*(2), 347–360. DOI: 10.1016/j.ccc.2025.11.003 PMID: 41825983

Shao, M., Chen, J., & Ma, C. (2022). Research on the relationship between Chinese elderly health status, social security, and depression. *International Journal of Environmental Research and Public Health*, *19*(12), 7496. Advance online publication. DOI: 10.3390/ijerph19127496 PMID: 35742744

Sharma, P., & Iyer, R. (2023). *Business Ecosystem Strategies for Ageing Markets in Emerging Economies*. IGI Global.

Sharma, S., & Sharma, S. K. (2014). Emotional labour and counterproductive workplace behaviour: Evidence from banking sector in India. *Journal of Organisation and Human Behaviour, 3*(4).

Sharma, V., & Krishnamurthy, M. (2025). Senior-friendly housing and the silver economy: A scoping review. *Journal of Population Ageing, 18*(2), 1–22. DOI: 10.1007/s12062-025-09495-8

Shen, J., Liu, N., Sun, H., Li, D., Zhang, Y., & Han, L. (2025). An algorithm based on lightweight semantic features for ancient mural element object detection. *NPJ Heritage Science, 13*(1), 70. DOI: 10.1038/s40494-025-01565-6

Siddiquee, N. A. (2016). E-government and transformation of service delivery in developing countries: The Bangladesh experience and lessons. *Transforming Government: People. Transforming Government, 10*(3), 368–390. DOI: 10.1108/TG-09-2015-0039

Singapore, M. O. H. (2023). *Agency for Integrated Care Annual Report 2022/23*. Ministry of Health.

Singapore, S. N. (2022). *Digital government blueprint 2020: Progress update 2022*. Smart Nation and Digital Government Office., https://www.smartnation.gov.sg

Singh, A.. (2025). Smart Contract-Based Crowdfunding. *2025 International Conference on Networks and Cryptology (NETCRYPT)*. DOI: 10.1109/NETCRYPT65877.2025.11102542

Sixsmith, A., & Gutman, G. (2023). Technologies for active and assisted living in ageing societies. *Gerontechnology (Valkenswaard), 22*(1), 1–14. DOI: 10.4017/gt.2023.22.2.six.08

Skublewska-Paszkowska, M., Milosz, M., Powroznik, P., & Lukasik, E. (2022). 3D technologies for intangible cultural heritage preservation—Literature review for selected databases. *Heritage Science, 10*(1), 3. DOI: 10.1186/s40494-021-00633-x PMID: 35003750

Smith, L. T. (2012). *Decolonizing methodologies: Research and indigenous peoples* (2nd ed.). Zed Books.

Social Finance, U. K. (2021). *Ageing Well Social Impact Bond: Impact report*. Social Finance UK Society of Actuaries. (2010). *Report of the Society of Actuaries Life Settlements Survey Subcommittee.*

Solmaz, T., & Altay, B. (2019). Yaşlılara yönelik evde bakım hizmetleri [Home care services for elder people]. *Sağlık Akademisyenleri Dergisi, 6*(2), 150-157. https://izlik.org/JA66FE63WK

Sons, T. (2022). *Corporate Social Responsibility Report 2021–22: Community and Mentorship Programmes.* Tata Sons.

Sorrentino, M., Fiorilla, C., Mercogliano, M., Esposito, F., Stilo, I., Affinito, G., Moccia, M., Lavorgna, L., Salvatore, E., Maida, E., Barbi, E., Triassi, M., & Palladino, R. (2024). Technological interventions in European dementia care: a systematic review of acceptance and attitudes among people living with dementia, caregivers, and healthcare workers. *Frontiers in Neurology, 15*, 1474336. Sorrentino, M., Fiorilla, C., Mercogliano, M., Esposito, F., Stilo, I., Affinito, G., ... & Palladino, R. (2024). Technological interventions in European dementia care: a systematic review of acceptance and attitudes among people living with dementia, caregivers, and healthcare workers. *Frontiers in Neurology*, *15*, 1474336. DOI: 10.3389/fneur.2024.1474336 PMID: 39416661

Southern Daily. (2022, September 5). The first in Guangzhou! Huangpu District to create a "sunflower parent-child hut," explore the community "mutual care childcare services" ! " ", " ". .

Stockland Group. (2024). *Stockland retirement living: Investor update.* https://www.stockland.com.au/investor-centre/announcements-and-reports/results-and-reports

Superannuation Australia & Association of Superannuation Funds of Australia. (2024). *How product layering can support retirement outcomes and address longevity risk.*

Suwanrada, W., & Sukontamarn, P. (2023). Should social pensions be universal or targeted? OLder persons' preferences over the old-age allowance system in thailand. *Journal of Aging & Social Policy*, *35*(1), 52–69. DOI: 10.1080/08959420.2022.2029267 PMID: 35067211

Swiss Re. (2025). Silver economy ushers in a new era of growth for life insurance. *Swiss Re Sigma Report*, (1), 1–48.

Tafoska, I., Bellazzecca, E., & Tropeano, T. (2026). Barriers and opportunities in outcome-based contracting for enabling social innovation: Insights from a collaborative, public–private pilot project in Italy. *Social Enterprise Journal*, *22*(2), 274–293. DOI: 10.1108/SEJ-07-2025-0154

Taga, Y. (2021). The Rise of Silver Dollars: Changing Pattern of Silver Use in Nineteenth-Century Vietnam. In Akita, S., Liu, H., & Momoki, S. (Eds.), *Changing Dynamics and Mechanisms of Maritime Asia in Comparative Perspectives*. Palgrave Studies in Comparative Global History. DOI: 10.1007/978-981-16-2554-1_3

Tan, C. (2019). Creative cocktails or toxic brews? Blended finance and the regulatory framework for sustainable development. In *Sustainable Trade, Investment, and Finance*. Edward Elgar. DOI: 10.4337/9781788971041.00023

Tanveer, U., Hoang, T. G., Ishaq, S., & Khalid, R. U. (2025). Public-private partnerships as catalysts for digital transformation and circular economy: Insights from developing countries. *Technological Forecasting and Social Change*, *219*, 124270. DOI: 10.1016/j.techfore.2025.124270

Thang, L. L., Yui, Y., Wakabayashi, Y., & Miyazawa, H. (2023). Promoting age-friendly community of support and care in Japan's aging neighborhood: The Nagayama model. *Aging and Health Research*, *3*(1), 100111. DOI: 10.1016/j.ahr.2022.100111

Thi, T. T. M. (2019). Institutional and cultural perspectives in elder care in rural Vietnam. *Wieś i Rolnictwo*, (3 (184)), 11–30. DOI: 10.53098/wir032019/01

Thi, T. T. M. (2024). Involvement of Vietnamese elders in economic activities in the lens of family ties, low institutional coverage, and gender identity. *International Journal of Asian Studies*, *21*(2), 284–303. DOI: 10.1017/S147959142300058X

Thurston, C. N. (2015). Policy feedback in the public-private welfare state: Advocacy groups and access to government homeownership programs, 1934-1954. *Studies in American Political Development*, *29*(2), 250–267. DOI: 10.1017/S0898588X15000097

Tomej, K., Garcia-Lozano, C., Vila-Subiros, J., Innocenti, A., Juvan, E., Le Pape, O., Arnoldussen, N. T., Verschuuren, J., Taylor, T., Huebner, G., Tollin, N., & Mernild, S. (2026). Enabling cross-sectoral transformation for coastal climate adaptation in Europe: Four directions for interdisciplinary efforts. *Environmental Science & Policy*, *177*, 104334. DOI: 10.1016/j.envsci.2026.104334

Topol, E. J. (2019). High-performance medicine: The convergence of human and artificial intelligence. *Nature Medicine*, *25*(1), 44–56. DOI: 10.1038/s41591-018-0300-7 PMID: 30617339

Trư ng Đ i h c Khoa h c – Đ i h c Hu . (n.d.). *Thông báo s 10330/TB-ĐHKH v k t lu n c a Hi u trư ng t i cu c h p xét ký h p đ ng lao đ ng đ i v i cán b có h c hàm Giáo sư, Phó Giáo sư, trình đ Ti n sĩ đ tu i ngh hưu.* [Notice No. 10330/TB-ĐHKH on conclusions regarding labor contract signing for retired professors, associate professors, and PhD holders].

Trư ng Đ i h c Y Dư c – Đ i h c Hu . (n.d.). *Quy t đ nh ban hành quy đ nh v h p đ ng lao đ ng v i ngư i lao đ ng cao tu i t i Trư ng Đ i h c Y Dư c, Đ i h c Hu .* [Decision on regulations for labor contracts with senior employees at the University of Medicine and Pharmacy, Hue University].

Tsega, Y. Tsega, G., Taddesse, G. & Getaneh, G. (2023). Leaving no one behind in health: financial hardship to access health care in Ethiopia. *PLOS ONE, 18*(3), e0282561. 10.1371/journal.pone.0282561

Tuan, N. D. (2023). Ti p c n d ch v chăm sóc s c kh e cho ngư i cao tu i Vi t Nam trong b i c nh già hóa dân s . T p chí Khoa h c Xã h i Vi t Nam, [Access to healthcare services for the elderly in Vietnam in the context of population aging]. *Vietnam Social Sciences Review*, (12), 5–13.

Turkish Statistical Institute. (2026). *İstatistiklerle yaşlılar, 2025* [Elderly statistics, 2025]. https://veriportali.tuik.gov.tr/tr/press/58231

Tyers, R., & Shi, Q. (2007). Demographic change and policy responses. *World Economy*, *30*(4), 537–566. DOI: 10.1111/j.1467-9701.2007.01004.x

UNDP. (2025). *UNDP Silver Economy Report Series*. United Nations Development Program.

UNESCO. (2003). *Basic Texts of the 2003 Convention for the Safeguarding of the Intangible Cultural Heritage*. https://ich.unesco.org/doc/src/2003_Convention_Basic_Texts_2024_version_EN.pdf

UNESCO. (2015). *Rethinking education: Towards a global common good?* UNESCO.

UNESCO. (2023). *Living heritage: Safeguarding without freezing* (Programme and Meeting Document CPE-2023/WS/10). https://unesdoc.unesco.org/ark:/48223/pf0000387872_eng

UNESCO. (n.d.). *What is Intangible Cultural Heritage?* UNESCO Intangible Cultural Heritage. Retrieved https://ich.unesco.org/en/what-is-intangible-heritage-00003

Ungerson, C., & Yeandle, S. (2007). *Cash for care systems in developed welfare states*. Palgrave Macmillan.

United Nation. (2024). *Asia-Pacific Report on Population Ageing 2022: Trends, policies and good practices regarding older persons and population ageing*. United Nationa. 10.18356/9789210021746

United Nations Department of Economic and Social Affairs. (2023). *World social report 2023: Leaving no one behind in an ageing world*. United Nations.

United Nations Development Programme, & Industrial Securities. (2025). *Financing the silver economy in China: Empowering an inclusive and sustainable ageing society*. UNDP, China.

United Nations Development Programme. (2025a). *A measurement study on multidimensional vulnerabilities of the elderly population in China*. United Nations Development Programme.

United Nations Development Programme. (2025b). *Enhancing the elderly care service system through the silver economy*. United Nations Development Programme.

United Nations Economic and Social Commission for Asia and the Pacific (UNESCAP). (2017). *Ageing in Asia and the Pacific: Overview*. United Nations.

United Nations Population Fund (UNFPA) & General Statistics Office (GSO). (2021). *Population aging and the elderly in Vietnam* [Già hóa dân s và ngư i cao tu i Vi t Nam]. UNFPA Vietnam.

United Nations Population Fund (UNFPA), General Statistics Office (GSO) & The Government of Japan. (2021). The elderly in Vietnam: An analysis based on the 2021 Population Change and Family Planning Survey [Người cao tuổi Việt Nam: Phân tích từ Điều tra Biên động dân sô và Kê ho ch hóa gia đình năm 2021]. UNFRA, *GSO,* The Government of Japan. https://vietnam.unfpa.org/sites/default/files/pub-pdf/nguoi_cao_tuoi_vn_report_18.3.pdf

United Nations Population Fund. (2019). *Ageing in Viet Nam.*

United Nations Population Fund. (2025). *Applying foresight to curate a care economy for older persons in Viet Nam.*

United Nations. (2019). *World population ageing 2019: Highlights*. United Nations Department of Economic and Social Affairs.

United Nations. (2020). World population ageing 2020: Highlights. Department of Economic and Social Affairs, Population Division. https://www.un.org/development/desa/pd/

United Nations. (2022). *World Population Prospects 2022: Summary of results*. United Nations DESA.

United Nations. (2023). *World population aging 2023*. United Nations.

United Nations. (2025). *World Population Prospects: The 2015 Revision*. Key Findings and Advance Tables. [Online Edition UN DESA, New York]

Urban Land Institute Asia Pacific. (2023). Kampung Admiralty Case Study, Singapore. Retrieved from https://knowledge.uli.org/-/media/files/case-studies/2023/kampung-admiralty-case-study.pdf

Van Hoa, H., Giang, H. T., Vu, P. T., Van Tuyen, D., & Khue, P. M. (2020). Factors associated with health literacy among the elderly people in Vietnam. *BioMed Research International*, *2020*(1), 3490635. DOI: 10.1155/2020/3490635 PMID: 32309429

Vera Zúñiga, J., Urbina Parada, F., & Cornejo Meza, D. (2026). Mapping semantic bias in UNESCO intangible heritage metadata through community detection in South America. *NPJ Heritage Science*, *14*(1), 133. DOI: 10.1038/s40494-026-02400-2

Vera-Sanso, P. (2023). Will the SDGs and the UN decade of healthy ageing leave older people behind? *Progress in Development Studies*, *23*(4), 391–407. 10.1177/14649934231193808. DOI: 10.1177/14649934231193808

Vietnam Association of the Elderly. (2023). Annual Report 2023. Hoi nguoi cao tuoi Viet Nam.

Vietnam National Assembly. (2009). *Law on the Elderly (Law No. 39/2009/QH12)*. Hanoi, Vietnam. Link < https://m.thuvienphapluat.vn/van-ban/van-hoa-xa-hoi/Law-No-39-2009-QH12-on-the-elderly-106095.aspx>

VinaCapital Foundation. (2023). *Silver Generation Initiative Report 2023*. VinaCapital Foundation.

Vu, N. C., Tran, M. T., Dang, L. T., Chei, C. L., & Saito, Y. (2020). *Ageing and health in Viet Nam*. Economic Research Institute for ASEAN and East Asia.

Vuong, Q. H., La, V. P., Vuong, T. T., Ho, M. T., & Ho, M. T. (2020). What have Vietnamese scholars learned from researching entrepreneurship? A Systematic review. *Heliyon*, *6*(4).

Wahyudi, A., & Paramastri, I. (2019). Ageism attitudes among young adults in urban Indonesia. *Jurnal Psikologi*, *46*(3), 189–201. DOI: 10.22146/jpsi.37561

Walker, A. (2002). A strategy for active ageing. *International Social Security Review*, *55*(1), 121–139. DOI: 10.1111/1468-246X.00118

Walker, A. (2006). Active ageing in employment: Its meaning and potential. *Asia-Pacific Review*, *13*(1), 78–93. DOI: 10.1080/13439000600697621

Wang, H., Coyte, P. C., Shi, W., Zong, X., & Zhong, R. (2023). Social governance and sustainable development in elderly services: Innovative models, strategies, and stakeholder perspectives. *Sustainability (Basel), 15*(21), 15414. Advance online publication. DOI: 10.3390/su152115414

Wang, L., Tang, Y., Roshanmehr, F., Bai, X., Taghizadeh-Hesary, F., & Taghizadeh-Hesary, F. (2021). The Health Status Transition and Medical Expenditure Evaluation of Elderly Population in China. *International Journal of Environmental Research and Public Health, 18*(13), 6907. 10.3390/ijerph18136907. DOI: 10.3390/ijerph18136907

Wang, Q. (2022). The Digitisation of Intangible Cultural Heritage Oriented to Inheritance and Dissemination under the Threshold of Neural Network Vision. *Mobile Information Systems, 2022*, 1–10. DOI: 10.1155/2022/6323811

Wang, W., Chu, Y., Cui, F., Shi, X., Zhang, X., Sun, D., Shi, J., & Zhao, J. (2025). Correlation between the online visiting time and frequency increase in telemedicine services offered by health care providers before, during, and after the COVID-19 pandemic in China: Cross-sectional study. *Journal of Medical Internet Research, 27*, e65092. DOI: 10.2196/65092 PMID: 40009835

Wenger, E. (1998). *Communities of practice: Learning, meaning, and identity*. Cambridge University Press. DOI: 10.1017/CBO9780511803932

White, H. C., & White, C. A. (1965). *Canvases and careers: Institutional change in the French painting world*. John Wiley & Sons.

WHO. (2023). *Decade of Healthy Aging: Progress report 2021–2023*. WHO.

WHO. (2024). *Aging and health fact sheet*. WHO.

Widiastini, N. M. A., Arsa, I. K. S., Prayudi, M. A., & Karta, N. L. P. A. (2025). Strategic collaborations and diversification: Pathways to sustainable growth in Bali's tourism village and business ecosystems. [Journal of Bali Studies]. *Jurnal Kajian Bali, 15*(1), 146–172.

Wong, J. H. C. (2018). *Disaster Social Work: From Crisis Response to Building Resilience*. Nova Science Publishers.

Wong, J. H. C. (2023). *Social Work in an Ageing World: Community Practice and Cross-Sector Collaboration*. IGI Global.

Wong, J. H. C. (2024). *Disaster Resilience and Community Social Work in Asia: Post-Pandemic Frameworks*. IGI Global.

Wong, J. H. C., & Ho, G. W. (2022a). *Cross-Sector Responses to Aging Populations: From Welfare Silos to Collaborative Ecosystems*. IGI Global.

Wong, J. H. C., & Ho, G. W. (2022b). Shielding without a shield—older people under COVID-19: A comparison of four cities. *Social Sciences (Basel, Switzerland)*, *11*(11), 498. Advance online publication. DOI: 10.3390/socsci11110498

Wong, J. H. C., Ho, G. W., & He, H. L. X. (2022). A safer world after vaccination against COVID-19. *Medical Research Archives*, *10*(8). Advance online publication. DOI: 10.18103/mra.v10i8.2987

Wong, J. H. C., & Leung, T. L. C. (2021). Trauma-informed practice during COVID-19. *Asia Pacific Journal of Social Work and Development*, *31*(1–2), 67–72. DOI: 10.1080/02185385.2020.1846604

World Bank. (2016). *Live long and prosper: Aging in East Asia and Pacific*. World Bank.

World Bank. (2021). *Vietnam: Adapting to an Aging Society*. World Bank Group.

World Bank. (2023). *Addressing the needs of an aging population*. World Bank.

World Bank. (2025). *World Development Indicators*. Washington. Retrieved 20/02/2026 from World Health Organization. (2021a). *Decade of healthy ageing: baseline report*. World Health Organization. https://www.who.int/publications/i/item/9789240017900

World Health Organization (WHO). (2015). World Report on Ageing and Health. Geneva: WHO. Retrieved from https://www.who.int/publications/i/item/9789241565042

World Health Organization. (2002). *Active ageing: A policy framework*.

World Health Organization. (2002). *Active ageing: A policy framework*. WHO.

World Health Organization. (2002). Active ageing: A policy framework. WHO. https://apps.who.int/iris/handle/10665/67215

World Health Organization. (2007). *Global age-friendly cities: A guide*.

World Health Organization. (2015). *World report on ageing and health*.

World Health Organization. (2015). *World report on ageing and health*. WHO.

World Health Organization. (2017). *Integrated care for older people: Guidelines on community-level interventions to manage declines in intrinsic capacity*.

World Health Organization. (2020). *Decade of healthy ageing 2020–2030*. WHO.

World Health Organization. (2020). *Decade of healthy ageing: Baseline report*. https://www.who.int/publications/i/item/9789240017900

World Health Organization. (2021). Decade of Healthy Ageing: Baseline report. WHO. https://www.who.int/publications/i/item/9789240017900

World Health Organization. (2021). *Integrated care for older people (ICOPE): Guidelines on community-level interventions to manage declines in intrinsic capacity*. WHO.

World Health Organization. (2021b). *Monitoring progress on universal health coverage and the health-related Sustainable Development Goals in the WHO South-East Asia Region 2021 update*. World Health Organization, Regional Office for South-East Asia. https://www.who.int/publications/i/item/9789290228936

World Health Organization. (2022). *Global strategy on digital health 2020–2025*. WHO.

World Health Organization. (2023). *Framework for integrated people-centred long-term care*. WHO.

World Health Organization. (2025a). *Global Health Expenditure Database*. World Health Organization. Retrieved 1/11/2025 from https://apps.who.int/nha/database/Select/Indicators/en

World Health Organization. (2025b). *The Global Health Observatory: Explore a world of health data*.

Wu, W., Ying, S., & Wu, Y. (2025). Silver economy industry market consumption characteristics research. *Journal of Modern Social Sciences*, *2*(1), 94–98. 10.71113/JMSS.v2i1.187. DOI: 10.71113/JMSS.v2i1.187

Xu, X., & Sun, Y. (2017). Study on the adoption of information technology in digital transmission of intangible cultural heritage (CN). *Library and Information Service*, *61*(6), 68–75. https://doi.org/https://doi.org/10.11968/tsyqb.1003-6938.2017124

Xu, K., Evans, D. B., Kawabata, K., Zeramdini, R., Klavus, J., & Murray, C. (2003). Household catastrophic health expenditure: A multicountry analysis. *Lancet*, *362*(9378), 111–117. DOI: 10.1016/S0140-6736(03)13861-5

Xu, S., Ho, F. F., Kwong, T. M. H., Li, A. S., Ha, E. H., Hua, H., Liong, C., Leung, K. C., Wang, B. H., Leung, T. H., Lin, Z., Wong, S. Y.-S., Pan, F., & Chung, V. C. H. (2025). Patient satisfaction with traditional Chinese medicine telemedicine service during the COVID-19 pandemic: A cross-sectional study. *Journal of Manipulative and Physiological Therapeutics*, *48*(6–9), 671–682. DOI: 10.1016/j.jmpt.2025.10.047 PMID: 41212126

Yang, C., & Zhang, C. (2026). Digital platform-led cross-border healthcare services for Hong Kong older adults in the Greater Bay Area: Regional integration in the digital age. *Cities (London, England), 170*, 106634. DOI: 10.1016/j.cities.2025.106634

Yang, H.-L., & Hsiao, S.-L. (2009). Mechanisms of developing innovative IT-enabled services: A case study of Taiwanese healthcare service. *Technovation, 29*(5), 327–337. DOI: 10.1016/j.technovation.2009.01.006

Yıldırım, H. H. (2012). *Sağlık sigortacılığı* [Health insurance]. Anadolu Üniversitesi Yayınları.

Yin, R. K. (2018). *Case study research and applications: Design and methods* (6th ed.). Sage.

Youtie, J., & Shapira, P. (2008). Building an innovation hub: A case study of the transformation of university roles in regional technological and economic development. *Research Policy, 37*(8), 1188–1204. DOI: 10.1016/j.respol.2008.04.012

Yuan, H., Li, Y., Wang, B., Liu, K., & Zhang, J. (2025). Knowledge graph-based intelligent question answering system for ancient Chinese costume heritage. *NPJ Heritage Science, 13*(1), 198. DOI: 10.1038/s40494-025-01776-x

Yun, J. J., Zhao, X., & Liu, Z. (2024). Regulation architecture of open innovation under digital transformation: Case study on telemedicine and for-profit-hospital. *Journal of Open Innovation, 10*(1), 100252. DOI: 10.1016/j.joitmc.2024.100252

Zaidi, I., Sharma, T., Chaudhary, S., Alam, A., Anjum, S., & Vardha, J. (2023). Barriers to access healthcare among the elderly population in rural regions of India. *International Journal of Community Medicine and Public Health, 10*(11), 4480–4484. DOI: 10.18203/2394-6040.ijcmph20233498

Zastrow, C., & Kirst-Ashman, K. K. (2016). *Understanding human behavior and the social environment* (10th ed.). Cengage Learning.

Zeng, Y., Fu, J., Cao, W., Chen, Y., & Yang, Z. (2024). Research Hotspots and Knowledge Framework of Digital Healthcare Service Management from the Perspective of the Silver Economy. Sustainability, 16(22), 9735.

Zheng, F., Wu, S., Liu, R., & Bai, Y. (2024). What influences user continuous intention of digital museum: Integrating task-technology fit (TTF) and unified theory of acceptance and usage of technology (UTAUT) models. *Heritage Science, 12*(1), 253. DOI: 10.1186/s40494-024-01365-4

Zheng, X., Wen, J., & Wu, X. (2026). Government linked companies (GLCs) and public private partnership (PPP) in the water sector in China: Political connection, utility performance and service quality. *China Economic Review*, *96*, 102650. DOI: 10.1016/j.chieco.2025.102650

Zhi, T. (2025). Safeguarding Intangible Cultural Heritage in a Knowledge Economy: Envisioning a Paradigm Shift of Chinese Economic Development. In Wong, J. H.-C., & Yu, P. (Eds.), *Driving Community Change Through Social Service and Business Partnerships* (pp. 59–96). IGI Global Scientific Publishing., DOI: 10.4018/979-8-3373-1852-3.ch003

Zou, C., Harvard, A., Qian, J., & Fox, B. (2023). A systematic review of digital health technologies for the care of older adults during COVID-19 pandemic. *Gigital Health, 9*. 10.1177/20552076231191050

About the Contributors

Johnston Hong Chung Wong, Professor in Applied Psychology, started his career as a youth worker in Hong Kong. His early academic interests focused on youth development, counseling, and family life education, branching out to psychological stress, unemployment, and industrial social services. In Hong Kong, he participated in various district and central government committees related to youth policies, education, social care, healthcare financing and hospital governance. Since 2005 he has been involved in many post-disaster social work and psychological interventions and become the non-executive director of the Social Workers Across Borders. In 2006 he joined BNBU (formerly UIC) as a Faculty member and helped to design the Service Learning Scheme and Emotional Intelligence Programs as parts of Whole Person Education. Later he was appointed the Chief of Student Affairs to strengthen the Personal Development and Counseling Center (PGCC). He taught courses like Management, Society and Life, Government and Society, Social Management Laws of China, Disaster and Emergency Management, Healthcare Social Work, Social Group Work, and Crisis Interventions. Recently his research interests included Services for Older People, Social Indicators and Social Integration, Healthy Villages and Cities, Social laws in China, Disaster and Healthcare social work, Distant counseling services, and Welfare Informatics. He has published eight books, co-edited one book, eighteen book chapters, and twenty-seven journal articles related to disaster intervention, student affairs in higher education, and services for older people. He received the International Crisis Intervention Leadership Award from ICISF and the Presidential Citation Award from ACPA while being recognized as one of the Outstanding Young Persons in 1990 by TOYPA.

Poshan (Sam) Yu is a Chinese-Australian professional with an astonishingly diverse background and an extensive collection of remarkable accomplishments. In the academic sphere, he currently teaches at the University of Victoria Program at Soochow University. Previously, he held the position of an external professor of financial technology and finance at SKEMA Business School. He also serves as a visiting researcher at the Australian Studies Centre of Shanghai University, a guest professor at emlyon business school China, and an adjunct faculty member at George Washington University's master (finance) program at Renmin University of China. As a visiting professor at Krirk University in Thailand and an EU-Asia research coordinator at the European Business Institute in Luxembourg, he brings a truly global perspective to his teaching and research activities. He is a member of the IP & Innovation Researchers of Asia (IPIRA) Network and the Global South Dialogue on Economic Crime (GSDEC), further enriching his academic engagement. His prior role as a casual academic at the University of South Australia Business School has significantly enhanced and diversified his academic portfolio. From September 2020 to February 2021, he held the position of visiting scholar at The Chinese University of Hong Kong on two occasions. His scholarly pursuits are extensive and multifaceted. As an editor for the European Academic Journal (Special Issue) - European Business Institute in Luxembourg, an associate editor for Humanities & Social Sciences Communications (an SSCI-indexed journal), and an associate editor for the International Journal of Interdisciplinary Research in Social Science, he plays a crucial role in the dissemination of knowledge. He is an ad hoc reviewer for a number of prestigious journals and academic presses, including Applied Economics, Applied Artificial Intelligence, Cogent Economics & Finance, Humanities and Social Sciences Communications, Journal of Chinese Economic and Business Studies, Journal of Digital Learning and Education, The Singapore Economic Review, ILMA Journal of Social Sciences & Economics, Journal of Environmental Issues and Climate Change, Advances in Global Economic and Business Journal, The Interdisciplinary Social Sciences Journal Collection, Common Ground Research Networks, Imprint - Xi'an Jiaotong-Liverpool University, Innovative Teaching and Learning, IBT Journal of Business Studies, Journal of Infrastructure Policy and Development, and Innovative Informatics and Artificial Intelligence Research. Moreover, he is an international editorial advisory board member for several edited books such as Advancing STEM Education and Innovation in a Time of Distance Learning (Scopus-indexed), Multidisciplinary Perspectives Towards Building a Digitally Competent Society (Scopus-indexed), Handbook of Research on SDGs for Economic Development, Social Development, and Environmental Protection, and Implications for Entrepreneurship and Enterprise Development in the Blue Economy. He has released more than 12 journal articles, among which 6 are listed as ABDC: B/SSCI. He has also contributed over 70 peer-reviewed book chapters imprinted by renowned publishers like IGI Global, Routledge, and Springer. He has edited 22 books, with 14 English-edited books indexed by Scopus and 6 Chinese-edited books. Notably, the book about Innovation & Exploration: The Development of FinTech in Jiangsu China has received the 14th Outstanding Achievement Award of

Philosophy and Social Sciences in Suzhou and the 3rd prize of the 2018 Jiangsu Provincial Education Science Research Achievement Award by Jiangsu Provincial Department of Education. His receipt of four Xi'an Jiaotong-Liverpool University (XJTLU) National University Teaching Innovation Awards from 2016 to 2020 and being recognized as a top contender in the same national competition in 2016 led to his appointment as the Institute of Leadership and Education Advanced Development (ILEAD) Research Fellow by XJTLU. In 2021, he received The Outstanding Contribution Award for Industrial Research Development in China, CIE100 issued by Wisdom China Magazine: Beijing. Beyond academia, he is actively involved in various industries. He is an entrepreneur and venture capitalist, collaborating with alumni and senior faculty members from Cambridge University. Additionally, he is a guest financial news commentator on over 30 media platforms in China. In the business world, he holds significant positions. He is a regional partner in China for FasterCapital based in Dubai, United Arab Emirates. He also serves as vice president at Tinbowah Investment in Beijing and as an honorary vice president of the Belt and Road Blockchain Association. Furthermore, he mentors businesses for AIC RAISE in Coimbatore, India, the Griffith Industry Mentoring Program in Australia, and University College London Innovation & Enterprise. In 2023, he was invited to act as a venture capital panel judge and mentor at 'Y&Archer A Stream 2023' conference in Jeju, South Korea. His research interests are broad and encompass financial technology, regulatory technology, blockchain, web 3.0 in financial services, generative AI, public-private partnerships, mergers and acquisitions, private equity, venture capital, startups, family offices, IoTs, supply chain finance, intellectual property, art finance, wine, back-door listing, intangible cultural heritage, and Chinese economy & policy. His extensive experience in international fintech, edtech, startup, social media, and cleantech companies across India, the UK, Australia, Hong Kong, and China is truly remarkable. His three-year tenure in significant leadership positions within the Chinese-Australian media marketing and public relations sector, along with his role as an OzAsia Festival Ambassador in Australia, has exerted a profound influence on his current modus operandi as an academic and business consultant. Additionally, it has considerably broadened his perspective within the international multicultural arts community and enlarged his business network. This multifaceted experience has furnished him with a more comprehensive and inclusive outlook on academia, industry, and research. He is fully dedicated to making substantial contributions in these areas and is keen on furthering his development in the future. Incidentally, Sam has an inclination towards wine, arts, and reading.

***

Chokri Arfa holds a Ph.D. in Health Economics from the Faculty of Economics in Tunisia and the IÉSEG School of Management in Lille, France, as well as a postdoctoral diploma in the Ability to Lead Research. He is a Professor of Health Economics at the University of Carthage. His academic and research contributions focus on promoting social inclusion, equity, and well-being in health systems. He has been actively involved in international initiatives and collaborations, contributing to innovative policy solutions and managing complex projects. He has authored numerous academic and technical publications.

Bayu Tri Cahya, Ph.D., M.Si., is a lecturer at the State Islamic University of Sunan Kudus, specializing in economics and accounting, with a strong focus on Islamic economics, sharia finance, and sustainable development. He is actively engaged in research and publications at both national and international levels.

Berra Cansız Kösesoy is an Assistant Professor in the Department of Social Work at Fırat University. Her research interests include social determinants of health, medical social work, public health, care services, aging, addiction, child welfare, social justice, and social inequalities. Her academic work particularly focuses on rights-based approaches, the empowerment of vulnerable groups, and the development of social work policies. She has conducted interdisciplinary studies on elderly care, integrated care systems, psychosocial support services, and the relationship between social welfare policies and public health. Her research aims to contribute to the development of inclusive, sustainable, and person-centered social service systems within the context of contemporary social policy challenges.

Yitian Chen from Soochow University focuses her research on finance, artificial intelligence, business analytics and telemedicine.

Adi Fahrudin, PhD is a Professor of Social Work under the Ministry of Higher Education, Science, and Technology of the Republic of Indonesia, currently seconded to Universitas Esa Unggul, Jakarta (since September 2025). He was Director of the Institute for Research, Community Service, and Publication at Universitas Bhayangkara Jakarta Raya (March 2022–August 2025). He also held academic positions at the University of Muhammadiyah Jakarta (2012–2022) and the Bandung College of Social Welfare (1993–2011). Professor Fahrudin holds a Doctorandus degree in Social Work from the Bandung College of Social Welfare (1991), a Master's (1996) and PhD (1999) in Social Work from Universiti Sains Malaysia, and a Bachelor's degree in Psychology from PASIM National University, Bandung (2010). He has held visiting professorships and research fellowships internationally including at Japan College of Social Work, Universiti Malaysia Sabah, Shukutoku University (Japan), and Universiti Sultan Zainal Abidin (Malaysia). He also serves as an external examiner for several universities worldwide and is actively engaged in international professional associations including the APASWE

Yunus Harjito, S.E., M.Si., is a dedicated academic and lecturer at the Faculty of Business, Universitas Setia Budi (USB) Surakarta, specializing in Accounting. Since joining the university in 2015, he has played a pivotal role in the academic community, serving as Secretary of the Faculty and currently serving on the Editorial Board of the Journal of Business and Entrepreneurship (JBK). As a doctoral candidate in Economic Sciences at Universitas Sebelas Maret (UNS), his research focuses on financial performance, carbon disclosure, and CEO characteristics, reflecting his commitment to integrating sustainability and corporate governance within the accounting field.

Ida Hindarsah is a professor in business innovation at the Department of Business Administration, Faculty of Social and Political Science, Pasundan University, Bandung, West Java, Indonesia. She graduated with a bachelor's, master's and PhD in business administration from Pasundan University. She has been active in academic and non-academic (business development, community service) areas, including the development of a cooperative model and business partnership.

Allen Hu is an independent researcher, graduated with a Master's degree in Social Work from Hong Kong Baptist University and completed an Executive Education Program in Business Administration for Mid-to-Senior Managers at Tsinghua University from 2022 to 2024. Since obtaining his postgraduate degree in 2013, he has been engaged in youth social work, geriatric social work, and elderly care services. In 2016, he joined Social Workers Across Borders, where he received professional post-disaster social work training. He participated in relief efforts following the Zhuhai typhoon disaster and provided online psychological support services to residents of Hubei Province during the 2020 COVID-19 pandemic. Over the years, he also has participated in various elderly care service projects, accumulating extensive practical experience in the field. He has led the operation of multiple projects including home-based care, community-based elderly care, "property + elderly care" integrated models, wellness and tourism integration for seniors, retirement communities. He has served as overall project director or general manager in both non-profit organizations and Fortune 500 companies.

Zisheng Huang is currently a lecturer in the School of Art and Education, Guangdong Polytechnic of Industry and Commerce. He received his PhD in Fine Arts from the University of Macau in August, 2024. Before his PhD pursuits, he had studied at the Accademia di Belle Arti di Roma in Italy for eight years, receiving his Master's and Bachelor's degrees with high distinction. For many years, he has participated in professional exhibitions both domestically and internationally, with his works being collected by numerous art institutions and collectors both within and outside China. His creative endeavours and research are grounded in the integration of Chinese and Western art, delving into the core of intangible cultural heritage, and exploring design innovation and sustainable transmission pathways for traditional crafts in contemporary contexts.

Do Huong Lan is a Vietnamese scholar specializing in innovation studies, digital transformation, international economics, and entrepreneurship policy, with a strong interdisciplinary orientation integrating economics, social sciences, and public governance. Born in 1976, she graduated from Foreign Trade University (Hanoi) and obtained her PhD in Economics in the Russian Federation. Over many years, she has conducted in-depth research on comprehensive Vietnam–Russia economic cooperation, international economic integration, and the institutional and political–economic dimensions of bilateral relations. From 2011 to 2017, she served as Deputy Head of the Office for Research Management at Foreign Trade University, contributing to the coordination of scientific research and academic policy development. From 2019 to 2024, she was Deputy Director of the Center for Entrepreneurship and Social Innovation at the National Economics University, where she played an active role in fostering innovation ecosystems, entrepreneurship education, and university–industry–society linkages. In 2024–2025, she served as Director of the Institute of Policy and Management at Vietnam National University, Hanoi. She is currently Director of the Institute of Innovation and Digital Transformation at the University of Finance and Marketing, under the Ministry of Finance of Vietnam. Associate Professor Dr. Do Huong Lan has an extensive record of research leadership. She has served as Principal Investigator of four national-level research projects, along with numerous research projects funded at ministerial and local-government levels. She is the author and co-author of ten academic monographs and has published nearly 100 scholarly works, including journal articles, book chapters, and conference proceedings. Her research interests encompass innovation ecosystems, social innovation, digital transformation of enterprises, digital society governance, entrepreneurship education and international economic cooperation, with a particular focus on transitional and emerging economies. She is currently serving as the Principal Investigator of a national-level state-funded research project focusing on the governance of digital society, reflecting her contribution to the development of both theoretical and applied foundations for digital transformation in Vietnam.

Lam Thi Le, PhD in Social Work, is a lecturer at the University of Science and Education, University of Danang. She has extensive experience in teaching, curriculum development, and supervising student internships. Her research focuses on school social work, child protection, and early mental health intervention. Her work has contributed to developing school-based and community-based programs to prevent violence, bullying, and sexual abuse against children. Dr. Le has led and participated in multiple projects on preventing violence and sexual abuse among children and adolescents, as well as training teachers and educational staff in counseling, student support, and safe school development. She has also been actively involved in community interventions to raise awareness and equip children with protective skills. Currently, her research emphasizes applying social work practices to promote early mental health interventions in schools, contributing to policy development and improving the wellbeing and protection of children in Vietnam.

Karen Yoon Fah Lee is an Assistant Professor at Beijing Normal-Hong Kong Baptist University (BNBU). Backed by over 20 years of senior financial industry experience, her research focuses on wealth management, ESG, and pension trust funds. She provides practitioners with practical longevity finance tools, including life settlement fiduciary disclosures and hybrid capital architectures for aging populations. Dr. Lee holds a PhD in Business Administration, an MBA in Finance, a Post Graduate Diploma in Financial Planning/Wealth Management, and credentials including ChFC and RFP. Beyond research, she has served as Associate Director of the Students' Affairs Office, secured a 2026 National Entrepreneurship Grant, and received the Guangdong Provincial Excellent Teaching Achievement Award. She also boasts nearly three decades of community service with the National Association of Women Entrepreneurs of Malaysia and Lions Clubs International.

Merve Nur Oktar is a faculty member in the Department of Social Work at Burdur Mehmet Akif Ersoy University. Her research interests include disability, disability welfare, disadvantaged groups, care services, gender, ageing, addiction, medical and psychiatric social work, and rights-based social work. In her studies, she focuses on the experiences of disadvantaged groups, the social participation of individuals with disabilities, social work practices, and the inclusiveness of social policies.

Ratih Paramitasari is a dedicated academic and educator at the Open University (UT) Surakarta. He has a deep focus on developing learning methods and actively contributes to supporting the distance learning system that is characteristic of the Open University.

Muhammad Usman Tariq is a strategic higher education leader and scholar with more than 18 years of international experience across academia, research, and industry. He holds dual doctorates, a PhD in Artificial Intelligence and a Doctorate in

Business Administration and has published extensively as the author of research articles, case studies, book chapters, and academic texts. His contributions also include several patents, reflecting his applied research in technology, business, and education. He is the Founder and CEO of TheCaseHQ.com, a global hub for professional certification programmes, narrative and video case studies, and digital learning innovation. In addition, he serves as President of the Gulf Higher Education Network (Gulf HE), an initiative dedicated to advancing academic practice, faculty development, and institutional collaboration across the region. He is a Principal Fellow of Advance HE (UK), Chartered Fellow of the CIPD (UK), Senior Fellow of SEDA (UK), and a Senior Member of IEEE, reflecting his standing as both an academic innovator and a global professional leader.

Nguyen Trung Hai is a PhD in Sociology and currently serves as a Lecturer at the University of Labour and Social Affairs, Vietnam. With a multidisciplinary educational background from the French Republic in Sociology, Ethnology, and Linguistics, he has accumulated extensive experience in teaching and empirical research. His primary research interests include social work, social security, social policy, and psychosocial intervention models for vulnerable groups, such as the elderly, traumatized minors, and people with disabilities. He is the author and co-author of numerous monographs and scientific articles published in prestigious journals, focusing on the refinement of legal frameworks and the development of the professional social work practice in the context of innovation in Vietnam

Hastin Trustisari is a Doctor in Social Welfare and currently serves as a senior lecturer.and researcher in the Department of Social Welfare at Universitas Binawan, Jakarta, Indonesia. Her academic work and research focus primarily on disability studies, social work practice, and inclusive education. With a profound interest in marginalised groups and community development, she actively explores social intervention strategies to empower vulnerable populations. Her contributions to the field aim to bridge the gap between social policy and grassroots implementation, fostering a more equitable society.

Andri Veno is an academic in the field of management and business who actively teach, conduct research, contribute to governance policy study projects, and contribute to the development of scientific publications.

Weixi Zhang is currently pursuing a Bachelor of Business Administration in Culture, Creativity and Management at Beijing Normal-Hong Kong Baptist University (BNBU). Her interdisciplinary work sits at the intersection of intangible cultural heritage (ICH) preservation, artificial intelligence technologies, and digital culture and creative industries.Weixi's ongoing research focuses on technology acceptance among ICH practitioners. She also leads a provincial-level innovation project exploring the integration of Cantonese storytelling traditions.

Tianhao Zhi is currently an Assistant Professor at the Faculty of Science and Technology, Beijing Normal-Hong Kong Baptist University. He obtained his PhD in Finance at the University of Technology Sydney, Australia. His main research interests include intellectual property valuation in a knowledge economy and sustainable development. His research works have been published and presented at a number of international journals and conferences, including Emerging Markets Review (EMR), Studies in Nonlinear Dynamics and Econometrics (SNDE), Social Development Issues, International Schumpeter Society (ISS) Conference, Computational Economics and Finance (CEF) conference, Workshop of Economics with Heterogeneous Interaction Agents (WEHIA).

Index

A

B

C

D

E

F

M

O

P

R

S

T

V

W

www.ingramcontent.com/pod-product-compliance
Lightning Source LLC
LaVergne TN
LVHW061531290926
849162LV00004B/747